From Oppression to Inclusion

From Oppression to Inclusion

SOCIAL WORKERS ADVANCING CHANGE

Gwenelle S. O'Neal

West Chester University

cognella® | ACADEMIC PUBLISHING

Bassim Hamadeh, CEO and Publisher
Amy Smith, Project Editor
Alia Bales, Production Editor
Emely M. Villavicencio, Senior Graphic Designer
Alisa Munoz, Licensing Coordinator
Gustavo Youngberg, Interior Designer
Natalie Piccotti, Director of Marketing
Kassie Graves, Vice President of Editorial
Jamie Giganti, Director of Academic Publishing

Cover image copyright © 2017 iStockphoto LP/MicroStockHub.

Printed in the United States of America.

ISBN: 978-1-5165-3781-5 (pbk) / 978-1-5165-3782-2 (br) / 978-1-5165-7096-6 (hc)

For Rondald, Eavvon, and Taila,
our extended families,
and our communities.

CONTENTS

DETAILED CONTENTS

Preface

The evolution of social work has essentially been on a progressive pathway in addressing the expressed needs of traditionally excluded groups, incorporating policy advocacy, and confronting continuing obstacles to social justice. Despite Jane Addams's and Mary Richmond's emphasis on assisting immigrants residing in Chicago neighborhoods, Becerra and Iglehart (1998) reported that social workers in many instances resisted the work of assisting people of color as they migrated after the Emancipation Proclamation, mainly because it was too hard. The forces against incorporating people of color into the social fabric in the 1900s were just tremendous. Barriers remain that obstruct the inclusion or restrict opportunities through policies and regulations of people of diverse class, ethnicity, abilities, and nationalities.

The tides have ebbed and flowed regarding social work and the communities served. Social work has maintained the emphasis on direct practice. However, advocacy within the profession has increasingly exposed the need to understand that all services are connected to macro realities—laws, regulations, organizational policies, mission statements, and the political inclination toward social injustice. The move to promote social justice and human rights encourages personal awareness, endorses citizen participation, and compels the supervision of social work leadership.

This text provides a framework for examining the history of oppression that perpetuates contemporary social divisions and maintains social injustice. The content promotes personal assessment regarding social work values of appreciating diversity, and it offers pathways for collaboration and capacity building across disciplines and with community citizens to advance change that fosters justice and well-being.

Multicultural socialization provides information and resources that inform of strengths and partnerships that work to help individuals and families develop potential and participate in our communities to benefit all of us. These goals derive from social work values and human rights.

The chapters encourage attention to these parameters:
- Multicultural history
- Cultural strengths
- Self-awareness and critical thinking
- Culturally affirming resources and strategies translated into information for service users
- Collaboration and service planning across micro, mezzo, and macro dimensions
- Prevention services across health populations
- Social justice advocacy and citizen participation

The larger view of transactions and interactions in the social environment suggests that not only would people of excluded groups benefit from an expanded provision of multicultural socialization, but so would members of the dominant cultural group. Integrating multi-cultural resources in communications in families, across school districts, and with service consumers can help promote healthy dynamics. College and graduate students often conclude that primary and secondary education are most important for disseminating multiple perspectives and cultural strengths.

From Oppression to Inclusion: Social Workers Advancing Change presents a platform to explore cultural strengths before colonization and assess one's awareness of multiple and multicultural perspectives. This base encourages students to evaluate the statistics of disparities and policies that stress and often penalize service users. Local, national, and international examples point to the various contexts that illustrate ways many persons are or become vulnerable to economic and social challenges.

The chapters may be used in totality or individually to spark conversations, raise questions, and facilitate further inquiry of content that can be used to teach social work practice, planning, and social policy analysis, as well as design approaches to enhance service-user confidence and performance.

Social work professional values and skills, identity perspectives of the populations we work with, and social and institutional structural realities form the environment within which we work.

Examples of literature, film, video, poems, music, and art by persons of various identity groups contribute to expanding mindsets to appreciate diversity. Used as a basis for critical thinking, conversations, lessons, and session planning with diverse and monocultural individuals, families, and groups, these examples foster information literacy.

Social workers and other helping professionals are responding to the contemporary challenges that exist. Through networking, partnerships, collaboration, and creativity, we have many opportunities to translate information and research, as well as advocate to enhance learning and advance change.

Acknowledgments

This project is the result of decades of experiences and observations of families, friends and foes, and other ordinary citizens in the context of multicultural survival. Workers, parents, teachers, students, and children further illustrate the participants in this social, political, and economic environment.

I am grateful to Naijian Zhang for steering me to this path, for the initial and subsequent support of Kassie Graves, the Acquisitions Editor, Joshua Perigo, at Sage, and the review of the early manuscript by my friends and colleagues, Janis Coombs Reid and Ann A. Abbott. The ongoing comments, questions and resources contributed by students and colleagues at West Chester University and my committee colleagues of the Columbia University School of Social Work alumni groups, including Jenn March, Brenda Sherman, and Mark Laster, have been especially meaningful.

Finally, I appreciate the editorial assistance of Amy Harris, and the expertise of Amy Smith and her team at Cognella who have brought this project to fruition.

PART I

Recognizing the Range of Identity Perspectives

There are 7.2 billion humans on our planet Earth. Social workers around the world are organized to assist people in their efforts to survive and thrive. Anthropologists have explored who people are by engaging with them to identify customs that are used to provide for and sustain themselves. People identify themselves in unique ways which do not fit into the generalized convenience categories presented by officials. These have usually been determined in ways to keep wealth and power by some and to exclude others. Social constructions promote minimal frames of description and tend to promote negative impressions of peoples who seem different. Critically thinking about the basic needs for food and shelter, and connections to family urge social work to appreciate all humanity and respect who they say they are. Exposure to the rich histories of cultural ancestry help us appreciate the range of identity perspectives.

CHAPTER 1

Social Work and Social Justice
Considering the Frames of Reference

CHAPTER OVERVIEW

This chapter introduces the context of the book: the purpose of the dialectic, the competencies to be addressed, and the social messages resulting from a history of oppression of Native Americans and enslaved Africans. Students will be expected to engage in reflection and conversations that address this past and consider potential pathways for improving services in diverse contemporary social environments.

LEARNING OBJECTIVES

- Social Work respects all individuals and communities.
- Persons pursuing social work credentials acknowledge the learning process to be interactive and engaging with diverse persons and communities.
- Social work practice builds on multicultural knowledge, critical thinking, reflection, and dialogue.

Benchmark: Students should be able to identify how social work competencies build interpersonal and task centered skills.

Helena is an 18-year-old graduate of a Midwestern high school in a suburban town of about 5 million people. Her high school of 500 students included about 75 students of visibly diverse adolescents. The curriculum was traditional, and the clubs she participated in were mostly composed of her cultural peers. She is a member of an all-white church. Some of her family members make derogatory comments about other people. Helena is aware of families in her community who have lower incomes and are often food insecure. She volunteers at the food bank. She wants to be a social worker to help people.

STUDENT SCENARIO 1

SOCIAL WORK AND SOCIAL JUSTICE

The profession of Social Work and the dynamics of Social Justice are inextricably linked because of the goals of addressing social challenges and upholding humanity. Reisch (2014) reviews the profession's evolving and expanded dialogue of multiple concepts, complex connections, and often contentious perspectives regarding the why and how of promoting social justice within existing institutional and political systems.

Social work and social justice are joined as a profession and a dynamic that impacts the value of humans. As the profession trudges through standards setting, discussion, research, practice, evaluation, and commentaries, it grows in ways that confront the challenges faced by those affected by crisis and vulnerable life circumstances, as well as incidents of daily aggressions. The examination of social work within a framework that promotes just, transparent, and democratic procedures presents a process established on paradigms that exclude many based on traditionally set labels and notions about other people. Becoming more legitimate as a purveyor of helpful change requires collaboration across group memberships, exploration of previous and contemporary opinions, and the inclusion of the broad array of people and perspectives.

Júlíusdóttir (2006) considers this development to represent the maturing of the social work profession.

SOCIAL JUSTICE AS A VALUE

Inequality exists and has created disparities that occur within social categories of race, gender, class, sexuality, nationality, and physical ability (Dill & Zambrana, 2009). The range of fields that social workers engage in practice is influenced by the value of social justice elements and efforts to overcome the disparate outcomes. For example, substance-use ideas of abstinence or nothing have been sidelined by options that address rigid labeling by considering more flexible and hopeful approaches. *Recovery* is the term that illuminates the step-by-step process of moving along a path of less frequent use of substances, thoughtful reflection of life's past and current episodes, and services that examine and appreciate historical trauma or adverse experiences on micro and macro levels. Coping methods that do less harm to one's body and social relationships are acknowledged and may be encouraged.

Another example of social work's value of context and justice is the use of psychiatric research that builds on knowledge of the brain and recognizes the impact of place and environment on brain architecture. The paths to schizophrenia and other diagnoses and the processes of genetics, family stress, and interactional dynamics encourage awareness of culture and biology within broad *environmental contexts* that connect intersectional identities (Stevens-Watkins, Perry, Pullen, Jewell, & Oser, 2014; Sutton & Kemp, 2011). These require understanding and skill development for multifaceted interventions. Appreciating the strengths in these examples rather than judging behaviors that don't fit into traditional paradigms offers more opportunities and fewer constraints on individual, natural, and community pathways for well-being. According to Putrie (2014), a mantra that is used more now is "What happened to you?" rather than "What is wrong with you?"

The contributions of social workers, other helping professionals, and researchers of various backgrounds and areas of interest are reframing, reconceptualizing, and expanding research— and thereby encouraging the *inclusion* of views and opinions largely ignored in traditional paradigms and networks. While most approaches are not entirely new, policy promotion for citizen participation in the planning and implementation process are continuing and have resulted in client-centered models of service delivery.

Exposure to perspectives about context and experience may offer opposing views yet create opportunities to mull ideas, consider options, and critically reflect on life. *Critical thinking* provides steps to consider alternative ways of knowing. The process also involves recognizing the emotions that lurk in our observations. As Freire (1997) has proposed, dialogue can be used to increase awareness of conditions impacting humanity and to progress through an engagement process to liberate communities. Social work pursues social and economic justice through micro and macro transactions and collaborative relationships.

The Council on Social Work Education's (CSWE) Educational Policy Accreditation Standards (EPAS, 2015) address these concepts. As the social work profession evolves, these educational elements are emphasized:

- Use critical thinking to inform and communicate professional judgments.
- Engage diversity and difference in practice.
- Advance human rights and social and economic justice.
- Apply knowledge of human behavior and the social environment.

The CSWE competencies are addressed within the chapters of this book (see Figure 1.1).

COMPETENCY	CHAPTER
1: Demonstrate ethical and professional behavior.	Chapters 1, 4, 9
2: Engage diversity and difference in practice.	Chapters 1, 2, 6, 13
3: Advance human rights and social, economic, and environmental justice.	Chapters 1, 4, 5, 9, 13
4: Engage in practice-informed research and research-informed practice.	Chapters 10, 11, 12
5: Engage in policy practice.	Chapters 8, 9, 13
6: Engage with individuals, families, groups, organizations, and communities.	Chapter 10
7: Assess individuals, families, groups, organizations, and communities.	Chapters 6, 10, 11, 12

FIGURE 1.1   Competencies Addressed in Chapters

COMPETENCY	CHAPTER
8: Intervene with individuals, families, groups, organizations, and communities.	Chapters 9, 11, 12, 13
9: Evaluate practice with individuals, families, groups, organizations, and communities.	Chapters 5, 7, 8, 9

This chapter introduces the broad context, the purpose of the dialectic, and the socialization that springs from the history and trauma of oppression, especially of Native Americans and enslaved Africans. The absence of the beauty of the Native American lifestyles before Columbus and the Moorish and African art, science, and social arrangements that have been buried and vehemently denied, is raised for consideration as sources of strength. Change.org (2014) noted the need for this information in a petition. Readers are asked to engage in critical reflection and conversations that address this past and consider potential pathways for integrating inclusive knowledge.

SOCIAL WORK AS AN INSTITUTION

Social work has been viewed as a representative of the institutional structure. Although the history suggests the connection of services to immigrants and persons challenged by community and family circumstances, a view of professional services tends to associate the work to traditional formal and informal boundaries. Several perspectives (Courtney & Specht, 1994; Wakefield, 1997) focus on the social control of institutions and the private practice goals of social workers. The institutional culture continues to impose controlling parameters. For example, agencies that continue to offer service hours only during the day without any evening or weekend slots speaks to addressing the needs of staff rather than consumers. Another example is the frequent absence of educational information about mental health diagnoses and complementary resources to consumers and their families. Information is often held by the institution rather than shared to benefit understanding.

Despite these sources of concern, members of the social work profession have continuously made efforts to consider and evaluate the pros and cons of the status and effectiveness of service delivery. The National Association of Social Workers (NASW) provides the NASW Code of Ethics that guides social work practice. The International Federation of Social Work (IFSW) also promotes ethical principles and human rights. Social work professionals are committed to follow protocols and educate students to do so to continuously learn, enhance our methods, and improve our services for the communities we serve. Social work is the practice of methods and techniques to engage with others for collaboration, problem-solving, skill development, and advocacy to benefit the social welfare of members of society, especially those needing the support of a social welfare system.

In a recent speech by Ana Lima (2017), president of International Federation of Social Work Europe, her remarks emphasized that social work is committed to defending people's rights. She noted that the future of fellow citizens depends on social work to seek a balance between human and social development and economic development.

As the social work profession evolves, promoting consumer and service-user capacity to represent social issues in the civic arena supports the inclusion of diverse voices and concepts and sustains the social work institution.

WHAT IS THE DIALECTIC OF OPPRESSION TO LIBERATION?

The *dialectic* is the mental, emotional, and cognitive process of reviewing ideas about the multiple concepts related to social justice with ongoing feedback and reflection. The social work profession values fair, just, and equitable paths for social and economic opportunities that support civil and human rights. Awareness of the extent of *oppression* for many diverse ethnic groups; lesbian, gay, bisexual, transgender, and intersex persons; those challenged by physical, emotional, and learning variations; many immigrants; and those with intersectional identities, is fundamental to engaging and developing relationships that motivate and support efforts to enhance well-being for all.

The dialectic of oppression to liberation is the process of ongoing review, evaluation, discussion, policy analysis, and policy modification to address the challenges of including multicultural voices for planning and implementing progressive steps for citizens using services or in need of assistance. By viewing the existing landscape of the social environment, we are aware of the separation and segregation of institutional and personal spaces. As we proceed in addressing social justice issues, tackling the challenges and obstacles that exist involve listening to perspectives that view issues in different ways. Various new viewpoints are often misunderstood by some participants. Tracing the sources of perspectives and integrating diverse information begins the student's journey of gathering knowledge, processing information, reflecting, and discussing the various views in order to gain insight.

The dialectic of oppression to liberation involves reading about the history of the world and the specifics of oppressive conditions and situations; discussing the multiple perspectives of what happened and what is going on now; analyzing the impact of the realities; and assessing strategies for embracing the diverse social landscape to assist people to cope, thrive, and progress toward potential.

The dialectic of oppression to liberation involves reading and engaging one another in the classroom, in-service settings, and in other forums to talk about and listen to reactions to information about oppressive situations and circumstances. This process requires *listening* to our inner voices, our intuitions, and those of others, as well as *developing* relationships that allow us to share and to work together to address the systems that often do more harm than good.

The process of dialogue is framed by theoretical considerations in moving through sequential and collateral phases for learning and change.

COMPONENTS OF THE DIALECTICAL PROCESS

The process of the dialectic of oppression and liberation involves stages. These include the reading of multiple perspectives, processing the information, reacting, critical thinking, reflecting, and dialoguing. Core themes include *oppression, restricted opportunity, privilege,* and *capacity building.* The dialectic involves engaging in conversations with colleagues, class-mates, community agents, activists, leaders, and consumers of various identities to broaden awareness and develop capacity to remedy tremendous obstacles. The goal is to improve democratic participation in decision-making to assist people to care for themselves, their families, and communities.

The basics of collaboration among individuals, groups, and organizations include bringing self-awareness and respect for others, both of which foster inclusion. Designing strategies for this process requires examining situations from multiple dimensions. Several skills are needed for the different participants and stakeholders:

- *Self-awareness* involves recognizing one's prejudices, biases, messages received, and messages shared and acknowledging the various perspectives that exist among the millions of citizens in the United States who do not accept narrow traditional media stories.
- *Respect for others* recognizes the value of people.
- *Ethical considerations* present ideas about what is right or wrong.
- *Critical thinking* is the process of selecting diverse perspectives, alternative paradigms, and research, considering their merits and limitations; connecting these ideas to one's own interpretations; and organizing a contemporary stance.
- *Advocacy* is promoting—through voice and action—attention to social justice concerns.
- *Capacity building* is working together to provide encouragement, informa-tion, resources, hope, and skills to establish meaningful and effective ways to achieve potential.

Students develop these skills in pursuing the social work curriculum and interacting with peers, faculty, agency professionals, and service users.

THEORIES

Using the theory of contextual fluidity as a standpoint, social work faces an ever-increasing panorama of people, perspectives, relationships, and problem-solving opportunities. This interpretation of the ecosystem involves emerging ideas of best practices, brain research, collaboration, prevention, and advocacy. Contextual fluidity accepts that behaviors and interactions occur across systems in non-predetermined ways, sometimes spontaneous, sometimes planned.

The parameters of context urge understanding of where we came from, contemporary cir-cumstances, and a need to be in the moment for understanding those with whom we have or are creating relationships. At the same time, workers should be informed of the forecast of trends and needs, with an emphasis on service evaluation, practice opportunities, and policy outcomes that may lead to higher levels of social and collective liberation.

Several theories may be used to help explain environmental, structural, and personal dynamics of oppression, discrimination, and progressive liberation. These are complex issues, and no single explanation provides a clear and complete picture. Oppression and reactions to it are complicated.

- **Contextual fluidity** describes awareness that incorporates the myriad circumstances and flow of environment and identity.
- **Ecosystems** acknowledge the interactions and transactions between and among subunits of our environments.
- **Restricted opportunity** describes the impact of discriminatory structures and actions.
- **Social construction** illustrates rigid perspectives connected to messages and experiences that tend not to include awareness of shifting or fluid identities and realities. Social construction theory denotes an emphasis on stereotypes and traditional views of people.
- **Structural functional theory** explains the tendency for organizations and systems to operate in ways that maintain the status quo and often penalize people who stand outside the box.
- **Social exchange theory** applies notions of fairness and win–win strategies in addressing social welfare issues. This theory promotes working with others.
-

Concepts related to the expanding acknowledgement of diversity include the following:

- **Identity** is used in helping to construct the multiple ways in which we see ourselves.
- **Ethnic sensitivity** is a term used by social workers in the early move away from the term *color blindness*.
- **Cultural competence** evaluates a state of awareness of the variations of cultural dynamics.
- **Cultural humility** addresses ethnocentrism and informs one's recognition of self on par with others.
- **Cultural relevance** accepts the significance of culture in connection to matters at hand.
- **Resilience** identifies mood, behaviors, and mindsets that progress in the face of ongoing or imminent struggles.
- **Self-determination** presents the faces of perseverance.
- **Hope** is the sense of optimism that moves toward the future.
- **Liberation** is the dual process of self-awareness and social participation to reduce and eliminate discriminatory, prejudicial, and minimizing attitudes, policies, and structures.
- **Change** is the flow of process from one state of being, awareness, and socialization to another.

Social work continues to evolve from traditional paradigms that narrowly value normalcy of white nuclear families and institutions that emphasize judgment and punishment to the broader awareness of the strengths that diverse people have used to navigate that system.

Interpretations of the social environment by analysts with bicultural experience are more included in the evaluation and development of services that welcome all persons, families, groups, organizations, and communities.

Competencies anticipated as a result of exploring multiple perspectives include foundation behaviors involving professional behaviors and oral and written communication skills (CSWE, 2015). The other significant competencies that flow from the orientation to inclusion include understanding one's intrinsic biases (Ross, 2016), gathering information about how institutions have operationalized oppressive structures and moved forward to advance social and economic justice, and human rights (CSWE, 2015).

The dialectical discourse encourages conversations across concepts and through critical thinking urges civic participation and helps develop understanding. Group work is an essential method in this learning process and also in the work of social engagement and development. It is through peer-to-peer conversations that people join, participate, and move from isolation to association. This process involves steps that come easily for some and not so easily for others.

IMPACT OF PHILOSOPHY THAT HOLDS PEOPLE IN SUBJECTION

> "Even when we feel we can't change things, it is important to have awareness
> of what has happened." —Alice Walker

Understanding the broad scope of history that comes before the colonies existed is important in appreciating the long view of human existence and development. The concept of oppression is tied to several ideas about being restrained as human beings and manipulated by social groups for the advantage of some over others. The history provided in typical elementary and high school classrooms has emphasized the idea of manifest destiny for the colonizers. *Manifest destiny* was a term used by John Sullivan in an 1845 article about annexing Texas. It essentially justified the expansion of the United States from the East to the West Coast by Indian removal and war with Mexico (History.com Staff, 2010). As this attitude of providential destiny grew, it normalized subjugation. However, there is another perspective that contests that idea and presents history from a broader and less ethnocentric viewpoint. That view denounces the violence associated with this destiny and addresses the human costs of decisions made by politicians and businessmen (Zinn, 2003).

THE MACRO CONTEXT

The macro context has a long view of historical and contemporary parameters. It presents points of reference that may or may not be acceptable to some readers, yet establishes themes that drive conceptualizing social issues. Let's establish a timeline.

World history documents the presence of humans for a very long time. Howell (2015) reports that humans have been around about 6 million years. Some research notes the presence of

Syrian Dynasty	Moors in Spain	Indigenous Civilizations	C.Columbus	Emancipation Proclamation	Depression
113 BCE	AD	1200	1492	1866	1930

Voting rights	War on drugs	Legalizing drugs	Sentencing reform
1965	1971	2014	2015

FIGURE 1.2

black and white Syrians in 113 BCE (M'Bantu, 2012). "The mysterious Olmec civilization prospered in Pre-Classical (Formative) Mesoamerica from c. 1200 BCE (Before the Common Era) to c. 400 BCE and is generally considered the forerunner of all subsequent Mesoamerican cultures such as the Maya and Aztec" (Cartwright, 2013, p. 1). Evidence of the Olmec describes the presence of African traders on the North and South American continents centuries before the colonists (Chengu, 2014; Coe, 1968). The colossal heads discovered in Mexico portrayed people with Negroid features.

Davidson (1966) describes the African genius he observed on several trips to Africa and extensive research on African kingdoms. Presenting evidence of unity, social charters, and other systems, he noted the insurgence of colonial industries that persisted in ways the existing societies could not overcome (Davidson, 1969).

Similarly, Chinese dynasties are reported to have been active since circa 2100 to1600 BCE (Columbia.edu, 2015; Gascoigne, 2003). *The Art of War* (Sun Tzu, circa 512 BC) establishes the presence of conflict, competition, and strategic interventions for thousands of years. The Terracotta Army, discovered in 1974 by a Chinese farmer, was dug up in rural China. It depicted a huge army with soldiers of various hues buried with the emperor from 210 to 209 BCE and whose purpose was to protect the emperor in his afterlife (Larmer, 2012).

Examples of ancient spiritual rituals, social arrangements and codes of conduct such as the Maat principle of ancient Africa, and the indigenous Native American people living harmoniously as a residential population (Dunbar-Ortiz, 2014) are not included in the usual history books. These brief examples of ancient history reveal civilizations and systems of mutual aid and trade that existed well before the presence of Columbus and European colonists.

There is much uncovered evidence of life on planet Earth over these millions (Ahlberg & Bennet, 2017) of years. Blumenthal (2015) recently reported on earthworks discovered in a 2007 Google satellite view of an area near Kazakhstan, a former Soviet republic that shares a border with China. There are figures built along straight lines on elevations, and early theories suggest they may be horizontal observatories to track the movements of the rising sun (Blumenthal, 2015).

Reports of the reasons and methods for the pyramids in Egypt and their architecture continue to be scrutinized but do offer evidence of sophisticated mathematics and astronomy and beliefs that tie life on planet Earth to connections with other bodies in the universe (Dash, 2015; Van Sertima, 1997).

It is this broad view of the rich heritage that many people of color are aware of that provides strength, and that communities rely on, that Western culture has ignored. There are other sources of information of which many may not be aware. The history that is presented to the world is so limited. Traditional media has associated negative stereotypes as rationales for terror and punishment of people who don't look like Europeans. This socialization—especially through educational institutions—has minimized historical traumas that remain in the minds and hearts of persons excluded from the social and economic growth of the time.

As more attention is drawn to multiple sources of historic information, educational curricula modifications are occurring. Recent changes in the Advanced Placement (AP) curriculum in high schools demonstrate the inclusion of historical truths. The College Board agrees that students taking a college-level history course should be exposed to multiple perspectives and viewpoints in the classroom. AP history courses are in the process of being redesigned to include increased coverage of Native American social systems and learning objectives that address interaction between Europe and the world, as well as consideration of multicultural perspectives throughout (personal correspondence, Thurber, 2015).

Substantive curriculum changes across disciplines that include historical truths and perspectives of multicultural authors and researchers can help students across grade levels become more informed and supportive of one another despite the past emphasis on exclusionary practices (Grant & Sleeter, 2013; Lee & Buxton, 2010). There are opportunities to seek and consider many more dimensions of knowledge than those to which we have been presented or exposed.

THE MICRO CONTEXT

Social welfare has a long history that includes charity-based approaches, needs-based approaches, and—more recently—rights-based approaches (Libal, Berthold, Thomas & Healy, 2014). Policies connected to contemporary service delivery spring from the early 1900s when women-run orphanages shifted toward male-run agencies that placed needy children in "home-placing agencies" managed by men (Encyclopedia of Children & Childhood in History & Society. (2015). Wh–Z (and other topics). Retrieved from http://www.faqs.org/childhood/Wh-Z-and-other-topics/White-House-Conferences-on-Children.html). It is within this 115-year time frame that we focus on as the beginning and evolving structure of the social work profession.

During this time, traditional and stereotypical frames of reference about diverse populations have tended to shape exclusive rather that inclusive policies and service systems.

Figure 1.3 offers an illustration of distinction between national, state, local, and personal-space communities. This separation is connected to the segregation that has historically informed residential patterns and the location of social and mental health services in the United States. By recognizing this environmental picture, we identify the situational context within which educators, practitioners, students, service users, and citizens live and negotiate daily activities. While the scenario does look segregated, there is, in fact, quite a mix of visible and invisible vibrations within and between the contexts. Becoming aware of these helps to evaluate and proceed.

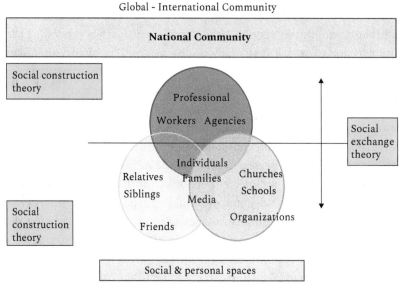

FIGURE 1.3   Social Environment: Segregated Spaces

THE ETHICS OF SOCIAL TRANSFORMATION

As we study what has been and engage in continuing work toward liberation from past constraints on identity and value, the use of evaluation research, self-assessment, and political activism take more prominent roles. Program evaluation that addresses contextual realities and includes potential service users can direct attention to needed policy modifications. In taking another look at the history that is bringing recognition of social injustice and a desire for moving forward, acknowledging human rights is required.

The projection of trends from current and evolving policies offers at least two potential scenarios. Choosing the one based on strengthening families; improving education; providing communication about nutrition, sexuality, other ongoing dynamics; and incorporating multicultural resources to build confidence and esteem among more children at an earlier age seems the priority. Funding to enhance learning at home and at school can assist families through conversations about relationships, family planning, financial planning, and public health. These elements support a prevention framework.

Social transformation is the movement from one state of affairs to another, presumably for improvements. Generally, social science understands this to be a progressive move in cultural dynamics from older-system traditions and addresses technology, economics, and politics (UNESCO.org, n.d.). The expectation is that the process should work to protect local and national communities against negative consequences of global change. However, there will be some upheaval of traditional status. An element of this movement involves how we see one another.

IDENTITIES ARE COMPLEX

In the construction of a comprehensive view of identity, Wetherell and Mohanty (2012) bring forth the huge frame of identity studies. The concepts of "names and looks," divisive categories, subjective interpretations, fluidity, and others contribute to academic resistance and discomfort regarding identity discourses. The reality of *identity* is complex. Some of us have knowledge of a diverse ancestral heritage and the strengths that come from that. Some perceive identity in the traditional binary formulation.

The binary view identifies two basic categories (i.e., Black and White, female and male). Others may perceive identity based on actions and behaviors that have occurred—some forced upon us and some entertained through curiosity. Identity realities involve a range of experience in our communities (Blow, 2014). Some communities may contain high diversity. Some smaller communities may be more homogeneous, but on a regional scale, diversity may increase. Inclusion involves learning more about one another and working on improving the democratic operation of our country. Pateman (1970) suggested that employing multiple opportunities to become more educated citizens and participate in our communities would likely benefit us all.

PREJUDICE

A traditional form of understanding identity is defined by the term *prejudice*. This understanding may be limited by a monocultural description of who is who. The nature of prejudice is *intrinsic*. It may exist even when we may think it does not. To move forward in thinking about transformation, it is essential to consider the nature of prejudice and its presence in how we operate. As a parallel to identity, some people are tied to messages from family and friends that are ethnocentrically based and that are connected to views of value and less value among humans. If we posit this, then those who are more tied to the appreciation of diversity are likely to be less prejudiced against those who may not look like them. Arriving at this conclusion is likely to occur through a process of experiences, conversations, education, reading, and work with diverse types of people and working on oneself.

According to Suzanne Pharr (2010), one of the key points in moving toward liberation is the need for progressive democracy. This involves "seeking ways to bring people together to work on common causes across differences" (p. 592). So the ethics of social transformation requires honestly confronting prejudices, greed, conflict, and the related variables that would occur in shifting focus from individual gain to more emphasis on benefits for the collection of families that comprise our communities. In the past, these changes have often been more incremental. In today's world, there is speculation that quick and unexpected change is occurring (West, 2016) and therefore impacting how individuals and communities adapt.

STEPS IN THIS PROCESS

Observations of people moving from views of people based on stereotypes to broader recognition of the broad range of people and personalities across groups tends to involve several characteristics:

- *Personal work.* Shifting gears for this requires increasing self-awareness and personal responsibility in transacting with others. This may mean calling oneself out with respect to behaviors that do not support, engage, or motivate for the greater good and calling out others. This is tricky and risky business; it can be scary.

While cultural competence urges starting with a focus on one's identity and working on building one's ability to listen to and understand people that we work with, Yan and Wong (2005) urge us to go steps farther. They propose that there is the need to "cocreate new meanings and relationships" across cultures (p. 186). Focusing on the difficulty associated with suspending one's cultural training, they point out contradictions in the cultural competence model. Pointing out the one-sided simplification of the existing cultural competence model, their perspective adds the reactions of the client to a more-informed worker into the process of transformation. This personal work includes the notion of cultural humility and is especially needed by helping professionals. It has also been proposed as a needed skill for workers in the Smart Machine Age (SMA) (Hess & Ludwig, 2017). Acknowledging the SMA as potentially as disruptive as the Industrial Revolution was, in its time, examining how to encompass being humble versus being arrogant (p. 15).

- *Cultural humility.* Intentional self-work is needed by diverse and white psychologists and other helping professionals working with diverse populations. Described by Gallardo (2014), cultural humility demonstrates self-work required to become more engaging, respectful, and effective in interpersonal communication and collaborative tasks. As a helping professional, a humble mindset brings a space for patience, listening, and mutual appreciation for the humanity of our work.

These foundation steps emphasize inclusion of diverse citizens and ideas in planning and developing more socially and economically just policies and move us to the step for a broadened perspective.

- *Community engagement.* Since civics has been removed from many school curricula unless families promote participation in community organizations, it is often left to people to discern this on their own. Social workers have a role in developing community relationships and in assisting service users coming together for the good of the community. Unfortunately, some local leaders may not pay attention to this component of leader qualities that speak to accountability to all.
- *Multicultural and prevention research.* This continues to be less funded than traditional research endeavors. The NIH Reporter (2015) is an online tool that provides access to reports, data, and analyses of National Institute of Health (NIH) research activities, including information on NIH expenditures and the results of NIH-supported research. Quick searches of the NIH Reporter show the range of projects that may address some cultural components or the use of peers in providing services. The impact of these efforts requires ongoing observation and evaluation.

Social work research that integrates multicultural perspectives, researchers, communities, and questions that address concerns of people of color, women, lesbians, gay men, bisexual and transgender persons, low-wealth groups, and persons often excluded from workforce opportunities by physical health and emotional challenges is critical to improving the effectiveness of service delivery systems. This kind of research requires collaboration and protocols that are continuously critically reflective, democratic, and sustainable of efforts toward social justice. According to a team of authors (Uehara et al., 1996), "the ultimate goal of multicultural social work practice and education is social justice and the transformation of contemporary sociocultural structures and processes that support injustice and inequality" (p. 614). Yet this remains limited.

- *Leadership.* In several domains, leadership is necessary to move toward the 22nd century. With projections of increasing demographics of older and more multicultural and multiracial populations (Shrestha & Heisler, 2011), it is likely that political and intellectual discourse will continue to be contentious. Research and management leadership in the social sector will play critical roles in the evolving scenarios. McKinsey's recent survey of nonprofit leaders revealed leadership teams lacking capabilities to be "effective in response to fast-changing demands" (Callahan, Gardner, Mendonca, & Scott, 2014). Leadership that simultaneously promotes enhanced performance by managers and service users in social arenas is critical.

EXAMPLE FOR CRITICAL THINKING

In exploring the potential transformation toward more inclusion, one area of examination is child welfare. Social work has a checkered image in the identity development of children who have experienced living in foster care arrangements. The authors of *Childhood, Youth, and Social Work in Transformation: Implications for Policy and Practice* (Nybell, Shook, & Finn, 2009) "present information that is chilling as we consider the impact of environment on identity development." The authors suggest irony in that current systems and the mid-19th-century industrialism both rely on the child for profit, one as a client and the other as a "homeless," outcast child. The criminal justice system has been analyzed to provide parallels and similar economic emphases (Alexander, 2012). The context this example offers for us is to consider then, now, and what is possible.

INFORMATION PROCESSING

Moving from the past to the future requires reading, thinking, and reflecting. The brain is considered to be the most sophisticated information-processing device there is. The Massachusetts Institute of Technology (MIT) introduces us to their courses on the brain and neuroscience in this way (MIT Open Courseware, 2017). Information processing theory, pioneered by Alan Mathison, examines how people select, attend to, and internalize information and subsequently use it in their behaviors or in making decisions (Kantowitz, 1974). Shiffrin and Schneider (1977) expand this process to include two modes—automatic and controlled—and link them to search and attention. Our framework for inclusion builds on a learning structure that directs attention to multiple and sometimes unavailable or underused information and encourages focusing on it (Dean & Fornaciari, 2014).

The review of several perspectives for consideration and analysis, discussion, reflection, and memory are steps in processing information that take us from existing ideas about oppression and privilege to views that may be somewhat broadened. There is a broad range of research regarding information processing theory that addresses cognitive and emotional elements and the stages of these processes over time (Kosslyn & Rosenberg, 2010). Considering critical thinking as a component brings in our understanding of ourselves, the people we work with, the people we serve, and the environments we all come from and live in. This background helps us appreciate the various routes that develop for recovery and capacity building. For our purposes, the steps in information processing build on the transformation process and include dialogue, reflection, meditation, critical thinking, and problem-solving. At the same time of the personal work, there is also the requirement for communication with others.

SOCIAL EXCLUSION AND MARGINALIZATION

Social exclusion and marginalization of people has been promoted through prejudicial attitudes (Van Wormer, 2004) that may separate and involve isolation. Laws, legislation, and policies regarding criminal justice, education, and housing have particularly contributed to restricted opportunities and obstacles to inclusion.

Higginbotham (1998) notes in *Shades of Freedom* the notion of racial inferiority was used by white colonists to subjugate African and Native descendants and to establish legal structures that maintained obstacles to freedom and opportunities. This is the basis for addressing social justice issues, as the NASW mission notes (NASW, 2017). The Black Codes (DuBois, 2014), an early set of regulations against freed slaves, prohibited education, prohibited assistance through education and employment, and obstructed people from working together to improve conditions for themselves. Subsequently, institutions that were established in their communities were denied resources.

Simultaneously, the limitations of many segregated educational systems often resulted in lower skills in abstract thinking and writing skills, and other academic performance. The explanations for this are complex and play out in black and white schools. Schmoker (2011) offers an evaluation of the limitations of academic rigor at the elementary school level. Second graders should be exposed to multicultural perspectives—should be required to write about the material, reflect on it, discuss it, and write on it again. The broader view requires acknowledging the dual levels of competency generated by invested educators on the one hand, but too often, teacher education does not actively address multicultural resources, recruitment, or multidimensional preparation (Cheruvu, Souto-Manning, Lencl, & Chin-Culubaquib, 2015; Cook, 2015; Milner & Laughter, 2015). The system should be held accountable. Looking forward to capacity building requires a foundation of academic, task, interpersonal, and communication skills, and multicultural resources.

MOVING BEYOND EXCLUSION AND SEGREGATION

Understanding oppression and privilege in the educational system assists in tapping into pedagogy that provides information for learning through complex intersectional dynamics.

Reading, thinking, and pondering lays a foundation for reflection, asking questions, contemplating reactions, and perhaps modifying perceptions in ways that inculcate revising ideas and ultimately policy options.

The reading, thinking, and pondering path for information processing is one that exists but may operate somewhat differently for young traditional students (those with limited work experience), students who have substantial work experience before beginning a graduate program, nontraditional students, and those students whose academic skills have been developed in less-than-rigorous institutions. This process is important for the personal, family, and professional development of students of the helping professions. It should also be available to people with whom we work, the service users. Consumers require exposure to learning to engage in dialogue, reflect, meditate, and participate in understanding the issues they are facing and the steps of recovery. The range and depth of the information contributes to the substance of the dialogue that builds capacity to tackle challenges. This involves practitioner skills that communicate the dynamics of this process and incorporates the trajectory noted in Figure 1.4.

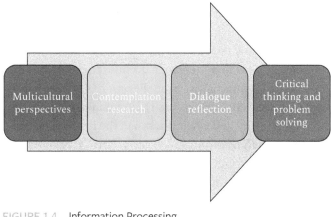

FIGURE 1.4   Information Processing

THE SOCIAL ENVIRONMENT FOR INCLUSION

The negative and stereotypical narrative is not the only narrative. The social environment contains multiple examples of strong social interactions that have supported people in surviving unacceptable situations and narrow paradigms. Understanding these ideas is fundamental to viewing the landscape of social work and efforts to continually progress toward enhanced civil and human rights.

Promoting the concept of inclusion requires considering the broader network and analysis of the field. If the network is limited by the absence of citizen participants at significant preparation points, strengthening it as a support system urges improving relationships for information development, knowledge sharing, and feedback.

The ecological framework presents a broad view of the systems and subsystems that exist in our environment. *Contextual fluidity* should help us understand the reality of how these components touch one another in history, in the current moments, and potentially in future times. The broadest dimension of environment must include the impact of the pollution of the soil, air, and water on our health. The use of toxic chemicals affects the safety of food. Diminishing quality of the air and water creates health hazards (Carson, 2002). Social work is concerned about environmental justice (Beltrán, 2016).

Restricted opportunity is the dynamic that has been shaped by prejudice, discrimination, and institutional structures and practices. Inclusion offers opportunities to become involved and to share information, feelings, actions through social exchanges that value fairness, righteousness, justice, and the creation of economic means for more of us.

The realities of exclusion, quality, and access across multicultural groups and locations have been addressed by individuals and families through generations. Social work is pursuing evidence, innovation, and collaboration to advocate, intervene, and demonstrate steps to move forward, improving prosperity.

INDIVIDUAL AND COMMUNITY PERSISTENCE AND FORTITUDE

The range and wealth of writing cannot be comprised into any one simple body of work. The invitation is to be aware of this wealth and be encouraged to seek materials from many sources to connect to communities and enhance understanding.

Points of view and stories that counter the "white racial frame" (Feagin, 2013) will be explored in advancing inclusion. Feagin has offered a significant view of racial ethnic theory in the United States. He argues that to understand American racism the analysis must focus on the what, why, and who rather than the inadequate concepts like prejudice, bias, stereotyping, and intolerance (Yancey & Feagin, 2015). He points out these concepts are based on white social scientists' views that have been connected to individual racial issues. He notes that the more informed analysis comes from African American analysts who have studied institutional and systemic structures in a more sustained fashion over time. He attributes some of this body of knowledge as coming from W. E. B. DuBois, Stokely Carmichael, Charles Hamilton, and others. Work by researchers of Native Americans descent, i.e., Tallbear and Sampson, and Latino descent such as Delgado, Aponte, and Gallardo, should be added to this list as the conversations about systemic discrimination and criteria for evaluation are expanded. Hardy (2016) has also added his substantial voice that highlights the knowledge people of color have about white behaviors, the impact of racial trauma, and the inclusion of this knowledge in strategies to shape theory and practice for health and human services.

LET'S EXPLORE!

Addressing this background lays the foundation for exploring and examining elements of socialization practices in the United States that promote the disparate side of the structural dynamics and restrict opportunities. To move forward, critically assessing the socialization process and including the strengths side can motivate interpretations and applications that support inclusion. The social work profession continues to evolve in recognizing multiple and intersectional social identities, seeing systemic barriers to realizing potential among citizens, identifying strategies to understand cultural dynamics, and participating in advocacy, planning, and implementing services for more effective outcomes.

Freire (1997) has challenged the oppressed and the oppressors to examine the environment more closely and talk about our experiences and observations. As more attention is brought to embracing the diverse populations that comprise our ecosystems, working to improve operations in complex systems of humanity, love, crisis, trauma, and conflict is involved. In moving from a color-blind stance of the early 1970s to hearing voices that explained the need to be respected and recognized, social work and other professional disciplines are inviting and listening to the elements that must be acknowledged to build a better environment. Thinking about inequality and reflecting on how this impacts people's lives and their ability to care for themselves and their family groups is crucial.

WHOSE MANIFEST DESTINY?

Manifest destiny has pervaded our history here and around the world. The art of war has been dominant. Stepping into a more inclusive world requires owning that history of subjugation and also acknowledging native belief systems based on kinship and collective responsibility to understand that everything is connected and that what occurs in one component affects the others (Hilliard, 1997). In reaching forward with interest in addressing injustice, it is necessary to own shame, guilt, and pain. Embracing the road of healing and recovery contains the presence of multiple voices that have pushed forward their perspectives and experiences. Including these voices and perspectives from early education to elementary and secondary education to higher education and professional development helps build capacity to manifest more positive destinies. Inclusive social work integrates multicultural education, diverse partnerships, and collective responsibility. The *Structure of Belonging* (Block, 2008) offers a proposal for contemplating and designing ways we engage with communities. Extending invitations and becoming more hospitable is fundamental.

SOME PERSPECTIVES INCLUDE ...

Persons of various identities, time periods, disciplines, religious or nonreligious entities, political connections, and families of origin have shared ideas about the environment and their experiences of oppression and struggle and of overcoming obstacles. Literature, poems, and research by people of color; lesbian, gay, bisexual, transgender, and intersex people; persons experiencing physical, emotional, and learning challenges; and people with various national origins have expressed strong belief systems and described many dimensions of struggle. Their stories and reports address challenges, offer hope, and have been available and accessed by those who are interested. The domain of literary studies is a broad one that encompasses regions, cultural and sexual identities, worldviews, and past, current, and future literature (Bost & Aparicio, 2013).

Kellogg (2015) pointing to Diaz's need to use more literature in education, acknowledges the work to explore racial matters in our culture, and notes the extreme pushback. The obstacles to works being published by multicultural authors (Hehrlich, 2015) and the constraints on teachers revising curricula (Stallworth, 2006) to include more multicultural literature are examples of the challenges to developing educational strategies to inform and assist socialization that promotes the knowledge of strengths across disciplines for all students. As social work stands to become more inclusive and assist in the facilitation of dialogues, the presence of strong opposition must be recognized. Strategies to listen and mediate are components of the engagement and collaboration process.

There are millions of voices to be explored, considered, and used to come to our own thinking about what is or is not, what is wrong, and what should be valued and validated. A few examples of life experiences and observations are posed here to ponder.

PEOPLE OF COLOR

Resources from the communities of color often intersect with other identity communities. These examples reference sources of the spirit of awareness and survival despite negative messages. The usual chronological path to today's society emphasized slavery to create and maintain horrible social conditions for people of color. The media messages promoted the implementation of laws to suppress, isolate, imprison, devalue, and psychologically distress persons of color, people of lower incomes, and those facing other challenges. As more research into genealogy and DNA strains occurs (e.g., genealogy sites such as ancestry.com and myheritage.com), it is apparent that humans often have various and multiple ancestral sources. These categories take that and the reality of intersectional identities into consideration.

Across groups, people rely on the resources available to them. They draw strength from history, support networks, and attention from those who are concerned and who reach out when there needs to be more assistance and understanding. Systems that create more obstacles than access require allies, bystanders, professionals, and others who appreciate humanity to work together to improve our structures for care.

AFRICAN DESCENT

Burrell (2010) presented the concept of brainwashing that critiques the media perpetuation of the myth of inferiority of people of color and white superiority. Repeated messages and administrative structures have promoted harsh penalties and financial burdens particularly for those of color and of low wealth. In raising awareness of malignant media representation that have programmed internalized marginalization he pushed for recognizing the need for steps against this. The need for more accountable journalism has also been expressed (McGowan, 2001). Efforts to recruit diverse reporters and journalists have been complicated by the intricacies of continuing prejudices, white frame expectations, and cultural groups members' efforts to make changes. Many situations have exposed or precipitated embarrassing and conflictual scenarios.

Strengths

The contributions of Africans before Christ and before Columbus have not usually been included in elementary school texts. There is relatively little information about America's first civilization, the Olmec. Archaeological finds indicate that knowledge of the discovery of the Colossal Head statues in Mexico prior to 1869 was suppressed until the early 1940s (Coe,

1968). On the one hand, authors may not be aware of these documents since this content is not typically found in references used in traditional classrooms. On the other hand, diligent scholars may be aware of this information, but the institutional managers may not support the inclusion of this information. Documentation of Biblical entries (Darkwah, 2000), African kingdoms (Davidson, 1966), and voyages by Africans around the world circa 13th centuries (M'Bantu, 2012) have not been shared through educational institutions.

Karenga (1984) builds his presentation of information regarding the place of Maatian moral ideals and the examination of these principles from work in the early 19th century and earlier. He points out that it is this tradition of learning from parents and ancestors that links to fundamental truths of nature and divine and cosmic connections (Karenga, 1984). Hilliard (1997) reminds us of these early tenets of life as rules for encouraging and behaving respectably with one another. To the extent that deep thought and insight occurs and is promoted within the African American community, the additional dimension of improved lives may occur (Karenga, 1984).

Virginia Hamilton's *The People Could Fly* (1997) sets the tone for the role of multicultural literature from the point of enslavement. This folktale depicts the dismal reality of the system that enslaved, yet it offers a testament to the spiritual strength that supported the survival of so many.

The insistence on humanity by those brought to the colonies as slaves, though absent in their daily lives on plantations, is heard through Frederick Douglass. He observed the arrangements to maintain the bonds of slavery by connecting the slave status to the children through the mother. He decries these circumstances as he seeks release from the physical and emotional prison this experience creates (Douglass, 1845).

W. E. B. DuBois (1903) is credited with presenting the concept of double consciousness—the reality of the color line—for academic consideration. His perspective was one of many that surfaced during this time. The experiences of people of color in walking the color line accounted for the myriad expressions of handling pathways to success from learning trades (Booker T. Washington), improving agriculture (George W. Carver) and railway travel (Elijah McCoy), and building businesses (C. J. Walker) to returning to Africa (Marcus Garvey).

Ida B. Wells' anti-lynching advocacy was motivated by the murders of her friends who owned the People's Grocery Store outside Memphis, TN, and were a source of competition for the local white businessmen (Giddings, 1984).

Ture and Hamilton (1992) raised the issue of institutional systemic racism and called for more unity among African Americans in recognizing and speaking out about oppressive conditions.

The contribution that documents strengths of black families builds on the recognition of systemic devaluation and humanity constraints. This knowledge is critical to reflecting on the ways people have survived and opened more pathways for human champions. Their perspectives (Gutman, 1977; Hill, 2003; Ture & Hamilton, 1992) are important references for illustrations of love and compassion within African American communities.

The issues that voices of color have consistently raised identify institutional dynamics that may obstruct education and employment, impact emotional health, and often push into situations of punishment. Ta-Nahesi Coates (2015) addresses the impact of policy formulation based on some of the ideas initiated by Patrick Moynihan that negatively impacted families of color in too many ways. Policies that estranged families and heightened penalties on African American men are connected to the ongoing strategies for incarceration. Coates's novel (2014) identifies specific dynamics that African American males in particular have had to weather. He shares the ways in which these experiences have impacted his life to inform and hopefully protect our developing sons.

Resistance

Despite the atrocious conditions, there were relatively few publicized insurrections. However, Aptheker (*American Negro Slave Revolts* referred to in Clarke, 1992) notes 250 slave revolts. Nat Turner, a literate and intelligent black man, initiated a rebellion in Southampton County, VA, during August 1831. A group of slaves killed about 60 people (more than in any other incident) in retaliation for the wrongness of slavery and the subjection of people. The rebellion was put down within a few days, and most of the participants were executed before or after a criminal proceeding (Apetheker, 2006). The publication of William Styron's fictitious version of the proceeding, *The Confessions of Nat Turner* (1967), was vehemently responded to by 10 black writers (Clarke, 1968). Their observations noted the pain of his derogatory description and maintenance of stereotypical myths. These critiques are important reflections on several dynamics of perceived and experienced oppression.

Berger (2014) addresses the negative accounts associated with black fathers by sharing positive information about fatherhood that receives less media attention (Cadet, 2014). In further research by Jones and Mosher, black fathers are noted to be contributing to positive interactions with children across a national database.

According to Danielle (2014) "although black fathers are more likely to live in separate households, Pew estimates that 67 percent of black dads who don't live with their kids see them at least once a month, compared to 59 percent of white dads and just 32 percent of Hispanic dads" (para 8).

Moving Forward

As more voices are bringing attention to the inaccurate information used in educational curricula that devalue and stigmatize the role of multicultural literature, data and analysis must be promoted to assist in strengths-based socialization processes that are more likely to benefit humanity. Burrell's (2010) perspective should be applied to all. Haven't we all been brainwashed to tolerate the injustices that exist?

NATIVE AMERICANS

Conversations with Chasing Deer (Kaltreider, 2003) raise observations by Native people of the hard-to-understand philosophy of the colonists to be destructive. Speeches by indigenous leaders forewarned of the destruction that would continue under the colonialists (Blaisdell, 2000). *An Indigenous People's History* (Dunbar-Ortiz, 2014) chronicles the mindsets of the migrants resisting Britain's Irish policies and latching on to "Westward movement" lingo that transformed them to conquerors of vast lands. However, many of them following this dream ended up as landless migrants. Through this trek, or way of war, with the purpose to destroy people by destroying their food and support systems, the sacred land of the people had immeasurable human, noncombatant blood spilled (p. 58). Efforts to terminate Natives over and over illustrates the U.S. government's approach with Native Americans.

Strengths

Dunbar-Ortiz (2014) and Horn (2000) share the legacies of collective thinking and mutual support that responded to invasion, enhanced their warrior capacities, and yet were over-powered. Horn (2000), in *The Book of Ceremonies*, shares the ways of appreciating nature and preparing for and implementing ceremonies that honor Mother Earth. Despite the warrior customs, their survival instincts sometimes resulted in less-than-expected outcomes. Wallis (2013) illustrates another dimension of the mutual-aid phenomena within a tribe with a story about two elder women who were left behind because the younger ones believed they would be a burden. Yet the wiser women managed the cold winter through their understanding of the earth. When the young ones returned, having met with misfortunes, the elder ones embraced them and addressed their needs with their resources.

Regardless of the variations of survival, generally their connection to the spirit of creation and the Circle of Life sustained them. Dreams and visions, intentions and actions are important elements. Trees, animals, stones, air, water, wood, fire, the sky, and the moon are appreciated. Prophecies are valued as probabilities to be considered. Their experiences of 500 years of encounters with Spanish, French, Dutch, British, and American aggressors have precipitated much outrage, sadness, and meditation (Blaisdell, 2000).

An early question by Powhatan (also known as Wahunsonacock) circa 1609 was, "Why should you destroy us who have provided you with food?" He continued with, "Why should you take by force from us that which you can have by love?" Circa 1620, Chikataubut (of the Massachusett tribe) asked how they could desecrate the grave of his mother by stealing the skins that covered the burial place (Blaisdell, 2000).

Resistance

Subsequently, their Native American public statements addressed the realities, as Blaisdell (2000) went on to discuss. Miantonomo (of the Narraganset tribe) said, "Brothers, we must be one as the English are, or we shall soon all be destroyed." Their game and fields were being decimated. Cornplanter, Halftown, and Big Tree (Senecans), said, "The land we live on our fathers received from God, was said in 12.1790 (Loc 611). In 1805, Red Jacket (also known as Sagoyewatha and also a Senecan) said, "You have got our country but are not satisfied; you want to force your religion upon us" (Blaisdell, 2000). The Native people were calling them out, but to no avail.

Building upon the lives and ways of knowledge of their ancestors, Simpson (2014) has been studying nationalism politics of the Mohawks since 1996. She reports on the position of the

Mohawks of Kahnawà:ke to "refuse to stop being themselves," which is an awesome standpoint. She speaks of past anthropological analyses of indigenous people and their embrace of ceremony, as well as the rule of Empire conquests that injected a legal form of land ownership/theft that disregarded the possession of existing tenants.

Moving Forward

Simpson's (2014) observations, analysis, and perspective documents nationhood and sovereignty that discount the settler state story. She affirms that the political work of Native people addresses the structure settler colonialism used to miscast and pathologically vanish people (p. 177).

Similarly, the Standing Rock situation depicts a new illustration of Native resistance. Tribesmen are trying to stop the construction of a 1,172-mile oil pipeline that will bulldoze sacred sites and risk potential contamination of the Missouri River. Yet this protest also clearly documents Native persistence in calling out the arrogant behavior of Energy Transfer Partners, which dismisses the environmental long-term concerns (Donnella, 2016).

LATINO/A DESCENT

The "tricky" place of terminology and language (Bost & Aparicio, 2014) is created by the U.S. inventions of the terms *Hispanic* and *Latino*. These terms omit the mixtures of indigenous and African people that characterize *mestizaje*. *Hispanic* has been connected to European definitions, while *Latino* is considered a more progressive description that incorporates the diversity of the culture (p. 1). References to Latina/o theology address the communal emphasis that is put forth despite the various viewpoints that actually challenge consensus. The case of *Aponte-Torres v. the University of Puerto Rico* is an example of litigation regarding suspicious files against minority group employees (Aponte-Torres, 2006).

Strengths

The House on Mango Street (Cisneros, 1991) is often used to introduce students to the Latina/Chicana family experience in transitioning into the culture of the United States. The range of Chicana/Latina voices and the mix of cultural ancestors and experiences has brought forth not only the reality of this range but also the interest in exposing geographic areas around the world to this diversity.

Isabel Allende's approach to her cultural perspective challenges the history of class and family. Some people criticized her approach and content. Her resistance to the patriarchal norms of class, gender, and ethnicity promote variable ideas for reflection (Martin, 2010). Her work raises the creative permutations of identity intersections and different interpretations of traditional hierarchies that provoke thinking away from traditional boundaries.

Junot Diaz offers illustrations of "family loss and masculine stupidity" in his work (Kellogg, 2015). In *Drown* (1996), Diaz paints a story of the immigration of a Dominican family. The father leaves his home and goes to the United States seeking a better life for his family, spending years in separation, and eventually reuniting. The situations this arrangement creates are portrayed as each phase is challenged by economics. The family has limited options for earning enough money to pay the bills. The narrative presents the collective household participation as they work as they are able to and contribute to cover expenses.

Breaking Ground and Barriers (Bonilla-Santiago, 1992) establishes a Latina perspective that incorporates the strengths of women in the Latina community. Her investigation of Hispanic women leaders as grassroots community leaders promotes spiritual beliefs and family values as community resources (p. 5). Community participation was associated with ethnic pride, and several gender and cultural themes were associated with the extent of participation. Bringing attention to the circumstances of Hispanic women workers has resulted in progressive outreach and increased leadership.

Delgado (1999) recognizes the reality of the myriad configurations of service needs and brings attention to the absence of social work outreach in urban communities. Effective work in communities that do not come to the agencies as they exist requires critical assessment and collaborative partnership to develop sustainable relationships. He recommends enhanced engagement strategies.

Resistance

DeSipio (2017) summarizes the development of Hispanic and Latino resistance over the past 150 years. Early efforts against colonial forces occurred in the late 1800s in New Mexico and Puerto Rico. "In New Mexico, the Alianza de Pueblos y Pobladores (The Alliance of Towns and Settlers) confronted federal and state authorities to enforce land claims by the descendants of Mexican residents" (p. 6). At that time, there were no large-scale organizing efforts. However, members of the Latino and Hispanic communities began to speak out individually and with others to pursue civic and political inclusion. After World War II and progressing through the 1950s to the 1970s, more individuals and groups began to speak out for equal protection under U.S. laws.

Of the efforts across time that Hispanic and Latina people have participated in, voter participation and recent issues regarding immigration are most pressing. According to academic research, Latina immigrants are less likely to participate in civic activities. However, other data sources suggest immigrants are in fact engaged in civic and political events (Seif, 2009). On the surface, this reveals a disconnect between traditional paradigms, researcher awareness, and knowledge of community connections.

Moving Forward

Not only are there the examples of the subtexts in Latina/o literature, but there are expressions of Latina contexts with Russia and other geographic areas that illustrate interest in pursuing cultural variations around the world. Themes such as border theory and environmental literary criticism have joined an expanding range of multifaceted interpretations that evolve from an interest in transdisciplinary studies in cross-border environments. A group of Trans-Baikal scholars is examining the literature of Mexican American writers by using the parameters of border time and space (Bost & Aparicio, 2014). Immigration issues related to

Mexicans and those of other countries are impacted by barriers to inclusion and are the basis of emerging collaborations for analyzing circumstances.

ASIAN DESCENT

Life on the Asian continent demonstrated significant organization through centuries of conquest and establishing civilization (Gascoigne, 2003). Asian American authors demonstrate their reflection and emotions from circumstances of national experiences and personal interactions of friendship, responsibility, and quest for higher levels of survival.

For example, Tan, in the *Opposite of Fate*, moves the reader into believing the tale to be true. She describes an incident of mother abuse on a daughter with an unacceptable boyfriend which triggers angst and understanding. Similarly, Can Xue (1997) offers a series of stories in *The Embroidered Shoes* with quite unpredictable content and perspectives. The characters are unusual in context, settings, and illustrations; they push readers to connect to lives of mania, filth, insomnia, and other troubled realities. The social environment and historical frame follows the death of Mao and the 1989's Tiananmen Square massacre.

Also, subsequent to the massacre of unarmed students in Tiananmen Square in 1989, Yiwu Liao expresses his connection to the Chinese prison system after being incarcerated for writing two poems that offended the Communist government (Rohter, 2013). His work described a system created by the rulers that replicated state bureaucracy in which "those in power enjoyed unlimited privileges."

Julie Osaka provides a view into the experiences of a Japanese family and the process of internment by the U.S. government. The family's feelings, the neighbor's hesitant roles, and the policy framework give a multidimensional context of the vagaries of an immigrant's status, despite legality (Otsuka, 2002).

By observing the broader immigrant environment, Vö and Bonus (2002) report on the roles that children of immigrant entrepreneurial families bring. They acknowledge the connections and complexity of the family and business needs. These children operate as problem-solvers, translators, and leaders in their ethnic communities. Appreciating them is important for community development planning.

WOMEN

Phyllis Chesler (1972) calls attention to the insistence that assertive women be silenced by incarcerating their creative female minds in attics or asylums. Elizabeth Johnson (1993) shares that all thinking begins with a cosmic relatedness, yet hierarchical dualism placed privileged rational man apart and above others. The relationships with women could be challenging within this context. Margaret Atwood in *The Handmaid's Tale* (1985) puts another spin on efforts to silence the assertive and creative female mind. The theme, similar to *1984* by George Orwell (1949) portrays a social narrative in which rights are denied under authoritarian regimes.

Recognizing a wide range of views about women, pregnancy and abortion the existence of examples of beliefs regarding the acceptance of rape, albeit in joking fashion, by national legislators presents appalling views (Brainwrap, 2015). Perhaps this state of limited awareness and respect for 51% of the population reveals the great need for more gender diversity in our governing bodies.

Nevertheless, often views that dominate policy formation are based on a narrow conceptualization of forces that shape life choices that promote the stereotype of a welfare queen and the absent father. Bezusko (2013) points to how motherhood has been criminalized as the media shows that "women continue to be responsible for maintaining the health and economic security of the nation via the consumer-driven household—and the state is invested in identifying those who uphold the ideal and those who do not" (p. 16).

The 1970s examples of women's consciousness have pushed the examination of women's roles across cultures and geography. From Geetha Ramanathan's (2012) *Locating Gender in Modernism: The Outsider Female* to Maria Shriver's report *A Woman's Nation Pushes Back From the Brink* (2014), narratives describe the reality of exclusion and family benefits of women's perspectives and financial support. Women and third-world authors help refine notions of family, community, and world issues. Women and policies that support them and children benefit society.

Resistance

Women's narratives of lived experiences demonstrate unique and familiar situations. On one hand, the discussion of women's rights involves decision-making about the meaning and commitment to their identity as workers and the meaning of care. While the respondents in Jolanki's (2015) study anticipated some moral blame, they sought a balance. In reality, men also operate as caregivers, and she includes recent studies that point to the role of work in playing out as a respite from caregiving.

There are other concerns of social interpretations versus individual and family decision-making. From women who served as abolitionists such as Grimké, (e.g., a woman who recognized the inhumanity of slavery in South Carolina) to Ali Hirsi, a Somali questioning her religion's treatment of women, women observe and think about social issues and their consequences. In *Infidel: My Life* (2006), Ayaan Hirsi Ali questions the rigid doctrines of Islam, including requirements of submission to men. Chelsea Shields has addressed the similar obstacles to women's participation in the Church of Jesus Christ of Latter-day Saints (the Mormon Church) in her TED Talk that addresses gender inequality in the Mormon Church.

Barbara Kingsolver (1998) paints an important view of the patriarchal rigid mindset that some men have that obstructs the freedom of women, of daughters, and others who think for themselves and have ways of knowing and being that should be respected. The *Poisonwood Bible* illustrates religious and gender oppression.

Bringing continuing attention to civil and human rights of women is critical. The human trafficking of women, described in *Half the Sky*, by Kristoff and WuDunn, also increased exposure of the extent of assaults of women on college campuses. This has become the focus for many women advocates. Notably, Jimmy Carter has spoken out on the negative manifestations against women around the world in the name of religion.

This discrimination, unjustifiably attributed to a Higher Authority, has provided a reason or excuse for the deprivation of women's equal rights across the world for centuries. At its most repugnant, the belief that women must be subjugated to the wishes of men excuses slavery, violence, forced prostitution, genital mutilation and national laws that omit rape as a crime. But it also costs many millions of girls and women control over their own bodies and lives, and continues to deny them fair access to education, health, employment and influence within their own communities. The same discriminatory thinking lies behind the continuing gender gap in pay and why there are still so few women in office in the West. The root of this prejudice lies deep in our histories, but its impact is felt every day. It is not women and girls alone who suffer. It damages all of us. (Salzilla, 2014).

Moving Forward

The participation of women in the social and political spheres around the world have changed in some ways but in others remain constrained. Hessini (2016) reports that gender equality and sexual rights strategies using an inclusive approach is occurring in Muslim-majority contexts (p. 69). Activists are documenting the diverse realities and challenging discriminatory laws and practices. Their work involves outreach to and collaboration with young women. The Fourth World Conference on Women, which was held in Beijing, China in 1995, is presented as the standpoint that identified women's rights as human rights and emphasized the need "to identify and challenge the many pervasive forms of gender-based violence."

Overall, Hessini points out, women from Muslim-majority countries are creating innovative research, advocacy, and practices that challenge conservative discourse nationally and globally (p. 78).

CARE's president, Helen Gayle (Carlyle, 2013), and Jackson Katz's TED Talk (2012) remind us that the way to better lives for women needs to involve men. Gayle speaks to the role of access to capital and finding one's passion. Developing strategies of coalitions and collective organizing must involve diverse membership. The challenges of gender bias impact the growth and development of our children and families.

LESBIAN, GAY, BISEXUAL, TRANSGENDER, QUESTIONING, QUEER, AND INTERSEX (LGBTQI) PERSONS

The multifaceted experiences of sex and gender reveal the social forces of labeling that affect all groups (Sisneros, Stakeman, Joyner, & Schmitz, 2008). Persons who may identify or come to identify themselves as LGBTQI often deny, camouflage, or resist disclosure to avoid oppression. Staceyann Chinn (2010) recalls her childhood and notes where supports existed and where there were not any. Coming out risks having the presence of support of family and community, love or not. At worse, it can trigger complete rejection, elimination of relationships, and continuing negative interaction at home, at work, and in other community situations. For the faith-connected LGBTQI, persons marginalized in their identities may also deal with complex metaphysical dynamics of love.

Despite significant LGBTQI civil rights gains, states have continued efforts to obstruct LGBTQI rights (Mason, Williams, & Elliott, 2016). Although public opinion has moved to support their rights (in 2015, 61% of those surveyed were supportive), the legislation tends to address protecting religious freedom.

Multicultural voices of family members who have been ostracized because they did not meet identity expectations usually present notions of talents and potential that might have been. The "Story of Kowalski" (Griscom, in Rothenberg, 2014) illustrates the deprecation of a partnership by a family at the time when care and love was most needed. It highlights the absence of understanding of relationships and the suffering that's connected to those that look different. Charles Blow's (2014) example of the complexity of identity formation connected to lived experiences and self-evaluation raises the dynamics of adverse childhood experiences and recovery that few people want to consider. Further observations and research demonstrate the array of backgrounds that lead to an individual's identity formation and development.

Resistance

Solomon's (2012) work on identities that are distant from customary binaries shares the terms *transgender, transsexual,* and *transvestite* and raises for more consideration the feelings and emotions of knowing oneself as they experience themselves. He describes gender dissonance that can manifest at very early ages—by 3 or 4 or earlier—and that may be responded to with a diagnosis. Acknowledging the rights of young people stigmatized because of their identities and the alarming rise in suicide related to this, some states are stepping up to disavow conversion therapy discredited by major health organizations while still allowing other forms of counseling to occur (Hauser, 2017).

Moving Forward

As advocates for and against LGBTQI rights continue, those who are concerned about the well-being of those in the community who are discriminated against participate in several strong groups working to protect. One example is the "It Gets Better Project," which aims to help adolescents transition through years where they may face significant exclusion and bullying (itgetsbetter.org). Local organizations and groups are available to provide services and support systems to benefit persons of diverse gender identities.

THE DEAF COMMUNITY

Children born into families with hearing parents or children born into families with parents who may be deaf or hearing impaired have the benefit of bicultural lives as they grow and are exposed to the educational experiences of the deaf community. American Sign Language (ASL) and possible cochlear implants offer supports for members of this community. Although some persons who are deaf or have difficulty hearing may experience labeling or exclusion in some places, Gallaudet University and its library provides many resources and deaf community-related materials.

Literature about families with deaf members may address the challenges placed on hearing members to help and the resistance that may also be felt because of the overwhelming responsibility. *Deafening* (2003) by Frances Itani reports on the adjustment required when hearing loss occurs unexpectedly. *Of Sound Mind* (2004) by Jean Ferris addressed the pressures of responsibility for the family members who cannot hear. Recognizing the paths to hearing loss and the types of resources may help to manage diverse needs.

Moving Forward

The term *inclusion* as referred to in the educational arena addresses classroom composition and delivery of instruction. Our interest in inclusion is to be respectful of all identities and perspectives and appreciate collaboration in developing mutually acceptable strategies for social and economic justice and appropriate service delivery.

PERSONS EXPERIENCING CHALLENGES

Traditional perceptions of limitations on people who may be labeled *disabled* minimize their talents and foster policy suggestions that take away education for students with disabilities, reduce employment opportunities, eliminate affordable health care, and reduce accessible housing (Diament, 2017). Unfortunately, these policy suggestions expose the absence of knowledge of legislators regarding the capacity of people to care for themselves and their families when opportunities for support are available.

Solomon (2012) delivered a substantial body of work on the range of identities connected to the vagaries of life and the impact on the parenting phenomena. Not only are we informed of the stressors on parents of children with disabilities that might account for divorce, but we simultaneously are informed that other research suggests the rate may be lower among these parents or that the rate is consistent with the rates of divorce across the board. This pushes to the forefront the biases of researchers and the reality of families trying to make the best of situations and traumas with which they are confronted.

A child brought into a family as the result of a rape compares with children experiencing Down's syndrome or other challenges with respect to the feelings of calamity and the questions of having reliable support from a partner or family members (Solomon, 2012). Often, moving around in a wheelchair, riding in a small bus, or being referred to a mental health clinic has relegated people to a label and an approach limited in understanding. Solomon acknowledges the processes that families may move through as they react to labels and adapt to the circumstances.

Similarly, labels regarding low income, mental health, size, and criminal justice all attract commentary by some that may promote punitive reactions by teachers, other parents, peers, and strangers. All people face challenges—some more than others—and many are mostly connected to social constructions that obstruct recognizing the humanity in us all.

Resistance

Ibrahim (2011) edited an anthology of literature by persons labeled *disabled*. From where they sit or stand, observations of many people illustrate scenarios of trying to go about daily activities with environmental obstacles on streets, in buildings, and by people who prefer to mistreat than to be respectful. In "Public Transit," John Hockenberry (2011) tells his story of traveling to Manhattan from Brooklyn in a wheelchair. It reveals the lack of compassionate attitudes of most passersby. It is easy to imagine that hundreds of people may have observed his struggle with the stairs to the subway trains. Yet only one woman (a person of color) assisted him. The sidewalks, stairs, and unresponsive passersby presented many barriers for his travel. He illustrates the need for accommodations for persons with other ways of being mobile.

Rachel Simon's (2011) *The Story of Beautiful Girl* is about a couple who escaped from an institution and sought refuge for their newborn with a retired school teacher. The support they experienced and the exposure of the institution's rigid and restrictive policies encourages reflection on people's rights to determine their life paths.

Moving Forward

The pressures of sharing information with parents and conforming to norms can be terrifying. Solomon notes that allowing transition often permits the resolution of anxiety and learning disorders. Building on family strategies for learning and access to community-based services (Diament, 2017) assists progress. Providing fact sheets about in-school bullying and cyberbullying (Berkowicz & Meyers, 2017), its impacts, and ways to prevent and resolve it is required through broader advisory and work groups. Bringing these ideas to the classroom and community offers opportunities to process information and move forward.

INCORPORATING INCLUSION INTO THE SOCIAL WORK FRAME

Building on social work values to incorporate multicultural education, resources, and participants and promote inclusion in collaborative opportunities to enhance communities operates within a reading, reflection, writing, critical thinking, and peers-and-others dialogue framework.

Inclusion has been used to refer to educating children with special needs in a classroom with students without special needs. Its use in this text involves many more elements. Essentially, the term refers to reducing discrimination by including people who may be identified in ways that could exclude them from participation in activities, services, and planning. Inclusion incorporates the participation of people who may have not been fully represented in planning, implementing, or evaluating services and their ideas that express alternative notions of what reality is. This concept expands the ecological framework to recognize the strengths of the visible and invisible components of community realities.

Principles for inclusion include the following mandates:

- All people matter.
- Observe all interactions.
- Listen to all ideas and viewpoints.
- Hold up strengths.
- Acknowledge and promote multiple roles for family bonding and support.
- Employ universal designs that engage and accommodate needs and styles of all types of learners and participants.
- Enhance capacity to improve relationships and connections.
- Acknowledge consensus decision-making for social justice.

These principles counter some beliefs and attitudes about interpersonal and task interaction and also involve

- Unlearning racism
- Appreciating survival strategies that are alternative or complementary
- Incorporating economic justice for sustainable solutions

Incorporating information that these principles introduce expands databases, sources of knowledge, and at the least encourages dual perspectives of history and contemporary problem-solving. Steps along this journey to improve social work services can advance inclusion and contribute to interprofessional collaboration and community development.

REFLECTION

Reflection is a tool used in social work to contemplate information and feelings. Gathering information, hearing stories, and considering alternative perspectives garners progressive understanding when reflection and application scenarios are added. Schon (1983) has commented on reflective practice and use of self in doing social work. Reflection here denotes the use of reading perspectives that may be unfamiliar. Acknowledging our reactions to these views, thinking about the multiple dimensions represented, and making sense of human behavior in various settings offers opportunities for proactive application and are useful in preparing to work with diverse consumers.

CRITICAL THINKING

Information processing includes data gathering, dialogue, reflection, mediation, and critical thinking that incorporate the broad frames of reference for social work and social justice. The starting point includes self-awareness and context. Assessing information and personal biases offers a baseline from which to operate.

Students are encouraged to write critical thinking questions (CTQ) related to the readings. This can be ongoing and used in class groups or study groups. Peer-to-peer discussion may be used with the CTQ and then discussed as a whole class to garner the range of ideas and to facilitate understanding of those that may be uncomfortable. Paul and Elder (1999) provide the basic primer of critical thinking tools.

The ecosystem's framework acknowledges existing structures of personal and community life—biological, psychological, social cultural, economic, political, spiritual, and technological. The personal framework integrates familial and friendship networks that bring emotional states to processing knowledge. Acknowledging the anxiety that may accompany verbalizing ideas about discrimination and prejudice in addition to facilitating the critical consciousness process are steps in helping students develop reflection that can be used in clinical work. Social workers do operate as agents of control, yet in social justice work, they are committing to advocate for those experiencing system obstacles (Bransford, 2011). Learning to tolerate and transcend this ambiguity is also a social work skill.

DIALOGUE

The classroom conversations regarding diverse literature that students engage in provide exercises in expressing opinions and weighing best ways to deal with uncomfortable topics. These opportunities offer experience for mediation skill building as well as participating in exercises that encourage expressing points of view and listening to other views. Structured activities may be used in groups to practice dialogue skills in exploring the meaning of key terms, especially *oppression*, *discrimination*, and *privilege* and how they impact lives (Humphreys, 2012). The framework is based on content from Schoen and Hurtado (2001) and activities from Zúñiga (2013).

Thompson, Switky, and Gilinsky (2012) suggest the use of impromptu presentations for boosting student engagement and learning. Predetermined questions, cases, or scenarios may be used to garner reaction to a discriminatory incident and offer discussion on how to handle the situation.

Several in-class and online discussion techniques and tasks (Watt, 2007; Yan & Wong, 2005) may be used to engage students in small groups and in peer-to-peer conversations about social justice issues.

PEER-TO-PEER INTERACTION: STUDENTS REFLECT ON THEIR AWARENESS

The process of reading, developing critical thinking, and dialogue can be eye opening, challenging, and enlightening. It can also be somewhat intimidating, especially for those who may resist ideas different from those with which they feel more comfortable. The use of peer dialogues, small-group discussion, and large-group discussion that incorporate citizens' views and commentary are essential for critical thinking. When this process is tied to potential conversations that may impact policies for sustainable food and employment, environmental justice, and other human rights, students often move to higher levels of consideration. These steps in student experiences are variable. Some are intrigued with the process of new learning, some hesitate, and some resist. Some struggle with replacing old messages with new ones valued by social work. Each step must be respected as the next step is taken.

SELF-AWARENESS: REACTIONS AND FEELINGS

This process of using a framework for reviewing knowledge of systemic obstacles and processing feelings and related knowledge has resulted in a range of reactions by students. Whether in classrooms with homogeneous student groups or more diverse classroom compositions, offering interesting points of reference for the students to be aware of have been observed.

> As a straight, white, cisgender [*cisgender* is a recent term that denotes a person whose identity conforms to their biological sex] male, one student indicated he had become able to acknowledge inherited privileges by referring to a course reading from Hardiman, Jackson, and Griffin (2007, p. 28) and the quote: "Nothing is gained by feeling shame about what our ancestors did or what our contemporaries do to different groups of people out of fear, ignorance, or malice." (p. 34) He concluded that socialization could be rejected in taking steps as a social worker to challenge the system and strive for social justice.

Another point of discussion included this:

> Feelings of being an oppressor because of traditional history content can be connected to the lack of exposure to others in all white schools and effortless access to resources. This highlighted the basis for taking privilege for granted and failing to realize that not everyone is not so fortunate.

Other students added thoughts that:
- *It is* hard to believe lies are taught about history in early school years.
- People with limited resources often face choices that aren't really choices at all.
- For example, being unemployed and seeking assistance for food may be stressful for a single parent if she must choose between a minimum wage job and losing food stamps. She will remain unable to afford enough food for her family. If she does not accept the job, the case manager may judge her negatively. If she accepts the position and does not report the income, she may be subject to fines and become ineligible to collect benefits in the future. None of these options is an actual solution.

ACKNOWLEDGING THE PROSPECT OF CHANGE

For those who have not been exposed to the wealth of multicultural resources in every discipline, this process of modifying our thinking about what has been learned involves adapting to the content of alternatives in information processing. For others who are informed of multiple social identities, cultural strengths, and strong voices of experience, we welcome opportunities to share and lift up these warriors, "sheroes," and heroes. This emphasis on intersectional analysis has emerged to highlight the complexity of human experience (Dill & Zambrana, 2009) rather than reduce perceptions to the single-lens views of the past. Gil's (1998) treatise on oppression recognized the radical nature of confronting the injustice, a concept that students over the years have often dismissed as being wholly unattainable.

STUDENTS SPEAK OUT ABOUT GAINING CRITICAL PERSPECTIVES = CRITICAL REFLECTION

The process of critical thinking, engagement, and collaboration has obstacles and rewards. Hearing about and acknowledging the injustices of our past create various reactions in students. Students have reflected on where these ideas take them in contemplating their interests in social work and social justice. Reaching for these feelings and working with them is part of the learning process.

Students' increased awareness and growth are typical. Helena in Scenario 1 progressed through the course work on civil and human rights and cultural strengths and proceeded into her field placement able to make positive connections and engage well with clients. However, there are some students who hold on to views of egocentrism, have difficulty pacing through new information, and may have some difficulty engaging with some service users at a professional level.

Consider Amber in Scenario 2.

STUDENT SCENARIO 2

Amber is an 18-year-old graduate of an eastern high school in a suburban town of about 50,000 people. Her regional high school of 1,200 students included around 175 students of visibly diverse adolescents. The curriculum was traditional, and the clubs she participated in were mostly composed of her cultural peers. She is a member of an all-white church. Some of her family members make derogatory comments about other people; so do her friends. In her first interview at the agency she was placed in, she struggled with a client who identified as a member of the LGBTQI community. Although she wanted to pursue social work, she realized she held some of the same beliefs she had heard growing up.

CRITICAL THINKING

Ask yourself this: Can I assess my thinking about people different from myself in an open, honest, evaluative way? How can I do this?

CRITICALLY REFLECTING: EVALUATING ROLES

Student discussions have also raised students' abilities to conceptualize the intersectional identity. Inequality viewed through experiences of members of different groups could shape their thought process and way of life. The intersectional lens focuses on how separate factors play a part in experiences. Consider how a gay black man or a white straight woman may be treated differently based on those identity factors. The intersectional lens helps to generate innovative ways to view and address group members.

This and other student reactions provide self-observations of reactions and feelings of bias and prejudice. Critical reflection takes one's knowledge of self and works through immediate responses and thoughts that occur upon more thoughtful assessment of one's perspectives. A student may begin by wondering if anything will change, if the people that are service users can do better. What can be done? How can government do what it is doing that penalizes humanity in so many ways?

Imagine Amber asking herself more questions. Imagine her working on putting herself in another's situation—rethinking self-stigma related to social historical trauma associated with discriminatory mechanisms and perhaps individual or family trauma. Student critical reflections offer visuals of steps of persistence and fortitude that service users also must tread.

Rodriguez notes cultures to be interested in "the healthy sustenance of the people, committed to the survival of the whole" (Aponte-Torres, 2006, p. 43). Inclusion promotes visions of a diverse community, appreciated and respected with citizen members working to achieve more humanity. From the macro view, change for the survival of the whole is a social work goal.

CHAPTER SUMMARY

This chapter highlights the process of gathering knowledge from various perspectives, scrutinizing the behaviors and thoughts students bring, and the learning process that operates simultaneously on personal and social levels.

EPAS AND CODE OF ETHICS

CSWE EDUCATIONAL POLICY & ACCREDITATION STANDARDS

Competency 1: Demonstrate ethical and professional behavior.
Competency 2: Engage diversity and difference in practice.
Competency 3: Advance human rights and social, economic, and environmental justice. (EPAS, 2015)

NASW CODE OF ETHICS

6.01 Social Welfare: Social workers should promote the general welfare of society, from local to global levels, and the development of people, their communities, and their environments. Social workers should advocate for living conditions conducive to the fulfillment of basic human needs and should promote social, economic, political, and cultural values and institutions that are compatible with the realization of social justice.

6.02 Public Participation: Social workers should facilitate informed participation by the public in shaping social policies and institutions. (NASW, n.d.)

DISCUSSION QUESTIONS

1. The big question is this: Why should social workers engage in dialogues about social justice?
2. Have you had an opportunity to engage in a dialogue about social justice at work, in your field, or with friends or family? What issues were raised? What authors/sources of information contributed to your points of view? Have you recommended any of these sources to family, friends, or coworkers?
3. Are your perspectives influenced by diverse authors or majority culture writers? Please list up to five sources that have been of interest to you. Discuss with classmates.

EXERCISES

Classroom and online formats and discussions are guided by recognition and acceptance of social work professional standards. All ideas and responses are to be respected. **Students experiencing challenges regarding any content may request a conversation with the instructor during office hours.**

1. Develop an ePortfolio. Information about developing an ePortfolio can be used to paint your journey of cultural awareness and to include work that may be used in the future. (Some Learning Management Systems have this feature. It allows the collection of assignments that may be used for employment applications.)
2. Select two readings and list answers for Discussion Question (DQ)1 based on the selections.
3. Instructor may develop a handout of selected quotes from multicultural resources that present perspectives. Students will list two key points regarding the handout. Students will reflect on a quote using the key points.
4. Have students list three qualities of leadership regarding diversity and inclusion. Focus discussion on comparing their ideas about leadership to one of the chapter references.
5. *Online format*: Have students post an answer to DQ1 on the discussion board. Students should include an explanation of criteria used to support their response. Students should select one of their groupmate's comments to respond to. Students may identify the pros and cons of the suggestion, conclusion, or judgment.
   In-class format: This discussion can be peer facilitated. The group could have the option to submit a summary of their discussion for class review and comment.
6. Have students write on an index card a scenario in which feelings of stereotype or bias were present. Collect and select a couple to read and react to as a class.
7. Select one of the CSWE competencies or one of the ethics codes listed previously. Create a scenario that illustrates your understanding of the selection. Discuss with a peer. Review as a class.

MULTICULTURAL RESOURCES

A & E. (2005). *Biography: Sitting Bull: Chief of the Lakota Nation.*

Ahlberg, P. & Bennett, M.R. (2017). Six million-year-old human footprint discovered in Crete raises major questions about our evolution. *Newsweek.* Retrieved from http://www.newsweek.com/trachilos-footprint-crete-human-evolution-million-658287

Alexander, M. (2012). *The new Jim Crow: Mass incarceration in the age of colorblindness.* Revised Edition. New York, NY: New Press.

Alfred, G. R. (1995). *Heeding the voices of our ancestors: Kahnawake Mohawk politics and the rise of Native nationalism.* Oxford, England: Oxford University Press.

Ali, A. H. (2006) *Infidel: My life.* New York, NY: Atria Books.

Aponte-Torres, A. (2006). United States Court of Appeals, First Circuit. Antonio APONTE-TORRES et al., Plaintiffs, Appellants, v. UNIVERSITY OF PUERTO RICO et al., Defendants, Appellees. http://caselaw.findlaw.com/us-1st-circuit/1438439.html No. 05-1534. Decided: April 14, 2006.

Atwood, M. (1986). *The handmaid's tale.* Boston, MA: Houghton Mifflin Harcourt.

Blaisdell, B. (Ed.). (2000). *Great speeches by Native Americans.* New York, NY: Dover.

Blow, C. (2014, July 30). Age of identity. *The New York Times.* Retrieved from http://www.nytimes.com/2014/07/31/opinion/charles-blow-age-of-identity.html? hp&action=click&pgtype=Homepage&module=c-column-top-span-region&region=c-column-top-span-region&WT.nav=c-column-top-span-region

Bonilla-Santiago, G. (1992). *Breaking ground and barriers: Hispanic women developing effective leadership.* San Diego, CA: Marin.

Burrell, T. (2010). *Brainwashed: Challenging the myth of black inferiority.* New York, NY: SmileyBooks.

Chengu, G. (2014, October 12). Before Columbus: How Africans brought civilization to America. *Global Research Newsletter.* Retrieved April 6, 2015, from http://www.globalresearch.ca/before-columbus-how-africans-brought-civilization-to-america/5407584

Chesler, P. (1972). *Women and madness: When is a woman mad and who is it that decides?* New York, NY: Doubleday.

Chinn, S. (2010). *The other side of paradise.* New York, NY: Scribner.

Cisneros, S. (1991). *The house on Mango Street.* New York, NY: Vintage Books.

Clarke, J. H. (Ed.). (1968). *William Styron's Nat Turner: Ten black writers respond.* Boston, MA: Beacon Press.

Coates, T. (2014). *Between the world and me.* New York, NY: Spiegel & Grau.

Coates, T. (2015, October). The black family in the age of mass incarceration. *The Atlantic Monthly.*

Darkwah, N. B. (2014). *The Africans who wrote the Bible.* Orlando, FL: HBC Publications.

Davis, A. (1998). Masked racism: Reflections on the prison industrial complex. *Colorlines.* Retrieved from http://www.colorlines.com/articles/masked- racism-reflections-prison-industrial-complex

Delgado, M. (1999). *Social work practice in non-traditional urban settings.* New York, NY: Oxford University Press.

Diaz, J. (1996). *Drown.* New York, NY: Riverhead Books.

Douglass, F. (1845/2002). *Narrative of the life of Frederick Douglass.* Boston, MA: Bedford/St. Martin.

DuBois, W. E. B. (1903/1994). *Souls of black folk.* Mineola, NY: Dover Press.

DuBois, W. E. B. (2014). The black codes. In P. S. Rothenberg (Ed.), *Race, class, and gender in the United States: An integrated study.* Basingstoke, United Kingdom: Worth.

Dunbar-Ortiz, R. (2014). *An indigenous people's history of the United States.* Boston, MA: Beacon Press.

Ferris, J. (2004). *Of sound mind.* New York, NY: Farrar, Straus & Giroux.

Gallardo, M. E. (2013). *Developing cultural humility: Embracing race, privilege, and power.* Thousand Oaks, CA: SAGE.

Gascoigne, B. (2003). *The dynasties of China: A history.* Philadelphia, PA: Running Press.

Giddings, P. (2007). *When and where I enter: The impact of black women on race and sex in America.* New York, NY: William Morrow.

Gutman, H. G. (1977). *The black family in slavery and freedom, 1750-1925.* New York, NY: Pantheon Books.

Hamilton, V. (1993). *The people could fly: American black folktales.* New York, NY: Knopf Books for Young Readers.

Hess, E. D., & Ludwig, K. (2017). *Humility is the new smart: Rethinking human excellence in the smart machine age.* Oakland, CA: Berrett-Koehler.

Hill, R. (2003). *The strengths of African American families: Twenty-five years later.* New York, NY: United Press of America.

Hilliard, A. (1997). *SBA: The reawakening of the African mind.* Gainesville, FL: Makare.

Hockenberry, J. (2011). Public transit. In C. Ibrahim (Ed.), *An anthology of disability literature.* Durham, NC: Carolina Academic Press.

Horn, G. (2005). *The book of ceremonies: A native way of honoring and living the sacred.* Novato, CA: New World Library.

Itani, F. (2003). *Deafening.* New York, NY: Grove Press.

Kaltreider, K. (2003). *American Indian prophecies: Conversations with Chasing Deer.* New York, NY: Hay House.

Karenga, M. (1984). *Selections from the Husia: Sacred wisdom of ancient Egypt.* Los Angeles, CA: University of Sankore Press.

Kingsolver, B. (1998). *The poisonwood Bible.* New York, NY: Harper Collins.

Kristoff, N., & WuDunn, S. (2010). *Half the sky: Turning oppression into opportunity for women worldwide.* New York, NY: Vintage Books.

Martin, K. W. (2010). *Isabel Allende's House of the spirits trilogy (Narrative geographies).* Rochester, NY: Tamesis Books.

M'Bantu, A. (2012). *The ancient Black Arabs.* London, England: Pomegranate.

M'Bantu, A. (2012). *Unmistakably black: Sculpture and paintings from ancient Syria and Anatolia.* London, England: Pomegranate.

Otsuka, J. (2002). *When the emperor was divine.* New York, NY: Alfred Knopf.

Simon, R. (2012). *The story of beautiful girl.* New York, NY: Grand Central.

Simpson, A. (2014). *Mohawk interruptus: Political life across the borders of settler states.* Durham, NC: Duke University Press.

Solomon, A. (2012). *Far from the tree: Parents, children and the search for identity.* New York, NY: Scribner.

Ture, K. (formerly Carmichael, S.), & Hamilton, C. (1992). *Black power: The politics of liberation.* New York, NY: Vintage Books.

Tzu, S. (2007). *The art of war.* Minneapolis, MN: Filiquarian.

UNESCO.org. (n.d.). Retrieved May 27, 2017, from http://www.unesco.org/new/en/social-and-human-sciences/themes/international-migration/glossary/social-transformation

Van Sertima, I. (1997). *Blacks in science.* New Brunswick, NJ: Rutgers University Press.

Vö, L. T., & Bonus, R. (2002). *Contemporary Asian American communities: Intersections and divergences.* Philadelphia, PA: Temple University Press.

Wallis, V. (2013). *Two old women: An Alaska legend of betrayal, courage and survival.* New York, NY: HarperCollins.

Watt, S. K. (2007). Difficult dialogues, privilege and social justice: Uses of the privileged identity exploration (PIE) model in student affairs practice. *The College Student Affairs Journal, 26*(2), 114–125.

West, D. M. (2016). *Megachange: Economic disruption, political upheaval, and social strife in the 21st century.* Washington, DC: Brookings Institution Press.

Wetherell, M., & Mohanty, C. T. (Eds.). (2012). *The SAGE handbook of identities.* Thousand Oaks, CA: SAGE.

Yan, M. C., & Wong, Y. R. (2005). Rethinking self-awareness in cultural competence: Toward a dialogic self in cross-cultural social work. *Families in Society, 86*(2), 181–188.

Xue, C. (1997). *The embroidered shoes.* New York, NY: Henry Holt & Co.

CHAPTER 2

Social Construction and Difference

This chapter defines the elements of social construction and outlines ways of thinking about self and others. This lays a foundation for critically thinking about human behavior in social environments. The presence of ego, fault finding, judgment, and criticism, as well as socialization via messages informs reactions to others and the process of learning, unlearning, and deeper learning.

Traditional paradigms often employ binary conceptualizations, yet realities depict multiple dimensions. World history, which is usually connected to simple categories and labels, illustrates the magnitude of oppression against people of color and people of low wealth. The intersections of color and LGBTQI, of color and differently abled, of color and immigrants and refugees often increase the oppressive circumstances.

The observations of oppression and discrimination, the lived experience of it, and expressed reactions may be framed in many ways. The contexts of these manifestations require considerable recognition and assessment, especially for collaborating and intervention planning. Institutional exclusionary components have led to service gaps and discrimination that require evaluation of outcomes and consideration of alternative approaches to provide more effective services.

Persons experiencing warm environments with knowledge of family and community strengths may be somewhat protected from toxic beliefs and attitudes. Helping students and professionals review and consider the range of perspectives is part of the learning process. Evaluating the socialization process—messages received, behaviors that occur, exposure, and experiences—contribute to the critical thinking process that moves toward understanding.

LEARNING OBJECTIVES

- Most people have strong feelings about the groups they are born into.
- Exposure to information and respectful dialogue tend to lead toward understanding others.
- Observing multicultural participants in various roles enhances the ability to connect with others.

Benchmark: Students should be able to recognize social constructions.

Jeremy had heard a few members of his family at holiday gatherings say that women should only take care of children, Black people are dumb, immigrants should go back to where they came from, and LGBTQI people are vile. He knew many girls and there were some members of other groups in his high school, but he did not really know anyone outside of his group. He was very uncomfortable with the prospect of having a Black guy as a roommate.

WHAT IS SOCIAL CONSTRUCTION OF DIFFERENCE?

The messages people receive as they grow up, attend schools, and participate in sports, clubs, religious organizations, and community activities shape thinking about themselves, those in their communities, and others. Traditional messages incorporate normal or abnormal, male or female, usual and unusual, typical and atypical, and other categorizations. However, depending on where you live, the views of the people around you, and the experiences you seek, you may be exposed to perspectives that are much broader. Mindsets that are tied to the importance of learning and thinking for yourself rather than following include recognition and respect of the composition of the diverse ecosystems within which we live and work.

DEFINITION

Social construction is the process of establishing a view of people, places, or some entity or concept based on the messages and experiences one receives over time. Social construction theory was not included in the 1993 publication *Dictionary of Theories* (Bothamley, 1993). At that time, constructivism was related to art and construction with real materials. Another explanation of constructivism was connected to philosophy and mathematics that determined that entities could be constructed "based on things we accept already" (p. 115). Social comparison theory offered the view of using other people to evaluate oneself. It notes the preference for associating with others who are similar (Kantowitz, in Bothamley). Over time, conceptualizing others has moved from the narrow view of self and others like oneself to the huge world of human variation.

Social descriptions or identities have moved from simple observations to explanations that include people's different experiences, messages, and beliefs that influence views they hold. Traditional messages often suggest a way of thinking that cannot be generalized to a family or to a large group of people. Nevertheless, stereotypes and myths tend to categorize people within parameters based on generalizations from limited information and negative depictions.

Glenn (2013) points out that studies about race and gender were focused on men of color and white women as the usual subjects but omitted women of color in each of the explanations. The absence of citizens from other groups in the social construction discourse is a principle variable in recognizing the limitations based on traditional ways of thinking.

Broadly speaking, social construction comes from one's family or caregivers, media messages (print, broadcast, and now Facebook, Instagram, Twitter, etc.), organizations the individual and family are associated with, and educational institutions. For example, an urban, intercultural, Universalist, religious, nuclear family may have more welcoming constructs of immigrants than a rural, homogeneous, Christian, blended family. But there would be no real way to know how either the individual family members or the family as a group construct their views unless one engages with the family members and discusses ideas related to social identities. The need to include others and additional information in conversations is fundamental to establishing understanding.

According to a quotation by Daniel Lende (in Brendtro & Mitchell, 2013, p. 7), decades of research in biological anthropology and cultural anthropology have led to the conclusion that race is biological fiction and is a social construction. As such, it was elaborated by white scholars, and the error was in denying that there is one race, the human race (Brendtro & Mitchell, 2013). From their view, "racism is an irrational commitment to ignorance which is fed by negative emotions like hate, despair, doubt ... and fear" (p. 7).

ROLE OF EDUCATIONAL INSTITUTIONS

The role of educational institutions and the culture of the dominant players must be pointed to as having tremendous impact on how members of various class groups may be perceived and treated. Stanton-Salazar (1997) studied the roles and behaviors of institutional agents, teachers, and counselors and their impact in obstructing access to opportunities and resources for working-class and racial-minority children and youth. His social capital framework brings attention to the middle-class network features that promote Anglo Saxon cultural standards and avoids discussion of the exclusionary dynamics that challenge young minority students. In discussing these challenges, he notes the liberal sociologists' resistance to address this. The preference has been to focus on the capacity of students and their families to build resilience to tolerate and overcome the obstacles presented by the institutionalized structures.

HOW DO WE SEE RACE?

By relying on information from limited sources, one's views are not likely to expand or may resist incorporating new and different resources. How we see race has essentially been tied to messages about Black people and crime that were used to justify slavery and continually used to justify harsh treatment and penalties on people of color. In a recent article, Scott (2015) presents research by Eberhardt and others that shows how pictures of stereotypically portrayed Black people were rated negatively. Eberhardt reported, "No matter what we controlled for, the black defendants appeared to be punished in proportion to the blackness of their features." Similarly, other researchers (Lehrman, 2006) and those from Harvard, University of Virginia, and University of Washington have established how ingrained attitudes are about African Americans, women, thin people versus fat people, and so on. The Harvard's

Implicit Association Tests (Project Implicit, 2017) have evolved since 1988 through research on visual association tests and demonstrate pro-white biases among most people, including some of color. The impact of socialization is amazing and of concern. There are also views that the tests are not completely reliable (Bartlett, 2017).

SOCIALIZATION

Socially constructed opinions of minority youth have emphasized aggression and delinquent labels. Gibson and associates (2014) identified a plausible theoretical remedy that captures the tendency of many racial and low-wealth youth to react to the dominant/inflexible education institutional norms with anger and rebelliousness. As they considered the perspectives of educators, caregivers, and community members responding to young people of color receiving disproportionate rates of suspensions, the researchers focused on understanding the youngsters' developmental responses to educators' racial bias. These authors suggest the racial bias and cultural differences connected to social constructions of minority children to be responsible for the frequent punitive interventions rather than understanding that the rebellious behaviors of some children are more likely reactions to the school culture that pathologizes them.

These authors speculated that "the key may be creating a context in which issues of racial understanding are viewed as developmental" (Gibson et al., 2014, p. 280). Perhaps in this way, people can move toward more understanding and address developmental issues with more proactive and sensitive approaches to child and youth academic performance.

Chimamanada Adiche offers a robust illustration of how social construction works. In the TED Talk *The Danger of a Single Story,* she explains how the influence of one point of view impedes a sensible and more intelligent recognition of others.

PREDOMINANT MESSAGES

Receiving repeated predominant messages is the process of socialization. This involves taking in and responding to information regarding context and content (Persell, 1990) and results in fairly typical social interactions in usual environments. This occurs over the life span. These messages are received via social media, television, radio, billboards, magazines, and newspapers and are shared in family or household groups and community connections beginning from infancy. French (2007) points out that children do not develop in isolation but rather in the broad context of family, neighborhood, community, and society. This also suggests that as children develop and are exposed to messages that may be different from those experienced in their homes they begin to consider and evaluate perspectives that are different from theirs.

These messages impact personal views of self, family roles, ways of seeing and valuing others, and ways of thinking. The primary messages may be posed in the household, but others are heard and spoken in the streets and schools. There are alternative messages and ways of thinking connected to broader-based experiences and realities. For example, families in somewhat homogeneous environments may be more likely to engage in less expansive conversations than some families with diverse variables and connections. Children in a white family in a white community where parents and peers are healthy, employed, and feel comfortable and safe may not be as likely to discuss the self-valuing, strengths-based, and protective strategies that some bicultural families may discuss.

VIEWPOINTS

Viewpoints about social construction provide different ways of thinking about social descriptions. The Gibson team's investigation illustrates this and the discriminatory behaviors that may be tied to the constructions. Wetherhill and Mohanty provide a handbook of social identities that incorporates interdisciplinary interpretations of social divisions, social solidarities, categories, roles, and locations, as well as the associated practices of marginalization, exclusion, inclusion resistance, denigration, and segregation related to belonging (2012, p. 4). We cannot number these permutations as they are simultaneously connected to biology, culture, economics, race, language, relationships, religion, gender, ethnicity, class, ableism, performative behaviors, sexuality, indigeneity, families, geography, siblings, groups, and communities. The emergent field of identity studies gives credence to the multiple ways of constructing who we are. Several authors recognize the descriptors as parameters of being that don't inevitably place judgment.

WHY PROMOTE DIFFERENCE?

The rationale for promoting differences has generally been associated with maintaining the status quo for those with privilege under the existing social structure. Another view proposed by Roediger and Esch (2012) establishes the rationale for the production of difference that is tied to an analysis of labor control that revealed deliberate administrative policies to segregate and manipulate workers across cultures to the benefit of capitalists. This may be conceptualized as an outgrowth of slavery and the preservation of privilege. Buck speaks about the absence of emphasis on color in the early days before slavery. She notes that teaching about the value of whiteness occurred in order to divide and rule the labor force (Buck, 2014, p. 33). This social construction of racial group stereotypes is important to acknowledge in moving forward the discussion of the politics of judging identity as an element of social justice.

As we analyze the nature and process of social construction, it is critical to examine how it occurs in persons striving to understand and work with diverse people. This process may be explained by structural functional theory, how society operates to maintain narrow views, and how it may continually impact the self-esteem of young developing children exposed to these views in educational institutions. Simultaneously, exposing this process to critical thinking moves one's conceptualization through stages that respect others and address the challenges to interdisciplinary and community collaboration.

CONFRONTING DIFFERENCES

Evaluating the differences that social construction presents requires confronting the views that promote narrow descriptions of people. Advancing social and economic justice, engaging in diversity and difference provides the scaffolding to support innovative methods for inclusion of others in planning and delivering services. The consideration of human similarities rather than prejudicial differences in ideas about social identity construction and pervasive stereotypes is a starting point. The mistrust that stereotypes create should be recognized. Using social work theory that promotes strengths and recognizes self-determination can assist multidisciplinary helping professionals establish broader inclusive frameworks of social descriptions.

The SAGE Handbook of Prejudice, Stereotyping, and Discrimination (Dovidio, Hewstone, Glick, & Esses, 2010) presents the huge body of attitudes, beliefs, definitions, and dynamics related to ways differences are perceived and promoted. These occur through visible and invisible legitimate and subliminal machinations. Marshall McLuhan, considered the prophet of the electronic age, coined "the medium is the message" through *Understanding Media* (1964). He described how influential messages could and would be. Acknowledging the place of messaging from early print mediums of colonial times to contemporary Twitter accounts is critical to evaluating how negative messages about people with different contexts have been portrayed and treated. Perhaps we should consider differences simply as cultural variations. We are all unique humans.

NATURE OF AND REASONS FOR PREJUDICE

Prejudice is connected to social construction. Allport presented a comprehensive review in *The Nature of Prejudice* (1954) as the country reacted to the Supreme Court's decision in *Brown v. Board of Education* (Supreme Court History, n.d.) that segregation in schools is unconstitutional. Although the court decided that desegregation should occur with "deliberate speed," we continue to react to the biases and resistance that exist at institutional, cultural, and individual levels (Dovidio et al., 2010).

The brief definition of *prejudice* is "thinking ill of others without sufficient warrant" (Allport, 1954). Allport's work began there and progressed through several connected concepts of prejudgment, categorization, in-groups and out-groups, discrimination, ethnocentrism, and other related terms. At that time in the 1950s, key examples were related to Negroes (the term used then), Jews, and Japanese Americans. Unfavorable attitudes and overgeneralized beliefs were considered the basic ingredients for negative views. Moreover, natural mind processes, generalization, and hostility link categorization to prejudice as a normal process. Nevertheless, research regarding education and viewpoints indicated that people with grade school or high school education were less informed and held more intolerant attitudes about others than people with college education (Allport, 1954, p. 78). This research may not have accounted for viewpoints held by people of bicultural backgrounds. Reviewing Allport's work provides a basis for comparing current perspectives and considering one's own perspectives.

Conceptualizing prejudice, stereotyping, and discrimination over the decades has taken on additional phenomena, such as social cognition, functional relations and identity, and a more sophisticated analysis of bias (Dovidio et al., 2010). Contemporary interests include several disciplines such as neuroscience. Cultural neuroscience is an interdisciplinary science that investigates cultural variations in psychological, neural, and genomic processes (Chiao, 2015).

Epigenetics research is tied to this work and demonstrates the impact of oppression over time and its genetic release in subsequent generations. Findings conclude that negative behaviors can be transformed (Brendtro & Mitchell, 2013).

EGOCENTRISM

The basis of social construction is tied to egocentrism and its connection to individual and personality elements, as well as group membership. Egocentrism notes attitudes and behaviors that regard one's self and culture as the center of it all. Hutchinson notes this as a preoperational dynamic in children (2015, p. 511), and it usually precedes the ability to recognize other perspectives. This attitude is generally promoted in environments of privilege and imposed on others. Bizumic and Duckitt (2012) connected these attitudes and behaviors to hostility toward out-groups and the conceptualization of ethnocentrism.

However, there are many homes and communities of interest to our work that encourage humility and understanding regarding persons who visibly appear different. Some families are aware of multicultural heritage that may help develop mindsets that embrace collective rather than individualistic focus. Many share beliefs in humanity and the welfare of all (Hall, 2014).

A review of the history (Bizumic & Duckitt, 2012) and discussion of ethnocentrism identities three major categories to be most prevalent: group self-centeredness, out-group negativity, and in-group positivity. Additionally, they create other categories or facets of ethnocentrism and differentiate constructs such as prejudice, xenophobia, nationalism, social dominance orientation (SDO), right-wing authoritarianism (RWA), and racism (p. 16). Despite these variables, in-group views can support cohesion across groups and should be considered in assessing and developing ways to collaborate for policy formulation.

In addition to the egocentric base, a basic human feeling or opinion that places a negative view on persons of certain groups different from one's own group is intrinsic to prejudice. Some interpretations of history and human behavior use flawed concepts of manifest destiny or being chosen people to support prejudicial judgments. This opinion may exist before one is informed or educated about multiple perspectives that go beyond stereotypes. The narrow view is often present before one has any multidisciplinary substantive conversation or experiences with others. As people are more exposed to others with diverse experiences, race, culture, gender expression, economics, and religion, they may become capable of extending themselves in new relationships and opportunities to become more aware, tolerant, and willing to engage and learn about individual character traits rather than hold on to stereotypes about visible differences.

SOCIAL WORK AND THE STRENGTHS PERSPECTIVE

The other side of prejudged ideas is information about the strengths of groups—the information that prejudice does not focus on. The 20 core beliefs of the strengths perspective that Glicken lists recognizes the client as the primary agent of change. Workers need to understand clients' internal coping systems, their external ones, and the obstacles that exist in both environments (Glicken, 2004). With the strengths perspective as the theme for inclusion, reviewing other constructs about people invites readers to explore multicultural references and sources of knowledge that may help consumers identify and pursue goals. Promoting strengths helps readers move toward the social work competencies. This knowledge enhances skills that lead to engaging with diverse communities to advance human rights and social, economic, and environmental justice. Developing these skills requires expanding one's awareness of literature, music, and art of multiple cultures.

CONCEPTS OF STRENGTHS

The strengths perspective proposed by Dennis Saleebey (2012) in the social work literature brought attention to moving away from labeling perceptions of pathology in service users to approaches focused on strengths. Glicken (2004) modifies the definition to place the problem area in second place and puts emphasis on the daily successful strategies. Within the cultural literature, strengths take on broader and specific contexts. From the imagined to the realistic, visible, and invisible, spiritual dimensions are frequently ingrained in these ideas.

The concepts that arise from traditional or diverse messages influence the ways we think about people. The use of negative language about people shapes how people respond and engage.

Examining the nature of socialization and impact of social construction helps to identify conceptual baselines from which helping professionals begin to assess self-awareness and proceed to explore appreciating diversity and inclusion.

One of the most basic ways of promoting strengths and survival is through the oral tradition of folktales associated with various cultural groups but generally useful to all readers. These tales share ideas or visions of moving above and beyond the tribulations of life. Virginia Hamilton's *The People Could Fly* (1993) is an excellent example. Despite the tragic reality of people being taken from their native home of Africa, the belief that some people were able to fly, to get beyond their immediate circumstances, was embedded in their mindset. So after the people were put onto plantations, with the help of an elder those who had the flying capacity were sparked to revise that power and escaped in response to the horrible treatment the overseers imposed.

LaFerriere (2008) presents another example of the strength of believing in who you are, regardless of what others may think. His novel *I Am a Japanese Writer* alludes to the identities people have over time and place and how they might present themselves.

Self-assessment provides a qualitative baseline. Reevaluating one's self in moving through an educational curricula and exposure to different service users assists in ongoing reflection, self-reflection and learning. Critical self-reflection is pursued in stepping beyond critical thinking (Shank, 2016). This continual learning process moves us to analyze more deeply our self-judgment and potentially a broader awareness for engaging with others.

RESILIENCE

The strengths perspective is also considered the perspective of resiliency (Marsiglia, 2015). Strengths perspectives involve reading and listening to ideas and concerns of persons from diverse environments that speak to their ways of knowing and sharing. Emerging research that demonstrates the impact of environmental conditions on brain development is relevant to developing an understanding of the impact of historical trauma, adverse childhood experiences, and the mediating impact of strong, positive family and community supports and interventions. The construction of our experiences, the awareness of alternative experiences, and the impact of this knowledge on vulnerability and resilience contributes to how we see ourselves and others. The multiple views that exist among social identities and the intersections of these stand as fundamental reference points in working to develop our understanding of human behavior.

ALTERNATIVE AND COMPLEMENTARY SUPPORTS

Diverse ways of being and knowing allow notions of magic and other special characteristics to be linked in several cultural stories and to superstitious customs. Although contemporary trained persons often dismiss superstitions, many are still influenced in some ways by these traditional ideas. The *Dictionary of Superstitions* (Pickering, 2012) notes that some of the ideas related to plants and foods do have some scientific and realistic connections. Herbalism, aromatherapy, oracle cards, yoga, and energy medicine are contained in the holistic view of how people connect and interact with others and generate hope.

SOCIALLY CONSTRUCTED SUPPORTS

The ways we think about services and intervention are also connected to the messages we have heard. Social construction has been applied to resist the cultural remedies that people may use at home and in their communities. Western medical training has ignored natural remedies used in many communities. However, the prevalence of these other ways used around the world have become more influential in understanding people's stories. How people tell the stories of what has happened to them (Claxton, 2014) and how they have handled it so far resists the medical frame of what is wrong with someone and elicits a rapport that often becomes more engaging. Although this approach has been around, the attention provided through trauma-informed interventions reveals and validates the consumer as knowledgeable.

The National Center for Complementary and Alternative Medicine (2017) recognizes the range of varied components in the service users' environment. Consumer interest in herbs, also referred to as plant drugs, has prompted more research in the United States. The European use of phytomedicine, mostly developed in Germany, is not considered alternative but is integrated in the array of medical services (Foster & Duke, 2000). More research is being conducted, and there is a push for more inclusion and integration of diverse wellness concepts in service delivery.

Stories that address this range of broader contexts demonstrate how authors suggest facing challenging circumstances. Connecting the place of strengths in the visualization of advancing social justice from the history of slavery to the pursuit of equal access denotes a pathway for appreciating diversity. Andrew Young and Jacqueline Woodson offer two intriguing examples in *A Way Out of No Way*. This phrase is associated with the experience of slavery: "The Lord can make a way out of no way" (Young, 1992). Young recalls the journey over his lifetime connected to his spirituality, his reliance on God, and his place as one with heaven and earth (p. 21).

Woodson (1996) refers to writing that inspired her as a young girl and shares the words of several writers to offer readers ways out of no way. Young and Woodson constructed views of their experiences using the same theme with similar yet certainly different images of black life that are often neglected in stereotypical frameworks.

MICRO CONNECTIONS AND AGGRESSIONS

These culturally derived interpretations operate in small and large ways. The strengths base reflects connections. They may be useful in the many instances of micro aggressions that people of various identities experience in the world in daily life activities. Resilience and the potential for success reside within the micro domains of individual and family life. Micro examples of growing, learning, and accomplishment run parallel to stories of struggle and punishment.

Generally, a micro aggression can be considered to stem from the influences of social constructions. The use of the term has evolved since 1970, and much attention is associated with the work of Wang and Sue in 2007 (Fisher, Moore, Simmons, & Allen, 2017). Sue (2010) defined *micro aggression* as "the brief and commonplace daily verbal, behavioral, and environmental indignities, whether intentional or unintentional, that communicate hostile, derogatory, or negative racial, gender, sexual-orientation, and religious slights and insults to the target person or group" (p. 5).

The impact of social construction on the micro level often plays out in the ways people may behave toward one another or in the things they might say that from another's view may be disrespectful or aggressive. Reactions to micro aggressions may range from invisible physiological changes to visible and audible comments of discomfort or anger. Harrell, Hall, and Taliaferro (2003) use specific physiological data regarding blood pressure and cardiovascular activity to illustrate the impact of social pressures on people of color.

The nature of prejudice—the socialization process and individual ingrained behaviors and attitude—has established a process of social categorization that provides the basis "for social biases to develop and persist" (Dovidio et al., 2010, p. 14). These are most readily visible in interpersonal transactions. Prejudicial attitudes or beliefs are evident as behaviors that may be translated into political frames that create policies and laws that discriminate and penalize through institutional structures. Individual and group behaviors give rise to system obstacles that restrict economic opportunities and intergroup relationships, such as pertaining to immigrants and host nations.

VIEWS FROM THE OUTSIDE AND THE INSIDE

The research on prejudice is huge, from different forms and origins of bias; cognitive, affective, and motivational processes; and intrapersonal processes, demonstrated in subtle to blatant interactions (Dovidio et al., 2010). There are views associated with all the groups typically considered marginalized, as well as broad race, class, and gender notions. The context of manifest destiny that contributes to egocentric biases is resisted not only in the United States but also in other countries around the world. As we consider the dynamics of prejudice, bias, and discrimination, we should also include the colonialism these ideas have perpetuated and the reactions that have occurred and still exist.

OUTSIDE VIEWS

Predominant views about people of color or non-white people, persons with physical and emotional challenges, immigrants, and lesbian, gay, bisexual and transgender persons have been established by people outside of these groups. So much of what has been taught excluded voices of people with bicultural or intersectional identities and experiences. Their stories have always been available, but they have been covered or neglected in mainstream media presentations. Typical construction by mainstream agents has been related to stereotypes about how people may behave and the places in which they live (Smith, 2013). These constructs have been based on monocultural perspectives.

The concepts that have framed some thinking about service users, patients, recipients, clients, or consumers tend to categorize people as *deserving* and *nondeserving*. Since people that social work works with may fall into the undeserving lot, it has been somewhat paradoxical that professionals must interact with them and somehow put out of mind the socialized ideas that abound. This contradictory context has influenced the extent to which social workers have become activists to modulate or eliminate the uncomplimentary notions. As multiple perspectives are expressed, the impact of socialization has resulted in emphasizing a key value of social work—that all people matter, but some people are marginalized more than others. Acknowledging these reveal impediments to social work's active participation in politics and advocacy.

INSIDE VIEWS

There are impressive examples of oppressive constraints regarding the major social descriptors. Frye's description of the trappings of a birdcage illustrates the duality of image and reality (Frye, 2014). She brings to our attention the forces that mold, flatten, and reduce—that restrict mobility and how difficult it is to get away from or bypass the wires of the cage. Moving beyond the traditional messages that have been incorporated in the socialization process involves digging deeper, reading more, listening, and understanding voices in order to help modify the messages about people and cultural variations. Advocating, respecting, and including voices with dual perspectives help in navigating the challenges to improving collaboration.

Work to develop strategies to counteract prejudice is occurring. Limited research on the impact of stigma on people and on their coping methods is in part lack of understanding about how stereotypes, prejudice, and discrimination affect those targeted by these behaviors (Dovidio et al., 2010). In addition to multicultural education in schools and reformed disciplinary and criminal justice procedures, several lines of research have emerged to address reducing prejudice and biased behaviors. Moving beyond theories that explain the normality of prejudice, new theories seek to explain possible mediating processes of inter-personal and intergroup context regarding gender and class as well as race and ethnicity (Dovidio et al., 2010).

VIEWS THAT UNDERSTAND

Social cognitive associative training is another path for reducing the application of stereo-types (Dovidio et al., 2010, p. 19). Ongoing research on the physiological manifestations of discrimination on people of color (Clark, 2001) is revealing more specific data that drive better understanding the impact of inequality and inhumanity. Micro and macro situations illustrate challenging conditions for people of color; women; people facing physical, emotional, and learning challenges; and older people. Expanding our awareness and multidisciplinary efforts is in process.

INDIVIDUALS AND FAMILIES—MICRO AGGRESSIONS

Addressing the micro issues of aggression and social and economic injustice with clients is needed to provide more effective practices with populations across cultural groups. Being aware of race, class, and gender expression in the practice office and the institution involves acknowledgment. Rather than being blind to color or other diversity, or ignoring differences, acknowledging personal and family characteristics and listening to narratives helps engage people to work on mutually discussed concerns and goals.

STEREOTYPE THREATS

What happens on the micro level often is camouflaged, played out in micro aggressive com-ments unrecognized by many white persons but recognized and felt by others. Sometimes this dynamic operates as a stereotype threat. Defined by Steele and Aronson (1995), this refers to being at risk of confirming, as a self-characteristic, a negative stereotype about one's social group. Stoesser and Good (2005) connect this to potentially reducing one's performance because of the impact the negative view may have on someone.

Research conducted under the auspices of the Russell Sage Foundation, an organization that supports the study of social science concepts, showed that stereotypes are connected to achievement barriers for women in math and for African American academic performance in schools (Deaux, Bikmen, Gilkes, Ventuneac, & Steele, 2007). Another study suggests that as a result of this dynamic, the second generation of West Indian immigrants fared not so well in comparison to the first-generation group (Steele & Aronson, 1997).

The dynamics regarding stereotypes about people of color, members of religious groups, and challenged people might not quickly come to mind, but almost everyone can be impacted by this. For example, stereotypes about women and math, white people appear-ing racist, men and sensitivity, and the like illustrate how perceived threats can affect one's self-efficacy (Stoesser & Good, 2005). These influences sometimes transform potential into non-actualized talent.

Speculation associates exposure in the socialization venue to ideas of reduced ability to actual reduced achievement. Research and observations over the years demonstrate that environments that promote potential and expect achievement have been more successful in helping develop growth (Miller-Lachmann & Taylor, 1995; Wilson, 1992; Wynn, 1992). High expectations exhibited in teaching and social encounters, interactions, and communication have more promising results (Saffigna, Church, & Tayler, 2011).

PROMOTING WARM, WELCOMING ENGAGEMENT ACROSS SETTINGS

Early research on prejudice, stereotyping, and discrimination focused on the typical presence of negative ideas about members of minority groups. On the individual level, evolving research incorporates multiple perspectives. But what about the prejudice and bias of members of the groups that have been the focus? Yes, people of color, women, and persons facing challenges also express bias. Yet it is noted that these more frequently occur in reaction to their exposure to episodes of disrespect or devaluation (Dovidio et al., 2010). The reality of reactions to biases by members of the groups and their ability to process and move beyond the experience of subtle or blatant devaluation or stigma needs to be considered as a legitimate issue in the structure of effective interventions.

Paying attention to the uniqueness of people and being aware of micro aggressions help developing practitioners address these issues in more specific ways. The following examples illustrate how these situations might look among citizens of diverse backgrounds.

WOMEN

Micro aggression or micro insults (Brendtro & Mitchell, 2013) against women may be observed in conversations that imply a woman should be married, should have children, or perhaps should not be pursuing major work or career goals. Or examples may involve some references to sexual innuendo. Although contemporary society promotes ideas of equality, there are daily incidents of insensitive comments, bullying, and stereotypical overtures in schools, workplaces, and social situations. These forces may present obstacles that hold women back, obstruct opportunities, delay progress, or send them onto destructive pathways.

Traditional constructs of women's lives have promoted marriage and caring for a husband and family. Although many do strive for conventional arrangements, the reality is that marriage does not happen for everyone; and for many that do get married, divorce may occur. According to Single Mother Statistics (Lee, 2017), about 49% of single mothers have never married, while 51% are divorced, separated, or widowed. Most of these mothers are White, next are Black and the smaller percentage are Hispanic. One third have a college degree, and one sixth have not completed high school (Lee, 2017). The Pew Research Center (Livingstone, 2014) reported that fewer than half of the children in the United States live in a traditional family.

Family arrangements that exist today have always been part of the array of household compositions, but the proportion that does not meet the traditional construction of family is much higher. This changed family construction is more complex and how this has come to be is not simply explained. The interplay of social, economic, and technological developments and local and federal policies have influenced personal and family decision-making. People are waiting longer to marry or are not marrying. Many children live with parents who live together but are not married. The economy accounts for many deciding not to marry or to delay, especially until their finances look better. According to CNN, 53% of women over 18 are single. Many are deciding that marriage is not the best deal for them (Schwartz, 2014). DePaulo (2018) presents recent research that touts the benefits of being single.

Jimmy Carter's *Call to Action* (2014) is a critical, radical, and sobering assessment of the interplay of social dynamics that have contributed to the creation of systems that promote violence, the denigration of women, and the obstruction of justice. His recent comments confronted the oppressive stance the Southern Baptist church has against women.

Vice Essentials (2017) *Ovary Action* reports that the United States is one of two countries that does not have guaranteed leave for mothers. They include information about the Swedish system. Their taxes are higher than some other countries. According to the interviewed couple, they are able to plan for their family, knowing there will be a system in place to help them. This helps moms and dads take parental leave, up to 12 months to bond with and care for their children. In the example presented, the mom continued working because she was offered a great career opportunity. The presence of a parent with the child was not obstructed. The child ultimately benefits in this arrangement. The parents have less stress, and the children are protected by the system.

The ability of individuals and families to develop and mature within strong protective families is associated with positive outcomes. Socialization that includes conversations about the value of women, the potential to become whatever they desire, and expectations for fair treatment from family members and other citizens supports resilience building.

LESBIAN, GAY, BISEXUAL, TRANSGENDER, QUEER, AND INTERSEX (LGBTQI)

The terminology regarding LGBTQI is substantial, with many terms coming into use in recent years. Green and Patterson (2003) developed a list of relevant terminology. Human sexuality is diverse. Social construction regarding sexuality based on Western thinking links it to procreation (Hubbard, 2014). Sexual or gender expression outside of the reproductive framework has been stigmatized and may result in aggressions toward persons who identify outside of the traditional binary (Meyer, 2013).

The conservative stance in some families about gender expression has been the basis for the increasing number of youth expelled from homes and relegated to homelessness (Wayman, n.d.). It is reported that increasing numbers of LGBTQI youth are locked out or abandoned by their parents. This population has been sexually abused by the age of 12 at double the rate of other teens. Social construction may obstruct the ability of some family members to love those who do not conform to their binary gender expectations. Additionally, some transgender persons may be mistreated and discriminated against by workers that are supposed to help them (Crockett, 2015).

Traditional identity work focused on individual feelings, thoughts, and behaviors about sexuality. Emergent thinking addresses the stressors of families with lesbian, gay, and bisexual youth as well as the sexual fluidity that may occur before youth label or decide not to label themselves (Chung & Singh, 2010).

Moving toward more tolerance, acceptance, and support of people who identify in ways that don't conform to binary or heterosexual expectations may be difficult for some. Yet people who identify as their experiences and life realities lead them are above all else members of the human race. Understanding requires stepping closer to appreciating diversity by working to engage through inclusion, to listen to experiences others have had in shaping who they are.

PEOPLE OF COLOR

The government's conception of identity as described by the census categories reflects social construction that many citizens have not been in agreement with. Early categories were white-not-Hispanic, Black, Asian, and Hispanic (U.S. Census Bureau, n.d.). Asian Americans spoke out in the 1960s and 1970s that they were more than this broad category. Native Hawaiian or other Pacific Islander was added. More recently as the Latino population has grown, some have expressed the disconnect between the demographers' categories and the way people identify themselves (Navarro, 2014). Their view of race is different. With mixed-race persons exerting their right to identify with more than one race, deciding to check *Other*, or to leave the race category blank, demographers and others are engaged in discussions on how to address this. Research has also noted the tendency for parents with Mexican ancestry not to identify their children as Latino. How the numbers are described or calculated is a political issue that can influence how some policy decisions are determined.

Immigration. The political context is an important one across civil and human rights issues. Immigration issues and social construction are especially concerning. Public officials' use of positive or negative constructions regarding Latino immigrants manipulates winning or losing policy resources (Magaña, 2013). The 1996 Illegal Immigration Reform and Immigrant Responsibility Act (IIRIRA) restricted access to social services even for legal immigrants. Over the years, the negative construction of immigrants was continued and resulted in several election wins for anti-immigrant candidates. Eventually, pushback occurred, as evidence of the harm to some states rather than positive outcomes was realized.

Economics. Social construction regarding people of color is especially connected to economic justice. A principle discussion of social construction regarding people of color, especially African Americans, was proposed by the sociologist W. E. B. DuBois in *The Philadelphia Negro* (1899). His study of the Seventh Ward in Philadelphia provided concise evidence to reject the messages of white sociologists about inherent racial differences. He noted that the social problems facing black citizens in Philadelphia were derived from the way they had been treated in the past and their relegation to the menial and low-paying jobs. He concluded that "capitalists" had an unbridled self-interest within the context of white supremacy that prevented their deeper efforts to assist lives of black citizens because that might impose some level of hardship on them (DuBois, 1899). For many persons of color, the absence of employment opportunities and low-income realities impact life choices, including decisions to marry and the ability to raise children.

Health. The health disparities show how the stress and stigma associated with racism and discrimination is evident by the physiological changes that occur in people's bodies. Research now shows changes in blood pressure and heart rates occur in response to micro aggressions (Clark, 2001). Access to income and insurance impacts health care.

Criminal justice. Descriptions of people of color that have emphasized crime and violence influence negative perceptions that account for racial profiling and disproportionate contacts with the criminal justice system. Moreover, there are disparities in how U.S. police use force against people of color (Crockett, 2015). Reports of the violence perpetrated by white officers on black citizens demonstrate high levels of animosity and hatred that we might speculate in part derives from the negative messages of the socialization process.

PEOPLE FACING CHALLENGES

Stella Young, in a 2014 TED Talk ("I'm Not Your Inspiration, Thank You Very Much"), described her experiences in being perceived as an inspiration to others just because she moved around in a wheelchair. She pointed out how this stereotype really did nothing for her but create a false image. She watched television, talked to her friends, and helped out in her mother's salon—routine, everyday habits of daily living. She wanted to dispel the stereotype that placed her in an inflexible box that suggested that in dealing with her challenge she had to be an inspiration. She actually called it "inspiration porn."

Disability. According to Baynton (2014), disability has been used as a justification for inequality. The concept of not having some ability has been used to justify discriminating against women and minorities. People who opposed women's suffrage, African American freedom and civil rights, and restricting immigration used arguments that introduced stereotypes of flaws, deficits, and other deviations from the white male norm (p. 94) as rational explanations for discrimination.

Mental health. Another concern for health and mental health professionals regarding social construction is the stigma and prejudice directed toward persons with mental health distress. In Pennsylvania, 448,000 residents were diagnosed with a serious mental illness (National Alliance on Mental Illness [NAMI], 2010). People who were incarcerated showed higher proportions than those in the general population: 31% of female inmates and 14% of males incarcerated were diagnosed with a serious mental illness (NAMI, 2010). Persons with a mental health diagnosis have been categorized via social construction to be *Other* and linked to descriptions as "violent, untrustworthy and incapable" (Holley, Stromwall & Tavassoli, 2015). The effect of labeling prevents many from seeking services.

Timander, Grinyer, and Möller (2013) add another dimension to construction by connecting mental distress to the *Disability* and *Identity* categories, especially as people move into the recovery phase. Some agreed that mental health should be connected to oppression; others rejected that, tying it to disability. Nevertheless, it offers another perspective to be included when conceptualizing the social influences upon people and how improving services has more to contemplate than the monocultural framework allows.

Addiction. Persons with *Addiction* labels also experience stigma and marginalization by socially constructed assumptions about their mental stressors, substance use, and the related behaviors. It is understandable that persons who may acquire labels if they seek services or who have already received a diagnosis may be reluctant to expose this information. In terms of using coping strategies, they may decide that concealing this identity is safer than revealing it. With increasing numbers of persons tied to substance use and suicidal ideations, it is imperative that more attention is paid to addressing stigma in the manner that services are offered.

Social constructs tend to illustrate limited abilities of persons who have experienced physical, emotional, or learning limitations. People who work in settings that serve this population are often stymied by limited resources. Some staff remain connected to social constructs that suggest these persons are capable of very little. Others adhere to concepts of recovery that have broadened their understanding of mental health and addiction and the circumstances that may lead people toward particular ways of coping. Volkow (2015) acknowledges that brain researchers bear some responsibility in failing to educate the public on addiction's complexity. Innovations that have changed ways of thinking about the challenges some people face have sustained important modifications in information about addiction's impact on brain chemistry and the inability to exert will and follow through (Volkow, 2015).

Aging. Age, gender, and race discrimination occurs in the United States and in countries around the world. Avalon's (2014) analysis of the European social survey indicates that young and old women and ethnic minorities report more discrimination than others across 28 countries in Europe. This study reported a higher prevalence of perceived age discrimination than previous studies. Life satisfaction is connected to perceptions of discrimination and their interpretation of events.

Ly and Crowshoe (2015) agree that the quality of care and the outcomes of health services are affected by dominant cultural attitudes. Since medical students in their study felt stereotypes are rooted in reality, they see the cultural gap between Aboriginal and non-Aboriginal people as a starting point to address issues of racism and health inequities and note research is needed in the area of impact of stereotypes.

There is a range of descriptions of people across cultures, groups, and locations. Simple conceptualization is not useful for professionals seeking to assist persons in need. The emphasis on labeling and negative generalizations adds to the challenges people may bring to settings in which assessment and resource management is determined. Understanding the dynamics of social construction and the impact on some citizens that come for services is crucial.

Consider this room of service users on your first day of beginning client engagement. This is an after-school walk-in quiet room designed by the school to address emotional health needs after students have been oriented to prevention messages over the first few weeks of school.

To prepare for this, you have been advised to imagine meeting someone for the first time and who will be seated behind a curtain. You will not be able to see the person, and the service user cannot see you. Write a brief script for how you would begin and move through a 5-minute interaction. Which cultural dynamics would you want to know about, and which ones of yourself would you want to share? Review your comments. Are any social constructions connected to your perspectives? Why? Why not?

MACRO CONNECTIONS = LIMITED ECONOMIC OPPORTUNITIES AND HEALTH DISPARITIES

The impact of social construction on the macro level is usually observed in the policies that obstruct access to rights or services. Institutional bias is recognized in the ways some groups gain economic advantage over others. Organizations produce inequalities, often through policies based on business justifications to discriminate (Smith, Brief, & Colella, 2010). Macro dynamics also account for policies that may penalize people in low-wealth categories more than others. Within the macro systems, we view ways traditional thinking is perpetuated and maintains social controls on the micro level.

The impact of prejudice and discrimination in the macro realm leads to recognizing and assessing discriminatory-related factors such as stress, stigma, and how people are enabled or hampered in the process of coping. Emotional reactions to the frustrations created by crisis situations challenge families, individuals, and communities. Often, policies are designed by persons who may not face these challenges and, deliberately or not, create ongoing barriers to healthier functioning. Educational, health and mental health systems are of significance in working to include diverse consumer populations in ways that address chronic needs and provide community education for prevention. A long-term strategy to support coping is to change the sociocultural context that fosters stereotyping, prejudice, and discrimination (Dovidio et al., 2010, p. 422).

COMMUNITIES: MACRO AGGRESSIONS

Macro aggressions may be defined as policies of institutional structures that restrict opportunities. On the broadest scale, illustrations of interactions around the world occur through daily media messages directed through companies owned by a few wealthy corporations. Conflicts exist in so many environments. Different media channels present an array of perspectives. Al Jazeera, BBC, Bloomberg, CNN, France 24, MSNB, and NPR offer various versions of issues. ABC, CBS, NBC, and Fox offer their views. Newspapers, blogs, podcasts, periodicals, magazines, and newsletters present other views. About 12 conglomerates are highlighted as the major media companies (Selyukh, Hollenhorst, & Park, 2017). There are various connections among them and there are conservative competitors such as the Sinclair Broadcast Group (De la Merced & Fandos, 2017) that vie for control of local television outlets. Some media are called alternative, emphasizing views not covered by the traditional outlets. This array of coverage includes traditional to diverse voices that address, report, and influence issues of civil and human rights.

Every situation that helping professionals face is shaped by system structures as well as individual and family situations. Examples of policies or macro concerns that impact women, people of color, persons facing challenges, and others are typically influenced by traditional exclusionary standards.

WOMEN

The American family structure has changed. Two-parent families have declined, families are smaller, and more births occur to women who are single or living with a nonmarital partner (Pew Research Center, 2015). Policies that urge increasing the minimum wage offer an option for the many single heads of households working more than one job and spending little time with their children because they are trying to feed and clothe them. Women in head-of-household positions need a higher minimum raise to care for their families.

According to Rampell (2013), data from the 2011 U.S. Census indicates the median family income for young, black, and Hispanic single mothers with less education is $23,000. For older, white, married women with higher education who earn more than their husbands, the median is $80,000. Women with higher levels of education have increased their capacity to attract higher salaries and add to the well-being of their families.

For residents of communities with lower-quality schools, access to education and policies that drive curriculum impact their earning potential. Similarly, policies that take away health care and reproductive rights jeopardize the health of low-income women. Statistics report the increased numbers of women who take to extreme and harmful home remedies to end unwanted pregnancies when access to appropriate care is not available (Levintova, 2015).

Another way of expressing this concern comes from Sister Joan Chittister, a Benedictine nun:

> I do not believe that just because you're opposed to abortion, that that makes you pro-life. In fact, I think in many cases, your morality is deeply lacking if all you want is a child born but not a child fed, not a child educated, not a child housed. And why would I think that you don't? Because you don't want any tax money to go there. That's not pro-life. That's pro-birth. We need a much broader conversation on what the morality of pro-life is. (Salzillo, 2015, para 1)

Elizabeth Warren has garnered attention to her focus on jobs that have been taken away from families and the wage gap for women. She endorsed the Economic Policy Institute's recommendations to "increase the minimum wage, increase pay transparency and codify equal pay"

(Caldwell, 2015). Education, housing, transportation, and health care polices impact women and their potential to care for their families.

PEOPLE OF COLOR

The issues involved in policy development that impact people on a macro basis are multifaceted. These examples may be contemplated for the systemic obstacles that exist because of socially constructed frames of reference that devalue or ignore the needs of many.

Finances. Kiel (2016) presents a news analysis that summarizes the financial setbacks that frequently occur against families of color because of debt collection policies. He describes how small financial problems can spiral into major expenses. He links this to historical racism but more specifically to low incomes and the high proportion of court judgments. His research revealed the rate of debt collection lawsuits and judgments were twice as high in mostly black communities than in mostly white ones. Revising policies for debt collection could ensure less-damaging results. Restrictions on how much of a worker's paycheck could be garnished or how much of a bank account could be seized could help people address legitimate debt recovery needs and also allow workers access to some of their income to care for their families.

The view that Asian Americans are the model minority refers to a generalized picture. Lui and associates (2014) present more detail about the economics of this group overall and within the Asian subgroups. They report that high income rates and high poverty rates exist, and there is a substantial range within the various Asian ethnic groups.

Voting access. The report that 20 Department of Motor Vehicles (DMV) offices were closed in Alabama raised concerns that it would obstruct mostly African Americans in rural counties from obtaining identification to be used for voting. The state's call that the closures were needed because of budget constraints was responded to by the community. Initial reaction was that the political machine wanted to limit black voters. Subsequent review by the governor allowed the community members to air their perspectives, and further review occurred to determine if some options might be available (Lyman, 2015).

Education. Several observers have noted the need for more effective educational systems and curricula in low-wealth areas. Kozol's *Still Separate, Still Unequal* (2005) follows up on *Brown v. Board of Education*. There continues to be segregation and limited financing in schools that serve predominantly minority communities. The You Tube *Shame of a Nation* (2014) summarizes his concerns.

Shyamalan (2013) reports on observations of the Philadelphia school system. He investigated some popular reform ideas, the would-be reformers, and the processes of the schools that resulted in successes. He points to the delays that summer breaks create. Placement tests were "powerfully changed" by what happened between June and September. He commented that the impact of ongoing summer break times affects performance gaps despite the best quality pre-school instruction. In reviewing several studies of educational achievement and the obstacles, these elements appear significant: Students need high-quality teachers, varied instruction, more hours per day, and more days per year of instruction.

Native Americans continue to seek methods to improve their access to resources in their environments. Children and youth in educational districts that serve students from American Indian (AI) and Alaska Native (AN) backgrounds are overrepresented in disciplinary exclusions from the classroom and incarceration. In a study by a team led by Sprague (2013), exclusions of Native Americans compared to those of White students revealed "strikingly" different exclusionary consequences of policy violations. Poor educational outcomes are linked to feelings of being unwelcomed in the schools, distant teacher–student relationships, and culturally irrelevant learning environments (Tallbear.com, n.d.). Since attendance is measured from a white perspective, the results might be different if attendance is defined by people from different cultural backgrounds.

Addressing the issues that contribute to poor student outcomes and seeking to meet goals for students' social and academic competence requires operationalizing procedures from culturally equitable positions. Social construction constrains educational opportunities and requires more information, assistance, and organizational decision-making that commits to addressing the failures to minority students inherent in the existing education system.

Zanoni and Mampaey (2011) acknowledge the attainment gap of students in Western educational systems and present ideas of how inclusion can result in higher achievement levels. They present the contradiction that schools must address not skirt;—that the goals of inclusion come up against the institutional pressures to exclude minorities in order to attract majority students. "Majority parents avoid ethnically diverse schools because they are influenced by the [social construction] that inclusion means lower quality education" (p. 2).

Their investigation and analysis focuses on loose practices—the use of language as a way to reconstruct social frameworks to create positive discourse. Using the case example of Flanders, Belgium (an exclusive district), specific recommendations for changing the dynamics include the following:

1. Modifying the internal relationships of the school and relationships with external actors via partnerships with stakeholders, including minority parents and universities
2. Enhancing the organizational culture to demonstrate commitment to student needs
3. Using minority students' cultural capital, which is devalued by the educational system (Zanoni and Mampaey, 2011, p. 3).

When schools maintain the rigid ruling-class culture, they perpetuate the systems that have been failing. Developing a representative model with quality outcomes can be publicized so the outcomes are valued. For example, Williams (2017) points to a statistic that shows the potential impact of black males being exposed to black teachers in elementary grades. It helps them stay in school and want to persist toward college. This is not new information. It affirms the need for diverse staff in schools where impressions can really impact students. How can its implementation be improved? Does this role representation dynamic apply in other settings? Can recovering persons in treatment facilities bring a different level of outcomes?

There is some data (Shaw, 2003) that suggests this. Teachers exposed to more positive methods of intervention with diverse students also have positive results. A team of researchers (Elder et al., 2011) using meditation with students resulted in increased academic performance. Administrators across disciplines can pay more attention to these examples to enhance personnel policies and recruitment toward this goal.

Criminal justice. Criminal justice statistics clearly reflect targeting young men of color for detention rather than alternatives has aided the economy of private investors. Community sentencing options generally are offered white youth rather than black or Latino youth. Alexander (2012) and others report that polices over the last 4 decades have put more people of color in prison. Davis (Davis, 1998) describes the prison industrial complex and highlights the private capital gains associated with the punishment industry. The construction industry has benefited from building new prisons, and military tech companies are also benefiting. She also notes that other businesses profit from prison workers, including IBM, Motorola, Honeywell, Nordstrom, and Microsoft. Davis (2016) also reports on the continuing struggle to speak out, organize, and resist the pushback for freedom and equality

Limited data on offenses committed in the Asian American and Pacific Islander (AAPI) communities is raised as an area of concern. Hu and Esthappan (2017) point out that despite the notion of privilege in this community, recent cases involving persons of Asian descent "illustrate AAPIs' ambiguous position in the criminal justice system."

Efforts to address these disparities are widespread, but analysts admit the task is colossal, given the existing mindsets about minority groups and punishment. Many states have made reforms and reduced prison admissions. In the 15 states the Urban Institute observed, no changes had been made, and many projections of increasing rates of reforms have not been implemented. (King, Peterson, Elderbroom, & Pelletier, 2015).

PERSONS FACING CHALLENGES

Macro aggressions against people with physical, emotional, and learning challenges are often associated with minds set against stable and long-term employment opportunities. Traditional sheltered workshops and vocational opportunities were connected to ideas about the capacities of persons who were labeled *Handicapped* or *Disabled.* Often, they received no pay or were paid less than minimum wage. Legislation was proposed in April 2015 to encourage economic self-sufficiency and competitive employment for people with disabilities (Diament, 2015).

Recent reports of high school courses show examples of integrating life skills and work skills into special education school and community activities. A Mississippi high school has used a student-run business to learn the food-preparation trade (Crawford, 2015). Students cooperate in decision-making about using funds for the business and for their participation in community events. An Arkansas High School (Middleton, 2015) is helping students learn skills and confidence through community internships. Heasley (2017) recommends using more actors with disabilities. These strategies promote understanding of persons with different capacities and help inform our communities of the strengths people have.

However, the intersection of ethnicity and special needs continues to be plagued by inadequate practices and resources for providing appropriate care. Fletcher and Navarrete (2003) brought attention to the Hispanic students at risk due to unprepared teachers and misused testing and assessment procedures. Concerns that are related to ways of thinking about disabilities involve second-language learners and outdated modes of diagnosis related to neurological dynamics rather than "instructional" frameworks that have obstructed learning for many diverse students.

Procedures for working with persons diagnosed with schizophrenia have resisted genuine efforts to collaborate with patients in determining their care. Standardized uses of medication and hospitalization have been the norm. Some alternatives are now being reviewed. A first-break program (Carey, 2015) is an approach to treating people who are experiencing their first psychotic break. Although it is called "new," it is a form of case management that is more client-centered than traditional hospitalization approaches. The service delivers a process that emphasizes "supportive services, sustained one-on-one therapy, school and work assistance, and family education, as well as medication" (Thoms, 2015). Therapists work to engage the patient as an equal partner in decisions about medication and dosages (Thoms, 2015).

Substance use. Cordova and colleagues (2015) examined ecodevelopmental factors—poverty, exclusion, post-colonialism racism, and their connection to alcohol and drug use among Latinos with physical disabilities. Noting the high rates of substance use among persons with disabilities, research and effective service provision is limited for this community. Their research used a Photovoice methodology that organized the participants' concerns of micro and macro influences of risk and protection regarding their substance use. The absence of culturally responsive health and mental health care jeopardizes the protection of these citizens.

Implementing approaches that involve mutual planning and decision-making contests old stereotypes and social constructions that emphasized persons' limitations. Innovation requires institutional systems and workers to develop broader understanding of human behavior and appreciation of diversity.

CASE SCENARIO 2

Consider this room of service users on your first day of client engagement. This is an after-school walk-in quiet room designed by the school to address emotional health needs after students have been oriented to prevention messages over the first few weeks of school. To prepare for this, you have been advised to inform the students of the phases of services that are available. You gather their interests on index cards and share a resource list of multicultural mentoring services, early vocational, and tutoring services. You indicate the first session will also include a peer-led engagement group that begins with listening to student participants' selected music. How would this be different from Case Scenario 1?

STRUCTURAL DYNAMICS AND POWER

Structural constructs associated with class and privilege set a framework by which individual, family, and community behaviors are critiqued. Although cultural group memberships may establish standards of ethics and family tradition that foster family protection and survival, the association of income and material possession tends to be the criteria of advantage. The ethical- or humanity-focused domain is frequently overlooked, as stereotypes tend to present notions that create devaluing and dismissal of diverse family life structures.

The traditional social constructs are limited by the emphasis on structural functional maintenance that neglects the consideration of context. The notions of exclusion, prejudice, and discrimination are ingrained. Such beliefs limit exposure to other people and can obstruct the capacity to be welcoming. Beliefs and community efforts for mutual support and collective problem-solving that drive many interventions are minimized. Nevertheless, this is the dimension that social work standards and goals direct continuous improvements.

Grimes and Slaughter (2006) call out parents of children of color and urge a deeper commitment to protecting children from the marginalization that has been perpetrated upon them. Resisting the frames that promote passive acceptance need to be acknowledged and confronted for the sake of the children. Observations often reveal that once opportunities to meet others, read from various genres, and reflect together occur, strong relationships, new ways of thinking, and higher levels of creativity can develop.

INCREASING THE STRENGTHS PERSPECTIVES IN THE SOCIALIZATION PROCESS

When we move to focus more on the stories of strengths and resilience, we have many examples to share of how people have continually met the struggles presented them with strengths, fortitude, and persistence. Promoting the strengths perspectives requires policy advocacy and practice implementation of strategies to build confidence, self-esteem, increased family engagement, community education, and citizen participation.

This concept of overcoming is intrinsic to strengths. This is the component of socialization that supports communities and leads to positive self-esteem, self-confidence, and community empowerment. Delgado's (1999) practice and research on youth development, community-capacity enhancement and nontraditional urban settings urges social workers to assess needs and locations of services to promote community skill sets for leadership and advocacy.

PERSPECTIVES FOR ADDRESSING TRADITIONAL DOMINANCE

The nature of prejudice has influenced ways of thinking and the resistance to people standing up for their rights. Civil rights activists were met with water hoses and police dogs in the 1960s and 1970s, as well as allies and supporters. Steps that people take to move forward must be taken, acknowledging that resistance and pushback may come from persons who feel threatened.

Our contemporary environment has created more division and intolerance of persons who face systemic obstacles. Activism is the strategy that must continue. Empowering those we work with is critical for helping families.

Another perspective proposed by Reeves (2017) acknowledges the American upper-class privilege and the opportunities they enjoy. Suggesting the upper classes need to give up rather than hoard opportunities or some of their advantage is challenging. Yet it does illustrate the bottom line in developing compromises that could expand opportunities. Perhaps appreciating humanity by reinforcing more humane criminal justice reforms and encouraging more comprehensive history curriculum could be promoted.

Issues of poverty and privilege, power and powerlessness are encapsulated in the presentations and interpretations offered to the public. Generally, news we get does not focus on strengths; however, public protests are giving more voice to the range of perspectives that do exist. Institutional channels construct how and about what we are informed. How we see situations and circumstances influences how we develop responses. Residential planning and development is an example. Community planning has been narrowly tied to bureaucratic organizations and processes that believed in tearing down old housing buildings in order to make new. This concept can be associated with urban planning as well as family life. Bulldozing slums and divorcing old partners could be used to reflect on this idea. Within these two endpoints, there may be several additional possibilities. Acknowledging the range of realities and the diverse package of options is becoming more of a strategy for change.

A recent exhibit at the Museum of Modern Art (MoMA) in New York demonstrates the diverse interdisciplinary interest in planning for and participating in efforts to address the increased income discrepancy and urban challenges (Gadanho, 2014) around the world. In the preface to Gadanho's *Unequal Growth: Tactical Urbanisms for Expanding Megacities,* Barry Bergdoll refers to the United Nation's projection that urban populations will swell to 67% of the world's population (p. 10). The museum's leadership is playing a role in changing the negative language used in urban renewal discussion of slums to an emphasis on illegal dwellings, informal cities, and efforts to ameliorate life for citizens in these areas. Activist architects and designers are committed to selective interventions rather than demolition and combining local knowledge and global expertise.

The MoMA exhibition offers an interesting landscape of six cities—Hong Kong, Istanbul, Lagos, Mumbai, New York, and Rio de Janeiro—that can be considered on the macro level as territories with their own histories of oppression and inequality, taking steps toward inclusion and social development. Social work's acknowledgement of macro work includes collaboration with service users on international and local levels. Engaging with families and organizational agents to modify language, incorporate multicultural voices, and participate in networks that transcend differences to promote social justice and fair exchanges demonstrates the values that social work holds. This is a huge task.

Social work and social construction. Several conceptual frameworks and related theories influence thinking about social work services, the populations served, and service delivery. Social work has acknowledged how social construction has framed difference with the emphasis on negative connotations about people. Historically, the social constructions have justified the privileges and disadvantages of people.

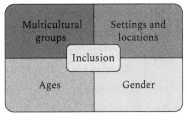

FIGURE 2.1   Inclusion

The social constructs that exist and that people have been comfortable with may be different or oppositional to some that emerging advocates present. Social work institutions, practitioners, and students are addressing the challenges. Advancing social justice issues requires us to listen to diverse service users and organizational representatives. Critical thinking requires identification of salient theories, appreciation of multicultural resources, and use of emerging areas of interest and collaboration skills. Critical reflection offers the opportunity to examine our past and current thinking and how it is influenced by family and friends—and to assess the quality of those ideas and beliefs. The road to integrating these can be rocky, sometimes a process of struggle, and frequently a process of enlightenment about oneself and others. Students pursuing social work careers must respect these goals.

IMPLICATIONS FOR SOCIAL WORK: SOCIAL WORK STUDENTS' REFLECTIONS

These different environments and ways of thinking are important for students of human behavior to become more informed to enhance their hearing, listening, interacting with, and working with people. The potential impact in social work and social welfare on professional thinking and planning for service users begins with recognizing the role of social construction on the planners and those for whom services are being planned. It is equally important to understand those who are unable to move to higher levels of understanding and how that occurs. Social workers, public health professionals, educators, and other proponents of the collaborative process must engage with people across levels of awareness and compassion.

Appreciating diversity and the obstacles to inclusion are recognized elements of social work expectations for engagement and collaboration.

STUDENTS COMMENTS

Student reflections about the socialization process and the messages received in homes and community settings point to what exists and their steps in processing the information to enhance the service delivery systems. The ideas presented in this class discussion indicate the students' grasp of key ideas:

> Promoting diversity is more complex than presenting members of different groups.
> It requires understanding how race permeates through all aspects of American life.

Social workers can reject traditional socialization to strive for social justice.

Examining the prison system more closely reveals that prisons are not the solution. Reading information and looking at statistics show how racism is masked.

Oppression reveals subordination of others on an individual level through dominant culture beliefs, at the institutional level via policies, and at a societal level by social downgrading of others.

Thinking through the reflection assignment helps to understand how white European men did not value anyone different from them. Some students noted how hard it can be to remain objective in reading about the horrible behaviors and systematic discrimination.

Yet, defensiveness and resistance occur in accepting the privilege white people can have because of these conditions.

Students of social work address their realities and those of others in gaining knowledge and understanding.

CHAPTER SUMMARY

Socialization leads to incorporating one's experiences, ways of knowing, family dynamics, institutional influences, and messages about understanding or dismissing others. Identifying our sources of information about others, the educational references we've been exposed to, and recognizing the realm of information we have not been aware of establishes a more distinct view of self.

Considering the range of ideas that challenge traditional social constructs is the next step.

As readers become able to provide examples of socially constructed illustrations, they are encouraged to identify messages that obstruct cultural appreciation and to generate ideas for reaching for the strengths in various situations. Developing a baseline of knowledge of messages received in context offers a setting for self-assessment. Cultural folktales provide an easy source of strengths and survival stories from which students and others can benefit.

EPAS AND CODE OF ETHICS

CSWE EDUCATIONAL POLICY & ACCREDITATION STANDARDS

Competency 2: Engage diversity and difference in practice.

- 2a) Apply and communicate understanding of the importance of diversity and difference in shaping life experiences in practice at the micro, mezzo, and macro levels.
- 2b) Present themselves as learners and engage clients and constituencies as experts of their own experiences.
- 2c) Apply self-awareness and self-regulation to manage the influence of personal biases and values in working with diverse clients and constituencies (EPAS, 2015).

NASW CODE OF ETHICS

1.01: Commitment to Clients
1.02: Self-Determination
1.04: Competence (NASW, n.d.)

DISCUSSION QUESTIONS

1. Complete Exercises 1 and 2. Discuss how you processed your thinking about them. What were your first thoughts?
2. Select three references and identify a key concept from each. With your neighbor, discuss the perspectives and your reflection on each. Why did you select the concepts? Compare your selection process with your partner's.
3. Select a group as an example base (e.g., race, ethnicity, class, ability, learning, diagnosis, etc.). What historical factors have shaped the basis for discrimination against this group today?
4. What are contemporary factors that create tensions regarding equality?
5. How does the history affect opportunities for social mobility?

EXERCISES

1. Write a brief identity of yourself. How did you decide on the components to list?
2. Consider the description. Did you incorporate family history and intersectionality? How are you classified by the powers that be? Gender, race, class, health/mental health? How has society influenced how you think and feel about the descriptions?
3. Have you ever wanted to be someone else? Write up to two paragraphs describing when this happened and who you wanted to be. Why did you want this identity?
   If you have not had such a memory, select one that you could work on. Why did you make this choice?
4. Describe a client situation that may be used to discuss intersectionality. What perspectives may be incorporated in analyzing the case?
5. Conduct the exercise located here:
   O'Neal, G. S. (2012). Teaching note: Self-assessment and dialogue as tools for appreciating diversity. *Journal of Social Work Education, 48*(1) 159–165.
   Ask students to reflect on their responses. Why do the columns look the way they do?

6. Have students assess the range of their connection to literature by diverse authors. Select a novel written by a person of multicultural identity—person of color, LGBTQI, differently abled (physical, learning or emotional), deaf community member, or immigrant—and discuss it from a social construction standpoint.

7. **Extra Credit**: Read the novel *I Am a Japanese Writer* by Dany LaFerriere (2010). Write a short essay (1–2 pages) on social construction, identity development, and one's place in society.

MULTICULTURAL RESOURCES

Adiche, C. N. (2009). *The danger of a single story* [Video file]. Retrieved from https://www.ted.com/talks/chimamanda_adichie_the_danger_of_a_single_story

Chin, S. (2009). *The other side of paradise.* New York, NY: Scribner.

DuBois, W. E. B. (1899). *The Philadelphia negro.* Philadelphia, PA: University of Pennsylvania.

Hall, T. (2014, March/April). The journey of Nishiguu. *Cultural Survival Quarterly.* Retrieved from https://www.utne.com/politics/the-journey-of-nishiyuu-zm0z14mazros

Hamilton, V. (1993). *The people could fly: American black folktales.* New York, NY: Knopf Books for Young Readers.

Kozol, J. (2014). *The shame of the nation: Public education still separate, still unequal* [Video file]. Retrieved Jan. 4, 2016, from https://www.youtube.com/watch? v=e7X3JI-aais

LaFerriere, D. (2008). *I am a Japanese writer.* Vancouver, BC: Douglas & McIntyre.

MSN.com. (2015, June 26). Key moments in LBGT rights history. Retrieved from http://www.msn.com/en-us/news/us/key-moments-in-gay-rights-history/ss-BBjXpV6#image=9

Tallbear, K. (n.d.). Research. Indigenous science, technology, society. Retrieved from http://www.kimtallbear.com/research.html

Wilson, A. N. (1992). *Awakening the natural genius of black children.* New York, NY: Afrikan World InfoSystems.

Wynn, M. (1992). *Empowering African-American males to succeed: A 10-step approach for parents and teachers.* South Pasadena, CA: Rising Sun.

Woodson, J. (Ed.) (1996). *A way out of no way: Writings about growing up Black in America.* New York: Henry Holt and Company.

Young, A. (1992). *A way out of no way: The spiritual memoirs of Andrew Young.* Nashville, TN: Thomas Nelson.

Young, S. (2014). *I'm not your inspiration* [Video file]. Retrieved from https://www.ted.com/talks/stella_young_i_m_not_your_inspiration_thank_you_very_much

FURTHER READING

Brodsky, A. (2005). *Children's books about disability: A bibliography—Teacher's guide.* Retrieved May 30, 2015, from http://www.state.nj.us/humanservices/documents/ChildrensBiblioDisabilityBooks.pdf

Horejes, T. P. (2012). *Social construction of deafness: Examining deaf language culture in education.* Washington, DC: Gallaudet University Press.

Witkin, S. L. (2012). *Social construction & social work practice: Interpretations and innovations.* New York, NY: Columbia University Press.

CHAPTER 3

Examining History

CHAPTER OVERVIEW

This chapter offers a framework of the history that has demonstrated oppression and discrimination, notably against Native Americans whose land was taken and Africans brought to the United States to serve as slaves and provide free labor in the colonies. It provides key points related to the exclusion of women, people of color, immigrants, and those challenged by life experiences, resulting in various physical and emotional outcomes. This history requires acknowledging the colonial pursuit of profits. As social work moves forward expanding the capacity of workers and communities, we appreciate the resilience of our communities and anticipate planning engaging partnerships to enhance opportunity for more citizens.

LEARNING OBJECTIVES

- Colonialism was built on horrible behaviors against humans held in captivity to advance economic pursuits.
- Traditions across cultures hold histories of moral principles and beliefs.
- Descendants of all cultures have resisted the tyranny of inhumane leaders.

Benchmark: Students should be able to identify moral traditions that have supported and encouraged people.

STUDENT SCENARIO 1

Russell attended elementary and secondary schools in a midsized school district outside of Pittsburgh, Pennsylvania. He did not learn anything about the agricultural innovations and female leadership of Native tribes or the presence of the Olmecs, who traded and lived in the Americas before Columbus arrived.

WHAT IS THE HISTORY OF THE UNITED STATES?

- History of greed versus humanity.
- Economic restrictions or obstacles for Native Americans, African Americans, Hispanics and Latinos, other immigrants, and persons with physical, emotional, and learning challenges.
- Social and economic restrictions for non-conforming gender expression, LGBTQI persons.
- Strengths knowledge minimized or excluded.
- Rich heritage of people from all groups succeeding in daily endeavors and overcoming obstacles.

The history of the United States is marked by the annihilation of native inhabitants and punitive treatment of Africans brought here as slaves. The cruelty is associated with greed for profit without labor costs (Zinn, 2009). The humanity of people was not a clear concern. Slaves were present in societies around the world. The cruelty of the behavior in the colonies has been described in several reports. Segal (2002) in *Islam's Black Slaves* discusses the variations of slavery under Christianity and Islam. He notes slavery in Islam was a social and cultural phenomenon in which the treatment of slaves was more benign based on religious faith rather than economic profit. The Atlantic slave trade was connected to the development of capitalism, which viewed slaves more as products for labor than as human beings. There are different views about this, but organized ledgers that document a process of capture, transport, and loss indicate that inhumane treatment by the colonizers occurred consistently.

Clarke (1998) agrees that the economic framework drove the surge for free labor and notes internal struggles in Africa contributed to the ability of the Europeans to exploit the villages. The history of Africa includes empire building and scientific advancements. Leakey (from *The Progress and Evolution of Man in Africa*, in Clarke, 1998), notes that most scientists are satisfied "that Africa was the birthplace of man, and that for many hundreds of centuries, Africa was in the forefront of all human progress" (p. 38). Despite this history, the officials of Protestant and Catholic churches referred to Africans as primitive in a way to denigrate their value and rationalize the inhumane treatment of slaves.

Dunbar-Ortiz (2014, p. 40) reports that "nearly all the populated areas of the Americas were reduced by 90% following the onset of colonizing projects." She states, "Settler colonialism is genocidal policy" (p. 6) in referring to the indigenous people's perspective of U.S. history. The loss of Native lives can be attributed not only to direct warfare but also the infectious diseases brought by the colonizers; the pitting of tribes against one another, as occurred in Ireland, Africa, and Asia; overwork in mines; malnutrition and starvation; and enslavement and related conditions. This mass destruction was not called genocide until recently. Lemkin (1944) coined the term *genocide* in his work, *Axis Rule in Occupied Europe: Laws of Occupation, Analysis of Government, Proposals for Redress.* The move to its interpretation as genocide was influenced by indigenous observers concerned about the methods of harm and the numbers killed by colonist invasions.

HISTORICAL CONTEXT OF OPPRESSION AND RACISM

The context of oppression and racism includes situations of trauma and survival. The exclusion of knowledge about the participation of people of Native and African descent in the development of world civilization reflects the setup of social construction that negates significant contributions by those other than Europeans and Christians. This socially constructed mindset has created tensions among groups that experienced trauma at the hands of the colonizers. This tradition continues to impact the contemporary landscape in economic, psychological, and cultural ways.

EXAMINING THE HISTORY

Examining how this has come about helps readers walk through the resulting range of perceptions that impact people becoming practitioners and how those who are vulnerable have come to be those that social workers serve. This examination also sheds light on how the professional development process is evolving, as practitioners work to include more evidence-based practices to speak up for social and economic justice. This occurs by sharing data that can be used to monitor system-wide performance and establish foundations for results accountability (Friedman, 2005).

As we review salient points for reference and offer sources for readers to explore, it is critical to consider the impact not only on individual groups but also on the intersection of diverse social identities and majority group members. The most critical group to reflect on is children. Whatever has happened to ethnic groups has affected children through the ways parents have been able to navigate their struggles. The ability to plan for children and protect them is affected by the macro environment that plays out in micro situations. Developing understanding that integrates these dimensions is fundamental to the inclusive context.

As the country became established, waves of immigrants weathered hatred, discrimination, and taunts to assimilate and discard their cultural "baggage." The existence of oppressive social dynamics has occurred around the world. India's caste system parallels the class hierarchies observed in other countries. Examples of brutal domination tactics can be found in the histories of China, Japan, Brazil, and others.

The emphasis on capitalism has promoted business operations supported by political connections that sought to limit and devalue persons deemed unworthy by those in charge. This way of thinking excluded or restricted Native Americans, people of color, women, persons with addiction problems, and others from participating in the evolving commercial enterprises.

The goal of maintaining the exclusion of persons who were exploited was strategically planned. Their positive heritage and contributions were hidden. The staging of stereotypes and punitive social dynamics from this view over time continues to influence social relations and impedes progressive attitudes and achievements across many sectors. These social constructions contribute to continuing adverse messages and experiences.

BEFORE SLAVERY: AFRICAN HERITAGE

Early documents report the presence of African traders in the Americas in the 4th and 5th centuries. The Olmec civilization existed before the Aztec empire in the Mexican area of the Americas. While researchers have feuded about the authenticity of the Olmec (Neff, 2006), recent evidence appears to confirm the well-defined and sophisticated African presence in art and science in the Americas, in Spain, in Asia, and on the African continent. Their civilization was established in multiple centers that traded and shared ideas (Lawler, 2007). There are photographs of the finds of 40 wooden busts with varied faces, similar to those of the Asian terra-cotta army (Williams, 2016), which also depict diversity.

> In a survey of medical students' views of aboriginal people, "student responses suggest they see the cultural gap between aboriginal and non-aboriginal people as being both a cause and a consequence of discrimination against them" (Ly & Crowshoe, 2015, p. 618).

Knowledge that the African continent gave birth to art, science, religion, and philosophy provides the basis of a reformation of contemporary beliefs and attitudes (Rollins, 1731). Further historical digging reveals that "[b]lack people can be found as indigenous populations throughout Asia from the western-most to the eastern extremity" (M'Bantu, 2012a, p. 1, Loc 8). It is interesting to view the terra-cotta army, found in 1974 by a Chinese farmer, with the depiction of "8,000 soldiers, 130 chariots, 520 horses and 150 cavalry horses" and consider the diversity of facial features that reflects various ancestries (umich.edu, para 1). This collection of life-size figures was created to defend the tomb of Qin Shi Huang, China's first emperor, and was completed around 209 BCE.

AFRICAN ACCOMPLISHMENTS

An examination of the history of the Bible by Darkwah (2014) presents an interpretation that runs contrary to what has been traditionally accepted. He raises questions about the origins of Christianity that connect to African roots. Early artistic portrayals of Jesus and his mother that are housed in the Vatican's Basilica show them as black.

Many of the relics of Christian churches in Ethiopia are still visible. Davidson (1966) presents a thorough examination of African kingdoms. He explains the role of religion and spirituality. He notes the goal of life was to live in the light of ancestors as the way of stability (p. 128). Using this as a reference point provides an easy connection to the turmoil observed by Nigerian author Chinua Achebe in 1958. His book *Things Fall Apart* describes the impact of missionaries on his family and community in his homeland.

The Songhai Empire ruled two thirds of West Africa from 690 CE to 1591. Education in universities, judicial law, and construction of monuments and palaces existed under several African dynasties in the major cities of the times (Walker, 2010).

The presence of Black people is documented in several text and visual examples (Davidson, 1966; Lawler, 2007; *Life*, 2015; M'Bantu, 2012; Huyghe, 1992). This history helps people recognize what has been hidden and ignored. Acknowledging this helps people understand what the world is all about. Recent changes in the Advanced Placement (AP) course curriculum incorporate more of this knowledge. Advocacy for changes in the regular education curriculum will assist teacher education and ultimately education across disciplines as it presents broader views of the world and the contributions before the European period.

Discussion of the origins of color and presence of people mixing in the Middle East and in South American locations such as Brazil are reported (Fleischer, 2013). From the report of the first instance of a Black scholar exercising his right to counter racism (9th century Uthman al-Jahiz, *Book of the Glory of the Black Race* [1981] or *The Pride Of The Blacks Over The Whites* [n.d.]) to contemporary opinions such as presented in Burrell's *Brainwashed: Challenging the Myth of Black Inferiority* (2010), the reality of strong, positive contributions by people of color to civilizations across cultures and across the world exist. Caribbean, West Indian, West African, and Latino writers, as well as those from American and European locations, have shared their experiences and documentation of the rich history of people of color.

THE ADVENT OF SLAVERY

Under Queen Elizabeth I, slave raids began in West Africa around 1592. The pervading philosophy in Spain sent Columbus to unexplored land with a mindset for pillaging and taking resources through war. While the true details of the early publication of *The Art of War* (Sun Tzu, 2010) are questioned [some note it may have been compiled around the 4th or 5th century], it clearly lays out a philosophy that perpetuates domination at any costs necessary. The subjugation of Africans as slaves required the denial of historic African accomplishments.

In the late 1600s, Europeans went to Africa from the colonies. Depictions of the depravity of the treatment can be viewed in the movies *Roots* (1977), *Amistad* (1997), and *Twelve Years a Slave* (2014). *Roots*, based on the book by Alex Haley, tells the story of Kunte Kinte, an African teen who was brought here and the impact on subsequent generations of his family.

Slavery was horrendous. Transporting the Africans here and their treatment was inhumane, as depicted in movies such as *Django Unchained* (2012) and *Lincoln* (2012).

The Willie Lynch Letter and the Making of a Slave (1999) provides an explanation of how plantation owners were trained to implement the slavery system (The letter has been criticized and dubbed fake, but nevertheless puts a frame on the perpetuation of inhumane treatment to arrive at avaricious goals. It notes the planned attack on families—their separation, the psychological torture of women and men, and their punishment—to inflict damage for years to come. Alvin Morrow's follow-up work, (2003), provides an example of the recognition of the impact of slavery on many families and the work needed to overcome the damage.

PEOPLE OF COLOR

Designated categories by demographers for census surveys have expanded from a few to several but these don't establish a a finite way of describing the diverse people with whom we work. The major race and ethnic groups derived from the U.S. Census are used for lack of a more respectful way of incorporating people's various social, political, and cultural intersectional identities. The presence of a rich heritage of people of color includes African, Caribbean, Native American, Latino, Asian, European and Middle Eastern ancestors. Some people may not claim being a person of color even if they claim a group that could be without known possible ancestral links. Understanding a person's relationship to their heritage and identity requires having dialogues of respect.

INDIGENOUS RESIDENTS—NATIVE AMERICANS

The history of Native Americans is broad and lengthy. From reports of the ancestors in Canadian and South American locations, there are many narratives regarding lifestyles and customs of tribes and family groups that were settled in community settings and those that were more nomadic.

NATIVE AMERICAN CULTURE BEFORE COLONIZATION

Native American civilization reveals hundreds of years of development. Their expertise was demonstrated by agricultural prowess, connections to plant and animal life, and methods of cooperative arrangements among men and women. There are 562 tribes recognized by the United States (Oklahoma, 2013). Descriptions of the Navajo and Apache reveal variations in gender and role responsibilities of these two well-known tribes. Documentaries about their cultures present a view of early agricultural pursuits and their responses to transactions with Spanish and Europeans settlers.

Narratives report their adaptation to conditions that occurred in their natural environments and through the invasions of their territory. From the use of corn in the precolonized lands to the presence of potatoes and sophisticated farming methods of indigenous people in Peru and Bolivia, villages maintained by the Arawak Indians who greeted Christopher Columbus thrived on corn, yams, cassava, weaving, and wore golden ornaments (Zinn, 1997). The use of buffalo, deer, and elk among many tribes in the 1400s began to be replaced by the use of horses after the invasion by the Spanish around 1540.

The culture of the Natives reflected cooperation between males and females, teaching children to work in solidarity with their tribal brothers, and the concepts of right and wrong. There were ways to discipline those who stole or acted without morals. Shame and ostracizing were used (Nash, in Zinn, n.d., pp. 20–21).

With colonization, naturally there was reaction and fighting back. The invasion from Haiti through the Caribbean and onto the contiguous land resulted in the loss of land and the lives of millions of Natives (Dunbar-Ortiz, 2014). Recent textbooks include information about massacres and invasions. Some cover issues of conflict and pushback on education and voting rights (Tindall & Shi, 2012). The massive enslavement and slaughter of Native Americans

(Romero, 2011) is not covered in detail in the typical American history books. The positive treatment of women, the reliance on the natural environment rather than buying and selling, or the range of their generosity may not be emphasized although it may be referred to. Their treatment by the invaders resulted in serious trauma. The choice of suicide by many rather than enduring the torture (Zinn, 1997) has not been presented as a reason for concern. The traditional focus has been on the settlers' relationship with Britain and the establishment of the government.

From the years of colonization through the writing of government treaties, the Native American and U.S. government relations have been conflicted. According to the 1783 Treaty of Paris that ended the American Revolution, the United States was given all the British land south of Canada and east of the Mississippi (Schmoop Editorial Team, 2008).

REACTION AND RESISTANCE

The following years (1792–1944) were marked by resistance to treaties the Indians felt were illegal or that were not abided by. U.S. invasions against Native Americans for their land were repeatedly responded to by force and, (usually) finally, surrender of the land. The realities, feelings, and experiences of reservation life illustrate the harsh policies of the U.S. government and the resolve of Native Americans. The perspective and strengths of the Native Americans are available in several novels and contemporary research. In *American Indian Prophecies* (Kaltreider, 2003), Chasing Deer shares dreams and prophecies of the Cheyenne. Sweet Medicine is described as a cultural hero who brings attention to the community and leads them to resume their ceremonial life.

The well-known Geronimo—real name Goyathlay (1829–1909)—stands out as a resistor and Apache warrior leader (Dembeck, 2011–2013). He sought revenge against Mexican troops after they murdered his wife, children, and mother. When settlers and soldiers invaded the Chiricahua Apache lands in Arizona, his tribe resisted the invasion and the government's efforts to put them on reservations. The angry white men called their resistance murderous and tracked them down.

The mythology about Native Americans suggests the land that Columbus visited was sparsely populated by Indians with limited agrarian resources. However, there is substantive evidence that precolonial natives were members of a diverse range of rich and sophisticated cultural social systems (Digital History ID 2908, n.d.). Indians lived in organized communities with moral, political, and communal land ownership structures. There were more than 2,000 languages across the land that was later designated the United States (Mintz & McNeil, 2013). Stories from indigenous leaders chronicle various confrontations from outside forces and the collective thinking and decision-making that occurred (Dembeck, 2011–13).

Contemporary indigenous researchers are concerned about the concepts of imperialism and colonialism that history books present. Linda Tuhiwai Smith (2012), notes "Columbus represents a huge legacy of suffering and destruction" (p. 2). In the traditional emphasis on manifest destiny, the settlers deny the realities of the existence of flourishing social communities. In this way, indigenous views are regarded as incorrect because the people resisted the mission of colonization. The settlers' purpose was to destroy and conquer. Voices of those with another perspective, other values and beliefs, have been obstructed and excluded and contested as barriers to the colonizers version of research. As we progress in efforts to become more informed of the diverse history of the United States and the world, revisiting history is considered a step toward decolonization (Smith, 2012).

UP FROM SLAVERY

Awareness of the politics and economics of the slave labor system was the fundamental basis for resistance and revolt. Goldstone (2005) has presented a compelling account of the contentious debates by those who supported the economics of slavery as representatives negotiated the Constitution in 1787 in Philadelphia. The voices that expressed resistance to the institution of slavery included men and women who spoke for their families and communities. Despite the misinformation that claimed a diminished family context, the underground relationships of people helping one another persisted.

REACTION AND RESISTANCE

Several examples of resistance included individual acts of sabotage, poisoning, fires, and organized uprisings to destroy property of slave owners.

Aptheker (1983) presented the first documented study of slave revolts. His careful research of the ongoing and common perseverance of slaves against slavery contradicted the myth of African American acceptance of slavery.

In 1712, about 25 slaves set fires to houses on the northern edge of New York City (Britannica, n.d.). They were killed and 18 other participants were brutally tortured using more violence than the slaves did.

In 1739, a group of about 80 slaves battled in Stono, South Carolina, resulting in deaths of 44 blacks and 21 whites (Apetheker, 1983).

In Southhampton County, Virgina, in August 1831 Nat Turner, led rebel slaves that killed between 55 and 65 people, the highest number of fatalities caused by any slave uprising. Although slavery was strictly enforced through mechanisms of control (Apetheker, 1983), the wives of slave owners, feared the slaves would retaliate.

In 1811, the largest uprising, which has received little attention until recently, occurred. Rasmussen (2012) reports that a well-organized revolt was planned with the intent of establishing a separate black state. The revolt was closer to succeeding than has been noted. The slaves had been reading the French Declaration of the rights of man. When their efforts expanded, federal troops and the militia took control. There was a trial, and the slaves were executed by firing squad. In an especially brutal move, their heads were cut off and posted along the river to warn others.

In 1822, Caribbean-born Denmark Vesey motivated up to 9,000 people to prepare to revolt. A slave informant notified the plantation owners, and the planned insurrection in Charleston, South Carolina, was squashed. Vesey and 20 others were executed (Robertson, 2000).

Multiple dimensions of the social environment aided the tides that resisted inhumanity. The forces of harsh treatment on the slaves certainly established the emotional context of resistance. The French Revolution with its push for Liberty, Equality, Fraternity, the Methodist church with about 20% Black participants, instilled concepts of equality and liberty, and the opinions of abolitionists provided social supports to continuing resistance (Apetheker, 1983).

ABOLITIONISTS

The abolition movement involved white and black people speaking out against slavery, eventually ending it through allies and advocacy. The obstacles were many. Sarah Grimké was the daughter of a plantation owner in South Carolina. She spoke against slavery, left the plantation, and moved to Philadelphia to further the cause. However, following several efforts, she was threatened with reprisals if she continued (Grimké, 1836).

> In 1833 in Philadelphia, the first American Anti-Slavery Society Convention convened. In a backlash, anti-abolition riots broke out in many northeastern cities, including New York and Philadelphia, during 1834–35. Several Southern states, beginning with the Carolinas, made formal requests to other states to suppress abolition groups and their literature. In Illinois, the legislature voted to condemn abolition societies and their agitation; Delegate Abraham Lincoln voted with the majority, then immediately co-sponsored a bill to mitigate some of the language of the earlier one. The U.S. House of Representatives adopted a gag rule, automatically tabling abolitionist proposals (Historynet.com, 2017, para 11).

Noted abolitionist John Brown was a radical supporter who advised outright war as the only way to overcome slavery. In 1859, he led an armed insurrection but was quickly captured, and a trial resulted in his being hanged.

OTHER GROUPS OF COLOR

Members of other groups of color are not specifically associated with slavery or genocide as the Native and African descendants are, yet they too have encountered discrimination, prejudice, and exclusion.

LATINO/HISPANIC HERITAGE

The use of the terms *Latino* or *Hispanic* has been confusing to some. The Latino population is comprised of people from Mexico, Latin and South America, and Puerto Rico. One site, Hispanic Economics, describes *Hispanic* as a broad term that includes persons who speak Spanish and those who do not. *Latinos* are referred to as American born with political interests (Nevaer, 2010, hispaniceconomics.com; Torres, 2009).

Valdeón (2013) states that considering the social, political, and economic connections of terminology are essential. His research addresses the consistency in the sociopolitical use of the term *Hispanic* in academic research. His work notes these definitions:

> *Latin American* refers to Mexicans, Central and South Americans, and was initially applied to countries where Latin languages were spoken. *Hispanic was* defined as being of Latin American descent living in the United States, especially Cuban, Mexican, or Puerto Rican. Latino is described as a self-chosen "pan-ethnic" identity (Valdeón, 2013).

Gutiérrez (n.d.) shares a summary of the Latino history through a National Park Service theme study. This history of Latino presence in the United States begins with the California Gold Rush. This period drew people seeking work in territory that belonged to the Republic of Mexico. The Treaty of Guadalupe Hidalgo (1848) allowed the United States to take more than one third of the area north of the current Mexican border. This included the states that are now California, Nevada, Utah, Arizona, and more. About 100,000 people who had come to the area were naturalized as citizens under the rules of the treaty. After the Chinese Expulsion Act was enacted, the number of Chinese laborers was reduced. However, as the economic development of the West continued, more labor was needed. This prompted an increase in migration from Mexico.

He describes a guest worker program implemented in the 1940s to hire contract workers to help employers as a policy to address labor needs. The number of unauthorized workers increased. During the Great Depression, a brief reversal of migration occurred when about 350,000 to 500,000 Mexican immigrants and their children were pressured or compelled by government officials to leave the country. Then, as labor needs developed again migration resumed. (Guitierrez, n.d.).

The issue of unauthorized residents while addressing the labor needs of U.S. employers is basic to the continuing immigration struggles. The population includes Mexicans, Cubans, Puerto Ricans, and the growing numbers of persons migrating from the islands to locations seeking employment. As Gutierrez summarizes past migration and anticipates continuing expansion of Latin people and the controversies surrounding immigration policy, he notes that about 50% of the people who are considered illegal immigrants actually came in through legal means but overstayed tourist permits and visas.

Literature of the history is found under Chicano and Latino descriptors. Lee (2003) refers to Anaya's work, *Bless Me Ultima,* as an example of Chicanismo built on memories in a similar vein as other writers such as Villarreal, Hinojosa, and Candelaria (p. 128). This novel addresses a child's development as he integrates environmental conditions and cultural healing practices.

ASIAN HERITAGE

As the slave population decreased, Asian Filipinos arrived as worker replacements around 1840. The British and Spanish used people from China, India, and the Philippines as workers in the Caribbean, Peru, Ecuador, and other countries in South America (Asian-nation.org, n.d.). Over the years, Asian immigrants came from the Philippines, Japan, India, the Pacific Islanders, Vietnam, and Cambodia.

As the gold rush developed and attracted people to the West, Chinese immigrants also came to seek their fortunes. They were hired to tend gardens or farm, many handled domestic and laundry work, and some became merchants. Many Chinese men worked to build the early railroad system (Asian Nation.org, n.d.). They worked many of the same jobs as European immigrants but were only paid 60% of the rate whites were paid. Their presence was responded to in gradually discriminating ways.

When the railroad line was completed, immigrants began moving into California, and they began to be seen as an economic threat. Retaliation occurred through violence against them, and the Chinese Exclusion Act was established in 1882. Immigrants already in the United States were not allowed to gain citizenship.

The history of discrimination against people of color has been tied to their use as laborers and the desire to pay low wages. Early immigrants in Chicago were provided services in settlement houses that catered to helping the newly arrived learn the language and gain employment. Iglehart and Becerra (1997) note the resistance of charity workers to provide services to people of color because it was difficult due to the discrimination against them,

WOMEN

The perspectives of white upper- and middle-class men generally predominate the socialization structure of Western culture. The place of women is typically presented to be secondary, based on European social standards. The value of women is illustrated in various ways. The existence of poor treatment, harassment, and violence speaks to the fact that women account for a substantial percent of persons that helping professionals work with. The social roles of women across groups may be similar but vary in traditional households and especially in single-parent ones. Even the history of women in the patriarchy-focused Chinese family includes illustrations of the reality of variations. Kinney's translation (2014) of *The Biographies of Exemplary Women* by Liu Xiang (79–8 BCE) is significant. There are many examples of the diversity of women's responsibilities across cultures.

DIVERSE FAMILY FORMS

The recognition of cultural behaviors that do not conform to traditional expectations draws on the reality of diverse family forms. Unfortunately, the media messages of the ideal family are not based on reality. Robbins (2017) explains that the narrow nuclear family description promotes blame and marginalization. She reports that this image accounts for less than one fifth of America's households. Using this to base policies on creates harm and waste.

Several scenarios of contemporary families note cooperative relationships and shared family work. There are examples of female tribal leaders—women queens in Africa and Native American chiefs in villages—that depict strong leadership that women across time have replicated. Women's activities among indigenous communities included contributions to the work life of the family as well as homemaking. The Buffalo Calf Woman introduced in Mother Earth Spirituality (McGaa, 1990) is a significant spiritual component of Native American life. McGaa proposes she should be respected just as spiritual stories of other groups, Israelites and the Red Sea, the Great Spirit and Moses, and others are recognized. It is a dynamic of empowerment for all members of the tribe. Wallis's *Two Old Women* (1993) and *Bird Girl* (1996) offer compelling examples of tenacity and skills beyond the stereotypes of age and gender.

Zinn reports on Nash's account of Iroquois society that the women were important and respected. Dunbar-Ortiz (2014) and Byrd (2011) also describe cultural environments that integrate women's participation. These cultures have operated with women in collaborative, leadership, and ownership roles. Iroquois women tended the crops and handled the village affairs while the men were hunting or fishing. He summarizes the difference between Native customs of shared power between the sexes versus the European idea of male dominancy and female subordination (Nash, in Zinn, n.d., pp. 20–21).

From the point of colonization, women's roles were categorized as distinct from men's. Victorian images of women generally involved images of married middle and upper-middle-class homes adhering to the male-dominated themes of life. Gender dynamics have been organized in terms of rights for men and limited ones for women. Traditional ideology recognized and supported women who conformed to family ethics—marriage and homemaking, regardless of their safety or their views about their interests. Marsiglia and Kulis (2015) presented the feminist notion that a traditional Western family conditions its family members to accept oppression as the way of operation. Challenges to the ideology have generally reformulated ways to continue subordination of women rather than facilitate concepts of work and behaviors that support their independent pursuits (Abramowitz, 1996) and share family responsibilities.

WOMEN'S CREATIVITY PENALIZED

The portrayal of women has essentially been tied to the masculine perspectives of women, marriage, and motherhood. Women have been harassed or penalized in the work force through obstacles for hiring when applying in certain fields or for being pregnant when these concepts have been challenged (White, 2015).

The Shriver Report (Morgan & Skelton, 2014) clearly addresses the realities of women as they respond to life issues and social pressures. Financial vulnerability, care responsibilities, and the need for policies to recognize our ultimate accountability to children and their futures rather than the unrealistic social construction of men are priority issues. Essays by Shriver, Beyoncé, Sister Joan Chittister, Jennifer Garner, Haskins, Sagawa, and more passionate voices claim the steps we are taking and goals we are pursuing.

As we have observed in the dynamics of maintenance of rule over others, harassment and violence are still present as means of control. Marsiglia and Kulis (2015) also point out women around the world continue to be a "sociological minority." The desire for independent work has been denigrated and mental health issues have been connected to women who didn't conform to the traditional ideology.

LESBIAN, GAY, BISEXUAL, TRANSGENDER, QUEER, INTERSEX (LGBTQI)

Social identities may be defined using several descriptors. Gender and sexual orientation have been tied together, but are separate entities. Awareness of a range of sexual activities is acknowledged to have existed over time, but reference to orientation having to do with the way people classify their feelings about who they are attracted to has been discussed more openly in recent years. Historically, two categories have been identified most visibly—heterosexual and homosexual. Diverse and intersecting identities include lesbian, gay, bisexual, transgender, queer, questioning, and intersex. However, the range of descriptions used by medical educators to address health needs of this diverse community also include gender nonconforming and those born with differences in sex development (Hollenbach, Eckstrand, & Dreger, 2014). Various sources may use or limit these categories.

The social objections to persons who identify as LGBTQI tend to be associated with the late 1800s. The history of homosexuality is traced to observations by European administrators (Ford, n.d.) in the 1860s and 1870s who began to recognize the organization of households around sexual activity rather than family operations. Approaches that categorized the behavior as deviant and in need of psychiatric and legal intervention had not previously been in place. Sizable groups of homosexuals are noted to have been recognized in Germany.

In the United States, homosexual communities have been connected to geographic locations, including New York, San Francisco, and Los Angeles, primarily as economic centers that attracted persons as they migrated away from farms and rural areas. The Mattachine Society, founded in November of 1950 in Los Angeles by Harry Hay, is reported as the first organized underground group to advocate for gay rights. Hay was a young musicologist who participated in the Communist Party (Infographics.com, n.d.).

Anti-homosexual beliefs were fostered via religious persecution, discrimination in employment, violence, and police brutality. In 1953, homosexuality was a status designated for persecution by discrimination in employment, endorsed by President Eisenhower (Infographics.com).

Baldwin's *Giovanni's Room* (1956) is referred to as a classic work describing a man's discovery of his sexuality in an era that was not kind to homosexuals. In 1952, homosexuality was listed in the *Diagnosis Statistical Manual (DSM)* as a personality disturbance. It was removed in 1974 as continuing research and advocacy demonstrated the use of labels as society's efforts to control nonconforming behaviors (Eckstrand & Sciolla, 2014).

PERSONS WITH MENTAL HEALTH STRESSORS AND PHYSICAL, LEARNING, OR EMOTIONAL CHALLENGES

While the images traditionally presented about these groups have been slow to change, there have been continual efforts to address the misconceptions. The history of services to people with mental health distress, physical assistance needs, with impaired vison or hearing, or with nuanced learning abilities has generally been stigmatized and promoted segregation. Economic class was associated with better outcomes, and poverty was associated with poor mental health outcomes (Pols, 2007). Rather than the asylum-level care people received in mental hospitals in the 1930s through the 1950s, persons with lower income often receive no treatment but do have homes. However, according to the National Coalition for the Homeless (2009), about 20% to 25% of the homeless population in the United States suffers from some form of severe mental illness.

Classic research as well as contemporary studies associate the presence of mental illness to income and the social environments that come with low income and stressful relationships (Gallo & Matthews, 2003; Pols, 2007). Services to the mentally ill were restrictive and limited. Szasz (1970/2011), though criticized for his anti-psychiatry stance, brought attention to labeling and questioned the use of confinement and coercion. Early research reported biological rationales for psychiatric symptoms. Emerging research connects the conditions of one's environment to adverse and nourishing experiences that impact developing brain architecture (Hoffman & Spengler, 2014).

Service for medical needs had the benefit of more progressive innovation, but ancillary accommodations were often not thought about. An ordinance for the use of white walking canes was established in Detroit in 1936 (Strong, 2009). Wheelchairs were used by the King of Spain in the 16th century (Scooters.com, n.d.). Curb cuts for wheelchair access on sidewalks sparked further thinking about universal designs for learning that would encourage multiple ways of presenting information for persons with different learning styles (Cast.org, n.d.). Children with special needs and learning differences have been bullied and made fun of in school settings. Often, they were institutionalized instead of being provided reasonable care. *The Story of Beautiful Girl* by Rachel Simon (2011) is a poignant example of a reality impacted by obtrusive institutional arrangements. White Cane day symbolizes the cane with a white tip as more than a tool for persons with low vision or are blind and other resources used by persons with challenges. This quote by Strong is used to highlight independence: "The only barriers against people with disabilities are discriminatory attitudes and practices that our society has too often placed in their way (Newedition.net, n.d, para 11.)." Solomon (2012) supports the experiences of families accommodating various living circumstances.

Schools and programs designed to assist families and their members with physical, learning, or emotional challenges demonstrated institutional constructions that minimized the strengths of persons to be served. Without the participation of persons to be served or their family members, challenges to discriminatory policies may be limited. Berry (2014) has us consider the nature of expectations:

> Living without expectations is hard but, when you can do it, good. Living without hope is harder, and that is bad. You have got to have hope, and you mustn't shirk it. Love, after all, hopeth all things. But maybe you must learn, and it is hard learning, not to hope out loud, especially for other people. You must not let your hope turn into expectation. (p. 1)

Expectations of pace or productivity may sometimes be connected to unrealistic assumptions (Bouton, 2013). Nevertheless, the establishment of Gallaudet College and their movement for a Deaf President Now (DPN) serves as an exemplary process of self-determination and empowerment despite situations that persons may face (Terry, 2015).

Identity politics that represent others who have been minimized historically and in existing institutions is stepping up its push to help those labeled in derogatory ways alter their self-conception and that publicized in society. Their work urges people to recognize that assumptions about different groups may be off target (Anspach, 1979). Old ways of thinking connected to assumptions built on egocentric frames need to be examined closely and require the participation of people from all groups to design and develop more effective ways to create productive communities for our future.

MAINTAINING THE STATUS QUO VERSUS POSITIVE MESSAGES AND ALTERNATIVE PARADIGMS

The status quo has evolved but retains essential characteristics that support the privileges of the dominant cultural group. Maintaining the interest of the power structure occurs through existing legal arrangements and through the wealth that this economic class owns.

The history reveals legal and illegal behaviors by dominant-culture members against groups (the adults and their children), which included obstacles to economic opportunities, lies, beatings, other forms of assault, and murder. When angry feelings against competition by members of the diverse groups grew strong, the tendency to go toward violence often prevailed. Wells-Barnett (2014), an advocate against lynching, protested. Her friends were lynched because they owned a grocery store (Giddings, 1984).

RESISTANCE

Moving beyond the traditional accounts of U.S. history to discover the real strengths and positive news has always occurred. Revealing this and incorporating strengths information to help shape more positive attitudes and beliefs across groups has not occurred easily or smoothly, but it has been consistent and continual. For all the uncovering of ethnic perspectives and the push for human rights, there tends to be pushback and dominant culture repeatedly blaming the victims. History also reveals numerous examples of dominant-culture members attempting to promote strategies that recognize humanity and work toward fair exchange and mutual development. Simultaneously, we observe rebellious, violent reactions and illuminating literary resources of the oppressive conditions that have impeded and frustrated individuals, families, and communities.

ROLE OF LAWS AND REGULATIONS IN MAINTAINING EXCLUSION

Laws and regulations created by local, state, and federal officials shape the opportunities and restraints on citizens and on undocumented residents. These are usually related to eligibility and access to formal organizational or institutional structures. Regulations are connected to the policies that guide our major government structures and the organizations that fall under this leadership.

LEGAL STATUTES—TREATIES, TAKING THE LAND, BREAKING THE CHILDREN

Relations with Native Americans were guided through treaties created by the European powers, U.S. agents, and Native American leaders. A key concept regarding Native American rights is that the tribes began with everything—their land, civilization, and governing institutions. The U. S. Commission on Human Rights (2014) notes this in pointing out the motivation of Indian society to retain their political and cultural distinctions (p. 501).

From 1778 to 1871, treaties were formed that described the sale of Native American land to "give up their rights to hunt and live on huge parcels of land that they had inhabited in exchange for trade goods, yearly cash annuity payments, and assurances that no further demands would be made on them" (Nebraskastudies.org, para. _1__).

In 1884, the Supreme Court ruled against Elk in *Elk v. Wilkins*. Elk was a Native American who wanted to vote as a citizen by laying claim to his right by the 14th Amendment. Despite the abolishment of slavery, this exclusion of the Native American from citizenship was upheld (Rothenberg, 2014).

As the U.S. government desired land more urgently and as Native Americans realized the value of their land over the minor items they received, they attempted to maintain their land. This led the government to move toward policies of Indian removal. A letter from Thomas Jefferson to Congress demonstrates their strategy:

> The Indian tribes residing within the limits of the U.S. have for a considerable time been growing more & more uneasy at the constant diminution of the territory they occupy, altho' effected by their own voluntary sales. ... In order, peaceably, to counteract this policy of theirs, and to provide an extension of territory which the rapid increase of our numbers will call for, two measures are deemed expedient. First, to encourage them to abandon hunting, to apply to the raising stock, to agriculture and domestic manufacture, and thereby prove that less land and labor will maintain them better than in their former mode of living. The extensive forests necessary in the hunting life will become useless and they will see advantage in exchanging them for the means of improving their farms and for increasing domestic comforts. (nebraskastudies.org, para. 3___)

Despite the language, the settlers were shaping interventions to take the land.

The pursuit of justice in the Georgia court system by the Cherokees against their forced removal was met by President Jackson and the state of Georgia ignoring the federal Supreme Court decision in 1831. The "Trail of Tears" refers to the forced removal of Native Americans to Indian Territory in Oklahoma (nebraskastudies.org, n.d.).

The description of legal status of Native Americans can be found through the documents of the U.S. Department of the Interior—Indian Affairs (n.d.). The Dawes Act was established to

promote rewards for Native Americans who adopted the civilized behaviors of the white settlers (Boxer, 2009). The concept of Native Americans having an inferior lifestyle to the white
settlers has been an assumption and used to fuel Christian missionary efforts to suppress
Indian ceremonial activities. This kind of thinking, connected to racism, was used to substantiate Indian education policies and promoted the removal of children from their native
homes. Furthering U.S. influences, from their view, was the removal of children from Native
families to boarding schools. Heape's (2009) documentary examines the educational system
in which hundreds of children died. He interviewed current and former students at schools in
Carlisle, Pennsylvania; Riverside California; Tahlequah, Oklahoma; Anchorage, Alaska, and
other locations. This system was maintained into the 70s and revealed haunting feelings of
child abandonment (Heape, 2009).

The steps to force assimilation of the Native Americans by taking their children were egregious. Consider the traumatic experience of a child being removed from the warm protection
of the traditional Sioux family where the child was never left alone to the legally sanctioned,
lonely separation in boarding schools administered by whites who imposed their ways, often
through beating. *Lakota Woman* (Mary Crow Dog, 1990) provides a woman's view of the cru-
elties imposed on her community and her journey through them. The poems of young Native
children compiled in *When the Rain Sings* (Francis, 1999) speak loudly of the pain and suffering
and other feelings of their lives. The personal and community traumas are apparent in the
ongoing health disparities (Health disparities, 2011) and discrimination many indigenous
persons continue to face.

LEGAL LIMITATIONS AND PENALTIES AGAINST BLACKS

Laws and policies that kept oppressive practices (Cooper & McCord, 2014; DuBois, 2014) in
place after emancipation have continued, and until recently, historians have maintained their
role in perpetuating the depictions of legitimacy. Increasingly, professionals across disciplines are evolving to become activists in revisiting what has been disseminated. Historians,
designers, and architects as well as social workers, public health community workers, and
others are increasing their participation in dialogues to assess continuing discrimination and
undue punishments to indicate interest in partnering with likeminded persons to develop
more proactive approaches to addressing social issues.

Higginbotham's (1998) treatise on the shades of freedom depicts how the laws were designed
to permit a little change. In fact, he illustrates how this has occurred via the Supreme Court
over the long history of race relations. From his African American view, the nine justices "by
their unnecessary legitimization of racism have caused far more systematic cruelty and grief
to African Americans than the hooded vigilantes wearing white robes" (Higginbotham, 1998,
p. xxx).

He points to the legal decisions that permitted people of color to be undervalued as people
and treated poorly and that laid the foundation for strategies to gain more equal treatment.
The *Dred Scott v. Sanford* decision (1857) declared that when the Declaration of Independence
and the U.S. Constitution were framed, Blacks had no rights which had to be upheld by whites.

In *Plessy v. Ferguson* (1896), seven justices legitimized the concept of treating Black people differently and more adversely than others. One justice dissented (Plessy v. Ferguson, 1896, in Rothenberg, 2014).

Subsequently, a couple of decisions began to move toward change. The *Gaines v. Canada* decision declared that it was unconstitutional for Missouri to refuse to admit a qualified African American to a state-funded school. In 1954, *Brown v. Board of Education* set the stage for eradicating the roots of slavery jurisprudence. However, there have been constant obstacles to the full implementation of this law across the United States (Higginbotham, 1998). In fact, Childress (2014) reported via *Frontline*, school segregation is back, more than 60 years after Brown.

The impact of the myriad regulations that may apply to Black people is perceptively contemplated in Claudia Rankine's *Citizen: An American Lyric* (2014). In an interview with Ms. Rankine (npr.org, 2016), she offers condolences to the families of the black men whose lives have recently been taken, and she wonders

> why a policeman would send a bullet in a car with a 4-year-old child ... when no one was firing at him. But that child—that black child—now has to behave and perform like an adult and negotiate a trauma for the rest of her life. What do you think?

LEGAL STATUTES AND IMMIGRANTS: ASIAN AND LATINO DESCENDANTS

Immigration policies have impacted the arrival of members of different Asian- and Hispanic-heritage groups. The variability of legal sanctions includes consideration of economics, environmental forces, and political climate.

ASIAN DESCENDANTS

The Chinese Exclusion Act passed by Congress and signed by President Arthur in 1882 restricted immigration of an ethnic working group into the United States (Lehigh.edu, n.d.). Following this legislation, several additional sanctions were implemented to deny property ownership, permit residential discrimination, restrict hiring in some occupations, and obstruct miscegenation. This exclusion resulted in Chinese living in communities where they developed their businesses to addresses their community needs (Asian-nation.org, n.d.). Despite this, these residents began to file lawsuits that contested the denial of their rights. This exclusion fostered their community organization into areas often called *Chinatown*.

In 1942, President Roosevelt ordered the relocation of about 120,000 Japanese because of fears that they might pose a security risk with a potential Japanese invasion (ushistory.org, 2018). Two thirds of these were American citizens (amhistory.si.edu/, n.d.)

Otsuka (2002) wrote the historical novel *When the Emperor Was Divine,* which describes a family's experience of being informed of the rule for becoming interned. This unwelcome reality involved the process of preparing, enduring the transition and relocation, returning, and adjusting to all that occurred. This legal action taken by the government as a means of protecting the country also put many citizens at risk to several unintended or unconsidered consequences.

Legal statutes regarding immigration and informal procedures regarding hiring by existing business impacted Chinese, Japanese, Korean, Filipino, Vietnamese, and Cambodian people as they settled in areas across the United States.

LATINO DESCENDANTS

Priority legal concerns of Latinos include immigration, language, and voting. Several states have introduced ordinances to profile persons of Hispanic or Latino descent if their documented status is in question. Local, state, and federal officials can create ordinances that address political agendas. The increasing immigrant population in urban and suburban areas has been recruited for low-wage labor. Portes (2014) urges the consideration of the consequences on the children of immigrants and their care as they grow up in environments of disadvantage.

The family situations and the discrimination that immigrants attract impact access to services that human rights demand—housing, education, and food. In most service settings, social workers will have to evaluate service needs for immigrant families. The U.S. penchant for selfishly seeking cheap labor, using it, and not thinking about the related details of human needs creates social problems.

As immigrants become integrated into communities, their need for education involves acknowledging their native language and their process of learning English as they seek paths to higher education (Wozniacka, 2014). As residents of the communities in which they reside, they become citizens and vote. Obstacles that officials may establish are likely to create more problems than solutions unless the view of labor and worker rights is examined in a more proactive manner.

Cisneros's *House on Mango Street* (1984) engages readers in the process of Esperanza's transitioning from Latino immigrant status to southwestern community resident and shares her experiences of pessimism, loss, and joy. *Soledad*, by Angie Cruz (2001), weaves her identity conflicts between Washington Heights and lower Manhattan. The family crisis that calls her home sets off her recall of family secrets and dynamics (Bost & Aparicio, 2013).

LEGAL STATUTES AND SEXUAL EXPRESSION

In late 1869, Karl Westphal proposed that homosexuality should not be penalized as a crime but should be noted as a psychiatric condition. In 1952, the first issue of the *Diagnostic Statistical Manual (DSM–1)* designated homosexuality as a "sociopathic personality disorder" (wikipedia.org, n.d.).

Following the Eisenhower statute, states established various laws against homosexual activities. Several countries and states have had laws that restricted or criminalized same-sex relations or discussions (lgbt-rights-hrw.silk.co/, n.d.). Human Rights Watch is also a source of information on this topic.

In the United States, regulations that stigmatize homosexual activity, associate HIV information with homosexuality, and penalize information in sex education classes that could be helpful to young persons have been passed in Alabama, Arizona, Louisiana, Mississippi, Missouri, North Carolina, Oklahoma, South Carolina, Tennessee, Texas, and Utah (Ford, 2014). LGBTQI rights have associated regulations regarding spousal benefits and employment discrimination. Limits in protection of concern include legal fragility of families, financial insecurity, housing, and eldercare (Knauer, 2009).

Advocacy against penalties for homosexual behavior and challenges to the legitimacy of the psychiatric interpretations resulted in revising the categories in 1974. In 1986, the category was removed entirely from the *DSM*. Contemporary concerns include the appreciation of gains the LGBTQI community has made but also ponders the discrimination that affects their lives and family members (Severson, 2017).

PERSONS WITH CHALLENGES

What kinds of challenges come to mind when you think of the social messages we have heard in various settings? Our history has essentially focused on reasons to restrict and exclude members of groups who differ visibly or in cultural orientation from those in the dominant culture that hold power. As we proceed with technology and the activities that have used resources, additional challenges have been created.

While we are creating methods to address basic SES (socioeconomic status) problems, there are also new problems arising. Persons experiencing a dry-eye condition are likely to have it because of the rising air pollution. Problems with lead in the water have been around, but clean water is questionable in more locations in the United States than one would think. Pollution in the soil (pesticide use) is harming bees, which impacts the natural ecosystem we depend on. Contemplating how the history of discrimination, prejudice, and privilege (Edsall, 2012b) have influenced the disparities and inequality that exist is also the basis for continuing to press forward.

THE PRICE OF INEQUALITY

The reality of the "self-replicating" (Edsall, 2012) establishment is the continual use of narrow views and approaches to addressing racial bias in our social environment. Stiglitz (2012) notes politics have shaped the market in ways that give advantage to those at the top at the expense of the rest. He makes it clear (Stiglitz, 2015) that without governmental regulation dominant interests use their leverage to make gains at the expense of the majority.

The economics of the recession and subsequent market activities have had the most impact on Black and Hispanic women. They have experienced job losses, limited job opportunities, limited access to health care, and limited resources for child care—potential situations that create less protection for their children. These circumstances exist in a political landscape that is hurtful to low-income people (Johnson, 2013).

As voices of every group have raised perspectives of humanity, the emphasis on self-awareness, acknowledgement of human rights, and need for reflection and growth also focus on themes of love, fairness, and moral obligation. Haidt (2012) raises essential questions about how we think about what is right and wrong. He targets comments about moral institutions, moral intuition, and morality that include variation of influences across cultures and acknowledges that these cannot be simply explained. Beliefs in individualism and collectivism add to this complex matrix. Students of social work and other helping professions are urged to recognize and to explore these dynamics in understanding their own ideas and those of others.

Victims of prejudice and discrimination are harmed as individuals, members of families, and of communities. As the trajectory of history illustrates, people who are hurt by practices and policies do speak out, and many others step up as abolitionists (Grimké, 1836), as allies (Ayvazian, 2010), and as supporters. We are observing more bystanders standing up as well (Katz, 2012). Our history has demonstrated ongoing inhumane behaviors. We are challenged to do more to make our social environment a healthy one.

DISPARITIES

The impact of the stressors on people is significant across many categories, and we examine five major categories to consider the disparities. The following charts provide some examples of summary data in economics/income, education, health, mental health, and criminal justice.

ECONOMICS/INCOME

All	$27,334
White	$28,661
Black	$17,569
Asian	$27,464
Native American	$15,671
Hispanic	$14,801

FIGURE 3.1   Per Capita Income

Source: U.S. Census Bureau. (2010). American Community Survey. Retrieved from http://factfinder2.censUS.gov/

The per capita incomes for Native, Hispanic, and Black Americans are low. This does not mean there are not members of all groups across all income categories. The Pew Research Center (2007) describes minimum incomes for individuals and families needed to qualify for income levels.

	ONE-PERSON HOUSEHOLD	TWO-PERSON HOUSEHOLD	THREE-PERSON HOUSEHOLD	FOUR-PERSON HOUSEHOLD	FIVE-PERSON HOUSEHOLD
Upper-Income	$66,000	$93,300	$114,300	$132,000	$147,600
Middle-Income	$22,000	$31,100	$38,100	$44,000	$49,200

FIGURE 3.2   Middle and Upper Incomes

Source: Pew Research Center. (2014). "Who Is 'Middle Income' and 'Upper Income'?" Retrieved from http://assets.pewresearch. org/wp-content/uploads/sites/12/2014/12/FT_14.12.16_middleIncome.png

Another way to look at income is to consider the working-class grouping. According to Wilson (2016) this group will become predominantly people of color sooner than the Bureau of Labor projected. She proposes more efforts in policy formulations across racial and ethnic groups to address inequality and raise living standards.

Continuing research regarding working-class groups, many of whom are service users in agencies that employ helpings professions, show that over the past 40 years "economic poli-cymaking has suppressed hourly wage growth and prevented greater improvements in living standards" (Cooper & Kroeger, 2017, p.). These researchers conclude the diminished income security is connected to employers stealing from workers in various ways such as "refusing to pay promised wages, paying less than legally mandated minimums, failing to pay for all hours worked, or not paying overtime premiums deprives" (p.).

Finally, the rates of unemployment among people of color is higher than among whites across the levels of education.

TABLE 3.1   Unemployment Rate by Race and Education Level

	BLACK	WHITE
No high school diploma	16.6%	6.9%
High school diploma	9.6%	4.6%
Some college experience	7.4%	4.0%
Bachelor's degree and higher	4.1%	2.4%

Source: Author's (Wilson, 2015) calculations based on monthly Current Population Survey data retrieved from http://www.epi. org/publication/black-unemployment-educational-attainment/. The 12-month averages include data for December 2014 through November 2015 and are calculated for people age 25 or older.

Black unemployment is significantly higher than white unemployment, regardless of educational attainment.

EDUCATION

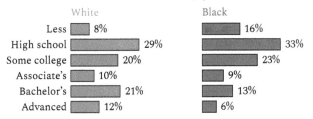

Educational attainment in U.S., by race (2013)

Advanced is master's, professional or Ph.D. Lindsey Cook for USN&WR:*Source:* Census

LINDSEY COOK FOR USN&WR; *SOURCE:* CENSUS

FIGURE 3.3   Educational Attainment by Race

Social and economic factors impact the level of education attainment.

Source: U.S. News. (2013). "Educational Attainment in U.S., by Race" [Blog post]. Retrieved from https://www.usnews.com/news/blogs/data-mine/2015/01/28/us-education-still-separate-and-unequal

HEALTH

Health disparity research shows that the physiological changes impacted by discrimination and micro insults or aggressions do affect how people feel and contribute to their health (Brodish et al., 2012; Williams, Neighbors, & Jackson, 2003) and mental health (Gomez, 2015). Emerging research notes the vulnerability of Black Americans to historical and current status. Gomez 's team (Gomez, Smith, Gobin, Tang & Freyd, 2015) argues that institutional betrayal, a concept similar to Freyd (2013) and L. T. Smith (2012) must be considered because of its role in condoning, perpetuating, and perpetrating micro-aggressive practices. We can speculate that the

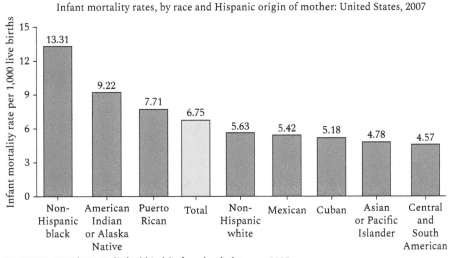

Infant mortality rates, by race and Hispanic origin of mother: United States, 2007

SOURCE: CDC/NCHS, linked birth/infant death data set, 2007.

FIGURE 3.4   Infant Mortality Rates

According to the CDC the infant mortality rates are of concern.

Source: CDC/NCHS. (2007). Linked Birth/Infant Death Data Set. Retrieved from https://www.cdc.gov/nchs/products/databriefs/db74.htm

current status of income, health, education, and criminal justice disparity rates are affected by the history of exclusion in services and institutional arrangements in the social environment.

MENTAL HEALTH

Mental health rates vary across groups and diagnoses or death rates.

TABLE 3.2   Suicide in Men by Age and Race

	AFRICAN AMERICAN MEN	NON-HISPANIC WHITE MEN	AFRICAN AMERICAN MEN/NON-HISPANIC WHITE MEN RATIO
15–24 years	12.0	22.4	0.5
25–44 years	14.3	31.7	0.5
45–64 years	9.9	37.1	0.3
65 years and over	8.9	36.1	0.2
All ages	9.4	25.8	0.4

Source: http://www.cdc.gov/nchs/data/hus/hus16.pdf OR https://minorityhealth.hhs.gov/omh/browse.aspx?lvl=4&lvlID=24

TABLE 3.3   Suicide in Women by Age and Race

	AFRICAN AMERICAN WOMEN	NON-HISPANIC WHITE WOMEN	AFRICAN AMERICAN WOMEN/NON-HISPANIC WHITE WOMEN RATIO
15–4 years	2.6	5.4	0.5
25–44 years	2.9	9.8	0.3
45–64 years	2.7	12.6	0.2
65 years and over	1.3	5.8	0.2
All ages	2.1	7.5	0.3

Source: https://minorityhealth.hhs.gov/omh/browse.aspx?lvl=4&lvlID=24

TABLE 3.4   Suicide in Adolescents

	NON-HISPANIC BLACK	NON-HISPANIC WHITE	NON-HISPANIC BLACK/NON-HISPANIC WHITE RATIO
Male	6.8	16.6	0.4
Female	2.2	4.8	0.5
Total	4.5	10.9	0.4

Source: https://minorityhealth.hhs.gov/omh/browse.aspx?lvl=4&lvlID=24

CRIMINAL JUSTICE

The trajectory of school suspensions leading to prison and incarcerations has been widely publicized. The Sentencing Project provides an interactive map of incarceration by state. The demographics of incarcerated populations is dramatically different from that of the United States as a whole. (Sentencing Project, 2017). According to the U.S. 2010 Census, Blacks are incarcerated five times more than Whites are, and Hispanics are nearly twice as likely to be incarcerated as Whites (Sakala, 2014).

Recent analyses and dialogues have raised more concern about disparities in the application of harsh penalties against young men of color (Alexander, 2012). People who were not informed of these situations are generally more aware now. The evidence for this stems from the legal codes enacted in slavery and post-slavery. Efforts by the court system and other major institutions to maintain control and push back against civil rights continue. The Sentencing Project (2000) published an analysis that shows how racial disparity influences several decision points in the justice system regarding law enforcement, arraignment, release and pre-adjudicatory decisions, adjudication and sentencing, probation and community-based alternatives to incarceration, jail and prison custody, and parole and reentry. The results of overt bias and traditional protocols appear to be reflected in the table of incarceration rates in Table 3.5.

The disparity data show that many people need to improve capacity in education and health to be more able to have financial security to handle family needs. Moving beyond negative beliefs and attitudes about people to foster skill building and vocational and academic pathways are considered likely to assist persons in moving forward. More work is needed. Disproportionate penalties and health disparities require continued focus, more research, and commitment to change. As the social work profession continues to address its ethics, values, and standards, inclusive social work offers a path.

TABLE 3.5   Incarceration Rates by Race
The racial and ethnic makeup of incarcerated populations is dramatically different from that of the United States as a whole.

RACE/ETHNICITY	U.S. POPULATION PERCENTAGE	U.S. INCARCERATED POPULATION PERCENTAGE	NATIONAL INCARCERATION RATE (PER 100,000)
White (non-Hispanic)	64%	39%	450 per 100,000
Hispanic	16%	19%	831 per 100,000
Black	13%	40%	2,306 per 100,00

Source: Prison Policy.org. (2014). "Breaking Down Mass Incarceration in the 2010 Census: State-by-State Incarceration Rates by Race/Ethnicity." Retrieved from https://www.prisonpolicy.org/reports/rates.html

CONSIDERING VIEWS AGAINST SOCIAL BARRIERS
AND ECONOMIC INEQUALITY

Progressive ideas about how to provide basic supports for people to help themselves and move forward are connected to the historical realities of our economic foundation. Moving from our history of greed and punishment to policies that address opportunity and collective decision-making is obstructed in many ways because of the socialization that has predominated.

Historians and activists are raising their voices to repeat and disseminate strengths-based information.

Emerging research and advocacy point to ways the focus on stereotypes can be shifted to alternative approaches that acknowledge the human developmental processes to resist oppressive circumstances and to move forward in recovery. Voices expressing resistance to this domination and urging efforts to improve our democracy require transparency and policies that promote higher education and capacity development.

The messages we are hearing from progressive groups in the community are refreshing. A lot of advocacy work involves pursuing substantive views of how changes can be made and the participants include voices with words that challenge the mechanisms that have restricted opportunities.

ASSESSING CULTURAL VARIATIONS OF GROUPS
IN THE COMMUNITY

Reactions to the situations of dominance and oppression in multicultural groups can be assessed with respect to economic, psychological, and cultural context. The legal sanctions generally are structured to maintain restricted economic opportunities. Examining the process of engagement and collaboration involves exploring place and location and encourages appreciation of diversity.

STRENGTHS INSTEAD OF STEREOTYPES

Behavior, beliefs, and attitudes that hold on to narrow social construction continue to be prevalent. Moving away from these mindsets requires challenging stereotypes, paying more attention to system obstacles, and exploring how elements of strengths can be highlighted in more ways. Persons of diverse descent groups have fostered positive contributions.

AFRICAN HERITAGE

The ways in which discrimination has been perpetuated are reflected in federal reports and regulations. *The Negro Family: The Case for National Action*, written in 1965 by Daniel Moynihan, Assistant Secretary of Labor, built the denigration of black mothers (Acs, Braswell,

Sorensen, & Turner, 2013) into socially constructed ideas about the culture in low-income neighborhoods. Like other ill-conceived ideas that put an official stamp on devaluing people of color, this 1965 document ignored the body of evidence that single mothers were largely the result of restricted labor and work opportunities for men of color. The economics of poverty were dismissed. Julius Williams's (1997) work, *When Work Disappears* presents a related perspective that reviews dynamics that address the specific economic issues involved in family struggles and the inability of a significant percentage of Black men to gain employment suitable to accommodate the needs of a family.

LATINO HERITAGE

The association of negative descriptions about Hispanics (e.g., lazy or dirty; Valdeón, 2013) and stereotypes about Latino men (e.g., absent dads that speak Spanish) can be connected to the usual devaluation by dominant culture to discredit people other than themselves. It is contradictory that these same descriptions are used with Blacks and Asians when it is that members of these groups have provided major sources of labor and supported the economy in jobs when others did not.

Singer (2012) points out that as the U.S. population ages, the labor force will increasingly depend upon immigrants and their children to replace current workers.

ASIAN HERITAGE

The influence of racial affronts that don't fall into the typical racial paradigm places the likelihood that when and where they occur, they often are not addressed (Appel, Ai, Huang, & Nicado, 2014). Discrimination may be obscured regarding color but is visible regarding accent, cultural practices, religion, and economic tensions.

The economics across Asian American groups varies by nationalities. The overall statistics suggest their standing at the top of economic rankings. However, a breakdown of income by national groups shows a varied income distribution (Lopez, Ruiz, & Patten, 2017).

It is critical for professionals who work with children and adolescents to become more informed of the strengths of different heritage groups in order to navigate their needs for role representations and culturally affirming interactions.

IMMIGRANTS

Immigrant workers play out different roles across industries. Anyone born outside the United States is foreign born. These include naturalized citizens, legal permanent residents, temporary migrants (including H–1B workers and students), refugees, asylum seekers, and authorized immigrants (Singer, 2012). Immigrants are overrepresented in some fields. In others, they may lack education. In some, their education keeps with the national trends of native-born residents.

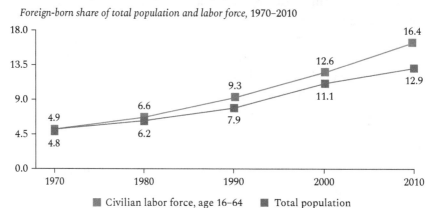

Immigrants are a growing part of the labor force

Immigrants make up 13% of the population but 16% of the labor force.

Foreign-born share of total population and labor force, 1970–2010

■ Civilian labor force, age 16–64   ■ Total population

Source: U.S. decemial census data, 1970–2000 and ACS 2010, accessed from IPUMS.org

FIGURE 3.5   Immigrant Education

Source: Singer, A. (2012). "Immigrant Workers in the U.S. Labor Force." Brookings.com. Retrieved from https://www.brookings.edu/research/immigrant-workers-in-the-u-s-labor-force/

STRENGTHS FOCUS

The American Historical Association's 2015 annual conference included a panel on which several points were made that emphasized the need for historians to become more involved in the dialogue. Heather Thompson, a panelist, described some contemporary backlash as virulent racism regarding the Trayvon Martin and Michael Brown police shootings that occurred in 2012 and 2014, respectively (Hawkins, 2014). The panelists acknowledged the need for history instructors to refine their approaches to better address connecting the past with the present tensions.

Post-racial is a term used to suggest that race is no longer an issue. However, continual events can be associated with the white racial frame that organized structural dynamics to maintain preferential treatment and opportunities to more privileged persons. There are millions across the globe for whom marginalization has not obstructed their progress. Nevertheless, the disproportionate numbers of those in need continue.

Marcia Chatelaine, on faculty at Georgetown University, discussed her work on the Michael Brown, case of 2014, in the Ferguson syllabus, which is available to schools to assist students in the discussions about the issues related to social justice (Clevenger, 2015).

Roediger and Esch (2014) proposed that history's focus on scientific management rather than the strategy of race in labor management demonstrates a narrow view. Analytical views that address race and income or capital access are more likely to tap into the source of some our country's pervasive social problems.

STUDENT SCENARIO 2

Christina is preparing to work with a community program that assists residents with basic needs. There is a substantial immigrant population in the area. Her peer supervision group has an assignment for today's session: Select a person from any one of the cultural groups and discuss the impact of the socialization processes that limits strengths-based information.

How do you think this discussion will benefit the participants?

CHAPTER SUMMARY

Laws and regulations related to economics, justice, and education impact mobility in our communities. The history of the diverse groups that comprise the United States is more than the promotion of manifest destiny and stereotypes about cultural groups. Readers will be able to select and investigate laws or policies that affect a group and consider the pros and cons of traditional messages about their history.

EPAS AND CODE OF ETHICS

CSWE EDUCATIONAL POLICY & ACCREDITATION STANDARDS

Competency 6: Engage with individuals, families, groups, organizations, and communities.

Social workers understand that engagement is an ongoing component of the dynamic and interactive process of social work practice with, and on behalf of, diverse individuals, families, groups, organizations, and communities.

- 6a) Apply knowledge of human behavior and the social environment, person-in-
- environment, and other multidisciplinary theoretical frameworks to engage with clients and constituencies; and
- 6b) Use empathy, reflection, and interpersonal skills to effectively engage diverse clients and constituencies. (EPAS, 2015)

NASW CODE OF ETHICS

1.05 Cultural Awareness and Social Diversity

- (c) Social workers should obtain education about and seek to understand the nature of social diversity and oppression with respect to race, ethnicity, national origin, color, sex, sexual orientation, gender identity or expression, age, marital status, political belief, religion, immigration status, and mental or physical ability. (NASW, n.d.)

DISCUSSION QUESTIONS

1. The system of separate but equal was put into full effect through several laws to punish behaviors that were inclusive, humane, or that involved marital relationships between whites and people of color. Consider this quotation that Buck (2014) used from Lerone Bennett's analysis of the differentiation between black and white in his work: "In a comprehensive campaign of mass conditioning, ... the severed heads of black and white rebels were impaled on poles along the roads as warnings to black people and white people, and opponents of the status quo were starved to death in chains and roasted slowly over open fires" (p. 34). Because of social norms and beliefs such as this, the "separate-but-equal" social ideology continued on for many years. Are there any norms that operate in this way today?
2. Are there current laws that pose intimidation and physical harm to limit human rights? Research and list three.
3. Using readings from this chapter, write a critical-thinking question (one that requires comparing one view with another) and craft an answer to it. Each student should share the question and answer with a classmate. How are the responses similar or different? Explain the variation or lack of variation.

EXERCISES

1. Write an opinion piece on an idea generated from this chapter's readings. Use *The New York Times* for examples.
2. Assume an identity of a member of one of the groups we have been discussing (i.e., immigrants, people of color, a woman of an early era, LGBTQI, physically or emotionally challenged, members of different religions, class, or age). Develop a conversation scenario that could be held in your family that would help socialize you to pursue your dreams despite the rigors of our discriminatory society.
3. Have each student write at least one statement of bias she or he has heard. Compile the list. Distribute as a handout. Have students discuss.

MULTICULTURAL RESOURCES

Bost, S., & Aparacio, F. R. (2013). *The Routledge companion to Latino/a literature*. Abingdon, United Kingdom: Routledge.

Bouton, K. (2013). Shouting won't help. Retrieved from http://www.npr.org/2013/02/15/172100123/npr-author-katherine-bouton-opens-up-about-going-deaf.

Burrell, T. (2010). *Brainwashed: Challenging the myth of black inferiority*. SmileyBooks.

Byrd, J. (2011). *The transit of empire: Indigenous critiques of colonialism*. Minneapolis: University of Minnesota Press.

Darkwah, N. B. (2014). *The Africans who wrote the Bible*. Henderson, NV: HBC.

Davidson, B. (1966). *African Kingdoms*. New York: Time-Life Books.

Francis, L. (Ed.). (1999). *When the rain sings: Poems by young Native Americans*. New York, NY: Simon & Schuster.

Geronimo (Goyahkla Chiricuhua), Dembeck, C. (Ed) (2011–2013). *Through apache eyes verbal history of the apache struggle*. CreateSpace Independent Publishing Platform

Kaltreider, K. (2003). *American Indian Prophecies: Conversations with Chasing Deer*. Carlsbad, CA: Hay House.

M'Bantu, A. (2012). *The ancient Black Arabs*. London, England: Pomegranate.

M'Bantu, A. (2012). *Unmistakably Black: Sculpture and paintings from ancient Syria & Anatolia*. London, England: Pomegranate.

Nebraskastudies.org. Native American citizenship: A long history of treaties. Retrieved from www.nebraskastudies.org/0700/stories/0701_0141.html

Oklahoma, T. (2013). *Native Americans before European civilization* [Video file]. Retrieved from https://www.youtube.com/watch?v=7FItlStGMY4

Rankine, C. (2014). *Citizen: An American lyric*. Minneapolis, MN: Graywolf Press.

Audio Interview with L. Neary, Poet Claudia Rankine On Latest Racial Violence, 7.9.2016. http://www.npr.org/2016/07/09/485356173/poet-claudia-rankine-on-latest-racial-violence

Simon, R. (2011). *The story of beautiful girl*. New York, NY: Grand Central.

Valdeón, R. A. (2013). The use of Latin American Hispanic & Latino in U.S. academics articles, 2000–2015. *Terminology, 19*(1), 112–137.

Walker, R. (2010). *If you want to learn early African history, start here*. London, England: Reklaw Education.

Wallis, V. (1997). *Bird girl and the man who followed the sun: An Athabaskan Indian legend from Alaska*. New York, NY: Harper Perennial.

Wallis, V. (2013). *Two old women: An Alaska legend of betrayal, courage and survival*. New York, NY: Harper Perennial.

VIDEO

Amistad, 1997. Director: S. Spielberg—Film

Belle, 2013. Director: A. Asante—Film

Django Unchained, 2012. Director: Q. Tarentino—Film

Ethnic Notions, 1986. Producer/Director: M.Riggs, Narrator: Esther Rolle [Video file]

Frontline Report: *School segregation is back, 60 years after Brown*. 5.15.2014. https://www.pbs.org/wgbh/frontline/article/the-return-of-school-segregation-in-eight-charts/

Goldhunting, History of Native American Indians—Documentary Parts 1–4, Retrieved 6/14/15 https://www.youtube.com/watch?v=28IAI6F0DZc

Health Disparities in the Latino Community, 10.12.2015; https://www.youtube.com/watch?v=2XWTgQeqRBg

Hidden Colors: The untold history of people of aboriginal, Moor and African descent, 2011. Director: T. Nasheed—Film

Katz, J. (2012). *Violence against women—It's a men's issue* [TED Talk]. Retrieved from https://www.ted.com/talks/jackson_katz_violence_against_women_it_s_a_men_s_issue

Lincoln, 2012. Director: S. Spielberg

Roots: The Saga of an American Family. January 1977. Producer, Stan Marguiles

Rules of racism, 2014. [Video file].

Trail of Tears—A Native American Documentary Collection. 2009. Rich-Heape films, Dallas TX, www.millcreek.com

Blacks and Native Americans

Twelve Years a Slave, 2013. Director: S. McQueen—Film

FURTHER RESOURCES

Bahn P. G. (Ed). (1999). *Lost cities: 50 discoveries in world archaeology*. New York, NY: Welcome Rain.

Jones, J. (2013). *A dreadful deceit: The myth of race from the colonial era to Obama's America*. New York, NY: Basic Books.

Jung, M. (2008). *Coolies & cane: Race, labor & sugar in the age of emancipation*. Baltimore, MD: John Hopkins University.

Nash, G. (1992). *Red, white and black: The peoples of early North America*. Carmel, IN: Pearson.

Pascoe, P. (2010). *What comes naturally: Miscegenation & law & the making of race in America*. New York, NY: Oxford University Press.

PART II

Exploring the History of
Oppression and Privilege: The
Impact of Oppression on Society

This section expands on the dynamics of social construction and the history of oppression and privilege. Chapter 4 presents the history of social welfare organizations that promote rights and services for all, especially those who are vulnerable or at risk and who face struggles with which they need assistance and support. Chapter 5 examines the broad social context of oppression, racism, and discrimination and its relationship to economics. Chapter 6 reviews the various identities that are traditionally connected to the exclusionary messages that social constructions describe.

CHAPTER 4

Social Work in Context

Values and Ethics

CHAPTER OVERVIEW

While the values and mission of social work have delineated the emphasis on assisting persons in need, helping them gain skills and connecting with resources, the reality of implementing this charge has faced continuous obstacles. Women's work has typically received a lower place in the social ordering of prestige, and work with people who are labeled as *needy* or *with problems* also creates tension. Charity Organization Society (founded in 1869) workers resisted working with African Americans because it was difficult—resources were meager, and those who were helped by the "friendly visitors" and the workers themselves faced stereotypes and biases (Iglehart & Becerra, 1995). Policies were framed for social control, and strict eligibility protocols were used.

As the landscape of social welfare expands to recognize micro, mezzo, macro, and global dynamics, the values context has also become enlarged. Values that respect diversity and human rights have expanded the critique of old binaries and urge evaluation of the impact of delivery, pursuit of accountability to service users, and the development of alternatives. This chapter acknowledges the restrictions upon social services, the participation of women of means, and the use of labeling in offering services that were perceived to be deserved. The challenge is about stepping up to the realities of social work practice in a multicultural, multidisciplinary environment where values of humanity and spiritual responsibility shake the existing frames.

LEARNING OBJECTIVES

- Impact of history on the profession, the communities, service organizations and potential social workers.
- Social work as purveyor of advocacy for services and rights.
- Social work advocates for women.
- Social work values human rights.

Benchmark: Students should understand the profession's evolving advocacy and practice for social justice.

CASE SCENARIO 1

A potential client, a person of color, is meeting with an intake staff person. As they proceed through the initial information gathering, the client says, "I'm aware that there is a tendency to treat white males with less penalty than black males in treatment facilities. Can you assure me that this won't happen here?"

What do you think about his statement and question?

FOUNDATION OF SOCIAL WORK

Social work is the profession committed to helping individuals, families, groups, and communities improve, restore, recover, and enhance well-being. The knowledge base is interdisciplinary and discipline specific. In examining the historical social context of the United States, we recognize its influence on current situations that citizens and social workers face and use the social work value frameworks of integrity and respect to move forward. Simultaneously, other helping professionals and people of the communities we serve share our value domains. Activists advocate the place of personal awareness and civic participation for collective capacity building.

The history of social work includes the development of components regarding the accreditation of social work educational programs, the establishment of the professional codes of ethical practice for practice, and the broad collaboration to advocate for global social welfare concerns. This history of the Council on Social Work Education (CSWE), National Association of Social Workers (NASW), and the International Federation of Social Workers (IFSW) demonstrates evolving presentation of principles regarding the treatment of people in need.

The Charity Organization Society and the settlement houses presented two dimensions of social welfare—one with focus on alms and services and the other emphasized theory and methods and affiliation with universities. Early workers of both groups believed they could be of little help to people of color for whom the denial of rights was so ingrained (Iglehart & Becerra, 1995). The substantive obstacles of discrimination and prejudice against people of color were not battles that workers in these organizations were willing to take on.

VALUE BASE

The social work value base has been connected to a Eurocentric paradigm and an evolving culturally and ethnic-sensitive social work model. The foundation model is based on individualism, competition, expertise, and materialism. The culturally sensitive model emphasizes family, education, individual enterprise, and hard work as well as mutual aid and concern for the welfare of the collective group. Reid-Merritt (2010) parallels Afrocentric approaches that begin with African history and culture, Nguzo Saba, and the principles of Ma'at: truth, justice, propriety, harmony, balance, reciprocity, and order. Similar emphasis on other non-Eurocentric principles by Puerto Rican and Hispanic social workers, Asian social workers, and Native American social workers are critical to appreciating the diversity and identity of the communities with whom we work. The mission statements for these organizations are located on their websites and are listed in the references.

Social work values were in place before the establishment of the key social work professional leadership institutions. These organizations grew from the Charity Organization Society and religious agencies that addressed the needs of the most vulnerable citizens. As such, they reflected the beliefs and attitudes of the dominant culture even as they reached out to those with low incomes. According to Iglehart and Becerra (1995), native-born, white, Anglo-Saxon Americans perceived themselves as superior to others, and this attitude was pervasive from the early arrival of new immigrants, Italians, Poles, Russian Jews, and Greeks through the contemporary arrivals from the southern Americas, Africa, southern Asia, and most recently Syria.

African Americans migrating to the North for employment received the most systematic and restrictive measures. They suffered poor housing conditions and were charged higher rates than other immigrants. Racial hostility and hatred played out in violence against people of color, in educational segregation, or in agencies' refusal to provide service. Mainstream social service agencies resisted inviting African Americans into the services.

Hull House was located in a community with the second-largest African American population. Although their annual report indicated there was a black mothers' club organized by Jane Addams in 1927, there was no evidence that any black mothers were on the mailing lists or receiving any services (Iglehart & Becerra, 1995, p. 119). There were a few settlement houses that welcomed African Americans.

Using Reamer's (2005) values framework, perceived moral standards offered the jumping-off point. Tensions between individual personal values and organizational ones were in place in early agencies. While there were perceived moral standards, the behaviors were connected to discriminatory attitudes that would rather exclude than work out new relationships. As the social service organizations developed, ethnic minority communities were also organizing and developing agencies that focused on strengthening families. These agencies emerged to fulfill residents' needs to feel engaged, welcomed, and appreciated. Mainstream agencies did not reach out to the broad community or embrace ideas of the workers who did want to improve their services. Despite the values of helping, in many respects the early agencies had underlying expectations to control members of the diverse communities.

CRITICAL THINKING QUESTION

What factors have shaped and continue to minimize rights of women, people of color, LGBTQI (lesbian/gay/bisexual/transgender/queer/intersex), and others?

THE SOCIAL ENVIRONMENT

The atmosphere of the social environment of the larger social system was not welcoming and fostered distrust in the ethnic minority communities. Asian Americans did not perceive themselves as one group and wanted their various nationalities to be recognized. The terms *Hispanic* or *Latinos* did not include Chicanos or Mexicans. Among the community usually referred to as African Americans, there were also several distinctive groups, including people from the Caribbean, Africa, and other regions. Social workers were not trained to focus on large system impediments to non-white citizens. The emphasis on casework was tailored to individual services, and traditional thoughts about people of color influenced an agency's lack of responsiveness to community needs. Agencies slowly began to evaluate their discrimination and recognize the need to train, hire and recruit workers from ethnic minority groups (Scott & O'Neal, 1981). Social work leadership agencies began to invite other relevant participants to the discussion.

COUNCIL ON SOCIAL WORK EDUCATION

PROGRAM ACCREDITATION

Social work education programs have been accredited based on professionally developed standards since 1952 following the joining of two organizations. The American Association of Schools of Social Work (AASSW) and National Association of Schools of Social Administration (NASSA) initiated the standards-based review of educational programs. The CSWE solicited participation of relevant stakeholders in developing standards that spell out the expected areas for performance and competency of trained social workers. The first standards were established through the Council for Standards in Human Service Education (CSHSE), which was established in 1979. The CSWE reported in 2015 this summary of accredited programs:

- 509 accredited baccalaureate social work programs
- 241 accredited master's social work programs
- 12 baccalaureate social work programs in candidacy
- 15 master's social work programs in candidacy (EPAS, 2015)

The Educational Policy Accreditation Standard (EPAS, 2015) addresses the social work value of ethics, professional behavior, and competent practice interventions. The set of standards provides guidelines for professional competence and curriculum content for values, knowledge, and skills for the social work professional.

Task force committees in the early 1970s gathered information and delivered reports on addressing curricula content regarding inclusion of women, African Americans, Asian Americans, Chicanos, Native Americans, and Puerto Ricans. Content for gay, lesbian, and transgender persons was initiated via the task force in 1980, and information has been updated since 2001.

International issues and opportunities for collaboration in the global arena are promoted and the Center for Diversity and Social & Economic Justice is working with communities regarding social needs.

ACCREDITATION STANDARDS

The accreditation standards, revised in 2015, presents these as fundamental components of training social workers. Programs should incorporate content that prepares students' social work degrees for nine competency areas:

- Competency 1: Demonstrate ethical and professional behavior.
- Competency 2: Engage diversity and difference in practice.
- Competency 3: Advance human rights and social, economic, and environmental justice.
- Competency 4: Engage in practice-informed research and research-informed practice.
- Competency 5: Engage in policy practice.
- Competency 6: Engage with individuals, families, groups, organizations, and communities.
- Competency 7: Assess individuals, families, groups, organizations, and communities.
- Competency 8: Intervene with individuals, families, groups, organizations, and communities.
- Competency 9: Evaluate practice with individuals, families, groups, organizations, and communities. (EPAS, 2015)

CURRICULUM CONTENT

Content about all the people we work with is extremely important. The Council has made consistent and ongoing efforts to engage with communities to gather and disseminate relevant materials for educators and programs. Early steps to inclusion involve addressing concerns of the diverse communities to become involved in the information available to students pursuing social work.

Since the 1970s, the NASW has promoted incorporating and advocating for diverse membership. As groups began to identify their population-specific needs, NASW responded to their interests. The Association of Black Social Workers, Association of Asian & Pacific Social Workers, Association of Puerto Rican & Hispanic Social Workers, and Korean Association of Social Workers began organization in the early 1970s. These groups and many individuals brought more attention to the needs of members of these populations to receive more effective services.

Members of Native American tribes have been members of the Council on Social Work Education from the early years and incorporating their cultural content has been emphasized (Weaver, 1999).

NATIONAL ASSOCIATION OF SOCIAL WORKERS

The National Association of Social Workers (NASW) was established in 1955 through the efforts of representatives of several organizations with mutual concerns for providing assistance and coordinating resources to people. Social workers with interests in the social work profession, group work, community organizing, medical and psychiatric services, school social work, and research consolidated their efforts into one organization (Virginia Commonwealth University, n.d.).

The primary function of the NASW is to promote professional development, monitor and maintain the established standards, advance social policies, and provide services to its members through its leadership and chapter organizations. (Socialworkers.org, n.d.)

SOCIAL WORK PRACTICE

Abbott (1987) identified key social work values in her study *Professional Choices: Values at Work*. These values are demonstrated through attitudes and behaviors. The key values derived from the study are respect for basic human rights, sense of social responsibility, commitment to individual freedom, and support of self-determination. Based on survey data of "beginning students, recent graduates, seasoned professionals, social work faculty, and field instructors, seasoned social workers scored higher than members of any other profession" (p. 83).

Akhtar (2013) connects values to the ways students must master skills through recognizing the complex accountability of social workers. The work of values clarification and the pursuit of value goals involves personal and organizational-level work. As we move to global issues and principles that advocate human rights, micro and macro circumstances involve private issues connecting to public policies. Values become more apparent and compelling as we seek desired outcomes.

In aiming to demonstrate the values within the practice arena, the NASW Code of Ethics was created in 1996 and revised in 2008. This code establishes social workers' respect for the profession, colleagues, services users, practice settings, and society. This code is relevant to the psychotherapeutic goals of practitioners and can also be applied as the profession expands its awareness of the role of advocacy by practitioners, organizations, and communities. The values that the ethical principles address include service, social justice, dignity and worth of the person, importance of human relationships, integrity, and competence.

REGIONAL SOCIAL WORK

As the profession is evolving, voices of people across the country and around the world continue to express opinions and data about service delivery to assist social welfare needs. NASW claims there are about 460,000 people with a social work degree (socialworkers.org, n.d.). The Bureau of Labor Statistics estimated 682,000 social work jobs with employment growth expected because of healthcare and social service needs (BLS, 2018).

Local chapters offer opportunities to network with social workers and gain information about local services and what social workers do in our communities. In addition to website information about professional development, advocacy, and social justice, support for one another in the jobs that we care about and the structures that challenge us is needed.

INTERNATIONAL FEDERATION OF SOCIAL WORKERS

The International Federation of Social Workers is comprised of 85 organizations from 70 countries and claims more than 460,000 members. It is a global organization "striving for social justice, human rights and social development through the promotion of social work, best practice models and the facilitation of international cooperation" (IFSW, 2014). The principles are generated by several documents contributed to and agreed upon by representatives of organizations around the world. These are used to shape policy development and service provision in a multicultural world.

The IFSW (2012) statement of ethical principles incorporates components from these documents that should be reviewed in offering social work services. Representatives to international conferences organized to address human, civil, and economic rights, forms of discrimination across cultural groups, and children established written proposals to put forth substantive values. This is a challenge to the profession and to related disciplines that espouse the goals of more effective services and prevention. The challenge goes beyond reflecting on the rights that are delineated. The parallel view begs the process and advocacy to incorporate the deeds and perspectives of multiple identities to achieve this kind of progress.

GLOBAL CHALLENGES

Healy and Wairire (2014) urge "social workers to tackle an ambitious agenda to contribute to the major social and environmental challenges" (p. 235). Referring to the Millennium Development Goals (MDGs), a set of eight goals adopted by the United States in 2000 that suggest a blueprint for social development, Healy and Wairire propose that social work educational programs incorporate the roles and tasks needed to promote awareness, lobby, and advocate in ways that would support and sustain social work values and commitments (p. 237).

An example of the awareness of social situations from a social work perspective includes media references to migrants as "swarms" to be managed, or migrants to be controlled. Wroe (2015) points out that they represent "the lives of real men and women, who have families, who have left jobs, who have made plans and paid money to come to the UK, and who are losing their lives in the most desperate of circumstances (para 2)." Migrants, despite their borders, are people with rights.

INTERNATIONAL OPPORTUNITIES

Social workers as professionals have a duty to speak up to protect human rights (Wroe, 2015). Addressing these value dimensions requires our consideration, reflection, and inclusion of migrant perspectives in designing collaborations and interventions that are respectful of these elements.

As the profession expands its awareness and interests, social workers become exposed to opportunities they may want to take advantage of by working in different regions of the world.

IMPLICATIONS OF HISTORICAL PERSPECTIVE OF RACISM IN THE UNITED STATES ON SOCIAL WORK PRACTICE

As social work leadership evolves, the reality of discrimination in the structures of services to persons needing assistance continues to impede the well-being of many citizens and requires examination. These obstacles have been identified all along the way and continue to require speaking up for accountability and transparency.

The history of social work is tied to the social climate of intercultural and interpersonal transactions and relationships. The country's segregated structure and restricted opportunities often presented huge obstacles for persons who did not visibly meet the traditional white male criteria of citizenship. People who responded to the need to work with citizens who were vulnerable against this network were typically women—white, middle-class women and women of color who valued all people and wanted to help people do better for themselves and their families. Certainly, men were also participants in this work to support human needs, albeit at times after the groundwork was accomplished by others.

In an 1863 publication, Benjamin Parham Aydelott began his book *Prejudice Against Colored People* (Aydelott, 1863/2014) with this statement, "The Bible clearly teaches the unity of the human race" (p. 1). He uses this to identify the basis of moral behavior, acknowledge the wickedness of prejudice against colored people, and note pride as the origin of prejudice. This short manuscript aligns Christian intent to overcome the prejudicial circumstances that exist and advocates for the use of power to overcome prejudice in churches and in the world since this prejudice has obstructed the rights of colored men.

IS IT ANTI-OPPRESSIVE OR IS IT RADICAL?

The ways social work has addressed discrimination, racism, and less-than-effective services have been conceptualized in different ways. Anti-oppressive social work does speak to affirming persons' rights to humane interactions that validate all, especially by social workers. Yet there are people pursuing social work credentials who have beliefs that devalue some people, especially those who are LGBTQI (Todd & Coholic, 2007). There can be some contradictions within these various service contexts and within the service delivery structure. Nevertheless, as doctors take the Hippocratic Oath to uphold ethical standards and do no harm, social workers are expected to value, support, and affirm all life, regardless of the service user's life circumstances. These concerns do require critical thinking and reflection as decisions are made about becoming a social worker.

The connection of morality to anti-oppression continued via liberation and theology movements developed in the 1960s in South America and continues. The exclusion of people of color, gender expression, and persons with physical, mental health, or learning issues maintains status quo protocols. The structures and behaviors that deny opportunities often create unreasonable penalties and more demeaning circumstances, which account for struggles and the spiraling impact many families face.

RADICAL SOCIAL WORK?

Is anti-oppressive social work just another way or describing radical social work? Bailey and Brake's (1976) work urged moving away from just seeing the individual to pursuing the development of new theories to address problems. Dalrymple and Burke (2006) suggest paying more attention to service users' lives, helping them use the process of appeals, and finding ways to reinterpret agency policies.

Similarly, calls to progress to a position that values equality are intrinsic on the path away from injustice and oppression (Gil, 1998). Social change has been occurring. Various representatives continually need to be included in having discussions that raise the questions we may not want to hear but challenge us to become better citizens in the process of planning and implementing services. Several films that have been produced over the years also offer perspectives of life and issues that can be contemplated regarding social work opportunities to be involved.

SOCIAL WORK AND EXCLUDED GROUPS

As the dynamics of oppression and exclusion impacted people of color, attitudes and laws that continued to control, penalize, and intimidate also influenced the attitudes and parameters of the social work profession. The concept of an American melting pot, used in the early 1900's to refer to the incorporation of immigrants, was not accurate. Social work values and mission statements identified and provided services to those in need as they transitioned and adjusted to new environments. Early work emphasized casework and subsequently group work and community organizing were used (McNutt, 2013). Yet, the socialization realities and structural dynamics impeded effective services across cultural groups. Some groups, when not visibly different, were able to mix or melt in. Others were not. For example, social workers in New York were often frustrated by the discrimination that obstructed work possibilities for people of color. New immigrant status affected most newcomers but there was more hostility, hatred and violence. Mobs of white people lynched, shot, beat and burned homes. Workers reportedly resisted providing services in these hostile situations (Iglehart & Becerra, 1995). However, advocates were speaking up and efforts to address juvenile conditions, mothers' welfare, and workplace conditions were taking place (McNutt, 2013). Given our past, contemporary research, and the social scenarios, these conditions continue.

UNCONSCIOUS BIAS

Ross (2016) clearly presents the fact that humans are biased and sometimes don't know it. But, on the whole, it appears we still have lots of work to do. The implicit association test (Project Implicit, 2011) measures attitudes and beliefs that persons may not want to reveal or may not be able to. There are opinions that support it's validity and those that question it (Kaufman,

2011). Greenwald and Krieger (2006), examined the mental processes research of the implicit tests project. Related studies suggest—that humans associate positive vibes to those with their in-group characteristics. Social construction marketing of negative vibes has worked. More confirmation of the dynamics is likely as bias measures are added to ongoing research regarding racial disparities.

Following the Civil War, the Freedmen's Bureau was established on May 12, 1865, to help newly freed slaves gain some resources for transitioning. Originally called the Bureau of Refugees, Freedmen, & Abandoned Lands, the agency dealt with issues about labor, education, relief, politics, and civil rights (Fitzgerald, 2004). But the slaves' transition into civilian life was complicated by personal attitudes that resisted the idea of emancipation of people of color. Similarly Bureau of Indian Affairs bureaucrats were observed to demonstrate similar attitudes of bias and resistance that resulted in trying to change Native Americans' cultural heritage.

SLAVES BECOME FREED PEOPLE

The expectations of the freed people, planning by agency bureaucrats, and the refusal of Southern whites to accept the changing status of slaves contributed to services that were not ideal. The freed people were disappointed by the Bureau's inability to protect their access to land and independent work life. The white Georgians obstructed the ex-slaves' ability to gain a better life during Reconstruction. Many agency officials were too timid to advocate strongly for the ex-slaves and tended to be on the side of arranging structures that maintained subordinate positions (History.com, n.d.).

The response to the ending of slavery and the need for education and employment was met by people of color in their own communities (Ross, 1978). The Atlanta University School of Social Work was founded in 1923 by E. Franklin Frazer. Churches played a significant role in building resources (Lincoln & Mamiya, 1990) for the community, including libraries, museums, schools, and other organizations. Clubs and community groups evolved in setting up social and business opportunities for community members.

As the professional social work responses gained attention on the broad front, the efforts of people of color within their communities was largely ignored. However, it was these internal community efforts that paved the way for broader attention and participation in the social welfare arena. Mutual aid efforts account for substantial community progress.

In Chicago, Jane Adams and others organized to help immigrants improve language skills and learn behaviors to assist their assimilation into the American culture by offering services in neighborhood locations called *settlement houses* from 1897 through 1905. These services generally responded to the perceived need to assist immigrants to become more like Americans to improve chances to integrate into the mainstream and to obtain employment (Iglehart & Becerra, 1995). These efforts were mostly applicable to European immigrants.

NATIVES—BECOMING CIVILIZED

Native Americans have vehemently expressed their distress about the removal of their children to boarding schools American Indian Relief Council. (2015). This was a policy established by employees of the Bureau of Indian Affairs in 1860 to educate children in white men's values as the way to civilize them (Native Partnerships, n.d.). Their values apparently did not include any assessment of the need to help families deal with the grief the policy caused.

Byrd, in *The Transit of the Empire* (2011), notes the continuing efforts of the U.S. government to undermine the Chickasaw tribe's value of their home, place, and belongings. She reports the need to examine the ways that geography, intimacies, and anxieties persist in colonized or formerly colonized areas. Her view of indigenous legacies illustrates a continuing pitting of groups against one another, obstructing the value of native boundaries.

SOCIAL WORK LIMITATIONS

In a keynote address about the history of social work to the Columbia University School of Social Work alumni, Barbara Simon (2015) said that while the social work profession has significant elements of compassion and support for people in vulnerable situations, the efforts for people of color were negligible. She noted that in 1902 white people were still referring to black people as "less than human" (Simon, 2015).

The *Moynihan Report* (Geary, 2015) was a description of the impact of the low proportions of employed black men in African American communities. This analysis categorized the family structure that resulted as a broken family (Coates, 2015). Frazier's The Negro Family in the United States (1966) also focused on community limitations in the face of discrimination and economic restraints. There were emotional reactions to this context within the African American communities and in government and political circles.

Gutman's (1977) work, *The Black Family in Slavery and Freedom*, 1750–1925, in large part addressed the negative connotations. His research, using data of occupational and household status, in several cities presented examples of the range of cultural and family structures. The experience of slavery weakened families. Yet many were able to maintain or reorganize family connections. He found many families headed by couples who managed to live together through the challenges they faced (Williams, 2015). Gutman (1977) concluded that "Frazier and de Tocqueville did not misperceive the oppressive nature of enslavement but underestimated the adaptive capacities of the enslaved and those born to them and their children" (p. xxi).

Social workers and public institution administrators didn't resist the policies that obstructed family reunification and family strengthening in any real way until the 1970s when advocacy groups outside the mainstream revved up their activities.

CRITICAL THINKING QUESTION
How has the social work profession evolved regarding social justice and human rights issues?

IN COMMUNITY SERVICES

The services offered to communities in many ways reflect the impact of the early forms of discrimination. Social and human services are delivered within professional ethics and competent practice guidelines. Yet the proportion of vulnerably labeled persons tends to be connected to those most marginalized in our communities. Children designated as special needs or needing special education, children with health risks related to toxic neighborhoods, adolescents who are suspended from school, young men who are profiled and punished disproportionally, older people who are ineligible for insurance benefits, or those receiving the least successful interventions continue to be associated mostly with low-income persons of color. Institutional services that are separate and unequal continue legacies of betrayal to many citizens.

CHILDREN, YOUTH, AND ELDERS

Access to services across the spectrum is in need of improvement. Most particularly, the influence of socialization on service delivery has been observed in services to children, youth, and elders. Choosing to emphasize these groups recognizes the role of young people in building our environments of tomorrow and respecting the elders of today as they represent what has been. Addressing the needs of children, youth, and elders is another way to approach concerns about the inclusion of representatives and voices of persons served by helping professionals.

BUILDING ON STRENGTHS

The nature of social services with children and families of excluded groups has tended to be toward the removal of the children and proliferation of penalties on the parents. The impression of socialized messages on dominant-culture folks and on members of the groups has been to foster decisions about family adequacy based on observations connected to material possessions or related ideas of sufficiency. Low income—or the more-often-used term *disadvantaged*—does not necessarily equate with family inadequacy. Decisions to remove children from families without resources to make repairs or cleanup in ways that money would provide is not a good decision in and of itself, if it does not address the love and familial interactions that may nevertheless be present and substantive.

RESOURCEFULNESS AND NATURAL RESILIENCY

Resourcefulness and natural resiliency exist among communities of color. Despite obstacles and constraints, many families have demonstrated their talents and interests to protect their families and to pursue dreams. Logan and Freeman (2004) identify frameworks to draw on these strengths to inform social work practice, research, and policy.

The activities among diverse social workers in the 1970s pushed NASW to begin to move from colorblind rhetoric to more direct efforts to address the alternative ideas groups raised. With the initiation of associations of Black, Puerto Rican, and Asian social workers, more attention was being drawn to the needs they identified in their communities.

The intersection of age, ethnicity, and gender presents other contexts in which discrimination appears. The potential for adverse childhood experiences to occur in family or institutional environmental settings must be evaluated, given the values and ethics in the interest of children. Keeping that in mind as we consider the intersections of identities adds another lens through which to consider the matrix of oppression and potential resource development.

COMMUNITY EDUCATION

Discussions related to children are particularly important and related to several policy areas. Children are at risk of mistreatment in their families, in institutions, and as refugees. Information regarding the rights of children as promoted in the United Nations Declaration of the Rights of Children may be offered as education in various local community organizations. Reports of continuing exclusion of children in the United Kingdom involve refugee and asylum seekers, gypsy traveler children, and those in local authority care (Ryder & Cemlyn, 2016). American criminal justice policies regarding the use of solitary confinement with children or youth are rightly being reexamined (American Civil Liberties Union, 2017; Wheeling, 2017).

THINK ABOUT PREVENTION AND CRIMINAL JUSTICE

The participation of children and youth in the design and decision-making of programs that are to assist them must first be assessed in terms of whether authorities can recognize the value of observations and feelings of this group of service users. In the webinar *Police and Community Trust* (2016) conducted by the Office of Justice Programs, Tracie Keesee discussed some basics of relationship-based policing. It is a component of a comprehensive approach focused on prevention and requires understanding that both sides may yell or be angry. It involves procedural justice and being respectful of one another in all encounters between police and citizens.

Another presenter offered an example of working to build relationships with youth from his work in White Plains, New York. A police officer gave an example of where the two sides started. The youth asked, "Why are you always chasing us?" The cops asked, "Why are you always running?" Their conversation began from there.

A 2016 forum sponsored by the Urban Institute reviewed the recommendation from the Colson Family Task Force. *Transforming Prisons, Restoring Lives: Final Recommendations of the Charles Colson Task Force on Federal Corrections* incorporates steps toward a reformed vision of incarceration and means of keeping the public safe. There are nine recommendations that encompass encouraging people to participate in planning while in prison to assist with reentry, options for learning while in prison based on specific service or learning requirements, addressing addiction, improving family visitation opportunities, and reinvesting the savings of these programs back into the services delivery system.

Kunen (2017) supports learning while in prison with examples from his experience that demonstrate positive results that extend to the children.

INCLUDING SERVICE USERS AND FRONT-LINE STAFF VOICES

Inviting youth, elders, and workers to participate in program planning has not occurred often until activists or whistleblowers exert tactics that contest the powers in place. These populations are the targets for various services and outcome trajectories. Their ideas should be considered as we continue direct interventions and develop prevention and resilience development. Shifting thinking in research acknowledges the relevance of research with and by children (Bishop, 2014) to gain better understanding of their perspectives and to enhance qualitative and quantitative research processes.

Suggestions from frontline workers note the ways that clients are viewed influences how they are treated. Social workers support structural explanations for poverty, recognize the reduced stigma of universal programs (Blomberg, Kallio, Kroll, & Niemelä, 2015), and admit to having to diminish relationships for organizational efficiency. People in this sample admitted sometimes having to be mean in their jobs rather than addressing "goals of mutual obligation and care" (Baines, 2006).

Problems associated with the traditional institutional system are clear. "Practitioners, activists and social policy analysts in Canada, Australia and other English-speaking industrialized countries are searching for new models to meet diverse needs, expand social justice and counter the growing inequalities that characterize the current sociopolitical environment" (Baines, 2006, p. 1). According to Baines's survey, if workers could have one wish, most would encourage proactive approaches and prevention.

RECOGNIZING AND MANAGING PERSONAL ATTITUDES AND BIASES

Examining U.S. history, its impact on opportunities, and its impact on social work means appreciating our value base, examining our personal attitudes, and extending our concerns through community education and capacity building.

Social work values that are spelled out in the NASW Code of Ethics, the CSWE's competency areas, and the IFSW's definition of *social work* embrace human rights. Recognizing the conflict that exists about what is desired and what operates in family and social communication is a step in continuing toward inclusion.

SOCIAL STRUCTURES CREATE BARRIERS

There is substantial evidence that persons who pursue social work are aware of the structural barriers that restrict opportunity (Blomberg et al., 2015). However, the broad frameworks of exclusion and conservative perspectives about individual sources of poverty have influenced how some workers perceive service consumers.

A broad view of multicultural realities in a monocultural-dominated society affected by power dynamics is described by Davidson (2012) as "cultural genocide." The goal of cultural genocide is to diminish a culture in order to undermine effective resistance (Davidson, 2012). He presents a framework that describes the planned demise of ethnic or cultural groups. He illustrates this through discussions of cultural genocide and the American Indians, Russia and Jews in the 19th century, Israel and Palestinian cultural genocide, and the Chinese assimilation of Tibet. The process occurs through "purposeful destructive targeting of out-group cultures to destroy or weaken them (p. 1). He proposes that this occurs as it relates to people primarily concerned about what happens to them in their immediate environments, a concept he calls "natural localness." His analysis of cultural genocide points to the illegality of physical genocide under international law but cultural genocide, occurring though existing institutions over time, is not yet illegal (p. 2). The local community meets most people's needs. The tendency is to treat out-groups with aggression.

Leaders operate from acquired stereotypes associated with their vested interests. So they present stylized or biased pictures of events, consciously or unconsciously (Davidson, 2012, p. 7). The socialization processes are carriers of hardwired emotions (p. 8). Thoughts about others not part of their group then get tied to stereotypes. The procedure for breaking out of this thinking would involve a group's willingness to listen and contemplate information about contexts that contradict the stereotypes. Integrating consideration of this process is needed to modify traditional procedures and incorporate innovation.

SOCIAL WORK: PROTECTING THE VULNERABLE AND AT RISK

There is no single social work ideology. Just as we have become more aware of multiple identifies, people have perspectives influenced by multiple ideas, facts, concepts, and experiences. The range of concepts associated with social work core values includes focus on protection of those vulnerable and at risk, as well as enhancing inner resources, social justice, and social control (NASW, n.d). The basic values tend to protect and strive for individual rights and freedom (Lum, 1986), and many assume these are accepted by all. The values of ethnic minorities generally are perceived to be somewhat different and not completely compatible with Western ideas. The emphasis on "family interdependency and obligation, metaphysical harmony in nature or religion, and ethnic group identity" (Lum, 1986, p. 29) are notions that many would like incorporated more into the planning of service delivery. There is some evidence of this inclusion. Services that emphasize family unification, recognition of elders and parents, and mutual responsibility recognize these values that are more inclusive and protective than individual psychotherapeutic themes.

IDEOLOGICAL VIEWS

People become interested in social work and other helping disciplines through various experiences and observations from many sources. Using the values that the social work profession is founded on—that people are innately good, valuable, and worthy of respect—we might agree that the range of views we have given our socialization contains conservative-to-neoliberal ideas about humanity. Our frames of reference range from psychotherapy or clinical social work to community education, and environmental justice may influence the perspectives we hold when we begin to become social workers, those we hold upon graduation, and those we express as we mature in the profession.

What is *ideology*? Within the context of social work and social welfare, ideology may be considered a definition, the body of doctrine, belief, or philosophy that guides an individual, social movement, institution, class, or large group (Dictionary.com, n.d.). And it may change from time to time.

How do we get it? It comes from our associations with representatives and the messages we take in to help us make sense of where we are and where we might want to go.

SOCIAL CONTROL OR SOCIAL DEVELOPMENT

Ideology guides the social work profession's efforts to channel practice and advocacy to address social and economic justice issues. It shapes how we challenge obstacles to the best practices for those we serve. Ideology also guides efforts to maintain social controls that allow and support the status quo. Margolin, in *Under the Cover of Kindness: The Invention of Social Work* (1997), presents some of the contradictions that social workers in institutional settings face with clients who experience service provision as a form of control. The discussion raises real concerns and awareness about clients' expectations from prejudicial attitudes. Simultaneously, there are concerns about workers' skills to promote empowerment within this historically exclusive context. The concept of personal and group self-determination can sometimes challenge one's ability to tolerate ambiguity and support the client's perspective when it is different from the practitioner's. Social workers learn not to reject a client's formulations even if they don't believe it is in their best interest. Providing clear, well-balanced information about options, choices, and consequences is a starting point.

Courtney and Specht (1994) point to the professional values of individualism and expertise to be ones that pose obstacles to the worker's capacity to help the service user. These early social workers embraced work to assist the community toward capacity development and resisted psychotherapy. The collectivist view encourages a process of human development that helps people focus on the capacity to grow and change over the life cycle rather than reliving past experiences in therapy. They promote the use of groups as the method of choice. There is room for the many approaches that exist. Assessment and evaluation are tools for working with service users to arrive at appropriate strategies.

BIOLOGY IDEOLOGY

Another way to consider ideology is linking it to biology. Hibbing, Smith, and Alford (2014) report that conservative ideology has been linked to personality facets that are connected to military, law enforcement, resistance to immigration, and guns. According to recent brain research, their findings are related to a threat-oriented biology (Mooney, 2014). Overall, the study results "consistently finds that conservatism is positively associated with heightened epistemic concerns for order, structure, closure, certainty, consistency, simplicity, and familiarity, as well as existential concerns such as perceptions of danger, sensitivity to threat, and death anxiety" (Mooney, 2014, p. 2). A 2003 discussion by Jost and associates of psychological studies on ideology suggested conservatives need certainty and are intolerant of ambiguity. Their view has the premise that subjective beliefs start from some rational source and satisfy some psychological need. While questions remain, the evidence offers another perspective on why people may think and react as they do to social and political circumstances.

ORGANIZATIONAL VALUES

Social work services are provided through organizations that reflect some level of acceptance of the traditional ideologies. Acknowledging the early limited management roles of women and the exclusion of people of color (Dressel, 1987; Iglehart & Becerra, 1997) helps us understand where the social work profession has come from. Human service management focuses on the service mission, eligibility requirements and guidelines, and effective practices. In order to address the needs of the broader service population, employee recruitment was an early example of inclusion. As more organizations seek to diversify their personnel, it is clear that diversity impacts performance (Hunt, Layton, & Prince, 2015). This research from McKinsey and Company (based on composite data for all countries in the data set) shows the likelihood of financial performance above the national industry median where the workforce is diverse.

There have been some improvements in recruiting and hiring diverse applicants, but historic employment exclusion continues in social services and other helping organizations. Social work values, embraced by those pursuing social welfare for citizens, operate within several different types of organizational and host settings. The organizational values should be examined within the framework of delivery and effectiveness.

TRADITIONAL THINKING

Employment opportunities are influenced by traditional structures and networking among the dominant culture. When competition by workers of ethnic groups is perceived as a threat to the employment of dominant-culture workers, discrimination and violence frequently result. *When and Where I Enter* (Giddings, 1984) captures the anger and resentment of white merchants played out against business owners of color. Rather than allow market competition, white men would kill. Giddings included Ida B. Wells-Barnett's advocacy against the lynchings that occurred to frighten people of color from pursuing business endeavors to care for and protect their families.

Organizational polices to help designated children in need have been criticized for their tendency to discriminate and penalize children of color and to disproportionately place them in special education classes, foster homes, and educational situations that often impede their development and capacity to obtain reliable careers and employment. Some parents resist services because they have observed the increased problems families may encounter when connecting to a governmental program.

Discriminatory attitudes that misdiagnose or render disrespectful interactions often exacerbate feelings of low esteem by children and their families. A report by the Franklin Law Group (2015) submitted to the United Nations observed that the "rate at which African American girls in foster care are prescribed psychotropic medication is nine times the rate prescribed to others" (p. 1). They requested an investigation into this as a violation of human rights. Several films depict community scenarios that portray discriminatory or oppressive challenges that people face and that hamper stable financial situations.

RELIGION INFLUENCES

Religion has played a major role in the structure of discrimination. It has been used to justify exclusion and to cover up violence and abuse. The perpetuation of oppression and imperialism as "manifest destiny" was connected to God (Scott, 2017). Religion has also been used to argue for the protection of human rights. Aydelott (1863) proposed to Christians that prejudice has robbed people of their rights (Kindle Location 53). He concluded that within the human family, regardless of complexion, all exhibit evidence of a moral nature. This offers a common heritage of inalienable rights and interests. He believed a moral being gains understanding of the relationship of things through a conscience and free will so the choice is for right or wrong (Aydelott, Kindle Loc 55).

LIBERATION THEOLOGY

The liberation theology movement connected social justice to the needs of those with the least economic resources. Subsequent thinking tied these ideas to the oppression of black people and to women.

Liberation theology expands on the religious aspect of the moral role of services for the poor and vulnerable. As a philosophy and theological movement, it emphasizes the relevance of work against social injustices and the misuse of political power (Boff & Boff, 2000). Early liberation theology work has been connected to Hans Kung (b. 1928) and Jurgen Moltmann of Germany (b. 1926), Samuel Ruiz of Mexico, and South Americans Gustavo Gutiérrez of Peru (b. 1928) and Camilo Torres of Colombia (1929–1966; Gutiérrez, 2012; Theopedia.com, n.d.). The emergence of this thinking in Latin America occurred in the 1960s and subsequently evolved into versions designated as black liberation theology and feminist theories (Christian, 2011).

The marginalization of women in religious denominations has also been recognized. Shields confronted gender inequality in the Mormon Church. "Religions can liberate or subjugate, they can empower or exploit, they can comfort or destroy," she says. "What is taught on the Sabbath leaks into our politics, our health policy, and violence around the world?" Her TED Talk (2015) addresses the recognition and the action to address it.

Contemporary thinking connects liberation to notions of peace building in regions around the world, including Palestinian liberation theology (Omer, 2015).

SOCIAL WORK ACKNOWLEDGES THE DIVERSITY OF SPIRITUAL CONNECTIONS

In social work, while Christian beliefs are associated with the recognition of needs for more humane systems there are other sources of belief to be respected. A recent study (Lewis, 2015) shows that social workers acknowledge the importance of spirituality in the lives of persons they work with regardless of its source or structure. However, the tendency is to overwhelmingly ignore this dynamic in addressing their needs. There are helping professionals and service consumers who do not claim any spiritual connections. This position is also recognized.

The place of clients' religion and spirituality has been found to be of importance in a substantial proportion of service users, with many citing positive connections to emotional health outcomes (Oxhandler & Pargament, 2014). In addition, there are ongoing discussions evolving among social workers with respect to religion, values, and contemporary social issues. The recent Supreme Court decision on marriages is one example. In some spaces, the discussion may be contentious. NASW provides position statements on major legal issues that should be consulted (NASW, 2013).

The connection of social work and religion is complex and requires engaging in more research, continuing education, and supervising conversations (Oxhandler & Pargament, 2014). The link to social workers' perspectives on religion regarding personal and professional identity forces separating these and bowing to social work values that support self-determination.

CASE SCENARIO 2

Ms. Johnson visited an agency to get help for her three children. It was near the end of the month, and her funds were nearly depleted. A worker visited the home and found broken windows and a stove that did not work. There was evidence that she used alcohol. The worker recommended the children be removed.

The supervisor decided to send out another worker, Mr. Rollins, for a second opinion. He offered Ms. Johnson some ideas. Would she be interested in learning how to do some of the repairs needed in her house? Would she be able to work on decreasing the use of alcohol if it meant she was more likely to keep her children? She agreed. They were able to come up with a list of needed repairs and a budget.

Mr. Rollins taught her how to replace a window. She replaced two on her own. He brought the supplies for her to paint the children's rooms. She had them painted before he returned the next week. They worked together for 4 weeks on repairs, cooking meals (he had the gas company come to repair the stove), and reducing her alcohol use. Her children were not taken away. They made plans for the next 4 weeks that included connecting her to a women's support group. What do you think about this case?

CULTURALLY AFFIRMING THINKING

Culturally affirming thinking moves beyond the narrow boundaries of traditional beliefs to include the varied contexts that service users bring. Considering Case Scenario 2 from an inclusive lens would embrace a strategy that would assign resources rather than cause further distress.

The approach to this case based on traditional thinking would likely rely on the organizational tendency to remove children rather than employ family development goals that use resources in innovative ways. The recommendations of family breakup and child removal tends not to benefit family repair or recovery. The TED Talk by Hillary Cottam (2015) gives an excellent assessment of traditional service delivery and the use of a more affirming approach. It is a U.K.-based example but is also representative of our system. Consider it in discussing this case.

Other examples based on monocultural assessment tend to neglect a substantive cultural picture and put more challenges on the family rather than identify strategic interventions that may be more relevant to family bonding than to meeting criteria that are punitive and crippling.

There are more examples of efforts to keep families together and to keep costs down (Barth, Chung Kwon, Wildfire, & Guo, 2006). Chester County in Pennsylvania has Turning Points for Children, which has requested support to develop and implement Family Strong, a preventative program that uses research-based Family Finding methods to prevent children in Coatesville, Pennsylvania, from entering into foster care.

There are examples of using key informants and advisory groups that include foster care children, adolescents, and graduates to design approaches that affirm the participants and connect them to support networks. Family and peer coaches who survived childhoods in boarding schools for Native American children provide content and perspectives for evaluating outcome pathways that address attachment issues in better ways (Alegria, Atkins, Farmer, Slaton, & Stelk, 2010).

Similar situations have been documented by child welfare workers in communities of color. Brian Cladoosby, president of the National Congress of American Indians, illustrates the group's interest in breaking the cycle of behavior connected to a group's historical trauma. Instead of allowing the Bureau of Indian Child Welfare to continue removal of children for irrelevant assessment, their group is advocating breaking this cycle of death and alcohol by increasing opportunities and supporting pathways to alcohol-free home environments and family participation in innovative ways to support children (Cladoosby, C-Span, 2015).

Sherman Alexie's *The Absolutely True Diary of a Part-Time Indian* (2007) offers a memoir of growing up in his Native American family with its rewards and challenges. An ingredient of Arnold's (the main character) development was his persistence and connection to his family of origin. Novels about the traumas of foster care also point to persist such as Stacey Patton's, *That Mean Old Yesterday* (2007) and Tiffany Haddish's *The Last Black Unicorn* (2017) and illustrate the emotional impact of separation and grief; and emotional and other forms of abuse that may be dismissed, ignored or not fully communicated and resolved. Alexis and Haddish added extra humor in their stories.

CULTURAL VARIATIONS ON INCLUSION

Going beyond the limitations of Western thinking means incorporating multidimensional ways of thinking and appreciating life. Protecting the environment in which we live is a concern for many citizens. Protecting our natural resources, especially water, though often associated with communities in other parts of the world, is also relevant to U.S. communities.

The Flint, Michigan (CNN, 2017), water situation exposed political cost-saving decisions that have resulted in major health problems for the residents. It has also made people more aware of the presence of toxins in our water and the vulnerability that exists in our neighborhoods. The concerns and ideas of the communities we work with should be included in reforming our institutions for an improved democratic operation.

COLLABORATION FOR GOAL SETTING AND DECISION-MAKING

Reamer's (2005) review of the social work profession's odyssey regarding values and ethics includes honesty, respect, trust, fairness, responsibility, autonomy, nonmalfeasance, beneficence, justice, fidelity, faithfulness, forgiveness, generosity, compassion, and kindness (p. 27). He categorizes the phases of concern in the values and ethics discourse to be morality, values, ethical theory, and decision-making—and most recently ethical standards and risk management.

Whiting (2015) presents another take on social work values and skills. He moves the discussion from an emphasis on principles and values that include nonviolence, confidentiality, and antidiscrimination to a deeper examination of social values and the integration of humanism. Using Erasmus's *De Civilitate, Handbook of Manners* (2008), the emphasis of note here is his argument for positive interactions with one another. Social work skills may be enhanced by the humanist perspective. Mutual aid has been a core concept of social arrangements over time, especially within cultural collective philosophies. Steinberg (2009) agrees that it is mutual aid that advances society.

CRITICAL THINKING QUESTION

What is *humanism*? Take a look at the magazine *The Humanist*. Compare your notions of social work values to your interpretation of humanism.

Social workers do make use of self-help or mutual aid groups, and some recommend expanding their use. As a means of addressing a limited workforce in some areas, task sharing, peer workers, making referrals, and using early screening has potential for connecting community members for further services through mutual aid (Shrinivasa, Janardhana, & Nirmala, 2017).

WOMEN AND SOCIAL WORK

Social work standards that emphasize engagement with individuals, families, groups, organizations, and communities advances the intent to collaborate with others and to include others in preparing to work together. Women predominate the profession and those who are served. The diversity of the service users is immense and includes class, gender, gender expression, race and ethnicity, religion, immigration status, and physical, emotional, and learning stressors. Our history has demonstrated intolerance for many who fit some of these descriptions. Our future seeks to work together to improve conditions and well-being for more of us.

Women provide the majority of roles in social work. The place of gendered work has been described as the epitome of the patriarchal ideology that the social work profession grapples with (Dressel, 1992). This ideology is also the source of struggle for many women who seek services. Dressel noted the stereotyped view of the profession emphasized nurturing qualities rather than the analytical, resource management, and creativity requirements involved in helping address the welfare needs of families.

The role of women in the children's conference in 1933, U.S. Children's Bureau's Child Health Recovery Conference on October 6, 1933, (Gale group, 2004) that brought attention to the needs of children and women has also been displayed in some references as secondary to the men's roles in administration at that time. Women involved in advocating for the need for a Children's Bureau included Lillian Wald, Jane Addams, Florence Kelley, Julia Lathrop, and others. They observed families' needs in the tenements they worked in. "They became adept at making clear concise statements of facts, of arousing communities and States to unwholesome conditions, of making specific proposals for action" (Bradbury, 2015, p.).

In the social welfare field, women have been and continue to be the dominant workers. Women-led interventions may promote traditional and conservative views, as well as innovative ones. Former CARE director Helen Gayle working in Africa emphasized that men must also be invited to the meetings to help arrive at methods that will benefit all. She urged planners and organizers to appreciate that women and men live together so we should all be invited, encouraged, and supported in contributing to making our social lives improved (Gayle, 2013). This should apply across geographic locations.

VIOLENCE AGAINST WOMEN

Men were often administrators in the government bureaucracy while women worked in social agencies and church-based services that helped people who needed help (Encyclopedia of Children and Childhood, 2015). The past influence of male authoritarianism in services ideology has not had women's needs at the heart of policy development. Men have certainly played significant roles in the helping professions and in service management. But there are many who continue to obstruct women's rights and who impose harassment and other ungracious behaviors. Jackson Katz's (2012) advocacy against domestic violence calls out the responsibility men have to address behaviors that demean or devalue women. Violence against women and exclusion of women in various settings are areas in which more women's leadership is needed.

The recent veto of a bill in New Jersey (Sullivan, 2016) to compel convicted domestic abusers to surrender their guns is an example of insensitive policy formulation. According to Jeltsen (2015), approximately three women are killed every day in a domestic-violence incident. When a gun is present in the home, the number goes up to five. Several states have enacted laws to provide protection from persons convicted of abuse crimes.

Former President Carter posed a key question regarding women in our society. "Must women be subservient?" is the title of a chapter in his 2005 book *Our Endangered Values*. He has been adamant in bringing attention to the need to end violence and discrimination against women. His advocacy for women's rights targeted the Southern Baptist church's resistance to including women leadership. In *A Call to Action* (2014), he lists 23 abuses against women, including female sex selection abortion, child marriage, and honor killings, and he urges leaders around the world to address the needs of women.

REPRODUCTIVE RIGHTS

Society has a range of views about family planning, including pro-birth, pro-choice, pro-life, and pro-child care (which ties appropriate finances to the care of infants for persons without adequate means). Recent attacks on Planned Parenthood appear to be male dominated (CBS News, 2016), and any considerations of providing resources for unprepared potential parents seem absent.

TRANSRACIAL ADOPTIONS

Transracial adoptions provide another source of family dynamics in which mainstream cultural thinking may often obstruct the cultural interest of adoptees. Maggie Jones (2015) presents voices of Korean adoptees who have questions about the process of international adoption and the impact on their development. They want their opinions to be considered.

Typical organizational procedures involve program managers implementing a program supported by state or private funds. Including service users in the program development phase is possible as agencies are considering service user participation (Dunlop & Holosko, 2016). However, we might speculate the probability of having Korean adoptees in this phase would be low.

Traditional adoption concerns have focused on the rights of the birth parents and the adoptive parents (Opper, 2005). Voices have been asserted regarding the rights of the adoptees. Darryl McDaniels and Zara Phillips have written and recorded a rap that promotes opening private adoption records (Boynton, 2009). Social justice issues require working from where we are to expand our conversations and contemplate the concerns that arise from the verbal interactions of many backgrounds and interests, particularly those for whom services are to assist. Transparent and persistent dialogue will uncover the assumptions that many traditional services are using that do not respect the opinions of those who the services impact. A more open process recognizes what has been operational and respects the need to modify pathways to reach goals to include previously unrecognized citizens (Pointer, 2010).

WOMEN WORKERS IN OTHER FIELDS

The contributions of women in all fields and communities must be recognized to have been present as social improvements have occurred. Developing more pathways for this to advance comes with presenting more information from women. The Conference to Explore Economic and Health Issues for Girls and Women held at Fordham University (Stolker, 2015) discussed obstacles that many girls and women face in trying to get education. For some, just traveling to school locations can be risky. Not only is this real in Latin American villages, but Stolker observed similar risks and danger in Camden, New Jersey, in the 1990s.

Sharing information about the achievements of women in all cultural groups helps girls and women become informed and participate in their communities. Bonilla-Santiago (1998) described the range of women of Latino backgrounds who were involved in major activities that we were unaware of. In chronicling the Hispanic women's movement, she sheds light on the white feminists' efforts as well. She notes some of their efforts were to clarify "their role by virtue of birth or marriage as appendages of power" (p. 34) and were not necessarily achieved by activist pursuits.

WOMEN OF COLOR

The white feminist movement did not engage minority women. Minority women, Latina, Black, and Asian women founded and developed their own organizations or actively participated in other community organizations to bring attention to the needs of their communities. Santiago (1998) identified women supporting the arts (Miriam Colón), farmworkers (Dolores Huerta), pediatrics (Helen Rodríguez), politics (Polly Baca), workers for peace (Marta Benavides), and many more.

Giddings highlights the work of African American women in *When and Where I Enter* (1984). Black women's efforts navigated the harsh realities of punishment on black families, lynchings of black men, denigration of black women by white men and white women, and abuse of their children. In 1832, Maria Stewart, a free-born woman, spoke publicly to people of color and made remarks to white women about "the external circumstances rather than natural law that determined character, morality and true womanhood" (p. 51). Activist women, sometimes called *race women*, included many: Sojourner Truth, Ida B. Wells-Barnett, Anna Julia Cooper, Mary Church Terrell, Mary McLeod Bethune, and others, including hundreds of club women. These women noted the potential of opportunity and environment and worked to help gain these resources.

VARIOUS CHALLENGES

The challenges facing Asian immigrant women include lack of equal access to public benefits and the human rights violations of women who may be involved in trafficking. Their exposure to labor and sexual exploitation is a critical concern. Asian women are speaking up about oppressive situations through grassroots organizations. Foo (2002) reports on the narrow stereotypical presentation of Asian Americans that misleads the public's awareness by neglecting the range of realities within the 24 subgroups of Asian descent. Their struggles pertaining to socioeconomic status (SES) include inhumane workplace conditions, sweatshop illustrations of low wages and long hours for women and children, exposure to toxic chemicals, involuntary servitude, and trafficking.

Several advocates have expressed their views of citizenship issues and rights. Helen Zia contributed to the civil rights movement for Chinese and Asian Americans and worked with Blacks, Latinos, and Asian Americans in speaking out about the breadth of racial issues, the Vietnam War, and the issues of internment. Her book *Asian American Dreams* (2000) formulates an account of issues and dynamics that brought together an Asian American historical panorama from the gold rush to contemporary taxi driver protests.

Children of Japanese parents who were interned brought voices to the civil rights movement (Wang, 2014). Others found their way to participate in advocacy for change. Grace Lee Boggs, a resident of Detroit, Michigan, described herself as a Korean American activist for civil rights, feminism, and labor. Her book, *The Next American Revolution: Sustainable Activism for the Twenty-First Century* (2012), encourages hope and creativity to establish alternative modes of work, politics, and human interactions.

Half the Sky: *Turning Oppression Into Opportunity for Women Worldwide* (Kristof & WuDunn, 2010) addresses the worldwide oppression of women and girls with particular attention to Africa and Asia. The authors document the complexity of non-Western cultures where different kinds of practices exist: "'This is our culture!' a Sudanese midwife declared angrily when we asked about cutting. 'We all want it. Why is it America's business?'" (Pande, 2009).

Piepzna-Samarasinha, in *Colonize This! Young Women of Color on Today's Feminism* (2002), puts a final touch on this segment of voices. She offers histories of young, queer, feminist, undocumented women who were not covered in Michelle Tea's (*Without a Net: The Female Experience of Growing up Working Class*, 2004) or Sarah Schulman's (*The Gentrification of the Mind: Witness to a Lost Imagination*, 2013) "white queer-girl life" (p. 3). She talks about her "browngirlworld," looking for love and understanding and the desire for family amidst a parade of changing lovers, friends, and circumstances.

These examples offer some history of women of color, as well as their resistance and efforts to ameliorate conditions in their communities. These voices share a value system with social workers and others to participate in the growing understanding of the human race.

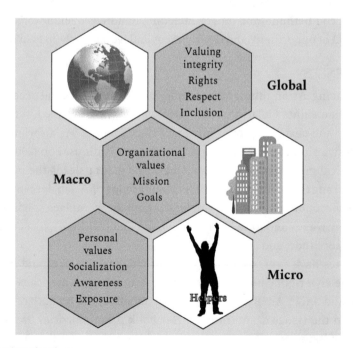

FIGURE 4.1   Social Work Values

SOCIAL MOVEMENTS AND SYSTEM IMPROVEMENTS

In some movements, social work has been absent as an organized group. As the profession evolves, its role is becoming more defined and visible, and many individuals are pursuing leadership in areas of concern to them. Yapa (2016) offers an instructive perspective in *Your Heart Is a Muscle the Size of a Fist*. His novel draws on the 1999 protest of a meeting of the World Trade Organization in Seattle. Protestors were motivated by trade deals and big corporation impact on ordinary citizens like the people who make shoes in Bangladesh and Sri Lanka. His evaluation of that historic event and recent controversies of police and protesters in Ferguson, Missouri, and Baltimore, Maryland, revealed a possible connection. "It's that when people feel cut off from decision-making … and aren't included in the decision, they take to the streets. … It's almost an expression of grief, people feeling powerless" (NPR, 2016).

The context of socialization that promotes discrimination has been exposed by activists from multiple social identities speaking up. These voices relate to social work values and urge work on the challenges that obstruct equality and human rights. As social work acknowledges the voices and encourages their inclusion in improving our democracy and the services delivered by social systems, we are advancing civic engagement and promoting the rights of the populations we work with.

The efforts of protestors over the years seem to reflect this sentiment. These are some of the protests and movements of the past (Shah, 2011):

- 1765—Anti-Tax Movement
- 1775—American Revolution
- 1830–1865—Abolition Movement
- 1848—Women's Rights
- 1851–1933—Temperance Movement
- 1930s—Labor Movement
- 1960s—Civil Rights Movement
- 1965—Anti-War Demonstrations
- 1960s—Environment and Pollution
- 2011—Occupy Wall Street

Generally, public protests occur when a substantial number of the population is affected by polices of the government or elite. Protests against G8, World Bank, International Monetary Fund (IMF), and the World Trade Organization have been connected to economics that don't help ordinary people. Engler (2014) reports that the 99% represent many who have lost jobs, who are working two or three jobs to pay bills and to pay back college loans for degrees that have not gotten them careers. Pickerill and Krinsky (2012) agree that Occupy Wall Street demonstrated resistance to capitalist inequality confounded by the unfairness of bank bailouts versus rising numbers of persons receiving decreased incomes. Occupy integrated the emphasis on place and occupation of space set aside for financial districts; the language emphasized the 99% of people who are not in the 1% wealthy group; and the movement recognized the areas for needed collaborations with labor unions and the difficulties that exist in working toward that kind of engagement.

BUILDING MOVEMENTS ON HISTORIC ISSUES

The issues posed in historic movements continue to be raised. Women's suffrage waged the reality of gender discrimination in the decision-making of the country. Protests by women to gain the right to vote occurred up until 1920 when the law was passed. Women's call for equal pay for equal work and obstacles to organizational leadership still exists, although many women have assumed significant managerial positions.

The civil rights movement has been in process since the 1865 Emancipation Proclamation, with voting rights not being secured until 1965. Current advocacy (2017) urges passing the Voting Rights Advancement Act (H.R.2978) to restore and amplify the process that supports citizen participation in voting. Continuing restrictions against men of color in unions and trades have made it difficult for many families. Some policies have changed since more media coverage exists of the broad scope of discrimination and the place of uncontested violence. Examples of efforts to address these occurrences demonstrate the strength of unified advocacy. Some places in New York are changing police officer training (Bochanski, n.d.) and Chester County, Pennsylvania, has also provided training in collaboration with police districts to enhance understanding issues for intervening with persons who may be experiencing mental health stressors (Personal correspondence and presentation, Smith, 2017).

The gay rights movement has progressed since the 1970s and includes many dimensions of protest, self-protection and perspectives of policy and legal implications. Conditions in local, state and federal contexts and international illustrations paint the tremendous energy involved in asserting voices for equality and human rights. From the raid on the Stonewall Inn in New York City (Green, n.d.) to the legal challenges regarding customer services (Williams, 2018), advocates are working across the landscape of social and economic justice to address LGBTQ protections.

The challenges to promoting the values and ethics of social work are huge. Yancy and Feagin (2015) note that social scientists have focused on single concepts related to racism, such as bias, prejudice, and stereotypes, but not on systemic racism. He acknowledges that the fullest analyses of racism come from people of color who have been affected by institutional racism. "To fully understand racism in the United States, one has to go to the centuries-old counter-system tradition of African-American analysts and other analysts of color who have done the most sustained and penetrating analyses of institutional and systemic racism" (p. 1., para 4).

PEOPLE WANT JOBS TO SUPPORT THEIR FAMILIES

If we examine our history and the voices reacting to the narrow policies of organizational systems, we realize that people just want jobs to support their families. Social work's early reluctance to assist African American families was tied to strong socialization against people of color. The need for jobs and community development and the hard work that must be done continues (Kirp, 2015).

The major emphasis in going forward from recognizing traditional socialization and service delivery appreciates the diversity of realities. This relies on listening and making adjustments based on the examples, stories, and perspectives of those who promote supportive interpersonal transactions. It requires engaging with respect to the interests, feedback, and advocacy of citizens to collaborate for more effective universal protocols.

SOCIAL WORK IN A MULTICULTURAL WORLD: MINDS READY FOR CHANGE

Moving into the 22nd century incorporates the social work values and ethics with others who share the profession's concerns about citizens and those most impacted by existing policies. Paying attention to Latinos who claim "they don't listen to us" (Cordova et al., 2015), Black Americans who identify institutional betrayal (Gomez, Smith, Gobin, Tang & Freyd, 2015) and Native Americans who urge operating from the critical indigenous model of communities and cultures look outward rather than operating from the colonial frame that negates their views (Byrd, 2011). These voices call for using alternative perspectives to examine the misidentification and placement of disproportionate numbers of children of color in special education (Fletcher & Navarrete, 2003) or other programs that confine their freedom, energy, interests, and ways of expression.

A major concept related to thinking about the reality of U.S. history and contemplating a move beyond the traditional auspices and structures is having a mind ready to be open to possibilities. Watts, in *Psychotherapy East and West* (1975), suggested that the move into liberation begins at the individual level where awareness progresses from the anchor of selfhood. Pope Francis in his Mass in Philadelphia (2015) urged us to move forward, not by maintaining structures that have brought us along, but by being open to possibilities that the Spirit opens to us in our daily lives. Meyers also refers to this dynamic in her 2014 devotional that a ready mind is needed to hear about our shortcomings in order to become able to be more inclusive in the work of addressing the needs of people around the world. Whether either of these authors are meaningful or any others of the multiple writers that may be consulted are accepted, examining concepts that encourage reading, thinking and helping others assist us in the examination of social work.

Groups typically organize in ways that separate or minimize disciplines and workers as well as bicultural partnerships, yet they are occurring. Unlearning racism is another huge task, when many people have been taught more about devaluing the worth of some than appreciating and valuing all (Brooks, 2012). Exploring models that we have not used (Hanna, Talley, & Guindon, 2000) and working toward moral ground we have not approached (Canda & Furman, 2009) can be tedious and painful, as well as enlightening.

CHAPTER SUMMARY

Social work values and ethics have progressed from resistance to assist African Americans as they migrated to the North seeking employment to inclusion via recruitment and modification of standards and codes. History offers examples of the rigid structures that maintain discrimination and the continuing efforts to raise moral obligations.

This chapter has outlined the values and principles that guide social work to continuously improve and learn. A mindset for change and an interest in unlearning racism involves understanding the nature of bias and ethnocentrism, the nature of establishing a "ready mind" (a positive mindset), and embracing the dignity of human life. Doing this will remind us to more fully take on the work of including our diverse representatives in improving our social fabric.

EPAS AND CODE OF ETHICS

CSWE EDUCATIONAL POLICY & ACCREDITATION STANDARDS

Competency 1: Demonstrate ethical and professional behavior.
- 1b) Use reflection and self-regulation to manage personal values and maintain professionalism in practice situations. (EPAS, 2015)

NASW CODE OF ETHICS

NASW Ethical Principle: Social workers' primary goal is to help people in need and to address social problems.

1.05 Cultural Awareness and Social Diversity
- (a) Social workers should understand culture and its function in human behavior and society, recognizing the strengths that exist in all cultures.
- (b) Social workers should have a knowledge base of their clients' cultures and be able to demonstrate competence in the provision of services that are sensitive to clients' cultures and to differences among people and cultural groups. (NASW, n.d.)

DISCUSSION QUESTIONS

1. How has the professional social work landscape addressed exclusion of minority group members from service delivery?
2. What have you observed about minority group recruitment in your agency?

EXERCISES

1. Gil states, "social work and social services, throughout history, [have] been to modify and fine-tune the intensity of oppression and injustice in societies, and to ameliorate their destructive consequences for human development" (Gil, 1998, p. 14). Describe an example of how you have observed this in operation.

2. Select a group. Research the history of its advocacy work.

3. Read the Op-Ed by David Brooks, (1.22.2016). The anxieties of impotence. *New York Times* Opinion Pages. List two ideas to reflect on regarding his opinion. Share with a peer and compare your ideas.

4. Select a historic social movement. Research a current event or news item regarding the issue. How do they compare?

5. Select one point from the chapter that was of interest. Locate a reference that you are unfamiliar with and read it. Present three key points.

MULTICULTURAL RESOURCES

Ahmed, S. (2012). *On being included: Racial diversity in institutional life.* Durham, NC: Duke University Press.

Alexie, S. (2007). *The absolutely true diary of a part-time Indian.* New York, NY: Little, Brown & Co.

Association of Asian and Pacific Social Work Educators. apaswe.com

Association of Black Social Workers. nabsw.org

Association of Puerto Rican & Hispanic Social Workers. napphsw.org

Association of Korean American Social Workers. kaswanyc.weebly.com

Boggs, G. L. (2012). *The next American revolution: Sustainable activism for the 21st century.* Berkeley: University of California Press.

Bonilla-Santiago. G. (1998). *Breaking ground and barriers: Hispanic women developing effective leadership: Organizing Puerto Rican migrant farmworkers—The experience of Puerto Ricans in New Jersey.* New York, NY: St. Martin's Press.

Cladoosby, B. (2015). State of the Indian Nations Address. National Congress of American Indians. C-Span. Retrieved from https://www.c-span.org/video/?323936-1/state-indian-nations-address

CNN (2017). Flint Water Crisis Fast Facts.

Foo, L. J. (2002). *Asian American women: Issues, concerns, and responsive human and civil rights advocacy.* Ford Foundation. Retrieved from https://fordfoundcontentthemes.blob.core.windows.net/media/1716/2002-asian_american_women.pdf

Frazier, E. F. (1974). *The Negro church in America.* New York, NY: Schocken Books.

Gates, H. L., Jr. (2016). *Who designed the march on Washington? The African Americans: Many rivers to cross.* Retrieved from http://www.pbs.org/wnet/african-americans-many-rivers-to-cross/history/100-amazing-facts/who-designed-the-march-on-washington/

Kristoff, N. D., & WuDunn, S. (2010). *Half the sky: Turning oppression into opportunity for women worldwide.* New York, NY: Vintage.

Lee, S. S. (2014). *Building a Latino civil rights movement: Puerto Ricans, African Americans in the pursuit of social justice in New York City (Justice, power & politics).* Durham: University of North Carolina Press.

Lum, D. (1986). *Social work practice & people of color. A process-stage approach.* Pacific Grove, CA: Brooks/Cole.

Piepzna-Samarasinha, L. L. (2002). Browngirlworld. In D. Hernández & B. Rehman (Eds.), *Colonize this! Young women of color on today's feminism.* Berkeley, CA: Seal Press.

Reid-Merritt, P. (2010). *Righteous self-determination: The Black social work movement in America.* Baltimore, MD: Imprint.

Scott, C. A., & O'Neal, G. S. (1981). *Supplying a critical need: Preparing ethnic minority doctoral social work students for leadership roles in mental health*. New York, NY: Council on Social Work Education.

Weaver, H. N. (1999). Indigenous people and the social work profession: Defining culturally competent services. *Social Work, 44*(3), 217–226.

Wells-Barnett, I. B. (1892 /2014). *On lynchings*. Mineola, NY: Dover.

Yapa, S. (2016). *Your heart is a muscle the size of a fist*. Boston, MA: Little, Brown and Company.

Zia, H. (2000). *Asian American dreams: The emergence of an American people*. New York, NY: Farrar, Straus and Giroux.

VIDEO

Katz, J. (2012). *Violence against women—It's a men's issue* [Video file]. Retrieved from https://www.ted.com/talks/jackson_katz_violence_against_women_it_s_a_men_s_issue

Pata, J. (2015). *Native American concerns*. Retrieved from https://www.c-span.org/video/?4008125/washington-journal-jacqueline-pata-national-congress-american-indians

Sue, D. (n.d.). *What does it mean to be white* [Video file]? Retrieved from https://www.youtube.com/watch?v=fonlNYdm0Hs

WuDunn, S. (2010). *Our century's greatest injustice*. https://www.ted.com/talks/sheryl_wudunn_our_century_s_greatest_injustice/up-next

FIGURE CREDITS

CHAPTER 5

The Social Context

Oppression, Racism, Discrimination = Economics

CHAPTER OVERVIEW

This chapter covers recognition of the social environment that contains oppression and discrimination. The role and impact of economics on these dynamics is described. The use of theories to explain the discriminatory context is associated with efforts of the social work profession to respond to needs for well-being by all people and to those who have been excluded. Theories are also needed to tailor interventions to people across cultural groups.

The different ways to think about oppression; racism and discrimination; and consumer resources, opportunities, and restraints is useful in planning service delivery. Examining the role of social work in transferring knowledge for empowerment is also a component of social work as action.

Social workers are employed in various types of settings. Criminal justice, foster care, mental health, public health, and education, as well as hospitals and family services attend to persons experiencing struggles, challenges, trauma, or other peace-threatening situations or circumstances. The observations of oppression and discrimination, the lived experience of it, and expressed reactions to it may be framed in many ways. The contexts of these manifestations have been established historically and require considerable recognition and evaluation. Acknowledging and implementing approaches based on theoretical conceptualizations provide structure to service delivery. At the same time, institutional exclusionary components have led to service gaps and unachieved outcomes. On the basic level, we can think about ameliorating attitudes to engage, embrace, and appreciate our diverse service constituencies. More sophisticated frames of analysis will conceptualize exclusion from legal and economic reference points. Both approaches involve a continual process and struggle.

LEARNING OBJECTIVES

- Our social context includes discrimination connected to identity and abilities.
- Macro theories offer explanations of the broad context and multidimensional nature of the environment.

- Micro theories include explanations that connect to biology, psychology, sociology, culture, anthropology, religion, spirituality, and economics to frame interpersonal interactions and family development.
- Power dynamics offer perspectives of the structure and regulations related to engagement, participation, rewards, and penalties.

Benchmark: Students will understand at least two theories connected to oppression and discrimination and responsive behaviors.

STUDENT SCENARIO

Anna and Brian are discussing the roles of scientists in the social work profession. Brian questions this possibility but suggests that social work is an art with some science. Anna agrees but argues that social work relies on science as the knowledge base so it actually leans more on the science side. Can there be an either-or?

SOCIAL CONTEXT INVOLVES DISCRIMINATION REGARDING IDENTITY AND ABILITIES

The social context in which we live reflects the myriad bases of observation and interaction across micro and macro dimensions. Discrimination impacts persons in groups that have not typically been embraced by major institutional systems. While many persons of diverse backgrounds survive and thrive despite the circumstances, access to capital and services is often obstructed by constraints on salaries, credit, and eligibility for educational and vocational opportunities.

Contemplating ways to improve our social environment requires examining existing ways of thinking and establishing a theoretical basis from which to evaluate and innovate. Evaluating theory choices involves determining the recognition of social and economic discrimination.

IDENTITY

Considering discrimination on the individual and institutional levels broadens the lens for developing alternative strategies. One way of conceptualizing the discrimination that many people experience may be tied to an acceptance of the labels that have been imposed through the socialization process. If these are rejected, there is likely a more positive self-evaluation. Examples of the impact of defining oneself on one's own terms rather than through the eyes of someone else are often the crux of multicultural resources. Asamoah raised the "what we call ourselves" element in multicultural social work (1991). The BBC News documentary, What Stands In The Way Of Women Being Equal To Men, (2014) offers opinions of adolescent girls from four countries. Generally, they expressed the desire to do what they want rather than conform to narrow ideas their fathers often suggest.

SELF- DEFINITIONS

Glover (2009) suggests the self-labeling and relationship competency of those who don't identify with the dominant culture may experience a different development path. Using a multidimensional model that accepts social identities, sexual orientation and abilities are not fixed but are more fluid would recognize the continuity of self-definition and perhaps reduce stigmatization. A social identity framework could potentially shift paradigms to the "human race" with cultural variations and offer more focus on the social and economic elements that would be of overall benefit.

Social identity theory offers a foundation for existing notions and emerging research that scrutinize in- and out-group exposure, segregation, bullying, and stigma resistance. Degner, Essiein, & Reichardt (2016) pose the possibility of creating alternative strategies connected to exposure to diversity vs segregation. Thornberg (2015) explores the structure of bullying in the binary, like us and not like us, of powerful and less powerful. Considering the peer culture of the children on both sides of this dynamic requires further research into social processes and how to co-create positive identities.

RESISTANCE TO STIGMA

The resistance to stigma is an important but minimally researched arena regarding discrimination and the use of traditional treatment services. Thoits (2016) calls identity deflection, the denial of mental illness, a form of stigma resistance that can be beneficial for persons with non-severe diagnosis. Participation in a support group that identifies a diagnosis may have some mediating effects connected to the support and esteem of persons with similar conditions (Crabtree & Haslam, 2010)

HEALTHCARE GROUP IDENTITIES

Social identity at the institutional level places professional groups at odds with one another in several ways and exacerbates the divisions. Munrouxe and Poole (2013) reflect on the inner world and outer world perceptions of how health group affiliates see themselves. Kreindler and associates (2012) explored the potential of the social identity approach to organize the literature and be useful in promoting integration and collaboration for system transformation. They note the literature emphasizes individual and interpersonal level interactions but propose a group level analysis using a social identity approach has the capacity to synthesize ideas across the discipline traditions. This approach would target the existing fragmentation and seek coordination and cost effectiveness. By applying this broader multidimensional approach to identities, the analysis might rise above personal biases to areas for substantive discussion.

ABILITIES

The discrimination of people based on abilities may be tied to low expectation perceptions of physical challenges, learning differences, class group, and emotional stressors or mental illness. Often, these are associated with media descriptions that label rather than interpersonal experiences that inform awareness of their lives. Paying attention to the strengths that exist can inform our methods of engagement. The Deaf community has a specific culture. Its identity involves a cultural understanding of being in the world (Delich, 2014) and individual abilities make evident their capacity to successfully operate every day in their social environments.

Micula (2014) examined the social perceptions and personal views of people with disabilities to test their acceptance. The source of bias and stigma was the interpreted deficiency. While no one expressed contempt, her survey indicated that most had very little interaction with any persons with challenges; even among highly educated respondents there was a low level of information about disability legislation, rights, network services or medical issues. The negative attitudes, stereotypes, and low expectations were created by those without disabilities.

Efforts to improve access and mobility involve addressing the obstacles they may encounter through support networks, training and educational achievement, family protection, and employment opportunities.

Perceptions about persons experiencing physical, emotional, or learning abilities have also been shaped by views that promote one way of being over others. Carlson (2001) refers us to several histories of mental retardation and notes the influence of gendered stereotypes. She addresses how the early definition of the word *feeblemindedness* came about and the history of the care of children and others in institutions (the word was used to label unmarried women giving birth and later to further marginalize and segregate "feebleminded women" in institutions).These interpretations have been imposed by outsiders.

Matthew Williams's 2016 TED Talk (*Special Olympics Let Me Be Myself—A Champion*) speaks to the context of exclusion. Overall, policy development has not included the voices of those most affected. Many people have resisted marginalization and the oppressive structures that have been established. People have written and spoken out against being labeled with negative descriptors rather than the ones that truly describe their spirits and fortitude.

AT-RISK POPULATIONS

When data suggests that some groups of people are more likely than others to contract a health concern, or fit a profile, they are designated as *at-risk populations*. Some examples of these populations might be those that are more likely to experience mental health distress, become homeless, contract illnesses, not graduate from high school, or become unemployed, detained, deported or incarcerated.

Groups at risk—especially those that have lower access to protections and who have greater exposure to risky behaviors—may be identified within most categories of health diagnoses. Generally, people are more at risk based on their low income, life stress, race; even stress during one's prenatal gestation can set one up for multiple lifelong stress-related pathologies (Lefmann, Combs-Orme, & Orme, 2017). Persons who experience adverse experiences during childhood (Choi, DiNitto, Marti, & Nathan, 2017) and youth are at risk for emotional health disorders (Garcia, Gupta, Greeson, Thompson, & DeNard, 2017). Chronic substance use, frequently used to self-medicate, often leads to various health disorders, psychotic experiences and multimorbid diagnoses (Cui et al., 2017; Degenhardt et al., 2017). Limited physical activity and diets with low plant and vegetable consumption also present risks for diabetes and heart disease (Lakerveld et al., 2017). Children with disabilities are frequently maltreated (Maclean et al., 2017), and children in families with parents who are incapacitated by serious emotional, physical or substance use conditions are often referred to foster care (Stein & Bever, 2017), and that puts them in harm's way of additional risks.

According to Chin (2005), the broad scope of populations at risk has not been well researched. Most studies about at-risk populations can be categorized into three groups: 1) description of disparities in access to care, quality of care, and outcomes; 2) mechanisms of disparities; and 3) interventions to reduce disparities. Data is available through the National Health Interview Survey (NHIS) and the Agency for Healthcare Research and Quality's (AHRQ) National Healthcare Disparities Report, but many groups and clinical areas remain relatively understudied. Further research is needed in these and related areas.

EDUCATIONAL SYSTEM

The impact of the educational system has been reported to have a negative effect on children of color and of lower-wealth communities. The Children's Defense Fund (2007) director Marian Edelman and others have urged more evaluation of the "pipeline to prison" that captures too many minority youngsters. The absence of diverse teachers, multicultural history, and affirming practices in educational settings neglects the need for inclusive role model representation in leadership and curricula. Studies indicate that a broadened framework and more integrative teaching strategies would support self-esteem and efforts toward higher-level academic performance (Mann, Hosman, Schaalma, & de Vries, 2004).

HEALTH

American Indians and Alaska Natives have disproportionately high rates of substance-use disorders. Most referrals come from the criminal justice system. The Center for Behavioral Health Statistics and Quality (2012) urges that improving understanding of the gaps could improve outreach and referral to offset the current pathways.

The **suicide rate** among American Indians/Alaska Natives between the ages of 15 and 34 is 19.5 per 100,000, which is 1.5 times higher than the national average for that age group and three times higher than the national average" (CDC, 2015). Suicide rates tend to be higher in rural states and lowest in highly urbanized areas (Stephenson-Davidowits, 2015).

The **mortality rate** increase in middle-aged white people has brought attention to health concerns among white communities as well as those of color. The study by Case and Deaton referred to by Kolata (2015) generated much speculation but basically presents an illustration of the complicated mix of social structure stressors and unhealthy coping responses. The researchers indicated the rates from 1999 to 2013 seemed to be influenced by several factors including alcohol and drug use, suicide, chronic joint pain, and emotional health issues.

The long-term **health impact of divorce, separation, and loss** on children and parents is also an area of concern. Some research in this area suggests that there is a connection to strokes in males whose parents divorced before they were 18 (Fuller-Thompson & Dalton, 2015). The health impacts are connected to the level and duration of the stress and the presence or absence of a strong support system (Browne, 2014).

Social work can draw on the use of mapping (Hillier, 2007) to locate health needs information. Geographic information systems (GIS) technology is a useful tool available to illustrate community demographics and to identity areas of need and resources. Kids Count (Kids Count. org, 2014) and other data sources provide excellent data on health and mental health needs.

> **CRITICAL THINKING QUESTION**
>
> What kinds of behaviors evoke physiological responses? Consider reactions to adverse experiences, family emotional abuse, social stigma, bullying, stereotype threats, or workplace harassment. Could any of these stress points become health or psychiatric diagnoses?

ENVIRONMENTAL INFLUENCES ON HUMAN BEHAVIOR

People often try to self-medicate and calm themselves through substance use or other risky behaviors. However, this tends to place them at risk for further health problems. The impact of stressors and unhealthy coping contribute to the differences in rates of health status across various groups. Not only are unhealthy coping methods of concern, but the prejudice and clinical uncertainty of health professionals working with minority groups also contribute to the disparate results in healthcare (Balsa & McGuire, 2003). Emerging research raises concerns about the negative influences of environmental and ecodevelopmental factors on the coping methods of all citizens, but especially on those with higher exposure to potential risks. There is pressure for coping that takes the form of alcohol and substance use by Latinos with physical disabilities (Cordova et al., 2015).

Several studies identify components of social stressors and emotional and physical responses. Teacher discrimination among adolescents is associated with their alcohol use over time (Fuller-Rowell et al., 2011). The impact of micro aggressions in a sample of Asian, Latino, Black and White children is highest among black children. Data on their physiological and psychological reactions to interpersonal and environmental intentional and unintentional acts of aggression (Forrest-Bank & Jenson, 2015) illustrate the range of intensity. The combination of racism and heterosexism influences unhealthy behaviors and emotional feelings of fear and helplessness among persons with intersectional identifies, especially of LGBTQI people of color to a higher degree (Balsam, Molina, Beadnell, Simoni, & Walters, 2011). Williams' team's examination of racial/ethnic discrimination summarized overall social pressures impact health indicators. They reviewed 53 studies from 2000 to 2003 on perceptions of discrimination which associated it to poor health status. They discussed the gaps in the literature and proposed areas for future research on discrimination (Williams, Neighbors, & Jackson, 2003). Community education translates research findings to become more aware of how poor health outcomes start and provide support systems to alter the trajectory. Prevention education needs to begin early.

INEQUALITY

The Economic Policy Institute (Mishel, 2015) points to the inadequate incomes as a damaging consequence of long-term pay stagnation. One of its major findings is that by raising the federal minimum wage to $12 per hour, public assistance spending would be reduced by $17 billion annually. The savings could offset other programs or education initiatives There are economists who agree that the history of capitalism has pitfalls. Stiglitz (2012) and Piketty (2014) offer perspectives that focus on the perils of current capitalism for the state of well-being of the country. In *The Price of Inequality* (2012), Stiglitz notes the absence of focus on class in the United States in the past but acknowledges that discussion of the arrival of the "99%" shifts attention to the population's economic divisions. He questions the moral compass of those in the financial sector and the political system that is obstructing the values of democracy. Piketty (2014) reminds us that economic inequality is not new, but the situation is getting worse.

A 2016 Princeton study says the United States now has not a democracy, but an oligarchy, in which the elite rule. Gilens and Page (2016) conclude from an analysis of over 1,800 policy initiatives from 1981 to 2002 that rich, politically active individuals influence the direction of national activities despite the ideas of the majority of voters. This results in a move away from a democracy.

ALTERNATIVE ECONOMIC FRAMEWORKS

Stiglitz (2012) believes, as the Princeton study pointed out, that the political system has warped the economic system into one that promotes and reinforces inequality. He proposes alternative frameworks that can lead toward more fairness. He does this by incorporating information from other disciplines. He examines the criminal justice system, the labor market, the unemployment rates, and the unemployment system (one of the least generous in the world). He notes that the capitalism game—as it is being played—involves people who skirt the law and who play unfairly to win. His recommendations for reform involve several steps, but especially emphasize a progressive income and corporate tax system with fewer loopholes (p. 273).

Piketty's (2014) *Capital in the Twenty-First Century* also tackles the unfairness in the economic system. Drawing on years of research on the past nature of capitalism regarding rates of growth, he recommends a tax on the wealthy around the world.

ANALYZING THE LIVED EXPERIENCES OF RACISM, SEXISM, HOMOPHOBIA, AND CLASSISM

Critically considering the existing explanations of human behavior and their connection to middle- and upper-class lives is the starting point for reassessing and evaluating service issues. Native American researchers have commented that white researchers tend to immediately dismiss the thoughtful contribution and alternative perspectives of indigenous persons (Byrd, 2011; Dunbar-Ortiz, 2014). White researchers tend to put down indigenous ideas that oppose their conceptualizations. However, Feagin's (2013) work that points to the need for using analysts of color to understand racism is a critical contribution for developing more objective methods and ways of analyzing the lived experiences of racism, sexism, homophobia, and classism. He notes those who have impacted his thinking include "major African-American social analysts of racism, like W. E. B. DuBois, Stokely Carmichael, and Charles Hamilton" (Yancy & Feagin, 2015, para 2).

This challenging work is continual. Addressing this matrix from one theory is impossible. Using the transtheoretical perspective involves the need to be pluralistic and critical in selecting theories to guide practice work (O'Neal, 2010). Reframing the structure for critical thinking and evidence-based formulas would integrate the transtheoretical concept on a multiple-tiered framework. It is necessary to use the research and data of multicultural researchers and analysts.

RESPONSES TO OPPRESSION

Individuals and groups react to social dynamics involving, racism, discrimination, homophobia, sexism, and ableism in various ways. Not only may historical traumas impact identity and policy formulation, but stereotypical ideas also challenge people, especially children and youth, as they develop (Davis, 1998; Deaux, Waters, Steele, & Thomas, 1999).

In *Post Traumatic Slave Syndrome* (2005), Joy DeGruy describes behaviors that some members of the black community may exhibit in response to the historical trauma of slavery. Her theory of post traumatic slave syndrome identifies patterns of insufficient self-esteem, feelings of hopelessness, destructive behaviors against self, others and property to be a consequence of multi-generational experiences of messages of inferiority and experiences of institutional racism. Her study guide is offered to work with groups to develop skills to address maladaptive behaviors and replace them with a strengths focus and positive behaviors.

INDIVIDUALS, FAMILIES, GROUPS, AND COMMUNITIES

Depending on the settings or situations, the range of responses to discrimination in organizational settings, or interpersonal aggression might include internalization, denial, withdrawal, hopelessness, anger, rage, violence, or understanding, hope, peace, overcoming, organizing, achieving, resilience, transcendence—or some place in between. There is a continuum of reactions and adjustment. Individuals and families may hold different perspectives of themselves in response to existing systems and structures. The expectation is that their views are valid and should be respected. How someone feels—culturally and emotionally—when a connection with a service user occurs should be considered in the assessment.

RESPONSIVE BEHAVIORS TO THE SOCIAL CONTEXT

The ways in which people respond to our social environment vary. Family environment makes a difference in shaping the capacity of family members to deal with life challenges. However, members of the same family or household may see things, situations, and experiences completely differently or may only see parts of what the other family members observe. The extent of communication between the household leaders and the children and relatives can all influence their interactions.

Families that operate with consistent structure, faith-based principles, and opportunities for the family members to express their feelings often move through the developmental process with confidence. In addition, if members of the family have household responsibilities and are supported, disciplined, and continuously nourished and protected, they stand up better to challenges of segregation, discrimination, and harsh systems. It is necessary to have networks that support and encourage discussion about the micro and macro aggressions that occur.

Nevertheless, there are so many experiences in the social environment that push people to quick emotional reactions that buy into negative messages. Psychological reactions include internalizing the negative stimuli, denying realities, and expressing the anger and rage that these conditions, coupled with other life struggles, can generate. Other reactions include withdrawal, depression, and lack of confidence and perseverance.

Encouraging service users to become involved in community organizations and places of worship, as well as seeking supportive teachers and other responsible adults helps establish relationships for sharing experiences and gaining wisdom.

INSTITUTIONAL RESPONSES

On an institutional level, responses to claims and observations of discriminatory practices may include task forces, committees, designated work teams, and mandates that are established to gather information and evaluate how the power dynamics play out in organizational settings. The work sets forth objectives to meet in making services more accessible. As contemporary events seem to promote the history of hatred and intolerance, the reactions of those who have benefited from the traditional methods are visible through various social media mediums, in comments, on television, and through interpersonal exchanges in workspaces. In some organizations, the administrators may not respond to staff or service users' requests for improvements. In some cases this could result in legal appeals or grievance complaints.

According to the Pew Research Center (2016), the majority of American citizens acknowledge the need to make changes to uphold equal rights for people of color. In fact, 86% of blacks and 53% of whites (up from 39% in 2014) say more needs to be done. The survey finds that black and white adults have widely different perceptions about discrimination as a reason for blacks not getting ahead (Pew Research Center, 2016). Figure 5.1 describes how skeptical people are that there will ever be racial equality in the United States.

SOCIAL WORK RESPONSES

The social work profession brings recognition to the multiple environments that affect people (Weick, 2009). Developing paradigms through evidence-based steps involves building relationships and collaborating with people who bring alternative ideas—indigenous and other non-establishment perspectives and approaches—to planning and implementing services.

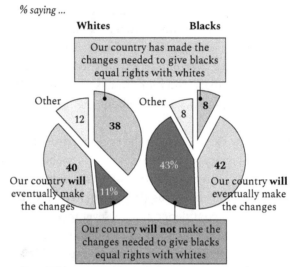

Many blacks are skeptical that the country will
eventually make the changes necessary for racial equality

% saying ...

Whites   **Blacks**

Our country has made the
changes needed to give blacks
equal rights with whites

Other — 12   Other — 8   8

38

40   43%   42

Our country **will**
eventually make
the changes   11%   Our country **will**
eventually make
the changes

Our country **will not** make the
changes needed to give blacks
equal rights with whites

Note: Whites and blacks include only non-Hispanics. Figures
combine results from two questions. The first asked whether or not
our country has made the changes needed to give blacks equal
rights with whites; the second asked those who said the U.S. had
not made the necessary changes if those changes would eventually
be made or not. "Other" includes voluntary responses of "Both" or
"Neither" in the first question and "Don't know/Refused" in either
question. Figures may not add to 100% due to rounding.
Source: Survey of U.S. adults conducted Feb. 29-May8, 2016.
Q6F2, Q6aF2.
"On Views of Race and Inequality, Blacks and Whites are Worlds
Apart"
PEW RESEARCH CENTER

FIGURE 5.1   Skepticism

THEORIES AND SOCIAL WORK

The knowledge base for social work incorporates information from several disciplines. Theories help us organize our experiences to understand and explain our environments. On the one hand, we need theories to provide structure and guide our practice (O'Neal, 2010). On the other hand, we maintain awareness and use critical thinking to balance the perceptions that may be shaped by the theories. In this way, theories are tools to help guide, develop, and critique efforts we make on behalf of others.

Based on the ecological framework, we operate from a macro lens, although the micro lens on human behavior is frequently the one that dominates ideas and theories about practice. As the profession evolves and more closely examines social and cultural dynamics and the process of change, theories about the science of learning, mobilizing and transferring knowledge, and implementing evidence-based approaches arise for discussion and reflection (Powell, Davis, & Nutley, 2017).

Theoretical concepts may be shared across macro and micro dimensions with context emphasizing various components. Theories and frameworks regarding professional interactions within and between organizations and across disciplines and professions include but are not limited to the following:

- Systems theory
- Emotional and social intelligence theory
- Management science theory
- Social justice framework
- Social action theory
- Social exchange theory
- Knowledge transfer theory
- Social change theory
- Implementation theory

Theories and frameworks focused on individual and group behavior include but are not limited to these:

- Attachment theory
- Developmental perspective
- Ecological perspective
- Conflict theory
- Empowerment perspective
- Feminist theory
- Crisis theory
- Risk/resiliency theory
- Social justice perspective
- Social action theory
- Social constructivist theory
- Social exchange theory
- Social learning theory
- Social systems theory
- Theories of social change
- Strengths perspective

Using a theoretical base connected to the relationship building necessary for community capacity should encourage co-creation with the diverse constituency.

MACRO THEORIES AND SOCIETY

Macro theories describe several ways of explaining *what is observed* in the broad view of society. These explanations direct how professionals scrutinize social issues and how services to families and individuals are delivered. The extent of thinking that embraces others, emphasizes strength, and promotes protecting the environment for generations to come takes on duality in theory development. The broad environment offers levels of context for systems thinking. Specific issues may align more with descriptors in a narrower field of theoretical boundaries.

Harari (2017) provides an even broader base for conceptualization. In *Homo Deus: A Brief History of Tomorrow*, the perspective of lost humanity urges views of artificial intelligence—how people will be treated by robots and how people adapt to it. People worry about what will happen to work as these technological advances occur. (Kessler, 2017). As social work evolves, it strives to handle those who become vulnerable and who may have difficulty keeping up with technological and evolutionary change.

Macro theories also describe how to make sense of all this information. Evolving social work protocols address interprofessional collaboration, transdisciplinary research, and community-based prevention. We may conceptualize other connections as well. However, if we use just these three as examples, knowledge transfer, translating research, and evaluating outcomes assume high priorities. All these elements should be addressed in planning for the co-creation of service interventions.

SYSTEMS THINKING

As we pursue increasingly sophisticated paradigms that integrate the variables of people with limited services, systems thinking is required. This involves theory, relationship building, and understanding the personal domains that impact our activities as change agents (Stroh, 2015).

Lack of coordination and the inability to work together wastes resources and impedes goal achievement of a healthier community. Systems thinking includes team learning, as well as building shared vision, mental models, and personal mastery (Senge, 2006). This model supports an organization becoming one that can learn. Ultimately, this should lead to improved service delivery.

INTERORGANIZATIONAL KNOWLEDGE TRANSFER

Szulanski (1999) refers to the needs and obstacles of transferring knowledge within an organization. Building on systems theory, every organization within the service delivery system has its own internal and external relationship networks. He points out that knowledge transfer and integration within the organization are complex. It is neither costless or expedient. Between and within subunits, there may be obstacles in communication and resources; those obstacles may involve people who do not want changes, thus requiring adjustments and training.

EXTERNAL KNOWLEDGE TRANSFER

Transferring knowledge within the external community has dynamics. Broner, Franczak, Dye, and McAllister (2001) consider the transfer of knowledge for policy-making and community empowerment as a consensus-building model. Recognizing that any knowledge exchange involves power relations, they suggest that the implication of their observation "is that a more efficient, effective, and democratic policy-making process should not rely solely on higher-level officials but incorporate those who actually implement policy decisions as well as those the policy ostensibly addresses" (p. 80).

The parameters of exchange become more complex the broader the effort extends. Yet the advancing labor of social work—if pursued using Sommerfeld's (2014) conceptualization as transdisciplinary action science—portends the capacity of social work to indeed promote action. His discussion presents a conception of social work as an action science, pursing scientific and technological knowledge within evidence-based approaches.

According to Bloom, Fischer, and Orme (2009), practitioners are committed to locating the best and most effective resources for service users for any issue in service planning. Can we do this? Is this being done? What have you observed?

Kelly (2016) confirms that the social, institutional, and power networks must be more thoroughly evaluated to understand and engage with the environments in which social workers work. It is clear that evidence-based practice is the goal in the United States, the United Kingdom, and other international locations. However, the implementation has fallen short and the need for more "participatory and democratic models of knowledge sharing" (p. 246) are required.

> ### CRITICAL THINKING QUESTION
>
> Which theories do you find useful in explaining the context of oppression and the basis for addressing disparities?

EVIDENCE-BASED PRACTICES

The emotional health affected by life circumstances is what brings people to social services. The social work profession and other helping professions are organized to assist those in need, address vulnerabilities, and contribute to work that builds individual and community capacity to support humanity. The evolving work seeks interventions that have been proven to be effective.

Originating in medicine, evidence-based practice (EBP) refers to explicit and judicious use of the best knowledge in decision-making about the care of patients (Gibbs, 2003). Drisko and Grady (2015) expand this to denote an integrative decision-making process aimed at more effective social work through better client outcomes. As the definition of *EBP* is evolving, the appreciation of client "attributes, values, preferences and circumstances" has been added (Drisko & Grady, 2015). Social workers may employ interventions from basic talk therapy to cognitive behavior therapy, dialectical behavior therapy, interpersonal therapy, and others. A designation of effective psychotherapies is available for review for planning and decision-making (Australian Psychological Society, 2010).

The clinical perspective continues to maintain a medical model connection. Social work practice, however, operates on a broader foundation. Weick (1983) acknowledged the resistance of changing from the model that holds expert power over a more inclusive paradigm of health service that involves workers' willingness to relinquish their power to enhance consumers' strengths. Social work's competency areas include social and economic justice, human rights, engagement, and collaboration, as well as direct practice with individuals, families, organizations, and communities.

To address the issues that are linked to historical trauma and stereotyping, services must go beyond the medical model.

MACRO EVIDENCE-BASED PRACTICES

Macro evidence-based practices could merge with existing clinical, organizational, and institutional models to elicit consumer participation at policy development levels. The best knowledge for macro practice implies the use of additional kinds of research. Quantitative and mixed-methods research has been conducted on community development, micro enterprise, citizen participation, social planning, and leadership. Qualitative studies, economic analyses, practice guidelines, systematic reviews (Thyer, 2008), as well as informant and ethnographic studies, incident analyses, consumer feedback evaluations, and GIS evaluations can be used.

As evidence-based or evidence-informed practice continues to evolve, the literature is expanding in the United States and other countries. There is a need for universities to conduct more useful social problem solution-focused research (Policy Press, 2009). In addition to replicable quantitative measures, ethics and practice expertise are added to the framework for consideration. The gap between the interventions and what the clients says they will do and what they actually do and what the helper estimates will happen is often inaccurate (Gambrill, 2008). How can that be addressed?

Similar issues of systematic identification of data, ethics, and service-user outcomes are relevant for evidence-based macro practice (Salcido, 2008). Selecting programs that have worked should be useful to program planners and administrators. There are several reasons for more structured use of evidence-based approaches in the social work profession (Roberts-De-Gennaro, 2008). These include legislation-mandated accountability, managed-care systems promoting efficacious approaches, consumer advocacy movements, and legal decisions that are connected to service outcomes. Select one for further study.

IMPLEMENTATION OF EVIDENCE-BASED PRACTICES VIA COMMUNITY INTERVENTIONS

The implementation of evidence-based practices via community interventions brings additional challenges. While there is already some research on evidentiary information regarding macro practices, substantial research documentation is needed to guide organizational and community policy development. Community organizations need the capacity to produce appropriate and sophisticated research to gather data on consumer values and participation (Netting & O'Connor, 2008; Ohmer, 2008).

The determination of EBP at the micro and macro level must also incorporate culturally sensitive protocols. A major critique of clinical EBP is the absence of diverse participants in the clinical trials.

The growing diversity of the U.S. population and the interest in providing services in settings around the world demand interventions that have been culturally adapted and tested for effectiveness (Castro, Barrera, & Stelker, 2010).

As we proceed in thinking about the history of groups we work with, readers may contemplate examining career interests, agencies' dynamics, and particular service interventions. Moving forward builds on theoretical ideas.

INCLUSION AND CONTEXTUAL FLUIDITY

This conceptual perspective that emphasizes inclusion is connected to contextual fluidity, social construction, restricted opportunity, and social exchange. The multiple-element projection offers a standpoint for evaluating service populations in their environment. Readers should develop their set of theories and identify related obstacles. The broadest (macro) frame may present issues that citizens participate in to help regulate their environments and their air and water safety. The next level may involve preparing citizens to participate in shaping safer neighborhoods and schools (macro and mezzo) with multicultural education and universal learning designs that encourage creative and scientific pursuits and the prevention of mental health problems. *And Still I Rise* (1978) by Maya Angelou and "Alright" (2015) by Kendrick Lamar offer cultural interpretations of the pressures of micro aggressions (Forrest-Bank & Jenson, 2015) and the energies of communities.

Social work involves perspectives regarding the environment and people and the interrelatedness of these. The service delivery system is the broad system of organizations and communities through which social workers and other helping professionals coordinate and provide services to inform and improve well-being. The context in the broadest sense encompasses global concerns about all human rights, particularly children and women's rights, and adequate food, shelter, and environmental preservation.

Documents That Address Human Rights

The International Federation of Social Workers (IFSW) notes that social work is guided by these documents:

- Universal Declaration of Human Rights
- The International Covenant on Civil and Political Rights
- The International Covenant on Economic, Social, and Cultural Rights
- The Convention on the Elimination of All Forms of Racial Discrimination
- The Convention on the Elimination of All Forms of Discrimination Against Women
- The Convention on the Rights of the Child
- Declaration of Human Rights of Indigenous Peoples (IFSW.org, n.d.)

These documents raise several variables regarding values of humanity. The economics of services funding, the dynamics of organizational leadership, and advocacy and community needs shape how organizations and staff build on theoretical frames of reference. Integrating the expectations of these documents will alter the existing frames of blame to reflect ones based on rights and respect.

PROFESSIONAL STRUGGLES TO IMPLEMENT NEW KNOWLEDGE

Some professionals struggle to engage with new research and are reticent to implement innovation. Social network analysis (SNA) can be used to scrutinize the flow of social and material resources within the human and organizational connections we are affiliated with. Information about the give and take can illustrate the capacity for delivering services. The assessment of culture should be part of the network analysis (Nair & Guerrero, 2014). Yasui, Potttick, and Chen (2017) point to the failure to adequately measure engagement factors as a contributor to the gaps in effective services.

The psychological, social, and material conditions that existed in the bureaucratic workforce in post slavery that obstructed implementation of culturally relevant services to Natives and to African descendants are likely still in play in many ways in our contemporary work. The factors that allow discrimination may be observed within the workforce itself and among the types of services provided.

CRITICAL THINKING QUESTION

An example of network-influenced behavior in an organization could look like this:

A white worker in the child service agency who returns to school and receives a master's degree in social work is quickly assigned clinical cases. A black worker in the same agency with more experience is asked to continue the work she was doing and not quickly assigned clinical cases. How would social network theory explain this behavior?

Social work is committed to producing knowledge that will help improve services. Theoretical and empirical knowledge is useful in designing interventions but more work is needed to implement services that are effective (Kreisberg & Marsh, 2016). In service applications, consumers of color may be offered interventions that don't incorporate increased opportunities but continue restrictions or penalties. For example, in the criminal justice realm, community service opportunities may be offered to some young white offenders but not to young black men (Sentencing Project, 2017). When knowledge about alternative paths exists, how is that implementation applied or ensured? Are education-based options prioritized? According to the findings from research regarding the implementation of knowledge production (Harrison, Spybrook, Curtis, & Cousins, 2017), there is a need for theoretical approaches. Knowledge production occurs through ongoing investigations and testing. It offers information, techniques and protocols that may promote better outcomes. Workers may need help understanding the professional culture of decision-making and how this knowledge can be translated administratively and via engagement across ethnic groups into shared knowledge (Nielson, 2015). Inclusion requires recognizing and incorporating the knowledge and experiences of those who are affected as workers and as services users (Kelly, 2017).

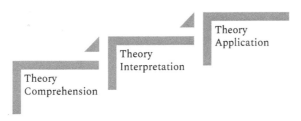

FIGURE 5.2   Thinking About Theory

WORKING WITH THEORIES

Designing a theoretically based approach to working with an agency, a community, or a system should include ways of explaining and intervening with the system and the people. Figure 5.2 urges processing ideas about theory in a variety of ways before developing the application.

Developing a palette of theories to shape an approach to practice is the beginning. There are three ways to work with theories in practice: theory comprehension, theory interpretation, and theory application. A review of the definitions of theories of interest should offer meanings that can connect to specific situations.

To grasp the explanation of a theory, try using it to express meaning of some of your basic activities. Can you *understand/comprehend the situation* via the theory's content? For example, social learning theory explains the cognitive process of gaining information.

Next, can you develop an *interpretation* of the theory? How and why does that explanation fit with your observations? For example, social learning theory would be useful in explaining the biological and psychological dynamics of using information to solve a problem.

How could this concept of learning be applied to a service user's scenario? Would one *apply it to a micro and macro* situation? How can the theory be applied to evaluate or improve an incident or interest in program development?

CASE SCENARIO 1

Jessica has completed a retail management training program and has been looking for a job. Her two children attend a local school where they are doing OK. Several parents have complained about the impact of some incidents related to violence near the school and the absence of a diverse history curriculum. The school is interested in revising its collaboration with the parent–teacher groups in the district.

Which theories would be useful in thinking through this scenario?

Theories that make sense in planning for Case Scenario 1 would include systems, social exchange, social learning, and cognitive development, trauma, and prevention. Motivational theory (Atkinson & Woods, 2017) would also be useful for thinking about how to encourage Jessica to take on some leadership in addressing the community's concerns Figure 5.3 offers a trajectory for considering a service user scenario and considering potential theoretical approaches.

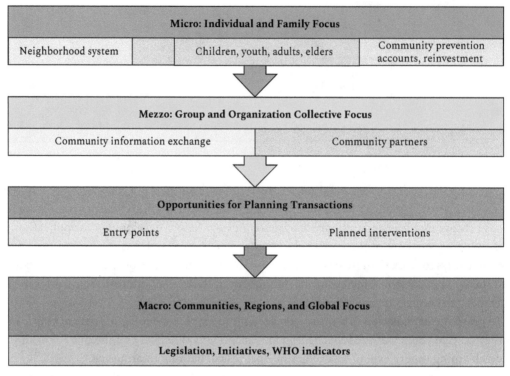

FIGURE 5.3   Contextual Landscapes

THEORIES AND PERSPECTIVES

Table 5.1 may be used to begin an analysis of existing conditions and potential steps for community building. Theories and perspectives that provide the broad foundation for the social work profession include but are not limited to the following:

Can walking through explanations of context help us think through designs that address the needs of a service user and the skills of the worker?

The *ecosystem* framework relies on *field theory to* offer a view of the territory or geography that contains social work's persons in their environments and links large and smaller systems and subsystems. *Think about Jessica in her neighborhood. What does she see? Who are the people that surround her and her household members? Will her children have access to resources*

TABLE 5.1   ⸻Explaining and Designing⸻

EXPLAINING WHAT IS	DESIGNING ALTERNATIVES
• Ecosystems	• Strengths
• Structural functional	• Contextual fluidity
• Restricted opportunity	• Social exchange
• Social construction	• Social change

within this space? Are there businesses that might hire her? Can she earn a living wage in within a 25 mile radius?

Contextual fluidity acknowledges our environment as is and as it flows and interacts between personal and collective experiences. "Helping is perceived as the central concept" (O'Neal, 2010, p. 34). This theory draws on the idea that people of the land, indigenous or born in the area, navigate to meet needs among kin and neighbors through mutual aid networks (Smith, 2010). Despite the challenges of aging in rural communities (Bascsu et al., 2014; Nelson & McPherson, 2004), there are examples of blended family–friend–neighbor care models of support for healthy and equitable interventions that apply in any environment. *Does this structure of her community offer childcare, opportunities for continual learning, opportunities to meet and interact with different community members in a ways that support the similar needs that families haves in positive ways?*

Restricted opportunity is a concept that describes the major dynamic of discrimination. Persons of some groups may be denied access or be obstructed in employment, housing, health care, education, or participation in civic engagement. *Does Jessica have access to affordable housing, (housing without toxins that affect asthma or water quality), healthcare, and resources for her aging parents? Does she know how to participate in her community to address the anger that exists in her community that sometimes occurs around the schools her children attend? Is she connected to spiritual supports?*

Social construction refers to general ideas about identity that are promoted by one group but may not agree with individual or other in-group self-interpretations. *Is Jessica affected by the names some of her community members are called or is there leadership that encourages all community members to use their strengths to make their neighborhood safer and smarter?*

Social exchange offers a basis for change that encourages win–win strategies. Is the community leadership promoting the strengths of its members to use education curriculum to allow students to contemplate role models that look like them, to use their skills to write, draw, or sing their answers and draw up learning plans of their own to meet academic performance goals

The *strengths* perspective is an element of the ecosystem framework that seeks to build on abilities and is the perspective social work uses for **building resilience and capacity.**

Other theories that have been used separately or in conjunction with others include the following:

1. *Field theory* was introduced in the early 1970s to illustrate the broad context for examining what is going on in specific environmental contexts.
2. *Systems theory* has been associated with Ludwig von Bertalanffy's biology-based description of entities and boundaries in the late 1920s to contemporary ideas of structures, interactions, and perceptions of the social environment's subsystems, participants, and roles (Friedman & Allen, 2010).
3. *Deviance theory* has been used to describe behavior that does not meet traditional views of proper behavior.

4. *Structural functionalism* is connected to the sociological and political organizational functions that maintain existing operations.
5. *Role theory* refers to expected patterns of social interactions.
6. *Critical race theory* ties the discrimination that impacts persons in need to the institutional systems that exist.
7. *Social change* is observed to occur over time with impacts of active voices and community reactions.

SELECTING THEORIES

In pursuing the mission of social work, perspectives regarding the practice focus and the standards of competency may guide one's selection of theoretical explanations or exploratory pathways. The tiers of context that affect communities or population groups include broad economic, environmental, and ecological conceptual frames as well as narrow specific paradigms that explain micro dynamics. A theory set may be selected to guide a session, a group, a series, or a program.

Evidence-based micro psychotherapies and macro-based practices may be connected to another theory to shape the multiple-level intervention strategy. There are several programs that have been designated evidence-based programs that involve mezzo- and macro-level components (Coalition for Evidence-Based Policy, n.d.).

Overall, the ecological perspective integrates the complex interplay of biology, neuroscience, and psychology with social, economic, cultural, and spiritual forces. Treatment approaches connected to administrative regulations and organizational culture dynamics (O'Neal, 2010, p. 32) are observed and evaluated as micro- and macro-level interventions.

POWER DYNAMICS IN THE SOCIAL ENVIRONMENT

Across environmental settings and along all points of the life cycle, power forces influence the maintenance of institutional systems for infants, toddlers, children, youth, adults, and seniors. Young people experience power by parents, guardians, and educational authorities. Older people experience power through workplace and income sources. Seniors frequently are guarded by caregivers, attendants, medical personnel, and grown children.

The dominance of middle-class values by teachers, counselors, and school administrators was discussed by Stanton-Salazar (1997) as a frequent impediment to educational success for working-class minority youth. He identified the social–capital framework of institutional agents to be problematic in that it neglects their life context and often penalizes them when their behavior challenges expectations of school personnel. More recent teaching strategies connected to inclusion concepts urge the use of multicultural resources and personnel recruitment across the diversity spectrum, especially people of color, bilingual, and those in wheelchairs or who use bionic apparatus and equipment. There are more actual sources of power in our environment. These need to become more visible in schools and other organizations that support children and youth.

SOCIAL WORK AND POWER

Dressel (1992) discusses the lack of attention to power in social work practice. He notes the tools of power of expertise and the use of persuasion. The impact of social constructs on the roles of women as workers in human service organizations, as well as the needs of women service users presents some contradiction. The social worker has a role in maintaining patriarchal service structures often managed via personal experience and consultants rather than management practices that are based on well-researched performance measures (Nair & Guerrero, 2014).

Women who come for services often do so as a result of "gendered and racialized power relations that have rigid and patriarchal capitalist workplace culture" (Wessels, 2003, p. 79).

SOCIAL CONTEXT OF TRADITIONAL THINKING

Traditional gender stereotypes put men in management or tout the ideal worker as single or have the woman at home caring for the children (Slaughter, 2015), but they do not address the reality of contemporary household composition. The model illustrated by *Mad Men* (Weiner & Lionsgate, 2007), the television series based on corporate advertising marketers, puts the job before everything. This model ignores the human needs of workers and families to operate in ways that integrate household and work performance planning. The tension of gender-based structures also contributes to the obstacles that become evident in pursuit of holistic strategies.

Slaughter (2015) contributed to recent conversations about workplace tensions for women that include Sandberg (2013), who urges women to "lean in". She suggests that women ask yourself, What would you do if you weren't afraid? Then do it. (p. 26) Blair (2015) has expanded the discussion to include men and whoever plays the more predominant role in conducting caregiving duties. She refers to the social message of value placed on the person that goes to the office. If the focus could move to the well-being of children, approaches for reforms would include more flexible work schedules and investments in opportunities to meet family obligations (Heathfield, 2016). These concerns move the focus to the well-being of the family group rather than to the prestige of the workplace.

The voices that bring attention to power express their observations of the exclusion of concern for others. Often, these voices come together as coalitions to seek, gather, and distribute resources.

SOCIAL CONTEXT OF ECONOMICS

The role of economics in the service delivery system must be recognized as the major force in how service delivery operates. The impact of economics on peoples' lives has always been apparent, but in the contemporary climate, it often regards food insecurity, access to health care, and homelessness, among other issues. Some situations involve people who have not grown up in low-wealth communities but may be as likely as low-income people to be unable meet their social, self-actualization, and spiritual needs (Gil, 1998). In the typical world, the reality of impoverished communities is that established structures and developing economic communities resist sharing resources with those who don't have access to multiple sources of income.

ABSENCE OF EMPLOYMENT

Within the social welfare field, the absence of employment opportunities is a significant area of concern. The unemployment rates overall may not look grim. However, statistics in many low-wealth neighborhoods have much higher rates of persons without jobs. DeSilver (2013) reports that the black unemployment rate has been twice that of whites for the past 60 years.

When work and opportunity were available via manufacturing and other businesses, there were productive communities in urban and the surrounding areas. As these sources of employment disappeared, families that were able to relocate for work did so. Those with more limited skills remain in areas that have become increasingly segregated (Wilson, 1996) and have higher unemployment rates. Research on neighborhood effects shows that these concentrated areas contain low-performing schools, inadequate housing, and negative peer pressures that are harmful.) have shown mixed results. Although moving to better neighborhoods can help, the quality programs that have addressed criminal activity and helped develop community interactions or "neighborliness" (Parry, 2012) of education and skill development appear to be the required ingredients for mobility.

Senator Elizabeth Warren's (D–MA) proposals for jobs and the economy speak to several issues that cut across the contextual landscapes (elizabethwarren.com). College debt (Berman, 2016) and job creation are important for social workers and populations that use social services. She has also made proposals for roads, water and other infrastructure needs that should assist families.

In the first of a series of conversations called *Degree of Freedom* that were presented by the McSilver Institute of Poverty at New York University School of Social, Hawkins (2016) presented an illustration of the economics of poverty. He pointed out that poverty is not just access to certain amounts of money. His description of the Katrina Hurricane situation reveals the macro context of poverty, which includes health, debt, devastated communities, violence, mental health issues, and a history of traumatic events, all related to the causes and consequences of negative life outcomes. As he reviews the improvements that have occurred in New Orleans since 2005, the picture is clear regarding where the economic investments have been made and returns realized. These have not been shared with the poorest parts of the community, but Hawkins notes that resources historically (or currently) have not been shared with people of color. Michaels (2015) agrees that the Ninth ward has been abandoned. There has not been a desire to share economic or political power in ways to improve the larger community. He recommends more work in building community coalitions.

SOCIAL WORK AND ECONOMICS

The resistance of economists to talk to other disciplines is discussed by Cowie (2016). He describes the field of economics as trying to protect itself while the current social climate is urging more activity in the market of ideas that examine more than the narrow intellectual discourse. He observes that the traditional focus on textbooks alone rather than the use of contributions of other disciplines goes against democratic theory and practice.

As social work tries to advance social and economic justice, paying attention to family income and financial literacy becomes a matter of concern. The living wage campaign is based on the notion that a full-time job should pay enough so that the family is not in poverty. This idea is an alternative to minimum wage (Devinatz, 2013). It is also an alternative to welfare (Bole, 1995). At the same time, there is more evidence that illegal and unethical behavior in a firm increases the levels of inequality and creates conditions that discourage unions (Hogler, Henle, & Gross, 2013)

Another example presents an innovative approach to encouraging fairness. A church-based organization, BUILD (Baltimoreans United in Leadership Development; 2017), pushed for an ordinance to require private companies with city contracts to pay a living wage. This group formed an alliance with workers and with the American Federation of State, County, and Municipal employees to advocate for the living wage. Although years of advocacy and electing supportive council members were moving towards better wages, owners of an outsourcing company, a tech firm, and a call center pushed back against the increases by saying they would move their businesses elsewhere rather than pay the increased amounts (Campbell, 2017).

LIVING WAGE CAMPAIGNS

Living wage campaign advocates have raised awareness about economic conditions that affect a broad range of workers and potential workers (Luce, 2005). They have helped pass legislation and achieve gains for new and existing unions. In some places there have been additional jobs created but the increase in service sector jobs with low pay continues to drive income inequality. Although they are counted as new jobs available, there is very low job security, high turnover, and practically nonexistent benefits (Simmons & Harding, 2009). Working with workers and community organizers is direct macro practice; building coalitions, pressuring politicians, and battling business lobbyists is work that helps create new relationships. When the partnerships result in community benefits agreements (CBAs), the work achieves broader effects and power for the groups and low-wage workers.

The living wage campaign at Harvard University involved janitors, security guards, and dining hall workers who earned as little as $6.75 an hour and worked up to 90 hours a week. Many worked two and three jobs. The group, Our Living Wage Campaign, demanded that Harvard implement a minimum $10.25-per-hour wage with benefits, the same standard enacted by the Cambridge (Massachusetts) City Council. It took 3 years for Harvard officials to agree to even talk with the group (McKean 2001). As of June 2002, an agreement increased starting wages for many union workers to $10.85 (Harvard.edu, 2002).

EXAMINE ECONOMICS FROM THE PAST AND FOR THE FUTURE

Perhaps the most significant economic indicator to consider in observing social and economic justice dynamics is the impact of discrimination on economics over time. Mazumder (2014) examines the legacy of slavery and segregation by questioning how long black Americans are likely to be disadvantaged because of this history. He uses several studies and datasets that measure black and white rates of intergenerational mobility. *Intergenerational mobility* is the ability of families to improve their position in income distribution from one generation to the next.

Mazumder (2014) uses data on parent characteristics, wealth, and marital history from the Survey of Income & Program Participation (SIPP); National Longitudinal Survey of Youth data, including test scores, personality traits, family income in both generations, and spousal data; Panel Study on Income Dynamics data; and large samples of black families. He analyzes the data within and between the datasets. Using this data from the 1950s to early 1980s, the overall conclusion is that black citizens are more downwardly mobile. The effects are most associated with education and family structure. The variables and variations are discussed. If the rates continue as they appear, mobility progress is unlikely. The kinds of policies that can potentially foster upward mobility and reduce downward mobility need to be determined and implemented. The potential seems to reside in economic and income policies, modern education interventions to address the achievement gaps, and other interventions implemented at earlier life cycle points.

Razgale, Kokarevica, and Belsteino (2014) raise the importance of social work for social and economic benefits. Conducting a fiscal analysis is a starting point to evaluate early intervention methods in social work with families. This is needed to determine steps toward long-term maintenance.

The power forces are clearly involved in economics and the application of theory to how services are financed and how economics impact consumers' lives. It is necessary to debate policy regarding cost-effective economic targets that can impact consumers' needs: minimum wages, food insecurity, home/shelter security, and education, among others.

INTERVENTION CONNECTIONS

Within these theoretical areas, readers may consider theories that address specific behaviors and stages of treatment. Minds Matter organized a chart that shows evidence-based psychotherapies for key health issues. The chart, Reference_Chart_Of_Disorders_And_Evidence-Based Treatments for Children and Adolescents, shows what works, what seems to work, practices not adequately tested, and what does not work (Mind Matters, 2014). Developing a theory set that begins with a macro view and explores possible interventions that could be connected to it is another step in selecting theories and examining the potential for implementation.

ENTRY POINTS

Interventions with service users occur at various entry points, at various ages, and may be connected to a range of events. The possibility for dual diagnoses or concerns is likely (O'Neal, 2010). Connecting a theoretical base related to the screening and assessment process may be connected to the agency's mission and services. The range of issues people may bring requires openness to initiate a conversation with a practitioner about what has happened.

There are several entry points for service facilitated by social workers (Oxhandler & Pargament, 2014). These points of entry are often ones that persons who have experienced stressors over the years are referred to or come on their own as they try to manage the struggles they may face. McWhirter (2013) states that "adolescents of color living in inner cities [often] have

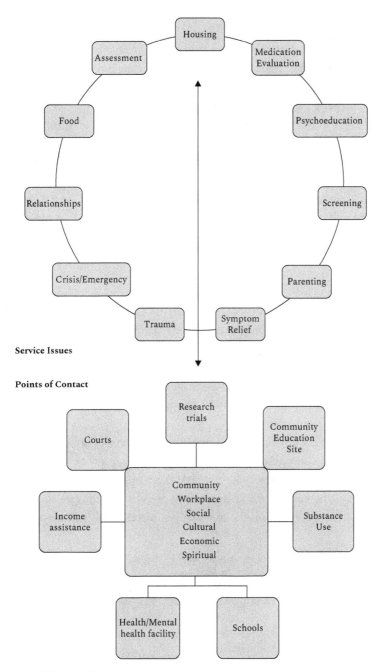

FIGURE 5.4   Issues and Points of Contact

much higher levels of personal victimization" (p. 229). Theory sets may be determined to move toward particular goals. Overall, we are striving to organize our thinking and planning from selected theories for resilience and capacity building. Figure 5.4 identifies issues that may bring citizens into a service agency through a variety of entry points.

PROCESSING

Processing service users' concerns involves using interview skills and analyzing the conditions from a standing theoretical point or one that develops from the information-gathering procedure.

Preliminary screening can start the process in different settings. Screening methods help service users become aware of their status regarding issues and be informed of service pathways. SBIRT (Screening, Brief Intervention, and Referral to Treatment) is a model that asks a few questions regarding substance use. It is considered a community intervention. It can be used in doctor's offices, emergency rooms and other settings. It has been found effective with adults (Communityguide.org, n.d.) and is one of the leading ways to help reduce the impact of unhealthy alcohol and substance use (SBIRT, 2016). It is also available for use with adolescents.

INTEGRATIVE AND PARTICIPATORY HEALTH MODELS

This contextual landscape seeks to encourage practitioners and managers to approach service delivery through an integrative and participatory health model. For example, not only are alcohol, tobacco, and other drugs (ATOD) a basis for service integration (Blankertz & O'Neal, 2010), but most areas of need involve some other, co-occurring dynamic. Children and adults are identified at various entry points where screening interventions may be conducted and where citizens may volunteer or be recruited to provide their perspectives on service user needs and evaluation of outcomes.

Using these preliminary notions about theory and environmental context lays the foundation for the theoretical approach. This contextual landscape process for designing a theory set can be illustrated via three theory levels. Figure 5.5 offers a frame.

Theories that address macro, mezzo, and micro dimensions may be further refined by the area of focus, geographic location, partners or potential ones, and by tools and resources.

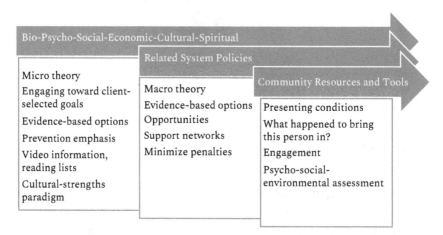

FIGURE 5.5   Theory Sets

For example, using the Reference Chart Of Disorders And Evidence-Based Treatments, the substance-use disorders category lists four treatments that could be selected for the micro level—cognitive behavioral therapy (CBT), family therapy, multisystemic therapy (MST), and motivational interviewing.

Depending on other issues of concern, a young person may also need assistance in support system development. Collaborating with community organizations to engage through evidence-based social programs would be a next or parallel step (Coalition for Evidence-Based Policy, n.d.). This example sets up a strategy for multiple theories, multiple resources levels, and encourages multidisciplinary professional collaborations.

NEW FACES OF OPPRESSION: GENDER OPPRESSION, TRAFFICKING, CHILD REFUGEES

Historical oppression has shaped present social concerns and is connected to efforts to expand awareness of rights and promote change. *What Stands in the Way of Women Being Equal to Men?* (BBC News, 2014) is a video about women's rights that points to the feelings and concerns of young girls and raises questions that can be applied to other cultural domains: Why? Why not? What occurs when these challenges are dismissed or escaped?

TRAFFICKING

Kristoff and WuDunn (2010) grab our attention with *Half the Sky: Turning Oppression Into Opportunity for Women Worldwide*, their book about human rights violations against girls in developing countries. The situations include cultural practices against women and sex slavery that demeans women. What other economic options can assist women?

CHILD REFUGEES

What Is the What is Eggers's (2006) novel of the journey of Deng, an adolescent from Marial Bai, a village in Northern Bahr el Ghazal state, South Sudan. After 13 years as a refugee in Ethiopian and Kenyan camps, he arrived in Atlanta at the Lost Boys Foundation and spoke about his life. This agency helped young boys from Sudan and was closed in 2014. But there are many refugees' stories. They tell of the harsh circumstances they face in the refugee camps and the chaos that led them there in the first place. Agencies and foundations—some sponsored by faith-based entities—have offered passage and support.

Social work is pushing for humanization through activism at the clinical and policy levels. Using history and theory are steps in the ongoing process.

FAMILY AND COMMUNITY DEVELOPMENT

The context of oppression and the movement to advance human rights is connected to serious, organized thinking, as well as discourse with those who have lived it, those working through situations, and those who want to help. Interventions that work tend to be inclusive

TABLE 5.2   Theory Set Example: Accessing and Referring to Formal and Informal Resources

	MACRO	MEZZO	MICRO
AGE	Theory of change	Network theory	Grief and loss theory
CONNECTIONS	Legislators, agency officials, and advocay groups	YMCA program	Teacher–student organization
CULTURAL RESOURCES	Community-based organizations	Book list Videos Music—What kind of music does he listen to?	Peer groups
TOOLS	Student organization Community service	Online research Library work	Mentor screening—Are there local mentors available?

of multiple theories, paradigms, strategies, and participants; Freire encouraged social workers to facilitate personal and societal-level transformation (Carroll & Minkler, 2000). This
requires taking on discrimination and exclusion, helping community members become
informed themselves, integrating existing community healing resources, and building on

---

CASE SCENARIO 2

Marcus lives in a suburban neighborhood with working-class families who have incomes that
range from a little above poverty levels to a middle-class level. His mother works a night shift,
and his grandmother has lived with them providing evening supervision since he was in elementary school. His grades have been OK, but he has just started to think more about his future.
Most of his peers don't have good grades and already have girlfriends. He has had Mom Mom
(his grandmother) to talk to, but she passed away last week. He enjoyed watching two programs
with her in the evenings. He really misses her when they come on. When he told his teacher that
she died, the teacher referred him to you. What approaches could you take to help him develop
confidence and take steps toward goals?

Select three theories to guide your thinking and reflection on this case. Consider the sample
theories and contextual issues to use for engagement and assessment.

Draft a theory set that includes contextual fluidity. Using the example above, would your process differ? Would your recommendations change based on the theories you choose? What ideas
would be connected to changing one of the theories? Include opportunities for reading, film/
video, website review, social network participation, screenings, and collaboration with at least
two service systems. Select specific variables that may affect process and outcomes: insurance, no
insurance, documentation, and no documentation, and so on. Compare and discuss with a peer.

innate resilience. Consider these variables and items in Table 5.2 to make a plan that includes consideration for micro, family and community capacity building for the Case Scenario below.

The translation of research and social work advocacy for social and economic justice anticipates more effective interventions and outcomes through use of anti-oppressive maneuvers and integration of indigenous and noncolonizing strategies (McMillin, 2014). The context for our research is broad. Innovative and rigorous research and evaluation based on multidimensional theoretical frames is required to substantiate the validity of our work and reduce the disparities created by the history of exclusion.

STUDENT COMMENTS ABOUT CONTEXT

Students selected excerpts from the readings or reflected on experiences they would use for conversations regarding the contextual landscapes in which some people have experienced harm, trauma or other discomforts.

- An excerpt from *Thurgood Marshall—Revolutionary*, by Juan Williams, prompted students to reflect on social work from a traditional micro view connected to criminal justice to the role of social work advocacy that is connected to social justice and the need for legal reforms to address the disparities of the justice system. Marshall was able to help gain advances that established protection of civil rights (Williams, 1998).
- Comparing an experience as a child in a white family
  After reading *The New Jim Crow* a student considered that a white family dealing with addiction, selling drugs, and neglecting their children might not experience the consequences of jail and removal of the children that occur for many black poorer families.
- Another class participant pointed to an excerpt from *the Color Purple*. "He beat me today cause he say I wink at a boy in church. I may have got somethin in my eye but I didn't wink. I don't even look at mens. That's the truth. I look at women, tho, cause I'm not scared of them ..." (p. 6).

Listening to voices from multicultural literature and to classmates' reflections broadens our understanding and our questions about the complexities in our environments.

CHAPTER SUMMARY

Building foundations to plan and implement services requires more than one theory. One approach is to select three different methods to address needs on the macro, mezzo, and micro levels. Using theories to consider oppressive or discriminatory conditions on any level offers a way to work with citizens to recognize these obstacles and to structure approaches for moving forward regarding other issues and health concerns. Students should be able to link at least two theories to views of oppression and strategies for improvement.

EPAS AND CODE OF ETHICS

CSWE EDUCATIONAL POLICY & ACCREDITATION STANDARDS

Competency 3: Advance Human Rights and Social, Economic, and Environmental Justice

Social workers understand that every person regardless of position in society has fundamental human rights such as freedom, safety, privacy, an adequate standard of living, health care, and education. Social workers

- 3a) apply their understanding of social, economic, and environmental justice to advocate for human rights at the individual and system levels;
- 3b) engage in practices that advance social, economic, and environmental justice. (EPAS, 2015)

NASW CODE OF ETHICS

Ethical Principle: Social workers challenge social injustice.

1.01 Commitment to Clients

Social workers' primary responsibility is to promote the well-being of clients. In general, clients' interests are primary. However, social workers' responsibility to the larger society or specific legal obligations may on limited occasions supersede the loyalty owed clients, and clients should be so advised. (Examples include when a social worker is required by law to report that a client has abused a child or has threatened to harm self or others.) (NASW, n.d.)

EXERCISES

1. Describe a scenario of observed or experienced oppression. Select a theory and explain how it can be applied to interpret the scenario. Discuss the selection and explanation with a peer. With a partner, develop two scenarios in which the theories can be used to improve some facet of service delivery to a specific age group. Use the theory comprehension, theory interpretation, and theory application model for the discussion.

2. Read the 2001 Licia Carlson article found at http://cr.middlebury.edu/amlit_civ/allen/2012%20backup/vsara/licia-carlson.pdf (Carlson, 2001). Consider the possible theoretical explanations that allowed the marginalization of women in early institutions. Select a theory that would eliminate that possibility in the current social environment. Review the theory choices of the class and discuss the interpretations and applications.

3. Consider macro evidence based practice. Locate research on one of these methods that is of interest to you to present in an upcoming class session: legislation-mandated

accountability, managed-care system promoting an efficacious approach, consumer advocacy movements, or legal decisions connected to service outcomes. Facilitate a 15 minute discussion on the content including a summary and issues for classmates to think about.

MULTICULTURAL RESOURCES

Angelou, M. (1978). *Still I Rise*. New York, NY: Random House.

Bascsu, J., Jeffrey, B., Novik, N., Abonyi, S., Osman, S., Johnson, S., & Marti, D. (2014). Policy community & kin: Interventions that support rural healthy aging. *Activities, Adaptation & Aging, 38*, 138–153.

Eggers, D. (2006). *What is the what?* New York, NY: Vintage.

Girma, E., Tesfaye, M., Froeschl, G., Möller-Leimkühler, A. M., Dehning, S., & Müller, N. (2013). Facility based cross-sectional study of self-stigma among people with mental illness: Towards patient empowerment approach. *International Journal of Mental Health Systems, 7*, 21.

Lamar, K. (2015). Alright. M. Kuhle & P. Williams (Producers). *To Pimp a Butterfly* [album].

Sandberg, S. (2013). *Lean in: Women, work and the will to lead*. New York, NY: Alfred A. Knopf.

Slaughter, A. M. (2015). *Unfinished business: Women, men, work, family*. New York, NY: Random House.

FURTHER READING

Ahmed, S. (2012). *On being excluded: Racism & diversity in institutional life*. Durham, NC: Duke University Press.

Dominelli, L. (2003). *Anti-oppressive social work theory and practice*. Basingstoke, United Kingdom: Palgrave Macmillan.

Tester, F. J. (2003). Anti-oppressive theory and practice as the organizing theme for social work education: The case against. *Canadian Social Work Review/Revue canadienne de service social 20* (1), 127–132.

Identity Development in the Context of Oppression

Race, Class, Gender

CHAPTER OVERVIEW

Chapter 6 raises issues to be considered regarding identity. Consumers' identities are multidimensional, connected to abilities, race, ethnicity, class, gender, sexual orientation, and location. Practitioners' identities are also connected to this range of categories. Identity involves perceptions of who one is and opinions regarding group and community membership are linked to several sources. These may include personal observations, behaviors, wishful thinking, notions of place, and ideas about how others see us.

Erikson provided a basic framework for the bio-psycho-social theory of development around 1959. He proposed eight stages of life challenges (1994) that individuals were expected to confront and achieve. Since then, theorists have presented additional influences of context and environment on development over the lifespan to foster the inclusion of social, cultural, spiritual, and economic status and challenges. As social culture changed regarding identity issues, Erikson added essays on race and women. Currently, life cycle components have led theorists and practitioners to move from bicultural and bilingual dimensions to multicultural ones. Persons who have different abilities, persons of color, immigrants, and others labeled in a way that may create stigma or discrimination can have a complex formative period. This natural evolution of awareness is central to expanding an individual's inclusion of people and ideas.

Identity development is influenced by several factors. There are elements of genetics, epigenetics, personality, family dynamics, environment, social and physical network components, talents, abilities, nutrition, role models, supports, and organizational and community agents. Racial socialization research suggests that children who are well supported in families that engage in extensive communication about negative and positive aspects of their environments and who are taught ways to navigate these realities are often protected from the negative impact of discrimination (Barrow, Armstrong, Vargo, & Boothroyd, 2007). Collaborating with clients regarding cultural and racial socialization, identity issues, reading assignments, and community support system participation can promote validation and progress toward goal achievement.

The next section will present identity-related views from across cultural groups. Traditional responses to nonconformists often involve some type of punishment or putdown applied via particular access points. Identity examples within major categories will be presented with a focus on the strengths and obstacles. In acknowledging the strengths of identity, possible pathways that embrace community development and support systems will be mentioned.

Readers should follow identity interest groups and research authors, artists, and musicians to enhance awareness. Resources and opportunities to support actualization paths for individuals, families, and communities can be investigated in local areas.

LEARNING OBJECTIVES

- Race, class, gender, and abilities impact persons' views of their identity.
- Identity is intersectional.
- Appreciating diversity is connected to awareness.

Benchmark: Students will be informed of multicultural resources that assert a range of intersections and perspectives.

> **STUDENT SCENARIO**
>
> Anna and Brian are continuing their dialogue about social work. She asks, "Can anyone be described using only a single identity frame?" Brian, a career changer who is moving from finance to social work, admits that a year ago he could identify as a white man. Now, he is more in touch with his intersectional qualities. What do you think about the question?

IMPACT OF RACISM OR EXCLUSION

Historically, people of color, to a large extent, have been influenced by their access to capital and education. The exclusion from access to opportunities to live and grow with adequate food, shelter, and family protection and relief from structural racism and discrimination is a significant variable to consider in developing strategies to support and strengthen vulnerable communities.

The following concepts should be contemplated in critically thinking about how racism, discrimination, and exclusion affect people.

HISTORICAL TRAUMA

Historical trauma is the cumulative memory of emotional and psychological wounding of an individual or generation caused by a traumatic experience or event. This has been demonstrated in relation to Native genocide, slavery, the Holocaust, and other experiences around the world.

Still grieving the loss of the land. Native Americans have most clearly been hurt and traumatized by the ambush of their homes, takeovers of their land, removal of their children, relegation to reservations, and dishonest treaty arrangements. These issues may be applied in some form to the experiences of many members of traditionally excluded groups. Loss and separation of any sort may influence biology, psychology, economics, and social environmental factors.

Obstruction of freedom, racial socialization, and monoculturalism to Nihilism. Family socialization denotes ways family leaders engage in daily endeavors and how they structure family members' understanding of who they are and how they fit in despite social messages. Feelings about racism may persist over the lifespan, or they may be adjusted as experience and communication dictate.

Adverse experiences without the presence of supportive messages may leave people with absent or limited relationships and reduced strategies for persistence. Interventions that foster awareness, resilience, and continuity promote recovery.

Escape from dictatorship. The range of life circumstances that pushes individuals and families to relocate, immigrate, or run away is diverse. The original colonists were running away from religious persecution and social pressures. Contemporary immigrants are mostly looking for better educational and economic opportunities for their families, and many are seeking refuge from areas of armed conflict.

Stereotypes or Stereotype threats. The prevalence of stereotypes in socialization messages influences persons across groups. It sets up prejudicial ideas that create negative beliefs and biases. Stereotypes may challenge self-worth. Sometimes they create self-doubt or legitimate paranoia. On the other hand, for persons with fortitude and resilience they create a life experience to overcome.

Multiculturalism, biculturalism. The message that all people matter, backed up by mostly positive connections across economic and social lines, is vital to strengths development and self-confidence.

Community development and overcoming obstacles. When persons of traditionally excluded groups participate in associations and organizations that support their needs, the results are usually positive. Mutual aid offers a process and results. Persons need to be willing to become a participant and look forward to benefits of engagement.

The impact of these variables takes shape in various ways over the life cycle. Experiences that mold people—whether distressing or enlightening—are the substance of change. Individual stories told by service users are the ones we must value and include.

IDENTITY

Goffman, in his book *Stigma*, noted that "identity is formed when people assert pride in the thing that made them marginal," (Solomon, 2012, p. 28). Social identity has been considered to be formed by a person's sense of his or her group membership. The field of social identity is enlarged by the perspectives that are tied to context and intersectionality.

The field of identity studies (Wetherill & Mohanty, 2012) has proliferated and emerged through broad contexts of us, them, narratives, emotion, binaries, categories, locations, fluidity, conflicts, and more ways of conceptualizing and knowing. The contributions in their text are interdisciplinary and international. There are theoretical formulations, formative conditions, traditional categories, and contextual dynamics that shape the perspectives that result.

Walters (1999) informs us that native people have survived the negative dominant group messages by internalizing the positive identity knowledge of their culture. She presents the Urban American Indian Identity (UAII) model that could be applied to other groups. The stages involve moving from the influence of negative attitudes to an awakening of the ethnic and non-ethnic world to integrating identity attitudes and adopting healthy psychological buffers. For some, the influence of positive identity may be in place in families as a factor of protection. For others, an intervention that provides positive identity resources may be useful.

IDENTITY MODELS

Identity models have been modified over time to reflect different forms of conceptualizations of appreciating our race, ethnic identity, and comfort or discomfort with our identity. A criticism of Erickson's model initiated in 1959 (McLeod, 2018), which focused on the white, middle-class male environment, was modified in 1974 to include some consideration of children and people of color. Cross's (1978) racial model and Phinney's (1989) ethnic development models have been used to examine and gain understanding (in Robinson, 2012) across diverse backgrounds and for adoption dynamics. The Helms model uses an interpretation that does not incorporate non-Western cultural experience (Cisneros, Stakeman, Joyner, & Schmitz, 2008). Cross (in Constantine, Richardson, Benjamin, & Wilson, 1998) and Sue and Sue (in Constantine et al., 1998) introduced models that brought attention to the range of self-acceptance in communities of color. Some variation of emphasis on color issues seemed to be influenced by gender, class, and education.

Hutchinson (2015) discusses research conducted with children regarding cultural identity that shows there was no substantive exploration of identity for many European Americans. However, for children of color, awareness of bicultural dimensions begins as early as age 3 or 4 and continues through middle childhood. Identity has been categorized by persons often outside of the groups being categorized. McAdoo (in Hutchinson, 2015) points out that children of nondominant groups are more informed of bicultural dynamics. Families that encourage children to explore their heritage and engage in conversations and supportive behaviors regarding identity tend to promote confident and healthy outcomes.

COMPLEXITY OF IDENTITY IS EMBRACED

Models of identity development for indigenous Americans, African Americans, Latinas and Latinos, other Hispanic groups, and Asian-heritage persons embrace the complexity that their identities involve (Cisneros et al., 2008). In fact, our identities are established in various ways, and current research is expanding the questions and approaches to enhancing our understanding of multiple and integrated or intersectional identities. For example, persons from Caribbean islands or other places not represented may use the *Other* box or refuse to check a category. Or consider Daniel Laferriére, a black writer from Montreal who was born in Haiti, presents an interesting interpretation as he contemplates *I Am a Japanese Writer* (2013), while observers see him as a Canadian Haitian.

Understanding who someone is requires listening. Understanding oneself requires seeking information, contemplating and reflecting on one's environment and experiences over time, and resolving issues of family dynamics and conflict. In the words of Buddha, "All we are is the result of what we have thought. ... Therefore the lesson is be careful what you believe for that is what you will become" (Green, 2014, Loc 409). Internal and external messages are gleaned from biology, psychology, environment, social place, culture, economics, and spirituality. So who are you thinking you are?

Identity is connected to an individual's claim on who she or he is. This claim is associated with the family context and/or the absence of family history. Some families have clear communication about paternal and maternal extended family members and their ancestors. Some families may have mixed and/or limited sources of information. Some families have been disconnected from parents, have absent or unknown parents, or have been raised in diverse households and may not really be aware of who their family is. Awareness of family history can be tied to the extent of family nurturing and communication. Family identify is often complex and sometimes very complicated. Figure 6.1 offers a starting point for reflecting on identity.

IDENTITY FORMATION AND DEVELOPMENT

Identity formation and development research suggests that racial and ethnic identity begins to occur around age 3. The connection of self-esteem to the selection of black or white dolls in young children of color has received much attention based on the findings that the children "preferred and identified" with the white dolls (Hutchinson, 2015, p. 155.) However, in a subsequent test when children were not asked to make a preference, they showed interest in Asian, black, and white images. It could be speculated that the selection of the white dolls in the past was related to the absence of dolls of color in the marketplace and children's increased familiarity with white dolls. Notwithstanding the research in this area, identity development and self-concept are not so simply explained.

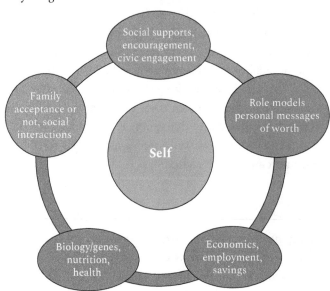

FIGURE 6.1   Influences on Identity Development

The impact of economics, biology, psychology, and social experiences influence child development, and the quality of family stability and communication assist the progression of identity formation. Adolescence is observed as a critical phase in reconciling and maximizing identity. Parental and community supports, as well as environmental and social climate conditions may support or hinder identity strengths and clarification.

CLASS

Identity related to class is generally derived from the family situation one is born into but may change over the life cycle. The terms used to describe persons who have access to a minimum number of dollars to live on usually include *poor, impoverished, disadvantaged, underclass,* and *undeserving.* Atwood puts it bluntly: "Inequality is the product of social class differences" (2014, p. 484). Social mobility is connected to the ability to achieve in educational institutions and gain employment. The class structure is reproduced through the educational systems (Crettaz & Jacot, 2014; MacLeod, 2009), with some variations across countries. Schools in hypersegregated communities with meager resources are likely to have overall performance rates that need improvement.

The identity taken on by students in schools may be shaped by the strength and leadership of the schools and the protective factors of the families and the communities. Some may take on low academic performance and some will not. Some will benefit from families that cultivate academic and social performance. Lareau (2011) suggests that middle-class families have time and resources to engage their children in the process of "concerted cultivation," and working class families rely on accomplishment of natural growth. It's not that simple. Many working families are able to encourage and support their children and youth. Watch the sitcom *Everybody Hates Chris* (Rock & LeRoi, 2005) for an example!

EMPLOYMENT RESOURCES

Over the past 20 years, the number of persons with very low incomes has swelled from about 475,000 to 1.6 million (Edin & Shaefer, 2016). The widened gap between rich and poor has always existed but has recently garnered more attention. The inequality of lower-class status affects adults and their children. The label of *working class* now describes more people who were expecting to be *middle class.* With the loss of thousands of manufacturing jobs to other countries and the scandals of banks and financial companies jeopardizing workers' pensions, opportunities for Americans to earn incomes to make them socially mobile have dwindled.

Chronic unemployment in many communities is not a new problem. The crisis of joblessness is connected to violence, despondency, and health problems (Editorial Board, 2016). This state of being can be associated to West's concept of nihilism (1996) and Anderson's *Code of the Street* (1999). It is associated with a social identity that is minimized in light of the environment. MacLeod (2009) observed young boys in a housing project and concluded that their optimism and pessimism stem in part from their perceptions of American society, their potential roles related to employment, and their future ability to move beyond the barriers of social mobility.

Macleod's work with the Hall Hangers and the Brothers offers a view of working-class youth's expectations and can be compared to Hostetter, Sullenberger, and Wood's (2015) study. Their work showed adolescents as more aware of the structural barriers that impact family economics. Adolescent awareness of the influence of structural barriers to social mobility urge improving paths to prospects for work (Atwood, 2014).

When opportunities for employment are absent, street hustlers offer options to provide income for family needs. Identity becomes associated with whatever income-producing activity one can get into. For young boys and men, this may be theft or the drug trade. For females, this may be prostitution work. Understanding the context of identity and the requirements associated with gaining employment puts another face on the dimensions of service strategies that might be needed.

ECONOMIC IDENTITY

Identity related to economics may be connected to different types of literature that speak to intersections of identity. The identity connected to economic resources is essentially tied to employment or unemployment. This establishes the basis of insecurity that may lead individuals and families to services. Not only are these systemic issues connected to the constrained opportunities of marginalized groups, but they appear to be connected to recent statistics of increased health problems, drug use, and suicides among middle-aged white persons. The context of oppression across groups has resulted in what Smiley and West call *The Rich and the Rest of Us* (2013).

While the emphasis on excluded groups has focused on people of color, when social dynamics are examined with respect to economics, low-income and working-class white people are also marginalized. Although rates of children of color living in families with low incomes are disproportionately higher, the *number* of white children in poverty is higher (NCCP, 2016).

The history of class in the United States describes low-income white people as the "original underclass" (Macgillis & Propublica, 2016). The impact of lost jobs and low optimism (Graham, 2017) is exhibited in fewer opportunities for mobility (Putnam, 2015) and increased use of substances and early mortality (Kolata & Cohen, 2016). Vance (2016), in *Hillbilly Elegy*, offers a cultural perspective on what the social environment he grew up in looked like and how the strengths perspective helped him overcome economic constraints.

The increased number of persons living with low-wage incomes is connected to the increased numbers who rely on organizations for food and other basic needs (Smiley & West, 2013).

IDENTITY INTERSECTIONS

When we consider economic identity as a baseline, other identities may take on other relevance. Social construction has highlighted color, other visible characteristics, and an idealized version of family to prejudge. Media presentations of family have emphasized a stable two-parent-led household (Robbins, 2017). This view accounts for fewer than one fifth of American homes. Acknowledging the broad range of family constellations and the strength and support of the diverse identities they have is a critical point of observation. Broadening the analysis to incorporate ways people are similar regardless of household composition and group descriptors could lead policy development to provide options that support everyone.

PEOPLE OF COLOR

Visual and literary images of people of color are innumerable. Every group has some spiritual tradition that is likely to assist in gaining their sense of worth and value. It is their choice to disclose or discuss this in a public agency setting. Professionals are working on ways to respect this dimension. Earth, Wind & Fire (Dunn, White, & Bailey, 1975) made this point in the their hit song "Shining Star": "You're a shining star, no matter who you are." This message is a good one for young children.

NATIVE AMERICAN HERITAGE

Sherman Alexie's *The Absolutely True Diary of a Part-Time Indian* (2007) introduces readers to a young person's awareness of the absence of people that look like him in the socialization process. Alexie has written several novels that speak to the impact of historical trauma and the intersection of those feelings and current ones regarding self and others in contemporary environments. *War Dances* (Alexie, 2009), a book of short stories, raises questions and contemplates the issues of mortality along with the conflict between self-preservation and external responsibilities in art, family, and society.

Covarrubias, Hermann, and Fryberg (2016) remind us of the importance of relevant role representations and the absence of them in social environments for Native Americans and Latinos. This applies across groups and is a starting point to discuss the need for positive group examples of underrepresented racial-ethnic minority youth and adults.

In *The Soul of the Indian*, Eastman (2014), of the Ohiyesa tribe, shares his memories of the qualities of tribal life. The respect of elders and the customs that supported family interactions allowed a peaceful intimacy for tent life. The unity of family and the sanctity of daily life were revered until the advent of subjection, starvation, and imprisonment from 1780 through 1914 (Porter, 1997).

AFRICAN AND CARIBBEAN HERITAGE

Scenes and narratives of the social environment have been captured by the artists and writers of the communities of African and Caribbean descent. Allan Rohan Crite, an African American artist, chronicled the social life of people of color in Boston's South End (Crite, 2015). *School's Out* in a painting of a busy community of parents and children.

Andrew Young's *A Way Out of No Way* (1994) informs us that he started out living his life the way his parents wanted him to live it. His parents, a religious dentist and a superintendent of Sunday school, and a school teacher, wanted good things for their son. He shares the steps he took to come into his own identity. His developmental process shows readers his family supports and strengths, as well as the community connections that led him on a spiritual journey and to work he found purposeful.

A Way Out of No Way is also the title that Jacqueline Woodson (1996) uses for her compilation of literary works to illustrate reactions and paths other black people have taken. From the novel *The Friends* by Rosa Guy (1995), we feel the pain that young people may feel in a classroom and on the street. Poetry selections—for example, "Latin" by Tim Seibles and "Big Bowls of Cereal" by Paul Beatty—open our ears to more life, living, and growing up (Woodson, 1996). "Latin" gives us words for particular things ... Honeysuckle, cicadas, wave; language and meanings. Beatty's bowl of cereal is full of adolescent meanderings of a genius boy at the corner arcade who wants to be Ellison's invisible man, and on some days needs to be excused from the atomic table!

Literature selections help us connect to the day to day as well as specific circumstances that have influenced writers. Woodson's choice of Toni Cade Bambara's "Gorilla, My Love" is a child's reflection of being in the navigator's seat with her grandfather.

Bambara's (1995) "The Golden Bandit" and its dual meaning is certainly worth exploring. It is another take on childhood stories and their reflection in an adult world—Goldilocks was a vandal!

Others' stories help us empathize with and understand people around the world as they struggle. Adiele and Frosch's 2007 book, *Coming of Age Around the World: Multicultural Anthology* illustrates the many experiences of biracial, multicultural folks in their families and communities as they grow older, help one another, and recognize the impact of biology, nutrition, and life on their appearances and health.

Adiele's life was chronicled in a PBS documentary *My Journey Home* (Tajima-Peña, & Portillo, 2004), as she described her lived experience as the only black member of a Nordic family. Her conceptualization of her development is connected to the men in her family and the absence of her Nigerian father, whom she goes to find. Her ability to connect the life of an uncle who suffered physical disfigurement to her identity as a black woman is interesting.

Those of African Caribbean descent present another dimension of identity that is often overlooked despite very clear variations. Sidney Poitier, a Haitian-born, American actor, describes the impact of his life and environment on the man he became. His autobiography, *The Measure of a Man: A Spiritual Autobiography* (2007) includes this: "As I've mentioned, a large part of my father's legacy is the lesson he taught his sons. He brought us together and said, 'The measure of a man is how well he provides for his children" (azquotes.com, para 1).

Biracial authors who express the trajectory of their lives were influenced in several ways. Mosley's *Fortunate Son* (2006) offers the example of two boys raised in a wealthy home until their mother dies. One reaps the benefits of a white father, and the other struggles because of his dismissal into a foster care life that leads nowhere. McBride's *The Color of Water* (1995) provides another version of struggle and accomplishment in a story about his Jewish mother surviving their social environment while married to a black man.

ASIAN HERITAGE

Asian American descendants include roots from China, Japan, Korea, the Philippines, India, Vietnam, Laos, and Cambodia. Takaki (1989) describes these immigrants as coming from a different shore than the European immigrants. They brought Asian history and a different visible appearance. They came to work as plantation workers, railroad crews, factory persons, cannery workers, and farm labor. Not only were they paid less than white workers, but Asian men who came to the United States to work on the railroads could not bring their wives or families with them. Women dealt with gender and class biases in a sharp patriarchal environment. Women of all classes were considered inferior to men and responsible for family and domestic needs—their bound feet served to keep them in their place.

Snow Flower and the Secret Fan (See, 2005) discusses the foot-binding process and related family and emotional context. The strength of friendship and context of female transmission of tasks among friends and relatives is laid out with cultural details. Amy Tan's *The Kitchen God's Wife* (1991) is among her novels that reveal the nuanced relationships of women and the impact of family history and marriage on older and newer generations of women who are adjusting to their lives in another culture and in subcultural communities.

Literature by Vietnamese writers shares portraits of women and the impact on lives under cruel and unjust leaders. The story of Kieu (Du, 1987) is one that demonstrates the force of family loyalty over individual love. With an emphasis on morality, there are vestiges of astrology, metempsychosis, and fortitude. Political allegiance, resistance to oppression, and personal relationships are revered by many readers of Du's work.

Within a different context, Yu Hua, a young boy in China, comes of age experiencing traumatic events and working to resolve his existence. Ha is now a noted Chinese novelist. This piece, *On the Road at 18* (in Adiele & Frosch, 2007) is about self-discovery.

Family heritage is interesting. Blending families and adoption may create complexity.

Transracial adoption can be controversial. Identity development among adoptees presents challenges for the youngsters who are adopted and for professionals assisting them and their families. Some studies note lack of identity, identity with an adoptive parent's identity, and some claim shame, stigma, and embarrassment of their cultural origins (Robinson, 2012).

Finding their identity is extremely important to 300 to 500 adoptees who have moved to South Korea—primarily from the United States but also from France, Denmark, and other nations (Jones, 2015). They recognize the stigma and pressure against single mothers in Korea that pushed them to place their babies for adoption. The activists in Adoptee Solidarity Korea, ASK, are pushing for legislation to help Korean families remain intact because they feel international adoption (and the removal of a child from his or her natural kinship networks) is cruel. Perhaps the Korean value of filial devotion, described in the folktales of *Chung Hyo Ye* (Diamond Sutra Recitation Group, 2007), reveals the history that speaks to adoptees who want to return.

HISPANIC AND LATINA/O HERITAGE

Narratives of the experiences of young people moving from their home to a new place often emphasize the loss of connections to grandparents and extended families and the customs they enjoyed. *How the Garcia Girls Lost Their Accents* (Alvarez, 2010) describes the lives of four sisters who moved to New York from the Dominican Republic when their father was suspected of antigovernment activity. Their wealthy lifestyle was replaced by more modest accommodations. The adjustments of the siblings and the parents varied in response to their relationships with one another and to the people they encountered in school and in their community. For two of the sisters, the stressors eventually were so overwhelming that they required mental health interventions. Incidents of discrimination, sexual harassment, identity questioning and validation, and marriage and family pressures were evident as they assumed places in the American environment.

The class perspective is noted in cases of immigration across groups. It costs to move from one location to another. For some who can afford it, there is the expectation of attaining equitable employment. This is achieved by some, but when it doesn't occur quickly, it may be difficult to fit in with lower-class Hispanic citizens (Arfelis, 1997).

Anaya is a Mexican American author whose coming-of-age story, *Bless Me Ultima* (1972), shares his connection to the midwife who delivered him and her presence as a *curandero*, a healer. As a 7-year-old, his story begins and moves through his observations of life and death, the influence of the Catholic faith, and issues of sin and faith. *Tortuga* (2004) finds him at age 15 in a hospital for medical care due to paralysis and weaves in the mystical presence of a mountain situated next to the hospital. The lives of the local children—with various tragic conditions—are interwoven in the work.

Justice Sotomayor's story, *My Beloved World* (2014), presents her life and achievements and presents her as a role model. Her story reveals hard work, taking care of health issues, and understanding family growth and transitions.

Prospero's Mirror: A Translator's Portfolio of Latin American Short Fiction (Stavans, 1998) is a compilation of seasoned and then-emerging writers. The Spanish and English translations expose readers to the language as well as the story. "Tres Tiros Na Tarde" is a hard-to-believe tale of a domestic situation gone awry. Questions about identity, rage, and selfishness can be posed for discussion with students about family dynamics.

Among the population of Hispanics and Latino/as is an Afro-Latino component. According to the Pew Research Center (Lopez & Gonzalez-Barrera, 2016), about 25% of U.S. Latinos identify as Afro-Latino, Afro-Caribbean, or of African descent with Latin American roots.

INTERSECTIONALITY

Using abilities as the foundation of identity for our work as helping professionals, adding each additional label, identity, or membership category expands the intersectionality. Intersectional identities may apply to basics: age, race-ethnicity, gender, and gender expression. These will be impacted by income levels, education, geographic location, neighborhood, language, and employment. Further identity details may be associated with health status, whether there has been some assault or adverse experience in their history, and survival. There are other variables that may be connected to the intersection of identities that may influence the context of one's environment.

Marsiglia and Kulis (2015) suggest that the basic theory of intersectionality would include white women in the gender category. As the term intersectionality evolves, it claims more association with black women and the multiple burdens linked to their identity (Bartlett, 2017).

Intersectional dynamics move beyond the binary approaches of race, ethnicity, and gender. The intersectional nature of identity has always existed but was not addressed in formal, empirical, academic research. The range of fluidity and identity complexity is what tends to come across in conversation and in literature. Contemporary emphasis on individualism and collectives, consumer lifestyle, new media, politics, and workplace and social place elements adds more to the identity mix. The content of Wetherill and Mohanty's (2010) work illuminates these vast areas of consideration about one's personhood. Intersectional, hybrid, and global identities describe the ever-broadening complicated versions of a person's identity and place.

An inclusive frame would not assume any one identity is more relevant than another. Workers have the responsibility to evaluate their identities and sense of validation. Establishing relationships, listening, and assessing service users' interest in working on identity issues and validation may also be a part of planning and goal setting on the micro level. On the mezzo or macro level, there may be other conceptualizations that a social worker might consider to enhance understanding. How the dynamics of intersectionality play out with respect to citizenship may present more than simple considerations. Developing confidence at the micro level builds support for civic participation and advocacy on the macro level.

Parisi (2015) speaks to migration politics and examines the matrix for exclusion and the naturalization system as a process of control. On the other side, "mixed couples and their intimate lives define resistance against bio-political power to control people" (p. 739). The role of intersectionality and created power impacts development work. The simple use of categorizations may be more complicated in remote villages where categories may be more complex within boundaries. People may differentiate themselves with more complexity within a binary category used by workers. Inquiring about identities may reveal how identities are silenced or obscured in ways that will affect how various stages of projects can go forward or not (Grünenfelder & Schurr, 2015).

Further investigations of intersections find the prevalence of nondominant group characteristics to be related to peer victimization, especially when disability is one of the intersecting variables (McGee, 2014). Preventing the abuse of persons connected to identity is of particular concern to helping professionals and community members in improving the social environments in which we live.

COMMUNITY DEVELOPMENT: USING MULTICULTURAL RESOURCES

Advancing the location and inclusion of human behavior knowledge involves increasing readers' access to information from writers and agents of various cultural groups. The focus is to use affirming information and share it in educational and socialization processes and in care pathways. Role representation is significant in motivating participation in social structures across the environment. People want to see themselves in what they learn and where they work.

The multicultural resources database (O'Neal, 2012) includes a wide variety of literature written by people of diverse backgrounds. The goal is to share titles and encourage readers to select some, research more, and refer others to develop their own reading lists. Selections referred to over the course of this text represent a minute sample of writers and artists. Use it to become more familiar with ideas and beliefs of people who may experience the world differently from you. Use it to assist identity development and become informed of positive identity constructions that show tribulation and demonstrate that all paths require perseverance.

CULTURAL CONTEXTUAL INFORMATION

Gathering information from multicultural sources expands community and cultural contextual information. Listening to consumers and their stories will help us understand who and how they see themselves. Reactions to some consumers may involve some bias, judgment, and expectation that are connected to generalizations from traditional socializations. As key players in assessing families and children, acknowledging the range of realities and strengths as well as risk requires social workers to use their power in relevant ways. Identifying children at risk is an issue in identity development and validation. Roets and associates (2015) warn that institutional practices may operate as "an ambiguous social construction" (p. 199) that is used at the expense of parents and often results in the use of more surveillance. The institutional focus on deaths of children under social work supervision in European countries, the United Kingdom, and the United States begs for improved assessment, documentation, and protection.

Literature, film, music, and art offer perspectives, dreams, nightmares, and illustrations of life across the contextual landscape. Examples from these resources can be used to increase our perspectives, raise questions, share reflection, and design approaches to incorporate these dynamics into our work. One way of focusing a search for materials that may be helpful to you and your clients is to explore some of these intersections.

Choose an intersectional identity and research resources that offer perspectives you may not be familiar with. Consider some of the examples posted in Table 6.1.

TABLE 6.1   Selecting Multicultural Resources in Identity Categories

IDENTITY AREAS	INDIVIDUAL	FAMILY	COMMUNITY/COUNTRY
ABILITY	*Seventy two Hour Hold,* by Bebe Moore Campbell	*Far From the Tree* by Andrew Solomon	*American Deaf Culture (1989)* by Sherman Wilcox, Editor
CULTURAL GROUP, HERITAGE	*Paradise of the Blind (2002)* by Duong Thu Huong	*Bird of Paradise: How I became Latina,* by Raquel Cepeda	*Hullabaloo in the Guava Orchard* by Kiran Desai
GENDER, SEXUAL ORIENTATION	*The Caged Virgin An Emancipation Proclamation for Women and Islam* by Hirsi Ayaan Ali	*The Blind Owl (1990)* by Sadegh Hedayat *Murder in the Name of Honor (2009)* by Rana Husseini	*Last Exit to Brooklyn (1957)* by Hubert Shelby

IDENTITY AREAS	INDIVIDUAL	FAMILY	COMMUNITY/COUNTRY
IMMIGRATION	*Iran Awakening* by Shirin Ebadi	*House of sand and fog* by Andre Dubus III	*The Cellist of Sarajevo* (2008) by Steven Galloway
CLASS	*House of Spirits* (2015) by Isabel Allende	*Modern Korean Fiction: An Anthology* by Bruce Fulton and Youngim Kwan	*Mark my words: Native women mapping our nations* by Mishuana Goerman

ABILITIES

There are many examples of persons with different abilities. Are we exposed to visual images that positively represent them? The television program "NCIS: New Orleans" (CBS TV Series, 2014) includes a cast member who is in a wheelchair. C.B. Strike, a series on Ciemax, includes a vetran that has become a P.I. and has a prothestic leg (Photo 6.1).

PHOTO 6.1

The prejudice of exclusion regarding abilities is broad. Rauscher and McClintock (1996) define *ableism* as

> a pervasive system of discrimination and exclusion that oppresses people who have mental, emotional and physical disabilities. ... deeply rooted beliefs about health, productivity, beauty and the value of human life, perpetuated by the public and private media, combines to create an environment that is often hostile to those whose physical, mental cognitive, and sensory abilities ... fall out of the scope of what is currently defined as socially acceptable. (p. 198)

Solomon, in *Far From the Tree: Parents, Children and the Search for Identity* (2012), uncovers family views of children who arrive and mature through realities different from parental expectations. He begins by focusing on differentiating the reality of reproduction. A newborn entity may share some traits with the parents but may also have traits very unlike those of the parents. As he analyzes the connections between what is usually described as "illness" or "conditions," he points out the parents' tendency to torment the child to be someone he or she is not. The ability of a parent to respond to their child in the earliest interactions with warmth and support, regardless of their special characteristics will aid how the child feels welcome and gains self-esteem. When the family is unable to support a child's immediate or emerging identity, emotional distress and anguish may exist until he or she finds acceptance within a subculture or until the family, through love and encouragement, becomes able to support and accommodate the child's identity.

The obstacles for people who use wheelchairs are described in the essay "Public Transit" by John Hockenberry (2011). Descriptions of irregular sidewalks, noncaring pedestrians (with one exception), and the train system's overall inaccessibility were clear. Transportation policy should include more attention to non-ambulatory citizens.

As helping professionals, the ableism view brings attention to what has been perceived as disability. The labels service users receive upon visiting "helping agencies" may set them up for another level of exclusion. Corrigan (2007) discusses the diagnosis as a stereotype that sets up stigma and discrimination. Once labeled, citizens may be perceived in ways that obstruct work, housing, or other life opportunities. So many people who could benefit from some type of emotional health services may refuse to seek help or will terminate early, in order to avoid being labeled with Diagnostic Statistical Manual (DSM) language, i.e depressed, bipolar, paranoid.

The presence or development of an illness or a variation of ability can lead to job loss and reduced earnings, so concerns for economic rights has led to advocacy to remove barriers to employment, education, and accessibility (Vallas, Fremstad, & Ekman, 2015). The impact of oppression through labeling requires increased emphasis on strengthening laws against discrimination in hiring, pay, and promotion (Davis & Gould, 2015).

Since the deinstitutionalization movement occurred in the 1960s in the United States, Canada, and countries across Europe, community-based services have emerged but with minimal success for serving persons with co-occurring mental illness and developmental disabilities (Kreitzer, McLaughlin, Elliott, & Nicholas, 2016). There are rights based approaches for mental health and disabilities based on nondiscrimination (Androff, 2016). Advocacy groups are needed that have persons with mental stressors in leadership roles who can represent persons living in rural or remote areas as well as those in urban areas. Anderson and Gittler (2005) report similar concerns for adults and especially for rural adolescents. Almost 64% of the adolescent population do not receive mental health and substance-use treatment, mainly because of how clients and families feel about the services the related stigma, in addition to issues regarding the finance, organization, and delivery of the process.

Critical disability theory proposes disability to be socially constructed; persons with a disability fall on a continuum of human variation. They have a right to self-determination, and their voices express their uniqueness (Rocco & Delgado, 2011). Disability rights legislation has made strides. In 2014, the Workforce Innovation and Opportunity Act (WIOA) and the Achieving a Better Life Experience (ABLE) bill joined the 1990 Americans With Disabilities Act (ADA) and the Individuals With Disabilities Education Act (IDEA) to support antidiscrimination, access to education, improved work opportunities, and the ability to have savings accounts (Vallas et al., 2015).

Wearing (2011) recognizes the marginalizing intersections of gender, racial, and disability identities. A focus on citizenship should frame the approach that "listens and responds to young people in research and practice" (p. 534). Social workers can share information with service user groups about rights and survivor group movements, peer support, and potential reforms that lead to reduced discrimination (Androff, 2016).

DEAF CULTURE

Citizens who are members of the Deaf community have a rich heritage in American Sign Language (ASL) and their unique patterns of cultural transmission. Solomon (2012) introduces his discussion of this community with a report of the protests against hiring a hearing CEO for the Lexington Center for the Deaf in Queens, New York, in April 1994. According to one of the student protestors, "a Deaf person's school is a primary model of self-identification" (p. 50).

The capitalized *Deaf* refers to the culture, while *deaf* is considered a pathological term (Solomon, 2012) and also refers to the audiological condition (Padden & Humphries, 1988). Until *Sign Language Structure* (Stokoe, 1960/2005) was published and described the grammar and logic of the signing system, hearing persons would push to have Deaf persons learn to speak rather than sign because they thought it would impede their language skills.

Examples of family life with deaf members described the harsh economic conditions and discriminatory feelings and behaviors of relatives. On the other hand, "members of the Deaf culture have their membership in a beautiful culture" (Solomon, 2012, p. 100). As in all cultural groups, there are persons who are extraordinary and who find their purpose in various careers and leadership opportunities (Nomeland & Nomeland, 2012). Deaf people are Deaf and deaf (Padden & Humphries, 1988). This sets up the dual perspective of their community membership. The triple dimension is represented by their geographical, historical, or political situations.

The identity claims by deaf or hard-of-hearing person may be responses to critiques by others as determined by their abilities to hear or be like hearing people and to be associated with members of the establishment (Padden & Humphries, 1988). It is somewhat interesting that there are several examples of prison guards moving into jobs as resident counselors in the dormitories. Their behavior with the children showed they sometimes assumed the children were like the prisoners—bad, mean, insane. However, with time and observation, the children were known to be kind, organized, and intelligent and the staff stopped using harsh treatment.

Members of the Deaf community resist the negative messages of hearers. They may derive power in their ability to separate themselves from others or to navigate the world in their own way (Benedict, n.d.; Wilcox, 1989). Stories in *Deaf Community News* (deafnewstoday.com) offer many perspectives of their experiences.

Socialization of members of the Deaf community occurs in classrooms, in dormitories of residential schools, and through their communities. Their intersection as members of African American, Hispanic or Latino, Asian American, Native American, Scandinavian, French, and German identities are embraced. It is important for schools to also recognize this diversity and incorporate multicultural education into the curricula (Nomeland & Nomeland, 2012).

Uniquely Human: A Different Way of Seeing Autism (Priznat, 2015) is another example of the strengths perspective and a view that accepts the voices of persons with their own sets of abilities, perhaps different from traditional notions but still valued.

NEURODIVERSITY

Neurodiversity is an emergent term that embraces the forms along the autism spectrum as identities, even when classified as a disability (Solomon, 2012). Some parents are frustrated by their child's adversity. Others are able to see their children in a positive light. *Neurotribes* (Silberman, 2015) recognizes the presence of neurodiversity. This approach urges respect and support in educational institutions and workplaces for the range of ways of thinking and being.

The autism spectrum disorder is an array of complex brain development disorders with subtle differences in symptoms and characteristics (NIMH.com, 2015). *Learning disabilities* is a term that refers to an array of areas in which a developing child may have difficulties with skills regarding reading, writing, and listening (helpguide.org, 2017). Temple Grandin, a woman with autism, raised awareness in her autobiography *Emergence* (1984).

The realities of a person with diverse abilities are a foundation concept for appreciating diversity and inclusion. Reaching out and addressing the need requires evaluating how *mental health* is defined (Fuller et al., 2000) for the people we want to assist. Those who we know are struggling with distress but do not come to our agencies require more welcoming strategies.

A 2015 reality television series, "Born this Way" about young people with Downs Syndrome won a Critics' Choice Award (Heasley, 2018). It also received Television Academy Honors, which highlights programs that "tackle complex issues and advance social change." (para 5) This program will enter its fourth season and shows that media messages are changing. Including real life portrayals rather than ignoring diverse people or using images that elicit pity should result in more helpful behaviors (Kamenetsky et al., 2016). Enhancing our understanding of lives ameliorates our abilities to reach out, to sit with, and learn about others.

DIAGNOSES

The diagnostic process is connected to the medical prototypes of classification and organization and is expected to offer a basis for developing treatment plans, being paid for services, and for steps to recovery. However, these steps are not infallible and in several ways obstruct individual and family connections and adherence to service recommendations. Daniel (2004) notes that labeling has a lot to do with attitudes and biases about mental illnesses not only among the media and the public but also among service providers.

The World Health Organization estimates about 20% of the world's general population suffers from some mental disorder. Especially in remote and rural areas, many people (both homeless or in homes who are not supervised or treated) may come into contact with police or family service workers, so these front-line personnel must make decisions about how to handle persons who may be demonstrating unusual behaviors. Although interventions may be determined after spending time gaining information about the person's life context and interrelationships, this may not be so forthcoming in crisis situations. Often, workers' responses may be tied to stereotypes that anticipate unchangeable behaviors rather than episodes that can be recovered from.

Mason and associates (2010) concur that attribution and labeling theories tend to be the basis for prejudgments regarding mental health and personality disorders. The manner in which staff intervenes may be tied to ways the consumer establishes trust or mistrust, as well as to levels of staff support and training to increase skills, confidence, and competence to work with particular diagnoses.

It is necessary to look at the diagnoses from another perspective. Longden (2013) presents a TED Talk that sheds a truly strengths-based consumer view. Acknowledging and supporting the support networks is an area that has not been well developed. Helping professionals also may initiate, modify, or shrink from relationship building with clients according to feelings, reactions, or experiences with persons we may categorize in various ways. New perspectives may help improve the appreciation of diversity.

Rocco and Delgado (2011) demonstrate the lack of attention to disability by showing the limited topics that have been addressed within disability from 1984 to 2010 and posing concerns about critical areas that have been ignored or suppressed. Their book contains perspectives that are exciting to consider.

IMPLICATIONS FOR CHILDREN

Social issues related to diagnosis do involve misdiagnosis, misapplied diagnosis, discrimination, and contested diagnosis (Jutel & Dew, 20014). Ruscio (2004) argues that despite the considered effect of stigmatization, diagnoses are relevant and suggests formulating other methods to combat stigma. The arguments that resist the validity of stigmatization appear to minimize the emotional context in which labels are received.

Early labeling is perceived as onerous for children but simultaneously early intervention can lead to better outcomes. There may indeed be some problem with attachment in the family. But the institutional means of dealing with it primed children for further problems. Noting that clinical work must involve classification, developing alternative strategies to enhance compassionate communication with parents and the community on the potential for care is recommended.

People with learning disabilities are especially vulnerable to negative perceptions. Adolescents with a learning disability and psychiatric illness (Barlow, 2001; Howland & Gibavic, 2010) get multiple diagnostic labels, and the impact on the child and the family is enormous. Abrams (2001) proposes examining the social context effects for norms that shape acceptable and nonacceptable expressions of distress and the presence of internalization. Her research acknowledges the social context as an important dimension to conceptualizing social work practice interventions.

The tendency to "genderize" disability is another concern. O'Toole (2004) points to the stereotype in the United States and the United Kingdom that has emphasized the disability movement related to white men in wheelchairs. There has been some move from accommodating structural access from men to white women in the workplace. She brought attention to the minimal inclusion of the diverse perspectives among academics in the disability field. Audre Lorde's legacy highlights the relevance of intersecting identities—"African American lesbian, mother, writer, cancer survivor or victim", (p. 296) and the responsibility for addressing this limitation.

The intersection of emotional distress, mental illness, disability, race, and gender faces several obstacles to constructing useful dialogues across disciplines and stakeholders. There are several authors who push the need to broaden the parameters of discourse. Jarman (2011) raises the resistance to traditional psychiatric models to consider and incorporate alternatives to their rigid and narrow interpretations of healthy assertiveness. She uses Campbell's final novel, *72-Hour Hold* (2005) to critique the institutional and social implications of helping an adult child navigate a bipolar world.

Hall (2002) uses *A Quiet Storm* to present a view of the religious connection to hiding manic depression as a family secret and obstructing care by professionals. Simon (2011) shares the impact of institutional barriers to love and family in *The Story of Beautiful Girl*.

Solomon's (2012) treatise on identity, *Far From the Tree: Parents, Children and the Search for Identity*, recognizes the paths of devastation of social labels. An area that he shows needs more attention is the social scene after the schooling experience. "You can't learn how to be in human society if you are separated from it" (p. 217). Peers teach one another in ways that teachers cannot. Educational inclusion acknowledges the multiple layers of socialization and engagement.

SOCIAL PARTICIPATION

Chang and colleagues (2016) address the marginalization of persons with serious mental illness. The value of social participation has been recognized more widely and areas of research identified that are needed related to variations of participation, age, diagnosis, social groupings, geographic locations, and so on. Their research sample validated an instrument to measure levels of participation in Philadelphia, but its use in more remote areas needs more exploration.

Howarth and colleagues (2014) promote social participation among persons with learning disabilities. Their review of social care interventions explores this issue with respect to isolation within social networks and presents several limitations within the existing studies, including quality and bias. The discussion offers approaches that capture the effects from the service user and provider points of view, as well as the need for reliable quantitative methodology. Effective interventions include person-centered planning, alternative activity patterns, semistructured group sessions, and supported-learning programs, with learning objectives and social skills.

IMMIGRATION AND REFUGEES

The stories of immigrants and refugees often follow families' efforts to escape from tyranny, war, famine, lack of educational or economic opportunities, or other situations that obstruct people from living lives that allow freedom and development. Linking their identity to where people have come from and where their dreams take them requires navigating rough terrain, such as complex immigration or adoptions; it might also vary by gender, class, and age.

Nesteruk and associates (2015) explore ethnic identity development among young adults of immigrant families. About 25% of children live in immigrant families across the United States, but some states have higher percentages (Kids Count, n.d.). Overall, immigrants account for about 13% of the U.S. population. Nesteruk et al. refer to Pinkney's three-stage ethnic identity-formation process, which includes ancestry knowledge. They point out the differences for immigrants of white ancestry and those of color. The lives of those of color will be impacted by how their minority group is perceived in the environment in which they are settling.

The Cellist of Sarajevo (Galloway, 2008) describes a harsh daily life as people of Sarajevo risk their lives to line up for resources and search for ways to meet daily needs. The impact of these conditions and the transition to new places to live when that happens have profound effects on the children.

The past experiences of immigrants are filled with issues that involve coping, adjustment, and adaptation (Chang-Muy & Congress, 2009). Elements to explore in assessing their journey will include the process of immigration as well as social power and its changes.

GENDER ROLES

Gender identify roles go beyond binary concepts. The expression of roles of females, males, lesbian, gay, bisexual, and transgender people demonstrate various ways of establishing households and caretaking responsibilities. Young people have been generally socialized to expect they will grow up, find a mate, and raise a family. Gender identity begins in early childhood as the internalized understanding of one's gender (Hutchinson, 2015). Gender roles associated with male and female have been connected to resource provider for the male and nurturer and child caretaker for the female.

From 1940 to 2016, 8 times more women have attained a college degree (The Statistics portal, 2018), and as more women have entered the professional workforce, tensions have risen regarding these roles. Women working full-time are challenged to manage their work, children, and household maintenance. Some men are willing to share in the household and caretaking duties, yet many resist this because of their identity expectations. Some women have fewer children or take jobs with fewer hours to accommodate the family needs (LePoire, 2006). However, many work full-time and adapt routines as needs require.

Relationships are impacted by the demands of developing a family. Campbell (2000) described some of the challenges of the dual-career marriage. In some cases, even before children entered the picture, couples were undergoing anger and withdrawal as the partners worked on their individual identities in contexts regarding the independence of the woman— they were experiencing role strain. New parents and step-parents may experience that same strain as they move into new roles.

Campbell addressed these tensions in *Successful Women, Angry Men* (2000) through surveys of dual-career couples. Coping with and reducing interpersonal threats were significant issues in handling housework, child care, and finances. These issues have continued, especially as men and women are marrying more as equals rather than women marrying up into higher income brackets (Miller & Bui, 2016). The contemporary views of marriage suggest some changes have occurred but still involve the basic issues. Miller and Bui suggest that people are marrying later and more for companionship, so they seek persons similar to themselves and therefore within similar economic brackets.

Brooks (2016) agrees that marriage quality has improved but believes the average marriage is weaker. Using three lenses to evaluate this, he lists the psychological lens, the romantic lens, and the moral lens. With a 45% divorce rate, he suggests that the 15% who maintain lifelong secure marriages reach for all three levels to have stronger relationships.

Current marriage rates have declined as young people have decided to delay marriage in order to better handle educational debt with lower-paying jobs (Collins, 2015). With fewer marriages occurring, and people adapting to the contemporary relationship needs, divorce rates have also declined. Class systems may offer various family adaptation and role performance based on family/household needs rather than middle- or upper-class expectations of entitlement.

On the other hand, many are satisfied with being single (DePaulo, 2018) or maintaining relationships without the push of marital expectations. Some determine that individual economics are more satisfactory than marital expectations and emotional stress.

GENDER EXPRESSION

Gender expression has to do with the ways people exhibit their construction through dress, manners, or general presentation (Hutchinson, 2015). The binary categories of male and female have been replaced by male, female, and transgender.

Emerging research is documenting the biological structures that support gender identity that does not fall neatly into the traditional paradigms. According to a recent research report in Endocrine Practice (Neporent, 2015), as many as 1 one out of 100 persons may identify their gender differently than their birth identity. Although some laws reflect this, some authorities think they can dismiss an identity from being accepted or recognized. That cannot erase the reality someone experiences.

The preconceptions that people bring are not reliable in pursuing efforts for engagement and relationship building. Locke (2015) suggests considering the concept of disruption for reorganizing, rethinking, and adjusting methodological tools to explore and reflect. Austin (2016) points to the need for more informed clinical work that shapes understanding the transgender and nonconforming (TGNC) persons as they transition in personal and social identities. Practitioner engagement will seek to support TCNC persons as they navigate possible resistance by family and friends and increase their ability to recognize transphobic and racist oppression while developing resilience and self-esteem.

CHILDREN IN HOMOSEXUAL HOUSEHOLDS

The development of children in lesbian and gay households is an area of study. Questions have been raised about the well-being of children in custody disputes, adoption cases, and assisted-reproduction births. As other new family forms resulting from scientific reproductive advances and surrogacy have emerged, research has become available to assist in responding to these questions rather than using assumptions and speculation (Golombok, 2015).

Key factors that appear to be required for child well-being in traditional nuclear heterosexual families are linked to child well-being in families with same-sex parents and with children derived from alternative methods. A supportive family environment is essential and includes psychological well-being of the parents, quality of the parent–child relationship, and quality of the marital relationship (Golombok, 2015). Several studies suggest that their children do not experience psychological or educational problems and there is not disproportionate teasing (Bosisio & Ronfani, 2016). The pressure of institutional discrimination does impact the families and children by presenting difficulties through law and politics. The impact of stigmatization on children of lesbian mothers was observed to include behavior issues in boys and low self-esteem in girls. Schools that exhibited more inclusive strategies for same-sex parents and parents that participated in their lesbian communities demonstrated more protection of the developing children's well-being. This finding contrasts with early child custody decisions that did not allow mothers visitation rights if they were involved with the lesbian community (Golombok, 2015, p. 63).

While there are limitations in the research, the overall findings of different methodological approaches indicate difference in parenting quality or child adjustment studies do show that children whose mother is experiencing personal or relationship difficulties are likely to have psychological difficulties similar to heterosexual families (Golombok, 2015, p. 67).

Children raised by gay fathers are different from those raised with lesbian mothers since they are raised by men. The research on this group is smaller, but there appears not to be any definite conclusion that mothers make better parents than fathers. Golombok's review indicates it is the quality of the fathers' relationships with their children—as with the mothers'—that is important. Children of gay fathers have exposure to stigma and discrimination that may be greater, and the children may exhibit fewer sex-typed behaviors with the absence of the female role model (Golombok, 2015, p. 165).

The reasons gay men want to become parents mirror those of heterosexual couples—they value family relationships and raising children. Some support adoption more than surrogacy because reconciling the place of the birth mother seems difficult (Golombok, 2015). Issues surrounding adoption involve potential of behavior issues that may be associated with pre-adoption circumstances, foster placement attachments, and relationships related to visitation by biological parents. Preparation of the children by the families to address stigma and other related issues requires substantial commitment. Reducing the stigma against children in same sex parent household can occur through institutional recognition of diverse family forms.

GENDER: WOMEN

The status of women differs in various settings, in relationships, in work spaces, and through diverse descriptions of who, what, where, when and why. Stories written by women about themselves include the joys, sadness, and tragedies of life. Walker's *The Color Purple* (2006) shows the lived experiences of a devalued status internalized, understood and overcome via relationships that bring women to awareness. Perspectives and toys that promote female strengths are important—Wonder Woman, black dolls, and other diverse dolls are crucial for helping girls develop confidence.

The Street (Petry, 1972) described a pathway from marriage to poverty and vulnerability for a woman and her son. Similar paths still exist, though women have established independence in many ways. Yet rights and economic sufficiency, especially where women must earn the income and care for the children, can often be an almost-impossible dream.

Persepolis: The Story of a Childhood (2004) by Marjane Satrapi reflects on growing up in Tehran during the Iranian Revolution. She offers a view of experiences that some immigrants may bring to the United States. Her work was written to express alternative images of Iran than the media presented and to identify women's concerns about sociopolitical issues. As an artist, her work through the comic strip medium is impressive.

GIRL CULTURAL STUDIES

Girl cultural studies are another area of focus on gender. Girl studies has examined socialization, gender expectations, media and empowerment (Lipkin, 2009) of white, middle-class girls. In the United States only 4% of teens from 16 to 19 are not in school (Kids Count.org). According to Herz and Sperling (2003), more than half the girls in Sub-Saharan Africa don't complete primary school. In South Asia only 1 in 5 complete 5th grade (p. 3). Worldwide 65 million girls are not in school. (ABC News, n.d.). Of 123 million people between 15 and 24 years of age who cannot read or write 75 million are women. Worldwide, 91 per cent of primary-school-age children were enrolled in school in 2015. The number of out-of-school children of primary school age declined globally from 99 million to 59 million between 2000 and 2015 (UNICEF, 2018).

The emphasis has been on how girls are shaped and how they are defined as this affects what they may become. Life experiences influence choices or set in motion ways of life there may be little control over. Schaffner (1998) discusses how the early sexual victimization of girls often leads to the types of crimes that lead them into the criminal justice system. Content in *Girlhood Studies: An Interdisciplinary Journal* addresses resisting and preventing violence, sexual exploitation and protection of girls with disabilities.

Social family circumstances often shape the paths women choose. Adiele and Frosch (2007) selections broaden the context of people coming of age around the world. Elisabeth Gille's (2007) *From Shadows of a Childhood: A Novel of War and Friendship* provides an example of women responding to atrocities and the experience of parental loss (Adiele & Frosch, 2007).

GENDER: MEN

The role of men in social work is understudied. In past decades, there have been substantial numbers of men in social work, but current statistics project fewer men entering the profession (Fischl, 2013). As many problems described in our communities involve men, the absence of facilitation of services by men needs more attention.

Stereotypes linked to men promote aggression, competition, and dominance. Data show that men commit homicide on men at a higher rate than homicide on women (WGAC, 2017). Yet intimate partner violence (IPV), domestic violence, rape, child sexual abuse, and dating violence are areas for social work prevention. Collaborating with communities should include more invitations to men to participate in discussion about improvement. In his TED Talk, Katz (2012) makes it clear that abuse is not a woman's issue, although discussion often places blame on the female.

Prevention services include going against stereotypes of men to recognize those with warm personalities that appreciate, are cooperative, loving, and collaborative. Women social workers are encouraged to invite men to participate. Outreach efforts to men, young boys, teens, and young adults could promote learning how to cofacilitate family meetings with mothers and increase interactions with children. Gilligan (2012) proposes assisting foster fathers to use skills to provide male foster children with more security in their homes. Gilligan (2012) explains that a

> meta-analysis of interventions seeking to influence parental sensitivity and parental attachment has found that interventions also involving fathers "appear to be significantly more effective than interventions involving mothers only" (Bakermans-Kranenburg et al., 2003). (p. 474)

LGBTQQI

Lesbian/gay/bisexual/transgender/queer/questioning/intersex (LGBTQQI) people contemplating coming out to their families is a source of emotion for many narratives from this community. The how-tos and what-ifs pose visions of acceptance versus denial, horror, and, at worst, dismissal from the place they have called home. Exposing one's identity in this context has consequences.

The literary voice presented by James Baldwin addressed civil rights, interracial relationships, and gay male relationships (Blasius & Phelan, 1997). In a 1949 piece, *Preservation of Innocence,* Baldwin's discourse on LGBT rights and issues includes comments and raises questions about the emotional energy spent on contemplating human nature and the unnatural. Salty Current (2015) proposes that discontent arises because the position destabilizes concepts of gender structure.

Chin's *The Other Side of Paradise* (2010) takes the reader through the Jamaican culture of mixed-race family heritage, loss of parents, the presence of Grandmom, and the revelation of secrets. Eventually, she comes out as a lesbian and begins to move confidently as a poet and activist. Her journey tackles the cultural community resistance to other sexual identities.

Gonzalez's (2006) *Butterfly Boy: Memories of a Chicano Mariposa* shares the pressure of coming out in a migrant, machismo, farmworker community. The loss of his mother and abandonment by his father confounded his coming-of-age but eventually allowed a coming-to-terms with his identity.

The resistance against LGBTQQI identities impact youth in seeking medical care. Shaddox (2016) notes that rejection by family, school personnel, and peers often pushes young people to risky behaviors that result in mental and physical health concerns. They often receive unwelcoming experiences by medical staff as well.

The Society for Intersex advocates against denigration. It estimates that "1 or 2 per 1,000 babies undergo surgeries to 'normalize' genital appearance at birth" (Guibard, n.d.). A botched circumcision or other medical errors could also account for identity variations that distress one's mental health.

Jeffrey Eugenides' novel *Middlesex* (2002) describes a family saga that begins in a small Greek town, migrates to Detroit, and then goes to the metropolitan suburbs. The story of Calliope Stephanides, who emerges as Cal during adolescence, reveals the gender identity transformation due to genetic processing over several generations. His female body did not coincide with his internal references about who he was.

TRANSGENDER

The 2015 transformation of retired Olympic decathlete Bruce Jenner to American TV personality Caitlyn Jenner brought newfound attention to the transgender community (Bissinger, 2015). The phrase *transgender*, developed in the 1960s by John Mooney, was noted as an "individual's internal sense of self as either a man or a woman (boy or girl)" (Fausto-Sterling, 2010, p. 169).

The root of gender identity discrimination is that "transgender people face a lack of understanding or affirmation of who they say they are. It can be difficult for many cisgender people to grasp the struggles transgender people face. Widespread misunderstanding continues to exist despite the recent media attention to transgender persons" (Levasseur, 2015). According to Levasseur the "simplistic understanding of sex, as two fixed binary categories, is medically, scientifically, and factually inaccurate" (2015, p. 946).

The treatment of transgender people generally involves observers and the legal system dissecting someone based on their socialization to the binary categories. Mistreatment, discrimination, harassment, refusal to respect the transgender person's identity denies their right to live without fear or shame. "Gender identity must be given primary weight, as the single most important biological determinant of sex" (Levasseur. 2015, p. 1004).

Shelby's landmark novel, *Last Exit to Brooklyn* (1964), is a classic representation of the harsh views of the characters living in low-income Brooklyn in the 1950s. The absence of acceptance by the larger community is offset by the internal community relationships.

CONFORMITY AND VARIATIONS

Conformity to male and female gender roles has been a long-standing socialization process connected to biological markers. The use of binary categories has emphasized male and female, although there have been variations of sexual orientation across time. Conformity to traditional role expectations is one pathway through younger years to adulthood. However, as people search for identity, meaning, and purpose; reconcile their experiences; and are informed by economic conditions, the range of diverse personalities, skill sets, and behaviors follow a huge continuum that cannot be contained in simple assumptions about conformity.

VARIATIONS IN PERFORMATIVE INFLUENCES

The huge continuum of identity would include the outliers as well the typical configurations of identity. Genetics, anatomy, and family dynamics offer bases for sexual variations. Experiences—selected or forced—establish incidents of performance that may impact how people see themselves sexually as well as via class, race, ethnicity, and other characteristics.

The anatomy of persons that don't conform to the typical male or female presents the intersex marker. When doctors discovered discrepant internal and external genitalia, they often made the decision to modify, choosing either male or female. In 2015, Malta became the first country to outlaw nonconsensual decisions (Reuters, 2015).

The theory of performative influences raises another realistic concept for consideration. Recently, performance situations in which sexual actions have occurred as imposed upon one or participated in by choice or curiosity have been reviewed. Chinn (2010) points out that the path to inclusion follows intense debates by philosophers, activists, academics, and linguists that connect sexuality and identity to power systems and a collection of sexual practices, desires, and partnerships.

In that vein, *Fire Shut Up in My Bones* (Blow, 2014) presents circumstances that call into question points of view that have been presented and forces us to think about other influences on personal choices and development. His discourse notes the trajectory of abuse, emotions, and experiences regarding the performative influences of homosexuality (then bisexuality). He concludes that it is up to him to come to terms with where he stands on this.

PUNISHMENT VERSUS REFORM

Traditional responses to nonconforming behaviors, punitive labels, and those who test social controls are to restrain people and jeopardize their access to opportunities. According to Mallett (2015), student suspensions and expulsions have increased due to "criminalizing typical adolescent developmental behaviors and low-level type misdemeanors: acting out in class, truancy, and similar offenses" (p. 15). Zero-tolerance policies and more police presence in schools have resulted in the disproportionate impact on vulnerable children, youth, and their families and their referral to punitive systems. This leads to the continuing growth in incarceration rates and also higher substance use and suicide (Data Spotlight, 2012).

Punished: Policing the Lives of Black and Latino Boys: New Perspectives of Crime, Deviance & Law (Rios, 2011) describes the pathways for so many young males of color that begin with parents struggling with economic handicaps, which leads to their children struggling with teachers who are not interested in them and who pass them along via detention and confinement to police and gang encounters. Marked as dangerous, they are under surveillance until something lands them in jail and the criminal jacket grows. Rios calls this criminalization "the youth control complex" and explains how it deprives these young citizens of respect and dignity and obstructs participation in pathways for employment and opportunities to establish themselves as effective adults.

Although a few incidents of violence in schools raised concerns that moved policy changes to be more restrictive, overall violence in schools is low (Mallett, 2015). But the emphasis on this unconfirmed violence has led to less-positive school structures, which have harmed students by diminishing teacher, student, and administration bonds and decreasing academic performance. Zero-tolerance policies mandate applying often severe predetermined consequences on student behavior infractions, regardless of mitigating circumstances (Mallett, 2015). These have added to the criminalization of the school system. Generally, these policies have negatively impacted persons living in lower-wealth communities with developmental contexts that are ignored by traditional and middle-class institutional practices.

There is also the need to examine students' rights with regard to schools with police (Bracy, 2010). Students in schools with school resource officers (SROs) are likely to have their legal rights compromised, especially their Fourth and Fifth Amendment rights. This is complicated by various arrangements that different types of schools have with law enforcement pertaining to situations in which student suspect information should or should not be reported to the police (Daggett, 2013).

DISMANTLING PUNITIVE PROTOCOLS

There are ways to dismantle the punitive protocols without sacrificing concerns for safety. Many schools have established improved systems that incorporate alternative paradigms and ways of respecting cultural ways of knowing and learning. An example of evaluation of existing problems and follow-up efforts is available through the Urban Institute. It has published substantial research on punishment reforms. In 2002, Travis reported on the increase in laws that limited the rights and privileges of ex-offenders. These obstacles constrained them in obtaining employment and addressing needs of their families. In 2016, the Institute presented a live webinar on "Effective Partnerships for Family-Focused Reentry Service." Of particular interest was their evaluation research on Fatherhood Reentry projects and discussion of community-based partnerships that can build on strategies to collaborate and assist people returning home or to establish themselves in other settings (Urban Institute, 2016). In Wake County, North Carolina, an analysis of discipline data shows that black students were suspended 5 times more often than white students but "there is no evidence that the black students act up more often or more severely than the white ones" (America Tonight Digital Team, 2014, para 7).

There are also examples of the use of meditation or yoga with children, which has had good results. A Baltimore program reports excellent results in sending students to a meditation room (Haupt, 2016), integrating yoga classes through the day to help children become more focused and address situations that in the past would have suspended them from school. This process teaches calming and recovery-focused coping skills.

Helping professionals have opportunities to be informed of culturally affirming representative programs and to share ways of participation that encourage support networks and alternative paradigms for strengthening vulnerable populations. Moving beyond the theme of punishment to strategies that reform is associated with improving our social environment.

ACCESS POINTS

A child's development is impacted by early-age assessment and detention. The points of jeopardy and confinement represented by connections to the criminal justice and foster care system dominate child labeling and negative consequences and outcomes. There are several points of entry: schools, social services, mental health services, emergency rooms, and medical clinics where need may be identified but follow-through is often incomplete.

Data on service dropouts suggest programs may not be engaging effectively with some service users. As de Haan and associates (2014) note, the dropout rate for youth in psychotherapy is high. The range extends from 16% to 69% (p. 1). The study results point to the variations of youth who complete services and those who do not and offers speculation of the more serious needs of those who drop out.

There are self-referrals by persons or families seeking sources through primary care. However, lack of trust or knowledge of discrimination will keep people away. Organizational assessment and individual practitioner assessment must occur to understand how biases and traditional practices maintain inequality and oppression (Dacres, 2016).

Listening to parents and other service users provides information that can improve services. The challenge to innovation using consumer involvement and feedback is for helping professionals to become more flexible and incorporate community recommendations to appreciate that consumers do not have to do it the way the practitioner suggests.

ALTERNATIVE ACCESS: PREVENTION, CAPACITY BUILDING

Work that respects identities and offers outreach and evidence-based services can assist persons in being validated, moving forward with identity development, and pursuing self-work that achieves goals. Community education through community-based prevention services offers a model of community practice in nonstigmatizing locations. This already works through interventions that inform about the perils of smoking, diabetes, harsh parenting, and low nutrition. The community education option offers ways of engaging with communities around quantitative and qualitative research translated to assist in health and mental health prevention and family development, to address isolation via support group and workforce development, and to offer employment endeavors.

Alternatives to referrals from institutional punishment sources would be through primary and universal entry points to eliminate stigma and discrimination and promote health. As social, health, and environmental issues continue to gain our attention, macro practices provide critical entry points for planning and service delivery. Community education in public spaces offers alternative places for providing information about health and mental health prevention and screening.

In order to reach citizens who may benefit from health services, providing access in community schools, libraries, community recreation centers, or places of worship should be considered. For service users, the first step—engagement—is key. Sanders (2016) referred to engagement as the best practice; the goal is to get the person to come for the second session. Broadening one's awareness of knowledge about cultural group members and sharing information with consumers demonstrates a higher recognition of others.

The National Network of Libraries and Medicine (NNLM) is promoting public health information at libraries. It recognizes low health literacy rates, especially among older adults, immigrant populations, minority populations, and low-income populations. Community library-based sessions inform residents of Medline information resources that will assist them in gaining health information (NNLM, 2017).

Listening to clients discuss their perceptions of identity before getting to the "what happened to you" or the "why are you here" steps could be useful. Having office space with decorations, reading materials, and art that demonstrates appreciation of diverse identities can make visitors comfortable. When sensitivity to these cultural recognition elements is absent, there is more likelihood that persons may not be comfortable, may not return, or may not become motivated to participate (Gary, 1996), and the professional outcomes are likely to be limited. These issues warrant social work's recognition of the ways persons who are not white, middle-class professionals perceive the social environment. Mackelprang and Salsgiver (2008) pointed this out:

> Oppressive social and economic forces must be acknowledged and social justice oriented policies and structures must be promoted in work at the micro, mezzo, and macro levels. ... Unless we develop compassionate and responsive systems, we will continue to fall further behind in this quest each year (p. 104).

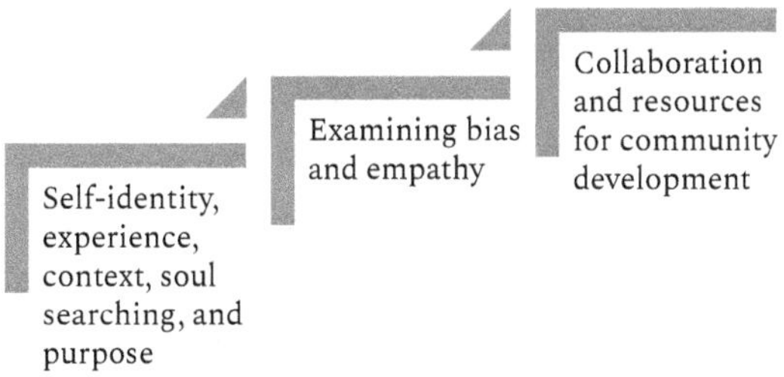

FIGURE 6.2   Building from Self-Awareness

Reading materials by multicultural authors, watching films/videos with diverse characters, and becoming familiar with role models of color, of gender identity, immigrant status, or religion/spiritual interest is a path to recognizing and respecting cultural variations. Sharing role-model role representations, images, and information across macro, mezzo, and micro levels can help validate personal experiences or situations and motivate movement to a next step.

ACTUALIZATION PATHWAYS

As the realities of privilege, exclusions, and the associated penalties become more publicized, there are ongoing efforts to tailor assistance in more flexible ways. The refined services build on identity affirmation and encourage confidence building. Figure 6.2 projects building confidence for civic participation.

What seems to be really important for self-development and recovery is the freedom to be who we are, to identify ourselves, think positive things about ourselves (we are what we think), and be free from stigmatic classification by others. Freedom from judgment is certainly not easy. As social work advances in the midst of governmental policy constraints, personal challenges, and social questioning, integrating recognition of self-identity, self-care, and compassion for others is critical to inclusion and community development.

PATH: SELF-LOVE, COLLECTIVE RESPECT, AND PREPARATION

Preparing for and planning self-care, improvement, and recovery builds on talents, family goals, self-love, and the science of mental health. Emphasizing recovery demonstrates the response to consumer resistance to traditional approaches by respecting their autonomy (Lukens & Solomon, 2013).

PATH: RELIGION AND SPIRITUALITY

Traditional views of religion have promoted discrimination against women and approved of slavery and intolerance. Bruni (2015) points out that we must note "the degree to which all writings reflect the biases and blind spots of their authors, cultures and eras" (para 5).

On the other hand, acknowledging the spiritual dimension that provides strength to many has not been routinely included in health and mental health status assessments or in treatment planning. Acknowledging the role this may have in the context of health and the use of complementary and alternative health practices is a component of understanding personal environments. The National Institute of Health's National Center for Complementary and Integrative Health (NCCIH, 2017) offers resources and research.

Nelson (1994) noted that "the modern culture of materialism since the 18th century has ignored the role of the spiritual and transpersonal dimension of human experience or the science of the soul" (p. ix). Western thinking about psychosis and altered states of consciousness has obstructed investigating and understanding the alternative sensory or extrasensory dimensions of reality. In *Healing and the Mind* (1996), Moyers spoke with physicians, scientists, therapists, and patients about the science and multidimensional nature of healing. Investigating these perspectives can be enlightening.

PATH: SCHOOLS AND COMMUNITY MULTICULTURAL EDUCATION

Student reactions to exposure to knowledge that has not been available to them at the elementary and secondary school levels often leaves them quiet, incredulous, and questioning why they have been educated with lies (O'Neal, 2012). Schmoker (2011) suggests that we could better serve all students by preparing them at the second-grade level to read more, think more critically, view presentation of multiple perspectives, and implement more effective teaching methods to improve student socialization and academic performance.

PATH: BUILDING UP THE COMMUNITY

In the Columbia School of Social Work's Tony Tripodi lecture, Dr. George Rupp, President Emeritus of Columbia University (2016), called on social work to press against the assumption that individualism and narcissism are the ways to proceed. The profession must not exclude the conviction of communities, and the goal is to include the collective perspective in pluralistic societies. Moving forward, planning, and collaborating with communities' members for more effective service delivery and for identifying potential leaders is needed.

The benefits of multicultural information for identity validation and development is clear. Colleges and universities are using innovative ways such as intergroup dialogue to incorporate race in the curriculum. This process has resulted in benefits for students of color, multiracial, and white students as they make sense of their experiences and observations of oppression (Ford & Malaney, 2012).

Providing multicultural information and education responds to the multiple identities and multiple talents of the people to whom helping professionals are committed.

STUDENT COMMENTS

Students analyses of multicultural book selections yielded several excerpts that could be used to generate conversations in individual or group settings to encourage awareness or spark further reading. The following are some examples of their choices.
- "You can only be destroyed by believing that you really are what the white world calls a nigger." (Baldwin, 1963, p. 4). Use in groups for self-esteem building.

- From Alexie, 2007, "It sucks to be poor, and it sucks to feel that you somehow deserve to be poor. You start believing that you're poor because you're stupid and ugly. And then you start believing that you're stupid and ugly because you're Indian. And because you're Indian you start believing you're destined to be poor. It's an ugly circle and there's nothing you can do about it" (Alexie, 2007, p. 13). This could be used in a group of young American Indians (or others to compare, contrast, and discuss) to promote self-esteem and to promote a hope for change for the future. It could be used to identify and affirm their feelings of the effects of oppression.

CHAPTER SUMMARY

Ideas about identity and the impacts of racism, stigma, and bullying are integrated throughout literature, art, and music examples that speak to the strengths and perseverance of people. Students will be able to illustrate a possible manifestation of oppression's impact on identity for persons with different abilities and diagnoses, women, persons of color, and those coming from other countries. At the same time, readers can share ways and reasons identity development can help build confidence and support people in achieving goals.

EPAS AND CODE OF ETHICS

CSWE EDUCATIONAL POLICY & ACCREDITATION STANDARDS

Competency 6: Engage with Individuals, Families, Groups, Organizations, and Communities
- 6a) Apply knowledge of human behavior and the social environment, person-in-environment, and other multidisciplinary theoretical frameworks to engage with clients and constituencies.
- 6b) Use empathy, reflection, and interpersonal skills to effectively engage diverse clients and constituencies.

Competency 7: Assess Individuals, Families, Groups, Organizations, and Communities
- 7a) Collect and organize data, and apply critical thinking to interpret information from clients and constituencies.
- 7b) Apply knowledge of human behavior and the social environment, person-in-environment, and other multidisciplinary theoretical frameworks in the analysis of assessment data from clients and constituencies.
- 7c) Develop mutually agreed-on intervention goals and objectives based on the critical assessment of strengths, needs, and challenges within clients and constituencies. (EPAS, 2015)

NASW CODE OF ETHICS

Ethical Principle: Social workers respect the inherent dignity and worth of the person.

1.05 Cultural Awareness and Social Diversity

- a) Social workers should understand culture and its function in human behavior and society, recognizing the strengths that exist in all cultures. (NASW, n.d.)

DISCUSSION QUESTIONS

1. What do you think are the key points regarding the existence of racism that society has to address? Which authors move you toward this conclusion?
2. Do these articles assist or obstruct conversations about how to address obstacles to our work?
3. How does the review of these articles help you evaluate the traditional messages or stereotypes of labeled people?
4. What other kinds of information would be useful (to you, your friends, or family) in evaluating your opinions about status quo situations?
5. How does identity development among at-risk populations impact social welfare structures or policy development?

EXERCISES

1. The instructor will prepare a list of diverse identities (e.g., person with autism who is black, from Puerto, and lives with a maternal aunt; young Latina with cerebral palsy; middle-aged, unemployed Caucasian woman living with her biracial grand-children). Cut up the list and put in an envelope. Students will each select one and complete a scenario about them, including their mezzo and micro circumstances—strengths and/or risks. A full class discussion can focus on what ideas were selected and why.
2. Using the theory set designed in Chapter 4, select a client/consumer identity and work up a care pathway.
3. Consider a case in a preliminary phase. How could the client benefit from a reading list regarding his or her identity and opportunities to develop from examples of positive pathways? Based on conversations with the client and her or his basic concerns, set up a reading and/or music list for three sessions, including areas for discussion.
4. Identity also includes one's political identity. How might social workers approach understanding the dynamics of multiple or intersectional identities among young Muslims in the West. Use three PowerPoint slides to create a set of concepts to be

explored in a youth group on understanding religious diversity. Be creative; add illustrations or photos to represent the ideas.

5. Using small groups, have each select a multicultural resource—a short essay or a story on identity. Each student should develop one critical thinking question and post it in an online discussion forum for each group member to respond to.

6. Request students to review their self-assessment grid completed in Session 1 or 2. Ask them to add, using red or some other color, information they have reviewed since then. Reflect on their learning and interests since then. Select a novel or non-fiction book written by a person of color, a LGBTQI person, or a person with different abilities for a reading analysis assignment. The multicultural resource analysis should:

   a. Reflect integration of course material from a social and economic justice perspective, demonstrate sophisticated critical thinking skills by thoughtful reflection from an ethical and professional perspective;

   b. Recognize structural dynamics (macro) and individual and family (micro) influences; and

   c. Indicate self-awareness that describes the influence of personal biases, values and experiences or lack of experience in working with diverse groups and includes ideas to address bias.

MULTICULTURAL RESOURCES

Adiele, F., & Frosch, M. (2007). *Coming of age around the world: A multicultural anthology*. Florence, MA: Free Press.

Allende, I. (2015). *House of spirits*. New York, NY: Atria Books.

Alexie, S. (2007). *The absolutely true diary of a part-time Indian*. Boston, MA: Little, Brown.

Alexie, S. (2009). *War dances*. New York, NY: Grove Press.

Alvarez, J. (2010). *How the Garcia girls lost their accents*. Chapel Hill, NC: Algonquin Books.

Anaya, R. (1972). *Bless me, Ultima*. New York, NY: Warner Books. Retrieved from http://www.neabigread.org/books/blessmeultima/readers-guide/

Anaya, R. (2004). *Tortuga*. Albuquerque: University of New Mexico Press.

Anderson, E. (1999). Code of the street: Decency, violence, and the moral life of the inner city. New York, NY: W. W. Norton.

Baldwin, J. (1963. *The fire next time*. Dial Press.

Bambara, T. (1995). The golden bandit. In L. Goss & C. Goss (Eds.), *Jump up and say: A collection of black storytelling*. New York, NY: Simon & Schuster.

Benedict, B. S. (n.d.). Communication considerations A to Z: Deaf culture and community. *Hands & Voices*. Retrieved from http://www.handsandvoices.org/comcon/articles/deafculture.htm

Blacks and Native Americans, On the Trail of Tears, DVD.

Blow, C. (2014). *Fire shut up in my bones*. Boston, MA: Houghton Mifflin.

Chin, S. (2010). *The other side of paradise*. New York, NY: Scribner.

Covarrubias, R., & Fryberg, S. (2014). Movin' on up (to college): First-generation college students' experiences with family achievement guilt. *Cultural Diversity and Ethnic Minority Psychology*.

Deafnewstoday.com. (2017). Retrieved from http://deafnewstoday.blogspot.com/

Diamond Sutra Recitation Group. (Ed.). (2007). Chung Hyo Ye: *Tales of filial devotion, loyalty, respect and benevolence from the history and folklore of Korea*. Flushing, NY: Yong Hwa.

Du, N. (1987). *The tale of Kieu* (H. S. Thong, Trans.). New Haven, CT: Yale University Press.

DuBois, W. E. B. (1903). *The souls of black folk.* Chicago, IL: A. C. McClurg.

Eastman, C. A. (2014). *The soul of the Indian.* Plano, TX: SMK Books.

Eugenides, J. (2002). *Middlesex.* New York, NY: Picador.

Galloway, S. (2008). *The cellist of Sarajevo.* New York, NY: Riverhead Books.

Gille, E. (2007). Shadows of a childhood: A novel of war and friendship. In F. Adiele & M. Frosch (Eds.), *Coming of age around the world: A multicultural anthology.* New York, NY: Free Press.

Gonzalez, R. (2006). *Butterfly boy: Memories of a Chicano mariposa.* Madison: University of Wisconsin Press.

Grandin, T. (1984). *Emergence: Labeled autistic.* New York, NY: Warner Books.

Guy, R. (1995). *Friends.* New York, NY: Laurel Leaf.

Ha, Y. (2011). On the road at 18. In F. Adiele & M. Frosch (Eds.), *Coming of age around the world: A multicultural anthology.* New York, NY: Free Press.

Haddon, M. (2003). *The curious incident of the dog in the night.* New York, NY: Vintage Contemporaries.

Hall, R. (2002). *The quiet storm.* New York, NY: Simon & Schuster.

Hedayat, S. (1990). *The blind owl.* Princeton, NJ: Princeton University Press.

Hix, L. (2013). Black is beautiful: Why black dolls matter. *Utne Reader.* Retrieved from http://www.utne.com/arts/why-black-dolls-matter

Hockenberry, J. (2011). Public transit. In C T. Ibrahim (Ed.), *An anthology of disability literature.* Durham, NC: Carolina Academic Press.

Husseini, R. (2009). *Murder in the name of honor: The true story of one woman's heroic fight against an unbelievable crime.* London, England; Oneworld.

Huong, D. T. (2002). *Paradise of the blind.* New York, NY: William Morrow.

ICMN Staff. (2017, July 21). Know the real Geronimo: Life of Native American hero in pictures. *Indian Country Today.* Retrieved from http://indiancountrytodaymedianetwork.com/2011/12/11/know-real-geronimo-through-literature-37876

Jones, M. (2015). Why a generation of adoptees is returning to South Korea. *The New York Times Magazine.*

Laferriere, D. (2008). *I am a Japanese writer.* Vancouver, British Columbia: Douglas & McIntyre.

McBride, J. (1995). *The color of water: A black man's tribute to his white mother.* New York, NY: Riverhead Books.

Mohanty, C. T. (2003). *Feminism without borders: Decolonizing theory, practicing solidarity.* Durham, NC: Duke University Press.

Mosley, W. (2006). *Fortunate son: A novel.* New York, NY: Back Bay Books.

O'Neal, G. S. (2014). Online multicultural resources database. Retrieved from http://subjectguides.wcupa.edu/socialwork?p=395263

Padden, C., & Humphries, T. (1988). *Deaf in America: Voices from a culture.* Cambridge, MA: Harvard University Press.

Petry, A. (1997). *The street.* Boston, MA: Houghton Mifflin.

Poitier, D. (2007). *The measure of a man: A spiritual autobiography.* San Francisco, CA: Harper.

Rios, V. (2011). *Punished: Policing the lives of black and Latino boys—New perspectives of crime, deviance & law.* New York: New York University Press.

Satrapi, M. (2004). *The story of a childhood.* New York, NY: Pantheon Books.

See, L. (2009). *Snow flower and the secret fan.* New York, NY: Random House.

Shelby, H., Jr. (1957). *Last exit to Brooklyn.* New York, NY: Grove Press.

Shin, K. S. (2011). *Please look after Mother.* New York, NY: Vintage.

Simon, R. (2011). *The story of beautiful girl.* New York, NY: Grand Central.

Sotomayor, M. (2014). *My beloved world.* New York, NY: Vintage.

Stavans, I. (Ed.). (1998). *Prospero's mirror: A translator's portfolio of Latin American short fiction.* Evanston, IL: Curbstone Press.

Tajima-Peña, R., & Portillo, L. (Producers). (2004). *My journey home.* Washington, DC: WET.

Takaki, R. (1989). *Strangers from a different shore: A history of Asian Americans.* New York, NY: Little, Brown.

Tan, A. (2006). *The kitchen god's wife.* New York, NY: Penguin Books.

Vance, J. D. (2016). *Hillbilly elegy.* New York, NY: Harper Collins.

Young, A. (1994). *A way out of no way*. Nashville, TN: Thomas Nelson.

Walker, A. (2006). *The color purple*. Boston, MA: Mariner Books.

Wearing, M. (2011). Strengthening youth citizenship and social inclusion practice—The Australian case: Towards rights based and inclusive practice in services for marginalized young people. *Children and Youth Services Review, 33*, 534–540.

West, C. (1996). *Race matters*. Boston, MA: Beacon Press.

Wilcox, S. (Ed.). (1989). *American deaf culture: An anthology*. Burtonsville, MD: Linstok Press.

Womack, Y. (2010). *Post black: How a new generation is redefining African American identity*. Chicago, IL: Lawrence Hill Books.

Woodson, J. (Ed.). (1996). *A way out of no way: Writings about growing up black in America*. New York, NY: Henry Holt.

Yiwu, L. (2013). *For a song and a hundred songs: A poet's journey through a Chinese prism*. Boston, MA: Houghton Mifflin.

Young, A. (1994). *A way out of no way: The spiritual memoirs of Andrew Young*. Nashville, TN: Thomas Nelson.

Young, S. (2014). *I'm not your inspiration, thank you very much* [Video file]. Retrieved from http://www.ted.com/talks/stella_young_i_m_not_your_inspiration_thank_you_very_much

MUSIC

Earth, Wind & Fire (1975). *Shining Star*. You tube. https://m.youtube.com/watch? v=rl-WsmryfSY

Tupac—*Mama Native American music,* http://www.canyonrecords.com/http://indiancountrytodaymedianetwork.com/2013/06/14/indian-hoUse-records-lifetime-sound-149909 https://www.youtube.com/playlist?list=PL3B7A9EDDD0BA4D6E

Black/Multicultural:

Positive images: http://ontheblacklist.net/top-5-films-handle-racism/?utm_source=rss&utm_medium=rss&utm_source=On+The+Black+List&utm_campaign=754b7575bd-OTBL_MC_DAILY_CAMPAIGN&utm_medium=email&utm_term=0_a3fec71fa1-754b7575bd-103652841

Art /Mural in Athens Georgia: https://www.socialworkhelper.com/2016/02/29/art-as-a-form-of-community-and-youth-empowerment/

http://www.defjam.com/

http://www.stlamerican.com/news/columnists/article_4d768f74-d3ad-11e2-9c19-001a4bcf887a.html

http://www.icrates.org/tag/african-american-record-labels/

Latino:

http://www.latinpopartists.com/rec_labels.htm

http://www.nacionalrecords.com/

http://www.npr.org/2012/08/27/160105693/latin-alternative-record-labels-we-love

Asian American:

http://www.fUSionmagazine.org/still-waiting-asian-americans-in-mUSic/

http://goldsea.com/Air/Issues/Pop/pop.html

FURTHER READING

Bildeau, B. L., & Renn, K. A. (2005). Analysis of LGBT identity development models & implications for practice. *New Directions for Student Services*, Fall, 25–40.

Szymanski, D. M., & Gupta, A. (2009). Examining the relationship between multiple internalized oppressions and African American lesbian, gay, bisexual, and questioning persons' self-esteem and psychological distress. *Journal of Counseling Psychology, 56*(1), 110–118.

FIGURE CREDIT

Source: Photo 6.1: Copyright © 2017 by BBC One.

CHAPTER 7

Impact on Anglo-Europeans and Others of Privilege

CHAPTER OVERVIEW

The range of ideas about how oppression, discrimination, and class issues impact people of Anglo and European descent has been expressed through various voices. These include examples of those who have operated as allies from abolitionists' times through activists of civil rights events to contemporary allies of the LGBTQQI community, autism advocacy, and families of people with emotional distress. Analysts from different countries have deliberated on observations of Anglo-Europeans feelings and reactions to concepts of oppression, racism, and privilege.

Generally, we may have the impression that white families do not have to think about racial socialization or consider it an issue for family discussion. There is more likely a range of possible sources for discussion that extend from serious contemplation of issues to more limited expression falling into traditional frames. Caucasian families with diverse members, through adoption, friendships, or intercultural relationships experience additional opportunities for reflection.

Examining one's family messages, observations, experiences, and relationships assists in understanding how identity has been formed and influences interactions. This knowledge provides a foundation for moving forward in working with colleagues and clients.

Some of the concepts that might be connected to conversations include the following:
- Lack of awareness, restricted information
- Color blindness
- Narrow socialization
- Denial
- Resistance
- Microaggressions
- Advocacy

Awareness or lack of knowledge of these concepts may have influenced people's desire to work in social work or related people-helping disciplines. In this contemporary time of sentiments of tolerance and intolerance, identity assessment regarding privilege is fundamental to examining the broad contextual landscape.

LEARNING OBJECTIVES

- Privilege affects the way we view and listen to others.
- Privilege affects our understanding of the lack of privilege.
- Blaming the victim is connected to the denial of structural oppression.
- Intentional and unintentional micro and macro aggressions occur.
- Abolition allies and helping professionals seek mutual concerns for justice.
- Commitment to service and acts of kindness are present in our environment.

Benchmark: Students will consider the feelings and reactions of people of Caucasian descent to people of color and others asserting their voices to the negative forces against them.

STUDENT SCENARIO

Emily and her best friend, Gina, have been assigned a case at the local re-entry program for incarcerated women. Emily worked here last year, but this is Gina's first week. Emily recognizes that some of Gina's early comments are reflecting assumptions about the women that are made from a point of prejudice and not of service. What does it take to move from this beginning point to one that provides high-quality interaction?

CONCEPTS OF PREJUDICE AND DENIAL

Maintaining the status quo essentially means buying into the structure that exists. As we examine the forces that have installed the past and current personal and institutional barriers to civil and human rights, the intent is not to foster blame or guilt but to more clearly understand why and how we have arrived at this point. The history of oppression has resulted in some people reaping more benefits and opportunities for economic, material, and social gains. Yet the typical response to the issue of white racism is pretense and denial. The response of Nazi officials was similar; they knew nothing about the inhuman practices in the concentration camps (Feagin, Vera, & Batur, 2001).

In the current social climate, it is a perceived change in status, access, and opportunity that has shaken the political timbers so much since the election of President Obama in 2008 and again in 2012. Foner (2015) and Staples (2016) compare these times to the Reconstruction era after the Emancipation Proclamation was signed and slaves were freed. After 1863, persons who justified slavery found it difficult to change their beliefs about access to citizenship and voting rights for black people. "The Southern fixation on denying African-Americans the right to vote was a direct response to the rise of black political power during Reconstruction. A similar backlash to positive community developments erupted during the modern civil rights movement" (Staples, 2016, para 5).

This response by white citizens developed into the rise of the Ku Klux Klan and acts of murder, assault and arson can be described as homegrown domestic terrorism against African Americans. Since the Trump election there have been similar responses. Far Right groups have killed

48 people since 2011 (Plucinska, 2015). The Southern Poverty Law Center (2017) identifies and monitors hate groups and radical anti-government militias. An annual census of these extremist groups is published including Ku Klux Klan, the neo-Nazi movement, neo-Confederates, racist skinheads, black separatists, antigovernment militias, Christian Identity adherents and others (para 1). In 2017, 917 groups were operating across the United States.

PREJUDICE

The use of stereotypical patterns of perception for discrimination and persecution is how prejudice operates (Knappertsbusch, Milbradt, & Kelle 2013). Prejudice based on beliefs and attitudes that have held European, Christian, healthy, persons to be superior, privileged, and normal has now shifted to focus on the institutional processes that legitimize this advantage. Some of the worst of the messages this attitude has derived from in history are reported by Gichuhi (2016) of images of Europeans putting Africans in zoos.

These ideas have been deeply embedded in a white-centered culture, major institutions, and daily life (Feagin et al., 2001). This has been operationalized through practices of white culture domination that target and exploit people of color and others who don't fit historically emphasized nationality, gender, and circumstance. The persistence of racism today is observed in continuing racial subjection language and messages that are reproduced through social mechanisms (McKnight, 2010; Urban Wire, 2016).

The day-to-day application of the historically instilled ideas influences how oppression impacts the overall white culture. It falls along a spectrum modified by personal and institutional socialization and exposure to persons other than those in the dominant culture. We could use Wingfield and Feagin's (2010) proposal that there are two versions of the white racial frame from which to consider impact. The hard version accepts blatant stereotyping, imagery, and interpretations that support prejudice and denies reasons for inclusion. The soft version prefers to approach racism from the colorblind stance. The broadest view incorporates human rights and respects and appreciates all people.

In a subsequent interpretation, Feagin (2013) examines racism from a broad white frame and points to the relevance of hearing from voices of analysis other than those who created the systems that are in place. In an interview with *The New York Times* (Yancy & Feagin, 2015), he explains:

> That white racial frame includes not only racist prejudices and stereotypes of conventional analyses, but also racist ideologies, narratives, images and emotions, as well as individual and group inclinations to discriminate shaped by the other features. Additionally, all whites, no matter what their racial prejudices and other racial framings entail, benefit from many privileges routinely granted by this country's major institutions to whites. (para 3)

Feagin's work moves the analysis to the macro level by viewing the deep layers that exist and manifest in various ways for those impacted by policies. Becoming more aware of this offers opportunities to resist maintaining the negative dynamics and encourages working for change.

Davidson corroborates the traditional framework in *Cultural Genocide: Genocide, Political Violence, Human Rights* (2012). He explains that governmental authorities have their own pictures that have been influenced by their limited awareness of others' experiences, their ideologies, religious and political connections, and their vested interests. These they promote through public media outlets because they have control of them. Simultaneously, there is no desire by those authorities to be more informed of the positives of other groups. The tendency is to deny that those of other cultures are excluded. The rationale is if they don't work hard and benefit from their own efforts; it is their own fault.

DENIAL

Denial is the concept used to respond to examples of privilege at the expense of other humans (de Montigny, 2013). A growing body of research on the "new racism" incorporates ways those who "wish to express negative views as justified, warranted, and rational, deny and excuse negative views toward minorities in order to position themselves as decent and moral citizens" (Augoustinos & Every, 2010, p. 252). The increased number of refugees has also fueled growing public debates. The relevance of contentious debates in the media around issues pertaining to race, immigration, and ethnicity, as well as the supportive yet critical analysis of these discourses must be reviewed by persons choosing to be helpful to persons of the various cultural categories.

The growing number of expressions of virulent, racialized discourse demonstrates the shared ground of Far-Right and moderate conservatives (Wood, Jakubek, & Kelly, 2015) who hold on to symbolic rural idylls that push against notions of humanist moral engagement with diverse populations. The Southern Poverty Law Center (SPLC) documents an increased number of active hate groups in the United States, fueled by the presidential election of 2016 (SPLC, 2016).

CONSTRUCTION OF RACISM AROUND THE WORLD

This prejudice and denial exists in other countries, too. Malhi and Boon (2007) report that tolerance and diversity norms flourish along with covert democratic racism on individual and institutional levels. South Asian Canadians have been present since the 1800s and have historically faced discrimination and resentment. They point out that old-fashioned racism has been replaced with newer forms. The conflict between a person's abstract values of equalitarianism and continued feelings that blame another for their unemployment is exposed. These authors use Tator and Henry's book *The Colour of Democracy* (2006) to highlight the dominant discourse of democratic racism—which is denial. In this text that addressed institutional racism in Canada, the authors focus on the impact and lingering dominance of group values.

The construction of racism in Australia (Dunn, Forrest, Burnley, & McDonald, 2004) is experiencing similar observations of social constructions that are associated with age and language spoken (Robertson, 2015). Intolerance of Muslim, Asian, and Indian students occurs. Constructed images of citizenship and managed mobility are ways that new norms may be developing that can create new barriers.

Early and continuing research on prejudice and racism examines the individual level, but more research is documenting the institutional barriers and the role that individual professionals play in maintaining the status quo structural oppression (Windsor, Pinto, Benoit, & Jessell, 2014) and in assisting the modification of policies and consumer participation.

Recognizing the historical manifestation of racism and privilege and the current evidence of pushback against human rights and inclusion efforts brings more awareness to the interest in pursuing antiracism or antioppression initiatives. What is new in the discussion is the subject of the white person—the white male—and the frame that no "longer grants immunity from social judgment, legal action, or stigma with regard to black life" (McKnight, 2010, p. 100) and other lives that have been excluded in policy measures.

Examining the micro-, mezzo-, and macro-level impacts of oppression history on Anglo-Americans raises the experience of privilege and the discomfort or disruption that may occur as persons are encouraged to reflect on whiteness and privilege.

PASSIVE INVOLVEMENT

A frequent description of awareness of prejudice and discrimination may be linked to passive connections to the social climate at large. Various polls that show active connections of discrimination by race show higher proportions of people of color being aware of racial dynamics, while the proportions of white people are lower. For example, situations regarding

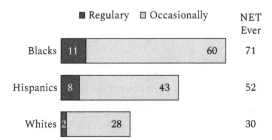

A majority of blacks say they have faced racial discrimination

% saying they have personally experienced discrimination or been treated unfairly because of their race or ethnicity ...

Note: Whites and blacks include only non-Hispanics. Hispanics are of any race. Those who said they had experienced discrimination were asked if they experienced it "regularly" or if it is something they experience "from time to time, but not regularly." "Occasionally" includes those who say "from time to time, but not regularly," as well as voluntary responses of "only one time" and "rarely." The "NET Ever" column was calculated before rounding
Source: Survey of U.S. adults conducted Feb. 29-May8,2016. Q27. "On View of Race and Inequality, Blacks and White Are Worlds Apart"

PEW RESEARCH CENTER

FIGURE 7.1

the recent attention to police murders of unarmed black men show perspectives coming from different standpoints. Jones (2014) reasons that it is difficult for whites to understand another perspective because most only talk to other white people who may share their opinions. He relates this to the reports that some white people didn't understand the outrage of the police killing of an unarmed back teen, Michael Brown in, Ferguson, Missouri, in 2014. There are also persons of Anglo-European descent who are engaged in identity formation who recognize the sources of white opposition and have reconciled their feelings and interests in civil and human rights, but who may not be activists.

ACTIVE INVOLVEMENT

Participation in dialogues regarding awareness of inequality, its impact on all of us, and collaboration with diverse persons in sharing broader-based perspectives can be perceived as active involvement. We might speculate that people who are concerned have examined their own lives, recognize the restrictive opportunities and policies on minority group members, and are interested in helping create more humanistic channels for well-being. This help often comes as offers of support, comments that address stigma and stereotypes and push for transparency and participation of those affected in the discussion and planning of improvements.

CONCEPTS OF PRIVILEGE AND ENTITLEMENT IN FAMILY, ORGANIZATIONS, AND SOCIETY

Increasing awareness of privilege and entitlement may occur through access and interest in diverse sources of information. Without opportunities for conversations and exercises that encourage thoughtful reflection and scenarios and facts that illustrate actual systemic barriers, denial may easily continue. The use of Jane Elliot's (2006) eye color class exercise for privilege awareness demonstrated the concept within the white community. Exercises that place persons in wheelchairs or that deny vision have been helpful in expanding understanding of other's experiences.

According to Dottolo and Kaschak (2015), studies of whiteness have been conducted by sociologists and critical race theorists, but they have been largely ignored by psychologists and psychotherapists. They refer to Fine, Weis, Pruitt, and Burns's (2004) critique of the absence of research on the hierarchy of whiteness that excludes and deprives its intersections (i.e., women and those with disabilities). An example of this is displayed by McCoy's (2017) observation of how low-income people who receive government assistance or who seek handouts over work are judged.

Dwyer and Jones (2000) propose the need to incorporate the study of race in geography to assess the regional and national contexts that operate via residential segregation and how forms of whiteness are established in this sociospatial frame. The segregation of communities has essentially been tied to historical policies and attitudes. The research has been limited regarding ways affluent, racially integrated communities differ from affluent, majority-white or majority-black communities and how they benefit residents (Swanson, 2004).

OPPORTUNITY RESTRICTION

An essential method for establishing and maintaining privilege is the restriction of opportunities to others; and the promotion of ideas that those who have it, have it through merit. Meritocracy demonstrates how restricting access is used to counter affirmative action in Australian education admission policies. Principles of individualism, merit, and egalitarianism are used to legitimate opportunity restriction and justify discrimination of Aboriginals (Augoustinos, Tuffin, & Every, 2005). Two hundred years of white affirmative action, white privilege discourse in discussion of racial inequality (Hastie & Rimmington, 2014), and inequality of women (Hastie & Cosh, 2013) have been maintained via structures of employment, education, and religion.

Durrheim, Greener, and Whitehead (2015) describe the difficulty of actually moving from the old frames. They suggest that race attitudes are not products of individual minds but are products of social interactions that operate to maintain the denial of outgroup constructions. So, even as an organization may purport to proceed forward, efforts to stay away from specific race language continues to produce divisions and discredit the other's interpretation. Their research demonstrates how the use of comments about race actually shut down reasonable discussions about white privilege. These behaviors are observed in face-to-face and online communications.

ESTABLISHING RATIONALES

Analyzing the maintenance of existing privilege mindsets, also reveals the place of responses that have been formed to obstruct the outgroup objections and evidence of other ways of thinking. A predominant rationale for maintaining the system using negative interpretations of behaviors include blaming the other (Ryan, 1970) for the problems they have; rationalizing that their problems and behavior justify punishment; and shaping stereotypes to make society fearful of people of color, especially men. Narrow socialization and limited opportunities for observing positive behaviors or interacting on equal footings permit the existing views to continue.

BLAMING THE VICTIM

Coles's (1972) review of Ryan's book (*Blaming the Victim*, 1970) introduces him as a political activist who perceives behaviors toward people of color as scapegoating. Ryan's classic book describes the processes in play that operationalize racism by blaming people for the circumstances that impact them. This reflects the individual and ethnocentric frames that people have used to denigrate others. Ryan urges readers to look inward and acknowledge the structural barriers that account for wretched housing, high infant mortality, unemployment rates, and discouraging schools.

Blaming persons with low incomes is associated with ways in which the media tends to individualize and dehumanize portrayals (Lugo-Ocando, 2014). Not only has blaming been used to rationalize the disadvantages for people of color, but also for women who have been assaulted. Rape myths have been used to shift the responsibility of a sexual assault from the perpetrator to the victim. Suarez and Gadalla (2010) show that men generally accept rape myths more than women, but hostile rape myth acceptance (RMA) is also linked to beliefs about racism, heterosexism, classism, and ageism. The adherence to these myths is observed by campus law enforcement officers and, in some instances, by helping professionals (Smith, Wilkes, & Bouffard, 2016).

There are other concepts that operate to support denial.

COLOR BLINDNESS

Color blindness seems to be an effort to push away from race talk in a positive way. It has been used to suggest the absence of prejudice or racism by avoiding color. Yet it immediately presents a lack of respect for the obvious part of a person's identity. This approach was used by the National Association of Social Workers (NASW) in the late 1960s. The announcement of color blind beliefs by NASW in the social work profession resulted in the development of associations for black, Puerto Rican, and Asian social workers who expressed feelings that people, and social workers, cannot be dismissed because of color. The reality of color has to be addressed (Britton, 2013).

Color blindness attempts a response that goes to the other extreme. A rationalization for not wanting to be discriminatory is to avoid it altogether by pretending as if everybody is the same—no colors, abilities, nationalities, and so on. By assuming to take the high road, this concept provides another dimension to consider as we peruse the process of moving beyond the parameters of segregation. However, ignoring differences that exist in social and institutional structures denies the opportunity to discuss the realities and move toward better solutions.

Bonilla-Silva (2010) describes the situation as no one wanting to be called racist but asks how do whites explain the apparent contradiction between their professed color blindness and the United States' color-coded inequality.

Ferber (2013) reviews the context of whiteness studies that has not included all the players but is moving toward recognizing how traditional frames have narrow views and why additional voices help shape a more substantial understanding of what has been pointed out and who else must be recognized. McIntosh (1988/2014) was influential in setting up examples that clarified privilege and discrimination.

Bush (2004) shares an analysis of the economic and political transitions in the discourse occurring within the United States and globally. What has been highlighted is the broader view of the numbers: statistics show that white people are affected by the economics even though people of color are disproportionately represented.

COLOR BLINDNESS IS A FORM OF RACISM

Color blindness is considered a form of racism as it couches discrimination based on projected fairness into a denial of realities related to color and exclusion (Williams, 2011). Color blindness is denial (Bonilla-Silva, 2010). The basic ideas connected to color blindness do not address gender (Ferber, 2013) or class, but these dynamics should also be considered in assessing the rationales against broad dialogues about the vestiges of oppression.

Fu (2015) addresses it as a training and supervisory approach that is unattainable and one that reinforces prejudice. Williams (2011) sums it up: "Color blindness creates a society that denies their negative racial experiences, rejects their cultural heritage, and invalidates their unique perspectives" (para 4). In dismissing color from importance, it also dismisses, ignores, and avoids whiteness as a factor. This use of the *color blind* term in some ways suggests that the civil rights movement has progressed enough to warrant dismissal (Brown et al., 2005). However, this is not the case.

Offermann and associates (2014) examined the color blind concept. Racial qualities of respondents were connected to endorsing the concept. People of color supported multicultural descriptors. White people held color-blind views and held attitudes that were OK with hearing derogatory comments. Racial group membership also reflected different perceptions of workplace discrimination. "The more people endorsed institutional discrimination, the less likely they were to perceive workplace microaggressions of all types, and those not acknowledging racial issues were less likely to perceive what should have been blatant examples of racism" (Offermann et al., 2014, p. 505).

THE COLOR OF FEAR

The Color of Fear, which is a documentary directed by Lee Mun Wah (1994), illustrates the ways men of color and white men view people of color. In a weekend retreat, they addressed ways stereotyping occurs via narrow socialization about people of color. The messages that are sent out to make white people afraid of people of color also make people of color afraid of white people because the reality of lynchings, murder, homes burned, and other examples are reasons for terror. Although messages that were presented suggested that people of color harm white people, the data indicate that there is more terrorism by whites against blacks, especially through lynching and police brutality. They refer to their fears of moving around in predominantly white communities where they could be assaulted. On the other side, one of the white men suggests that people could do better if they just work harder. The discussion moves to the system limits on access that have nothing to do with personal fortitude.

Ethnic Notions (Riggs, 1986) also shows the early thinking of media workers trying to impose a positive image of slavery accepted by whites and African Americans. This video chronicles the reality of the opposition that always existed against social discrimination and became most vocal with the March on Washington in 1963 also known as the March on Washington for Jobs and Freedom.

Another example of the use of social fear is apparent in the murder of a white, pregnant woman in Boston in 1989 (Feagin et al., 2001). The murder of Carol Stuart was linked to a black assailant, and the terror that was incited in the Boston area was huge. The overall association of criminality with people of color is the basis for the perpetrator thinking that his lie would be believed; he could lay blame on a black man.

Research in the United States shows that people of color in low-income neighborhoods have disproportionately experienced proactive policing strategies and forms of police misconduct. Observations have been made of the impact of police behavior on suspects but very little research has examined the perspective of those stopped by the police (Brunson & Miller, 2006). Brunson & Miller's (2006) research suggest that minorities typically experience inordinate surveillance and stops, arrest, disrespectful treatment, and verbal abuse and sometimes react to this negativity in negative ways. The rough police intervention with Dr. H. Louis Gates in Boston (Pilkington, 2009) when he had to break into his house was a well-publicized item demonstrating the tendency of people of color to suspect police rather than expect protection from them (Staples, 2011). There is research that shows when officers treat young males with respect and exercise authority fairly, the males are more likely to perceive more police credibility and perhaps respond more calmly (Brunson & Miller, 2006).

Fear may also be considered a factor in the decision to intern Japanese Americans during World War II. "Over 127,000 United States citizens were imprisoned during World War II. Their crime? Being of Japanese ancestry" (U.S. History, 2016, para 1).

ROLE OF MEDIA IN CONTINUING NEGATIVE MESSAGES

The role that media plays in perpetuating stereotypes and promoting feelings toward persons who are not white, heterosexual, Christian people must also be recognized as an obstacle to improving relationships between diverse people. The messages that we receive through various communication mediums have essentially presented negative or incomplete frames of reference across different groups.

Gabler (2016) presents a discussion of why media coverage often misses the realities that most Americans experience. People who report the news in major cities don't look like the average person. Journalists are typically white males, members of the press elite. He sums up the press disconnect this way: "A country that is increasingly younger, darker and half female is being reported on by a press corps that is older, whiter and more male" (para 8). Journalists live in more urban areas than the broad geographic range that citizens live in; and many, if not most, of the major network anchors live with upper incomes when the U.S. mean income is about $52,000. So the people who report the news tend not to have friends, networks, interests, or discomforts that more average citizen's experience.

Senden, Sikström, and Lindholm (2015) present a study on the use of the words *she* and *he* in 400,000 Reuters news messages. Using a latent semantic analysis (LSA), a data-driven method, they discovered that *he* was used 9 times more than *she* and was used more positively. They concluded this seemed likely to maintain and reinforce gender stereotypes.

The labels used to represent out-groups influence the way people think of them. Saleem (2016), in a lecture at Emory University in Atlanta, presented research that indicated the role the media play in promoting negative views of Muslims. She noted that despite demographics of Arab Americans—35% are Catholic, 24% Muslim, and 10% Protestant—most assume all Arabs are Muslim. Her work noted the primary ways that people move toward understanding others is through contact. Often, this occurs in college classrooms, as prior references have indicated that fewer hate crimes are associated with more diverse campuses (Stotzer & Hossellman, 2011). But more routinely, there is not much intergroup contact unless people are willing to step into opportunities to meet different people.

Holland, Blood, Thomas, and Lewis (2015) discuss the politics of obesity and examine the ways stereotypes promote negative views of people who are large. Although we want to promote healthier nutrition, respecting body diversity is another element for inclusion.

Scharrer and Ramasubramanian (2015) report on the very limited study of the role of media literacy education in reducing stereotypes. In one of the few studies they described, a lab-based experiment that addressed white Americans' implicit racial prejudice regarding African American and Asian Indians. A combination audience-centered and message-centered approach resulted in some prejudice reduction. The potential for positive depictions and exposure of nonstereotypical and favorable portrayals by media to play a progressive role in intergroup dynamics is huge. Interdisciplinary social science research and interprofessional collaboration are needed.

ANGER, FEAR, AND RESISTANCE IN CHANGING CONSTRUCTIONS

Despite the effectiveness of the rationales regarding denial, color blindness, and blaming, the idea of confronting past social traumas continues to generate feelings of anger and fear. Steps toward improved engagement and acknowledgement of civil and human rights involve potential economic compromise, assessment of personal esteem or status, and disruption of the status quo. Consequently, the resistance is understandable. For some, there has been and will be growth and understanding in relation to others on the planet. For others, the path may lead to participation in associations that build on hate.

A discussion of humanism and the Black Lives Matter movement raises a salient component of the impact of oppression on white lives and those who have privilege under the existing system. Driscoll (2015) refers to "uncertain humanism" as a way of privileging human possibilities for flourishing that embraces uncertainty, not knowing, feeling anxious, insecure, and unsettled. Although he is speaking to the humanist audience, the idea applies to all who have been comfortable in their identity and their place in the world being informed that there are other ways of knowing and being that might put that place in jeopardy.

Religious dogma and governing policies often obstruct paths to equality. The atmosphere that does not seriously repudiate old stereotypes continues to stir up fears. Activism on all fronts is raising awareness about existing obstacles and ways bias and discrimination operate to reduce potential.

MICROAGGRESSIONS

Everyday communication that manifests as verbal comments or behavioral incidents that operate as disparaging messages are considered *microaggressions* (Sue, 2010). Generally, these comments are made against others, especially related to members of traditionally excluded

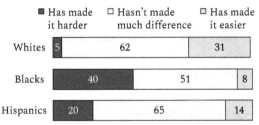

Blacks more likely than whites,
Hispanics to see their race or ethnicity
as hindering their success in life

*% saying that overall their race or ethnicity___ for
them to succeed in life*

	■ Has made it harder	□ Hasn't made much difference	□ Has made it easier
Whites	5	62	31
Blacks	40	51	8
Hispanics	20	65	14

Note: Whites and blacks include only non-Hispanics.
Hispanics are of any race. Voluntary responses of
"Both" and "Don't know/Refused" not shown.
Source: Survey of U.S. adults conducted Feb. 29-May8, 2016.
Q15a.
"On Views of Race and Inequality, Blacks and Whites are Worlds
Apart"

PEW RESEARCH CENTER

FIGURE 7.2

groups, but such transactions may occur within personal relationships. Sue (2010) lists *modern racism*, *aversive racism*, and *subtle racism* as terms to describe nonblatant racism.

Microaggressions often surface in college and work environments. The environment of denial, color blindness, and hatred impacts social work and other helping professional students as they navigate personal feelings and reactions, while at the same time acknowledging the systemwide and structural obstacles that do exist. Students may be able to recognize the variables involved in accepting the privilege they hold, but some may react with other feelings (Ambrosio, 2014). Whatever feelings erupt should be accepted, processed, and worked with in order to gain sense of their identity and establish points from which to grow. Some potential helping professionals struggle with expectations of appreciating diversity and may decide that the profession is not for them. However, the preferred outcome is the understanding of embedded feelings and the desire to pursue paths for civil and human rights. Figure 7.2 describes continuing feelings of exclusion.

INTENTIONAL OR UNINTENTIONAL

Microaggressions may occur unintentionally as micro assaults, micro insults, and micro invalidations (Sue et al., 2007 in Gonzales, Davidoff, Nadal, & Yanos, 2015). Generally, these have been observed regarding racial and ethnic groups, gender, sexual orientation, and physical disability. Research has documented the social rejection of people with mental illness, but there is very little discussion or research on microaggressions against people diagnosed with mental illnesses. The study sample of mentally ill clients and college students, (Gonzales,

Davidoff, Nadal, & Yanos, et al., 2015) was small, N = 38,—four focus groups with 38 participants. The results included descriptive experiences of microaggression that included invalidation, feeling minimized, having normal feelings labeled as *symptoms of an illness*, and patronization (being assumed to be inferior and dangerous). These microaggression incidents made the persons feel ashamed, frustrated, and stigmatized. These feelings could jeopardize therapeutic alliances and family relations, as some of the incidents were reported to have occurred by family or friends.

Further research on intersectional microaggressions (Nadal, Davidoff, et al., 2015) is moving beyond single racial aggressions toward people of color, Asian Americans (Nadal, Wong, et al., 2015), Latinos (Torres & Taknint, 2015), and Native Americans (Jones & Galliher, 2015). Nadal and Wong et al.'s study of 107 Asian American women and 50 men found that racial microaggressions predicted general mental health problems. Torres and Taknint (2015) noted the limited research on the impact of subtle and covert forms of discrimination on Latinos. In their sample of 113 Latino adults, they found indirect effects were most robust where there was low ethnic identity and low self-efficacy. Jones and Galliher (2015) investigated 114 Native American young adults and found links between microaggression experiences and their ethnic identification.

Nadal and Davidoff et al. (2015) examined studies of the impact of microaggressions on racial groups and noted the absence of studies that used multiple identifiers to classify the interactions. They suggest that respondent categories of race, i.e. Asian American, would not gather accurate microaggression data if did not also include other identifiers such as sexual orientation, expression, class, religion.

It is widely acknowledged that much of the existing research has been based on monocultural frames that limit the scenarios within which people actually exist and live with aggressions by dominant-culture people.

VIOLENCE

Violence ranges from angry individual messages or individual murders to hate crimes against members of other groups, against their organizations, and against larger and public groups. These crimes often make headlines and demonstrate the intensity of feelings and reactions some people have against others. The history of these actions has been mentioned in previous chapters. Recent incidents illustrate continuing episodes.

The impact of oppression on white people incudes reactions connected to feelings of dislike from ethnocentric self-views to reactions of anger. Subsequent behaviors include microaggression, rudeness, disparaging remarks, overt verbal aggression, and more violent acts of homicide, arson, and assault. The use of slurs and insults may not only be the result of anger but may also be used strategically to manipulate others' views of someone without "explicit impoliteness" (Archer, 2015, p. 1). The impact of socialization has resulted in this range of paths to awareness and maintenance of old ideas and stereotypes, as well as beliefs and attitudes about humanity and equality. The expression of views against nonwhite people include the use of racial profiling to justify discrimination and brutality (Da Silva, 2001).

ACTS OF HATRED

When the most ingrained feelings about others exist, reactions may reach the level of violent acting out against members of other groups perhaps in a school or workplace or in the community. From using a hand to depict a gun pointed toward a person on a street to violent incidents against individuals or groups, hatred plays out in different ways, places, and times and for clear or unclear reasons.

THE SOUTHERN POVERTY LAW CENTER (SPLC)

The Southern Poverty Law Center (SPLC) has documented hate groups and activities in the United States since 1971 with a mission to seek justice for vulnerable people. The center monitors actions that include hate and extremism, children's rights, immigrant justice, LGBT rights, economic justice, and mass incarceration. Their website lists current legal fights they are working on. Their group fights racism and bigotry through legal means by calling out ways institutions demean people with low incomes to justify their agendas. After the 2016 U.S. presidential election, the SPLC conducted a survey with 2,000 schoolteachers about the negative effect the campaign had on schoolchildren that have been related to increasing bullying (2016). Key findings of the study include the following:

- More than two thirds of the teachers reported that students—mainly immigrants, children of immigrants, and Muslims—have expressed concerns or fears about what might happen to them or their families after the election.
- More than half have seen an increase in uncivil political discourse.
- More than a third have observed an increase in anti-Muslim or anti-immigrant sentiment.
- More than 40 percent are hesitant to teach about the election. (SPLC, 2016)

HATE CRIMES

Hate crimes are considered offenses against an individual, a family, or property that are precipitated by bias against a race, religion, dis/ability, ethnicity, nationality, origin, gender, sexual orientation, or gender expression (Swignoski, 2006). According to Swignoski, most offenses are verbal abuse against lesbians and gay men, reports or threats of violence and physical violence against gay men, and physical violence against lesbians (p. 366). Reasons people move to act on prejudicial thoughts against others include fun and self-protection. For some, violence is perceived to be a valued weapon against differences.

GENDER IDENTITY

Reactions to gender identity and gender expressions range from microaggressions to various methods of violence that express animosity. The treatment of lesbian, gay, bisexual, and transgender people in the United States often takes on abusive and extreme punitive conduct by police (Amnesty International, 2015). The history of criminalizing same-sex sexual behaviors and failing to protect LGBT people against discrimination in domestic situations, in the street, at work, in housing, and in health care has led to the denial of their human rights in today's environment. There are 76 countries that continue to criminalize same sex relations, and six of these implement the death penalty.

Microaggressions. The microaggressions associated with sexual orientation are related to overt heterosexism and the psychotherapeutic relationship (Shelton & Delgado-Romero, 2011). In this research, themes were identified via two small focus groups of white participants. These included messages that avoided their sexual orientation, assuming the problem was related to their sexual orientation, overidentifying with the client orientation, making stereotypical assumptions, and being warned against their orientation.

In a study of LGBT people of color (Balsam, Molina, Beadnell, Simoni, & Walters, 2011), the microaggressions were associated with racism and heterosexism. Their experiences of microassaults, microinsults, and microinvalidations were linked to poor mental and physical health. The limited work on the impact of intersectional and multiple stressors for lesbian, gay, bisexual, and transgender people of color (LGBT-POC) points to the need for a scale to assess the stressors. These authors note that persons who employ a microaggression might not recognize it as such but the target often reacts with feelings of anxiety and helplessness. These feelings over time and experience contribute to poor mental health. Exposure to these kinds of circumstances in the context of romantic or friend relationships may also harm that dynamic.

Harsh violence. Despite the Matthew Shepard and James Byrd, Jr. Hate Crimes Prevention Act of 2009, or the Shepard-Byrd Act, "LGBT people—particularly black transgender women and gender-nonconforming gay men—are victimized, persecuted, and murdered at alarming rates" (Mitchum, 2013, para 1). Violence against perceived gender identity has increased over the past 10 years, although research in these areas has been limited. The reporting system is inconsistent across states, and the legislation across states is also not standardized. Tracking and prosecution level data are not accurate. Stotzer's (2008) review of data on violence against transgender people in Los Angeles County showed the confusion and complexity of gathering data connected with gender and sexuality and race. The connection of class and hate crimes is also limited but raises a significant area for review because workplace violence and harassment impacts the socioeconomic status.

RELIGIOUS GROUPS

Religious bullying is repeated aggressions in the name of the institutional religion. Aggression against religious groups has taken the form of intersectional targets, people of color in their religious environment, and religious minorities. Dupper, Forrest-Bank, and Lowry-Carusillo (2014) note we are seeing more tolerance, but the reality is that "racial and ethnic oppression and religious intolerance have been at the root of some of the worst atrocities in the US and world history" (p. 37). In 2011, there were 1,400 antireligious incidents—for example, youth being bullied and assaulted by other teens questioning whether they believe in God and if they are Jewish or Muslim. Another well-known example is the terror attack on African Americans during their Bible study class at Emanuel African Methodist Episcopal Church in South Carolina (Eversley, 2015).

COLLEGE CAMPUSES

The presence of hate crimes on college campuses is an observed reality. Campuses with larger numbers of people of color tend not to report frequent incidents as campuses with lower diverse enrollments (Stotzer & Hossellman, 2011). Their research suggests that the more connections between diverse people, the more likely improved relationships occur. The enactment of criminal laws against offenses is important in penalizing inappropriate words and acts. There are hate crimes laws and hate speech laws. (NPR, 2011). Most countries have laws against hate crimes. Social work has expressed its support of laws against hate crimes. More discussion is needed to ferret out the tangles and controversies of which behaviors and speech constitute inappropriateness.

IMMIGRANTS

Immigrants are often targets of negative stereotypes. In some circumstances, they have received serious harm and mistreatment. Keeton (2012) describes the use of strip searches in the case of minor offenses. O'Leary (2012) observed mistreatment of Latinos in eastern New Haven as common and traced it through communities of Irish and European immigrants. Those groups were able to assimilate based on color, but those not invisible are at more risk. However, with the assistance of advocacy groups and the FBI, the community is taking strides to resolve it.

Nevertheless, the push against undocumented immigrants is increasing. Jeff Sessions, the current U.S. attorney general, has announced that new rules will increase prosecutions (Sarana, 2017).

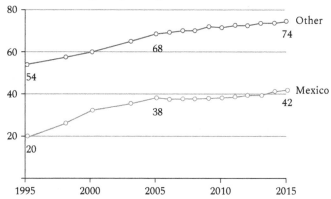

Naturalization rate of Mexicans vs. other immigrant groups, 1995 to 2015

% naturalized among immigrants eligible to become U.S. citizens

Note: Naturalization is the process through which U.S. lawful permanent residents who fulfill length of stay and other requirements become U.S. citizens.
Source: Pew Research Center estimates for 2005-2015 based on augmented American Community Survey (IPUMS); for 1995-2003 based on March Supplements to the Current Population Survey.
"Mexican Lawful Immigrants Among the Least Likely to Become U.S. Citizens"

PEW RESEARCH CENTER

FIGURE 7.3

ON THE OTHER SIDE: AWARENESS AND INFORMATION

Despite these enduring manifestations by individuals and institutions, there is also a broadening of the perspectives to move forward against inequalities and obstructed human rights. *Uneven Growth: A Speculation on Tomorrow's Cities Today* (Gadanho, 2014) is a presentation of efforts across continents and disciplines that illustrates how cities, their design and development, are important sites for addressing everyday struggles. A telling statement by Gadanho (2014) suggests what is needed to move forward:

> Uneven growth can only be solved through politics, but politics is broken when left in the hands of poll-driven politicians and screaming extremists. The New City Reader is a tactical newspaper installed in a public space that asks us to slow down, stop looking at our electronic devices, and once again read and discuss matters civilly in public. (p. 78)

For persons who have some responsibility in the development of children and youth, recognizing the impact of negative socialization should be addressed by modifying policy in ways to promote the strengths of all. The attitudes and behaviors of persons in authority positions have direct impact on how children respond. On one hand, children exposed to discriminatory words and behaviors may be hurt, but the moral demeanor of authority should speak to the positives regardless of personal feelings.

PURSUING INFORMATION

Students pursuing careers in the helping disciplines must be exposed to a variety of information to frame the history of exclusion and the voices and reactions across cultural groups. The typical student may not be informed of the multiple perspectives these voices present. Adjusting to the expanded sources of information is often intriguing for those committed to understanding and change, and willing to listen and critically reflect. Weis (2006) compares the developing research on masculinities and identities to a study of white college males whose precollege and college environments were highly segregated. Cabrera's (2012) findings reported that males with this limited exposure to others minimized racism, expressed being victims of multiculturalism, and blamed racial antagonism on minorities. These views were reflected in the white male fraternity groups. Guillem (2014) chooses to highlight her insights about whiteness, foreign privilege, and performativity through an autoethnographic reflection, as a way to make sense of it. She evaluated her privilege as she traveled from Spain to New Mexico by observing how responses to her visible appearance were based on her access to medical care. This was connected to whether her insurance coverage for her and her daughter was accepted. Depending on her insurance, not being a resident of the location would pose privilege or the absence of privilege.

Another view presented by Petersen (2015) suggests that white privilege is a myth. His perspective cautions increased "race talk" and suggests that by extending the conversation on privilege, especially in elementary and secondary levels, it can encourage more resentment and discomfort for children and youth of all ages. This notion is connected to themes in Berchini's (2014) dissertation that agrees with the need to understand our painful past and the need to discourage continually emphasizing racism. However, she observed that English teacher education is constructed with a whiteness frame that should be reconstructed or reframed to benefit all.

The exposure of majority-culture members to diverse resource information is usually limited. Their connection to history has generally been through a narrow racial frame. Sources of information have not provided any reason to question the status quo. But, for example, how much content about Africa or Asia is in the American curriculum (Kelto, 2015)?

This narrow socialization then, allows the natural ethnocentrism to wage and establish intrinsic biases against people of color, women, and people of diverse sexual orientation, gender identity, and physical and emotional circumstances. Project Implicit (2011) attempts to show how ingrained stereotypical information is with its Implicit Association Test (IAT). "The Implicit Association Test (IAT) measures the strength of associations between concepts (e.g., black people, gay people) and evaluations (e.g., good, bad) or stereotypes" (Project Implicit, 2011, para 1). Researchers at University of Washington, University of Virginia, Harvard University, and Yale University have participated in this research but make no claims about the validity of the interpretations.

DEVELOPING AWARENESS OF FORMATIVE INFLUENCES IN CHILDHOOD AND ADULTHOOD

Social work students and those of other helping disciplines connect with service users at various entry points. Becoming more informed of how human behavior operates on children during their learning years as well as on adults with various beliefs is important to developing strategies to address this range of feelings. Evaluating how the delivery of services may create additional problems and challenges, as well as diminish the restorative impact is a component of policy analyses. There may be eligibility requirements which support continuing negative performance rather than provide complementary support services as people gain self-knowledge, awareness and recovery steps are taken. For instance, a job offered with low pay and no health benefits would be a job and meet work requirements but would jeopardize the family's health care and recovery maintenance.

A substantial share of white respondents (31%) say their race or ethnicity has made things easier, a view that is more common among whites with at least a bachelor's degree, higher incomes, who are younger than 50, and who identify with the Democratic Party (Pew Research, 2016).

ATTITUDES: AVOIDANCE, DENIAL, DISMISSAL, OR CHANGE?

The impact of the history of oppression has resulted in attitudes that are most likely developed since childhood and manifested in prevailing stereotypical conditions. These allow and encourage continuing bullying, stigmatization, harassment, and adverse experiences for others. In his book *Dear White America: Letter to a New Minority* [2012]) and YouTube speech (*400 Years Head Start and How White Wealth Was Created* [2015]), Tim Wise, an antiracist activist, calls us to examine more closely social ideas about race that many have.

Changing attitudes that have moved from avoidance, denial, and dismissal have likely occurred through expanding knowledge about U.S. history, history of the world and opportunities for conversations and working with diverse people. Students need exposure to multicultural content and multicultural educators. There is a range of reactions to course content on white privilege, to different race and nationality of teachers facilitating discussions about white privilege (Sisneros, 2003). There is also variation on how students reflect their bias through their teaching evaluations (Smith, 2007). Nevertheless, helping professionals need to own these feelings and reactions as steps in the process of becoming more aware.

UNDERSTANDING OURSELVES IN RELATION TO OTHERS

Gaining understanding of the social work profession and our individual awareness of identity in the face of a history that has been violent and traumatizing to many is a step in assessment. Social work professionals' participation in dialogues, interprofessional collaboration, and advocacy involves psycho-social–based interventions that have the potential to inform, assist, and mediate people from various arenas. These interactions can address invalidation and promote nurturing. Behaviors may be prescribed through micro practice strategies. However, the conditions that impact all people exist at the institutional level and require evidence-based macro practices.

This micro and macro work is taking place in the United States, Canada, the United Kingdom, and other countries. Several countries are testing their support of antioppressive policies and cost-benefit concerns, especially regarding immigration. Evaluating the research on the individual, professional, and agency levels contributes to establishing the big picture of macro evidence and the implementation of changes.

Gallardo begins his book, *Cultural Humility,* (2012) with the example of organizational resistance by the American Psychological Association to provide an opportunity to discuss social justice values in a social/discipline/economic mixed venue. Discomfort or tension is likely to occur in conversations among people with lack of previous contact. When there are no clear precedents for having a culturally affirming and socially just conversation, preparation and planning are required. The discourse is imperative.

UNDERSTANDING OURSELVES WITHIN THE INSTITUTIONAL CONTEXT THAT PERPETUATES EXCLUSION

The expansion of ideas about racism and race, privilege, sexuality, gender, immigration, and the intersection of any of these components lays the broad framework for listening to and hearing diverse experiences and perspectives. There may be contention when the discourse urges dissecting the impact of existing views and policies on human rights and proposals arise to modify thinking and behaving to promote win-win dynamics and compromise rather than privilege and power take it all.

Muhammad (2012) describes the history of race illustrating the one-sided context of crime, where the social climate has been, and where it is. Some people of color may deny racism or privilege. Some white women may deny sexism or privilege. Some people with a mental illness and a low income may not feel stigma. Some people may react with anger to suggestions that they have, should, or might feel some ways about the implications of these kinds of challenges. It is what it is through different eyes. It is what it has been. Recognizing and appreciating the multiple views helps to build skills to respond to service needs appropriately.

SOCIAL WORK LEADERSHIP

The role and potential leadership of social work lies in the awareness of issues and continuing steps toward change that are already in place. Social work has listened to the various cultural groups and constituencies and has been progressively moving forward to listen to and stand up for all people. Social work has also taken a hit on its image. Typical stories related to child abuse or neglect elicits emotion by the public and focuses responsibility on social workers. More proactive relationship building with the media may assist in gaining community understanding (Warner, 2015). In recognizing how we have been influenced by the history of privilege and focusing on outcomes, professionals and consumers must observe, encourage, recruit, research, and collaborate (CSWE, 2016; Jacobson, 2012; NASW, 2016).

Different interpretations rising from various sources of concern require our attention. In the current climate of political commentary and divisions, claims for and against exclusionary procedures take on moral and scientific stances. Stanton (2016) raises his take on a candidate's presentation from a moral view. What are the principles involved? Overall, choosing to care about others has costs—money, energy, time, and effort (Meyer, 2011). Advancing change can be a life's work.

WOMEN

Although we know there are women in all kinds of jobs, the tendency remains to have narrow expectations for women. Jardine (2016) presents a video that illustrates the expectations of young children regarding jobs. This reflects the tendencies that usual socialization encourages. Jude Kelly (2016) presents a broader view in the TED Talk, "Why women should tell the story of humanity". There are many examples of the diverse goals women seek to achieve. Being able to use these examples helps progress toward greater understanding and inclusion.

DIVERSE CONDITIONS

Silberman (2015) uses the advances in neurobiology and neuroscience to explore evidence that people with conditions like dyslexia, autism, and ADHD are examples of a wide range of human variation that should not be denigrated but appreciated as another form of human vitality.

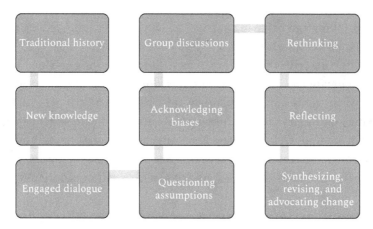

FIGURE 7.4   From Absent Knowledge to Integrated Information

Acknowledging the range of feelings, behaviors, and interests of persons opposed to getting to know others better, to working with the many advocates who want to enhance civil and human rights, is a start. Duhaney (2010) describes the Canadian analysis, which recognizes that in their educational system everyday practices and ordinary interactions continue to be obstructive. The brief video *Students Learn a Powerful Lesson About Privilege* (Buzzfeed Video, 2014) illustrates how access to privilege is easily unrecognized. Understanding the range of ways to recognize privilege and oppression is critical to analyzing how we might all move forward. Social work practice and interprofessional education for prevention moves across barriers as Figure 7.4 illustrates.

STUDENT COMMENTS

Students raised questions about moving beyond stereotypes. Using Sharon Flake's (2010) work identified the discomfort experienced when reading examples of social constructs of reality relative to the young black community. Questions arise—Am I racist? Can I make meaning through reflections? What do I need to do to move beyond this old construction?

CHAPTER SUMMARY

The history of oppression against women, people of color, and persons experiencing physical and emotional challenges has more frequently been illustrated in negative ways in media. The increase in hate crimes and negative vibes about people illustrates the social and class divisions that do exist. The social work professional is tackling the way things are and has increased advocacy efforts to challenge social and economic injustice. Assessing our own humility and respect of others provides the foundation to become more respectful of others and to push our organizations to do the same.

EPAS AND CODE OF ETHICS

CSWE EDUCATIONAL POLICY & ACCREDITATION STANDARDS
Competency 9: Evaluate Practice with Individuals, Families, Groups, Organizations, and Communities
- 9a) apply knowledge of human behavior and the social environment, person-in-environment, and other multidisciplinary theoretical frameworks in the evaluation of outcomes;
- 9b) critically analyze, monitor, and evaluate intervention and program processes and outcomes; and
- 9c) apply evaluation findings to improve practice effectiveness at the micro, mezzo, and macro levels. (EPAS, 2015)

NASW CODE OF ETHICS
Value-Service
Ethical Principle: Social workers' primary goal is to help people in need and to address social problems.

Social workers elevate service to others above self-interest. Social workers draw on their knowledge, values, and skills to help people in need and to address social problems. Social workers are encouraged to volunteer some portion of their professional skills with no expectation of significant financial return (pro bono service).
Dignity and Worth of the Person
Commitment to Clients (NASW, n.d.)

DISCUSSION QUESTIONS

1. After completing Exercise Question 1, discuss how the graph of the students' scores compares with their perspectives of the class as a socially conscious group.
2. What ideas does Chinn bring to the way we think about sexual orientation labeling?
3. How can policy reform address statements such as "We made it, why can't you?"
4. How can practice interventions address statements such as "We made it, why can't you?"

EXERCISES

1. Assign students to complete an IAT and bring in their results on an index card. Create a graph of the scores for the class. Discuss. (See Harvard Implicit Project at https://implicit.harvard.edu/implicit/)

2. Select white, a gender construct (e.g., female, male, gender, nonconforming), and another descriptor (e.g., autism, LGBT, and/or a medical/mental health diagnosis). Would this intersectional construct influence the white identity and the view of oppression and discrimination? Explain.

3. Refer to one of the articles in the special 2015 issue of *Women and Therapy* [*38*(3–4), pp. 179–184] at http://www.tandfonline.com/toc/wwat20/38/3-4. Read one article and select two key points to share in small-group discussion in class or online.

4. Select a current or recent news item about potential service users. Discuss these questions with your neighbor:

    a) Is there any prejudice embedded in the news item?

    b) What might be the impact on different persons? Why?

    c) Are there other ways this message could be interpreted?

    d) Discuss where the range of feelings, reactions, interpretations may come from.

5. Your instructor may have a set of articles for students to choose from. Apply the points for review from Question 4. Discuss.

MULTICULTURAL RESOURCES

Chinn, S. (2010) Chapter 6, Performative identities: from identity politics to queer theory In: *The SAGE Handbook of Identities* Edited by: Margaret Wetherell & Chandra Talpade Mohanty.

Flake, S. G. (2010). *You don't even know me: Stories and poems about boys.* New York, NY: Disney Hyperion.

Lee, R. A. (2008). *Multicultural American literature: Comparative black, Native, Latino/a and Asian American fictions.* Jackson: University Press of Mississippi.

McIntosh, P. (2012). *Mirror of privilege: Making whiteness visible* [DVD]. Retrieved from https://www.youtube.com/watch?v=8KYJ10PECv8

Wah, L. M. (2009). *The color of fear: A documentary.* Retrieved from https://www.youtube.com/watch?v=vBSImagHK8c

Williams, M. T. (2011, Dec. 27). Colorblind ideology is a form of racism. *Psychology Today.* Retrieved from https://www.psychologytoday.com/blog/culturally-speaking/201112/colorblind-ideology-is-form-racism

Wise, T. (2008). *On white privilege* [Video file]. Retrieved from https://www.youtube.com/watch?v=J3Xe1kX7Wsc

FURTHER READING

Britton, J. (2013). Researching white mothers of mixed-parentage children: The significance of investigating whiteness. *Ethnic and Racial Studies, 36*(8), 1311–1322. Special Issue: Mothering across racialized boundaries.

PART III

Systems, Organizational Culture, Status Quo Dynamics, and Change

Part Three brings our attention to how institutional structures that host or provide direct services to community citizens operate. Data illustrates that within national, state, and local systems there are usually some range of public services. Access to services, the quality, and the quantity of them frequently have to do with income and geographic location. The range of services, eligibility, disparities, and program evaluation data that reflect evidence-based social policy may be associated with strategic planning and the incorporation of consumer participation and feedback. Chapter 8 provides data that describes key institutional structures, economics, housing, education, health and mental health, and immigration. Chapter 9 describes social work practices to provide the services, and Chapter 10 offers strategies to reach out and engage with communities.

Reflection in Social Institutions
International, National, and Local Examples

CHAPTER OVERVIEW

This chapter considers the global view of poverty, along with some international and U.S. systems and disparities data. It presents views on why the disparities exist and persist. The role of dominant culture media agents is highlighted as a continuingly limiting and mitigating source of perspectives about the situations that affect our society. Major institutions of concern include employment, housing, education, health and mental health, criminal justice, environmental protection, and immigration.

LEARNING OBJECTIVES

- The Global view—Conditions we observe in the United States exist around the world.
- The social structure contains systems and subsystems.
- Service populations have assets.
- Disparities can be viewed from various viewpoints.

Benchmark: Students will be informed of systems, goals, and disparities.

CASE SCENARIO 1

Eric has been working in a homeless shelter in a large metropolitan area for 5 years. He describes the wide range of program initiatives his agency uses to reach out to persons of diverse sexual identity, sex workers, persons who have been in the military, and those previously incarcerated who have difficulty finding steady employment and stable housing. His interest in obtaining a master's degree will help him move up in the hierarchy. He is interested in moving into other leadership roles that may assist his role in policy formulation to address structural issues that have forced people onto the streets. What are the organizational entities he may have to contend with to provide quality interventions to the service population?

GLOBAL VIEW OF POVERTY

According to the World Bank Group (2016), the main source of global poverty data, a person is considered poor if his or her income is calculated to be less than $1.90 a day. It is difficult to accurately measure consumption levels across countries (Roser & Ortiz-Ospina, 2017). However, the measure has been tied to industrialization. Improvements in material wealth, health, and education have been connected to decreasing poverty. Some areas have progressed more than others. Higher proportions of poverty exist in rural areas, where access to food, good schools, health care, electricity, safe water, and other critical services is limited (World Bank Group, 2016).

Disparities around the world fall into several categories. Here are a few to consider:

- Life expectancy varies across countries. For example, a child born in Malawi can expect to live for only 47 years, while a child born in Japan could live for as long as 83 years (WHO.org, 2017).
- In Chad, 1 in 5 children die before age 5, while in Europe it is 13 in 1,000.
- American men are more likely to die of suicide than females.
- African American men in the United States are more likely to develop cancer.
- More than 1 billion people live with hunger around the globe.
- More than 50% of the workers around the world are in vulnerable employment with no social security or health benefits. (World Bank Group, 2016).

INTERNATIONAL EXAMPLES

Privilege and disparity exist around the planet. The Credit Suisse report (2014) notes, "Wealth inequality has continued to increase since 2008, with the top percentile of wealth holders now owning 50.4% of all household wealth" (Grandhi, 2015, para 7). It defines *wealth* as the value of assets, including property and stock market investments, but it excludes debt (Treanor, 2015). This report notes the higher income levels in the United Kingdom, the United States, and China. There are now more individuals in the middle classes in China (109 million) than in the United States (92 million; Credit Suisse, 2014). Data from this Global Wealth Report notes that India dominates the world's poorest 10%, while China dominates the global middle class, and the United States dominates the world's rich.

Most public opinion from around the world shows worry about the rising inequality (Pew Research Center, 2013). Figure 8.1 illustrates the opinions.

Inequality a major problem

	System Favors wealthy*	Rich-poor gap ... Has increased past 5 years	Is very big problem
Meadians for ...	%	%	%
Advanced	74	80	53
Emerging	70	59	67
Developing	70	70	74

* Data not available for China.
PEW RESEARCH CENTER Q21c, Q24 & Q56.

FIGURE 8.1

DISPARITIES

Disparities occur in similar ways around the world. The United States and Canada have similar statistics regarding the impact of racism. In both countries, people of color and indigenous people are somewhat more likely to have lower incomes and less wealth, are underrepresented in higher-level positions in government and business, and are more likely to have "bad" jobs. They are more likely harassed by the police, convicted of offenses, and sentenced to prison (Camfielo, 2016).

Existing structural components and organizational cultures maintain the ways work has been done and relationships initiated or established. As agencies respond to disparities, critics of service effectiveness, and the need for outreach to consumers, administrative leadership is under review. Regions around the world have different management and implementation methods (Best, 2007). There is a move to incorporate more expertise in social and cultural dynamics (Ananthram & Chan, 2013). In the United States, employees have gained more attention via the recruitment and hiring protocol (Abrams, 2013; wsj.com, 2017). More recently, companies also want to manage their reputation in response to employment reviews (O'Donnell, 2017).

INDIA

India has a staggering wealth gap. The difference in the wealth share held by India's poorest 10% and the richest 10% is enormous; India's richest 10% holds 370 times the share of wealth that its poorest hold (Rukmini, 2014). Popular sources of information on India offer a range of conservative-to-liberal perspectives on current events and include The Times of India, Aaj Tak, The Hindustan Times (Ranchi), and Indian Express.

INADEQUATE PUBLIC SERVICES

Barry (2016) reports that the uncontrolled growth in India is accompanied by the city government's inability to provide appropriate health care, water, transportation, and security services. Privatization of shelter has occurred in a way that sells places to sleep on the street that can cost 30 to 50 rupees (46 to 77 cents) each night. A documentary film, Cities of Sleep (Sen, 2015), uncovers the sleep vendors who have risen up where there is inadequate shelter. Those who can't pay for the night build fires, sometimes out of plastic. The number of homeless is vast, and many die early as a result of the wear on their bodies. The police report about 3,000 unidentifiable deaths every year. Many of the people, usually men, are day laborers. The documentary raises the question of the morality of the practice of exploitation for blankets and overnight space.

Sengupta's book *The End of Karma: Hope and Fury of India's Young* (2016) speaks to the mindsets of young Indians contemplating their lives and the structure of the institutional world they live in. Reflecting on the history of the cultural traditions and the ideas of the maturing young people, she integrates her immigrant experiences with family/household dynamics and anticipation of the community potential. She refers to her experience but emphasizes the realities of those living in India who want accountability from the government to provide the education they need. The political world affects the ideas and stories she shares. Another story that is useful in understanding the class system is *The Space Between Us* (Umrigar, 2007) a novel that illustrates the bottom line of economics: Class matters may override humanitarian ones.

ASIA

Asia is home to about 60% of world's population. There is no well-structured system of birth or death registrations (Irin, 2013), so many people are unaccounted for and vulnerable to exploitation in the world's two most populous countries (China and India, home to more than 2.5 billion people). Because there are few birth registrations, there is little civil protection, and that leaves children and adults without information needed for health planning. The World Health Organization (WHO, 2017) reports on the need for functional registration systems. The impact offers the basis for disparity:

> Unregistered children and adults from ethnic minority groups such as Myanmar's Rohingya, who are de jure stateless under Burmese law, by default have limited access to food and health care, leaving them susceptible to preventable diseases and malnutrition. Many are prevented from attending school and used for forced labour. (Irin, 2013, para 14)

China experienced a similar problem as an offshoot of the one-child policy (begun in 1979 but phased out starting in 2015); many families had more than one child but did not reveal this to the government (Gordon, 2015). Access to education and other services may be limited to members of that vulnerable population.

AUSTRALIA

Australia's situation is similar to other countries under review. Above-average economic performance of the 1990s did not trickle down to lower-income households and in some ways contributed to higher unemployment and adversely affected work incentives by limiting participation in the labor force (Ramakrishnan & Cerisola, 2004).

Dart (2016) reports for the World Health Organization (WHO) that vast disparities of the Aboriginal communities are largely associated with high unemployment and incarceration. The government is proposing to tackle these social concerns to address the challenges that members of their communities face.

All Ginibi's Mob (2007) shares stories and poems of lives in the close Bundjalung community of Australia. Ruby Ginibi uses the voices of her family members to express their observations of health, illness, incarceration, low incomes and love.

EUROPE

The history of the European countries brings various political and economic scenarios. The European Union and its regional status versus individual countries are of more interest in recent times. In 2011 (Ranesh, 2011), the Organization for Economic Co-operation and Development (OECD) reported that income inequality in the United Kingdom (UK) had risen faster in Britain than any other, but the wealth gap is observed in Germany, Denmark, and Switzerland also. As wealth has grown, the tax rate on the wealthy has fallen. The analysis attributes the inequality to the incomes of people working in financial services and the labor and social policies that helped the wealthy.

An October 2009 report by the European Commission, Solidarity in Health: Reducing Health Inequalities in the European Union (EU), serves as the foundation document regarding the EU's policy statements on approaches to disparities. This report addresses several variables connected to the health disparities identified across Europe. The disparities are linked to lower income status and the associated levels of education and occupations. In acknowledging the health problems are also a result of economics, the Commission recognizes that to make improvements social policies would need to be created in a way that would accommodate groups who have not benefited from current economic growth (Commission of The European Communities, 2009).

Docteur and Berenson (2014) compared the United States and European policies for eliminating disparities. While some conditions are similar, the U.S. emphasis on racial health disparities does account for many social determinants that impact health. Yet, the growing health problems among white citizens the United States raises more concern. The European strategy to collect data that is not linked to racial groups but to geographic location seems to offer a sensitive approach to establishing a commitment to the economic and social strategy for healthcare.

PROTESTS

The proliferation of protests around the world is tied to the many citizens who feel disenfranchised and neglected with respect to their needs for employment. In most countries, except the United States and Japan, 50% of the people say inequality is too high. In the UK, 65% agreed with this (Ranesh, 2011).

In a study comparing the health disparities in the United States and the European Union, (Docteur & Berenson, 2014) the way the health differences are framed presents the paths for efforts to make improvements. The Institute of Medicine (IOM) publication *Unequal Treatment: Confronting Racial and Ethnic Disparities in Health Care* (2003) compiled evidence that demonstrated lower quality of care and access by racial and socioeconomic factors. Ongoing research provides evidence that in addition to economics, environmental-, behavioral-, and education-related conditions play even more important roles as determinants of health.

The political landscapes in Europe and in other countries raise conservative and pro-human rights perspectives about inequality. The U.S. policy recommendations in the IOM (2003) report present racial and ethnic disparities as key, along with advocacy for vulnerability related to income, geography, disability, and sexual orientation; but it limits emphasis on socioeconomic factors. It did advise the potential of cross-cultural education for training health care professionals to improve provider–patient communication.

HISTORICAL CONTEXT OF OPPORTUNITY IN THE UNITED STATES

Institutional discrimination allows persistent policies and behaviors in our social structures—the labor market, schools, residential access, healthcare—to restrict and obstruct opportunities to members of some groups more than others. The history of the United States presents the context of opportunity. The mantra has been if you work hard, you'll make it. You'll get a job and can buy a nice car and home. For many, this has occurred, but for many others, it has been more difficult to achieve. As a capitalist country, wealth and power are concentrated in 1% of the citizens. James (2014) refers to Martin Gilens and Benjamin I. Page, who argue that as some people in the Unites States have gained wealth and power, they have influenced the political systems in ways that have diminished the democratic process. The key conclusion of their research is that these elites have organized and used their funds to direct policies on their behalf. Organizations representing average citizens have little impact against them.

EXCLUSION AND DISPARITY

The historical exclusion of some types of people is connected to the disparities that exist in institutional policies and practices that minimize and challenge many citizens. The democratic process implores equality. The reality of voter suppression (Ollstein, 2015) and obstruction of human and civil rights by those with wealth is the nature of our social landscape. The complicated context of the contemporary social climate presents professions invested in assisting vulnerable populations with the need to be informed about the range of diverse elements, the institutional resistance, and self-awareness. Work in this area helps build enlightened considerations.

Macro and micro practices are available to social welfare practitioners. We are concerned about the levels of ineffectiveness that exist in several programs across the country. Simultaneously, we are pleased that more attention is now placed on the strengths that communities demonstrate. Helping residents become more aware of them and capable of accessing them when needed contributes to community capacity building.

There is polling data that shows the "views of a majority of Americans—including affluent Americans—can be described as conservatively egalitarian, in that they are concerned about inequality to the point of being willing to make personal sacrifices to address it" (Docteur & Berenson, 2014, p. 7).

INSTITUTIONAL DISCRIMINATION

When we consider the full scope of what racism does, it influences all major systems in ways that obstruct the opportunities of many. Granted, life is not fair and is full of challenges.

In many ways, when people demonstrate concern for one another and work together rather than foster discrimination, some challenges can be limited and more people may be helped by assisting one another.

Let's not minimize the accomplishments that U.S. citizens across cultural groups have made. Many efforts are going on to help those who need food, family, and health care. However, there are people struggling every day. Edin and Shaefer (2016) describe the destitution in the United States that resembles that of developing countries. Social work, public health, education, counseling, and other related helping professionals exist to assist those for whom opportunities don't exist or are limited, those who are not members of the networks that get the jobs, or those whose identities, circumstances, and adverse experiences constrain the development of their talents. There are opportunities and obstacles in every area.

PRIVATE NEEDS AND PUBLIC ISSUES

Identifying private issues as the beginning of concerns that move to policy discussions and subsequent formulation has occurred for decades. Connected to early calls for social welfare and welfare reform, the pressures families faced regarding income became highlighted to address family and child capacity to purchase food and attend to medical needs. Today, families having to provide care to children or aging family members strains finances and employment options (Hunt & Reinhart, 2015). This attention to the developmental needs of citizens, health disparities, aging issues, and family caregiving needs have revived the concept. Levitsy (2014) describes this as "the process of reinterpreting longstanding 'private' needs as matters of public deliberation and decision-making" (p. 1). Contemporary concerns around the globe identify food security; environmental conditions that impact the quality of water, air, and soil; education; and the capacity of families to address family caregiving needs as elements in the forefront of enhancing social development.

CHANGING DISPARITY ISSUES

Disparities have been typically associated with groups traditionally excluded. Recent data reflecting the growing pattern of poorer health among white Americans along with their shorter life spans (with many dying at younger ages) was reported by the National Research Council (Docteur & Berenson, 2014). This does not fit the typical frame of health disadvantage. The expected example of poor health has been associated with low income persons rather than those with more advantage via education and health insurance.

Friedman (2017) refers to a report by Anne Case and Angus Deaton that describes how

> middle-class whites in particular have experienced an alarming increase in midlife mortality since the 1990s, driven largely by "deaths of despair" involving suicide, alcohol and drugs. These addicts did not suddenly lose their moral fiber. Instead, they faced poor job prospects, a steady erosion in their social status and, consequently, mounting stress. (p. 6)

RELIGIOUS ORGANIZATIONS

Religion has played a strong role in influencing how some services are structured and offered. Policies that exclude may be translated as absences of women, people of color, and persons with challenges in religious leadership roles. Shortly after the 1963 March on Washington Martin Luther King, Jr., said (Smietana, 2015) that the most segregated hour is the Sunday 11:00 a.m. hour in churches across the United States (Stetzer, 2015). Since then, according to the 2010 Faith Communities Today report that surveyed more than 11,000 congregations, the number of multiracial congregations nearly doubled (Roozen, 2015). Mega churches are reporting more diverse congregations, and so are non-Christian churches that include Buddhist, Hindu, Muslim, and other faith traditions. Some churches are promoting their diversity outreach to include persons of Deaf communities, LGBTQQI persons, and others.

RANGE OF RELIGIOUS AND FAITH ORGANIZATIONS

The Interfaith Calendar (interfaithcalendar.org, 2016) shows the expansive range of religious and faith traditions that are observed around the world today. Religion statistics indicate there are up to 4,200 different religions. Of these, there are 19 major denominations and 270 subdivisions (adherents.com, 2017).

The existence of many variations of religious and spiritual traditions speaks to the importance of religion. Women participants in faith exercises dominate that of men, especially in the Western hemisphere (Pew Research, 2016). Acknowledging the difficulty in measuring religious commitment around the world, their research noted that in 61 of 192 countries, women are more likely to have a religious affiliation.

The religious diversity of the United States has expanded in recent years with the influx of immigrants and Americans modifying their traditional religious activities. Emory University's Candler School of Theology is using a model that trains emerging Christian leaders to be prepared for engagement with other faith traditions to "reach across deeply held differences to help tackle concrete problems all people face" (Spirited Thinking, 2013). The Claremont School of Theology, in Claremont, California, is educating leaders of other faiths along with Christian leaders.

Views about religious groups have changed over time. The Pew Research Center (2014) reports on groups feelings about one another, shown in Figure 8.2.

EXAMINING RELIGION

Questions about religions are being addressed in many venues as people wrestle with contemporary issues and divisive realities. The 2017 National Geographic Channel series The Story of God with Morgan Freeman presents six episodes that examine religion and history and God's influence on mankind (Babcock, 2016). Contemplating the role of religion on human relationships and its place in the helping professions acknowledges resources that some clients use or don't use. Recognizing and evaluating the role of religion and its influence on perpetuating marginalization is relevant in our pursuit of evidence-based macro practices. Simultaneously, its significance for consumers' shared decision-making should be recognized.

Religious group's ratings of each other

| | Most negative | 0 to 33 | 34 to 66 | 67 to 100 | Most positive |

Mean thermometer ratings given to ...

Ratings given by ...	Jews	Catholics	Evangelical Christians	Buddhists	Hindus	Mormons	Atheists	Muslims
Total	63*	62*	61*	53*	50*	48*	41*	40*
Protestant	64	60	73	45	44	47	32	36
White evangelical	69	63	82	39	38	47	25	30
White mainline	63	62	62	54	50	52	41	37
Black Protestant	59	55	73	41	42	42	30	44
Catholic	61	80	57	55	53	51	38	40
Jewish	89	58	34	61	57	48	55	35
Unaffiliated	58	52	41	64	56	44	60	45
Atheist	61	47	28	69	58	39	82	44
Agnostic	58	49	37	70	60	47	66	47
Nothing in particular	58	54	45	62	54	45	53	44

Source: American Trends Panel (wave 4). Survey conducted May 30-June 30, 2014, Respondents were asked to rate each religious group on a "feeling thermometer" ranging from 0 (coldest, most negative) to 100 (warmest, most positive).

Note: Respondents were asked to rate "evangelical Christians" on the feeling thermometer; the question did not ask specifically about white evangelicals or about evangelical Protestants.

PEW RESEARCH CENTER

FIGURE 8.2

The religious freedom laws present areas for discussion in our process of study, reflection, and collaboration (American Civil Liberties Union, 2017).

Kujawa-Holbrook and Montagno (2009) propose even more specificity to the examination of religion. *Injustice and the Care Of Souls* helps to inform those entering pastoral care of the realities of people of color and members of marginalized communities. Selections in their book highlight the connection of justice to compassion.

ECONOMICS AND EMPLOYMENT

Racism, discrimination, and exclusion have a major impact in disparities regarding employment and income. The rates of employment and the economic situations of persons in groups that have been excluded from employment opportunities and access to capital is a key indicator of family well-being. The research clearly concludes that low income particularly affects child development and their mental, emotional, and behavioral health; it is a strong rationale for prevention based on poverty as a risk factor (Smith, 2013). Related research shows that when families are able to move out of poverty the family well-being improves. For couples with low incomes, the stressors connected to their struggles with finances and substance use would benefit from preventive and supportive resources.

A Brookings Institute report prepared by Reeves and Rodriguez (2016) refers to the economic disparities gaps. A chart describing the state of wealth illustrates a drop in the median black family income of $19,000 in 2007 to $11,000 in 2013. The median decline among Hispanic households dropped from $16,000 to $13,700 (Kochhar & Fry, 2014). By comparison, the median for white families in 2007 was 192,500 and 141,900 in 2013.

The median Asian household income was reported to be higher than all other minority groups (Pew Research Center, 2013) at $66,000 in 2010. By some measures, Asian family wealth grew faster than the median income of white families since 1989 (Federal Reserve Bank of St. Louis, 2015). However, some views respond to concepts of Asian wealth by identifying the range of Asian ethnic groups, family sizes, and use of family retirement monies on education that the growing children are expected to repay as variables involved in addressing class descriptions (Wessler, 2015).

The actual range of incomes across groups is variable depending on education, location, and employment opportunities. Some areas have educational and vocational pathways for people of color and persons with challenges.

The Pew Research Center report (Kochhar & Fry, 2014) describes the impact of the recession on all families and notes existing savings and other resources would also account for households' abilities to recoup from losses due to the crises in the housing and financial markets.

Figure 8.3 describes this.

Respondents generally say policies since the 2008 recession have helped (Doherty, 2015) higher-income people rather than lower-income people. A note about the sampling procedure

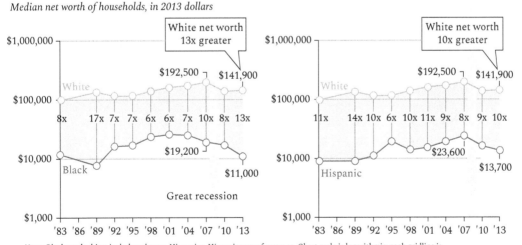

Racial, Ethnic wealth gaps have grown since great recession

Median net worth of households, in 2013 dollars

Notes: Blacks and whites include only non-Hispanics. Hispanics are of any race. Chart scale is logarithmic; each gridline is ten times greater than the gridline below it. Great Recession began Dec. '07 and ended June '09.
Source: Pew Research Center tabulation of Survey of Consumer Finances public-use data

PEW RESEARCH CENTER

FIGURE 8.3

for this survey is that contacts via cell phone, landlines, and a combination of each are used in gathering a sample. The variation in access to survey participants has changed with increased cell phone use. More information on the sampling technique and survey construction is available from http://www.pewresearch.org/methodology/u-s-survey-research/.

JOB CREATION AND EMPLOYMENT

The status of employment conditions in the United States is being more closely reviewed by economists, sociologists, and labor scholars. About 44% of jobs created in the aftermath of the recession were low-wage jobs. These are now a central component of the job structure. These jobs pay low salaries and do not have worker protections or opportunities for advancement (Cordero-Guzmán, 2015).

Recent graduates are looking for jobs in an environment with fewer higher- and middle-wage opportunities. It is taking longer to find jobs, and the pay is low. Many high school graduates are struggling to find employment (Abel, Deitz, & Su, 2014). Greenstone & Looney (2011) note that persons with a college degree are more likely to be employed and are making more than those with less education. The jobs projection through 2018 (Carnevale, Smith, & Strohl, 2010) note the highest level of education and technology skills will garner the highest salaries.

MINIMUM WAGE CAMPAIGN

The minimum wage is a controversial topic. On one hand, it assists lower-income families to support their families. It is contested as an effective strategy for fighting inequality and a means to correct labor market imperfections (Muravyev & Oshchepkov, 2016). Research shows that as youth unemployment increases others are pushed into more informal jobs with less protection and security.

Social work has a history of valuing the needs of low-wage workers as a step toward structural change or "societal reconciliation" (Reisch, 2009). However, there is also a history of not supporting wage (Chandler, 2009) campaigns. Recent leadership efforts are geared to promote economic policies for minimum wages. This is a step toward helping persons with lower incomes improve their circumstances. The Economic Policy Institute (Mishel, 2017) is promoting data that urges pushing the minimum wage to $15 by 2024, predicting 41 million people (30% of the workforce) would benefit. Draut (2016) predicts the working class will push the change process.

CASE SCENARIO 2

Jason has been working in an agency that recently opened a walk in clinic. They get people from the surrounding rural area and sometimes people who are commuting from nearby areas to the urban city about 3 hours away where the jobs are. Situations that have come to him include lack of child care when parents commute long hours to work; problems with children afraid when the parent is not available; and lack of food in the home when the money runs out. This week he talked to a man who was living in his car because he could not afford a dwelling. Although he is employed and trying to save money, he does not have an address and needs one to handle business and inquiries. He has been parking at a camp site but just received a police citation that warned against overtime spent there. What are the municipal regulations or local ordinances Jason may need to research and what government agencies does he need to reach out to for these kinds of circumstances?

HOUSING

The influence of housing in the status and potential of children and families has taken a more visible place in research in the past few years. Specifically, housing is connected to income, health, and education. Income and access to capital impacts the financing capacity families have to purchase housing. Housing marketing strategies also impact families' access to quality housing and to future financial situations. Researchers from Boston Medical Center, Boston University, and partner agencies have developed a child opportunity index that is linked to various sources of child data in the region. The data is being made available to help agencies do a better job in providing regional data to local community residents and agencies to address prevention steps for improving child well-being (Boynton-Jarrett, 2017).

HOUSING ECONOMICS

The dynamics of housing economics should be reviewed as indicators of access to mortgages for home ownership. Black borrowers are denied mortgages more than whites, but the data shows denial rates decrease as house prices rise (Wheeler & Olson, 2015). Advocates for a holistic approach call for improving housing for all target cities and zip codes to create a culture of health. Increased attention is focused on rental housing, cross-disciplinary collaborations that urge identifying common goals, and bringing in financial representatives for more innovative investment strategies (National League of Cities, 2017).

LEAD EXPOSURE

Low-quality housing and homes in disrepair sold through unscrupulous financing arrangements have put more children at risk for cognitive difficulties because of lead exposure (Hawthorne, 2015). The impact of housing on education is clear but not well addressed. According to Rothstein (2013), the segregation that exists in neighborhoods is a result of planning and zoning connected to federal and state policies implemented in local regions pertaining to access to mortgages, construction, housing, and law enforcement (Rothstein, 2013; Santow & Rothstein, 2012).

POLICIES THAT PLACED FAMILIES AT RISK

Housing policy in the United States was guided (Voborníková, 2014) by redlining and other specific regulations noted in the Federal Housing Authority's (FHA) *Underwriting Manual*. The policies established in 1934 (Madrigal, 2014) stipulated that housing communities were to be racially segregated. Well-known white suburbs in Levittown Long, Island and Levittown, PA were built in the late 1940s to 1960s and excluded non-whites. The *Shelley* Supreme Court decision was passed to stop racial restrictions, but the FHA continued to exclude. Methods used in rental and sales markets call block busting and steering illegal practices but have been and continue to be used to discriminate potential buyers. For example, Willingboro, New Jersey, was set up to be an integrated suburban community (Wood, 2003), but over time, it became troubled. Wood discusses the role the *Burlington County Times* played in shaping the public view of Willingboro as a black town with problems. It also suggested that integration was not desirable.

As the United States has become more diverse, the traditional demographics of people of color in the cities and whites in the suburbs have declined (Badger, 2013). Of 200 neighborhoods across the country, African Americans live in 199 of them; however, communities with few people of color tend to be located in rural areas (Isaacs, 2012). Badger's report of a study of the 10 major metropolitan cities shows that all except New York City have become less segregated. This trend masks the actual demographics in different areas. For example, Atlanta is more integrated primarily because of the increase in Asians and Latinos. The number of majority-black neighborhoods has increased (Pooley, 2015).

ACCESS TO HOUSING

Access to housing continues to be influenced by housing policies and the ability of people of color to obtain loans and mortgages. The U.S. Department of Housing and Urban Development has put forth a rule that instructs applicants that funding will be based on applications that do not support or encourage discrimination or housing segregation (Kusisto, 2015).

Housing costs for lower-income citizens rose by more than 50% between 1996 and 2014. The cost did not rise as much for those with higher incomes. Families without sufficient safety nets can lose their homes. The impact of eviction and homelessness includes negative health outcomes on mothers and children especially. A 2016 report from Children's Healthwatch and the National Housing Conference shows that public investment in housing for homeless families and rental assistance for food-insecure families would make a tremendous impact in improving health and lowering health care spending (Imbery, 2016).

PUBLIC HOUSING

The key housing programs have been public housing where citizens are placed, and housing vouchers (Leung, Sarpça, & Yilmaz, 2012).

> Voucher recipients are not restricted in terms of their residential choices.
> They reside further away from unskilled households, obtaining larger lots

and increasing their leisure proportionally. Even though they work less than the typical unskilled resident living at the same distance in baseline equilibrium—a result of the income effect caused by the voucher—they work longer hours than they would if they lived in public housing. (p. 319)

Public housing tends to discourage the labor supply and vouchers seem to support workers thus confirming the research that in-cash benefits work better than in-kind.

HOMELESSNESS

Another consideration of disparity in housing can be measured in the numbers and types of persons who experience homelessness for short- and long-term episodes. The economics of housing includes the supply of housing, price ranges, access to mortgages, and the number of affordable housing units. Housing needs in urban and suburban areas get frequent attention. Affordable housing availability in cities and the surrounding areas has been hard to find. The rising costs of rentals have impacted low-income citizens in ways that frequently result in household members becoming homeless.

The lack of affordable housing in rural areas is also critical. Only 21% of the population lives in rural areas. Much of the existing housing is old and needs repair (White, 2015). Older people who live in these areas cannot easily pick up and move away. The use of prefabricated manufactured homes or trailer homes is an option, but these have stigmas attached. Revitalizing these areas is challenging for local governments.

For people who have lost jobs or who have health or mental health needs, being able to afford a home is impossible. Rural homeless may be more invisible, as people may live in tents or cars. States with limited budgets work with nonprofits that try to provide services (White, 2015). Many people in rural and urban areas are undercounted in U.S. Census efforts, which impacts funds that could be made available (Wiltz, 2015).

Sandal and colleagues (2016) expand on the research regarding the devastating impact of homelessness on children's health. The reductions in the federal budget since 2010 permit fewer than one in four eligible households to receive housing assistance.

COMMUNITY CONCEPTS FOR HOUSING

The role of housing needs for immigrants has not been addressed widely. Yet the meaning of *home* and *environment* (Choudhury & Mahood, 2012) before immigration and their sociodemographics bring attention to the need of designers and planners to explore home ownership, neighborhood enclaves, and consider the macro-level topics within community planning.

The potential of community development is clarified by this Syrian example that describes an effort to develop safe spaces for women and provide services.

> Jasmine Tents are to be places of healing and development for women who have been impacted by trauma, loss, hunger, sexualized torture, and other effects of the Assad regime's assault on civilians. In particular, Jasmine Tents

are places where women can say "no"—no to the Assad regime and no to the jihadists trying to replace it. No to aging oppression, repression, censorship, and violence. (Jouejati, 2013, para 6).

AGING IN PLACE

The gap in housing of different demographic groups persists despite some efforts to reduce disparities. A community-spirited idea comes from Grace Kim to promote co-housing in *How Co-Housing Can Make Us Happier (and Live Longer)*, a 2017 TED Talk (Kim, 2017) that addresses the isolation that some traditional neighborhoods foster. Rethinking architecture urges more discussion about planning communities and including older people in this process. Blancato and Ponder (2015) note that social security keeps millions of older adults out of poverty, but lack of congressional interest and sexist and ageist attitudes have obstructed progressive ideas and the renewal of the Older Americans Act, which could address end-of-life policy needs.

More research on housing policies and citizen behaviors is needed to help understand why some members of the Hispanic and Asian demographic have responded to policies that are thought to target them (Narine & Shobe, 2014). Further research is needed to analyze the multiple economic and social dynamics and discriminatory practices that may influence decisions regarding homeownership.

EDUCATION

Disparities that occur within educational institutions result from longstanding individual attitudes and beliefs, institutional policies that promote opportunity for some and obstruct opportunity for others, limited awareness, and deliberate exclusion of social interactions that would contribute to social capital development. The absence of curriculum that includes multicultural researchers, authors, and analysts and promotes strengths across cultures can be attributed in part to ongoing unawareness of the contributions diverse people make to the world every day. There are also administrative behaviors that hinder diversification of teacher workforces.

Education is key to future opportunities. Most strive to gain knowledge in order to pursue interests, economic capacity, and innovation. The makeup of residential areas affects educational resources of local schools. Access to high-quality education in lower-income communities has been impeded by policies that tie school financing to property tax revenue. Areas with low-income housing generate fewer dollars for school services. Property taxes are the form of revenue that finances most neighborhood schools.

Brown v. Board of Education in 1954 provided legal rights for all children to receive education, but the reality of administrative regulations and public attitudes have obstructed the law in several ways. Following the *Brown* legislation, according to Middaugh and Perlstein (2005), there were efforts to encourage curriculum development that embraced forms of schooling that were consistent with America's democratic ideals. They report on a project directed by

Hilda Taba that addressed the campaign to integrate schools and bring in intergroup relationship building. She "developed new materials, approaches, techniques, and ways of mobilizing school and community resources for improving human relations and fostering intergroup understanding" (p. 235). These efforts to charge teachers with reforming social studies to involve clear student evaluation and assessment and holding schools accountable offers an important framework that is useful in today's environment.

Still separate, still unequal (Kozol, 2005)—referring to the continuing segregation and low-quality educational system many children of color experience—is a phrase that is old yet remains current. According to the Hamilton Project, "the majority of public school students, over 27 million, attend a high poverty school" (Whitmore, Schanqenbach, Mumford, & Nantz, 2015, p. ii).

PUBLIC POLICIES

The effects of public policies on public schools have endured and are interconnected. Santow and Rothstein (2016) report that the public schools faced with enormous challenges are doing as well as they can. Although many children who attend public schools in low-income neighborhoods live in warm and protective homes, collateral issues facing many others include

> health problems, parental unemployment, family crises related to lack of rent or mortgage payments, loss of instructional time because of moves to address housing and the stress of violence in their communities. These pressures reduce academic success (p. 1).

With school segregation continuing to increase in some areas (Toppo, 2016), many of the children are often isolated from the positive peer and family influences of middle-class environments. Situations with higher incomes provide children access to more books, reading, professional role models, and parents or caregivers who are knowledgeable of the procedures to monitor and hold educational professionals accountable for their instruction (Santow & Rothstein, 2016, para 1).

IMPACT OF STIGMA AND DISCRIMINATION

The impact of stigma and discrimination is approached directly in several descriptions of efforts to improve school quality. Howarth and Andreouli (2015) provide a framework that promotes intergroup cultural relations in the United Kingdom. There are specific guidelines for educational and community settings that begin with an appreciation of context. They acknowledge that discrimination and exclusion cannot be handled solely within schools but actually requires local and national initiatives "in order to engage with the complexity of the social context that creates and shapes these problems" (p. 190).

TEACHER EDUCATION

Teacher training that has maintained biases against children of color, children with special needs, and immigrant children is difficult to change. As the proportion of children of color increases, it become even more critical that education approaches address the gaps and improve student retention, reduce disproportionate expulsions as disciplinary approaches, and include multicultural research and text materials that validate the belongingness (Strayhorn, 2015) of all children in schools.

Teacher education is working on developing curriculum to support and engage children of color, those with special circumstances, and immigrants in order to retain their participation. The goal of the Zinn Education Project series *If We Knew Our History* is to introduce students to a more accurate, complex, and engaging understanding of United States history (zinnedproject.org, n.d.). The project offers substantive content of multicultural perspectives.

Teacher preparation that includes multicultural materials in the various disciplines and individual teacher/student planning is reviewed in teacher certification programs. The Educative Teacher Performance Assessment is evaluated as a tool to encourage more capable teachers. Yet proponents of diversifying the teacher candidates wonder if the certification process will obstruct teachers' historically underrepresented groups (Ratner & Kolman, 2016). Some fear that "the new tests will result in significant numbers of students leaving or never applying to teacher preparation programs," but also question the appropriateness of encouraging candidates with limited finances to "pay the costs of taking these state certification tests that many need to take over and over again in order to pass" (p. 21).

COMMUNITY AND SCHOOL CONNECTIONS

The place of community engagement and interaction is a social capital factor that also impacts children's educational development. Shoji and associates (2014) identify the types of social interactions that need to occur between and among parents, teachers, and program staff in low-income, predominantly Latino schools. The Harlem Children's Zone (2017) approach connects the micro and macro dimensions for academic performance.

The role of education in setting the foundation for economic opportunity is clear. A *U.S. News* report (Cook, 2015) notes that more children of color (black, American Indian, and Hispanics) are retained in grades, despite the growing research that suggests retaining is not the best way to address academic needs. More children of color drop out and do not graduate. Lack of attention to pedagogy needs of diverse students also includes the absence of student-centered methods of teaching math and science, courses needed to further educational interests and performance.

States vary in the graduation rates of non-white and white students. For example, in a comparison of New Jersey and Pennsylvania, the rates of Hispanic graduates are better in New Jersey than Pennsylvania (Kids Count, 2016). New Jersey rates are higher for all student racial groups, white, Hispanic, Black and Asian, than Pennsylvania (Governing, 2011–2012). Intervention steps are needed by the institution through innovative teaching and disciplinary policies and through outreach for family engagement to tap into their strengths in becoming more helpful to children in the academic learning process.

Students require opportunities to build relational connections that will produce social capital. Lee and Lam (2016) found a "strong association between academic achievement and positive social relationships with friends and teachers" that is a critical component for immigrant adolescents as well as adolescents of other groups (p. 144). Respondents that noted institutional discrimination were more likely to be low achievers. Paying attention to the need for peer interaction and opportunities to engage positively with teachers should be included in strategies developed by educators and policymakers.

DISPARITIES

An example of disparities related to education is the unlawful denial or delay of education to undocumented children (Mueller, 2016). An investigation of the Westbury (Long Island) school district found a "pattern of schools violating state or federal law by asking about children's immigration status or diverting them into alternative, non-degree-bearing programs" (p. 1).

The disparities that are connected to organizational structures that exclude have become areas of concern as more immigrant and refugee children arrive in schools. The level of their literacy skill (Hudson & Casey, 2016) may be impacted by their absence from schools in their home places because of strife and conflict. They may have experienced trauma and other adverse childhood experiences. If they come with second-language needs, another dimension of literacy must be addressed. Educators should collaborate with other helping professionals to address the literacy and trauma impact needs that may require substantial attention. Planning to appreciate students' native languages, assess assets, and the range of literacy skills they bring will be helpful in their transitioning to a new learning environment.

GRADE RETENTION

The role of grade retention in disparity or assistance in academic performance is a controversial area. There is little research on whether or how retention impacts performance, high school graduation, or college attendance (Warren, Hoffman, & Andrew, 2014). A major consideration is the measurement of retention and the lack of consistent measures over time. Their method of measurement is used and finds disparities in grade retention by sex, race/ethnicity, geographic location, and socioeconomic circumstances. They note the retention rates have declined since 2005.

OTHER INFLUENCES

There are other dynamics that impact the quality of education and the ability of students to persevere. Intersectionality not only influences identities but also affects health status. Educational disparities and disability requires further evaluation. The prevalence of chronic diseases contributes to disparity and the disabling impact among lower socioeconomic (SES) groups (Klijs, Nusselder, Looman, & Mackenbach, 2014). More effective treatment, rehabilitation, and opportunities for employment are needed.

REFLECTION FOR TEACHING STRATEGIES

King and associates (2010) discuss the use of reflective practice strategies that encourage teachers and students to consider situations from the view of persons with particular challenges. Students were able to consider the need to talk to people rather than assume they know what is needed. The case vignettes and discussion with Deaf community members helped students understand their need to read lips or operate in ways others may not be aware of. The levels and type of structure provide—such as precourse foundations, course/classroom assignment, and instructor fit—are areas found to facilitate excellent work.

Emdin (2010) refers to the need to address students' affiliation and alienation within the educational structures as a path to tapping into their academic performance and goals. Adenika-Morrow (1995) called attention to this as building self-esteem. Students who have been marginalized in the educational system need to be more welcomed and approached in ways that respect them, then encourage, support, and motivate.

Monroe (2013) indicates the need for more research in areas that would benefit teachers of all cultural groups. She points to the limited research of geography and discipline. The need to increase the number of minority teachers and the increased presence of diverse children, especially in the southern states that have growing demographic changes, requires more understanding of what steps and behaviors teachers use who are able to establish successful discipline in their classrooms (Monroe, 2013).

EDUCATIONAL FINANCING

Economic resources are basic to providing adequate and higher-quality education. According to the Department of Education (2016), states and localities are the primary sources of K–12 education funding. There are implementation variations that impact the sources and levels of funding and the schemes that maintain inequities related to race and class. Hinson (2015) examines how Title I of the Elementary and Secondary Education Act distributes financial aid and argues that it is ineffective. She advocates for an evaluation of the policies at the state level to assess the adverse impact on equality of opportunity by bringing attention to various effects. "High-poverty schools may appear to receive the same basic education resources as low-poverty schools within a single school district when in fact they do not" (Hinson, 2015, p. 387). This article argues that

> because the United States has included no measure on the effects of disadvantages such as race, ethnicity, national origin, and cultural isolation, and no measure on child poverty, in both the ESEA and the NCLB Title I funding scheme, the United States has failed to address educational funding inequities in public schools. (p. 382)

There are other ways that financing shortchanges schools. The role of parents in fund-raising in public education has not been well documented via research. Parents who have chosen public education often operate as economic participants by fund-raising through their high-income capacity and connection to social networks that can contribute to provide additional resources that support their students' needs. Posey-Maddox (2016) explores how school-based parent fund-raising can exacerbate resource and opportunity disparities.

CHARTER SCHOOL COMPETITION

The situation regarding charter schools and their role in diminishing opportunities for public school students is another concern regarding educational inequities. Karp (2015) reviews the school reform controversy in Newark and Montclair, New Jersey. There is some evidence that pro-public education coalitions are organizing across urban, suburban, race, and class lines with some emphasis on undoing racism. The corporate education reform side is pushing proposals that lean toward privatization; reducing pay for aides, custodians, and cafeteria workers; weakening teacher rights; and increasing test-based evaluation of students, teachers, and schools of education, among other policies that replace local-citizen governance with mayoral and state forms of authoritarianism.

Practices in charter schools, considered vehicles of improved methods, often reflect punitive procedures that violate state laws. In some cases, schools violated procedures for suspending children with disabilities and suspended students without hearings (Karp, 2015, p. 8). The question is raised that although the charters promote open-door policies through the lottery, the rigid discipline and high expulsion rates leave hand-picked students that contribute to higher achievement scores (Rich, 2016). So what does this mean for public education?

Kids Count provides visuals of the comparative data (2016). For example, at www.datacenter.kidscount.org, compare the median income of households with children in states near you. How do families compare regarding housing and education in these states? According to their data,

> high-quality prekindergarten programs for 3- and 4-year-olds can improve school readiness, with the greatest gains accruing to the highest-risk children. Head Start and the expansion of state-funded programs since the 1990s have greatly increased access to preschool. But many children, especially 3-year-olds, continue to be left out, exacerbating socioeconomic differences in educational achievement. (para 1).

This indicator is included in the Kids Count Child Well-Being Index. Examining the data per state regarding children placed in families other than their own shows how states' resources for children are being used.

HEALTH AND MENTAL HEALTH

Global initiatives for better health and mental health have evolved from work on global health and mental health concerns. In 2003, the National Institute of Mental Health partnered with other health leaders to establish a set of 40 challenges to facilitate efforts to mesh mental health and health services in a way that more effectively address the multiple issues citizens bring to service settings. In 2007, planning added goals for more health-specific health issues including noncommunicable disorders (NIMH, 2016). These were met with more funding and new programs.

HEALTH

According to Bradley and Taylor (2013), the United States spends more on health care but has poorer outcomes than other developed countries and members of the OECD. The impact of social determinants of health, income, education, housing, education, stress, and social relationships affects overall well-being. Without investments in economic, environmental, and social supports, health goals are more difficult to achieve. Evidence that supports this effect has led to the call for a holistic approach that requires a cross-disciplinary system that urges local and federal government to operate as a catalyst for innovation in housing, employment, and food security that also fosters application and inclusion across all SES groups.

AWARENESS

Awareness of risk factors for hypertension, hypercholesterolemia and weight, and indicators related to cardiac risk were found to be low among foreign-born English speakers and non-English-speaking immigrants. Immigrant status affected persons' awareness of prevention possibilities regarding immunization, dental care, cancer screening, and knowledge of diabetes (Langellier et al., 2012). Overall, there are efforts emphasizing the disparities in pediatric mental health and the enormous toll the lack of access and low-quality services take on children, youth, and their families. Recommendations include acknowledging the need to hear from minority youth and their families about their preferences (Alegria, Vallas, & Pumariega, 2010) and ensuring collaboration that recognizes that some traditional practices will have to change.

Disparities in health and mental wellness are frequently associated with income levels and personal habits. To a large extent, services are driven by access to insurance plans and technology. As more pushes for natural and complementary approaches are expressed, evidence of environmental toxins, circumstances, and policy impacts have also been revealed. These bring more attention and awareness to the dynamics of macro systems of personal and community well-being.

Healthy People 2020 defines a health disparity as a "particular type of health difference that is closely linked with social, economic, and/or environmental disadvantage. Health disparities adversely affect groups of people who have systematically experienced greater obstacles to health based on their racial or ethnic group; religion; socioeconomic status; gender; age; mental health; cognitive, sensory, or physical disability; sexual orientation or gender identity; geographic location; or other characteristics historically linked to discrimination or exclusion." (SAMHSA, 2017, para 8). A basic definition of Health is the state of being free of illness or injury. Generally, this has referred to well-being of one's body. The National Institute of Health works to prevent disease and improve health. Disparities in health and mental wellness are frequently associated with income levels and personal habits. To a large extent, services are driven by access to insurance plans and technology. As more advocates push for natural and complementary approaches evidence of environmental toxins, circumstances, and policy impacts have also been revealed. These bring more attention and awareness to the dynamics of macro systems of personal and community well-being.

The Department of Health and Human Services (HHS) and the Joint Center for Political and Economic Studies note the multiple impacts of health and disparities and the costs of health inequalities and early deaths. The emphasis has shifted to effective prevention treatment and services for diverse populations (SAMSHA, 2016). The planning by SAMSHA includes five strategies to improve behavioral health equity: data, communication, policy, workforce development, and customer service/technical assistance that is connected to a data-driven approach separated out by ethnic groups and sexual orientation, where possible.

The planning by SAMSHA includes five strategies to improve behavioral health equity: data, communication, policy, workforce development, and customer service/technical assistance that is connected to a data-driven approach separated out by ethnic groups and sexual orientation, where possible.

A 2016 report—The Impacts of Climate Change on Human Health in the United States: A Scientific Assessment (U.S. Global Change Research Program, 2016)—describes how impending climate changes will impact public health. The report is based on over 1,800 published scientific studies and new federal research and was reviewed by the National Academies of Sciences (U.S. Global Change Research Program, 2016). Forecasts of more heat waves and higher pollution predict increasing numbers of potential respiratory episodes and heat-related deaths. Governmental agencies need to modify plans to address projections for communities.

DISPARITIES

The disparities in health care are also apparent in the connection of injuries to kinds of work performed. Studies show Hispanics have a higher number of work-related injuries (McCoy et al., 2015). Workers in lower-level jobs have more work-related injuries.

Another issue of concern about health service access is the influence on medical doctors of traditional stereotypes about black people. According to Tweedy (Mock, 2015), 25% of medical student respondents in a major survey indicate they believe that African Americans don't feel pain as much as white people and that their skin is thicker. Using these beliefs, which are not based on medical facts, many doctors do not address pain management in appropriate ways for patients of color.

Women's health care needs and their reproductive rights involve disparities, especially for those without insurance. Women's right to birth control should not be connected to an employer's religion. They should be able to make choices for their own reproductive health (NASW, 2016, para 4).

Sullivan and Eagel (2005) address reasons for the glaring gaps in the health status of blacks and whites. Low income certainly impacts the lack of access to best medical services, but there are also biological factors and the health behavior of individuals and groups (p. 5). The way resources have been focused also attribute to the continuing disparities. An Institute of Medicine (1999) report, The Unequal Burden of Cancer, notes the miniscule budget allocation of research monies for the study of cancer among the nation's minority citizens.

Limited English-proficient patients are less likely than English-proficient patients to use any remote medication refill system (Moreno et al., 2015). Patients with chronic conditions who are not English proficient may risk medication non-adherence, which increase disparities within this group.

AGING ISSUES

Disparities exist for the elderly, elders of color and LGBTQQI groups, and those with other health diagnoses (Dilworth-Anderson, Pierre, & Hilliard, 2012). This has been established through the ways that planners have neglected including representatives of all groups of citizens in designing service delivery. Their case study of Alzheimer's disease is presented as an example of social injustice. Dementia is often undiagnosed or misdiagnosed among racial/ethnic minorities. When it is diagnosed, antidementia medication may not be prescribed (Zuckerman et al., 2008).

Of great concern is the use of dominant service models that pose ethical dilemmas (Lee, 2015) by the exclusion of persons in need who do not commit to the traditional service model. This is particularly apparent in abstinence-only addiction programs. "The abstinence-only service delivery model is a barrier to the majority of substance users who need services" (Lee, 2015, p. 62). The moral, disease, and abstinence models have been shaped by paternalistic and authoritarian frames. Harm reduction and recovery models are flexible and work by engaging with individuals and their families to meet them where they are.

MENTAL HEALTH

The disparities in mental health care are stark. Mental health is the state of well-being of one's mind and emotions. Mental health involves how we feel, think and behave and our sense of well-being, confidence. "Approximately 25% of people in the UK have a mental health problem during their lives. The high incidence of mental health disorders over several years has been documented in the US despite increasing treatments (Jorm, Patten, Brugha, & Mortubai, 2017). According to SAMSHA (2016) health disparities exist at concerning rates among communities that tend to experience stress and discrimination such as racial and ethnic groups; lesbian, gay, bisexual, transgender, and questioning (LGBTQ) populations; people with disabilities; transition-age youth; and young adults (SAMSHA, para 3).

The National Institute of Mental Health is promoting global initiatives to address mental health service needs (NIMH, 2016). The goals that they have identified have been developed through the use of community practice methods and techniques to gather ideas from the communities and recommend priorities. Constituent groups suggest that mental health services personnel should consider the impact of methods, collaboration, funding, staff recruitment, transportation, housing and employment. In 2010, the Grand Challenges in Global Mental Health initiative was launched to focus collective efforts on these issues (nimh.nih.gov, 2016).

RECOVERY

SAMSHA (2017) defines *recovery* as a process of change that includes evidence-based clinical treatment and social supports. Recovery acknowledges the process of healing that includes the identification and use of a range of events, activities, and services that offer some type of assistance. These include education, employment, housing, peer services, illness care, or other clinical service. According to SAMSHA, services delivered by professionals and peers are offered in various settings including formal and informal service settings. High schools are also designated for specific recovery options and have been reported to have high retention rates (SAMSHA, Recovery, para 13).

According to the *Global Burden of Disease Study 2010*, "mental and behavioral disorders are the leading causes of disability worldwide" (Collins et al., 2011, p. 1). The traditional paradigms have supported funding for the medical profession to conduct research on diagnoses related to biology and genetics—emphasizing nature over nurture. Very limited research has been financed that explores the social environment impact on mental health and its support of other health behaviors. More effort in this area is needed and is expanding. This is particularly relevant for social work, mental health, and family policy development and service collaborations.

STIGMA ASSOCIATED WITH MENTAL HEALTH

The stigma against persons with mental health distress is strong, and it is very difficult to change attitudes and beliefs about it (Makowski et al., 2016). Yet there is a relationship between stereotyping, discrimination experiences, and mental stress as well as between childhood adverse experiences. It is not difficult to conclude that the ways in which dominant culture impacts those who have been excluded interferes with their interest to seek services in the traditional formats (nami.org). Attention is urged to design access points for young people already associated with child welfare and juvenile correction, and those in low income households that will attract them and demonstrate benefits of employment and family supports (Jiang, Ekono, & Skinner, 2015).

CHILDREN'S EMOTIONAL WELL-BEING

According to the National Association of Mental Illness (NAMI), one in five children ages 13 to 18 experience or will experience a serious mental health episode. About 20% of youth live with a mental health condition. The services delivery for children and youth is inadequate for the level of need that exists. (Stagman & Cooper, 2010).

Although there has been an emphasis on reducing disparities since 2000, serious questions remain about the effectiveness and ability to provide quality services to racial/ethnic minority children (Alegria et al., 2010). From a broad view, "all professionals who interact with children on a regular basis are well positioned to learn from and implement science based strategies that prevent and address the impacts of toxic stress" (National Scientific Council on the Developing Child, 2005/2014, p. 7).

Much of the disparity observed in mental health care appears to be related to access (LeCook, Manning, & Alegria, 2013). Some evidence suggests that the absence of encouragement by providers or suggestions and recommendations for youth to seek services could account for the youth's being less likely to use specialty care sectors (Alegria, Lin et al., 2012). Innovations in screening, community education for families, and emotional task-sharing protocols may aid in providing community-based prevention services that can address the resistance to traditional services.

NEUROSCIENCE

Emerging brain and neuroscience research offers significant knowledge on the impact of stress in the roots of mental health in children and urges more financial and programmatic supports for early intervention. This research (National Scientific Council on the Developing Child, 2005/2014) describes the impact on the developing brain structure of children who live in stressful and adverse circumstances and the potential for repair via early and ongoing positive and nurturing interventions.

Working Paper 3 of the National Scientific Council on the Developing Child (2005/2014) points out that healthy development "can be derailed by excessive or prolonged activation of stress response systems in the body and the brain" (p. 1). Yet there is no credible evidence that the exposure of early adversities cannot be repaired. Research has typically focused on negative impacts and unfounded speculations. Macro-practice evidence in the areas that connect science and policy is especially needed. Disparities that result from the effects of toxic stress on parents and children in low-income households could be addressed through targeted early intervention policies, TANF- (Temporary Assistance for Needy Families), ADA- (American With Disabilities Act), and Medicaid-related requirements, and services for screening, assessment, and pediatric collaborations that involve foster care, school sites, and other universal (nonstigmatizing) locations (Shonkoff, Boyce, & McEwen, 2009).

Social justice is the idea that persons should not be denied their rights because of perceptions of inferiority by those with power and influence. These habits have brought us to where we are. There is tremendous evidence that our complex problems can be tackled. The work demands accepting an added level of effort and working with persons who resist. The pathway to serious improvements continues to be a challenge.

WELFARE: FOOD AND WATER

The welfare of the populations we serve is tied to their economics and survival. We cannot ignore the broad spectrum of people in the world of various identities and their basic needs and rights for food and water. There are high-wage earners, middle-range employees, and low-range wage workers. There are wealthy and healthy citizens, but social work and public health especially face citizens who may need assistance in tackling daily living requirements. In several ways, micro-oriented planning has emphasized personal-problem diagnosis rather than macro-service planning. Emerging ideas call for macro practice to emphasize attention to clean water and nutritional food.

Generally, access to water has been taken for granted. Recent incidents have introduced the status of water cleanliness (e.g., Flint, MI; Newark, NJ). There is a developing awareness of the extent and possibility of water contamination, air pollution, or climate influences. These are areas which community residents should be informed. There should be opportunities for residents and agencies to work together to modify and plan reasonable strategies regarding the impact of global warming. Gina McCarthy, chief of the Environmental Protection Agency

(EPA), notes climate change also affects mental health and helping community members understand these links is needed (U.S. Global Change Research Program, 2016).

Stanford and Taylor (2013) acknowledge the association of social policy and professional practice to the persistent social problems in Australia. They connect a white perspective to the way welfare dependency is framed and argue that frame rationalizes the way the victim is blamed. They believe that moving away from that frame will enhance better responses to welfare issues.

TANF (Temporary Assistance for Needy Families) (USHHS, 2017) shifted the safety net in 1996 to require employment of mothers with young children. Rather than provide support for new moms to attach and nurture the children to begin a healthy relationship, the pressure to be employed has led to children being unsupervised while mothers work two or three jobs. Despite requests for data and accountability regarding this program, (Hildebrandt & Stevens, 2009) there is evidence that poverty and family crises have been exacerbated because of the policy change (Floyd, Pavetti & Schott, 2017).

The welfare of humans includes these several aspects we are reviewing, but the place of food insecurity and security belongs here as well. Research shows that Supplemental Nutrition Assistance Program (SNAP) "is one of the single-most effective pieces of legislation in protecting the health of young children and promoting their cognitive, emotional, and social development (Ewing, 2014, para 3).

The multiple-dimension landscape urges social workers to be less passive and step up to actively pursue policies that address the economic and social welfare access realities of the populations served by the profession. Integrating more poverty-aware knowledge into social work education can help students be informed of the range of welfare needs, gaps, and opportunities to conduct interprofessional and consumer collaboration. Skills needed in the curriculum to address these myriad issues include multidimensional and multicultural knowledge and techniques. Establishing relationships across social statuses and using geographic information systems (GISs; Chronicle of Social Change, 2016), data, and mapping will move us forward in advocacy and realization of rights.

CRIMINAL JUSTICE (CJ)

The United States has the distinction of being the top jailer in the world with the longest sentences and appalling rates of imprisonment disparity (Suk, 2016). According to Gopnik (2012), "there are more black men in the grip of the criminal-justice system—in prison, on probation, or on parole—than were in slavery in 1850" (para 3). Institutional policies and practices are the operating channels that allow or encourage discrimination and disparity in the application of criminal justice. We are aware of the huge absence of parity in suspensions, expulsions, detentions, arrests, and incarceration of young men and women of Native American, African American, and Latino descent.

Not only are we informed of the disparity that exists, but the profit and cruelty that accompanies the prison industry should also be mentioned. The scale of brutality or zeal for punishment captured in the U.S. system includes the extent of solitary confinement, the magnitude of rape, and the conceptualization of prison as a slave system—cheap labor for major corporations (Gopnik, 2012).

The for-profit status of prisons exacerbated the dynamics. Evaluation of the prison industrial complex by Davis (1998) and Schlosser (1998) includes the profit motives and compares the sentencing methods to other countries. Davis reviews the prison construction bonds and contracts tied to the backs of typically low-income people by the corporations seeking huge profits. Several companies, such as Westinghouse, IBM, Motorola, Boeing, Texas Instruments, and others, reaped benefits through investments and the sales of products at high rates. MCI charged high telephone rates to inmates and their family members for telephone calls.

Schlosser (1998) noted the large prison population numbers could be explained in part by sentencing procedures for drug offenses. Over the past twenty years it has been recognized that crime rates have decreased and factors for the high rates include higher rates in black neighborhoods, racial bias, and use of past criminal records (Lopez, 2016). Although there is a move to reform sentencing in ways that address non-violent offenders those who have committed violent offense pose a more difficult road to policies.

In many countries, these drug offenses would be dispensed through community service, fines, and drug treatment (Law Library of Congress, 2016). In the United States, young people of wealthy families often do receive sentencing decisions that limit destruction to their lives.

The increase in incarceration occurred over time even as crime rates declined and continue to decline. Now, the number of incarcerated persons has dropped for the third year and is attributed mostly to removing or reducing cash bail (Bellafante, 2018) in several states. As policies continue to be reviewed other dynamics are revealed that impact the ability for released offenders to be maintained in the community. Lack of housing is critical and the need for continual employment remains.

IMPACT ON FAMILIES

The Urban Institute (Peterson, Fontaine, Kurs, & Cramer, 2015) documents several ways the criminal justice (CJ) system disparately impacts families and communities of color. Not only do the disproportionate numbers show how many are affected, but the related context expands the considerations of challenges. Researchers conducted site visits in New York City, Pittsburgh, Pennsylvania, and the San Francisco Bay area to examine the impact of incarcerated parents on children's trauma and subsequent practices to address the family's needs.

Their report shows that one fifth to one third of children with an incarcerated parent are present when the arrest occurs. The extent of challenges, the unknown impact on this "hidden" population requires more research. Yet there is expectation that the range of interventions may help mitigate, repair, and strengthen family connection. Policies on making an arrest of a parent, parenting and mentoring for children would assist the families in handling these circumstances.

There are two major types of crime data: crime victimization and crime reported by law enforcement (Bureau of Justice Statistics, 2016). The data across these areas is extensive and bears more investigation depending on one's interest. The disparity data tends to be linked to the extent of bias that exists in determining offenses and procedures for penalty setting.

Social workers are working in communities with police and there is also a designation of police social work (Patterson, 2008). These partnerships have the potential to assist families in viable ways.

LACK OF ATTORNEYS

Greenagle (2016) notes that many from low-income households are especially influenced by the lack of access to defense attorneys. The role of pretrial intervention, conditional discharges, and probation alternatives are available to those with resources. Peña (2015) reports that the situation in both Ferguson and St. Louis, Missouri, illustrates this. His review of 33,000 cases over 3 years documents the presence of one public defender for 394 cases in a year and the negative effect that has on persons arrested and detained without representation.

RESTRICTIONS ON VOTING

Imprisonment is one component of involvement with the CJ system that results in voting restrictions. All states except two, Maine and Vermont, will not allow an incarcerated person to vote. All States have regulations about how justice system–connected people can exercise voting. Illinois and Pennsylvania don't allow inmates to vote. California and New York don't allow inmates or parolees to vote (McDaniel, Simms, Monson, & Fortuny, 2013). These regulations impact ex-offenders' ability to resume civic participation in his or her community.

ADOLESCENTS IN JEOPARDY

The trajectory of school to prison (Children's Defense Fund, 2016) notes that "1 in 3 Black and 1 in 6 Latino boys and a significant number of girls born in 2001 are at risk for imprisonment" (para 1). Many of the juveniles detained have disabilities. It is estimated that emotional and learning disabilities comprise a significant proportion but without actual evaluations it is difficult to be accurate. (Hagner, Malloy, Mazzone, & Cormier, 2016).

The intersection of developing adolescence and residence in low-incoming housing areas adds to the pressures young people may feel and the risky behaviors that may lead them to criminal justice or mental health conditions (Jordan, Mireles, & Popkin, 2013). A proportion of young people are pushed from their homes by parents who don't like who the children have become or find their behaviors uncontrollable. Some LGBTQQI youth may become involved in commercial sex to meet their survival needs. An Urban Institute (Dank, Yu, & Yahner, 2016) report found that most youth care for themselves by using protection against sexually transmitted diseases and pregnancy by visiting service providers. However, youth respondents indicate they need help with employment and housing, which most agencies don't provide.

REDUCING DISPARITIES

The U.S. Department of Justice (McDaniel, Simms, Monson, & Fortuny, 2013) and Urban Institute (Jordan, Mireles, & Popkin, 2013) are reviewing the laws and agency enforcement policies that have led to mass incarceration and family vulnerabilities. Norris (2012) reports on efforts that states are taking to analyze and reduce disparities in the criminal justice system.

Observable institutional policy implementation appears to emphasize punishment and enforcement options. Traditional responses have focused on individual and micro interventions. However, according to national surveys conducted in 2001 by Cullen, Vose, and Jonson (2007), public opinion favors dealing with the causes of crime through prevention and rehabilitation. Support for job and vocational training, family counseling, and use of local community centers for young people is recommended. Advocacy, research, and interventions for community-based implementation are needed.

IMMIGRATION

Immigration issues are of concern to helping professionals and educators who work with or are likely to work with immigrants or refugees. Local workers are often in conflict or are ambivalent about the course of action that should occur in providing services, and the laws regarding services can be confusing.

The Immigration Act of 1924 limited immigrants to a yearly quota of 3% of individuals from a country residing in the United States, based on the 1890 census (Ewalt, Freeman, Kirk, & Poole, 1998). The largest numbers of immigrants came from northern and western Europe. Asian and Pacific country residents and those from eastern and southern Europe were restricted. Immigrants from Africa were excluded.

In 1965, the Immigration and Nationality Act shifted the policy by abolishing the national origins quota system. It restricted the number of people that could enter, favored family reunification of relatives of U.S. citizens, and aimed to recruit immigrants with jobs skills that would benefit the United States (Brookings.edu, n.d.). Amendments to the law regulated the worldwide admission quota to 20,000 per country. Special admission policy was established for refugees (Ewalt et al., 1996, p. 120.). Current policies seem incomplete, confusing and inhumane.

The contemporary situation is an ongoing discourse with sentiments involving racial and ethnic biases and economic concerns. Family members are being deported, children need to work to care for themselves and siblings if their parents have been taken away and cities are trying to figure out what to do (Villavicencio, 2018).

FAMILIES REACTING TO LIFE CIRCUMSTANCES

A refugee is fleeing a situation of war and has not had the time to prepare to emigrate to another country (Libal, Berthhold, Thomas, & Healy, 2014). These circumstances often have families reacting to peril.

Over the years, changes to the law have included discussions of family reunification, employment, concerns about adding to the welfare numbers, and banning inner-city blacks from employment (Drachman in Ewalt, 1998). One's immigrant status determines what level of services she or he is entitled to.

The Universal Declaration of Human Rights supports the 1949 Geneva Convention, which states no one should be subjected to inhuman treatment and gives the right to asylum. Current refugee crises have put pressure on countries that resist taking on the economic requirements of helping those flee from armed-conflict areas. Several countries have been criticized for human rights activist treatment procedures of asylum seekers.

HUMAN RIGHTS

With the advent of an increased focus on human rights, more attention has been called to the broader range of rights that are involved. Human rights include the right to participate in civil and political activities (Libal et al., 2012). Exclusion can be measured by participation in party-based activities, voting, participation in community groups, and other community-building events.

As immigrants adjust to a new environment, some groups have established organizations to assist. Credit unions in the Latino and Korean communities offer support to new arrivals. Being excluded from resources in the broader community illustrates the lack of power to participate in discourse regarding their needs.

Some media reports that immigrant sentiment has increased in the United States and in several countries. Recent debates on immigration have been tense and reveal continuing prejudices and resistance to broader immigration policies that would respond to human rights expectations. While the basic arguments against immigration have to do with threats to employment, reactions tend to relate to rationalizations or justifications of anti-immigration reactions to outsiders in European countries (Cihodariu & Dumitrescu, 2013), as well as in the United States.

West (2010) suggests that it is time for a new immigration policy that integrates the real contributions immigrants make to U.S. society and well-being. This view appears to be supported by the Pew Research Center. Over the past 20 years (Jones, 2016), opinions about immigrants have shifted from views that say immigrants are a burden to views that say they strengthen the country. However, despite the positive contributions of immigrants the US is facing a restrictionist policy climate (CAP, 2017) that will increase the costs through detaining, deporting and harming families.

The disparities that are generated in the context of immigration and refugee populations are similar to those of the other excluded groups. There is a lack of access to resources. A review of research regarding the impact of immigration policies on health status describes mental health stressors that include depression, anxiety, and post-traumatic stress disorder (Martinez et al., 2015).

PERSPECTIVES FOR REFORM

Information about the wealth and disparities of the world involves myriad efforts to address human struggles. The values and principles of the social work profession attend to global concerns, promotes rights as stated in the Convention on the Rights of the Child and the Declaration of Universal Human Rights, and advocates for the rights of all. There are certainly obstacles in the pursuit of continuously improving services. The impact of negative media messages and political power that negates humanity is a reality.

CONCERNS FOR NEGATIVE IMPACTS

Nonprofit agencies, advocacy groups, and grassroots organizations have missions to address needs of persons who face life challenges. There are vast social work opportunities to advocate as a profession and to collaborate with client citizens and through interprofessional coalitions.

The existence of pushback by those who stand on old ideas—who espouse xenophobic, anti-immigrant, and racist ideologies to the point of violence—are acknowledged as forces to be informed and aware of and to collaborate with around common goals. Conceptualizing approaches that pull together multiple ethnic, religious, and class needs is beyond the experience and the thinking for many citizens. Yet it is this terrain that those who advocate for citizen rights must labor. As we explore multiple identities as well as micro and macro evidence-based practices and as we reflect on personal awareness and congruence with civil and human rights, social work stands to participate in policy development and implementation.

DEVELOPING SUPPORT FOR SOCIAL JUSTICE

As the major associations for service delivery present strategic plans for reducing poverty and addressing the major areas of concern across the needs, dialogues are occurring within and across professions and academic disciplines. A recent statement by the American Association of Group Psychotherapy (AAGP) includes the inclusive framework of the helping professions. Their mission includes

> promoting dynamics of belonging, protecting the scapegoated, healing the wounds of exclusion, facilitating constructive dialogue, and maintaining physically/emotionally safe environments. These principles apply for all regardless of nationality, ethnicity, race, gender identity, sexual orientation, religion or cultural background. Exercising these principles fosters groups that support healthy communities, reduced conflict/violence and basic human connection. (AGPA Statement on Inclusion, 2017, para 3).

FROM THE DUAL PERSPECTIVE TO MULTIPLES

As social work has evolved, so too has it modified the lens through which students have been encouraged to approach work with clients and especially clients of minority groups. In 1978, Norton proposed via *The Dual Perspective: Inclusion of Ethnic Minority Content in Social Work Education* that content about ethnic minority groups should be included in the content of social work education programs. This concept referred to the social work theoretical knowledge of human behavior and the knowledge of minority-client systems. This dual perspective allows for assessing the immediate family environment and the broader institutional environment, which in many ways maintains structural barriers and disadvantages. This duality may also be perceived as a bicultural lens that includes bilingual elements. It may be connected to religions, immigrants, and those with diverse abilities. This lens urges helping professionals to assess individuals and families in the macro context as well as in the micro one.

By examining the social work professional pathway from dual perspective to current concerns regarding inclusion, the additional ways of knowing and thinking related to experiences and cultural traditions lead us to considering a triple perspective. This frame layers onto humanity the cultural intersections and the broader macro context of life.

FROM DUAL TO TRIPLE PERSPECTIVES FOR INCLUSION

From this foundation of duality, developing a triple perspective seems to be the next step. Being aware of the consumer's micro and mezzo environments would be the basic levels for assessing the primary surroundings and institutional connections of a service user. The micro level includes screening and selection of evidence-based therapies in conjunction with the other dimensions of care. The broader macro dimension incorporates the range of existing and potential participation in social, civic, and prevention activities that address safety and protection, as well as enhance living spaces and health knowledge.

This macro dimension assesses institutional opportunities and barriers. Implementation factors related to financing, organization, and delivery of care pathways requires a diverse skill set (Nair & Guererro, 2014). The mezzo level recognizes the existing support system and network, management and professional leadership, and opportunities or barriers to promote social participation and friendship networks (Howarth et al., 2014). Becoming more informed of community resources and referring service users to them links the clinician to the macro resources.

The social worker's application of the triple perspective would allow professional assessment of the three primary contexts, related perspectives, and potential resources. Collaboration for information sharing of micro-/clinical-, mezzo-, and macro-level screening, interventions, opportunities, and barriers provides a framework and foundation for more-personalized and precision-focused interventions.

CENSUS BUREAU MODIFICATIONS

The preliminary work by the U.S. Census Bureau to incorporate revised questions for the next census survey recognizes the variation of human identities and the reality of many persons who do not live in standard housing or typical communities. Their efforts to reach people are commendable. They were studying how to allow multiple identities, how to ask about their racial and Hispanic identity and wanted to add a new Middle East-North Africa category (Cohn, 2016). In January it was decided that there would not be any major changes, some adjustments would be tested in a sample distribution to occur in Rhode Island, and further study is to occur (Wang, 2018).

STEPS TOWARD INCLUSION

Broadening the ways we accept people's self-views helps us appreciate diversity. This multidimensional view does not rely only on theoretical knowledge and academic sources about psychiatric diagnoses and life cycle conditions but invites the use of consumer voices. A triple perspective encourages integrating multicultural perspectives and resources to enhance engagement efforts, community education, and service interventions. This framework reaches out for consumer feedback through regular agency focus groups, community meetings, and structured mobile or survey methods to impact institutional decision-making about service programs and delivery locations.

By reviewing the statistics on people impacted in some way under existing institutional service strategies, it is clear that policy modifications in line with evidence-supported techniques can be examined more closely and implemented. Research in areas uncovered before needs to be conducted. Appreciation of existing community methods and structures should be incorporated into development. Stevie Wonder's insight applies to all service populations who need assistance: "We need to make every single thing accessible to every single person with a disability" (Kircher, 2016).

CHAPTER SUMMARY

In major systems of social services—mental health, health, education, and criminal justice—there are pathways to gaining more positive outcomes across groups. The procedures that result in low efficacy for disproportionate numbers of people of color, LGBTQQI persons, persons with physical and learning challenges, immigrants, and many with intersectional identities illustrate the ineffectiveness of many contemporary interventions. The basis for the disproportionate exclusion or lower quality of care appears to be linked in large part to continuing negative attitudes and beliefs about diverse people. Limited research about methods and ways of connecting that include ideas and feedback from these citizens. Their input has been ignored, resisted, and excluded from the service-planning process.

Readers are reminded of the significance of housing and household income on quality of life and access to services in the United States and other countries. Students should also be aware that as quantitative and qualitative data are collected for implicit and explicit measurements, specific issues of social and economic injustice require observation and discussion for clarification and ongoing pursuit of improvement.

Members of the various social groups who live in their spaces, who have surmounted obstacles, and participate in protecting their families and communities must be welcomed into the broader community to address the civil and human rights we want for one another.

EPAS AND CODE OF ETHICS

CSWE EDUCATIONAL POLICY & ACCREDITATION STANDARDS

Competency 8: Intervene with Individuals, Families, Groups, Organizations, and Communities
- 8b) use inter-professional collaboration as appropriate to achieve beneficial practice outcomes;
- 8c) negotiate, mediate, and advocate with and on behalf of diverse clients and constituencies. (EPAS, 2015)

NASW CODE OF ETHICS

Value: Social Justice

Ethical Principle: Social workers challenge social injustice.

Social workers pursue social change, particularly with and on behalf of vulnerable and oppressed individuals and groups of people. Social workers' social change efforts are focused primarily on issues of poverty, unemployment, discrimination, and other forms of social injustice. These activities seek to promote sensitivity to and knowledge about oppression and cultural and ethnic diversity. Social workers strive to ensure access to needed information, services, and resources; equality of opportunity; and meaningful participation in decision making for all people. (NASW, n.d.)

DISCUSSION QUESTIONS

1. Think about agencies you have worked in or where you have had a field placement. Is there any organizational policy that could be considered discriminatory toward staff or service users? Explain.
2. People respond to issues of oppression around the world. Advocates for human rights overall or for more specific interests (e.g., women, ethnic groups, sexual orientation) have expressed their concerns in many ways. Select an area that you have little information about. Present a brief paragraph about the topic or perspective on the discussion board. Explain why you selected the issue.
3. List three reasons that may impact the extent of mental health problems in the United States.
4. What references support your ideas?

EXERCISES

1. Select a topic from the chapter. List three points of view that may be associated with a relevant policy area. What would be in a first draft of ways to address service needs for persons experiencing the disparities?
2. Consider an international example: Select a country and research disparities within an ethnic group. How does that compare to how the United States perceives that group?
3. Select a news source about an international example of disparity. Research their coverage of the disparity. What are your conclusions?
4. Review the tables of the U.S. strategies and the EU strategies in the Docteur and Berenson (2014) article. Select two from each that you would present as priority steps for addressing disparities.

MULTICULTURAL RESOURCES

Abrams, D. A. (2013). *Diversity & inclusion: The big six formula for success.* Amazon Digital Services.

Ahmed, S. (2012). *On being included: Racism and diversity in institutional life.* Durham, NC: Duke University Press.

Harlem Children's Zone. (n.d.). Retrieved from http://hcz.org/

Jouejati, R. (2013, Oct. 3). Syrian women organize for security. *Utne Reader.* Retrieved from http://www.utne.com/politics/syrian-women-organize-for-security.aspx

Sen, S. (Director). (2015). *Cities of sleep* [Documentary].

Sengupta, S. (2016). *The end of karma: Hope and fury among India's young.* New York, NY: W.W. Norton.

Umrigar, T. (2007). *The space between us.* New York, NY: Harper Perennial.

Williams, W. E. (2011). *Race and economics: How much can be blamed on discrimination?* Washington, DC: Hoover Institution Press.

FURTHER READING

Brunst, K., Wright, R. O., DiGioia, K., Enlow, M. B., Fernandez, H., Wright, R. J., & Kannan, S. (2014). Racial/ethnic & socio demographic factors associated with micronutrient intake & inadequacies among pregnant women in an urban U.S. population. *Public Health Nutrition, 17*(9), 1960–1970.

Urban Institute. (2014). Families and parenting: Father involvement. Retrieved from http://urban.org/family/involvement.cfm

U.S. Department of Labor. (n.d.). *History of federal minimum wage rates under the Fair Labor Standards Act, 1938–2009.* Retrieved from http://www.dol.gov/whd/minwage/chart.htm

CHAPTER 9

Examining Professional Issues

This chapter raises issues that have evolved over the years from our history of oppression and service structures that need improvements. Continuing disparities and ongoing pressures on low-wealth persons and families suggest needed attention. Increasing awareness and efforts toward cultural competence in the macro system is pushing more attention to evidence-based practice and integration of culturally affirming resources.

Concepts that are relevant to this examination include:

- Social struggles: civil rights, gender rights, disabled rights, human rights
- Antioppressive, antiracist practice
- Agency policies
- Practice interventions
- Global perspectives

As we tell our clients, negative thinking needs to be reviewed and evaluated. As advocates, taking on the positive strengths, promoting these through various approaches in practice, and building on strengths—as Saleebey, Delgado, Hill, and so many others employ us to do—is the basis of capacity building. Reaching for partnerships across numerous types of stakeholders and disciplines is encouraged through the Grand Challenges Social Work Initiative (GCSWI) (Nurius et al., 2017). The authors point out ongoing evaluation of disparities and service gaps and the examination of potential successful outcomes requires a concerted inter-professional workforce collaborating with community citizens. The twelve grand challenges identify needs across policy groups including but not limited to homelessness, health care, education, and criminal justice.

- Social work values drive our observations and evaluation.
- Interprofessional collaboration is key to addressing the Grand Challenges to social work initiative.

- Service user participation highlights innovative partnerships.
- Continuing improvements through teamwork are connected to transformative solutions.

Benchmark: Students will be able to identify challenges and obstacles to social innovation.

Bryan is working with the local health department to develop workshops that community residents described would be helpful to them in trying to plan nutritional meals and help family members lose weight. They are hesitant to go to clinics that have been disrespectful to them in the past. He has designed a series of four weekly sessions as community-based prevention workshops for families to learn about family planning and nutrition. They will be held on the weekends at the local community recreation center. Parents and youth assisted in the planning of cooking classes (for children and youth) and parenting sessions.

At first, the health department administrator, an MBA executive, resisted the Saturday planning meetings, but members of the local social work student organization encouraged him at a community partnership meeting to give it a try.

What kind of evaluation tools would you suggest to use at each of the workshops? How could the data be used?

WHERE DOES THE EXAMINATION BEGIN?

As social work pursues its mission, values, goals, and evidence-based interventions, it must also be open to recognizing the issues that bring many people to us for services. The Grand Challenges document emphasizes the potential of interdisciplinary teamwork that uses the collective impact model (Nurius et al., 2017). There are several disciplines represented in providing services that address social and economic justice. These include anthropology, economics, education, psychiatry, psychology, criminal justice, sociology, rehabilitation, neuroscience, and nursing. Economics, education, and health care stand out among the disciplines for inclusion here. The ability to gain skills for people to work, fair treatment as workers, education that prepares citizens for jobs and careers, and access to healthcare are major pillars for individual and family development.

SOCIAL WORK AND OTHER DISCIPLINES

The standard setting associations for helping disciplines have developed guidelines for equality and continuous improvement. Social work's leadership through the Council on Social Work Education educational standards and The National Association of Social Workers Code of ethics demonstrate the connection of educational preparation and practice. Continuing to move forward in the work of delivering more effective services must involve high standards across disciplines that purport to assert values for humanity.

We urge helping professionals to stand with other disciplines to integrate data-driven evidence and the inclusion of diverse students and service users in training and service delivery. Advocacy for recruitment of staff and faculty of color, of those with physical challenges, and of other diverse characteristics across the helping professions is vital for the discourse of services examination and refinement of delivery strategies that ensure trust and provide effective family supports.

ECONOMICS

Economics involves the capital that allows access to resources that help families and children. Anna Rosling Rönnuld (TED Talk, 2017) describes her work using photographs of people and their homes around the world to illustrate the ways dollars translate to household utilities. Dollar Street (gapminder.org, n.d.) shows how similar families around the world are. Money itself is not the finite answer for family life. Policies that protect workers and access to jobs are relevant to the challenges social work acknowledges must be addressed to move toward the reduction of disparities and poverty.

Recent discussions of economic policy highlight the ways policies impact persons' capacity to help themselves. Bivens and associates (2018) discuss 10 actions passed in the past year that hurt workers. The tax law, elimination of overtime protection and weak tip protection make low income workers more vulnerable. Karsten & West (2015) refer to a comment by Hillary Clinton which questions the merit of an economy that doesn't protect workers.

Researchers at McKinsey.com (Ilanes et al., 2018) describe the need to refine workers skills as the major effort needed regarding workforce preparation. They compare this shift to the move from agriculture to manufacturing and believe it is the responsibility of business to provide the training and reskilling of workers.

Social workers participation in establishing a presence in the discussion of skills and education is needed.

EDUCATION

Education, attention, and resources available to children impact confidence and the development of talents and skills to assist people as they mature. The quality of education through school curriculum and the capacity of teachers and other professionals in the education network foster performance on their own influences learning.

Teacher preparation programs are accredited through CAEP, The Council for the Accreditation of Educator Preparation, a recently formed organization. This council was established in 2010 through the consolidation of recommendations of the boards of the National Council for Accreditation of Teacher Education (NCATE) founded in 1954 and the Teacher Education Accreditation Council (TEAC) founded in 1997. The standards include assessments connected Content and Pedagogical Knowledge, Clinical Partnerships and Practice, and Candidate Quality, Recruitment, and Selectivity (ncate.org/) Standard 10 urges collaboration with learners, families, colleagues, other school professionals, and community members.

Social work and education can benefit from developing collaborative learning opportunities for students that prepare them to work together in communities.

The Sourcebook for school services (Franklin, Harris and Allen-Meares, 2013) includes content that offers strategies and resources to support students with interpersonal and social problems, health, mental health, and education diagnoses. This text also shares strategies for working with families.

PUBLIC HEALTH

Public health describes the parameters of the social environment in which people work to promote and protect health in communities. The social and economic context of a globally racialized society denotes stress on the quality of life. Canada, Europe, the United Kingdom, Australia, and other countries report exclusion of members of underrepresented groups in the major institutional hierarchies and decision-making opportunities. The value base of the social work profession takes on the social injustice that is perpetrated through these systems. Public health also uses a framework that draws on evidence, values, and ethics (Carter et al., 2011). The Office of Minority Health has established National Standards for Culturally and Linguistically Appropriate Services (CLAS) in Health and Health Care (thinkculture.hhs. gov). This resource identifies the need to include language in cultural dynamics and ways to advance, implement and sustain the standards.

EXAMINING PRACTICE AND POLICY

Practice interventions have been influenced by the medical model that holds the expertise of medical professionals in highest regard. Medical research is important, yet the ongoing provision of family nurturing is essential and must be supported and enhanced especially in situations of crisis and need.

In *Lakota Woman* (1990), Mary Crow Dog and Richard Erdoes present a dynamic of oppression that is crucial to understanding some of the foundational damage that has harmed many people of color. She describes the historical center of Sioux society as the *tiyospaye*—the extended family group of uncles, aunts, in-laws, second fathers, other well-thought-of relatives, and medicine men. These folks were the warm protective family that also operated as the basic hunting band that provided food and security. But, she says, white people "destroyed the tiyospaye, not accidentally but as a matter of policy" (p. 13).

Policies established during slavery to isolate, break, and penalize African people and their families had the same intent and effect. Policies were also established to penalize white people who recognized this inhumane behavior and wanted or attempted to help (DuBois, 2014). The resulting psychological and mental health ramifications (DeGrury & Johnson, 2016) and low economic successes continue to prevail (Campos, 2017).

Similarly, contemporary health care policies that restrict or remove humane considerations regarding women's reproductive rights are designed to harm women. Kristof (2017) pointed to the high maternal mortality rates in the United States). Martin and Montagne (2017) report that this rate has been rising in the United States and decreasing in other countries. Funding has not been directed to the health of the mothers.

The facts must be understood, reflected on, and addressed as we work on creating services and strategies to reduce the disparities created by our history. The examination does not request blame or anger but must be honest about where we are and how much work is needed.

SOCIAL WORK STRUCTURE IN ORGANIZATIONS

Social work services provided through direct practice may occur in profit or nonprofit agencies and they may be considered primary, with social workers as the main discipline, or secondary, in which the professional staff is interdisciplinary (Kirst-Ashman, 2014). These agencies or departments of large institutions, such as hospitals, may offer mental health, behavioral health, food, or other ancillary services. Sources of funding may link designated services and eligibility requirements. *Ethics in Health Services and Policy A Global Approach* (Harris, 2011) and *Dark Money: The Hidden History of the Billionaires Behind the Rise of the Radical Right* (Mayer, 2017) present different views on how funding sources may influence service delivery.

PUBLIC AGENCIES

Public agencies are typically managed by governmental employees regulated by policies and laws established via state and federal procedures. Funding comes from tax revenues and other sources. These are considered nonprofit institutions, but some of the financing may involve cost-effectiveness strategies that allow methods to address cost benefits (Kirst-Ashman, 2014). Accreditation may be obtained for public or private organizations through The Council on Accreditation (coanet.org). Standards were revised for public agencies in 2016.

PRIVATE, NONPROFIT, OR FOR-PROFIT AGENCIES

Agencies that are owned by nongovernmental entities or private citizens may be set up to provide services and not make any financial gain in doing so, making them nonprofit facilities. Agencies that are set up to provide services and make a profit are proprietary. These rely on a board of directors to formulate policy and mange agency operations (Kirst-Ashman, 2014). Board members are expected to guide policy development and advocate for the organization's mission (National Council on Nonprofits, n.d.).

THE EXAMINATION PROCESS: SERVICE USERS AND SERVICE PROVIDERS

The Community Mental Health Centers Act (1963) proposed a strategy to monitor its services through mandated staff and consumer methods for participation. A consultation and education unit coordinated design and collaboration with community organizations. Although this component was quickly eliminated from mental health budgets, some organizations and state level mental health planners have addressed the need in different ways.

The California Mental Health Act of 2004, amended in 2012, includes community education as a key element to helping communities help themselves. "The Act addresses a broad continuum of prevention, early intervention, and service needs and the necessary infrastructure, technology and training elements that will effectively support this system" (dhcs.ca.gov, California Mental Health, 2016, para 1).

Other examples indicate policy initiatives to involve service users have been resisted in some organizations and by professionals (Bee, Brooks, Fraser, & Lovell, 2015). Issues of user philosophies, expectations, feelings of exclusion, and professional accountability created tensions. The lack of a well-defined structure and implementation steps appeared to obstruct the potential of this collaboration.

Concerns for the rights of women, people of color, and people who have been labeled in ways that minimize their value continue to be expressed across the globe. Research concepts related to the dynamics of exclusion have expanded. Examining professional issues uses assessments of the issues and strategies to move forward for goal setting and outcomes focus. Overall, these concerns build on the social struggles and social movements of the past.

The examination process involves assessing oneself, the profession, and the organizational relationships within major institutions that impact human well-being. This exposure can be messy. Frequently, there will be pushback, barriers, and challenges. Questions are raised about how to implement strategies that are effective or may be effective, which may include representation of those who have been actively constrained from participating. We wonder, then, how good is antiracist social work when the structures continue to operate and perpetuate white constructions of the way to do things (Jeffrey, 2005).) The examination process is one of peeling back the layers of constraint, contemplating what is revealed, and continuing the commitment to pursue relationships that benefit. Part of social work's responsibility is working to inform community citizens of 1) information to benefit their health and their children, 2) of options to foster healthy behaviors, and 3) opportunities for civic participation that keep elected officials accountable for policies to assist the social welfare of all.

CRITICAL THINKING QUESTION

What behaviors and practices have the social work profession used in response to oppression and discrimination?

EVOLVING PRACTICE DYNAMICS

As the disciplines involved in health and mental health care evolve, changes can be observed.

Social work 's relationships with service users and related disciplines is shifting to include alternative and complementary approaches that integrate multiple approaches and the strengths perspective. Probst (2010) notes this paradigm shift to recognize strengths, introduced by Saleebey (2012), is emphasized in some practice settings and some curricula content but an empirical analysis of its systematic incorporation into instruction has not occurred. Concerns about helping service users evaluate what has happened to them rather than what is wrong with them demonstrates an aspect of implementing this changing mindset. The ongoing examination of social work helps guide the development of evaluation and service delivery.

EVOLVING EDUCATION DYNAMICS

Examining the use of models is occurring in education. Zhao (2016) calls for the need to move away from the deficit based model to one to enhance strengths. He describes the existing model as one that emphasizes what students can't do or don't have rather than what they can do. Shifting to classroom approaches that capture and strengthen talents and interests through school policy and learning plans can help prepare students for emerging workforce skills and support their emotional health.

EVOLVING HEALTH DYNAMICS

Changes in health delivery are especially linked to access to insurance and research in the health sciences. Research findings about the role of the social environment in brain architecture and recovery and social determinants on well-being have contributed to evolving behavioral health service. Rigard, Laracy, DuPaul, Shapiro, et al. (2015) suggested that neither service users nor service providers paid attention to the connection of past traumas to social challenges. Recognizing this has led to protocol recommendations to improve services through trauma informed care especially in schools. Bowen and Murshid (2016) note the trauma informed model can help transform the policy development process to become more transparent and inclusive.

EVOLVING POLICY CONSIDERATIONS

Policy formulation is influenced by national, organizational and personal ideas about professional services. Increasing awareness through professional education across disciplines has fostered more attention to cultural variations, the impact of stigmatization of service use, and the ways organizations respond to community needs.

Reaching toward collaboration with those with similar interests in social welfare invites the need for rigorous and multilevel reviews and diligence in following up professional interests and engaging more effectively with the citizens we deliver service to. In order to reach the goal for families to behave differently with their children, professionals may need to behave differently than we have in the past, and our institutions have a responsibility to help our work achieve better outcomes by rethinking policies and how they are implemented

Providing opportunities for workers and work teams to debrief encounters and implement approaches that have evidence of resulting in desired outcomes will help policy modifications and development. The process of change to address disparities needs to challenge work conditions because we are doing more challenging work. (McNoll, 2016).

Service user participation (SUP) is acknowledged to be limited in use around the world, but it is necessary to increase dialogue and collaboration for evidence-informed planning (Dunlop & Holosko, 2016). Recommendations for growth and for change emphasize focus, motivation, and mastery of goals. Social workers can and do create opportunities to help citizens persevere.

THE SAFETY NET

The evolving concerns of research in social work education and healthcare operate in the political context. Lind's (2016) opinion speaks to his political assessment of our country's democratic status. He notes that the United States and Europe are experiencing a democratic deficit that has resulted in backlash. He sees the politicians being chosen by donor-based groups rather than neighborhood party machines. He suspects this contributes to voter apathy and disenfranchisement that can be addressed by reforms that give non-elite voters more power to affect policy outcomes. His solution is more democracy, not less.

Congresswoman Rosa DeLauro (D-CT; 2017) speaks to the vulnerability of working people in the face of business indifference. She describes the development of the safety net as "legitimate actions of a democratic government" (p. 8) and defends the needs of children, women, working families, the hungry, the sick, and the unemployed.

ACKNOWLEDGING ATTITUDES AND POLITICAL POSITIONS

Acknowledging attitudes and political positions of one's own and of those with whom we want to engage is a first step. Lind (2013) reminds us that evolving social environments have accompanied the steam engine, electricity, the internal combustion engine, computer technology, and now additional technologies, media, and climate changes. As technology-driven change leads to misaligned economics, laws and political structures will push us toward negotiations that can bring about innovative behaviors and structures.

UNDEREMPLOYMENT AND UNEMPLOYMENT

Unemployment, exclusive networks for good employment, and limited work opportunities urge affirmative policy initiatives. The need for socio economic strategies to improve access to wealth for members of underrepresented groups tends to create backlash because white people feel intimidated. While that feeling may be somewhat natural, the evidence indicates it is not underrepresented people threatening or jeopardizing economic access. The Upshot, a section of *The New York Times* (Irwin, Miller, & Sanger-Katz, 2014), shows clearly the source of dwindling income access. The increasing wealth gap shows shifts in the members of the higher and lower income groups. One of the results of this is that more ordinary people have become less able to find long term employment or jobs with salaries that can pay bills. Some reports suggest ordinary people are buying less and retail businesses are feeling the impact of that. More adult children are living with their parents (Domonosoke,

2016). People with higher incomes are not the backbone of local establishments. Retailers are important to our economy, but slower US retail growth may extend beyond the next five years, becoming the "new normal" (Lind, 2013; Mackenzie, Meyer, & Noble, 2013). The economic impact on middle and lower income citizens is of importance to social work because service users tend to fall into these income groups. According to Campos (2017), for the past 5 decades there has been a consistent income gap between black and white Americans across the economic spectrum. He notes "the historical pervasiveness and contemporary persistence of racism in America offer more than adequate explanations for what should be considered a scandalous state of affairs in regard to race-based economic inequality" (para 7).

He calls out the connection of racial and economic justice against people of color and people with middle and lower incomes "Between 1980 and 2014, the post-tax income of the bottom 50 percent of the population grew by 21 percent, while that of the top .01 percent grew by 424 percent. (Campos, 2017, para 13)

MOVING FROM INDIVIDUAL WORK TO CO-CREATION PROCESS

As the social work profession evolves in promoting the value that all people matter, it simultaneously confronts values that resist this idea. The presence of disparities is evidence of system resistance to full access. Health disparities are pervasive among racial and ethnic groups (Brooks, 2016). Social work professional missions and the global declarations of human and children's rights hold in common the value that working toward these goals is desired.

Social work organizations are pushing for policy actions in areas of importance to the profession. Depending on where one works or wants to work, the issues are wide. Practice performance and theory development have moved from casework and clinical practice to a greater emphasis on system views and collaboration. Early theories on management emphasized the science of optimizing worker routines and specific steps. Subsequent thinking introduced organizational goals and leadership styles that integrated emotional and social intelligence for systems thinking and approaches that relied on co-creation (Maisano, 2016). Partnerships in the community expand the notion of co-creation.

WORKERS AND SERVICE USERS

The bottom line to assisting persons whose incomes make them vulnerable to other experiences of hardship and adversity requires structured economic changes. Stiglitz (2015), a Nobel Prize economist, has spoken up over the past few years about ways our economy could be improved to assist more than just the upper class. Warren (2014) has advocated for consumers regarding Wall Street reform and college affordability. Their ideas address ways to help people tackle household needs.

Understanding the economic dimension brings us to the necessity of examining the class stratification and relationships of capitalism and how they cannot be separated from racist oppression (Spector, 2014). Spector raises uncomfortable and difficult-to-answer questions that are meaningful yet disquieting about classism, racism, and privilege.

Factors for persons deciding to seek help or not include fear of stigmatization, feelings of incompetence, lack of confidence, and survival fatigue (Wimer, 2016). Although some nonprofit agencies could help with some emergencies, most people are unaware of them. In uncovering more information about people's feelings about help seeking, forms and approaches of outreach may be modified.

New solutions and finding ways to develop them are required to have democracies resist instability. Giving workforce support through evidence-based policy development and developing citizen-informed education and procedures for more voter rights and citizen participation are ideas that promote strategies built on coalition building (Anderson, Adeney, Shinn, Safaranek, et al., 2015) and data use for designing improved services.

WORKING WITH OTHERS WHO WANT TO DO BETTER

Co-creating and collaborating organizational partnerships and coalitions involves setting up opportunities for dialogues. Different settings will bring various attitudes and political positions in the move toward innovation. By establishing relationships with individuals, families, organizations, and communities, the process is to observe, evaluate, and modify. As the social work profession surveys the landscape of the past, contemporary circumstances, and projections for the future, we will encounter pushback from conservative tenets that resist inclusion. The other side is the disruption potential of collaborating with community and indigenous voices that call for more qualitative work and interventions within the academic quantitative political environment (Symon, Buehring, Johnson, & Cassell, 2008). Sharing information in ways that address institutional parameters from heretofore excluded workforce members requires another level of management sensitivity.

SOCIAL WORK PRACTICE: EXAMINING MICRO AREAS

The frequent discussion of social work practice starts at the micro level. The strength-based perspective (Windsor et al., 2014) presents a platform for health that must be connected to economics. Their work relies on the resilience that communities, despite the challenges, have demonstrated by addressing the structural dynamics that contribute to health problems. They propose that individuals and families cannot be treated effectively without integrating the socioeconomic and political contexts. Their framework, Community Wise, examines the concentration of disparities in low-income, segregated communities with substantial crime, incarceration, and substance use and the limited service access they experience despite the elevated need. Their model allows participants to address their frustrations regarding oppressive and traumatic events and gain knowledge about critical thinking, civic participation, and personal and family development.

DIFFERENTIATION AND INTEGRATION IN TRANSFORMING ONESELF, ORGANIZATIONS, AND GROUPS

Transition beyond micro level work embraces the co-creation process. This requires understanding our socialized views of the world and the context of others' socialized experiences as we work with service users and colleagues. Evidence-based practices (EBP) are presented as well-researched and appropriate interventions. Using definitions of EBP, we expect these methods to have been properly investigated, evaluated, proven to be effective, and promoted for use by clinicians. Yet sometimes narrow views of the perspectives and supports of others neglects appreciation of the various ways of knowing, sensing, and coping that many people use with their daily struggles of family issues, especially when surviving with low incomes. Graham (2015) notes the high cost of low-income survival is often measured by the levels of stress, pain, and worry that impact performance and health. Several critiques point to the lack of research with substantial multicultural populations that would validate cross-cultural effectiveness.

Social workers have promoted and continue to pursue research that uses approaches that value multicultural dimensions and employ reflection and collaboration (Uehara et al., 1996) and that is based on client and worker communication and negotiation (Yan & Wong, 2005). Yan and Wong point out that in the traditional view of service, social workers continue to operate within a professionally accepted culture that wants clients to change their culture to assume one based on the intervention mindset. The better outcome in this scenario is that the social worker is "open to the influence of the other" as well, and this co-creation establishes new meanings and ways of navigating needs and change. Generally, funding and research have supported monocultural views of interventions (Lee & Bhuyan, 2013). Indigenous ways should also be respected and considered in shaping pathways through recovery.

EXPANDING STUDENT AWARENESS OF THE POLITICAL CONTEXT

As practice is examined, the role of social work and politics has become clearer. Past surveys given at the start of community practice courses over the years indicated students did not consider participation in community politics important (O'Neal, unpublished 2009). But by the end of the course, those numbers changed. Exposure to research and essays about what works, what doesn't, and what could be considered with respect to sharing information with consumers helped enhance their understanding. Strong feelings seemed to be associated with socialization but often not connected to actual experiences.

As awareness of disparities and the environmental context is examined. The process of examination should help us decide to remove the negative language that tends to be associated with the people we serve and want to collaborate with. The role of politics illustrates how service delivery is influenced. There are pros and cons to every element of the examinations and resolutions. As readers consider and reflect on their interests in social work and their areas for participation, all assumptions require examination, reexaminations, reflection, and planning.

INTERVENTIONS THAT COULD BE BETTER— IDENTIFYING THE OBSTACLES

Identifying obstacles or limitations is a crucial step during the evaluation phase. Since we can refer to indigenous communities' perception that Caucasian researchers often reject or consider alternative perspectives to be wrong (TallBear, 2014), the need to examine from various lenses and perspectives provides benefits and challenges and should be integral to the process.

ANTI-OPPRESSION AND ANTI-RACIST

McLaughlin (2005) points out that early on anti-oppressive social work was considered radical, but it has, to some degree, become institutionalized. In this way, it moves from being a challenge to being a way for the state to reposition and uses the anti-oppressive social worker to enforce reimagined moral codes on welfare recipients. A similar analysis conducted by Ali, McFarlane, Hawkins, and Udo-Inyang (2012) describes the principles of anti-oppression advocacy shaped by social justice ideals that also are challenged by the complexity of racism and the longstanding methods of training helping professionals that fail to equip with tools to actually counter oppression.

Anti-oppression social work has incorporated the lens of dual perspectives and awareness of "racecraft" (Fields, 2014) in evaluating the challenges faced as a profession. In the 1970s, Norton (1978) noted that social work needed to understand the dual perspectives of people of color and that this concept is important for working with clients as well as working in service institutions. There are many models and frameworks that promote more in-touch or high-touch communication with persons of underrepresented groups in institutional settings. Anti-oppression or anti-racist practices are forms of discourse about moving forward from the impact of exclusionary practices and policies on institutional and individual attitudes, structures, and behaviors.

While there are anti-oppressive sentiments and principles, the actual implementation of changed behaviors is minimal, especially in public social services (Strier & Binyamin, 2014). The institutional context of public social services has been censured by the neomanagerial perspective, discontent of the service users, and privatization interests. These parameters often diminish opportunities for anti-oppressive principles to become viable.

INTERVENTIONS THAT COULD BE CONNECTED— ALTERNATIVE AND COMPLEMENTARY APPROACHES

As we strive to be more inclusive, broadening our awareness and acknowledgment of strategies people use to help themselves has become part of the conversations. Holistic and integrative health care strategies require appreciation of people's networks in order to collaborate across multiple dimensions.

Using community-based interventions would be helpful. Partnerships with organizations and agencies within and external to the mental health and health systems are occurring and offer examples of potential collaborations. Barriers to these arrangements exist, but the trend across Europe (McDaid, Oliveira, Jurczak, Knapp, & The Mheen Group, 2007) demonstrates mindsets that recognize the benefit of balancing institutional- and community-based services that promote mental well-being and that tackle the consequences of poor mental health. Their examples include variations in funding and entitlements for mental health–related social care and housing services outside the health care structure.

The National Center for Complementary and Integrative Health (NCCIH, 2017) is responding to the acknowledged presence of alternative health measures. It begins the federal interest in establishing how some other therapies and means of coping may be integrated with the more-established care methods.

There is very little research on how astrology, acupuncture, gemstone therapy, card reading, herbal therapy, reiki, chakra balancing, energy medicine, palmistry, reflexology, and other alternative sources of emotional support have been helpful. However, these facets of culture are garnering more attention that may lead to future investigation. There is now funding support for research activity regarding mindfulness and yoga. Preliminary work on yoga suggests that it may be effective for low-back pain (Saper et al., 2016), increasing attention and focus with children (Thompson, 2013), easing depression in older adults (Behrmann & Tebb, 2009), and helping preschoolers self-regulate (Razza, Bergen-Chen, & Raymond, 2015).

When examining alternative measures, one approach to defining these suggests that there is more an emphasis on preventing or caring for conditions rather than waiting until one is sick. Harrison (n.d.) refers to the medical model as "sick care" rather than health care. He lists more common alternative health care therapies to include the naturopathic, chiropathic, Ayurveda, homeopathic, and herbalistic methods, as well as acupuncture, acupressure, massage, movement, and nutrition. These promote maintaining healthy behaviors and practices for emotional and physical mobility and health.

IDENTIFYING OPPORTUNITIES FOR CAPACITY BUILDING

Despite the resistance of institutional systems to support the needs of vulnerable citizens, there are progressive effortsacross fields of service. Examining perspectives from institutional status, organizational missions, and personal views provides multidimensional information for critical thinking.

WOMEN

Strier and Bershtling (2016) point out an integrated view of resistance contains gender, cultural, and social contexts. Women are still perceived to lack official roles in social change. "Gendered conceptions of social work and colonized views of social work in oppressed communities constitute a major challenge for professional resistance (Abramowitz in Strier & Bershtling, 2016, p. 116.). Their recommendations include 1) refusing to cooperate with managerial dictates, 2) actions aimed at identifying and assisting clients, groups, and communities in their resistance to oppression, and 3) confronting dominant professional and social discourse to deconstruct beliefs that maintain unequal power relations at the institutional and social level.

DeLauro (2017) reports the fastest growing segment of the U.S. population is single, divorced, separated, and widowed women. Women are the primary breadwinners for two thirds of American families, account for two out of every three minimum-wage earners, and live in "the only advanced economy without paid maternity leave" (p. 67).

Services to women are often inadequate because women generally are responsible to children and elders. Services for them require thinking about how the household will operate without her if the program is residential. Substance abuse programs often neglect the special needs of women, yet Alcoholics Anonymous actually offers benefits for older women that have not always been emphasized. Ermann, Lawson, and Burge (2016) found that major benefits regarding relationships with other women and support in additional activities could be generated through AA participation.

There is data regarding high levels of smoking among women, yet there is a lack of specific tobacco cessation programs for women (Heming, Greaves, & Poole, 2015). Using data for planning based on areas of need could be more developed. As women experience transitions that create anxiety, services might be targeted to be of assistance.

The Shriver Report (Morgan & Skelton, 2014) focused on women's needs in response to life circumstances and highlights services to support women achieving resources and skills for family progress. Many of the photo entries describe women and children experiencing divorce and separation. Women's situations could result from no paid leave to care for a child or lack of employment where a worker can earn paid sick days. Some organizations provide family-friendly scheduling, but many people working in lower-income jobs don't have this flexibility.

REPRODUCTIVE HEALTH RIGHTS

Women's health needs encompass the needs of herself and those of her children and her family. The absence of universal health care especially affects lower-income women and children. Concerns about a motherhood penalty describe lower wages for mothers over childless women (Gough & Noonan, 2013). Legislation and employer practices that punish women and do not protect children seems to be unbalanced. The proponents of pro-choice and pro-life have beliefs that support their points of view. But the concerns of women regarding their reproductive issues are more than a social issue; they are rights to their own body and self-determination to consider economic security for family planning (Naral.com, 2017).

Feminism may look somewhat different based on viewpoints or inequality oppression (Anyikwa, Chiarelli-Helminiak, Hodge, & Wells-Wilborn, 2015). The push for better training, especially for women (Brown, 2014) in lower-paid jobs who often support young children and older people, is an area of increased advocacy. Shriver's program points to these needs. *I Am Malala* (Yousafzai, 2013) and *Reading* Lolita *in Teheran* (Nafizi, 2008) speak to the traditional education obstacles for women in some countries.

SEXUAL ORIENTATION

Difficulty in gaining access to members of lesbian relationships is an obstacle to understanding the range of health benefits and challenges to the health of this community. There is sensitivity to needs of LGBTQQI community members, but the resistance of lesbian women to participate in research studies constrains access to controlled studies regarding service needs and participation.

Concerns range from attitudes of nonacceptance to services that do not address stigma or the relationship of discrimination to their mental health issues. McIntyre and associates (2011) report increasing evidence that the medical model contributes to the disparities experienced by sexual minorities. Recent sexual minority research points to even higher rates of stigma against bisexual people and notes the higher levels of stress they experience (Flanders, Robinson, Legge, & Tarasoff, 2016). Affirmative services—culturally sensitive interventions that affirm and validate their identity—are important.

CHILDREN—EARLY INTERVENTIONS AND PREVENTION

Opportunities for improving services to children emphasize dialogues and visually engaging research information for direct access by children. The results of qualitative and quantitative observations and research are opening doors to ways of knowing and doing that are beyond the narrow parameters of the traditional medical model.

Addressing stigmas that feed restricted opportunities, bullying, and related trauma feelings impact student performance. From using better language to describe diverse, nonwhite, diagnosed, or nondiagnosed persons to creating pathways for persons who may not meet traditional expectations require broader macro thinking. Recruitment of qualified diverse and bilingual staff and support services needs to be in place to help move young people from preK through high school graduation and into productive occupational endeavors.

Early intervention cannot occur unless access to screenings is improved. People of color and immigrants experience fewer screenings and may not be connected to services until children are older and exhibiting chronic behaviors. Research from the New Jersey Statewide Network for Cultural Competence (NJSNCC) reviews some of the reasons. Some immigrants and others are not aware of the developmental milestones or the need for screening. Some don't expect access. Some are unclear about coverage. Many may be scared or hesitant given the current anti-immigrant messages. Some do not have insurance. Some have had negative experiences with providers that they do not want repeated. The lack of diversity among providers does not promote trust.

There are ways to overcome these barriers. There needs to be a commitment to work with communities to establish relationships that involve trust and help families become connected to resources. The SPAN (Statewide Parent Advocacy Network; n.d.) framework in New Jersey offers information and strategies for customizing for diversity and inclusion and may be a stepping stone for other states to develop a similar framework.

DEAF COMMUNITY

Recognition of sign language of the Deaf moved social awareness to a broader understanding of communication. Interactions, gestures, and kinesic behaviors developed through interpersonal transactions sustain the survival of persons with hearing or speaking variations (Stokoe, 2005). The development of awareness and comprehension of other forms of communication has helped the world as well as the Deaf community.

The need for resources appropriate for deaf children is an area for review in creating more opportunities for outreach. Students with various learning dynamics require resources to support them. Strategies to help teachers of the Deaf and hard of hearing address social and emotional needs would be helpful (Norman & Jamieson, 2014). Young and associates (2016) refer to the need for deaf participants in clinical trials to have sign language access.

There is also the availability of cochlear implants (approved by the Federal Drug Administration in the 1990s) to restore hearing. Opponents addressed the impact this appliance would have on the existence of sign language and the cultural role of signing in the Deaf community. In a *Radio Times* NPR broadcast (Whyy.org, 2016) hosted by Mary Cummings-Jordan, a discussion panel, including Louise Montoya, a licensed counselor; Melisa Draganac-Hawk, director of the early childhood center at the Pennsylvania School for the Deaf; and Judy Sexton, director of Clarke Schools for Hearing and Speech in Philadelphia, presented the tools used in helping children and families decide on courses of learning that include hearing implants, hearing aids, and speaking. There is room for a variety of interventions and services.

MULTICULTURAL EDUCATIONAL APPROACHES

Miller-Lachmann and Taylor (1995) promote approaches to multicultural education that appreciate the broad range of identities that children bring into the classroom. They describe activities, multicultural materials, and strategies that can be supportive in expressing views, being heard, being informed of multiple perspectives, and being encouraged to reflect as the way of learning. These steps along with developing a diverse workforce—people of color, those in wheelchairs, others with prosthetics, and so on—are needed in service delivery centers.

M. Night Shyamalan's (2013) 4 years of research concluded that the basic ingredients for schools to improve are the following:
- No "roadblock" teachers
- The right balance of leadership
- Feedback
- Smaller schools
- More time in school

Shyamalan believes the needs of the student must come first. If that is addressed, there will likely be more student success.

Several examples over the years have demonstrated the successes of students in schools that pay attention to them and their social environments and customize approaches and programs (Collins & Haley, 1990; Perry, 2013; Tough, 2009). These success stories describe educators who get close to the students and motivate them to pursue their potential. They are supportive disciplinarians that use positive strengthening approaches rather than judgmental and punitive communication. *Lean on Me* (Schiffer & Avildsen, 1989) is a film starring Morgan Freeman that offers another example of efforts to turn around a school beset by its stressful environment.

What works to improve educational quality and inclusion is the preparation of curricula that reflects the diverse students' population and the strengths they all bring. Further, that curricula provides learning opportunities for all types of learners and encourages interactions with the information and with classmates in ways that are respectful to all.

SOCIAL POLICY: EXAMINING MACRO AREAS

Social policy—rules and regulations that guide federal, state, local and agency operations—can be associated with the values and beliefs of those who participate in the decision-making. Students often enter social work programs without a clear focus on how shaping their views of politics and policy may influence their work for the benefit for service users in their field placements. Given the disparities and the organizational culture that is frequently more obstructive than remediating, social work is exploring ways to assist students and service users.

Social work programs may work with agencies through field placement events to develop macro assignments that have student's research the organization's policy issues that impact them and to plan events to gather their feedback. Munro emphasizes the goal for social services is to reform organizational constraints and include observations from the children and youth who are being protected (Munro, 2011). Refining policies through community-based conversations and collaborative efforts can build creative partnerships and cultural supports.

WORKFORCE DEVELOPMENT

Implementing change that addresses the gaps in services, the attitudes, and the structures must also involve the recruitment, training, and activation of bicultural workers with informed training and skills. Policy analysis and policy development includes a range of steps identified for becoming an effective advocate. Depending on the context, there may or may not be a reference to jobs, job creation, or workforce development. Social workers can help advocate and develop programs that incorporate job opportunities at various service delivery entry points.

Economic concerns drive employment possibilities and enhanced strategies for training social workers, other professionals, and talented community members. Overall, the examination of disparities, new paradigms of social construction, and understanding economics are leading social work education to continue to include people and ideas, and to streamline our efforts to address social disorder on micro and macro levels.

Social policy parameters include the specifics of the policy issue, the incorporation of voices that speak to the various social identities, the process of fund-raising among stakeholders, the role of workforce development, and the potential for influencing preK and family development. Researchers are urged to investigate the impact of discrimination on Native American employment outcomes. Strategies include better maternal and child health and high-quality education from early childhood programs through high school that retain and assist students through graduation. The emphasis on better education for groups that have had lower-quality education is of essential importance.

IDENTIFYING CHALLENGES

The movement of social work practice through awareness and recognition of past and contemporary examples of exclusion can lead to contentious discourse in classrooms and meeting rooms. Or it may promote the silence of persons whose personal values and religious values create discomfort. There is sometimes tension between how social work values anti-oppression and affirmation of diverse persons (Todd & Coholic, 2007).

On the one hand, social work's anti-oppressive and inclusive themes do at some level exclude those with fundamental religious views that discriminate. Social workers are trained to examine and assess environmental context that denies and denigrates and seeks to affirm and validate. At the same time, acknowledging realities of personal experiences and religious or spiritual context also calls to question the potential harm that religious judgment presents for segments of service users. The authors deftly note: "Canda and Furman (1999) stated, perhaps our greatest challenge is how we can be inclusive of exclusivist spiritual perspectives" (p. 10).

RELIGION AND GENDER IN DISCRIMINATION

Al Gharaibeh (2016) proposes another view of the role of religion in discrimination. His research seeks to help us understand the role of custom, religion, and law in honor crimes. What are the implications for social work in respecting religious views that allow this level of discrimination? Honor-based violence (HBV) involves a family member killing another family member, usually a female, because the family judges her actions to denigrate the family's honor. Gender issues are involved in the range of religious reasons for discrimination and murder. When women and LGBTQQI people speak up about this from within their groups, there is pushback, but there is also support (Ali, 2007; Husseini, 2009; Lewis, 2015). The use of anti-oppression tactics has a goal of forcing conformity. Practice of these actions dates back to tribal societies before Islam and has been connected to cases in non-Muslim countries. This tends to be associated with patriarchal control of females.

As more emphasis is paid to human rights across genders, the ideas and attitudes connected to these traditions are called into question and the relationship to violence and harm to others is critical. Lewis (2015) describes the traditional role of support in the African

American community by their churches. The HIV/AIDS epidemic produced a response that pulled supports away from members of the LGBT community, exposed Bible-connected moral indignation and homophobia, and fostered increased stigmatization. His study highlighted the presence of some black churches that engaged with and supported the LGBT community and provided leadership for other churches. Social workers can participate in this sort of collaboration.

Ellis-Petersen (2016) reports on the Amen Projects town hall meeting that included a panel with Catholic, Jewish and Muslim speakers. Panelists presented ideas to think about. The group proposed dialogues to move to new paradigms that could allow collaborations that promote spiritual strengths separate from traditional perceptions of gender roles.

Drabble, Trocki, and Klinger (2016) note the protective factor of spirituality. The inclusion of spirituality and sexual minorities is an area of research that can be helpful in reducing hazardous drinking and drug use. Lewis (2015) notes in an online bio: "I discovered that spirituality is by its very nature inclusive, while religion can tend to be exclusive, but it doesn't have to be that way."

CRITICAL THINKING

The call for critical thinking has been presented to improve social education at the baccalaureate, masters and doctoral levels to equip students to create, test and translate solutions to practice setting (Nurius et al., 2017). Developing engagement strategies can incorporate a secondary level that draws on service user talents to translate information in ways to expand their knowledge of resources and community support networks.

Social workers in faith-based organizations must reflect on their support of social work values and their religious views. Navigating the challenges of referring individuals who want religion-connected agencies, social workers can help service users consider the potential of discrimination and their ability to speak up for themselves if they experience discrimination or stereotype threats (Tangenberg, 2005). Some faith-related services are offered only if the client agrees to participate in religious practices and commit to faith activities. From the basis of self-determination, clients should be informed of these requirements in the process of assisting them meet goals.

SOCIAL POLICY: WHAT WORKS? WHAT DOESN'T?

Work to address disparities and improve services across settings for vulnerable people includes several routes for intervention and advocacy. Examination of references across disciplines regarding anti-oppression and inclusion reveal at least three areas of focus across social and economic disparities:

- Professionals' self-awareness of cultural humility and institutional patronage

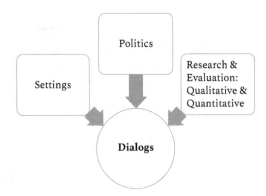

FIGURE 9.1   Dialogues for Designing Innovative Interventions

- Acknowledgement that social work, public health, psychology, and education need to enhance inclusion knowledge and steps to employ this knowledge in field and practice settings
- Promotion of the integration of indigenous and community voices that incorporate innovative and alternative modes of well-being

The *UNESCO (United Nations Educational, Scientific and Cultural Organization) World Report* (2009) refers to the myriad issues around culture and communication that relate to various levels of policy development. On the broader landscape, the report refers to cultural approaches to development, poverty eradication, and environmental sustainability. They note that mainstream messages that typically label societies as *underdeveloped* often fail to recognize that these societies have been living sustainably for generations.

According to the cultural context model (Hancock, Kiedaras, & Waits, 2012), persons who become critically aware of the dynamics of oppression come to see themselves as players in the oppressive structural arrangements. Their study explored the attitudes of BSW and MSW students after engaging in a course that addressed oppression. More BSW students remained focused on individualistic reasons for oppression than structural barriers. But 84% of the MSW students and 65% of the BSW students demonstrated a change orientation that would allow them to work with and advocate for members of excluded groups (p. 17). The process of change for persons interested in social work as a profession brings attitudes and beliefs that may resist more macro-level understanding, especially at the undergraduate level. The higher rates of connection to the structural dynamics of inequality appear with respondents who, perhaps, have been in the workforce longer and have had more opportunities to reflect and interact with service users.

ECONOMICS: WHAT WORKS? WHAT DOESN'T?

Social work cannot move toward more effective services without examining the economics that support and obstruct the ability of families to care for themselves. As social work has examined the areas of need, it continues to push those pursuing work in the field to participate in macro dimensions to benefit consumers. Research from the Columbia University School of Social Work, Population Research Center (Wimer, 2016) has expanded poverty measures to include income, food, housing (material hardships), and health. Using the Robin Hood Grant Foundation poverty tracker, survey data shows that in the state of New York about 21% are under the poverty line. Of all the respondents, 53% experienced some form of disadvantage; 23% experienced some severe health problem that limited their ability to work; and 37% experienced severe material hardship. These hardships included loss of job, loss of partner, emergencies that affected their ability to pay rent or utilities, evictions, loss of child care, and other hardships that caused change in ability to manage life situations.

The economics picture requires considering what works and what doesn't to enhance services regarding employment, the workforce, job creation, and housing.

EMPLOYMENT

Economics influence the employment scene. The status of the workforce and its capacity to find suitable employment at wages that can sustain families is of critical importance. As Wilson (1996) pointed out, when work has disappeared or is not available, the impact is felt in multiple ways. Substantial numbers of U.S. jobs have been replaced by countries that pay lower wages, and poverty has been experienced in more locations than just urban ghettos. Smiley and West (2013) document the increased number of middle-class persons moving into lower income levels, and Shafer and Edin (2016) connect stories of hardships to the equivalent of living on $2.00 a day in the United States.

THE JOB MARKET

The May 2016 employment numbers revealed weakness in the job market (Greenstone & Looney, 2011. The job market is tough, more so for persons without a post–high school degree. Porter (2016) concurs that these circumstances are being observed around the world, and they have made people angry. The anger is connected to how the wealth of the elite comes at the expense of ordinary people working to make ends meet.

Current economic and employment circumstances are not working as well as they did in the past. Employment strategies are needed and are being formulated based on disparities research. There are improvements occurring within tribal territories based on community capacity building that are developed through collaborative partnerships (Austin, 2013). Researchers are urged to investigate the impact of discrimination on Native American employment outcomes. Strategies include better maternal and child health and high-quality education from early childhood programs through high school that retain and assist students through graduation. The emphasis on better education for groups that have had lower-quality education is of essential importance.

WORKFORCE DEVELOPMENT

Implementing change that addresses the gaps in services, the attitudes, and the structures must also involve the recruitment, training, and activation of bicultural workers with informed training and skills. Policy analysis and policy development includes a range of steps identified for becoming an effective advocate. Depending on the context, there may or may not be a reference to jobs, job creation, or workforce development. Social workers can help advocate and develop programs that incorporate job opportunities at various service delivery entry points.

Economic concerns drive employment possibilities and enhanced strategies for training social workers, other professionals, and talented community members. Overall, the examination of disparities, new paradigms of social construction, and understanding economics are leading social work education to continue to include people and ideas, and to streamline our efforts to address social disorder on micro and macro levels.

Social policy parameters include the specifics of the policy issue, the incorporation of voices that speak to the various social identities, the process of fund-raising among stakeholders, the role of workforce development, and the potential for influencing preK and family development.

HOUSING: WHAT WORKS? WHAT DOESN'T?

At one end of the spectrum regarding housing is the lack of affordable housing, the geographic environments of low-income neighborhoods that contain dilapidated structures, and toxic conditions regarding water and lead. There are concerns for availability of housing related to LGBTQQI needs and housing for youth and elders. Some assisted-living facilities discriminate in placing transgender persons

HOUSING IS MAJOR FOR CHILD DEVELOPMENT

Housing is noted to be one of the major factors for appropriate care for children and youth and for addressing needs of persons who may have limited access to resources over the life cycle. McCarty (2008) observed that social workers are most engaged with families living in low-income and subsidized housing. Yet social work participation in the development of housing policy has been limited and is largely developed by economists and housing activists who may not be connected to social welfare services. The decades-old governmental policies of concentrated segregation in public housing has only led to isolation in high-poverty areas. Research studies on Section 8 housing vouchers have shown positive effects of families moving into other areas. Hypersegregation is a result of several factors, especially the pervasive housing discrimination against low-income minority group members (O'Neal, 1998) and exposure to joblessness.

Stanhope and Dunn (2011) address the dynamics of housing policy and elaborate on the presence of evidence and policy. A major point they inject is the absence of evidence and values in policy deliberations. It is in this context that social workers from practice areas that have significant relevance for citizens impacted by policy need to be involved. Evidence-based policy is a macro component. Their discussion is linked to the example of Housing First (Stanhope & Dunn, 2011), which is a policy solution for homelessness.

HOUSING FIRST

The evaluation research on the Housing First initiative that goes to providing housing for the individual or family immediately has demonstrated a reduction in psychiatric hospitalization in comparison to the control. The research also documents cost savings per year in more than one location. A criticism of the program is that it did not reduce substance use problems, but although it was not designed to address addiction, it did show improvements in that area. Other research (Parsell, Petersen, & Mouton, 2016) studies are encouraging the use of supportive housing rather than crisis-based and transitional housing. The debate on single site versus scattered locations includes tenant perspectives of contact with other tenants and development of the home and community context.

One of the observed differences in the use of public housing or scattered locations is the tenants' perspectives of the presence or absence of support. Within public housing, there may be options for child care and food sharing if needed. But when in scattered locations, the ability to replace such supports may not exist (Keene & Geronimus, 2011). For younger people, eviction and loss of income assistance may exacerbate conditions regarding violence and multiple vulnerabilities, as well as loss of connection to social services (Zivanovic et al., 2016).

SUPPORTED HOUSING

Hickert and Taylor (2011) also observed reductions in jail bookings and residential substance abuse treatment following implementation of supported housing. There is evidence that supportive housing programs for the vulnerable aging can help those who face health issues and homelessness. Brown, Thomas, Cutler, and Hinderlie (2013) outline the reasons aging citizens become homeless. Some often experience personal challenges from a young age, including mental illness, health problems, and substance use that continue and for which emergencies take up any financial resources. Persons who may have lived in conventional circumstances may be confronted with the death of a partner or relative, divorce, sale of the residence by a landlord, or eviction that created a financial crisis that resulted in loss of residence. These persons at older ages are unlikely to regain employment.

Supported-housing policy is needed for young people who are reaching the end of their coverage in foster care. Many families have not fully prepared their youngsters for independent living. There have been some improvements in the Victoria, Australia, policies and legislation (Mendes, Baidawi, & Snow, 2013), but they are discretionary rather than mandatory. Their research categorizes *care leavers* as groups of youth moving on, survivors, and strugglers. The recommendations urge higher-quality services that form positive attachment to help them overcome their early adverse experiences, as well as more gradual and flexible transition plans. These would also be useful to U.S. youth aging out of foster care. Using their narratives, the losses, disconnected relationships—with siblings especially—and other insecure relationships illustrate the limited support networks available. Supported housing would provide a fundamental base for them to build from, gain confidence, and be able to see some possibility. The service user stories (Cunningham & Diversi, 2016) of their trajectory in adverse experiences and continued experiences should offer social work and child care advocates communications training for transitions, endings, and developing next-level relationships within foster homes and in their communities.

UNDERSTANDING PLACE

Understanding place is important for helping professionals working to benefit service users. Place has more relevance for behaviors than office settings. Research on place is a significant element in people's conceptualization of themselves and their spaces (Burton, Kemp, Leung, Matthews, & Takeuchi, 2011). Sutton and Kemp (2011) point to the spatial policies and practices that guarantee profits for developers and property owners, while substandard housing, employment, schools and services, unwanted land uses, and lack of adequate access to healthy foods are relegated to areas of residence for low-income persons.

GENTRIFICATION

Gentrification (Benz, 2013) is the process of middle- and upper-income people using their money, power, and prestige to move into working-class or poverty-stricken areas of a city and taking over the real estate. This impacts all the residents. Young people describe their emotional trauma of being forced to move, connect to new schools, and be impacted by the financial situations this may incur for the family and their loss of connections. Older people may or may not be able to recoup, especially since the payment they receive for their properties may not be sufficient to replace their homes. Adams (2016) explains these various contingencies in his recent article "The End of Black Harlem." He describes how gentrification is destroying the historic capital of African American culture.

AGING POPULATION

Public health strategies of the future must take into account the projections that double persons over 65 by 2050; people of color over 65 will triple (Vega & Wallace, 2016, p. 1). Lower-income adults become more financially insecure as they age, and concern for affordable housing is of critical concern because other costs, especially health care, will also rise and affect household budgets. Formulating policy for affordable housing and the use of alternative interventions (Behrmann & Tebb, 2009) would be better options to assist this population into the future.

EDUCATION: WHAT WORKS? WHAT DOESN'T?

Traditional policies and approaches have resulted in miseducating many children and youth of color and labeling them in ways that have obstructed their ability to obtain employment. Woodson (1933/2010) called attention to the absence of proper Negro history and indoctrination to follow and not think for themselves or seek high challenges. The labeling process stigmatizes and isolates young ones or places them in spaces that jeopardize their development. Lauryn Hill's 1998 song "The Miseducation of Lauryn" is a reference to this.

At the typical interface of micro and mezzo events, social work engages in the mental health status of children and youth in schools. Concerns about educational quality must also include children and youth who may be experiencing myriad social, health, and emotional circumstances that can make it difficult to participate successfully in the traditional classroom routine. Shonkoff an advocate of infant mental health, (Deruy, 2016) offers some examples of innovation and early education. With life circumstances impacting their performance, alternative measures and programs can be designed and customized for young people (Uretsky & Stone, 2016).

The assistance of social workers in schools involves collaboration with various school personnel and community stakeholders for program design and service implementation with individuals, groups, and families. On the broad macro level, consultation and education within communities for health and mental health education taps into a channel for assisting citizens with resource identification and strategy development for prevention and change.

SPECIAL EDUCATION

The problem with special education viewed from members of minority groups has been that it was a place to send children of color rather than teach them well in regular classrooms. The data show that this is the case in most schools across the country; the answer is tied to socioeconomic status and race (Zorigian & Job, 2013). Examining the data regarding special education enrollment raises a few approaches to considering the issues and trends. Samuels (2016) notes that after several years of decline in special education numbers there appears to be an increase. More money is being targeted for training (Heasley, 2016). The sources of this may lie in increase in numbers of children diagnosed on the autism spectrum and the inclusion of students with other health impairments, especially speech and language, and those with attention deficit hyperactivity disorder (ADHD). Data is available from the Department of Education, Office of Special Education Program's (OSEP) 37th Annual Report to Congress (2016) on the Implementation of the Individuals With Disabilities Education Act.

Stein (2011) reports that a Southern California school has an increasing number of English learners, with an overrepresentation of minority students needing special education services. Addressing the English learners' skills as they enter and modifying service as they proceed can be helpful in tailoring programs for their needs. The need for more professionals to work with children with disabilities is being addressed by the federal administration in the distribution of funding to enhance training programs.

MENTAL HEALTH: WHAT WORKS? WHAT DOESN'T?

Young people are less likely to receive mental health services than adults, and many without insurance do not seek care (SAMSHA, 2016). The lack of mental health professionals in many parts of the United States and in areas around the world leaves care to one's own efforts or folk healers. Research presented at the World Bank and World Health Organization conference in Washington (Carey, 2016) referred to the need for investment in treatment programs for depression and anxiety—the most common mental health problems—to bring significant returns via years of healthy life and social contributions. Psychiatry as we know it is not as effective as it wants to be (Davies, 2013).

The impact of poverty is also understood to affect the health of growing children, which results in chronic conditions that are likely to develop in later ages. There are many families that live with low incomes and manage their households within their means. They are able to provide structure, resources, and nurturing and raise confident and secure children. In other families, the impact of stressors on children living in households with low income and the related expressions of feelings, anxiety, and anger may create unhealthy physical responses. Taylor and Wade, pediatricians in Philadelphia, discuss how poverty affects children's health (*Radio Times*, 2016). The higher the number of adverse childhood experiences one has, the more likely the child's health is affected.

COMMUNITY-BASED PREVENTION

The tendency for persons with psychological distress to not go for care is frequently associated with stigma and lack of insurance (Reuters, 2017). Considering use of alternative approaches offers options for improved access and outcomes.

Emerging mindfulness strategies and recent poverty research (Wimer, 2015) calls out survival fatigue that obstructs the ability to deal with various agencies to get help. The impact of students' emotions on their achievement should be a clear variable, though not many researchers have chosen to pursue this area. Those who recognize that continual worry about their situations is harmful do offer interventions to modify these feelings and note that ways of control were beneficial (Sparks & Viadero, 2016; Valiente, Swanson, & Eisenberg, 2012). Some noted skepticism that cognition and emotion are connected. If we expand the consideration of emotion (especially anger) with the capacity to be focused on the impact of historical trauma on males (of color, particularly), it may be more conceptually feasible to recognize the influences that obstruct achievement in different contexts.

The limited engagement of young Aboriginal men in Australia parallels experiences of young men of color in the United States. Many are not in school or employed. Whiteside and associates (2016) worked with a sample and surveyed their self-assessment pre and post interventions that exposed them to opportunities and support to become more engaged. The evaluations indicated their participation in the Family Wellbeing Empowerment (FWB) program "enhanced self-awareness, sense of hope and optimism, family and community relationships, and an overall capacity to take control of their lives" (para 1). The content of the FWB included a 5-stage program of vocational educational training that earned the participants a Level II certificate.

When everyone does not have insurance or cannot access ongoing services, engaging with the community through community organizations such as libraries, special projects, and alternative approaches can also lead recovery and growth.

TASK SHARING IN THE COMMUNITY

Another option for services in the community involve task sharing. Vikram Patel, a psychiatrist (Patel, 2012), shares his research of the inclusion of the whole community in assisting the improvement of mental health. In a world of few psychiatrists and mental health professionals for all the needs that there are, he and others train community members to connect with their community and assist in ameliorating emotional distress. The macro level involves being informed of local and federal legislation that can help provide resources to help families.

Task shifting, or task sharing, involves provider education, supervision, and partnerships with local communities, but it also incorporates teaching community residents about self-care, family nutrition and exercise, and options such as telemedicine and telephone supports in some locations (Hoeft, Fortney, Patel, & Unutzer, 2016). These strategies help community residents become more informed of ways to foster encouraging and supportive strategies at home and teach them when to reach for more professional help.

Trauma-informed awareness and information interventions are great if persons will go to an agency. Training through community education has the capacity to touch many more.

HEALTH

It is somewhat surprising that the research on the links of mental health and education are limited. The improvement of health and mental health services relies on the examination and evaluation of existing services. Gaps in services tend to reflect connections to attitudes about the target groups and policies regarding supports. Health education and polices regarding diabetes, nutrition, healthy food consumption (Roberto, Pomerantz, & Fisher, 2014), and falls has been provided in community settings with some positive results. Concerns about food security and food affordability (Lee, Kane, Ramsey, Good et al., 2016) are related to the need for advocacy in food-pricing policies. As awareness of disparities is examined, broader areas needed for research are exposed. It has become clear that screening and treatment in an office does little to reduce the prevalence of chronic diseases and disparities in communities (Burton et al., 2011).

HEALTH EDUCATION

Awareness of information regarding approaches that may enhance health should be shared with communities. Resources for health may be provided by public, private, or faith-based agencies. The socioeconomic inequalities associated with outcomes offer approaches to address health needs. Martinson and Reichmann (2016) conducted secondary data analysis on low-weight births in the United States, the United Kingdom, Canada, and Australia. U.S.

and UK inequalities were similar, but there is better overall health in the United Kingdom, Canada, and Australia. These countries have more generous health care and social support systems. The highest infant mortality rates were found in the United States, and the better outcomes were associated with the higher quality of care in the other countries.

Price and affordability is pointed to as an important variable in helping populations improve their diets. Data on comparable food pricing is not readily available. Lee and associates (2016) examined food prices in local areas and compared them with household incomes. Results suggested that healthy diets could be made available via appropriate policies.

Falls and the fear of falls are associated with a reduced quality of life in older citizens (Vieira, Palmer, & Chaves, 2016). There were several conditions linked to risk for falls—pain, fear, rushing, cognitive flexibility, diabetes, and the use of multiple types of medication, called *polypharmacy*. Home-visiting services and other local connections for getting residents information appear to have great potential.

JUSTICE: WHAT WORKS? WHAT DOESN'T?

Social work via prison work has vacillated over the years. It has moved from service in the 1800s to reluctance in the 1940s and back to including correction in the social work curricula, led by CSWE in 1959 (Matejkowski, Johnson, & Severson, 2016). Social work in prisons has been limited in part by fear for the workers' safety. The lessons learned from observations and analysis of injustices against people of color, women, and persons facing challenges has led to advocacy for reform of the punitive system to procedures that allow for rehabilitation. Questions are raised regarding most dimensions of the criminal justice system. From the disproportionate numbers of arrests to punitive use of court costs for low-wealth people to charges against having a small amount of substance versus laundering drug money, the punishment is least for those with more money (Marshall, 2014).

The policies and attitudes that resulted in the prison industrial complex (Davis, 1998) and mass incarceration (Alexander, 2012) have been examined, and voices to liberate and establish more sensitive programs are in discussion. State policy makers have been influenced by the research that shows mass incarceration is not effective. "Forty-six states made 201 changes to their sentencing and corrections laws in 2014 and 2015" (Silber, Subramanian, & Spotts, 2016, p 9). Some worry that discharge of prisoners is the right way to go, but they fear it will go the way of hospital deinstitutionalization—too many citizens and too few appropriate and effective community resources.

The ineffectiveness of juvenile justice detention centers is a critical concern. Youngsters referred to as being "on the pipeline from the cradle to prison" have a high proportion of comorbid conditions. Difficulties include mental health, substance use, addiction, school-related problems, special education issues, maltreatment experiences, and court involvement (Mallett & Boitel, 2016). Some states are improving policies for juveniles, including raising the juvenile age (Childress, 2016) and are planning improvements in treatment for substance dependence and addiction.

WHAT WORKS—TEACHING SKILLS AND CRITICAL THINKING

Garrett (2016) refers to the data regarding increased rates of incarceration and the related costs to citizens and the inhumanity involved in the conditions. His advocacy pushes the growth of the state of incarceration to be an essential concern in social work's social justice agenda. Ireland's case study of their prison crisis reports similar happenings in other national settings. The Urban Institute (2016) has taken a leading role in producing research regarding incarceration, sentencing reform, creating community partnerships to assist reunification with families, and efforts to find housing and employment for persons recently released from prison.

The need for further research and the potential of social work participation in prisons is a step to address the costs of imprisonment for low-level crimes for spouses and children. The Annie E. Casey Foundation-led Juvenile Detention Alternatives Initiative has helped courts decrease their use of detention and improve recidivism rates. While some lockup facilities are needed for more serious offenders, the programs found to be most effective include interpersonal skills programs, anger control, family-style group homes, multiple service agencies, and community residential programs (not juvenile justice).

Eliminating the use of solitary confinement in juvenile and adult facilities has been recommended. Isolation is suggested to be used only as a temporary strategy. Research indicates that solitary confinement is more damaging and does little to enhance safety (Casey Foundation, 2016).

Several organizations and coalitions are working together with juvenile justice systems to improve juvenile corrections. Some states are also revisiting other policies that do more harm to young people. Many states have raised the ages of adult responsibility. Evidence shows that putting juveniles in lockup with adults leads to more crime rather than deterring or reducing it, makes it more difficult for them to re-enter their communities, and puts them at more risk for physical and sexual violence and a higher risk of suicide (Childress, 2016).

While more research and evaluation is needed, the evidence strongly supports juvenile courts to reassess punitive and nontreatment detention designs.

COMMUNITY ORGANIZATIONS

There is some evidence that voluntary community organizations help reduce crime. This relationship is not substantial (Wo, Hipp, & Boessen, 2016) but offers another strategy. This requires more long-term investment in research that further examines the agency interventions' impact on crime reduction.

Although there are signs that a decarceration era is blooming, incarceration incentives established over the past decades have built substantial obstacles. Eisenberg (2016) points to the empowered interest groups that are invested in maintaining the system. Public correctional officers, their unions, and private prison management will require changes in compensation and assessment structures to modify criminal justice procedures. Her analysis of the issues related to reform targets the stakeholders who staff, manage, and operate the prisons.

SUBSTANCE USE AND ADDICTION

Conversations regarding the potential changes in the justice system also involve substance use. As policies are modified regarding drug use classification and sentencing, relationships of social work to probation (Burke, Teague, Ward, & Worrall, 2016) and community supervision are also considered. The thousands of persons who have been incarcerated with addiction or mental illnesses will also likely be released and require housing, medical and psychiatric care, social services, and social and vocational care, which has already been limited in community settings (Lamb & Weinberger, 2014).

Social work has increased its emphasis on social justice, but literature on its participation in criminal justice reform is limited. The literature from the United Kingdom appears to be more focused on advocacy in areas that impact service users. Federal and state agencies are continuing strategies to reduce jail and prison populations while simultaneously seeking to design related services to address alcohol, drug, and mental health needs. Persons released from jails and prisons are at high risk of physical and behavioral health morbidity (Begun, Early, & Hodge, 2016). Existing policies may be incomplete for coordinating services to inmates and recently discharged persons that involve comorbid concerns. More attention is needed for outreach and outcomes protocols.

PLANNING: TECHNOLOGY AND COMMUNITY ADVOCACY

Planning as a term has not received much attention in recent years except as a component of various fields of service. Yet its history in social welfare services is long and rich. It has been a component of social work education and continues to evolve. Kahn (1969) presented a key question that our work has to address: Are Americans willing to plan to meet the requirements of democratic values? In arriving at what has been observed, examined, and evaluated, prioritizing and organizing requires implementing steps to translate social goals into effective programs.

Davies (2013) presents the view that psychiatry is not the best solution. Specht and Courtney (1994) warned social workers that moving into psychotherapy and away from community work was not the best pathway for the true foundation of social work. Moving forward involves understanding the history of care for persons in need and planning services needed to address current and emerging conditions affecting social and economic justice. This work requires continuing educational and technological preparation and awareness of self in working with others, involving service users, community representatives, and providing leadership.

PREPARATION—INTERPROFESSIONAL EDUCATION & ADVOCACY SKILLS

As the profession continues to examine traditional policies and emerging data on demographics and services outcomes, it becomes clearer that efforts across disciplines and within organizations will benefit from increased collaboration, advocacy, and services coordination.

Achieving health care improvements cannot occur without working across professions. As a profession based on interdisciplinary knowledge acquisition and committed to multilayered and multicultural interactions with individuals, groups, organizations, and communitie uniquely qualified to provide leadership (Jones & Phillips, 2016). Social work skills in ment, communication, group facilitation, empathy, engagement, and community bui assets to the development of interprofessional practice (IPP) and education initiatives

For example, not only is direct instruction of importance with children and their families, but advocacy skills are also required. Gottfried and Conchas (2016) provide examples of policies that backfire when schools close and the community feels betrayed by the closures. Ng and associates (2015) propose that rehabilitation professionals may become more involved in change as they are more informed of advocacy for children with disabilities in order to enhance competency frameworks and continuing education. Students and their families have feelings about the way they are treated by school personnel who are following school policies that discriminate or penalize, often in arbitrary ways.

Research is limited on the connections of emotions to achievement (Valiente et al., 2012). Some of the observations and research regarding the impact of stigma, discrimination and reactions regarding achievement, perseverance are offered in the resilience research. However, Gottfried and Conchas (2016) provide case stories that compel our thinking about how the policies are harmful. For the most part, we can speculate these policies are prepared from the perspectives of nondiverse administrators who are focused on their bottom line, not on the needs of the community they are serving.

Simultaneously, macro practice builds on system-level theories (Guererro & Nair, 2014) and perspectives for strategic planning and advocacy. Social change to improve the health of vulnerable populations (Stroh, 2014) and to promote social and economic justice (Libal, Berthold, Thomas, & Healy, 2014) is connected to social work goals for transformative expertise (Yliruka & Karvinen-Niinikoski, 2013).

SERVICE USER INVOLVEMENT

Consumer involvement includes participation in planning, community education, advocacy, and peer services. The community involvement component (O'Neal, 1984) of the 1963/1975 Community Mental Health Centers Act proposed this strategy through a consultation and education unit that was quickly eliminated as budgets were cut over the years. Originally, the participation of staff and consumers in planning and decision-making was mandated. Organizations and states have addressed the inclusion of these component in different ways. The California Mental Health Act of 2004, amended in 2012, includes community education as a key element to helping communities help themselves. "The Act addresses a broad continuum of prevention, early intervention and service needs and the necessary infrastructure, technology and training elements that will effectively support this system" (California Mental Health, 2016).

The policy initiatives to involve users have been resisted in organizations and by professionals (Bee, Brooks, Fraser, & Lovell, 2015). Issues of user philosophies, expectations, feelings of exclusion, and professional accountability create tensions. The lack of a well-defined structure and implementation steps appear to obstruct the potential of this collaboration.

There is growing attention to service user involvement. The concept is integral to improving services. However, its implementation continues to be resisted by institutional and professional cultures and some individuals. Laging and Heidenreich (2017) examine the need for its incorporation into the social work curriculum in Germany and recognize that in order to do this careful reflection and planning are important.

Comparing services from the retail perspective offers another view for consideration (Mackenzie et al., 2013; Mowbray, Robinson, & Holter, 2002). Beyond the historical use of consumer involvement is the comparison of service users to retail business. The phrase "the customer is always right" has not been respected very much in social or health services. Yet the customer expects quality and deserves respect if he or she is purchasing a service. Moving from the frame of "I know, as an expert" to "I am here to work with you" and "I understand that you are paying something for this service" puts another spin on the relationship.

LEADERSHIP: COMMUNITY AND POPULATION HEALTH AS A RESULT OF PROFESSIONAL EXAMINATION

Reaching for a "culture of health" (Heathy People.gov), recommended by Healthy People 2030, encourages professionals to think outside of the box and work across disciplines in dialogues with staff and service users or potential consumers.

Social workers in organizations have opportunities to help enable participants to enhance productivity through social work practices to develop leadership and management strategies. Guerrero and Nair (2014) note the potential of evidence based macro practice, total quality management—evidence-based macro practice—to influence structure and capacity to address social worker values and skills in organizations.

Adding a reflective structure through dialogical leadership will enable the process to foster staff well-being, motivation, evaluative dialogues, and retention. This will allow evaluation of primary tasks to build on for a next level for innovation. tools (Yliruka & Karvinen-Niinikoski, 2015).

Designed through working with practitioners, managers, service users, and political decision-makers, social work tasks can facilitate the incorporation of models that increase multidimensional strategies.

Expanding attention to education for girls and women benefits children and families (Brown, 2014). Gray and Price (2014, p. 78) illustrate partnering for screening through the enhanced engagement model, which was designed with the specific intent of addressing the unmet mental health needs of women participating in home-visiting programs through the Maternal and Child Health Bureau. The enhanced engagement "model is a culturally informed and responsive brief intervention that integrates existing theory with empirical evidence that is currently under investigation. The model offers social work practitioners a structured approach to the delivery of brief mental health intervention based on working components of integrated product teams (IPT) and cognitive behavioral therapy (CBT) while offering consumer choice among evidence-informed modules."

Pérez and Martinez (2008) promote the role of community health workers in engaging with people and collecting information within excluded communities that can be used in developing health policy. The real status of water pollution and lead contamination in communities across the country (Wines & Schwartz, 2016) should be a concern in our communities before it becomes a crisis. Rosner (NPR, 2016) reminds us that Flint, Michigan, has a long history of environmental injustice related to the automobile industry in its region. Are our elected officials being accountable to the needs of communities? Is corruption and greed (Ingle & McClure, 2010) at the center of some of the disasters or ineffective policies we experience? Can we participate in ways that show professional and community collaboration to address these challenges?

This examination of the issues that affect our profession reveals the broad-based social context that impact our lives daily. The findings are leading those who want better quality of services to research informed and data-driven options that include representatives of all our communities in the planning and implementation.

STUDENT COMMENTS

Students who participated in a class discussion agreed on the theme of vision and leadership for planning social work and criminal justice collaborations. They selected a quote from Alexander. "We should hope not for a colorblind society but instead for a world, in which we can see each other fully, learn from each other, and do what we can to respond to each other with love. That was King's dream—a society that is capable of seeing each of us, as we are, with love. That is a goal worth fighting for." (Alexander, 2012, p. 244)

A facilitator could use this quote in a group session with individuals suffering from societal constraints and frustration, particularly centered on race and identity. Reflecting on the social justice values of fairness and compassion for all individuals is not just necessary for social workers, but for everyone. This reflection could lead to an understanding of client values and social justice values, to inspire leadership in challenging times.

CHAPTER SUMMARY

This chapter acknowledges the challenges the social work profession faces from institutional racism and traditional service approaches. The status of services in micro and macro context are examined. Some examples of what contributed to disparities and ideas for improvements are highlighted. Students should be informed of the range of obstacles, including the impact of whiteness, on continuing interactions with clients of diverse realities. Students should be able to consider accessing various approaches for improving service user relationships and communication.

EPAS AND CODE OF ETHICS

CSWE EDUCATIONAL POLICY & ACCREDITATION STANDARDS

Competency 4: Engage in Practice-informed Research and Research-informed Practice.
- 4a) use practice experience and theory to inform scientific inquiry and research;
- 4b) apply critical thinking to engage in analysis of quantitative and qualitative research methods and research findings; and
- 4c) use and translate research evidence to inform and improve practice, policy, and service delivery

Competency 8: Intervene with Individuals, Families, Groups, Organizations, and Communities
- 8c) use inter-professional collaboration as appropriate to achieve beneficial practice outcomes;
- 8d) negotiate, mediate, and advocate with and on behalf of diverse clients and constituencies (EPAS, 2015)

NASW CODE OF ETHICS

Ethical Principle: Social workers' primary goal is to help people in need and to address social problems.
Ethical Principle: Social workers challenge social injustice. (NASW, n.d.)

DISCUSSION

1. Define *stereotype*. Describe a scenario in which you think the threat of being a stereotype occurs for some people. Who would you choose? Why?
2. Review the following article (Steinmetz, 2014) from *Time.com*: "Kansas Bill Allowing Refusal of Service to Gay Couples Moves Forward" (http://nation.time.com/2014/02/11/kansas-bill-allowing-refusal-of-service-to-gay-couples-moves-forward/? xid=newsletter-weekly). Write an appropriate comment as a social worker.
3. How does the reality of class and income affect service interventions?
4. List three questions/social issues you would raise for discussion at a community meeting.

EXERCISES

1. "I'm worried that students will take their obedient place in society and look to become successful cogs in the wheel—let the wheel spin them around as it wants without taking a look at what they're doing. I'm concerned that students not become passive acceptors of the official doctrine that's handed down to them from the White House,

the media, textbooks, teachers and preachers."—Howard Zinn Using this quotation as a starting point, how would you begin to analyze the contemporary employment possibilities for persons of historic exclusion?

2. In a speech to social work students at West Chester University in 2010, Stacy Patton challenged them to be more attentive to the needs and possible resources for children in foster care and to go beyond accepting the stereotypes assuming that they can't make it. How might the concept "power of words" impress you to work with foster care children?

3. *Hard Earned* (2015) is a six-series documentary (www.kartemquin.com/films/hard-earned). Watch one of the episodes. List concerns that are illustrated. What policies or services address their needs? What kinds of policies might be helpful? Are there any legislative policies impending that might be helpful?

4. Select two states to compare using the *Children in the States Fact Sheets 2015* databases on the Children's Defense Fund site (http://www.childrensdefense.org/library/data/state-data-repository/cits/). List three questions about the outcomes of services the state provides.

5. Select an area for you to continually examine over the remaining time in this semester: housing, workforce issues, wages, unions, addiction, interventions (or any other issue you might be interested in). Select at least two websites to monitor regarding social work and your area of interest. Choices may include *The New York Times*, NASW, IFSW, CLASP, Talk Poverty, Maternal and Child Health, SAMSHA, Utne Reader, and so on. Class participation will be linked to comments from your selected sites.

MULTICULTURAL RESOURCES

Ali, A. H. (2007). *Infidel*. New York, NY: Free Press.

Chavous, K. P. (2011). *Voices of determination: Children that defy the odds*. Piscataway, NJ: Transaction.

Collins, M., & Haley, A. (1990). *Marva Collins Way*. New York, NY: TarcherPerigree.

Collins, P. H. (2012). *Intellectual activism*. Philadelphia, PA: Temple University Press.

Crow Dog, M., & Erdoes, R. (1990). *Lakota woman*. New York, NY: Grove Weidenfeld.

DeGrury, J., & Johnson, U. (2016). *What is cognitive dissonance?* [Video file]. Retrieved from https://www.youtube.com/watch?v=ucN12khyfSU

Delgado, M. (2008). *Youth-led community organizing: Theory and action*. New York, NY: Oxford University Press.

Hard Earned. (2015). Chicago, IL: Kartemquin Films and Al Jazeera America. Retrieved from https://kartemquin.com/films/hard-earned

Husseini, R. (2009). *Murder in the name of honor: The true story of one woman's heroic fight against an unbelievable crime*. London, England: Oneworld.

Nafizi, A. (2008). *Reading Lolita in Teheran*. New York, NY: Random House.

Norton, D. (1978). *Dual perspective*. New York, NY: Council on Social Work Education.

Patel, V. (2012, June). *Mental health for all by involving all* [Video file]. Retrieved from https://www.ted.com/talks/vikram_patel_mental_health_for_all_by_involving_all

Patton, S. (2008). *That mean old yesterday*. New York, NY: Washington Square Press.

Perry, S. (2013). Magnet school principal: Steve Perry, a rebel with a cause. Retrieved from http://articles.courant.com/2013-11-24/news/hc-steve-perry-education-reform-1123-20131124_1_school-reform-efforts-diane-ravitch-hartford

Schiffer, M. (Writer), & Avildsen, J. G. (Director). (1989). *Lean on me*. Burbank, CA: Warner Bros.

Woodson, C. G. (1933, 2010). *The mis-education of the Negro.* Amazon Digital Services LLC.

Yousafzai, M. (2013). *I am Malala: The girl who stood up for education and was shot by the Taliban.* Boston, MA: Little, Brown.

FURTHER READING AND RESOURCES

Montoya, I. D., & Vocci, F. (2007). Suggestions for future research. In T. Geary (Ed.), *Medication treatments for nicotine dependence* (pp. 293–301). Boca Raton, FL: CRC Press.

Moyers, B. (2013) *Michelle Alexander—Locked out of America,* http://billmoyers.com/segment/michelle-alexanderlocked-out-of-the-american-dream/

Townes, G. (2009). Report: Cities' racial disparities in access to life-saving pharmaceuticals. *New York Amsterdam News,* *100*(25), 27–30.

Community Competence

Building Strengths

CHAPTER OVERVIEW

Chapter 10 will review cultural heritage knowledge that offers sources of strength. This knowledge is useful for helping professionals, members of groups, and others. This chapter emphasizes appreciating multiple perspectives and intersectional identities. The knowledge base draws on natural resources for self-care and collective strength. Reflecting on these ideas encourages knowledge building personally, within families, and in organizational development. Recognizing community assets leads to capacity development.

LEARNING OBJECTIVES

- Visible and invisible dynamics operate across communities.
- Families, communities and professions require education and material resources through the triple perspective of micro, mezzo, and macro dimensions.
- Beliefs, attitudes, and mindsets exist in all community entities.

Benchmark: Students will be able to identify strengths and assets across micro, mezzo, and macro levels.

A VIEW OF THE WORLD

On the broadest level, maintaining awareness of developments around the world regarding the civil and human rights of minority group members, women, religious groups, and those with identities traditionally excluded from mainstream attention is needed. Groupwork is especially important as a social work practice method. Using the knowledge gained to establish relationships, promote dialogues, engage in collaborative transactions, and build partnerships offers paths to improving quality of life.

Not only is incorporating research, literature, art, and music of clients important in broadening our understanding of people we work with, but it is also important for designing strategies to investigate the relationships of groups within the broader dominant culture. Seeking knowledge through ethnographic interviewing may involve discussions of music appreciation and lyrics that are meaningful. Stoute (2011) points out that through musical connection millennials are presenting a dimension that incorporates more common interests and concerns.

Racial and cultural socialization builds confidence in community membership. It occurs through the dynamics of communication and support. Socialization has been linked to the development of interpersonal protection and intrapersonal resilience. These dynamics have been identified in families and institutions such as historically black colleges and universities (HBCUs), American Indian controlled colleges, women's colleges, and Latino-serving institutions (Smith, 1997). The content and behaviors used by professionals in these organizations have contributed to the development of strong personalities and academic achievement. Content includes cultural heroes and *sheroes* (a term connected to Johnetta Cole's tenure as a Spelman College president) and examples of how to handle discriminatory and intimidating situations. Resource materials help identify role model behaviors that readers may contemplate and imitate in their lives.

Building upon exposure to the multicultural resources enhances steps in macro work to use intervention strategies that engage clients and consumers for capacity building and community development.

Maria and Esnad have just met in their social work practice class. They read about the spirit-calling ceremony, the Yuwipi, (McGaa, 1990) used by an individual as he prepared to go to Vietnam. In this ceremony, a small stone was given that he wore in a pouch during combat missions. They wondered about the relevance of this kind of information in planning a conversation for a service user. They compared this to ceremonies or rituals they know about. What could you contribute to this discussion?

STUDENT SCENARIO

BUILDING SERVICE USER CONFIDENCE THROUGH CULTURAL HERITAGE KNOWLEDGE

Awareness of the ecological frameworks that influence communities helps professionals validate a range of pathways for consumer participation in their communities. Simultaneously, social workers and other counselors and allies may join social and economic justice conversations and activities. Community competence builds capacity through the participation of constituents to contemplate their purpose and create welcoming interactions.

VISIBLE AND INVISIBLE DYNAMICS

The visible and invisible dynamics of a community present knowledge and structures people have used to support themselves and to offer mutual aid. *Visible dynamics* refer to the architecture, artifacts, books, and art that record events and activities and people's interpretations about their living arrangements and interpersonal transactions over time. Historical information that illustrates strengths should be used to offset historical trauma information.

Invisible dynamics refer to the attitudes and beliefs associated with mind and spirit that may be tied to individual, family, and community strengths and resolve. Thinkers, writers, and artists have presented interpretations that urge getting to know oneself and to identify one's purpose as steps to enlightenment and compassion. Trine (1933) acknowledges that we all dwell in the inner kingdom—mind and spirit—and the outer one—the body and physical universe around us (Kindle Location 1, p. 1). The zen experience, encourages understanding our own minds (Hoover, 1980). The Native American wisdom appreciates the natural state of vegetation and questions actions that diminish natural resources—trees, water, air (Kaltreider, 2003, Loc 109). Early African civilizations emphasized a holistic socialization process built on a spiritual foundation (Hilliard, Williams, & Damali, 1987).

Community supports and strengths address pain and remedy conditions that people have experienced and offer hope. Ceremonies and rituals connected to communities play out the mutual support and collaboration it takes to get through the journey of life. The path of appreciation of others—using compassion rather than being judgmental and conflictual—is also identified as a beneficial mindset and way of living.

WHAT IS CULTURAL COMPETENCE?

There are several sources of definitions of *cultural competence*. The National Education Association (NEA) describes the fundamental rationale for cultural competence is to address the increasing diversity of American classrooms so educators can be effective with young people from cultures other than their own. Their statement refers to scholars' desire to provide an environment of respect and reciprocity to ameliorate student outcomes by incorporating racial and ethnic minority contributions in curriculum and diversifying pedagogical practices (NEA, 2017).

DEFINITIONS AND VALUES

The health care messages posed by Substance Abuse and Mental Health Services Administration, (SAMSHA, 2017) describe cultural competence as the capacity of professionals to be responsive, respectful, and to interact effectively with people of various cultures regardless of race, ethnicity, age, gender, sexual orientation, disability, religion, income level, education, geographical location, or profession. The Office of Minority Health of the U.S. Department of Health and Human Services webpage (2017) has posted the National Standards for Culturally and Linguistically Appropriate Services in Health and Health Care (the National CLAS Standards). These expand the previous competence standards by including language and comprehensive principles that point to providing services in which the standards are addressed in governance, leadership, and workforce and accountability.

For social work, culturally competent practice builds on awareness and emphasizes continuous learning (Lum, 1999). The meaning of *culture* refers to ways, styles, customs, language, and values that people use to get about their lives. For students of social work and related professions, cultural competence involves "cultural awareness, knowledge acquisition, skill development, and inductive learning" (p. 3). This operates with respect to service users, practitioners, agencies, and communities. Appreciating the diversity that exists on each of these levels and the interactions and transactions that transpire reveals contexts within which we need understanding.

PROFESSIONAL ROLES

Health professionals are engaged in culturally competent work in a variety of ways. Lum (1999) sets up the early framework that illustrates knowledge acquisition of culture from arenas of practice to those that involve research and writing. Historians, researchers, educators, and others have long called for the need for appropriate role representation in the institutions that provide services for people. Our attention is focused on roles involved in analyzing the sources of ineffective services connected to the absence of cultural respect and understanding. Simultaneously, we are respecting who and what has been excluded and practitioner roles that support inclusion and seek innovation. *Awakenings* (Marshall, 1990), a mental health film that offers an interesting view on health care participants and change, demonstrates knowledge development and implementation.

There are several traditional helping professions and emerging fields that promote ways of learning about how humans operate with various ways of approaching and coaching toward improvements. Teamwork and collaboration are fundamental for managing and implementing these ideas. Team decision-making (Crampton, Crea, Abramson-Madden, & Usher, 2008) is challenging due to complex relationships of the street-level workers, organizational constraints, and family participants, and the use of technology.

RACIAL, ETHNIC, AND NATIONAL GROUPS HAVE THEIR OWN RESPECTIVE CULTURES

All cultural groups have various forms of cultural heritage and customs. While there may be some that members of shared groups hold in common, individuals and families are unique in what these customs may be or how they may be expressed. In recognizing the intersections of identity, it is paramount that mental health diagnosis and treatment consider these dynamics by listening and assessing people's stories of their lives, their beliefs, and what has happened to them over time. As important as it is to recognize the range of cultural schemes of service users, it is even more important to examine the cultural frames of our personal and professional lives. These two dimensions overlap. Each has history. For those born in more recent years (i.e., post-1970, or even 1980), the history across cultural groups and disciplines may be fuzzy, if not unknown. Yet it remains significant to understanding cultural history and baggage. It is the knowledge of positive cultural history that contributes to the academic success of children and youth (Okeke-Adeyanju et al., 2016).

ROLE OF TECHNOLOGY AND SOCIAL MEDIA

The historic role of social media has been explained as the significant purveyor of stereotypes that incense racism and discrimination. Fake news or narrow interpretations or messages that present the point of view or those who are paying for it marches on. For example, Katznelson

(2017) asks "Who really got handouts?"—a question that raises concerns that parallels the erroneous message that whites have diminished income because of people of color. Data shows higher wealth among Caucasians and Asians.

The Justice Department under Jeff Sessions suggests that college admissions deny whites access because of affirmative action (Katznelson, 2017). What the message hides is the fact that most affirmative action has provided for white people. American social policy has conferred substantive benefits to white folks who needed assistance while effectively excluding most southern black people.

Technology is also fueling messages for people who don't think deeply or read, compare critically, and analyze. The fast pace of access via the Internet, Google, Facebook, and Amazon pushes people to immediate emotional reactions and to draw on old and new messages. These entities offer convenience, and while beneficial in many ways, they also shortchange our connections to reality. According to Taplin (2017), the dominance of these monopolies promotes their values and rules. Their camouflaged autocracy excludes all of us. He asks us to "consider the role they play in our lives." From his view, by giving them control we obstruct our future freedom. We need to become more thoughtful about our democratic values and asserting our voices for more accountability.

SKILL AREAS

The skill areas that will assist in navigating the community competence territory are those that recognize assets, share that knowledge, and build strengths on that foundation. Identifying discipline-specific frameworks that target ways of knowing and doing among groups allows us to begin. From this view of community practice, key skills include awareness, establishing *community geography identification* and context, *interviewing* for qualitative data of the context, *network analysis,* group *facilitation, knowledge of cultural resources, listening, mediation and negotiation, community organizing, research sharing,* and *goal setting.*

The ecological framework attracts ethnographic interviewing, which draws on anthropology and expects an interview process that requires engagement and immersion in the interviewee's knowledge of the context. As the knowledge base expands from association with community members, skills require working with smaller to larger groups and engaging via methods and techniques that seek internal leaders and foster broad motivation for information- and health-seeking behaviors.

Social workers have opportunities to translate research in ways that service users can understand the situations and trauma that may be associated with issues their families face and restraints that may compel them to disintegrate or destruct. Professional services are available to help persons implement strategies to recover and progress. Practitioners should share with service users specific multicultural resources that show through reports, examples, and stories the successful outcomes of individuals and families that rely on their heritage of strengths.

Kirp points (2015) out, "To improve poor neighborhoods, the people who live there must have a hand in deciding their own fate" (para 3). Social work interventions and community organizing offers prevention and encouragement for participation in nonstigmatizing arenas. Our opportunity is to use skills and methods to bring in community members to help plan improved services and community education.

ASSESSING CULTURAL VIEWS

Enhancing relationships between helping professionals, organizational managers, and service user networks involves acquiring knowledge of cultural groups, ancestral heritage, and contemporary perspectives. Being informed of cultural history encourages listening and engaging from a potentially more comfortable point.

Cultural assessment guidelines orient practitioners to professional cultural activities and segments of the service users' cultural picture (UMD, 1981). The employer has expectations for the service provision and the types of data to be gathered and used in assessing needs and planning services.

BEING INFORMED OF CULTURALLY AFFIRMING
INFORMATION TO DEVELOP CONNECTIONS

As the social work profession continues to observe and reflect on issues confronting our citizens, using the person-in-environment context encourages appreciation and respect of our communities. Sutton and Kemp (2011, p. 1) expose the basis of work regarding inclusion by exploring "place." They began with "Place matters to the quality of human existence." This statement is essential to contemplating social work's continuing efforts to reach communities with evidence-based practice. Examining the context of the communities within which we work urges more outreach in the process of inclusion. Using data that shows who is being left out may embolden next steps for engaging with those who are not served. At the same time, we must acknowledge that research is limited regarding the forms of information useful in preparing students for multicultural competency. The effectiveness of different types of multicultural training and the demonstration of the use of diverse resources requires further evaluation (Cates, et al., 2007).

OFFICES OR COMMUNITY SETTINGS

The practice of having clients come to an office where the experts live somehow diminishes the reality of where people come from and how their environments may be perceived in the recovery and resilience process. Angela Blanchard (2011) describes her programs that build on neighborhoods assets. Her approach, similar to Delgado's (2007), demonstrates working together in the community to develop strategies.

Drawing from the ancient use of ceremonies and rituals, these offer structure for families and individuals to associate the importance of one's self-seeking to being a part of the environment. John Nelson (1994) suggests the absence of this is associated with mental illness. Healing that split is how he recommends we think about the invisible dynamics in order to help. Helping professionals can spend time visiting in the communities in which they work. Figure 10.1 suggests a process for community members and professionals to think about connecting learning to acts of kindness.

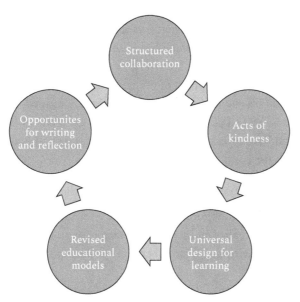

FIGURE 10.1   Sharing Acts of Kindness

RECOGNIZING AND RESPECTING CULTURAL HERITAGE STRENGTHS

An important basis for respecting communities is the awareness of the strengths that have been used to support one another. The association of cultural heritage knowledge to the educational curricula of diverse students is linked to higher self-esteem and academic performance (Atkinson & Stiglitz, 2014; Davis-Maye, Davis, & Jones, 2013, Kanaʻiaupuni, Ledward, & Jensen, 2010).

At the same time, traumas that many have experienced have been linked to society's denigration of groups and planned oppression and from negative interactions that often transpire within relationships. Trauma is frequently analyzed from the micro view. Moving forward in understanding the pursuit of community competence, it must be also be acknowledged on the macro level. DeGrury (2005) discusses what is involved in the healing process of posttraumatic slave syndrome. Yellow Horse Brave Heart (n.d.) speaks to this for Native Americans.

The heritage of multicultural people includes healing remedies and supports within various contexts. Being aware of broad areas of influence helps consider the variables that people draw on. As social environments have evolved, "every culture accumulated a vast historical and cultural sourcebook of proven cures" (Buchman, 2005, p. 9). These sources of information have been retained more or less throughout families. For many, they provide strong foundations for health and nutrition. For others, not so much. Being aware of these sources of knowledge can be helpful to professionals as they engage with diverse communities.

THINKING ABOUT THE FOLKTALES

Linking folktales to irrationality and primitive thinking may have been the perspective of some psychoanalysts (Boyer, 1979), but our purpose in including folk literature is to add to a body of creative expression to draw on.

Across cultures, there are likely to be strengths associated with plants, hands/touch, water, earth, breath, movement, animals, and the mind (Buchman, 2005). Mindfulness can be tied to calming oneself and communities. The attention to deep thinking within communities and their use of natural resources is one form of being focused in times of stress. There are also public demonstrations of strength that appear as festivals, parades, and other outdoor and community demonstrations. Delgado's *Celebrating Urban Community Life* (2016) is a refreshing look at the joy communities express. A sample of principles and folktales, from selected major groups offer some ideas for contemplation.

AFRICAN HERITAGE

One of the early forms of spiritual guidance from the African continent is called Kemetism. Early beliefs connected spirituality and science to basic principles that fostered right relationships with one another and with the spiritual creator (Hilliard, 1998).

Moral and Spiritual Heritage

Early books that should be reviewed for the ancient moral and spiritual heritage of those of African descent include *The Teachings of Ptahhotep: The oldest Book in the World* (Hilliard, Williams, & Damali, 1987) and *Selections From the Husia: Sacred Wisdom of Ancient Egypt* (Karenga, 1984).

These contain instructions according to one's power, authority, and leadership in how to behave and speak in the company of those more powerful and those with lesser authority. These include being excellent, listening, respecting women, and, above all, guarding against greed.

Martin (2008) discusses the use of Maat as the principle of order that informs the creation of the universe. The relationship between individual action and communal consequence is fundamental among African cultures. This connection is central to implementing development and recovery strategies (Davis-Maye et al., 2013; Martin, 2008). People make mistakes and make efforts to improve in several ways over long periods of time. Tupac Shakur presented himself in his poem, "The Rose That Grew From Concrete" (Shakur, 2009). Wells-Wilborn, Jackson, and Schiele (2010) used this as an example of a young man growing up, displaced by social oppression, who articulates the experience through his poetry: "these are my damaged petals don't ask me why, Thank God How?" (Tupac Shakur, 2000, Track 12). Traditional leadership and protection roles of men and boys have especially been trampled by discrimination of males of color.

Karenga has argued that the key crisis is the cultural crisis. "Liberation as human possibility must express itself as both an intellectual and social situation and practice" (Hilliard, 1998, p. 124). Hilliard proposes those who teach children have the responsibility to hear, understand, and acknowledge (HUA) cultural knowledge to inform and help students understand the context of African heritage.

Karenga sets the framework for those who may have become contaminated by years of racism and oppressive strategies with the introduction of Kwanzaa in 1966 as the first specifically African American holiday (p. 2). Kwanzaa comes from a Swahili phrase *matunda ya kwanza*, which means 'first fruits of the harvest." The holiday "was established as a means to help African Americans reconnect with their African cultural and historical heritage by uniting in meditation and study of African traditions and Nguzu Saba," the seven principles of African Heritage (kwanzaa.org, 2017). The principles celebrated over the 7 days from Dec. 26 to Jan. 1 are as follows:

Day 1. *Umoja* means unity.
Day 2. *Kujichagulia* means self-determination.
Day 3. *Ujima* means working together.
Day 4. *Ujamaa* means supporting each other.
Day 5. *Nia* means purpose.
Day 6. *Kuumba* means creativity.
Day 7. *Imani* means faith, especially faith in ourselves. (africa.upenn.edu)

The use of African heritage knowledge has been demonstrated to enhance and sustain parental involvement and family engagement in educational and service models (Harvey, McCullough-Chavis, Littlefield, Phillips, & Cooper, 20; Mickel, 2002), in juvenile justice interventions (Harvey & Coleman, 1997), and in counseling (Moodley, 2005). These models offer examples that exist in other cultural descent groups. These tend to be upheld in local community organizations and now on social media platforms. Black Girls Gather, sponsored by For Harriet, a blog community for women of African ancestry, is a nationwide event held in different cities that brings black women together for an evening of conversation in support of community building and sisterhood; it is guided by For Harriet's editor-in-chief, Kimberly Foster (Foster, 2017).

Principles

The African mind has been connected to the principle of *MAAT*, a Kemetic term that represents concepts of truth, justice, order, righteousness, balance, reciprocity, and harmony (Hilliard, 1988). The association of the history of the Ankh (considered the key to long life or eternal life) to energy, frequencies, and electrical magnetism holds symbolic knowledge depicted through the power of spiritual and electromagnetic worlds (Amen, 1999). The science surrounding the ankh relates to electricity, chemistry, astrophysics, and light and is connected to spirituality.

While contemporary academics don't openly claim the science/spirituality connection, these ideas offer support for those who investigate early life concepts and hold beliefs of nature and healing as fundamental to life. Beliefs about nutrition, movement, fasting, and the use of plants continue to be shared. For many, these provide direction in raising children, supporting families, and healing (Afua, 2002).

MAAT

MAAT, a key concept of African culture, is built upon the pursuit of knowledge and happiness offered through stories of humans striving to harmonize with the divine. MAAT set the standards for behavior for uniting with divinity (Hilliard, 1998, p. 16). Without deep African thought, the educational system would not truly prepare those of African heritage. Affirming respect for African traditions can support community efforts for becoming healthy and well.

The focus on heritage was highlighted in Hamilton's article "Education in the Black Community: An Examination of the Realities" (1968). His analysis of what schools needed to be legitimate pointed to the absence of assessment of the curriculum by the community. By including cultural knowledge he expected payoffs in academic performance and positive self-image (Hilliard, 1998). He thought schools should belong to the community, and both school and community activities should be conducted there. The Harlem Children's Zone is an example of this community school model (hcz.org/).

Folktales

Folktales are typically stories told about situations that ordinary people experience—every cultural group has some (American Folklore, n.d.). They offer guidance about life struggles, usually within the context of the social environment. *The King's Drum* (Courlander, 1962) is a compilation of stories from a region in southern Africa. Many are stories of humans disguised as animals. The simple tales camouflage stories of being foolish, of having positive relationships between father-in-law and son-in-law, and about eternal life.

Another book, *African Proverbs* (Leslau & Leslau, 1985), sorts stories by tribes. The Yoruba note, "A wise man who knows proverbs, reconciles difficulties." Folktales are often used with children in classrooms and as daily reading content. The stories are brief and can be used to help children develop their thinking about getting along with others. Folktales, legends, and fables come from the African continent as well as the Caribbean islands, Haiti, and South American sources. Wolkstein's (1980) collection speaks to the harsh realities many Haitians experience, paralleled by a sense of order, life, and richness that comes across in the stories, songs, and proverbs. "The Singing Bone" is a story of the mean stepmother—it alludes to proper care for children. *Tower to Heaven*, told by Ruby Dee (1991) an Ashanti tale, speaks to the community about links to the sky god who helps find solutions.

NATIVE/INDIGENOUS HERITAGE

The history of Native Americans and other indigenous populations highlights their emphasis on collective identity and respect for the natural world over generations. Their perspective on the control of their community by dominant society speaks to obstacles to their community's self-sufficiency and their well-being.

The indigenous mind also has a history of the beginning of Earth. Eastman, of the Ohiyesu tribe, reflects on the denigration of their spiritual origins by white men who wanted to push their religion aside. He describes their attitude of the eternal as the Great Mystery that surrounds and embraces us and is respected through wordless adoration. Their religion forbade the accumulation of wealth and fostered sharing the fruits of skill and success to be shared with less fortunate brothers and sisters (Eastman, 2014, Loc 206). Daily recognition of the Unseen and Eternal occurs through daily prayer; it is more necessary than food. Eastman is noted as the first Native American author to write American history from the Native point of view.

Principles

The place of nature and ceremonies is central to the spiritual environment of Native American philosophies. Water, earth, air, and fire are intrinsic to the spiritual base and are included in the six powers of the universe: the setting sun, West, the rising sun, East, North, South, Mother Earth, and Father Sun (McGaa, 1990). The key principles of Native American culture include the belief of the physical and spiritual dimensions, maintaining harmony and the sense of community that builds on sharing among all.

Prophecies

The place of prophecies is common among Native American tribes. The beliefs of holy men and holy women have called attention to visions of losses, land, food, and life (McGaa, 1990). Concern for natural resources is paramount. Greed, corruption, dishonesty, and selfishness are rejected and have no place in the ecology of natural life and social fulfilment.

Stiffman, Brown, Freedenthal and their associates (2007) note that researchers often ignore the internal and family strengths that people possess. Community assets are perhaps more important than they are given credit for. Recognizing the strength of Native Indian youths builds on the resilient foundations of their environment (McMahon, Kenyon, & Carter, 2013). Recognizing the impact of historical trauma on the traditional expectations of protection of the community by the males requires investment in and respect for healing ceremonies and the inclusion of Native mentors to honor the traditional role of boys and men across generations (Brave Heart, Elkins, Tafoya, Bird, & Salvador, 2012).

Folktales

An interesting set of folktales, myths, and legends of the native people of North America are presented in *American Indian Myths and Legends* (Erdoes & Ortiz, 1984). Stories from many tribes speak to powers and spirits connected to animals, birds, land masses, water—natural phenomenon. As a young man Black Elk, witnessed Custer's Last Stand, and eventually became a Lakota holy man. He shared the vision of connections of all through the circle of life including the four directions, Grandmother Earth, Grandfather Sky and Wakan Tanka. The stories and tales are used to teach children many values—especially to use vision, feelings, and thinking in going through life.

Ramirez (2004) uses a tale about Spirit Boy to introduce parenting techniques that are to encourage a child's development while simultaneously fostering one's growth as a parent and human being. As a white woman married to a Native American, she addresses the critiques she sometimes receives. Her acknowledgment of the values and their place in understanding that life is a prayer and respect of the sacred illustrates parenting behaviors as a nod to the sacred in the way in which you raise your children.

The legend of two old women demonstrates the strength of older women. Wallis (2013) tells the story of two older women left behind by the tribe because the younger ones thought they would hold them back. The women went about preparing for the winter in a way they knew would take care of them. The tribe returned to find the women—through their wisdom and preparation—had fared much better than they had. The young ones learned from this so they would think twice about dismissing the elders.

ASIAN HERITAGE

Asian strengths are derived from several spiritual sources. Over the course of time, religions in India, China, and Japan have offered explanations for life and continuing life. Coward, Neufeldt, and Neumaier (2006) offer an introduction to Hinduism, Jainism, Buddhism, Confucius thought, Taoism, Mao Tse Tung, Shinto, and new religions that are called Tenrikyo and Soka Gokjari. Connections that persons may have to ones for strength likely vary with respect to family beliefs and customs. Hinduism has a long history and includes community as a central influence (Hodge, 2004). Buddhism, which was established around the 1st century, emphasized moral duties and illustrated material world as fleeting.

Principles

Several philosophers of the Asian and Eastern geography offered principles for people to live by. The basic principles taught by Chinese philosopher K'ung Fu-tzu, who is known by the Western name Confucius, include kindness, righteousness, sobriety, wisdom, and trustworthiness. The teachings of K'ung Fu-tzu concern striving to be a good human being and appreciating the relevance of rituals (Puett & Gross-Loh, 2016). His ideas about behavior included the following:

Always be considerate to others.

Respect your ancestors.

Try for harmony and balance in all things.

Avoid extremes in behavior and emotion.

If you live in peace and harmony, then you will be in contact with the spiritual forces of the universe, including nature.

From another view, Mencius espoused the need for cultivating one's inner self (Puett & Gross-Loh, 2016).

Religion

The Hindu religion is not traditionally connected to any one proponent but is recognized as the spiritual basis for over 900 million adherents around the world, though it is primarily seen as the religion of India (compellingtruth.org, 2017). The concepts upon which Hinduism is established include community, interdependence, and divinity (Hodge, 2004). The foundation of well-being is considered to be based on human interdependence and interconnectedness. The principle of dharma may be understood as the unseen, metaphysical, moral order of the universe. The basis of family order is connected to this and to the three paths of liberation—meditation, selfless actions, and devotion to a deity. Sacred writings are used for devotions, and spiritual mythology is useful. Support within the family is connected to practices of close communication to the children and discussing issues that arise within the family unit led by the parents.

Volumes contain confession texts, prayers, and invocations to the sun, moon, waters, and fire. The ethics include honesty, truthfulness, generosity, and moderation. Behaviors that are to be avoided are crookedness, deviousness, deceit, and greed. The care for the poor, fairness, and moderation are essential values (Achari, 2012).

The breath of history and thought about Indian religion and its influence on Asia cannot be summarized briefly. In some areas, Hinduism and Buddhism have different meanings in different countries. Some perceive personifications of natural forces, the sun, wind, and fire. Some refer to the veneration of the dead and ancestors. There are ideas about austerities, ethics, effort, and emotion (Eliot, 1921).

Folktales

Desai's (1999) Hullabaloo in the Guava Orchard technically is not a folktale but expands on the usual suspects in a tale of a situation with social norms. The novel explains customs and expected conformity but presses the reader to acknowledge self-determination. An excerpt from Karma Yoga (Vivekananda, 1896) offers guidance about the social expectations: "The life of every individual, according to the Hindu scriptures, has its peculiar duties apart from what belongs in common to universal humanity. The Hindu begins life as a student; then he marries and becomes a householder; in old age he retires; and lastly he gives up the world and becomes a Sannyasin. To each of these stages of life certain duties are attached." (p. 22).

LATINO/HISPANIC HERITAGE

Persons of Latino/Hispanic descent have many cultures to draw from. As the demographics have increased and expect to trend higher in the next several years, taking the cultural assets approach is the one that must be promoted. The cultural assets paradigm is needed to enlist understanding the diverse community and to operationalize interventions and organizational protocols (Delgado, 2007). Across the groups that include Latino and Hispanic ancestry, family and community are paramount strengths for adaptation despite reactions they may have to struggle with as immigrants. Delgado applauds celebrations and festivals in the Latino community (2016).

A recent addition to matters to be celebrated is Random Act of Mendez. On September 16, 2017, a tradition was initiated to celebrate Random Act of Mendez (NHMC, n.d.). This marked the 70th anniversary of the civil rights case that ended school segregation in California. This preceded the well-known 1954 Supreme Court decision, Brown vs Board of Education.

Principles/Proverbs

Persons of Hispanic and Latino heritage bring reliance on traditional religion and on variations that have sprung from efforts to make a way in another and to assist their children in ameliorating the change of place and circumstances. Delgado (1999) draws on his experience in defining indigenous caring as the natural wealth of people being able to care for one another when trials and tribulations are so oppressive that ability may be overwhelmed.

Díaz-Stevens (1999) reports on the place of tradition in the configuration of spirituality among Latinos in the United States. She refers to Shil's definition of tradition to describe how in the Latino community "tradition transmits itself to human actions as implied or actual patterns, or as images, as well as the beliefs requiring, recommending, regulating, permitting or prohibiting pattern reenactment" (p. 4). The religious tradition, while deeply associated with Catholicism, is shaped by Latino experiences of place and experiences. The role of women in the spiritual arena is particularly important and is a factor in the presence and promotion of resilience within families.

Differences among Latinos reflect the disparate cultures and histories of the countries from which people migrate. Mexicans, Puerto Ricans, Cubans, and South Americans bring various traditions and connections to religious beliefs, as well as connections to supernatural and psychosocial dynamics (Caplan et al., 2011). The religious and spiritual principles offer grounding and sustenance in understanding a broad framework that helps make sense of the world (Musgrave, Allen, & Allen, 2002).

Language

Heritage language also depicts a source of strength among Latino and Hispanic immigrants (Oh & Au, 2005). Among adult learners including college students who may not speak language, assisting them in learning the language, connecting to their cultural identification, and participation have implications for their learning and confidence. The impact of the Hispanic literary heritage should also be a reference point in establishing cultural cognizance (Kanellos, 2012). This project, *Hispanic Immigrant Literature: El Sueño del Retorno,* (Kanellos, 2011) presents the rich experiences through lived voices of tradition and experiences.

The source of strength connected to language is described as parents seek bilingual classes for their children (Farruggio, 2010). Delgado's Celebrating Urban Community Life: Fairs, Festivals, Parades & Community (2016) also presents sociocultural festivities and participation as examples of community strength and support. Community is the foundation principle through which strength and resilience evolve.

Delgado (2007) highlights the assets of the Latino community; they have respectful and trusting personal relationships; geographical, psychological, cultural, and operational views; and natural supports, self-help, and mutual support groups and community capacity.

Folktales

Latin American folklore contributes to the cultural knowledge with examples of life and possible consequences. The Armadillo's Song, a Bolivian legend retold by S. E. Schlosser (Texas Trails, 2014), tells of aspirations despite roadblocks and possible outcomes.

Other tales address the stories of marrying types that don't look appealing but that turn out to be great (Texas Trails, 2014) and stories of working with people who do not appear to be what's expected but that end up helping build wonderful partnerships. Figure 10.2 highlights these notions.

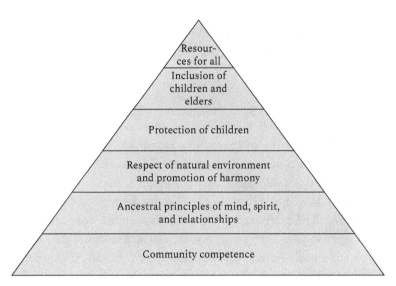

FIGURE 10.2   Competence Builds Upon Respect of the Principles and Assets of Communities

Cultural traditions involve symbols, artifacts, animals, and art, such as a medicine wheel, ankh, a totem pole, broom, dream catcher, elephants, and practices such as prayer and fasting. These may assist in their patience and ability to address their needs and to care for family members as they experience challenges (Hinton, Tran, Tran, & Hinton, 2008). Justice Sonia Sotomayor said: "Experience has taught me that you cannot value dreams according to the odds of their coming true. Their real value is in stirring within us the will to aspire" (Sotomayor, 2014). Health professionals can benefit through increasing awareness of some of the ancestral thoughts embraced by members of communities with which we interact. Not only does this enhance readers' knowledge, it also provides resource examples that may be shared with service users.

INTERSECTIONS

On one hand, intersectional identities have been associated with the possibility, if not prevalence of multiple risks. However, another view would propose that reactions to exclusion, bullying or micro aggressions might be counteracted when their connections to sources of strength are amplified through strategies and support networks (McGovern & Vinjamari, 2016).

LGBTQI: HERITAGE INTERSECTIONS

The strengths of members of LGBTQI communities are inherited from the broad and diverse intersection of many cultures and from their skills in surviving their environments. Whyy.org has an interesting video called *The Pursuit* (2016). The atrocities of inhospitable and egregious behavior and bullying many experience draw on their survival strengths and are to be recognized.

LGBTQI HISTORY

The history of social movements includes stories of persons disclosing their sexual identities in a world of potentially negative and assaultive reactions. The history of gay and lesbian thought and behavior presents observations and social discourse regarding the prevalence of sexual orientation that did not fall into binary parameters. Blasius and Phelan (1997) edited a volume that encompasses the prehistory through inclusion of LGBTQI contexts in contemporary institutions. The plethora of themes, perspectives, conflicts, and antagonisms presented in their work *We Are Everywhere: A Historical Sourcebook of Gay and Lesbian Politics* (1997) conceptualize the basis for anxiety that can occur for LGBTQI community members. As this discourse blossomed, it gained academic recognition through organized gay and lesbian studies.

MICRO AGGRESSIONS

The typical framework regarding LGBTQI concerns has focused on the micro aggressions, discrimination, and alienation of members of their communities (Nadal et al., 2015). Recently, the stressors regarding LGBTQI communities of color (Sutter & Perrin, 2016) point to higher rates of mental stress and suicidal ideation. LGBTQI members are twice as likely to have suicidal ideations, especially in families that are not supportive. Long-term mental stressors are likely to precede self-harm thoughts, and discrimination likely exacerbates this within the intersection of LGBTQI and POC (people of color) Sutter & Perrin, 2016). Asakura and Craig (2014) point to the emerging recognition that it is imperative to use the strengths view to address at-risk vulnerabilities. Young people who live with families that accept a child's nonconforming gender identity and promote family connectedness, have supportive teachers, have a safe school, and have friendships with similar peers benefit from this strengths trajectory. These factors are protective.

DIFFERENTLY ABLED PEOPLE: HERITAGE INTERSECTIONS

A woman attending the 2016 annual NASW conference in Washington, DC, stood up to make a comment after a plenary talk and described herself as a "differently-abled" person. The description illustrates the strengths view from within this community. People who have different abilities have phenomenal strengths. Although public media has focused on how someone's appearance may differ in a minimized view of humanity, folks who see themselves and their family members in ways that support and love tend to build rich lives. However, not all people with physical and emotional challenges embrace the differently abled phrase. Some folks embrace themselves and the labels that may describe them—for example, "autistic and proud" (Brown, 2013). Persons who may be labeled disabled in some way have diverse heritage backgrounds. They may have DNA from various backgrounds, and their experiences and beliefs shape the strengths they draw on and the pressures to which some may succumb.

DISABILITY PREVALENCE

Statistics on disability prevalence report 22% incidence among American Indian and Alaska Native populations. Complex federal regulations make it difficult to assess and intervene based on the Individual With Disabilities Education Act (IDEA), and many who might benefit from some resources may not get them (National Council on Disabilities, 2003).

Native American culture—deemed largely misinterpreted by Caucasian scholars—presents a worldview that does not allow translations of words such as crippled, disabled, or handicapped. The individual is not seen as others based on a "disability" but continues to be valued and an integral part of the community. Assistance may be offered by the community, and it may or may not be accepted.

Disabilities within the African American community are archived in an exhibit in the Museum of disABILITY History (2014) in Buffalo, New York. The museum is "dedicated to advancing the understanding, acceptance and independence of people with disabilities. The exhibits, collections, archives and educational programs create awareness and a platform for dialogue and discovery" (para 2). A consortium with Historically Black Colleges and Universities (HBCUs) was created to identify ways to provide culturally responsive disability services and classroom instruction to black and African American college students with disabilities on all campuses, while also trying to increase black and African American students with disabilities going to college and graduating with undergraduate and graduate degrees (Museum of disABILITY History, 2014).

The range of reactions to the high proportion of African American children in special education is predominated by concerns of the tendency toward stigmatization and negative influence on children labeled as not normal (Gold & Richards, 2012). While the process of assessment is argued to be for the benefit of the children, there is substantial evidence that this is not necessarily the outcome. Moreover, transition to postsecondary and employment opportunities (Banks, 2015) may be extremely challenging. Similarly, the overuse or lack of use of appropriate medications among children of color for controlling behavior in schools and foster care residences is a concern. Existing practices of labeling and segregating those whose behaviors may not be well understood and for whom current practices conducted by majority group teachers and practitioners may not be customized for the needs of these families and their children. Use of programs that have demonstrated a more supportive network orientation and use of Afrocentric dynamics have demonstrated positive results that encourage development of the workforce as well the children and their families (Harvey, Loughery, & Moore, 2002).

The care of persons with disabilities in India and different countries and within the Hindu community may vary depending on traditions. Pinto and Sahur (2001) suggest that persons in the Indian culture see the birth of a child with some disability as something to be ashamed of. The disabled may be shunned or pitied. The belief in karma fosters an understanding spirit that accepts what fate has brought. Families then tend not to invest in the care for those with atypical needs. Economics, transportation, and education may impact families' efforts to access services.

Recent situations suggest there may be more appreciation of the diversity in Indian communities. Bhatnagar (2017) reports on the mission to get more people out to vote by providing Braille-enabled voting machines, women-friendly polling stations, and wheelchairs to transport voters. Situations and emerging concerns are influencing social responses to citizens' conditions. Cordova and associates (2015) refer to the belief that the authorities don't really care about Latino communities as an explanation for services that do not adequately address their needs. That belief is shared by others. Cultural beliefs in the role of God and traditional customs have been acknowledged to be of relevance in caring for persons in the Latino community (Jurkowski, Rivera, & Hammel, 2009).

Bogosian and associates (2015) note that the parents' emotions and mood rather than the multiple sclerosis disability per se impact the development of their adolescents. The ability of the parents to deal with their challenges appeared to be most influential. The levels of resilience that persons with physical or emotional challenges experience vary. The role of spirituality across diagnostic groups and age groups has shown to be beneficial to many (Harris, 2015; Hodge, Andereck, & Montoya, 2007; Sternthal, Williams, Musick, & Buck, 2012). Consideration of more culturally supportive steps in working with families and children to enhance strengths suggest increasing potential for improving outcomes.

A special issue of Family Relations contained reports that conclude that across diagnostic groups, parents felt successful in their ability to assist their children's development. Parents of children with Down syndrome perceived fewer communication difficulties among their children than parents with children with other differences (Farrell & Krahn, 2014). Intersectional identities draw on principles of inclusion, life values, and supportive relationships that offer protection and strength.

There are lots of examples of Deaf community members working together to address intimidation and discrimination. The resilience of members of that community offer ways for imitation and for leading one another:

> Deaf people construct their world around the resources of movement, form, and sound. The metaphor of silence has explanatory power for hearing people, emphasizing as it does what they believe to be the central fact about deaf people. However, it is clumsy and inadequate as a way of explaining what Deaf people know and do. The lives of Deaf people range from silent to very loudly click, buzz, swish, pop, roar, and whir. (Padden & Humphries, 1988, p. 109)

CLOTHING NEEDS FOR DIFFERENTLY ABLED PEOPLE

The clothing needs for differently abled people are being addressed by a company, Runway of Dreams, that listened to the comments from this community. A survey found there were three major categories that affected their issues with clothes shopping:

Closures—buttons, snaps, zippers, hooks and eyes that are hard to use

Ability to adjust the clothing—waistbands, pant lengths, sleeve lengths are difficult to change

Method to get into clothing—putting a shirt/sweater over one's head and getting it down requires some type of strength and dexterity (Goldman-Schatell, 2015)

As the voices of diverse people get heard, more manufacturers have come forward to be helpful.

REACTING TO NEGATIVE STIMULI FROM AUTHORITIES

The code of the street on reservations, suburban, urban, or rural areas may take various forms as persons address survival needs. The high rates of suspension in schools and incarceration in communities of color continue to demonstrate the institutional structures that constrain people of color. As more efforts shine on policies that exacerbate stigma and discrimination, efforts are made to promote the strengths focus instead of pathologizing. Gangs tend to develop along ethnic lines in communities with high unemployment, food insecurity, limited incomes, single-parent households (Starbuck, Howell, & Lindquist, 2001), and other characteristics that emerge where trauma and stress occurs.

Families may warn young people against participating in underground economies or gang activities—to keep away or to run away from the enticements. But so many sometimes do not or cannot heed that advice. Gangs, despite public reputations, often meet material and emotional needs in some communities and may be categorized as assets (Venkatesh, 2008).

EMOTIONS AND WITHDRAWAL PROTECT AGAINST TRAUMA EXPOSURE

In *Last Night I Sang to the Monster* (2009), Sáenz describes a young man's escape into alcoholism following a traumatic family incident. The residential treatment process of creating friendships and relationships of support builds confidence, hope, and resilience so that he is able to face his past and recover. Sáenz's character Zack takes us through the resistance, pain, protection, and hope in the process of addressing a situation that he has blocked. Again, there is hope.

The literature from voices that live in crushing situations demonstrate how blossoming can occur. This kind of literature exists in every culture, of every race, in all geographies. Recognizing and appreciating these lives should motivate social workers and other care planners to invite them to work together.

EDUCATION—CRITICAL THINKING

Expanding the conceptualization of practice to the multilayered panorama offers the opportunity to consider multiple sources of strengths, knowledge, practice methods, and critical thinking by students in preparation to work with diverse service users. Service users also require information about multilayered learning opportunities.

Depending on the age of the users and developmental stage (Erikson, 1994), their level of thinking may be preabstract thinking. If this is the case, opportunities for thinking reflectively about circumstances, consequences, and options are imperative. Pointing this out in education classes for inmates in a New York prison has also concluded that these kinds of experiences have potentially positive outcomes (Kunen, 2017).

SURVIVAL

The strengths of cultural groups attend to the realities of everyday life and create subsystems that attempt to compensate for oppressions that deny participation in dominant economic systems.

The protective factors for youth and families come from cultural heritage, tradition, language, and kinship systems. These components require more use and exploration rather than continuing the focus on pathology and intrusive deficit-based measures (Kelley & Small, 2015). The risk factors exacerbated by the negative focus and the barriers of the existing service systems often counter the trust needed to establish long-term relationships that motivate and promote change.

Native researchers have also brought attention to the need for innovative economic development tools in determining the future paths of tribal societies. "When tribal development plans are conceived externally by members of the dominant culture, no matter how good the intentions, they tend to reflect the beliefs, aspirations and values of their authors rather than those espoused by tribal cultures" (Smith, 2000, p. 94). The strategic planning process that invites representatives from reservation and nonreservation tribes seeks to create a vision that enlists economic, cultural, community, and other endeavors.

TRAUMA INITIATES BEHAVIORS FOR SELF-PROTECTION

In evaluating the influences on young Native American suicides, substantial adverse childhood experiences are recognized. A study of American Indian/Alaska Natives and Two-Spirit people who attended boarding schools or who were raised by persons who attended boarding schools found they were more likely to have attempted suicide or were more likely to show symptoms of anxiety or traumatic disorder (Evans-Campbell, 2012). Previous studies have reported similar findings. (Trafzer & Weiner, 2001). These conclusions suggest the boarding school experience has not only affected individual and families but the entire community and the researchers recommend services that are based in cultural tradition and community based (Evans-Campbell et al., 2012). Preliminary findings from a culturally sensitive prevention intervention, New Hope, demonstrate that delivery by American Indian paraprofessionals and continuum of care initiated in emergency departments show great results. The community-driven participatory approach shows some success in high intervention exam scores, participant satisfaction, improved outcomes, and increased capacity of the local workforce. There were limitations and areas revealed that could increase effectiveness with the inclusion of elders, trusted friends, and local community-based locations (Cwik et al., 2016).

NATIVE AMERICANS' SURVIVAL

Smoke Signals (Eyre, 1998) is a film with the screenplay written by Sherman Alexie, author of several important novels about Native American lives and their intersections with the environment. The story illustrates young friends, their family lives, and the interplay of social connections, school, dreams, and frustrations on a reservation.

The rise of gangs among Native American youth has been associated with the increased separation of children from parents through the boarding school system. In the past, youth learned ceremonial ways and links to the spiritual nuances of the community through partnerships with their parents (Henderson, Kunitz, & Levy, 2001).

The means of surviving the daily discrimination system involve the strengths gained from the community heritage and communities of support. When the larger society weighs in on criminal behavior and employs the need for self-control theory, the inclusion of the absence of jobs and lack of other opportunities often relegates adults and young people to the underground economic level to put food on the table. If the people who made the laws had experience in trying to locate income for family needs when stakes are against them, there might be more incentive to gain perspectives of how policies impact people in different contexts.

AFRICAN DESCENT SURVIVAL

Within communities of support not legitimized by broader society, there are codes of behavior. In *Gang Leader for a Day,* Venkatesh (2008) presents a view of the financial and political life of a major Chicago gang. Anderson, in *Code of the Street* (1999), poses the strategy of the criminal activity and violence in Philadelphia, but also notes the decency and moral themes embedded in the social climate.

GANGS OFFER FOOD SECURITY

Predating these gang scenarios, the Black Panther Party (BPP) was founded in October 1966 by Huey Newton and Bobby Seale to provide "patrols in Black communities to monitor police activities and protect the residents from police brutality" (AAR, 1966, para 3). The BPP organized to meet basic needs of the community by modeling efforts to improve conditions. The organizers were open to working with white allies who also wanted social change. The Federal Bureau of Investigation launched major activities against them in response to their political efforts." (African American Registry, Historic events). Their early activities included social services, meals for children at schools, medical clinics, help for the homeless to find housing, and free clothing and food. External pressures and internal conflicts led to the Panthers' demise. Many women held leadership roles in providing social service interventions in the communities across the country in which chapters were located.

ASIAN AMERICAN SURVIVAL

Ling (2016) reports on the second wave of immigrants that have come from Southeast Asia (e.g., Vietnam, Laos, and Cambodia) and from harsh political situations. They have come expecting better opportunities only to find limited opportunities, and many have difficulty gaining employment in legitimate businesses.

GANGS OFFER ECONOMIC SUPPORT

With costs of $15,000 to $35,000 per person to get into the United States, persons deposited in New York and California may become connected to smuggling enterprises of cars and humans. Some of the gang activity may also involve legitimate business (Ling, 2016). There are efforts to get young people linked to school and community programs that offer alternatives to illegal activities. The Strategy Against Gang Environment (SAGE) programs teach residents to recognize potential gang activity and recruit students into the educational options (Ling, 2016).

Huang (2007) offers a typology to analyze gangs that goes beyond the single dimension approach. His discussion identifies several constructs that may be used to examine gangs but distills the variables to delinquent groups, ordinary street gangs and organized crime blocs. Law enforcement targets their activities to reduce crime and violence.

Wang (2014) reports on the Queens-based Chinese American gang that smuggles heroin and traffics Chinese immigrants in the film *Revenge of the Green Dragons*. Most people interviewed in the process of the filmmaking indicate if they knew then what they know now, they would not have immigrated here.

The Tiananmen Square situation in 1989 created a social climate that created enormous reaction within China about the government shooting its own citizens (Zhang, Nathan, Link, & Schell, 2008). Yiwu (2013), a poet and writer who was jailed after he wrote a poem about the massacre, wrote about the situation and the jail conditions. He expressed himself about the need to keep writing, and that can be applied broadly as people react to situations in their environments:

> Having gone through these sufferings has become part of my capital as a writer, and the experiences I shared with others and what I learned from other people has become my capital as a writer too. I've learned that one can go through very difficult and troubling experiences that could put one into despair, but still be able to survive, and even beyond that, find there is a need, a necessity to survive. (Yiwu, 2013, Loc 6319, Translator's note.)

LATINOS/HISPANICS SURVIVAL

As pointed out before, all communities have strengths, and people excluded from dominant economic streams have survived through creative and often underground or illegal means. The street codes of young men and women combine these variations to take care of families and to address daily possibilities of assault from within their communities and from the policing system of the larger city. There is also love and support within the communities by parents, relatives, and friends who understand the duality and ambivalence of the survival system.

GANGS OFFER PROTECTION

Participation in gangs has been considered a way to be protected in the street environment. The likely probability of becoming a victim as a gang member is high. Yet this seems not to trump the expected emotional protection that organizational membership should provide. Two examples illustrate the range of issues and dynamics that this faction of communities attends to.

Always Running (Rodriquez, 1993) tells the story of harsh realities and struggles of Chicano men in Los Angeles trying to survive. He describes brutal experiences that occur. With high odds against special or desired outcomes. By continuing illegal activities, possible injury, incarceration, and or death can become the future. Yet his life shows this potential future can be overcome.

Rodriquez presents another example in *The Buddha Book: A Novel* (2001), an intriguing examination of young people living in the south Bronx. On the one hand, there is exposure to occupational options outside of the drug economy and the desire to move away from a family business built on illegal drug sales. Then, there is the day-to-day reality of adolescent life in school, the street, and family that bring challenges via relationships with friends and relatives. It is an illustration of sociocultural influences on cognitive development and social-emotional movement.

Punished: Policing the Lives of Black and Latino Boys (Rios, 2011) reveals the incredible strengths of young men who grow up in environments that obstruct potential and emasculate visions through systems of denigration and denial. Some do transition and breakout.

PRACTICE AND SUPERVISION

Issues that are presented in sessions frequently involve crises connected to emergency situations, relationships, children in trouble, partners in dispute, loss and grief, substance use, and financial struggles. The reactions and responses may be perceived as steps taken to survive. At the same time, the behaviors probably violate another's safety or property. Professionals may benefit from examining scenarios that service users bring from the structural rather than individual context.

Decisions regarding removing children from a home are often connected to blaming a parent rather than examining the conditions regarding rental cost, landlords that don't repair properties and who penalize persons who have been evicted (Desmond, 2017). It may help a worker or supervisor to think about a situation from points of reference that show who benefits rather than who comes in need. Thinking about what comes before the housing without heat, the antecedents, may contribute to understanding the broader dimensions that may be operating. Stokes and Schmidt (2011) investigated this and observed that the structural issues that influence child safety are invisible and often are not considered in the decisions of social workers.

The tendency remains to hold parents responsible despite their inability to protect their children from vulnerability of social and organizational policies that create the marginalization. Individual and case work often focuses on individual presentation rather than institutional dynamics. The case for housing as a basic need is gaining attention as a major concern for assisting families' health, behavioral health and safety.

> **CRITICAL THINKING QUESTION**
>
> If a worker is accustomed to indoor plumbing, dishwashers, and neat interior design, would her or his evaluation of a home with broken windows, a broken toilet, and peeling paint blame the substance-using parents or the local agency policy? Discuss the situation and how criteria should be determined.

COMMUNITY-BASED ORGANIZATIONS

Practice settings are likely to be perceived as formal institutional places. Community-based agencies more likely to be nonprofit and welcoming of people in ways not expected in formal organizations. A formal setting may offer out-patient services. A community-based organization may offer behavioral health or family counseling and it may also help a family move from one home to another one. Community organizations represent cultural-group associations for arts, law, college preparation, apprentice programs, and business groups. These entities often emulate the strengths perspective of people their mission supports.

The strengths of diverse families, denied or camouflaged by descriptions written by Caucasian academics, have been identified and applauded. Community-based organizations operate in most culturally defined communities. The work of community-based organizations such as the NAACP, the National Urban League, Congresso, the African American, Latino or Hispanic Chambers of Commerce, La Communidad Hispana, and others are conduits for positive self-image and discipline.

The Asian Women in Business in Philadelphia (AWIB, n.d.) and Latin American Economic Development Association (LAEDA, n.d.) in south Jersey are community based organizations that similarly are connected to the positive images and capacities of their constituents. Economic development associations are community–based organizations in many cities or regions that assist in networking and business growth.

Mander (1999) discusses the role of media in shaping the messages we receive. We are certainly aware of the disparities that exist. Yet, there are youth from single-parent households in every community who are likely to attend college and achieve in more ways than the media generally present. There are many other examples of community productivity in community organizations that reach out to young people offering resources, supports and connections.

Social workers seeking to implement change are encouraged to connect with these agencies to foster opportunities to address economic needs, reduce isolation and emphasize the strengths of the communities they serve.

LOCATING CULTURAL-SPECIFIC RESOURCES IN THE COMMUNITY

As social workers seek ways of improving community connections, recognizing local organizations and seeking to establish partnership with some groups who have relationships in the community can be indispensable. Most cultural communities have several types of local or national profit and nonprofit organizations with missions to benefit their constituencies. Near Native reservations, there are usually art councils, business associations, college fund associations, bar association, and women's groups (DiversityBestPratices.com, 2017) that offer programs and services.

There are Deaf-specific organizations or faith-based groups that welcome all cultural groups and provide accommodations as part of their outreach. The Americans With Disabilities Act (ADA) requires employers to provide reasonable accommodations for qualified applicants and employees with disabilities" (Taylor & Weisberg, 2015, p. 1) and defines discrimination as the absence of accommodations.

Some areas may have culturally specific LGBTQI or Deaf community specific agencies. There is a Directory of LGBTQ People of Color Organizations and Projects in the U.S. (2009). There is a directory of agencies that serve the Deaf and hard of hearing community in Philadelphia, PA (Garb, 2008).

These entities, often nonprofits, may have special funds to help people move or meet other obligations that formal agencies won't touch. In planning field placements, perusing a community website to locate community-specific resources adds to the knowledge of community resources. Locating more community specific resources could occur through dedicated exploring and reaching out to community organizations. Speaking with community residents and staff in local agencies can help.

The limited research on social work partnerships with community organizations indicate this is an area that needs to be explored. Cleland (2014) notes that an effort in the United Kingdom to increase ethnic minority participation in sport events is an effort on their part to become more inclusive in community sports.

CLINICAL ISSUES: RACE, GENDER, AND CLASS

Traditional contact with community members is more likely to occur via a case management system. While issues that clients bring to an agency may be perceived by the organization to fit into neat diagnostic boxes, from the client's view they may look different. Van der Kolk (2017) helps us understand that trauma experiences create brain architecture changes that result in different ways of perceiving situations related to their recall of danger. Talk therapy may work in some situations, but approaches that increase activities and help people become more focused away from uncomfortable memories can be helpful in maintaining calmness rather than anxiety.

Community-wide prevention approaches that help people understand these connections may offer evidence and encouragement for monitoring health numbers, establishing exercise routines and improving nutrition.

ADDRESSING RACISM AND OPPRESSION IN PRACTICE SETTINGS

There are ways that people in the street deal with racism and oppression reactions that don't fit neatly into a clinical-practice setting. The ways that people of color respond to being disrespected often lead to some miscommunication, anger, and perhaps violence. The disrespect plays out in policies that put people at risk. The Health and Human Services decision to eliminate reproductive health programs restricts opportunities to prevent teen pregnancies across cultural groups, including young white women. The Office of Population Affairs (HHS.gov) has a Title X program for family planning that provides a locator for family planning clinics. Some may be close by and some may be quite a distance away. When transportation is an issue the service may not be available but contacting the office is a start.

Clinical interventions meet specific guidelines. Some have been evaluated with specific evaluation tools and have been found to meet standards. The research on effective culturally informed interventions have not been conducted in any comprehensive fashion. Yasui, Pottick, and Chen (2017) provide substantial evidence that consistent research has not investigated models that would be effective with minority clients or immigrants. They note that despite the acknowledged central role of culture in mental health disparities, existing measures "have failed to integrate culturally specifically factors that shape families' engagement with mental health services" (p. 1).

SYMPTOM RELIEF

When people seek health and mental health services, they need some intervention to help them address situations in their lives that need immediate attention. Medical and emotional issues are generally co-occurring to some extent. Depending on the structure of the agency, there may be routine strategies for clients or expectation of ongoing services for a short period of time.

Situations that involve trauma impact the service user and the treating professionals. Across the board, young people need options for strength and confidence building in safe environments. Collaborations with the treatment team will pose interventions and screening for related conditions.

TRANSFERENCE AND COUNTERTRANSFERENCE

Transference and countertransference are generally descriptive of emotional feelings and reactions of service users and therapists or facilitators in mental health settings. Transference issues have to do with a range of feelings, conflicts, and expectations projected onto a service user (Smith, 2007), typically in a mental health agency. Countertransference, which occurs when a therapist transfers emotion to a person in therapy, is often a reaction to transference (Goodtherapy.org, 2017).

Several examples of transference are tied to feelings about clients in palliative or hospice care (Farnham, 2008; Giamportone, 2015). While professional boundaries are essential, many situations mimic personal experiences with the care of children and seniors. The issues around race and class may create tension but can be facilitated using careful processing and discussion.

SNARES

As workers on the front lines of "childhood abuse, domestic violence, violent crime, disasters, and war and terrorism, secondary traumatic stress (STS) is becoming viewed as an occupational hazard of providing direct services to traumatized populations" (Bride, 2007, p. 63). Cases that draw on compassion can be draining. Countertransference has been joined by such emotional reactions as traumatic stress, burnout, traumatic countertransference (TC), vicarious trauma (VT), and secondary traumatic stress (STS)/compassion fatigue (CF) to describe the feelings many mental health professionals experience in their work (Kanno & Giddings, 2017).

Building confidence in others and competence as professionals draws on our knowledge of cultural heritage, and it also continues to integrate the intersections and confidence of professional helpers. Zufferey (2012) clearly illustrates the tensions that arise when workers and privilege present in the expert domain in her reference to Anne Barton's words:

> As a white Australian, I can only become part of the solution when I recognize the degree to which I am part of the problem, not because I am white but because of my investment in white privilege. (Anne Barton, 2010, the great-granddaughter of Australia's first Prime Minister Sir Edmund Barton [p. 659])

Our acknowledgement of privilege, wherever it comes from in agents of the profession, should be foremost in our interests and enthusiasm to help others. There are race, class, and gender issues in our practice settings. Our work in this arena involves the invisible, the policies, and our mindsets as we reach out to others, without defensiveness (Trevithick, 2011) or denial when the client is not young, with income, white, or articulate or similar in ways of the practitioner.

CRITICAL THINKING QUESTION

"The basic sources of happiness are a good heart, compassion, and love. If we have these, even if we're surrounded by hostility, we'll feel little disturbance." —the Dalai Lama. Do you think this is true? Why or why not?

FOCUSING ON THE STRENGTHS

Kelley and Small (2015) explored establishing validity and reliability of strengths-based resources for Native Americans. The project team captured sources of strength within the resilience continuum and offered recommendations for moving beyond the existing deficit paradigms. As Watts and colleagues observed, "When young men begin to take an interest in the sociopolitical dimension of their lives, acceptance and resignation give away to a growing awareness of and concerns about how inequality is established and maintained" (Vera & Kenny, 2013, p. 21).

NETWORKS AND PARTICIPATION

Overall, community members and the support system networks have influence on resource access, recovery, and improvements. The impacts of mentoring programs have been found to be substantial in assisting young people to follow less-destructive pathways than those without caring adults. The success of Big Brothers and Big Sisters of America is an example. NAMI, the National Alliance on Mental Illness, advocates for public policy and provides family education and support. Other major community organizations, sororities and fraternities, and others demonstrate mezzo level opportunities for engagement and program activities. The need for volunteers is great.

MULTIDISCIPLINARY AND INTERPROFESSIONAL RELATIONSHIPS

The steps to inclusion involve people of all types coming together. While we have presented strengths information of cultural heritage points and intersectionality, we also recognize economic groups that are included in multidisciplinary and related professional groups collaborating and promoting policies that benefit us all.

Ramirez's contribution of her perspective of developmental psychology and Native philosophy offers an example of integrating cultural philosophies and health professional knowledge to benefit communities. Her take on assisting children is illustrated by the use of the Spirit Boy and the Gift of Turquoise. Strong spirits should be used in service of the people (Ramirez, 2004, Loc 236). Sharing books and stories that parents can read to children or children can read to parents is a way to build links within families, sibling groups, and child-centered programs or schools. These can be integrated across disciplinary interventions and promoted by several professional roles. The *A to Z of Groupwork* (Doel & Kelly, 2014) offers several concepts for facilitating discussions.

COMMUNITY PARTICIPATION AND DEVELOPMENT

Growth opportunities may be created from existing professional organizations and situations and may be established through coalition building. Vera and Kenny (2013) point to interventions aimed at large systems via deep structure modification as well as through culturally relevant social justice–oriented prevention that emphasizes developing community member strengths (p. 20).

Advancing efforts for social justice involves enhancing opportunities for inclusion and engaging with communities. Recognizing and respecting the micro to macro conditions that federal, state, and local policies have framed where many low-income persons have grown up or been displaced from need to be recognized in order to consider and plan for establishing opportunities for community transformation.

Igniting citizen participation is significant for developing community competence and joining in social justice efforts in communities. Requests for proposals (RFP) over the past few decades have required more federal money applicants to partner with other agencies to plan and develop service programs. Ewalt and associates (1996) presented a comprehensive review of programs from around the country in the 1990s that represented partnerships. For example, the Model Cities programs, community mental health centers, prevention programming, and family and child development have set precedents in inclusion. The NASW Smart Brief continually reports on innovative partnerships and programs being conducted across the states. For example, a New Jersey special service proposes the use of family specialists (SPAN, 2018) that follow up with parents after screening families with children with indicators for autism spectrum conditions. Reviewing these examples and others reveals positive efforts and opportunities to create and establish additional avenues for working together across disciplines, citizen groups, and age groups.

BUILDING COMMUNITY CONNECTIONS FOR COMPETENCE

Building community competence within professional and community settings must raise up the importance of appreciating diversity and expanding the political activism that encourages policy to foster accountability in agencies and in families. Moving to respect the words and comments of persons in their environment can build on the ideas presented by Bloc (2008) that emphasize hospitality in reaching out to engage with local communities. The connections that assist family, individual, and community capacity building on micro, mezzo, and macro levels involve practical and spiritual models.

Michael Jackson's *They Don't Care About Us* (2009) video sums up interpretations from our diverse communities. Appreciating diversity requires acknowledging what has been the structural arrangement and inviting the voices of community strengths to participate in alliances to establish better mechanisms. More effort in including these voices in the planning and development of ways to become more effective is promising. New partnerships can help facilitate workforce creation and policies that help develop and sustain the educational and occupational capacity of families.

CULTURAL COMMUNITY COMPETENCE

Cultural competence need not be defined by strict adherence to any set of ancestral principles. Families or individuals may use ways of doing and being by drawing on the strengths of various philosophies. Many people who may claim one religion or spiritual connection may also use other resources. For example, those who believe in Christianity may also use meditation, Chakra calming techniques, crystals, and herbs.

Community competence requires respect of the principles and ideas that people bring even as they seek assistance outside of their communities. As Bicakci (2013) describes in his work with refugees from places of active war, what may help people recover from traumatic situations is their worldview, or their ways of doing, surviving, and treating others. Acknowledging their strengths in making it so far and recognizing their power and potential in overcoming the past emphasizes their reality. They don't need to be reminded of the circumstances that may bring them to a professional office. They need support in moving beyond this point. Starting with their strengths, appreciating them, and initiating engagement can lead to effective collaborations.

INCLUSIVE PARTICIPATION

Inclusive participation for community development (Sutton & Kemp, 2011, p. 93) ameliorates regions for the people who live there (Kirp, 2015). Issues around gentrification raise concerns about the traditional methods of removing persons, usually people of color, from their communities to other places so that people with money can come in to revitalize the area. How can social workers and other concerned professionals work in the areas to stimulate growth and include the people who have been living there? Coalition building, grassroots organization, newly formed associations, and long-standing community nonprofits are agencies within communities committed to listening to community needs and garnering support through more informal mechanisms. Their work tends to respond to the broader community landscape and advocate for or provide supports that formal agencies often miss. The Coalition of Human Needs (CHN.org) is an alliance of organizations that follows legislative activities that impact low income and vulnerable people and advocates funding for human needs programs.

The Century Foundation renamed the Twentieth Century Fund is a progressive public policy research institute that promotes fairness and opportunity in education, labor practices, technology and democracy. Locating organizations whose research and advocacy efforts address the issues related to social work competencies and other social justice issues will offer opportunities that can assist our work and involve our service users.

Given emerging research and policy concerns, we should also include additional arenas for social justice applications in probation and offender reentry, schools, after-school centers, food security, environmental and climate concerns, banks, and financial counseling centers.

ADDRESSING OPPRESSION AROUND THE WORLD: MOVING TOWARD SHARED DECISION-MAKING

Not only are we to become more informed of strategies around the United States that are more engaging, but examples from other countries are also useful in advancing human and civil rights. The issues facing England have illustrated the social issues, emotions, and critical needs that economics and collaboration tactics have generated. Innovative ideas and coalitions are continuing to pose ways to offer help and hope. In some places, communities are coming together with refreshing, revitalizing, and creative worker strategies that support work productivity and family needs.

On the micro level, sharing decisions is linked to service paths. According to the Council on Social Work Education (CSWE.org, n.d.), shared decision-making is an approach to reduce the overrepresentation of persons with serious mental illness in the criminal justice system. The use of strengths model case management (SMCM) and shared decision-making are offered to develop better support and alternative strategies for establishing more comfortable life options.

CHOICE, OPTIONS, AND DECISION TALK

Elwyn and associates (2012) propose a model that is based on choice, option, and decision talk. It incorporates what is important to the person and moves forward from there. This model might be applied with service users who are immigrants or those from communities not traditionally served in some local facilities.

In the case of an Arab American marriage, customs that family members may bring are likely to impact an organization. Although Western views may label some cultures *oppressive* (Dahinden, Duemmler, & Moret, 2015), to be culturally sensitive and respectful we should be informed of ways that families may interpret their principles and family traditions and defer to their perspectives. Al-Krenawi and Jordan (2014) describe the increased numbers and the diverse identities to include Arabic and regular or fundamentalist Christian or Islamic identities along with other Westernized identities. Some may be seeking to assimilate on some level with more or less attention to maintaining Muslim discipline. Many Arab Americans are Christian. There are two major forms of Islam—Sunni (main) and Shia. There may also be Arab Christian people who may be "Maronite Catholic, Melkite Catholic, Syrian Catholic, Chaldean Catholic, Roman Catholic, Antiochian Orthodox, Syrian Orthodox, Coptic Orthodox, or Protestant (Abudabbeh)" (p. 116). There are gender roles and varying ideas of freedom.

Social workers and other care professionals and the organizations that serve diverse communities should acknowledge the variations of immigrants' identities. At the same time, the inaccurate views that some U.S. citizens hold must also be recognized so there is space to work out better understanding. The intersections of family, gender, sexuality, honor and stigma, economics, and divorce influence communication on both sides. Rather than make assumptions or neglect appropriate process, cultural mediators may be requested.

ORGANIZING INFORMATION FOR CONSUMER BENEFITS

As efforts to refocus and expand discourse on macro conditions and opportunities for service users to participate more actively in our democracy, integration of geospatial technology (GST), participatory methods, and asset-based procedures are needed. There is evidence that this framework along with updated tools will produce effective programs and outcomes in communities (Kelley, in Sutton & Kemp, 2011, p. 2).

The wealth of information from different arenas is available for social workers to use for developing creative, engaging, and effective interventions, collaborations, and means of service delivery. Smyth informs us that she tries to keep up with innovation in other areas as well (2017). Tweets and blogs provide access to new ideas and innovations.

CONNECT SERVICE USERS TO RESOURCES

The key to improving services is to connect service users to resources in ways that assist their trust and build confidence. Ideas about traveling medics in Ghana could be translated into redesigned home-visiting approaches (Green, 2016). Bornstein (2017) reports on a fascinating program, the Family Independence Initiative, that does not provide direct service or advice. It offers a structure and platform for families to strengthen social networks and track their own behaviors toward selected goals. They share this data with families to show what works and to help one another. The results have been great illustrations of how people can work together for their own benefit. This perspective respects people with low incomes and supports them.

The work of Doctors Without Borders through the Nobel prize–funded Drugs for Neglected Disease Initiative (DNDI) demonstrates the success of a multipartner group that has removed issues of profitability from drug research (Quigley, 2016). This group includes private sector participants. The work of these partners is to get resources to help without the overcharge element.

New ideas and discussions to create innovation are needed among professionals, between nonprofit and profit programs, among low- and high-income people; everyone should be listening to one another to push forward for all of us. Positive community identities (Born, 2014) can be fostered in many ways with all the people who are earnestly headed in that direction. Social worker education is preparing students with skills for facilitating and mediating communication in this macro environment.

STUDENT COMMENTS

In reflecting on the strengths and principles of the African community, student participants referred to Achebe's comment in *Things Fall Apart*: "We have been sent by God to ask you to leave your wicked ways and false gods and turn to Him so that you may be saved when you die." (Achebe, p. 145.)

Acknowledging that this kind of statement is disrespectful highlights how some past behaviors of missionaries were troublesome. Becoming a facilitator involves taking steps to gain understanding of the feelings and cultural beliefs of the client, family, and community before a mutually developed plan can be implemented.

CHAPTER SUMMARY

Principles of strength have been established in the ancestry of citizens across cultures in the United States. Recognizing these and appreciating that people draw from these offers a foundation for helping professionals as well as service users. Students should become more aware of the bases of cultural strengths and consider integrating community assets into the collaboration process. Using the triple perspective lens solicits plans to integrate strengths on three levels to support, motivate, and build confidence. Students will be able to identify resources for strength.

EPAS AND CODE OF ETHICS

CSWE EDUCATIONAL POLICY & ACCREDITATION STANDARDS

Competency 6: Engage with Individuals, Families, Groups, Organizations, and Communities
Social workers understand that engagement is an ongoing component of the dynamic and interactive process of social work practice

- 6a) apply knowledge of human behavior and the social environment, person-in-environment, and other multidisciplinary theoretical frameworks to engage with clients and constituencies; and
- 6b) use empathy, reflection, and interpersonal skills to effectively engage diverse clients and constituencies

Competency 7: Assess Individuals, Families, Groups, Organizations, and Communities

- 7a) collect and organize data, and apply critical thinking to interpret information from clients and constituencies
- 7b) apply knowledge of human behavior and the social environment, person-in-environment, and other multidisciplinary theoretical frameworks in the analysis of assessment data from clients and constituencies. (EPAS, 2015)

NASW CODE OF ETHICS

Value: Dignity and Worth of the Person
Ethical Principle: Social workers respect the inherent dignity and worth of the person.
Value: Competence
Ethical Principle: Social workers practice within their areas of competence and develop and enhance their professional expertise. (NASW, n.d.)

DISCUSSION QUESTIONS

1. Building competence confidence among professionals and service users is connected to self-awareness, cultural awareness, and services design that frequently involve feelings that cause tension and conflict. Have students read Zufferey (2012) and Trevithic (2011). Identify their notes regarding key points and discuss ideas of how these issues may need to be addressed to move forward.
2. Consider the role of spirituality in service delivery.
3. List up to three pros and cons for using a conversation about spirituality in a family session. What kind of additional skills would be needed?
4. How can the use of a community newspaper or ethnic website assist in the engagement process with clients?
5. Crystals, prayer beads, and rosaries: Do they have anything in common?

EXERCISES

1. With your neighbor, design a group module to provide community education about a local issue. Use community newspapers or websites for references.
2. In small groups, build an agenda for planning an interprofessional group to work on a prevention module for families. Who would be invited from the community? Where could it be offered? How could it be funded and marketed?
3. Design a brief discussion tool to evaluate attention to cultural dynamics in a service session.

MULTICULTURAL RESOURCES

Afua, Q. (2002). *Heal thyself for health and longevity.* Buffalo, NY: Eworld.

Amen, N. A. (1999). *The ankh: African origin of electromagnetism.* Buffalo, NY: Eworld.

Blaisdell, B. (Ed.). (2000). *Great speeches by Native Americans.* Mineola, NY: Dover.

Blasius, M., & Phelan, S. (Eds.). (1997). *We are everywhere: A historical sourcebook of gay and lesbian politics.* Abingdon, United Kingdom: Routledge.

Brave Heart, M. Y, Elkins, J., Tafoya, G., Bird, D., & Salvador, M. (2012). Wicasa Was'aka: Restoring the traditional strength of American Indian boys and men. *American Journal of public Health, 102*(S2), 177–182.

Brown, L. X. Z. (2013). How "differently abled" marginalizes disabled people [Blog post]. Retrieved from http://www.autistichoya.com/2013/08/differently-abled.html

Cap4kids.org. (2015). Philadelphia resources. Retrieved from http://cap4kids.org/philadelphia/parent-handouts/immigration-refugee-services/latino-resources/

Cleland, J. A. (2014). Working together through sport? Local authority provision for ethnic minorities in the UK. *Sport in Society, 17*(1), 38–51.

Compellingtruth.org. (2017). What is Hinduism? Retrieved from http://www.compellingtruth.org/what-is-Hinduism.html

Courlander, H. (1962). *The king's drum and other African stories.* San Diego, CA: Harcourt Brace, & World.

Davis-Maye, D., Davis, D. J., & Jones, T. B. (2013). Who's got next: SOTA's Kemet Academy as a model to improve the community college to PHD pipeline. *The Journal of Negro Education, 82*(3), 243–254.

Dee, R. (1991). *Tower to heaven.* New York, NY: Henry Holt.

DeGrury, J. (2005). *Post traumatic slave syndrome: America's legacy of enduring injury and healing.* Portland, OR: Joy DeGrury.

Delgado, M. (2016). *Celebrating urban community life: Fairs, festivals, parades & community.* New York, NY: Oxford University Press.

Desai, K. (1999). *Hullabaloo in the guava orchard.* New York, NY: Grove Press.

Díaz-Stevens, A. M. (1999, January). Memory, imagination and tradition: Diasporic Latino spirituality. *Union Seminary Quarterly,* 1–19.

Eastman, C. A. (2014). *The soul of the Indian.* New York, NY: SMK Books.

Elders Peaks. (2007). Indigenous Native American prophecies. Retrieved from https://www.youtube.com/watch?v=g7cylfQtkDg

Erdoes, R., & Ortiz, A. (Eds.). (1984). *American Indian myths and legends.* New York, NY: Pantheon.

Erikson, E. (1994). *Identity and the life cycle.* New York, NY: W. W. Norton.

Eyre, C. (Director). (1998). *Smoke Signals* [Film].

Farruggio, P. (2010). Latino immigrant parents' views of bilingual education as a vehicle for heritage preservation. *Journal of Latinos and Education, 9*(1), 3–21.

Foster, K. (2017). For Harriet [Blog].

Harvey, A., & Coleman, A. A. (1997). An Afrocentric program for African American males in the juvenile justice system. *Child Welfare, 79*(1), January/February, 197–211.

Harvey, A., McCullough-Chavis, A., Littlefield, M. B., Phillips, A. D., & Cooper, J. D. (2010). A culturally competent family enhancement and empowerment model for African American parents. *Smith College Studies in Social Work, 80,* 70–87.

Hill, N. S., Jr. (Ed.). (2013). *Words of power: Voices from Indian America.* Golden, CO: Fulcrum.

Hill, R. B. (1997, July 21). A strengths perspective on black families. *The Baltimore Sun.*

Hilliard, A. G., III. (1998). *SBA: The reawakening of the African mind.* Gainesville, FL: Makare.

Hilliard, A. G., III, Williams, L., & Damali, N. (1987). *The teachings of Ptahhotep: The oldest book in the world.* Atlanta, GA: Blackwood Press.

Hinton, L., Tran, J. N., Tran, C., & Hinton, D. (2008). Religious and spiritual dimensions of the Vietnamese dementia caregiving experience. *Hallym International Journal of Aging, 10*(2), 139–160.

Jackson, M. (2009) *They don't care about us* [Video file]. Retrieved from https://www.youtube.com/watch?v=QNJL6nfu__Q

Kaltreider, K. (2003). *American Indian prophecies. Conversations with Chasing Deer.* Carlsbad, CA: Hay House.

Kanellos, N. (2011). *Hispanic immigrant literature: El sueño del retorno.* Austin: University of Texas.

Kanellos, N. (2002). *Recovering the U.S. Hispanic literary heritage.* Houston, TX: Arte Público PR.

We Are Everywhere: A Historical Sourcebook of Gay and Lesbian Politics.

Karenga, M. (1984). *Selections from the Husia: Sacred wisdom of ancient Egypt.* Los Angeles, CA: University of Sankore Press.

Kelley, A., & Small, C. (2015). Establishing the reliability and validity of the sources of strength in one American Indian community. *American Indian and Alaska Native Mental Health Research, 84.*

Kunen, J. S. (2017, Summer). Opening minds behind bars. *Columbia Magazine, 20.*

Kunjufu, K. (1978). *Developing positive self-images & discipline in black children.* Chicago, IL: African American Images.

Kwanzaa. (2017). Principles. Retrieved from http://www.officialkwanzaawebsite.org/7principles.shtml.

Martin, D. (2008). Maat and order in African cosmology: A conceptual tool for understanding indigenous knowledge. *Journal of Black Studies, 38*(6), 951–967.

McGaa, E. E. M. (1990). *Mother earth spirituality: Native American paths to healing ourselves and our world.* San Francisco, CA: Harper.

McQuiston, & McQuiston. (Creators & Producers). (1994). *Nature in Native American Art.* San Francisco, CA: Chronicle Books.

Mickel, E. (2002). African centered family healing: an alternative paradigm. *Journal of Health & Social Policy, 16*(1/2), 185–193; and Disability and the black community. In S. D. Miller (Ed.), *The Haworth Press* (pp. 185–193).

Moodley, R. (2005). Maat: An African centered paradigm for psychological & spiritual healing. *Integrating traditional healing practices into counseling & psychotherapy.* 210.

Museum of disABILITY History. (2014). About us. Retrieved from http://museumofdisability.org/virtual-museum/

National Council on Disabilities. (2007). *Empowerment for Americans with disabilities: Breaking barriers to careers and full employment* [Letter to the President]. Retrieved from https://ncd.gov/publications/2007/Oct2007

National Council on Disabilities. (2003). Understanding disabilities in American Indian & Alaska Native communities: Toolkit guide.

National Education Association. (2017). About National Education Association. Retrieved from nea.org.

National Hispanic Media Coalition. (2017). Retrieved from http://www.nhmc.org

Oh, J. S., & Au, T. K. (2005). Learning Spanish as a heritage language: The role of sociocultural background variables. *Language, Culture and Curriculum, 18*(3), 229–241.

Padden, C., & Humphries, T. (1988). *Deaf in America: Voices from a culture.* Cambridge, MA: Harvard University Press.

Poussaint, A. (1974). Building a strong self-image in black children. *Ebony Magazine,* 138–143.

Ramirez, L. M. (2004). Keepers of the children: Native American wisdom and parenting [Kindle Locations 104–106]. Retrieved from http://www.parenting-child-development.com

Rios, V. (2011). *Punished: Policing the lives of black and Latino boys (new perspectives in crime, deviance, and law).* New York: NYU Press.

Robbie, S. (2017). Random act of Mendez. Retrieved from https://www.randomactofmendez.us/?%20utm_campaign=8.17%2BRandom%2BE-Blast&utm_medium=email&utm_source=8.17%2BE-Blast%2BRandom%2BAct

Robinson, R. (1999). Defending the spirit: A black life in America. New York, NY: Plume.

Rodriquez, A. (2001). *The Buddha book: A novel.* New York, NY: Picador Press.

Rodriquez, J.L. (2005). *Always running. La Vida Loca: Gang Days in L.A.* Touchtone.

Sáenz, B. A. (2009) *Last night I sang to the monster.* El Paso, TX: Cinco Punto Press. (Listen to the first pages read by the author at https://www.youtube.com/watch? v=i5I7flSOF6M)

Shakur, T. (2000). *Thank God how?* Track 12.

Skjærvø, P. O. (Ed. & Trans.). (2011). *The spirit of Zoroastrianism.* New Haven, CT: Yale University Press.

Smithsonian Institution: National Museum of the Native American. (2016). Strong women/strong nations: Opening song and introduction. Retrieved from https://www.youtube.com/watch? v=XTGQ8PrEYKA

Stoute, S. (2011). *The tanning of America: How hip hop culture created a culture that rewrote the rules of the economy.* New York, NY: Penguin.

Texas Trails. (Ed). (2014). *Magical folktales from old Mexico: A collection of 14 famous Mexican legends and myths.* Retrieved from http://americanfolklore.net/folklore/2010/07/the_armadillos_song.html

Trafzer, C. E., & Weiner, D. (Eds.). (2001). *Medicine ways: Disease, health, and survival among Native Americans.* Lanham, MD: Altimara Press.

Venkatesh, S. (2008). *Gang leader for a day: A rogue sociologist takes to the street.* New York, NY: Penguin Books.

Vivekananda, S. (1896). *Karma yoga.* Retrieved from http://www.vivekananda.net/PDFBooks/KarmaYoga.pdf

Wallis, V. (2004). *Two old women: An Alaska legend of betrayal, courage,* and survival (20th anniversary ed.). New York, NY: Harper Perennial.

Wells-Wilborn, R., Jackson, N. D., & Schiele, J. H. (2010). Lessons from the Maafa: Rethinking the legacy of a slain hip-hop icon Tupac Amaru Shakur. *Journal of Black Studies,* 509–526.

Whyy.org. (2016). The pursuit. Retrieved from http://www.whyy.org/specials/pursuit.php

Wilson, A. (1992). *Awakening the natural genius of black children.* New York, NY: Afrikan World Systems.

Wilson, A. (1978). *The developmental psychology of the black child.* New York, NY: African Research Publication.

Wolkstein, D. (Ed.). (1980). *The magic orange tree and other Haitian folktales.* New York, NY: Schocken Books.

Yiwu, L. (2013). *For a song and a hundred songs: A poet's journey.* New York, NY: Harcourt.

Zhang, L., Nathan, A. J., Link, P., & Schell, O. (2008). *The Tiananmen papers.* Available at https://katateag.files.wordpress.com/2014/10/the-tiananmen-papers.pdf

FURTHER READING

Community Newspapers

Asian American History: http://www.asian-nation.org/index.shtml

El Sol Newspaper: http://elsoln1.com/

Metro Chinese Weekly, in Philadelphia: http://www.nmspress.com/metro_chinese_weekly.htm

The Philadelphia Tribune: http://www.phillytrib.com/

Gay City News: http://gaycitynews.nyc/

Community Impact Newspaper: https://communityimpact.com/topics/differently-abled-children/

Books

Allen, P. G. (Ed). (1994). *Voice of the turtle: American Indian Literature, 1900–1970.* New York, NY: Ballantine Books.

Brauen, Y. (2011). *Across many mountains: A Tibetan family's epic journey from oppression to freedom.* New York, NY: St. Martin's Press.

Hale, J. C. (1998). *Bloodlines: Odyssey of a Native daughter.* Tucson, AZ: University of Arizona Press.

Jefferson, M. (2015). *Negroland: A memoir.* New York, NY: Pantheon Books.

Pinto, P. E., & Sahun, N. (2001). *Working with people with disabilities: An Indian perspective.* Center for International Rehabilitation Research Information & Research.

PART IV

Integrating Research, Multicultural
Resources, and Citizen Involvement

P art IV builds on the history of oppression in the United States and the
role of the social work profession to understand the social environment
that impacts people and practitioners. Existing research has limitations in
areas that address the disparities. However, there are many examples and
basic knowledge regarding how to create inclusive environments to help
foster confidence. There is much work still to be done. Continuous endeavors
to educate and support practitioners and service users are in play!

Facilitating Inclusion

Using Research and Developing Interventions / Micro

CHAPTER OVERVIEW

Chapter 11 helps professionals seek resources to affirm, validate, and offer examples for future use from early intervention throughout adulthood. Incorporating multicultural resources across professional disciplines through curriculum development and service strategies using the triple perspective (macro–mezzo–micro) framework will address needs for expanding community agent recruitment, student retention, and global citizenship. Prevention programs that provide culturally relevant, socially just interventions must be expanded to include peer mediators and role models to offer approaches to broaden the resources available.

LEARNING OBJECTIVES

- Ecological systems and environmental components impact the contexts within which persons live and develop.
- Multiple viewpoints shape awareness of discrimination and justice.
- Translating interdisciplinary research for consumer use requires multicultural and bilingual participants.
- Implementing effective interventions build on community strengths, including spiritual and theological tenets.
- Ongoing learning, reading, and critical thinking is recommended for service providers and service users.

Benchmark: Students will be able to develop and facilitate inclusive service strategies.

Ralph and Pedro are working with a group of young males in a foster care home. In their discussion group, they will address the issue of how to move from "walking on the wild side" to being more focused so they can get a job when their time at the foster home has ended. How can they translate the research on high school graduation, vocational opportunities, and problems that may occur after foster care into a discussion-oriented format that incorporates personal and family accountability?

STUDENT SCENARIO

MACRO CULTURAL COMPETENCE

Macro cultural competence involves awareness of ecosystems that incorporate subsystems that may impact the presenting issues of individuals and families that seek services. There are high-context and low-context cultural dynamics that also operate with fluidity across macro to micro dimensions. Using this broad view of systems—visible and invisible, natural and those created by humans—paints a clearer, yet more complex, version of what is involved in the lives of people we work with.

Low-context cultures (e.g., North America [sajan.com, 2013] and Britain) are described as ones that use precise verbal and visual communication, teach by explicit instruction, and use arguments to make a strong case. High-context communities value collectivist ideas and are oriented toward collective survival so more background information is needed (Neese, 2016).

Indigenous people bring an even-broader frame in that they have never forgotten that non-humans are beings engaged in social relations that shape human lives. In addition, for many indigenous peoples and those of various ancestries, their nonhuman others may not be understood in Western frameworks as living beings. "Objects" and "forces" such as stones, thunder, or stars are known within indigenous ontologies to be sentient and knowing persons (Tall-Bear, 2013). African, Asian, Arab, Latin American, and those cultures associated with native communities are high context and tend to conceptualize in this manner.

While we may assume a culture is one way or another, there is also the bicultural context that incorporates high- and low-context features. This concept introduced by Edward Hall, an anthropologist, in *Beyond Culture* (1976) has been used for intercultural communication and marketing. Although definitions associated with high context suggest traditional and collectivistic behaviors and low context associates with individualistic and explicit communication (Frost, 2013), there is variability. The tendency is that high-context folks often also have low-context skills, given their educational experiences and social integration in multiple communities over their lifespan. Modeling has an important role in working with one another to learn how to use a little of this and a bit more of that in different settings. Assuming a common understanding and fostering intuition, ambiguity may exist, and interactions may be integrated. Allowing for these variations may aid in appreciating that variables may not be consistent or definite.

THE GLOBAL ECOSYSTEM

As communication systems have expanded, people around the world are more informed of what is going on. Of course, many countries present controlled information, but the interplay of environment, social, and political situations can be explored through various sources. If we can imagine a global ecosystem, the economic and political subsystems would have tremendous impact on how people in various regions operate, interact, and manage together. In reality, these subsystems generate cooperative and conflictual interactions.

ECOLOGY AND THE ENVIRONMENT

Moving forward in social work and becoming inclusive acknowledges diverse sources of knowledge, perspectives, and the participation of stakeholders often excluded in the past.

The ecosystem perspective puts the natural environment and the structures that organize people at the forefront of macro thinking. Becoming more aware of social welfare issues across populations invites recognition and integration of the work group members have done to express their ideas and advance causes over several decades. Noting the visible and invisible components of communities and the need to become more informed of diverse resources may enhance the collaborative projects for social workers, other helping professionals, and service users.

Recognizing specific and regional cultural dynamics and building upon existing strengths and assets is essential for capacity building and social change. Most important to respecting communities is the need to address economic and employment issues. The ability to handle many stressful conditions is often related to family economics. As social workers broaden their view of the landscapes that impact and influence service users, attention to academic performance and employment needs for population health becomes a priority for capacity building. Macro practice techniques can be used to help inform families about the relevant policies that guide the educational and health services they receive.

Examining the big picture, the environmental landscape in which services are offered and the geography of where people live sets up more understanding of location and place and how micro engagement occurs. Although the traditional view has started with the individual and the family, to refine strategies that are more useful for people we need to use the broadest lens rather than the narrow view.

POPULATION HEALTH

Population health emerged as a concept in Canadian health policy. While it sounds inclusive as a planning tool for social, economic, and environmental issues, its approach is limited with respect to equity and social justice (Olivier, 2003). The definition follows:

> As an approach, population health focuses on the interrelated conditions and factors that influence the health of populations over the life course, identifies systemic variations in their patterns of occurrence, and applies the resulting knowledge to develop and implement policies and actions to improve the health and well-being of those populations. (Olivier, 2003, p. 26)

The simple solution for health care needs of vulnerable people (Lantz, Lichtenstein & Pollack, 2007) proposed by policymakers is access. But this route is not effective. The recommendation that addresses the real impediments to health is "community based policy responses that will improve neighborhood social environments for children that will address discrimination and forms of psychological stressors over the life course" (p. 1253).

This approach is proposed as an avenue for social work to proceed in discussing limitations and opportunities for shaping paths to improved income equality, health, and social inclusion. Individuals and families that have been able to manage in their social environments have drawn on cultural strengths as well as personal and family resilience. Persons in need of services within the professional network often seem to need access to their cultural networks as well as access to formal agencies.

We can relate population health to community capacity building. The conceptual foundation recognizes community strengths and institutional obstacles. Professionals and service users must navigate the alligators in the water and work to get more people safely to shore.

OPPRESSIVE STRUCTURES AND LIBERATING MANEUVERS

The essential facts about racism and sexism are the links to economics. People of color and women often earn less than others. The average income by race is highest among people of Asian descent and lowest among Black people (Semega, Fontenot, & Kollar, 2017). Being aware of this invisible dynamic is fundamental to change. The messages and the ways the structures camouflage these dynamics influence peoples' behaviors. Some hear and internalize the demeaning and devaluing messages, become frustrated and depressed, and may behave in destructive ways. Adverse experience in their environment can make it more difficult to move out of this pattern. Interventions that encourage self-awareness, goals setting, and personal accountability build confidence, skills, and resources.

Simultaneously, interventions that promote the development of multiple participants in coalitions to address employment opportunities, housing conditions, health care, and environmental standards are required. Policy formulation that emphasizes worker and parent development through alliances with helping professionals, activists, and concerned citizens target human and civil rights.

Colonists, conquerors, and oppressors have stolen resources and created mental anguish in ways that many people without the benefit of collective mutual aid have become unable to care for themselves. Justice comes through replacing resources and establishing alternative means for human survival.

Social justice involves process and goals (Bell, 2010) to address unduly punitive institutions and procedures. As we reflect on the examples of oppressive historical influences on people of different groups, the light at the end of the tunnel arrives through the validation of experiences, acknowledgement of the protective factors, and use of skills and networking to connect helping professionals, service users, and community. The outcomes should result in actualization of untapped talents and resources.

For some pursuing social work, the emphasis on service to the poor stems from a religious context. For others, the social work mission includes attention to the vulnerable, oppressed, those in poverty as well as others across class groups who seek assistance for needs regarding their and their families' welfare. Deines (2014) reminds us that the social work profession at times has resisted standing up for the poor and oppressed. When slaves were freed, they resisted providing services; during the Depression, they issued lower benefits to African American families than to white families; and after the Social Security Act passage, social work representatives wanted to avoid teaching about relief funds (p. 3). Beginning with our own sense of accountability, we can help others advance change.

MULTIPLE SYSTEMS IMPACT HEALTH

Health care involves several systems and subsystems. The multiple systems that impact service users include environmental, economic, social, cultural, spiritual, and political entities. Environmental systems address natural resources, housing, and food. Often, people who come for service bring some connection to a religious viewpoint that helps them. Some are adverse to spiritual connections. Despite these potentially strong beliefs, social work and other professions have resisted respecting them in their service planning. Ignoring or avoiding the history of the cultural dynamics of service users excludes a critical component of their human spirit.

Service delivery extends from these systems and incorporates ethics and spirituality. Improving service delivery and facilitating inclusion can establish recognition of the intentionally designed obstacles against service user values. The traditional uses and misuses may impact the health and well-being of community residents. Following a snapshot of this macro landscape, we will consider a few key themes.

ENVIRONMENT: NATURAL RESOURCES

The quality of the air, water, and soil impact the health of the human and animal residents of a community. The ecological perspective includes knowledge of the built and natural environments (Teixeira & Krings, 2015) as well as the social environment. Knowledge of this should be shared with the community. Where quality is low, residents should participate in holding officials accountable. Social workers can play a more active role in assisting residents in becoming more informed about their environment.

GEOGRAPHIC DYNAMICS

Urban, suburban, and rural areas suggest a basis for context description and for appreciating the demographics of an area. The history of the location helps us understand the current existence of jobs, sources of labor, and potential for future workforce development.

As we expand the areas to evaluate, implementing mapping and geospatial techniques to identify assets and the areas that need monitoring become clearer.

Gathering information about the communities in which services are delivered requires review of local demographics and assessment of community assets. Service delivery systems are connected to the geography, location, and population.

The pathways for improvements become visible and available for inclusion. Social workers informed of the research regarding the geography of places may be able to organize advocates to speak up, use data, and contribute to planning. This data may also be useful in connecting residents to resources for emergencies and advocating for infrastructure needs.

NEIGHBORHOOD PLANNING

Traditional approaches in planning large developments are shifting to more neighborhood-sensitive projects based on small community (Meares & Riggs, 2016). As environments evolve in this way, so do the composition descriptors, demographics, and context. The better approach, derived from some examples, seems to be addressing local context and encouraging adaptive planning and responses (Kirby, 2014). Walkability and access to goods and services, especially where vehicle ownership may be problematic, is resulting in positive influences in the Louisville, Kentucky, community, for example. (Farber & Shinkle, 2011).

In the United States, many think most public service systems are in place, but some need repair and others need development. Examining other geographic processes can provide perspectives that may be innovative in bringing together working communities, technology, the human network, and management strategies. Helpful resources include the Sustainable Cities Institute (National League of Cities, 2017) and William McDonough and Michael Braungart's (2002) *Cradle to Cradle: Remaking the Way We Make Things*. Modifying planning to increase green spaces would be beneficial in the long run.

The challenges of Lagos, Nigeria (Gadanho, 2014), pose an example of urban development and offer dimensions for consideration. The basic challenges are energy supply, water supply, and transportation. As they proceed to understand the context, they have configured "a database with examples of inventions, situations, compromises and players" (p. 100) to visualize proposals that integrate day-to-day skills of informal bottom-up initiatives with formal top-down ones. Schiller (2016) ties the need for network and scaling analysis to the study of cities and energy use to connect human behaviors and social institutions to approaches that address sustainability. Dunlop and Holosko (2016) describe the procedures for increasing service user participation.

NEIGHBORHOOD ASSOCIATIONS

Some communities have organized neighborhood or homeowner associations. Block captains and neighborhoods associations can play roles in gathering and sharing data among residents (*New York Amsterdam News*, 2009). But citizen participation at a higher level has brought controversy. The misuse of federal funds designated for low-income communities (Bonds & Farmer-Hinton, 2008) has obstructed some efforts for improvement.

Respondents in a survey of neighborhood associations indicate many are working on similar problems and express interest in working with other associations. However, the absence of actual collaboration suggest these groups have trouble engaging with one another within this network (Knickmeyer, Hopkins & Meyer, 2003). Student projects in macro practice could begin to take on intercommunity collaborations such as this.

COMMUNITY BUILDING: INCLUSIVE DESIGNS

Moving to more inclusion in planning community development involves rethinking ways and agendas used in how we work. Conference planners are organizing meetings of discipline groups to gain knowledge, discuss and reflect on issues, and identify calls to action. The Cambridge Workshops on Universal Access and Assistive Technology used feedback to extend presentation times to carry on discussions through plenaries and meals to generate a more cooperative and informative experience (Langdon, Clarkson, Robinson, Lazar,

& Heylighen, 2012). In this way, conference attenders could be more engaged in sharing ideas and opinions regarding the theme and planning by the professional associations.

Responding to the needs of older people, their cognitive impairments, and visual issues would push strategies and knowledge needed to design inclusive systems. Cities can do things to develop sharing economies. Zoning can be modified to rally against social and economic segregation and improve human settlement patterns (Talen, 2005). This concept offers jobs with flexible hours, opportunities to earn cash, and access to bikes and cars (Urban Institute, 2016a). While the idea holds promise for low-income people, current statistics indicate they have not reached out for these services as much as upper-income people have. There appears to also be inadvertent discrimination associated with them.

Greene and McGinty (2016) suggest ways cities could influence inclusive economies in planning cities. Instead of using outdated regulations and penalties, cities can bring together city leaders, community groups, businesses, researchers, and sharing-economy firms to develop a roadmap for an economy to work for more of the citizens. Their ideas include these key points:

- Protect workers with more work flexibility and independence.
- Provide seed capital and training and reduce licensing and permitting barriers.
- Require sharing-economy firms to expand into low-income neighborhoods or reduce prices for low-income consumers.
- Support peer-to-peer lending to help people build credit.

The National League of Cities (NLC) has also introduced a campaign to reach for a culture of health that supports leaders, agency representatives, community members and stakeholders working together and sharing data that can promote city decision making for positive health outcomes (Barnett, Dailey & Polis, 2017).

Not only can social workers present information regarding needs they may observe in their settings, but they should also be able to represent community groups in local government entities to assist in sustaining their service users and improving their well-being.

Service user participation in civic activities may not be at the top of the goal-setting list in individual or case management sessions. However, sharing information about the lived-in environment is a goal to be included as we assist people to examine the bigger picture for themselves.

AIR

We have known of the problems pollution has created for many years. In the 1990s, advocacy promoted the need for change by 2005, and Goldemberg (1990) proposed a carbon tax and a shift from fossil fuels to use of ethanol produced from sugarcane. However, in 2018, there continues resistance to doing what it takes to improve air quality. The clear need to cut emission by half in 1990 was not addressed. Environmental economics involves the effects of local and national environmental policies on social welfare (Nie, 2015). Air pollution affects child asthma conditions, other respiratory health conditions (Lewinson & Bryant, 2012), the prevalence of obesity in Chinese adults, especially women (Li et al., 2016), and most recently an increase in dry-eye symptoms (Goodman, 2013). Climate change and air pollution are areas of concern for public health and social work with respect to the implications for health care needs, prevention, and morbidity (Madaniyazi, Guo, Yu, & Tong, 2015).

WATER AND LEAD

Citizen concerns about environmental and water pollution have increased in 2016 as more information about toxins has been reported (McCarthy, 2016). Water quality is impacted by the amount of lead and copper contained. According to CNN, (Ganim, 2016) a report by water experts shows 18 million Americans live in 5,300 communities where the water systems are in violation of the law. The federal agency responsible for oversight is aware of the issues but has only addressed the problems in 88 communities.

Many water utility companies are cheating, using practices that hide the real quality of the water. Philadelphia is an example. A class-action lawsuit (Mitman, 2016) alleges that Philadelphia water main construction and repairs have created contamination. The city responded that the Environmental Protection Agency (EPA) language is guidance and there would be improvements in 2017 (Ganim, 2016).

Not only are traditional methods used to measure lead levels, but the impact of toxins on birds is reviewed. Pigeons have been used in Europe and the United States to monitor the evocation and prevalence of pollutants. A New York study of pigeons (Fell, 2016) discovered levels of lead in the birds track with neighborhoods where children show high levels of lead exposure. The New York City Department of Health and Mental Hygiene screens children in areas recognized for high lead contamination.

FOOD

Food justice issues range from access to food among lower-wealth citizens to concerns about GMOs (genetically modified organisms), pesticides, and the impact of emissions on air quality in agricultural settings. Conway and Lassiter (2011) describe an opportunity for community social workers to partner with food justice practitioners in Tennessee to get a transportation service from the public housing units to the farmers' market.

Food security is an issue that is addressed in social work education. Food insecurity among families is raised in the *Rich and the Rest of Us* (Smiley & West, 2013). More recently, Walsh (2016) identified trading sex for food as an issue among American adolescents. Social worker strategies in schools include assessing children who are in need of food, families that may need help in applying for nutrition assistance (Fram, Frongillo, Fishbein, & Burke, 2014), and helping to educate school staff in ways food service may be more accommodating. Another side of the food revolution has to do with the real cost of creating cheap food. Robbins (2012) speaks up about the chemical agribusiness systems that are destroying rural communities, polluting water, eroding soil, causing animals to suffer, emitting greenhouse gases, and contributing to the rising diabetes statistics. There is also concern about the transparency of companies lobbying for their products with respect to health consequences. For example, there is evidence that in 1967 scientists at the Sugar Research Foundation were paid to overlook the role of sugar in heart disease (De Graaf, 2016).

FOOD LOCATION

The connection of food security, or the "grocery store gap," has been described as one involving geographic access. Not only are food safety and access of concern, but providing information about community gardens, kitchens, and food rescue and redistribution is also relevant. Recent research with community residents found the lack of disposable income and the high price points of healthy foods to be a substantive barrier (Myers & Caruso, 2016). Their work concludes that using incentives to bring grocery stores into low-income communities will not succeed without increasing the incomes of residents or lowering prices of produce.

The alternative is offered through the creation of a robust public infrastructure, such as public education, public transportation, municipal water and sewer, fire, Medicaid, and so on. Within this context, they propose creating state-run grocery stores based on the commissary and state-run alcohol store models (Myers & Caruso, 2016) that would be located in neighborhoods without privately established food markets.

There are opportunities for social workers to help inform communities about the industrial food machine and how it is affecting us and to urge citizen participation in resolving some of the issues. Social workers can also be hired in the industries that are posing threats to well being as project participants who can provide social welfare analyses.

HOUSING CONDITIONS

Several categories of literature report the impact of neighborhoods on child development. Low-income neighborhoods may be associated with smoking, substance use, harsh parenting, and toxic levels in air, soil, and water. Many decisions about child custody have to do with the conditions of the homes in which they live. On low-income budgets, homes are frequently found with lead or in need of repairs. An example of an intervention in a Louisville, Kentucky, Families First case years ago observed the caseworker teaching a mom how to caulk windows and do minor repairs to the home so the children would not be removed. Current projects of the Kentucky Center for Women and Families address awareness and education (2017). Some states are participating in experimental programs that are examining how different areas impact one another.

Brennan (2016) describes the physicality of young children's behaviors (e.g., crawling on the floor) to be of special concern in fostering healthy cognitive development. This research addresses not just the potential of lead exposure, but speaks to housing policies regarding code enforcement, foreclosure prevention, and neighborhood revitalization. She suggests the negative effects of poverty can be mitigated in part if housing developers play a bigger role in supporting healthy development. Desmond (2017) increases our awareness of the negative impact of evictions on health and mental health of the parents and children; and the resulting moves to even more dilapidated housing conditions. More information is available at just-shelter.org.

Housing assistance to service users is not simply scheduling repairs and teaching maintenance. Housing counseling has guided clients through loan modification and foreclosure prevention. Theodos and Seidman (2016) reported only 2% of loans in foreclosure during the first quarter of 2016. They propose that housing counseling and coaching along with financial coaching can help prepare people for homeownership and for other financial benefits regardless of whether they ultimately decide to purchase a home. Informing consumers of financial details and guidelines can help them become more aware of several financial improvement strategies (Theodos & Seidman, 2016).

ECONOMIC CONCERNS FOR WORKING FAMILIES

The broad scope of economics is fundamental to the well-being of the populations that social workers are committed to. Liu (2016) brings attention to the need for policy development to generate more forward thinking in promoting public policies. She notes: "It's time to shift and broaden the purpose and practice of economic development to generate continuous growth, prosperity, and inclusion" (para 2). Her report analyzes 100 major cities and observes the growth that is occurring but emphasizes the growth is not better for all residents. She encourages planners to be innovative and deliberate about workforce development. A goal is to help residents increase their skills to enhance income and be able to remain in their communities as growth improves the environments.

CRITICAL THINKING QUESTION

What is your immediate thought about an older person? Consider your opinions of older people. Do you reflect on examples of capacity and strengths or do your thoughts engage ideas of fragility? What about their housing needs as you add intersectional identities? When you consider an older person as a coworker do your opinions change? How does reflecting on persons in context affect your ways of evaluating them?

CSWE has promoted financial social work as a component of helping people. Links to relevant information are available on their website (cswe.org). On a micro level, this involves addressing finances and helping to teach financial literacy (Karger, 2015). The broader social justice issue has to do with advocacy for minimum wages, flexible conditions for working class people, and support of educational programs in high schools and community colleges. On the micro level communities need to help graduates become employed, and legislation that addresses structural policy support that would assist low-income families. These sorts of concerns impact caregivers' abilities to address family needs—caring for children, being able to attend school programs, and so on.

Major economic concerns for working families include housing, child care, educational access, and criminal justice. Financial stressors and unemployment are also linked to depression and substance use (Grant et al., 2017). Economic concerns for older persons impact working families who must care for older relatives who may have insufficient retirement funds and are part of the low-wage industries that will hire them.

Advocates for living wages and minimum wages have wondered about social work's responsibility for the working poor. While the participation has been varied over states, social workers contributed to the work that won an advance in wages in Nevada (Chandler, 2009). In another example, the union rights organization Jobs With Justice promotes work-related issues and advocates for wages equity and working conditions (Johansson, 2017).

Social work participation in the minimum wage or living wage campaigns have gained more attention. Consider the needs of restaurant workers getting minimal shifts that keep them from earning meals, and parents facing inflexible hours that make it difficult to get regular wages or to be able to plan in order to cover children's care. These are major impediments (Golden, 2015). Not only do these result in struggles for the parents but also for the children.

SAFETY NETS OR INTEGRATED ELIGIBILITY

Concerns about human and civil rights pose challenges to social work in different ways in different countries. One negative result of globalization that many social workers agree on is the social impact of macro-economic changes. Cutbacks in safety-net programs or welfare provisions have introduced market discipline toward efficiencies and away from care, justice, and self-determination (Rowe, Hanley, Moreno, & Mould, 2000).

There are eight large assistance programs that serve low-income families:

- Supplemental Nutrition Assistance Program (SNAP)
- Temporary Assistance for Needy Families (TANF)
- The earned income tax credit (EITC) and the child tax credit
- Supplemental Security Income (SSI)
- Child Care and Development Fund (CCDF)
- Housing assistance
- Unemployment insurance
- Medicaid and the Children's Health Insurance Program (CHIP; Combi, 2013).

These programs address needs of families but in a fragmented way. Some are national programs with standard rules, and some are state programs that have variable rules and may not be available in every state. The use of the programs shows SNAP as the most received because as an entitlement program more people have become eligible for it as incomes dropped (Combi, 2013). TANF is not an entitlement, so help does not necessarily expand with family needs. In fact, the Safety Net Almanac (2015) describes the program to have low benefits that don't last very long and don't help very much.

The 2015 U.S. Census data annual report showed improvements on several poverty indicators, including a drop in poverty from 14.8% of Americans in 2014 to 13.5% in 2015; fewer people were uninsured than in 2014; and about 1 million fewer children were living in poverty, with the child poverty rate improving from 21.1% in 2014 to 19.7% in 2015 (clasp. org, 2017).

Policies from the 1930s through the 1990s shifted financial support to white suburbs via mortgage, transportation, and development strategies away from low-income Black and Latino communities with urban renewal, neglect, and planned shrinkage. These changes contributed to the wealth gap that currently limits education and employment opportunities and buying power in lower-income communities (Myers & Caruso, 2016).

LOW-INCOME WORKERS' RIGHTS

In a panel sponsored by the Urban Institute (2016b), Uma Ahluwalia, director of Health and Human Services in Montgomery County, Maryland, discussed increased service needs for students who change addresses several times over the school year. This is associated with rising housing costs and families seeking another home when they can't afford the current one.

Ahluwalia and the panel on "Reducing Poverty and Increasing Opportunity: Envisioning the Next 20 Years" (Urban Institute, 2016b) introduced a macro-oriented approach that would eliminate hurdles and challenges of the current systems.

Based on assessment of resident family needs, an integrated eligibility process would allow access to multiple services at once. A two-generation poverty approach would address the characteristics that exacerbate poverty. Supplemental programs have aided low-income families, but the existing system does not allow a mother time to address child care needs and get training to find sufficient employment. The system should incorporate the ability to hire and train natural community leaders for place-based and neighborhood-based work. Blending services over at least 5 years could operate in tandem with early childhood focus on preK education and training mothers during that phase as well.

Women without husbands are at risk for poverty as they age. Caregiver credits have become a component of public pension systems in high-income countries (Munnell, 2016) and are being explored in the United States. This would give women credit for the years they spend caring for children instead of being in the workforce.

The Economic Policy Institute has created a library of resources regarding the American workforce. Their research documents the impact of policies and proposed rules on workers' wages. (Economic Policy Institute, *State of Working America Data Library*, 2016). Worker's wages and protection of their rights can help families or increase their risks and vulnerability (Shierholz, et al., 2018). Social worker awareness of the connection of macro policies to service users should influence our participation in advocacy for economic justice in policy formulation.

ASSESSING AGREEMENTS AND CONCERNS

Impending legislation in these areas that affect service users is being raised for more attention in the case management and micro realm. The Trans-Pacific Partnership would hurt black and Hispanic workers more than white workers (Scott, 2016). According to this analysis, it would push downward the already low wages of non–college educated Black and Hispanic persons who suffer high unemployment. Unemployment rates in low income communities are typically higher than the overall unemployment figures, however December 2017 data indicate the lowest rate since 1972 (CBSNews, 2018). Cities are making a difference in reducing the rates (Perry, 2018). Examining these in assessing and planning services is an important step.

The decline of unions accounts for lower wages of nonunion workers. According to Rosenfeld, Denice, and Laird (2016), wages stagnation has occurred over the past 30 years because people without a college degree are not union members. While there is some variability in wage determination, the effects of union decline since the late 1970s appear to have influenced annual wage losses. Rebuilding unions and worker participation are ways to protect organizational responsibility to the workforce.

The connection of feelings and opinions about race relations to economics is unclear. While people want jobs, conditions related to police killings of black people and other social conditions impact opinions (Irwin, 2017).

SOCIAL SYSTEMS

As we have seen from a strengths view of heritage, people across cultures tend to have principles of life that emphasize doing what is right, engaging with one another for the benefit of the community, and raising children within that community context. Unfortunately, media presentations have promoted negative news in a clear strategy to divide and restrict opportunities of people who have been excluded primarily because of complexion differences,

Shifting or transforming these dynamics must involve the participation of members of all groups in ways that appreciate diversity and that bring attention to the power forces in the media industry. Recently (Emery, 2017), the Sinclair Broadcast Group garnered a deal to increase its holdings and increase corporate leadership of its political bias. More diverse representation in media spokespersons and justice systems will expose the social system to voices from all cultures of U.S. citizenship. It benefits everyone to broaden awareness of the macro environment through the lens of globalization as well as local dimensions. This can be done through the use of minority owned websites and newspapers, recruitment through culturally diverse community organizations, steps to emphasize positive news, reduction of accent discrimination (Guerin, 2016), and soliciting ideas from bicultural and multicultural representatives of diverse organizations that have not been approached through traditional approaches.

Research on the ways providers approach their work in welcoming immigrants in Maine and in Washington (Clevenger et al., 2014) offers beginning information on how workers shape their integration into cities. The ethics of refuge and views of respect of the immigrant's resilience were observed. Nguyen (2015) shares a fascinating interpretation of post war in Vietnam. More research is needed on the emotions and techniques of inclusion of new arrivers. The potential for social work leadership to creatively reframe the process by highlighting assets can bolster the social system of the city from a human rights lens.

MATTERS OF ENGAGEMENT: PROFESSIONALS IN MICRO WORK

The primary social work role through individual work, case management, or psychotherapy involves the translation of research into interventions. Assessing and designing interventions or using those established via the organizations help shape the practitioner's and service user's ways of thinking. As noted in the previous sections, people connect with social workers from a variety of standpoints, crisis situations, and places of need. Social workers have expanded their awareness of these influences. There are many opportunities to assist citizens in addressing their immediate needs and moving forward to make community improvements.

ETHICS IN THE MACRO DIMENSION

The ethical principles for macro and micro work across the world are influenced by conditions of different regions and countries. The IFSW (International Federation of Social Workers) offers basic guidelines for making ethically informed decisions while recognizing that social workers often find themselves challenged in situations of conflict between local and higher-level authorities, impacted by budget constraints and conservative agendas.

The Federation respects the codes of ethics of all member countries and has an international code of ethics. Its statement of ethical principles and social work definition upholds human rights, human dignity, social justice, and professional conduct. The principles from these documents are incorporated in the IFSW goals.

Universal Declaration of Human Rights

The International Covenant on Civil and Political Rights

The International Covenant on Economic Social and Cultural Rights

The Convention on the Elimination of All Forms of Racial Discrimination

The Convention on the Elimination of All Forms of Discrimination Against Women

The Convention on the Rights of the Child

Indigenous and Tribal Peoples Convention (ILO convention 169; IFSW, n.d.)

These documents represent attention to the multiple dimensions of life and behavior toward persons of diverse geography, heritage, religion, and life customs. Integrating and translating information from these resources in planning our sessions will enhance our communication with consumers and help them understand the landscape of services and their participation. This orientation of the macro to the micro promotes the value of inclusion. Reviewing the documents of our profession as we move along in developing relationships and interventions helps to maintain our focus.

CODE OF ETHICS

Social work emphasizes professional ethical standards. "The *Code* is designed to help social workers identify relevant considerations when professional obligations conflict or ethical uncertainties arise" (Code of Ethics, p. 2). Social work's duty is to understand the impact of ethical decision-making on the ability to assist those in need (Reamer, 2005). The definitions of *ethics* include "views of morality regarding what is right or wrong" (dictionary.com); "basic concepts and fundamental principles of decent human conduct" (Business dictionary.com); and "moral principles that include doing unto others what you would have them do unto you" (Resnick, 2015). Resnick points out that some principles may be commonly accepted, but individual interpretations are likely to differ. So, maybe we should consider the phrase 'do unto others in ways they prefer'.

INTEGRATING DIVERSE PROFESSIONAL ROLES AS VISIBLE REPRESENTATIVES
Continuing to work within the macro context presents organizations, professionals, and community agents with many entry points through which to offer opportunities to seek, find, and apply strategies and resources informed by basic social work concepts and emerging research. By expanding knowledge of multicultural resources through research and communication, broader databases become available to design and adapt interventions for services and social problem solutions.

Integrating awareness and interest in multilevel aspects of lives draws on the positive forces of the environment. This moves us away from the narrow perceptions and expectations of people who have traditionally been dominant in the literature and allows us to include the voices of variety that have existed but are frequently omitted. Resilience comes from family and community allegiance, problem solving, supportive relationships, and encouragement. Improving the visibility of diverse roles supports children in identity development, and confidence building helps improve their understanding of the world around them.

MICRO CULTURAL COMPETENCE
Micro cultural competence is recognition that everyone is a unique human being influenced by biology, genetics, and the environment. Evidence from these and related research areas illustrate positive and negative influences on one's development. Biology and the unfolding research and evidence of brain development reveal that it is not nature or nurture—it is both. The quality of interactions of the two may shape, misshape, or redirect one's abilities to find security and trust in a world of ongoing, changing, emerging, and transitional moods and phases.

MICRO WORK AND COMMUNITY ENGAGEMENT
Block (2008) encourages citizenship that is more than just being a voting person. Voting in a democracy is essential, but beyond this, citizenship is our work to "build the capacity of citizens to be accountable and to become creators of community" (p. 64). Not only is the work of helping professionals to engage and intervene in culturally affirming ways, but it also involves helping community members become more aware of their responsibilities for accountability to their children and neighbors.

Helping service users become more informed of the macro parameters that influence professionals and consumers can be approached in several ways. It includes gathering information about the status of policies that may affect them and their use of mutual aid and community supports. Social workers can become informed enough to refer persons to community associations and resources, as well as link them to traditional institutional services. This moves worker–user relationships to the mezzo level for service planning.

EDUCATION

Many social work interventions at the micro level occur in education. Some may be applied in the classroom environment and others may tap into content areas. Emdin (2016) reminds us that teachers and others who want to become more effective in assisting higher student achievement need to become more immersed in the culture of others. Art, music, and literature support, relax, and stimulate. Educators have been trained to perceive the "neoindigenous" customs as "inherently negative" (p. 13). People who may not look like or speak like white, middle-class Americans, despite their fewer resources, have found ways to live within these limits and maintain dignity and identity.

Interventions implemented through interprofessional and interorganizational partnerships tap into many spheres. Dorothy Day was a social activist who began the Catholic Worker Movement for social justice (Fresh Air, NPR, 2017). Several projects in different states bear her name and provide integrated services. Projects in New York have developed from abandoned lots to housing with education, training, and child care. In St. Paul Minnesota, the Dorothy Day Center is expanding to become an opportunity center with housing, employment, health and mental health counseling and training. Projects that are multilayered and target two generations are identified in several communities (Schumacher, 2013) that connect early childhood education to housing, parenting and to community development. School-based interventions are also considered effective approaches for improving student behavior and academic performance. Implementing programs without a controlled experimental setting requires further review and discussion of social work systems of maintaining fidelity to the delivery structure (Anyon, Nicotera, & Vech, 2016). Evaluation of outcomes at the child, family, program and community levels must occur.

INCLUSION IN EDUCATION

There are several areas of information that would enhance social and emotional learning in communities. Responding to Yasui, Pottick and Chen' s report of the absence of cultural frameworks in service delivery providing lessons in community-based settings on nutrition, in community based settings would be helpful (2017). Nutrition and home-work help conducted with bilingual and culturally affirming resources would be encouraging.

Teaching nutrition education is considered an area to help to young children prevent weight gains. A study in two provinces in China explored the influence of socio-demographic variables on their eating behavior. The findings suggest improvement in parent education would impact implementation of nutrition knowledge (Qian, Zhang, Newman, Shell, & Du, 2018).

After-school program (ASP) snacks is another area of effort to improve children's nutrition (Beets, Weaver, Turner-McGrievy, Huberty et al., 2017). The distribution of healthy fruits and vegetable occurred and showed that improvements could be made. The obstacle was the lack of storage space for the perishable foods and the delivery schedules.

Planning for nutrition education for Latino children emphasizes the need to involve the parents before implementing a program (Diaz-Rios, Muzaffar, Meline, & Chapman-Novakofski, 2016).

Including special needs students in class projects would help students work. A Georgia elementary school unified its Physical Education classes to include the fourth-grade students with the special needs class to play together. Observers noted they learned (Booze, 2017) from one another (Booze, 2017).

Field internships assignments or projects could support agencies by working with community groups to identify types of information needed. Students would develop collaboration, facilitation, and mediation skills, and prioritize community concerns for goal setting.

Providing research informed community education is an alternative to medical and mental health settings. Informing parents in community-based organizations of the research regarding nutritional meals to keep weight down as children grow, early education at home to foster good reading skills, parent engagement with teachers as children move through school and importance of after school clubs and church group participation could be emphasized through community partnerships.

POLITICAL SYSTEMS

To a large extent, political influence shapes policy implemented in the economic and social systems. The impact of political power players is clearly visible in the policies that diminish or restrict employment, educational opportunities, and access to food and energy resources. Economics and politics are closely linked in determining the policies that are developed and passed into legislation and who benefits from them.

As a representative democracy, citizens in the United States elect delegates to the national, state, and local government. These representatives establish bills to review and vote to become laws. Although only individual citizens can vote, special interest groups and lobbyists organize and raise funds to influence elections. Politics is connected to privileged groups using power to promote their interests and gain laws that support their financial goals. The influence of rich people to shield them from taxation has raised questions regarding the validity of the government as a democracy (Winters, 2014).

Social work macro concerns include voter information, rallies to increase voter participation and projects to encourage social workers to run for office. Community practice and political participation strategies are also used by those who do not support civil and human rights. Stevenson's point that justice helps address poverty (Chambers, 2018) encourages advocates to seek protection of the court system from political influence. This idea is being tested in Columbia South America through a citizen survey of community input regarding living conditions, access to public services, food security and legal problems. These data should help shape innovation. A Sao-Paul effort involves finding ways to explain public policy in the community and building inclusion through collaboration (Tendolini, 2018; Lewis, 2012). The Southern Poverty Law Center reports on hate group activity across the United States and fights against instances of organizational discrimination through legal means (SPLC, 2016). Community awareness of hate groups may encourage service users to join with associations that work for justice and equality.

AGE GROUP NEEDS

Acknowledging the needs of different age groups urges more consideration of how local and state committees include these dynamics in the data analysis and planning. There are ways to involve older participants and older researchers (Cormes et al., 2008). When residents attend the local municipal governing meetings, such as city council meetings, school board meetings, town information meetings, and church and temple meetings, they may realize the need to speak up about what is needed for all in the decision-making process. Health and mental health needs for toddlers, children, teens, adults, and older adults vary and require responding to particular key indicators.

MINDSETS OF THE PROFESSIONALS: SOCIAL WORKERS, COUNSELORS, PUBLIC HEALTH, PSYCHIATRISTS, PSYCHOLOGISTS, PARAPROFESSIONALS, ADVOCATES

Each professional discipline has literature and professional jargon that are connected to the work they do with people. Traditionally, these professionals have used discipline-specific knowledge and research findings to work with clients. But as all professions have been touched by racism, sexism, and homophobia, more paraprofessionals, allied health personnel, and advocates have emerged as informed but unlicensed workers. More importantly, advocates have accompanied service users or spoke up in their absence about the methods and quality of service on their behalf. Over time, there has been movement across disciplines toward listening to the service user for guidance and feedback.

SOCIAL WORK

There are several views of social work. Social work, in its originating framework, helped people with limited monetary resources, immigrant heritage, language needs, and often housing issues. While also influenced by colonial beliefs and attitudes, the profession specifically identified the needs of the poor and established ethical and performance guidelines to respect all service users, one another, and society's humanitarian principles.

Social workers have been victims of stereotypes connected to our work in child protection that involves removing children from families. This media representation is similar to the negative depictions that have been presented for all the excluded groups we have discussed. Similarly, social workers have strengths and spiritual connections that warrant illumination. In open chapter meetings of social workers, they express what being a social worker means. They feel rewarded through their micro work with individuals when goals are met and they observe the process of change. The role of spirituality has received increased attention, but in many cases, neither the service user nor the social worker mentions it (Furness & Gillian, 2014)

The narrative that Murray (2015) highlights is that social workers save lives. "We are not child-snatchers or do-gooders. Social work helps many and there are stories about improving lives of those vulnerable. Yet many [social workers] do not last long because of the workloads." *Critical Social Work*, a journal of human capacity and social justice presents a framework for interdisciplinary work to examine and promote the potential of social justice efforts. Social work operates in many fields across a range of obstacles and opportunities. Continuing discussions, competency goals, and service user involvement is fostering more accountability and inclusion.

SERVICE DELIVERY

According to Nair and Guererro (2014), service use and delivery may vary for different clients and types of services to be delivered. There may be a single point of contact and departure. There could be multiple points of entry and continuation. Simultaneously, as Bornstein (2007) illustrates, there is also an emerging landscape of paths for providing services. Social entrepreneurs are advancing innovative solutions to the ongoing problems that plague our social scenes.

As communities are observed, delineated by geospatial technology and analyzed via increasing enlarged dataset, fiscal analysis examines funds that are available and methods of payment for different levels of care. Advocacy for prevention has increased and recent findings indicate it does not reduce spending for healthcare. It does improve outcomes. (Carroll, 2018). That is a good thing!

CONTEMPORARY CONDITIONS

Higgins (2017) reports that emotional health diagnoses are rising. He refers to an analysis by the U.S. Burden of Disease Collaborators that examined increased suicides, substance use, and premature death and disability. Lack of specificity in some diagnoses, absence of new treatments, and reductions in neuroscience and pharmaceutical research account for some of the discouraging news. Nevertheless, outreach and innovative strategies are enhancing care in others. The role of exercise in improving physical health and depression is a significant finding (Jabr, 2017).

Social work involves direct practice interventions with individuals, families, groups, and organizations. Understanding the path to service needs frequently results from the situations related to one's economic class status. Limited personal capital is associated with "factors related to "unemployment, underemployment, displacement and fears related to individual and family finances. Often, these are connected to feelings, behaviors, and expectations. Short and long-term coping responses and the impact of these on relationships can lead to suicide, homicide, overdosing, heart attacks, hypertension, cirrhosis of the liver, arrests, imprisonment and mental illness" (Yates, 2008, para 10).

The awareness of policy impact on services and the tremendous role of social work in politics has emerged as the critical connection of macro and micro dimensions of services for community members. There are opportunities to advocate for specific policies to reduce disparities and to encourage voter registration to increase political clout. Helping professionals can inform communities of ways to proceed against political efforts to keep service users underserved (Abdul-Jabbar, 2016). Federal health agencies have strategic plans that urge community partnerships to achieve more effective and equitable care (National Conference of State Legislatures, 2017). Working to reduce disparities to improve services, to listen to consumer interest in upgrading weekend health services and outcomes is the overarching goal of health and allied professionals.

OPPORTUNITIES FOR MICRO BEST PRACTICE

Several theories may be used to frame the provision of direct social work practice. Psycho, social, cultural, biological, cultural, and economic research offers the prevailing explanations of individual and family behaviors. Using themes of strengths and resilience, processes of recovery from damaging psychosocial dynamics, and working to build capacity in families and communities, social workers can add contextual fluidity to the theories that inform the multidimensional panorama for culturally affirming services.

As students build toolkits for their professions, they also learn from the perspectives of other disciplines. Opportunities for social work students to work with traditional disciplines such as nursing, education, public health, counseling, criminal justice, and public adminis-tration exist. Developing relationships and partnerships in other settings, especially libraries and community recreation centers, and businesses and apprentice programs will need to occur and be integrated in the professional schools (Held, Mallory, & Cummings, 2017). These new connections offer ways to build innovation that stretches the context for addressing the Grand Challenges.

In moving from the realities of restricted opportunity constructed by oppressive structures to the acquisition of cultural strengths-based knowledge and citizen participation, learning theory can be applied to enhance the roles of helping professionals and service users. Figure 11.1 presents areas of research to sustain micro practice.

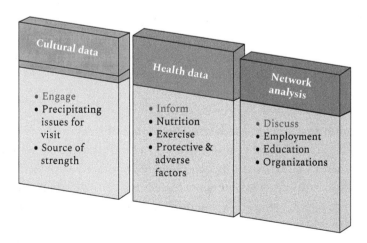

FIGURE 11.1   Pillars of Capacity Development

RESPECTING COMMUNITIES

> "Those who feel appreciated may work harder in ways not anticipated."
> Anonymous

Respecting communities involves using a welcoming approach; providing screening, health and emotional well-being information, and symptom relief; and offering nutrition and movement education, along with goal setting, resources, and follow-up framework. The triple perspective strategy broadens the agenda for assessment and providing interventions. Service planning for micro, mezzo, and macro issues occurs by collaborating with individuals, families, service teams, and community groups. Social workers and other health care providers have opportunities to enhance family awareness, development, and civic participation. Providing resources to connect to cultural heritage and family history may be areas of interest to service users. Operating from the broader macro landscape provides additional areas for consideration and mutual planning for goal setting over a longer time frame.

ENGAGEMENT

A welcoming process can begin in the community or in an office. Using "Mr." or "Ms." until desired names are determined shows respect. An orientation to the service process could involve brief information about health as the well-being of body and mind (Chopra & Tanzi, 2018). Offering an explanation of how emotions and physical fitness affect one another and that greater understanding of these dimensions can influence recovery from crisis. Challenging situations require discipline in managing healthy social and emotional routines. Engaging with service users includes finding out what music, TV, films, books, and poetry they like and using this information to design creative interactions and session planning.

SYMPTOM RELIEF

Social workers and other health care providers have opportunities to engage discussions about symptom relief, what the agency offers and ways to cope that avoid medication when possible. The use of evidence-based therapies and complementary approaches—such as recommendations for healthy meal planning, exercise, and meditation—should be discussed with the treatment planning team and the service users.

EVIDENCE-INFORMED EDUCATION

Introducing mindful moments at the beginning or end of a session can offer a hands-on experience for self-care and be an example to use in a family setting. Mindfulness and yoga have been examined as alternatives or complementary practice approaches (NIH, 2017) in research settings with positive outcomes for depression (Uebelacker et al., 2017), low back pain, (Whitehead & Gould, 2017), and other conditions. Meditation has also resulted in positive results when used in schools instead of detention (Gaines, 2017). Studies of the use of yoga have concluded with participants reporting relaxation and improved anger management (Brown, Eubanks, & Keating, 2017). We can provide service users with research fact sheets and homework for strategies based on multilayered health and mental health assessments.

Research pertaining to child development, nutrition and movement, and complementary health is useful, as are books, films, and websites regarding cultural support and history. Multicultural selections that target age groups might also be shared. Screening for health issues and cultural heritage interests can provide helpful guidance to draw on cultural strengths. In reviewing and determining service plans, social workers need to include discussion about cultural heritage, family history, family development, anger management, education, and vocational approaches. Sharing information about the potential and relevance of spirituality and the potential of local church, temple of other worship sites for support system development may also be included in research evidence sharing (Benson & Roehlkepartain, 2008).

GOAL SETTING

Goal setting includes a myriad of options that may expand the components of the clinical picture. Family history, cultural heritage, and strengths identification through narratives in addition to other areas of discovery linked to service needs are identified. Service user interests and concerns, assessment of specific diagnoses, and the presenting issues will drive the collaborative goal-setting discussion. Cultural processing will be helpful in engaging with different groups; group therapy with references to native themes will be more engaging (Warner, 2003). Significant others should also have an opportunity to review research-informed information and participate in goal setting and decision-making.

The location of the practitioner and the places that the service users have access to will also impact goals. Mezzo-level assessment and planning should evaluate the impact of social conditions, discrimination, and stigma for children and youth in school settings (Alvarez, Juang, & Liang, 2006). How children work to resolve stereotyping and stereotype threats could be an issue for discussion and planning (McKown & Strambler, 2009). Conversations with adoptive mothers about the cultural dynamics of their children and the relationships they are experiencing (Johnston et al., 2007) are important to include in developing plans. Collaboration with the other systems that service users are involved with may require developing and integrating multicultural resources and referrals across systems.

POSITIVE OUTCOMES

While some research shows evidence of effectiveness and positive outcome, the lack of research on culturally specific interventions continues to be a major limitation. There is a dearth of minority researchers or others interested in various aspects of culturally competent applications.

There is evidence that agencies can improve efficacy in treating specific problems. Addressing the goals of funders and local stakeholders, partnerships between organizations and university researchers are influencing changes in the organizational culture to support and sustain an evidence-based model of treatment. A case example of a university and agency collaboration (Letendre, 2016, p. 326) describes transforming a mutual aid (MA) model of group work into an evidence-based model that showed efficacy in preventing substance abuse with adolescents.

Collins and Sapiano (2016) report on the results of a diffusion project that involved disseminating evidence-based interventions (EBI) for HIV prevention over 15 years. These projects have identified interventions that are effective in meeting the higher-risk populations at lower-delivery costs:

- Community PROMISE (Peers Reaching Out and Modeling Intervention Strategies)
- Empowerment
- d-up Defend Yourself!
- Popular Opinion Leader
- CLEAR (Choosing Life: Empowerment! Action! Results!)
- Partnership for Health
- Healthy Relationships
- WILLOW (Women Involved in Life Learning from Other Women)
- CONNECT
- START
- Sister to Sister
- Many Men, Many Voices
- Personalized Cognitive Counseling
- VOICES/VOCES (Video Opportunities for Innovative Condom Education and Safer Sex)
- Safe in the City Interventions (Collins & Sapiano, 2016)

While limitations remain, overall these and other disease prevention and health promotion projects are demonstrating that users are able to obtain similar outcomes to the experimental research.

MINDSETS OF CONSUMERS/SERVICE USERS

The attitudes of many people, especially those for whom disparities are disproportionate and persistent, resist mental health services, special education, and other professional services. Their needs, comments, and feedback are frequently at odds with the existing structures but can be addressed at the micro level.

PEOPLE OF COLOR

Racial socialization messages have often posed assumptions of limitations, presented controversial stories or generalizations, or have blatantly ignored people. People resisting oppression have drawn on spiritual principles and associations based on mutual aid. Early mutual aid among those of African descent established forms of insurance and health care (National Humanities Center.org, 2017).

One the one hand, it is always best not to make any assumptions about how someone is, or what their beliefs, values or experiences may be. Analysis of theology and the realities of persons of color have come from experiences contrary to European traditions. The early connection of oppression to liberation is derived from the work of Gutiérrez (1973) in *A Theology of Liberation*. This work ties theology to the liberation of dispossessed people around the world. Subsequent work and questioning by other people of color and women raised the major focus on the care and treatment of the exploited. Liberation was presented as freeing oneself from internal and external encumbrances to more fully operationalize one's potential.

Breton (1993) pointed out that the historical reality of liberation is the social emancipation of the oppressed. She emphasized the core goal is liberation of the oppressed and commitment is needed about the concrete lives of people. She acknowledged this challenged the church and the professional and institutional powers, but she continued that people have been oppressed for centuries and their having a say has always been denied (p. 259). So having a say is a priority in taking control and shaping their destiny.

Cone (2010) also introduced ideas that contested Western views of the church and Christianity. He proposed that theology grows out of the experience of the community. He was criticized for ignoring women in this initial treatise, but other voices quickly took on this issue. The struggle—en la lucha—responds to the needs of the poor and oppressed. Isasi-Diaz (1993) presented the lens of theology from the Latinas' vantage point. Her treatment is based on humility—recognizing that "understanding is always limited." It encompasses steps of self-discovery, rituals, the birth process, and her experience with changing her place from Cuba to the United States. She brings attention to *kin-dom* (p. 166) rather than *kingdom* by noting the sexist connotation.

Among groups with intersectional identities, poorer mental health is often reported (Jackson, Williams, & VanderWeele, 2016). Situations among young people where bullying occurs in schools and in the street regarding different abilities and sexual identities urge further research (Chang et al., 2017) on coping strategies and ways organizations can intervene.

WOMEN

Further discourses from women's perspectives broaden the concerns. *Mujerista Theology* (Isasi-Diaz, 1996) aligns with womanist concepts and offers safe space for Hispanic women working in the struggle. *Womanist Theology: Black Women's Voices* (Williams, 1987) addresses the definition of women in the struggle that offers safe space for black women reluctant to connect with the limited perspective of feminism (Walker, 1974).

Asian feminist theology is called that because there is "no language or concept in common they can share when standing in multiracial, multilingual, multicultural, and multi-religious contexts" (Kim, 2014). *Inheriting Our Mother's Gardens* (Russell, 1988) and other work are noted in Kim's discussion that describes the influence of Christianity through stages and the strides to identify the feminine perspective.

According to Kim (2012) Kyung Chung describes the method of Asian feminist theology to be han-pu-ri. The process involves the "*kut* ceremony to release *Han*, the accumulated anger caused by experiences of injustice and oppression" (para 16). Listening to women's stories, analyzing the sources of oppression, and reflecting on these help reveal the woman's heart. She also raised concerns Asian, Asian American, and Pacific Island women have regarding their roles in the church.

DIFFERENTLY ABLED

Ways vary to engage with children and adults with different abilities. Families who care for children (Salkas, Magaña, Marques, & Mirza, 2015) often use spirituality to conceptualize and cope with disability. As persons with intellectual and developmental disabilities age, spiritual expression may change, and opportunities for rituals and practices may be considered by individuals and their families (Moody, 2005). The role of spirituality is a dimension of the macro context that may or may not be of interest to families and may be offered as an area for their consideration.

Individuals and their family members may not be aware of what kinds of treatment are available. In special education with children and adults and vocational training, there continues to be discrimination or unprofessional behaviors that should be changed. The Portland, Oregon, school district (Barnes, 2016) has been called out for ineffectual special education practices. Taking students out of class 5 to 15 minutes before the last bell rings to get on the bus has resulted in 15 to 30 hours of lost instruction time over a school year. The parent, Vanessa Smith, who filed the complaint was not aware of her son being taken out of class early.

The parent expecting to get appropriate care for a child beginning to display behaviors that need therapy and counseling discovers that school administrators were not abiding by the 1975 law (Individuals with Disabilities Act) that required school to provide specialized education to all eligible children (Rosenthal & Barned-Smith 2016).

Some schools are experimenting with programs that target specific occupational areas—retail, horticulture (Wong, 2016). There is criticism that these programs may pigeonhole students in to low paying areas but others support the work force plans. In India, there has been a movement toward community-based rehabilitation to assist greater independence and self-sustainability (Mehrotra, 2016). There is more awareness and identification as well. Agencies in the United States and other countries have examples of supportive services.

Issues of bullying special ed students pushed the 13 families in King county, Washington state, (Blanchard, 2004) schools to file an NAACP lawsuit to prevent cruel punishment such as handcuffing and pepper spray by security guards for minor infractions by children of African descent, such as talking back, having a cellphone, or disrupting class. The suit says a child has the right to punch back to protect themselves in self-defense if someone has started an assault (Rowe et al., 2014). Instead of zero tolerance the school officials have begun alternative practices such as using the safety officer for mediating situations and using in school suspensions rather than using month long out of school penalties. This is an improvement over past unfair treatment choices to write up white children with no loss of time but to remove children of color and create more disruption in instruction time.

CRITICAL THINKING QUESTION

Do your values support standing up for social issues?
Which social issues claim your attention?

Sharing information with families about local agency and school policies can help motivate family members to hold officials accountable, as well as help them educate their children of appropriate behavior. Use of instruction in innovative ways to encourage skill development can help build self-esteem, confidence, and motivation. There are several areas for macro critical thinking and advocacy for service delivery with any policy area you select.

THE DEAF COMMUNITY

Working with spirituality within the Deaf community is especially limited (Barclay, Rider, & Dombo, 2012). The literature on spirituality among people with hearing differences presents major themes at the macro, family, and micro levels. At the macro level, lack of cultural sensitivity in many world religions is clear. There is lack of access or outreach to serving or communicating with deaf and hard-of-hearing members (Delich, 2014). At the family level, there may be issues of maternal grief and stress and internal family and sibling relationships that could be connected to spiritual messages and opportunities for support. At the micro level, loneliness, grief, identity purpose, and other concerns could be impacted by spiritual variables in the social work practice. Much of the literature is presented by hearing people, so further research would benefit from the participation of Deaf community members. McLaughlin, Brown, and Young (2004) used their agency's efforts to consult with the Deaf community as an example to assess the issues and challenges of social control and empowerment.

There is interest in making accommodations for Deaf persons via visual communication and interpreters; some churches and mosques already offer sign language.

Operating with the mindset of strengths must appreciate learning, teaching, and service that stems from where people come from and what they want to talk and read about. Stein (2012) acknowledges that to make classrooms more democratic spaces "the forms of representation through which students make their meanings" must be accepted, appreciated, and implemented.

ADDRESSING INSECURITIES

Addressing the insecurity that doing something differently brings—conceptualizing from the parallel perspectives of strengths and the ongoing crisis of fear—challenges underachievement. Burrell (2010) notes brainwashed people have been led to believe in their limitations. A *in't no making it* (MacLeod, 2009) summarizes feelings of many young men who live in an ethnically diverse neighborhood in Britain that keep them in their place. For many, there have been incidents that create and sustain insecurity. Members of the working class encounter significant obstacles to achieving and progressing economically because of institutionally installed barriers and their limited expectations. The internalization of prejudices impacts people across groups. Alperin (2016) adds Jewish self-hatred to the range of issues that need dialogues, conversations, reactions, and supports.

DeGrury (2003) supports Burrell's interpretations of brainwashing. She notes, "When African Americans accept the depreciating accounts and images portrayed by the media, literature, music and the arts as a true mirror of themselves, that allows socialization by a racist society" (p. 175).

Professionals are working to understand how obstacles have influenced how they see members of working-class communities; their roles in maintaining the status quo; and how their changing steps will be required to assist in community capacity building. Sharing DeGruy's (2003) chapter on "Healing" is a good place to begin.

On the other hand, there are strengths that come from free thinking and rely on freeing oneself, and perhaps family, from the demeaning propaganda. Assisting people, professionals, and allies to think freely and critically to move beyond the negative messages and experience is part of the process. Listeners and supporters know stories of survival that help build confidence, motivation, and resilience.

ROLE OF CRITICAL THINKING

Critical thinking in social work continues to be evaluated and definitions repurposed (Mathias, 2015). Assessing the broad context, the traditional context, and gaps in effectiveness and planning are some of the goals of critical thinking in social work education. Developing reading lists and databases for ourselves enhances our personal understanding of others and helps raise questions that we may continue to contemplate; identifying reading for service users can likewise enhance their personal evaluation and offer examples of community strengths from which they may also benefit. Selections such as *The Last Tortilla and Other Stories* (Tronsco, 1999); *The Sympathizer* (Viet Thanh Nguyen, 2015) or *The Other Side of Paradise* (Chinn, 2010) for consumers of any culture simply offer opportunities to become immersed in a story they may have not known about before. Music selections that play on beats (O'Neal, 2013) offer suggestions to help folks relax. Doesn't all music do that? Levitin (2007) suggests that we can use more music in *This Is Your Brain on Music*. There are culturally specific websites, videos, and fashion sites that foster self-esteem and could be shared in case management sessions Group work with young people could include exercises to make music CDs to share as creative efforts to deal with emotional issues.

CRITICAL SELF-EXAMINATION

The broad landscape of the macro environment requires critical self-examination, thinking, and reflection. There are disagreements on how to proceed with practical reasoning in social work (Mathias, 2015). Barnard notes the self in social work involves awareness as an individual and as one involved in therapeutic work that engages a separate professional self.

Examining the citizenship role, civic beliefs, and the personal cultural experiences and status in community development are important categories to evaluate. Establishing a view of one's personal connections to the work of helping others is one step. Reflecting on the answers to these questions is the next step. Reconciling concerns and testing one's ability to apply the ethical standards in client interactions requires careful thought and behavior.

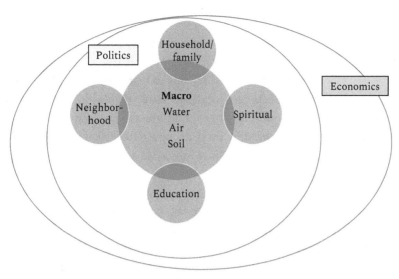

FIGURE 11.2   Macro Systems in the Natural and Social Environment

Block (2008) recommends that we move away from the "existing view of community as a problem to be solved" (p. 32). He refers to a breakdown in the capacity to create a safe space and promotes strategies to affirm a context of gifts, generosity, and accountability. Figure 11.2 emphasizes the natural environment.

MULTIDISCIPLINARY AND INTERPROFESSIONAL RELATIONSHIPS

One of the most significant realms of social work leadership potential is in helping other disciplines consider the person-in-the-environment perspective that social work applies. Caldwell's (2012) assessment brings the observation that legal education omits perspectives that would improve their analysis of the complexities of poverty and inequality that affect client's lives. Partnering with criminal justice and education, especially, to modify the traditional frames that continue to use minimalist views rather than the broader strengths views of people's lives may offer opportunities to share our framework for more effective strategies.

Examining the macro environment exposes students to the relevance of advocates for service users in multiple locations. The landscape is broader than teaming with educators, public health workers, substance use counselors, and hospital and medical care personnel. As social work curricula integrates knowledge of the natural resources of communities, the impact of air, soil, water, and climate change—along with human behavior—brings awareness and interest in working on teams with urban and rural city planners and economists. These potential relationships suggest working to direct policies toward values to promote sustainability across groups and ages.

Community linkages involve initiating and establishing relationships with schools, community centers, libraries, and churches. These connections will place social workers as service representatives and facilitators in planning and service delivery in nonthreatening and nonstigmatized social settings.

COLLABORATION WITH OTHER PROFESSIONALS

Connecting with other helping professionals in community settings, academic departments, and community locations may offer interdisciplinary teams that could be more accountable. It requires moving beyond working with old friends to learning how to listen to and respect different team members. The reluctance to call out water regulators by environmental regulators is an example of how accountability has sometimes not worked in the past. People who work with one another may resist holding them accountable for keeping the truth of environmental conditions away from the public. The Flint crisis and a situation in Philadelphia are examples (Ganim, 2016).

Kiehl (2016) suggests that facing climate change taps into feelings of anxiety regarding disturbing news. Anticipated losses bring along fear and associated psychological dynamics among populations and the authorities in charge. Contemplating change can bring on challenges to job security and personal comfort in addressing agency demands and expectations. Considering innovative team building will also present the possibilities of interorganizational relationships and issues of defining territory. We should welcome opportunities to participate in developing creative learning communities.

RESOURCES

Resources may include referral to specific service providers, community organizations, and self-help and support groups. Research regarding local groups will be helpful to pass along to services users based on their interests and needs. Wang and Lau (2015) report on the cultural differences of social support. Their study demonstrates benefits of mutual and nonmutual connections among East Asian Americans and European Americans. Perceptions of the role of support in families of adult children of alcoholics vary and indicate all don't struggle with problems as a parent did (Hall, 2010), suggesting that social supports do assist in their stability.

To address the needs of African American men who resist using the health care system, there have been recommendations for the provision of online social support for early stages of psychological distress (Watkins & Jefferson, 2013). A community collaborative intervention for HIV prevention among African American men who have sex with men and women (Operario, Smith, Arnold, & Kegeles, 2010) and who do not identify with the same-sex community has demonstrated successful social supports through implementing a four-session outreach facilitated by African American men.

Community-based prevention builds on resilience research and practice. Emphasizing protective factors offers optimism and several opportunities for active learning, cooperation, and inclusive activities (Benard, 2007). Including service users who go through training and can identify as experts (Toikko, 2016) adds a significant level of quality to community services. Organizations that identify and refer to apprenticeships (Bulanda, 2015) can support potential staff from the service user population, demonstrate responsible leadership, and also accommodate need for social mobility.

LINKING WITH HEALTH PROFESSIONALS: PHYSICIANS

Physician awareness of cultural competence has been changing, albeit at a glacial pace—although now we know glacial timing has sped up due to climate changes. Involving patient perspectives in research in the health system has revealed variations in how focus group members distinguish feeling about research and the level of trust they may feel regarding the trust of their physicians (Kelley et al., 2015). An emerging view, according this team, is that some are admitting that medical care is not always evidence based (p. 4). Patient views of approaches to risk assessment, use of stored samples, oversight, and informed consent and medical practices were studied. Patients value the patient–physician relationship and shared decision-making. Building a learning health system as an infrastructure is deemed important for research within usual care.

LINKING WITH PUBLIC HEALTH

While social workers have often assisted similar populations in delivering services, the recent increase in MSW/MPH programs suggest the emergent concern for gaining skills to address the system crises that exists (Ruth, Marshall, Velasquéz, Bachman, 2015). Public health professionals have worked with social workers in many capacities over the years.

LINKING WITH CRIMINAL JUSTICE

Efforts to reduce the effects of mass incarceration have occurred in the past few years (Alexander, 2012). Recent announcements to eliminate private prisons, efforts to reform sentencing for nonviolent offenses, and culturally competent approaches to working with young men of color who are more often targets for detention are gaining attention based on research that suggests these methods to be effective. Several reports indicate police departments are hiring social workers to create teams that may offer improved methods for improved community relationships.

LINKING WITH EDUCATION

School social workers are clearly identified as helpers in school settings. There are many ways social workers could develop opportunities to work with school personnel, students, and families and with the community in providing direct practice and community-based prevention (Fram et al., 2014).

Social workers also provide assistance to teachers and families with children with mental and learning challenges to integrate into mainstream schools (Romilă & Roman, 2015). Transitions for young children require specific services for the point of entry and as foundation for continuing supports and interventions (Rosenkoetter, Hains, & Dogaru, 2007). Teachers, social workers, and other workers are helpful in the transition of immigrant children (Matthews & Mahoney, 2005).

Social work and education students would benefit from graduate course opportunities to participate in team based learning seminars to prepare them for post graduate work settings. Using print or video cases of children or adolescents in a school setting for analysis from the social work and education perspectives would offer opportunities for interdisciplinary discussion and co-creation of service planning. From sharing multicultural resources for curriculum development to school-based-social and emotional learning exercises, there can be significant interventions for children and youth to help improve academic performance and self-care.

MOVING THE WORK INTO THE COMMUNITY: COMMUNITY-BASED PREVENTION

In recognizing the significance of the macro environment and building on the strengths and assets of communities, recognizing the need to move from our traditional micro work to inform communities of evidence-based research enhances the ability of the community to expand the participants and ameliorate outcomes for population health. Bornstein (2016) discusses the economic inequality of the Highlands, a town in Washington state hit hard by job losses in the timber and manufacturing industries. As a result of the economic downturn, the town plummeted into family breakdown and drug use; disease and crime surged. The good news is that from 1994 to 2012 community networks were organized to cultivate leadership and partnerships. They used evidence to make decisions and educated themselves about adverse childhood experiences, risks for social and health problems, academic obstacles, abuse, and violence. Some communities experienced challenges and setbacks, but in 12 communities, there have been significant outcomes and reductions in dropouts, suicide, and arrests.

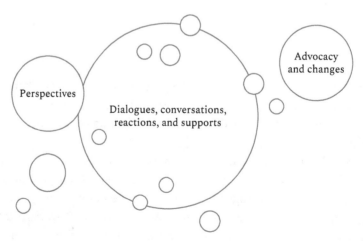

FIGURE 11.3   From Oppression to Innovation

This case clearly illustrates the potential of community-based prevention. Operating from a proactive stance was valuable for the community in ways that informed individuals and families of what steps help protect themselves and their children. "Moving upstream" (Cohen, Chávez, & Chehimi, 2007, p. 4) is the concept of taking action before a problem arises rather than waiting for problems to become chronic and more expensive to treat. Primary prevention requires including the community in developing an understanding of cultural strengths and research evidence of what helps to prevent health and social problems and dilemmas.

TAPPING INTO COMMUNITY STRENGTHS

Moving from that micro place encourages stepping out to make new friends and expand relationships. Recent research regarding prevention and participation research, from this perspective, indicates the need for decolonized approaches, changed focus, and integration of opinion and procedures that center on understanding theory from participants' standpoints (Monchalin et al., 2016). Developing practitioner skills to connect with resistant service users is of particular concern. Attachment is gained through engagement and navigating interpersonal process to reach a level of trust that will allow further growth (Shemmings, Shemmings, & Cook, 2012). The experiences of people in coming of age around the world (Adiele & Frosch, 2007) and Alexie's character in the *The Absolute True Diary of a Part-Time Indian* (2007) and so many others illustrate context and strategies people have used to navigate their experiences. Voices call for supporting educational processes through broadened worldviews and respect for knowledge, language, traditions, and practices that come from African, Asian, Latino, and Native homes and communities. Social work education and practice are in a key position to disseminate information and strategies for innovative work with individuals, families, organizations and community prevention (Hawkins, Shapiro, & Fagan, 2010).

CASE SCENARIO GROUP DISCUSSION

Refer to the Service User Planning Worksheet

You have just landed a job as a community field organizer for the regional community development association in a southeastern area of the United States. During the first week, five community people come to the office concerned about a rumor they heard about their water. They also wanted information about an apprentice program they want to get into; a street the children have to cross that needs a street light; and the homeless teens that are sleeping under the bridge.

Considering the triple-perspective planning approach, draft an outline of what kind of information you need to locate to share with these residents about their concerns.

Macro: Identify organizations with jurisdiction of the areas, current or pending legislation related to their concerns, numbers of complaints, services provided related to these areas, and a GIS map with relevant business identifiers.

Mezzo: Coordinate a community meeting to share information; encourage residents to join small focus groups for discussions. Check local data on Kids Count, Coalition on Human Needs, and Census.gov. websites. Encourage joining at least one local organization. Locate a buddy or peer mediator from the school to accompany you to the meeting.

Micro: Collaborate with schools and mental health agencies regarding other services teens may be using or in need of. Provide information about the EBP available in the community or consider developing a community intervention where you would present information that responds to their concerns.

TABLE 11.1   Service User Planning Worksheet

ISSUES	DISCUSSION	SUGGESTIONS/ PRIORITIES, TIME FRAMES
PRESENTING CONCERNS	**Micro**—Short-term/ symptom relief	
	Nutrition	
	Movement/Exercise	
		Interests, activities
SCREENING	Developmental/age appropriate resources	
	Alcohol or Substance use? SBIRT (Screening, Brief Intervention & Referral Treatment)	
FINANCES -FCAB		Acknowledging injuries related to unemployment, underemployment include: feelings of low self-esteem, consideration of harming oneself or others, physical reactions, destructive choices
RELATIONSHIPS - POTENTIAL		
INTEREST		School clubs, community recreation,
INVENTORY	**Mezzo**—Extra curricular	Neighborhood tutoring, church, synagogue, temple events
	Career interest inventory	
	School Performance—Grades	Meetings with teachers

ISSUES	DISCUSSION	SUGGESTIONS/ PRIORITIES, TIME FRAMES
	Macro—community organizations	Local government meetings, legislation related to services needs Letter writing—thanks and concerns
READING	Books about persons experiencing similar situations	
VIDEOS		
WEBSITES		

CHAPTER SUMMARY

Students are encouraged to view the broad landscape of environment and people within locations. Understanding the macro parameters of local, state, federal, and international domains offers a basis for community organizing to include citizen roles, responsibility, and participation in asserting accountability from officials to offer culturally affirming transactions in institutional settings. Students can identify individual and family profiles within community profiles and group concerns about service access and respect of cultural norms and concerns. Social workers evaluate their views of macro and micro dynamics. They must separate their personal views from the professional territory to allow and support service users' freedom of religion and self-determination. Respect of cultural variations, strengths, and religions is fundamental.

As the macro landscape is evaluated, there should be ways to create new partnerships that will foster creative application of social work skills for innovative endeavors. Micro work happens within a macro context. The mezzo level connects the two.

EPAS AND CODE OF ETHICS

CSWE EDUCATIONAL POLICY & ACCREDITATION STANDARDS

Competency 4: Engage in Practice-informed Research and Research-informed Practice
- 4a) use practice experience and theory to inform scientific inquiry and research;
- 4b) apply critical thinking to engage in analysis of quantitative and qualitative research methods and research findings; and
- 4c) use and translate research evidence to inform and improve practice, policy, and service delivery

Competency 8: Intervene with Individuals, Families, Groups, Organizations, and Communities
- 8a) critically choose and implement interventions to achieve practice goals and enhance capacities of clients and constituencies;

- 8b) apply knowledge of human behavior and the social environment, person-in-environment, and other multidisciplinary theoretical frameworks in interventions with clients and constituencies;
- 8c) use inter-professional collaboration as appropriate to achieve beneficial practice outcomes;
- 8d) negotiate, mediate, and advocate with and on behalf of diverse clients and constituencies; and
- 8e) facilitate effective transitions and endings that advance mutually agreed-on goals. (EPAS, 2015)

NASW CODE OF ETHICS

Value: Service

Ethical Principle: Social workers' primary goal is to help people in need and to address social problems. (NASW, n.d.)

DISCUSSION QUESTIONS

1. Select an immigrant and the country he or she is migrating from. Locate information about the background demographics of the home country. Select a United States location that has accepted the immigration application. Using the most recent census reports, describe possible similarities and differences of the two communities. Where would the immigrant possibly meet a social worker? What concerns would need to be addressed? Refer to the Table 11.1 Service User Planning Worksheet for ideas.
2. What are the waves of immigration? Select two of them. Compare the circumstances involved and discuss the characteristics of the immigrants: Who? How many? What kind of costs were involved? What were the jobs and housing opportunities for them?
3. Create an opportunity with a class in another academic department, education, counseling, public health, to have students from each meet to discuss a video case that reflects cultural dynamics. The video may be up to 20 minutes. Students should be in interdisciplinary groups. Design questions to be discussed in each group. Share the discussion issues, perspectives and questions raised through this interdisciplinary analysis of the same case.

EXERCISES

1. Community exercises:
   - Map the demographics of the area in which you live.
   - Where are the grassroots activities occurring?

2. Which advocacy groups address needs in your community?

3. Create a reading list (at least five references) from the Multicultural Resources Database that would be helpful to an individual, a family, or a group about their community assets, strengths, and role models for achieving positive outcomes.

4. Create a short database of videos and websites from multicultural people that promote self-esteem. Share them with the class when they are complete.

MULTICULTURAL RESOURCES

Adiele, F., & Frosch, M. (Eds.). (2007). *Coming of age around the world*: A multicultural anthology. New York, NY: New Press.

Alexie, S. (2007). *The Absolutely True Diary of a Part-Time Indian*. Boston, MA: Little, Brown.

India.Arie (2002). *Voyage to India* [CD]. "Talk to Her," "Slow Down," and "Healing."

Burrell, T. (2010). *Brainwashed: Challenging the myth of black inferiority*. New York, NY: Smiley Books.

Chinn, S. (2010). *The other side of paradise*. New York, NY: Scribner.

DeGrury, J. (2005). *Post traumatic slave syndrome: America's enduring legacy of enduring injury and healing*. Portland, OR: Joy DeGrury Publications.

Franco, Sr., J., Sr. (8.7.142014, Aug. 7). Ruben Salazar and the martyrs of the Chicano Moratorium [Blog post]. Retrieved from. http://www.latinopov.com/blog/? p=10622http://www.latinopov.com/blog/? p=10622

Isasi-Diaz, A. M. (1993) *Mujerista theology:. A theology for the twenty-first century*. by Ada María Isasi- Díaz *Journal of the American Academy of Religion*, Vol. 66(, No. 4) (Winter, 1998), pp. 953–955.

Jackson, M. (2010). They don't think about us [Video file]. Retrieved from https://www.youtube.com/watch? v=QNJL-6nfu__Qhttps://www.youtube.com/watch? v=QNJL6nfu__Q

Kim, H. H. (2017) *Asian feminist theology*. Drew University. Retrieved from https://www.drew.edu/theological/2012/03/30/asian-feminist-theology/https://www.drew.edu/theological/2012/03/30/asian-feminist-theology/ Retrieved 8.25.2017.

Nhà văn Phan Hồn Nhiê. (2012). *The last tortilla and other stories*. Vietnam: ChiBooks.

O'Neal, E. S. S. (2013). Indigoism music beats [Video file]. Retrieved from http://pitchfork.com/tv/6-selector/732-the-underachievers-break-down-indigoism-beast-coast/? utm_campaign=search&utm_medium=site&utm_source=search-achttp://pitchfork.com/tv/6-selector/732-the-underachievers-break-down-indigoism-beast-coast/? utm_campaign=search&utm_medium=site&utm_source=-search-ac

Russell, L. (1988). *Inheriting our mothers' gardens: Feminist theology in Third World perspective*. Louisville, KY: Westminster John Knox Press.;

Staples, M. (2014). Newport folk festival. Retrieved from http://www.npr.org/2014/07/21/333725707/mavis-staples-live-in-concert-newport-folk-2014? utm_source=npr_newsletter&utm_medium=email&utm_content=20140804&utm_campaign=MUSic&utm_termhttp://www.npr.org/2014/07/21/333725707/mavis-staples-live-in-concert-newport-folk-2014? utm_source=npr_newsletter&utm_medium=email&utm_content=20140804&utm_campaign=MUSic&utm_term=

TallBear, K., (2013). Native American DNA: Belonging and the false promise of genetic science. Minneapolis: University of Minnesota. Retrieved from http://www.kimtallbear.com/research.html. Retrieved 9.23.2016 http://www.kimtallbear.com/research.html.

Vargas, Jose Antonio,J. A. (2014). *Documented* [Documentary]. CNN. documentary, regarding immigration.

Walker, A. (1974). In Search of Our Mothers' Gardens: The Creativity of Black Women in the South (1974). Retrieved from http://www.msmagazine.com/spring2002/walker.asp

Welland, Sasha Su–LingS. S. L. (2007). *A thousand miles of dreams: The journeys of two Chinese sisters*. Lanham, MD: Rowman & Littlefield.

Wilkerson, I. (2010). *The warmth of other suns: The epic story of American's great migration.* New York, NY: Vintage.

Williams, D. S. (1987). Womanist theology: Black women's voices. Retrieved from http://www.religion-online.org/article/womanist-theology-black-womens-voices/http://www.religion-online.org/article/womanist-theology-black-womens-voices/ https://bycommonconsent.com/2013/03/08/womanist-theology-black-womens-voices/

FURTHER READING

Bryant, J. (2014). Immigration to the US: Yale–New Haven Teachers Institute: Contents of 1999 Volume III. Available at http://www.yale.edu/ynhti/curriculum/units/1999/3/99.03.01.x.html

Daniels, R. (2002). *Coming to America: A history of immigration and ethnicity in American life.* New York, NY: Harper.

Suarez, R. (2013). *Latino Americans: The 500-year legacy that shaped a nation.* New York, NY: Celebra.

Waggoner, L. (2013). Immigration reform 2013: 3 waves of immigration that changed American policy. Available at http://mic.com/articles/44183/immigration-reform-2013-3-waves-of-immigration-that-changed-america

Facilitating Inclusion

Developing Humility and Agility for Partnerships / Mezzo

Chapter 12 presents a range of cultural dynamics to be considered with humility by professionals working in government and community organizations. Ideas for interorganizational, interprofessional, and community collaboration are needed to enhance mezzo-level resources and opportunities for support. Students will work from multilayered paradigms to plan partnerships to deliver efficient and effective interventions for direct practice, prevention, early screening, and support system development. Assessment of individual, family, group, and community issues at the micro level leads to recognizing how network participation might assist the availability of resources and expansion of interactional skills. Expanded networks can contribute to building resilience and overcoming social system obstacles. It is critical to move to more dialogues about service delivery systems based on cultural competence, cultural humility, and critical thinking. These skills are useful in facilitating conversations within and between organizations in the process of partnering to establish a more encouraging environment for child and family development and civic participation. Enhancing our skills to facilitate difficult conversations can promote social work leadership in interprofessional, interorganizational, and community development.

LEARNING OBJECTIVES

- Facilitating inclusive collaborations and interventions requires a triple perspective that embraces macro, mezzo, and micro dimensions.
- Locating or establishing relevant culturally affirming associations involves subsystems within institutional entities.
- Recognizing the strengths of all people is needed, especially when the persons seeking help may be more vulnerable than strong.
- Seek knowledge of invisible systems and resources; engaging interpersonally with representatives of various disciplines and types of organizations and link them to traditional institutional services.

Benchmark: Students will contemplate humility, flexibility, and skills in reaching out to establish relationships and partnerships.

Nancy has been working with persons addicted to substances. In a staff meeting, someone used a colloquial term to refer to a substance user. She spoke up and asked the group to consider using better language about the people they work with. The group agreed to use *person in recovery* as the reference point. Have you observed situations where the use of language has been insensitive and no one spoke up about it? What skills or resources did Nancy have that let her assert her voice?

HUMILITY AND AGILITY

Engaging with existing and potential service users involves using foundation and advanced social work skills along with broadened cultural knowledge and resources. Evaluating services builds on technical skills to develop ways to communicate with service users (Toikko, 2016). Their responses to services are needed for practitioners and researchers to rate intervention success, devise methodologies, modify language and intervention steps that result in positive outcomes.

Cultural humility and agility evolve as students and practitioners become increasingly aware of themselves and others, the nature of community strengths, the concepts of triple perspectives, and population health. These offer the range of contexts social workers and other helping professionals communicate and work with. Self-assessment as a helping professional raises questions about one's humility, or existing awareness of more than one's own ego or group. Building on this introspection will guide the desire to become more informed and flexible in appreciating others and promoting opportunities that encourage wellness. The day-to-day survivors, self-help group participants, peer leaders, mentors, and advocates are examples of people making it through daily challenges. There are many celebrated people who demonstrate tenacity who are motivators and offer visuals for clients who may need encouragement.

CULTURAL HUMILITY

> "Humility is nothing else but knowledge and awareness of oneself as one really is." —The Cloud of Unknowing

Humility enables recognizing the ordinary in humanity through respectful engagement and continual self-reflection. In helping people feel secure in who they are and structure how they try to work with their talents, we draw on ways to use their data to move the process along. Fisher-Bourne and colleagues (2015) propose a move from the focus on cultural competence—knowing about others, to focus on practitioner accountability. Using this frame, humility pushes the practitioner to continually assess biases (Charles, Holley, & Kondrat, 2017) and confront the power differentials of the institutional status quo.

CULTURAL AGILITY

Cultural agility is connected to flexibility in operating with individuals and families, in organizations, and within the broader community. Working on the mezzo level involves recruiting and hiring diverse staff and communicating in ways to enhance organizational performance and address accountability. Humility and agility support personal professional behaviors and allow organizational adaptation to uphold rights to self-determination of service users. These qualities also produce interactions that facilitate mutual goal setting, decision-making, and partnership developments.

Randall (2012) notes that cultural agility is a skill set to promote and develop business growth and offers exercises that can be helpful. She includes being able to appropriately respond to different behaviors and worldviews to build strong working relationships. The skills include awareness of self and the environment, adapting to ambiguities, being authentic, and acquiring knowledge of different cultures.

According to the Financial Times, cultural agility is the competitive edge (Financial Times. com, n.d.; Abrams, 2013) concurs and describes the inclusive workplace—one that contributes returns to shareholders and to society—is destined for greater success. This inclusive space includes women, African Americans, Latinos/U.S. Hispanics, Asian Americans and Pacific Islanders, LGBTQQI, and seniors. He calls diversity and inclusion a business strategy.

Turner (2000) discusses the diverse landscape of the United States, where traditional researchers used white, middle-class persons as the basis for gauging and delivering services. Despite the argument against culturally sensitive approaches because of lack of empirical evidence for them, it is clear that many members of minority groups are not well served by the typical service structures. The evidence has grown that demonstrates better outcomes when approaches that respect cultural strengths and integrate cultural resource knowledge are employed (Chao, 1992).

The literature on cultural agility in the helping professions is sparse. We are familiar with cultural competence and work intently on this. Social workers do have the deep skills as described by Randall. What we may not be well acquainted with is the business culture. In pursuing ways to work within our organizations to encourage innovation and to seek protocols to engage with other organizations in our environment, enhancing our business savviness has become more important. Integrating our knowledge base and fiscal analysis should promote organizational performance and multilayered benefits.

FACILITATING INCLUSION ON THE MEZZO LEVEL

Facilitating inclusion is a concept for social work professionals to frame assessment and intervention planning to address human rights, social and economic justice, and individual and family service needs. It speaks to reaching out and engaging on multiple levels to motivate collective participation to improve our living environments. The actions that facilitate inclusion begin with direct service on the micro level. Mezzo-level work involves collaborating with organizations that engage with community residents for social interactions and skill development opportunities. The mezzo level is the village that it takes to raise us all!

Activities on this level may operate collaterally with macro efforts, addressing agency accountability, advocacy legislation support, and policy development; with the micro level, they include intervention specializations. This ongoing process of structure and implementation builds on cultural and individual strengths using social work methods for community organizing, coalition building, group work, and clinical skills. Together, we are all working to promote resilience and capacity building.

Starting with recognition of the larger dimensions within which we are raised sets up appreciation of the context we ultimately focus on in individual and family work. Using a picture of the geography from which a Vietnamese family has migrated to flee political persecution (Pham, 2007) and examples of their literature that describe a related scenario can be especially helpful in understanding family dynamics. Diverse experiences of immigration, adoption (Johnston, Swim, Saltsman, Deater-Deckard, & Petrill, 2007; Mohanty, 2013; Rienzi, 2009), and other family transactions bring various sources of information and cultural nuances. Respecting this view, and listening to the service user, helps plan for identifying cultural resources at the mezzo level. Community organizations, spiritual groups, or other cultural-related resources could add support for a family experiencing trauma in the migration experience.

Similarly, the migration of millions of African Americans (Wilkerson, 2010) from the outrageous Jim Crow environment of the South to the North in search of jobs presents a framework somewhat different from ones we may more likely conceive if we begin only with the individual. Beginning with a rural context and moving to an urban one may also establish an alternative view of how the broader community context helps shape the contemporary local environments in which we work and live.

MINDSET: CULTURAL HUMILITY

Cultural humility develops from a mindset that is open to new ideas, multiple perspectives, and awareness that one's work in the helping field requires critical thinking about self as well as others. This awareness grows from taking time to investigate the work of members of cultural groups and using mainstream research regarding physical, social, and emotional health issues. The multiple views of sources of evidence are relevant in the transactions of service users and agency personnel. Age group content and research are also especially salient in listening and collaborating for improvements and effectiveness.

FLEXIBILITY

Engaging with others involves flexibility to be respectful across variable languages, behaviors, religions, dress, music, art, and ways of knowing. Emdin (2016) points out that to assist students in improving academic performance, teachers must be able to respect and appreciate the "neoindigenous" ways some children interact and add those to their teaching tools rather than dismissing them.

Integrated health care also proclaims the need for an approach that interweaves physical and behavioral conditions and calls for various care models and financial procedures to operate differently. The researchers explain that "truly integrated healthcare involves a radical shift in conceptualizing care and challenges providers to function in ways that often contrast sharply with how they were trained to work" (Held, Mallory, & Cummings, 2017, p. 435).

People's strengths are not necessarily tied to what the experts think they know. The Outline for Cultural Formulation (OCF; Fernández et al., 2013) for gathering cultural information emphasizes taking information from clients. The subsequent revision attempts to address more specific cultural details, such as religious affiliation, sexual orientation, their interpretation of the illness, and their observations of racism and discrimination on the clinician–patient relationship.

Work on the mezzo level incorporates understanding the cultural dynamics recognized at the micro level and seeking conversations and deal making with organizations.

DEVELOPING CONNECTIONS: MATTERS OF ENGAGEMENT WITH ORGANIZATIONS

The existing institution structure is often called *the silo system*. Organizations are designed to do one thing, often for only one group of people. As we examine what is needed to be competent with service users, the way management operates becomes a key focus of attention.

Thinking about this from a systems view encourages the need to invite representatives of outside agencies to work with staff members. Becoming aware of the organizational cultures and the staff leaders also suggests the need to operate collaboratively in more than one way. Organizational connections of this type are built on the acknowledgement of services to a particular health population. Working through the development requires a two-pronged approach: a clear focus on the human relationships and the business operation.

RECOGNIZING THE MEZZO COMPONENTS: STANDARD OPERATING PROCEDURES

Preparing to work with professionals, staff representatives, and consumers of organizations other than the one of current employment requires doing some homework. Organizational culture is linked to its status as a profit or nonprofit entity. Its mission and values are tied to the revenue base. Revenues received through taxation and legislative mandates have bureaucratic standards and regulations for internal operations and for affiliating with other organizations.

Independent organizations may be guided by social entrepreneurs, boards of directors, or advisory boards. Talking to identified agency representatives will help guide the process of reaching out for collaborative opportunities. Information about an agency's history can offer an understanding of the agency's service types, community representation, and traditional or innovative interests.

Questions the partnership seeker might ask include the following:
- Are there staff who handle community relations?
- What kinds of community events have been offered?
- Has the agency worked with other agencies before? How? Why? When?
- Have any community surveys been conducted?
- Has a GIS map been prepared?
- Is there a consumer advisory board? Has there been one?
- Are different age groups represented?
- Is the organization a member of any local or national coalitions?
- Whom should you talk to?

Organizational mission statements and local, state, and national strategic plans should be useful in planning how to engage for collaboration. A view of an interorganizational operation conducted in an emergency department illuminates micro, mezzo, and macro social work (Moore, Cristofalo, Dotolo, Torres, et al., 2017). This qualitative content analysis of services provided to trauma patients in an urban trauma center identified macro-contextual influences, including socioeconomic barriers to health; mezzo-level forces, including limited resources, lack of health care coordination, and the medical model pressures to discharge; and micro-level complexity of worker–patient stressors such as strain and lack of closure as a realistic view of inter- and intrapressures and constraints.

Power forces and bottom line factors will influence partnerships, especially regarding ways the financing and cost effectiveness will transpire. Research is needed to clarify interprofessional and interorganizational service innovations and outcomes.

ACCOUNTABILITY

The logic of the democratic process that addresses inequality as well as the interest in improved services outcomes pushes the idea of social and economic development to improve the public service-delivery system (Frączkiewicz-Wronka, 2013). From a theoretical basis of resource management, social ecological parameters, and network theory, the need for efficiency and citizen participation has led to interest in interorganizational collaborations. Social services are within the scope of local government and public management. In this context, the provision is a result of social policy and implies stimulating interorganizational linkages.

There are examples of collaborations that engage public and private sector spheres that show how these diverse hybrid forms operate (Quélin, Kivleniece, & Lazzarini, 2017).

Boyd (2016) raises the need for accountability in the social science discipline. Responding to Prewitt's question (*Can social science matter?*), Boyd addresses transparency and accountability. He says, "If we want social science to matter, we need to be more thoughtful about the questions we ask. What is more? How respectful are we in asking? And what are we giving" (Boyd, 2016, para 18).

There are several discipline areas that are studied with respect to relationships with helping professionals. Drawing on identity within one's family and place, city environments (Fullilove, 2013, Gadanho, 2014; Sutton & Kemp, 2011), and our awareness of working-class issues, service user spiritual concerns, and business strategists offers emergent areas for consideration.

MEZZO ISSUE—COORDINATING SYSTEMS OF CARE

The mezzo level involves the coordination of services across systems of care and integration of community resources. Problems that have become more visible as outcomes are analyzed and feedback considered include the following:

- Traditional institutions resist making changes promoted by service users and advocates for inclusion.
- Lack of systems coordination occurs because different professional groups have views they don't want to change and have difficulty engaging with and discussing changes with one another.
- Helping professionals are often unaware of community resources that would benefit service users in addition to formal services.
- Self-help resources are frequently dismissed, ignored, looked down on, or are not available.

These observations are simply part of the mix in the complexity of service provision, delivery, and evaluation. There are also observations that see each of those arenas differently:

- Many traditional institutions are telling staff to adopt innovative strategies.
- Some groups are taking steps or are engaged in projects that are interdisciplinary, intraorganizational, multicultural, and technologically savvy.
- Collaborations are occurring among community organizations, faith-based groups, self-help groups and service users.

As we examine the examples, we expect to reflect on the connections to our experiences and consider how we may shape the ideas through critical thinking about potential applications.

COORDINATION INCLUDES FORMAL AND INFORMAL ORGANIZATIONS

Coordination is the essential idea that emerges in analyzing ways to address disparities and offer more effective care among groups of different professionals. Service users face organizations resistant to changing their procedures to accommodate multicultural and interdisciplinary approaches, and social workers are well aware of the tensions the systems they work in present. They frequently face the combined stress of working in resistant traditional bureaucracies and with stressed-out community citizens.

Sitshange (2012) points out that social workers have often reached out to collaborate with others because the needs of their clients push them to initiate resource pooling and management within structures that are not meeting their needs. These actions occur along a continuum of interactions where network is the simple form and collaboration is more intense.

A team presenting at the International Conference on Integrated Care in Barcelona (Sarquello et al., 2016) noted the trending interest by European governments of the need for integrated health care and social care. They recognize the huge barriers to service interventions because it is difficult to get the groups to work together. In the United States and in Europe, there are examples of teams making some accomplishments in this, but there are continuing examples of the challenges. Public social service networks resist the shift to patient-centered care (Riera et al., 2016).

De Camargo (2011) adds that the systems of care coordination should include health, education, and social welfare in order to achieve optimal results for the service users. He uses the example of assisting adolescents with disabilities transitioning. Several professional groups support guidelines for services for the youth, but politics remain a barrier to implementation.

ENGAGING WITH ORGANIZATIONS

Traditional funding flows from taxes to fund-raising. Resource management and identification can include a civic engagement agenda. Helping identify local officials connected to the systems that impact their lives can support building confidence to hold officials accountable for public services. Service users can be directed to reading materials and legislative offices to help understand their rights as humans and citizens.

Collaborations may be initiated for methods of referral to an agency after the basic services have been provided. They may build data-sharing systems that will support proposals to address the gaps that exist in certain locations.

NURTURE THROUGH SUPPORT SYSTEMS

The application of warmth and validation offers a manner of nurturing individuals and families within the various contexts in which people live. On the macro level, an environment of racism and discrimination may affect persons living in this context; here, strategies that encourage individual and family abilities to use strengths, resilience, and protection are critical. On the micro level, adverse experiences that are traumatic may be recovered from when nurturing and validation occurs in a consistent manner over time. Recognizing the impact of broad social themes as well as personal and family situations requires that nurturing be framed to address both dimensions. The institutionalization presence observed in behaviors and justifications for the racial status quo impedes change (Bonilla-Silva, 2010).

Adverse experiences that frequently occur between close family and kin relationships exposes an important factor that may be resisted in the policy arena for service planning and delivery. Recent research on brain elasticity, the changes that trauma, and harsh parenting may impose on a child's brain architecture, and the recovery the brain makes through positive nurturing is a tremendous discovery. Seita (2014) urges practitioners and parents to be aware of behavior challenges that occur in the process of recovery and operate beyond personal affronts by a young person's behavior to "show acceptance and set expectations." In the song "Healing" by India Arie (2002), she notes that pain is often caused by kin.

The science of hugs offers an illustration of how embracing one another not only can help ward off stresses of the day but are literally found to help ward off colds (Killiam, 2015). These results corroborate the importance of social networks for maintaining good health and portray more clearly how isolation and loneliness exacerbate poor health outcomes.

EXPANDING COMMUNITY ORGANIZATION RELATIONSHIPS

Pursuing a more service user-friendly picture of cultural and individual variants suggests different steps in relationship building. Helping professionals could work on becoming more informed of others' strengths so we can share with service users and not always take from them. Code switching, the concept that describes bilingual or bicultural folks switching their interactions based on who they are interacting with (Demby, 2013), occurs among many bilingual persons. The role of religion (Whitley, 2012) is also a cultural dynamic relevant for deeper understanding of people but is often not recognized or addressed in sessions. These are invisible dynamics that helping professionals could reflect on to incorporate into friendlier interactions.

Mezzo work builds on micro work and assists people to gain confidence, address challenges, and set goals to expand their networks and systems of support. Agencies are now developing strategies to expand their supports in similar ways. Funding applications encourage collaborating with organizations with similar missions to provide collaborative programming. Staff duties include developing ways to maintain service users and to reach new and potential consumers. To help service users progress from direct practice to more social integration and development of higher-level skills, agency efforts to develop partnerships and collaborative service planning will require paying attention to different cultural variations among professional populations.

Using more culturally appropriate designs also increases the marketing aspect of social services.

COLLABORATION

Collaboration opportunities have expanded as the competency expectations encourage new partnerships. Social work, counseling, public health workers, pastoral counselors, students, and practitioners connect with one another and other helping professionals and various academic departments to provide services. Collaboration involves creating relationships to foster research with emerging academic areas such as gender and queer studies, information processing and cultural studies. Scholarship interests of faculty show networks developing for more interdisciplinary research (Victor, Hodge, Perron, Vaughan et al., 2017)

Connecting with service users to motivate and encourage efforts to move toward their higher capacities requires the incorporation of their resources. Collaboration with non-traditional agencies and businesses also presents potential for innovative urban, rural and suburban arrangements that address housing, transportation and workforce development as well as traditional healthcare services.

Vanhanen & Heikkilä (2017) report on examples of working with the police department to support immigrant integration and to work in the schools. The reluctance of the service users in these cases was expected. However, the planning looked at the overlap of services, the potential of their expertise, pooling resources, and reducing cost. Navigating the multiprofessional relationships in a transparent manner was the approach. Outcomes in the police-school collaboration created a long-term safety plan, a protocol for bullying and reduced truancy rates were reported to be positive.

In the United States several cities are reporting efforts to partner with police departments for training and hiring social workers. In Chillicote, Ohio a Post Overdose Response Team (PORT) (Woodruff, n.d.) has been set up to follow-up persons who overdose.

Introducing culturally affirming approaches in schools is particularly important when improving graduation rates is a goal. The Native families in Browning, Montana, face obstacles to getting through high school. The American Indian and Alaskan Native school students are second-least likely to graduate on time, similar to black students. Culturally affirming instructional methods could impact student engagement and retention.

Integrative social work practice models based on ecological theory promote community practice (Lightburn, 2005). Expecting service users to come and develop a therapeutic alliance is unlikely without the implementation of additional steps, outreach, resource identification, and attention.

Multidisciplinary and interprofessional partnerships can help bolster the resources and interactions to be more helpful to young people of color. However, collaboration is not always easy to operationalize. Often, it does not work. When offering it as a path to change, it must be acknowledged that while aspects of it may be inspiring, adults may not want to cooperate. DeWitt (2016) spells out some of the reasons it doesn't work. Developing collaborative projects requires attention to power issues, costs and benefits, impact on the intended service participants, and multiple methods of evaluating the outcomes.

MULTIDISCIPLINARY, INTERPROFESSIONAL, AND INTERORGANIZATIONAL RELATIONSHIPS: MEZZO

Why do people select professions such as social work, public health, and counseling? Some people feel they are called to a helping profession. They have experienced situations in which they have followed their desires to help. For some, they have been helped by a professional themselves.

Becoming more informed of the mezzo-level situations and circumstances that bring people for services (Cheung & Leung, 2009) continues to reinforce the implementation of better-designed approaches. Incorporating global mental health goals and multicultural practice themes raise the economic and political issues. For social work and counseling, globalization "refers to the development of a greater sense of community commitment that expands the scope of human services to promote social justice" (p. 15).

Mezzo-level work involves social workers engaging with other professionals in organizations to develop and implement service strategies. Social workers may become involved in or initiate discussions with persons in other organizations to collaborate and build partnerships for ancillary or direct services. Social workers also can play key roles in identifying and joining with community-based entities to foster relationships to help build community capacity through stronger support systems.

SOCIAL WORK RELATIONSHIP BUILDING

Acknowledging the realms of strength and the existence of problematic or unsafe scenarios present platform for social work to engage with likeminded organizations and to listen to and encourage leadership among constituents. Simultaneously, there is interest in connecting with organizations social work has had minimal contact with in the past but could be a viable relationship given contemporary concerns. Identifying ways in which social workers can join with various organizations will model community behaviors. The importance of ethics in social work may differ in other professions. Social work education includes substantial attention to values and ethics and their application and testing in field settings (Papouli, 2016). Developing partnerships across professional groups will present opportunities and obstacles in the expanding professional ethics arena (Banks, 2016).

BUSINESS

People who come to service provision from a business perspective bring innovative ideas. The Alliance for Downtown New York (Lappin, 2016) reports on taking an approach to homelessness in the business district by partnering with Trinity Church and the Bowery Residents Committee to engage and motivate homeless men and women to accept services and move forward.

A business in Brazil—ABN AMRO (Kanashiro & Starik, 2016)—provided a social program that was able to significantly improve living conditions in a poor area that had high rates of violence toward children. The project ended, but it offered an example of a business being a part of an integrated approach.

The addition of social entrepreneurs, social firms, social ventures, social cooperatives, and social purpose businesses are similar to for-profit firms, but they focus on social goals as well as economic goals (Krupa & Lysaght, 2016). Some of these companies assist people who have emotional stressors to garner work identities. Diament (2017) reports similar observations. According to the American Association of People with disabilities and the U.S. Business Leadership Network, more businesses are embracing inclusion.

Another perspective of business models and systems is an approach some firms are using to hire persons is having them work on advocacy for the firm through social media. It stimulates growth for the company (Frederiksen, 2016).

PHYSICIANS

Social workers are encouraged to consider physician approaches to bioethics. Paasche-Orlow (2004) observed that the cultural competence literature did not include a substantive discussion on the role of ethics. He points to conflicts in medical training that limit an endorsement of pluralism and accommodating diverse, and for some, unacceptable cultural practices. From a Western medical ethics viewpoint, he encourages self-evaluation of moral traditions and intuitions and reflection on acknowledging it as significant, in whatever form it takes, in people's lives.

Listening carefully to patients who may have different value systems is an area in need of further research. If there is a large population of similar persons within the hospital radius, special efforts should be made to connect with their community. Identifying the types of trust patients (Padela, Pruitt, & Mallick, 2017) bring to the healthcare setting is helping shape the care that should be available.

EDUCATION/TEACHERS

Education has been identified as a relevant system to be included in an integrated or coordinated system of care, especially for children and youth. Barnett (2015) offers an example of the impact of religious beliefs in a teacher's efforts to eliminate negative interactions with students and simultaneously identifies the need to also examine teachers who do not bring strict religious frames to their transactions in roles of authority. The beliefs and values the students, as well as the teachers, bring are fluid and changing. Paying attention to both is complex, and addressing the structure has been continually resisted except in experiments with committed participants. The discussion takes many sides, and there are no clear stances. The teacher education curriculum could benefit from some discussion of how to address this context.

The interagency collaboration between education and social work appears to be one that is important for working with preschool children (Farmakopoulou, 2002). The complexity is shaped by aspects of social exchange, interorganizational relations, and the political economy. Collaboration in this area has been poor, but the author encourages pursuit of a strategy for this collaboration would be beneficial for these students.

WOMEN'S HEALTH

Women's health issues involve a range of concerns from personal decision-making about contraception and family planning to availability of immediate need and prevention education services for young and older people to relationship development and maintenance. Education about sexual health, HIV, sexually transmitted infections, consent, and rape (Pinsky, Shepard, Bird, Gilmore, et al., 2017) may not be available. The availability of education in schools and support for sexual minorities' (Brewster, Velez, Foster, Esposito, & Robinson, 2016) screening opportunities for cervical and breast cancer in rural and urban areas vary (Orwat, Caputo, Key,

De Sa, Jean, 2017), and other culturally specific health and mental health information often has not been researched in many studies.

For some, political views obstruct women's rights to self-determination about their bodies. Legislation that penalizes women by removing services or criminalizing their substance use behaviors (Hui, Angelotta, Fisher, & Carl, 2017) miss the humanitarian aspect of service.

Multicultural women experience various stressors that impact skin health, alopecia, and immune system problems that are not often addressed in mainstream health research (Johnson & Miteva, 2017). Stress-related conditions regarding bicultural experiences in biracial families (Robinson-Wood, 2011) may be addressed through herbal methods not well understood in traditional settings.

Access to care for women experiencing stillbirth (Huberty, Matthews, Leiferman, Hermer, & Cacciatore, 2017) is limited, and postpartum evaluation and education are needed in more locations. The use of telephone support interventions at 6 weeks and 6 months for those likely to experience postpartum depression (Ngai, Wong, Chung, & Leung, 2017) indicates positive results. Consideration of a women's physical and mental health before deployment for women military personnel offers a plan for addressing possible stress reactions.

Increased awareness of aggression against women in its many forms, including domestic violence, in the face of natural and human-related disasters (Houston & First, 2017) is needed to promote safety planning and care for the women and children in these circumstances.

As women's health concerns are viewed across the life cycle and within areas of potential distress, many ideas are likely to be considered for collaboration and resource development. Women who move into the sandwich generation and become caregivers of young children and older persons have interests in receiving practical assistance (Evans et al., 2017) from support system members. Program developers need to hear from women who are juggling several obligations, care for immediate and extended families and trying to pursue improved employment situations. Service users across age groups should be included in these conversations. Askheim, Beresford, and Heule (2017) advise more service user involvement in social work education.

POLICE

A study of police organizational culture found five perspectives that revealed disparities in officers' views and outlooks of their profession (Bayerl, Horton, Jacobs, Rogiest, et al., 2014). The study identified potential pointers for interorganizational collaborations. Police departments across the country already have social workers, and others are hiring them. Their duties vary but do assist in community relations. In several locations, police departments are hiring social workers to help teams improve cultural understanding and consider procedures for calling in a mobile-crisis team instead of taking people with mental problems to jail (Smith, 2017, class presentation Chester County MH).

SOCIAL WORKERS AND MENTAL HEALTH

Social workers play a substantive role in providing direct practice services in emotional and behavioral health care and substance use disorders through community organizing and advocacy for policy development that impacts service users. Already one of the largest professional groups for mental health and substance use, the Bureau of Labor Statistics (BLS, 2018) projects an increasing need as the demand for healthcare and social services grows. Wodarski (2014) proposes the move to an integrated system of health and behavioral health care involves the fiscally responsible use of social workers for screening and assessment on interdisciplinary health care teams. Knowledge of insurance and entitlements is significant in this delivery system.

Significant efforts have been made to increase service coordination and integration, but there is limited evidence for effective approaches for holistic care. Multiple barriers continue via bureaucratic obstacles, interprofessional challenges, and inadequate resources (Guerrero, Aarons, & Palinkas, 2014).

Substance use services are included in the mental health services continuum. Addiction policy, interventions and delivery systems are complicated. Tobacco and alcohol use have high mortality rates and the influence of substance use across individual and family health situations involve social workers in several different roles (Daley, 2013). The first concern involves establishing partnerships to deliver services through an integrated services model that addresses emotional health and substance use. Creating services that recognize co-occurring disorders may require policy modifications or legislation that would support flexible parameters that include recovery and harm reduction models. Delivery systems are moving toward distributed settings such as retail clinics and free standing service sites that are experiencing high returns on investments (Singhai, Latko, & Martin, 2018). Social workers are being hired in government agencies, nonprofits and businesses.

The second level requires establishing partnerships in community settings to provide related supports that persons require to address the circumstances that substance use may bring.

Social work roles are needed at the mezzo level to collaborate with community organizations, develop programs and connect service users to opportunities for reducing substance use and learning other coping skills for maintaining recovery.

Collaborative care team training and community education for citizens regarding legal rights and justice system issues are also needed. Projects through experiential learning can benefit students and community residents (Jewell & Owens, 2017).

As the social work profession navigates the growing health care industry, not only are we concerned about the ethics and social justice framework of social work, but that imposed by the broader health community is important as well. Working toward a more coordinated system that accommodates these new entities will offer additional complexity to this service system and offer opportunities. Breaking the hold of status-quo events in disciplines and organizations takes time and specific strategy planning for implementation.

TABLE 12.1   Integrating Mezzo Resources

PROFESSIONALS	SERVICE USERS	COMMUNITY MEMBERS
Service delivery	Household structure, information sharing	Community education, prevention information
Continuing education	Education, self-help	Task sharing, peer mediators
Research	Civic participation	Neighborhood associations
Advocacy	Advocacy	Advocacy

COLLABORATIONS WITH CONSUMERS

The communication regarding service eligibility and quality begins with the service users and extends to the workers who will shape opportunities for comments and feedback as well as contributions for program types. Network operations can offer ways to offset social exclusion as well as assist construction of agency interventions that meet specific consumer needs.

The place of self-help in our communities has been significant for a while, but social work has resisted incorporating referrals and using them with service users. Often, people may choose these resources. Steinberg reminds us of the significance of group work as mutual aid "the intent of mutual-aid practice as empowerment precludes oppression. It seeks to help people to identify, develop, and exercise their strengths, making both an antioppression focus a natural fit and antioppressive behaviors essential" (2017, p. 59). Hyde (2013) agrees that the mutual aid group is valuable. His work in Australia emphasizes recovery in mental health as a component of mutual aid.

A study conducted in Brazil (Nickels, Arvaiza, & Valle, 2016) explored perceptions of the effectiveness of a self-help program in El Salvador. The results found benefits across micro, mezzo, and macro social levels. However, mezzo-level improvements will include collaborations and partnerships that include locating and conferring with community-based organizations and self-help entities to work together. The process of working with members of the communities we serve, planning for developing capacity to work with business and government agents, requires knowledge and agility in focus and communication to improve spaces for people to lessen isolation and engage in activities for wellness.

AWARENESS OF INEQUITY AND RACISM

The awareness that people's experiences with inequity and racism are probably different from a service provider is a starting point for engaging with diverse families and communities. Inequity appeared to be a factor in a study of Latina/o youth decision-making about educational preparation and vocational development. Incorporating boundary crossing parameters for the school and community enhanced participation of the students (Achinstein, Curry, Ogawa & Athanases, 2016). Increasing partnerships that recognize the impact restricted opportunities have had on individuals and families is important, as is working to help parents recognize and plan for families and the expenses that come along with them. Helping parents prepare children for school and demonstrating how they can enhance their reading and math skills, communicating about coping measures to calm themselves, and thinking about fiscal supports for future education are critical to their futures. Neighborhood tutoring programs are in place in some community churches (Miller, 2015). Social work students and workers may find opportunities to join with these new programs.

McWhirter and McWhirter (2016) speak to the potential value of critical consciousness for educational persistence and vocational development. This component is valuable for students in underrepresented groups having access to career development information (Staff, 2013) earlier in their education to help them plan and foster pathways for future employment. Caregivers need information to assist their family planning (Gibson & Haight, 2013).

Information about the impact of secondary school choices and employment on mental health should also be available. Symonds and associates (2016) examined the anxiety and depression of adolescents and the fit of school, employment, or training connected to a job demands–resources model. Their mental health improved after support and self-enhancement steps and transfers to options they believed to be more compatible with their interest. A survey of young people in the United Kingdom revealed 93% of the 14- to 25-year-olds surveyed believed they had not been provided with information they needed.

COLLABORATION WITH FAITH-BASED ISSUES AND SERVICES

The role of social work and spirituality continues to be the subject of research and discussion. Organizations are setting policies regarding its recognition. For our purposes, spirituality and faith-based services are community resources. Acknowledging that people may or may not include these in their support system is a reference point to include in our assessment. When they are available, they may be included in the package of community-based components to be considered.

INTERCONNECTEDNESS OF SPIRITUALITY AND FAMILY

Alternative models from cultural communities often challenge Western models that cater to the individual person. This perspective integrates spirituality with cultural identity and place and is relevant for children separated from their birth families (Sharley, 2012). The Maori cultural perspective views people as part of the natural environment so viewing the child's identity as interconnected helps shape a more positive self-image to children who show low self-worth as a result of their experiences. The view seeks to remove preoccupation with adversity and risk but emphasizes values of surviving adversity and the ability to overcome.

Examples of communities' reliance on spiritual domains can support student recognition of this aspect and guide respectful conversations.

ASIAN OR PACIFIC ISLANDER DESCENT

The diversity of families of Asian descent is extensive. Families from India, Indonesia, Philippines, Korea, Vietnam, Japan, China, and other locations may adhere to traditional Buddhism or to other forms of spirituality. Local communities often have a variety of places for connections to these traditions. Nguyen (2015) describes a historic proposal for the Vietnamese government to include social work centers to partner with Buddhist temples. The temples are active as informal sources of community attendance for emotional health needs. The formal psychiatric hospitals are resisted. This proposal would link people through working with the monks to assist people with family conflicts, mild distress related to grief and loss and disabilities and illness. This demonstrates a cultural affirming process for planning and implementation.

LGBTQI AND SPIRITUALITY

The controversies regarding diverse sexual orientations extends to perceptions people have about lesbian, gay, bisexual, transgender, and those who identify as queer, questioning, and intersex (LGBTQI) persons. Generally, research suggests conflict with this group regarding religion and spirituality (Beagan & Hattie, 2015) due to high levels of intolerance by Christians. There is some research suggesting that believers in Judaism, Native spirituality, Buddhism, and Hinduism are more welcoming (Beagan & Hattie, 2015; Hodge, 2004). There is some debate about the cultural and legal regulations regarding male homosexuality and lesbianism in different places around the world. Same-sex intercourse carries a death penalty in five Muslim nations. The impact of religious and cultural intolerance across religious groups can damage the psychological and emotional well-being of LGBTQI individuals (Beagan & Hattie, 2015). Extensive research confirms the oppressive dominance of religion to subjugate indigenous people and others and has led to the consideration of correlations of religion and obsessive-compulsive symptoms, anxiety, and other topics related to sexual fulfilment (Liboro, 2015, p. 1208).

Spiritual Supports

Beyond the oppressive nature of the religious structures, the nature of spirituality to provide meaning to existence helps the well-being of LGBTQI persons. Acknowledging this offers a platform to help persons experiencing identity incongruity through customized affirming interventions. A study of heterosexual and gay Orthodox Jews indicated spirituality may be the source of emotional benefits rather than religiosity (Harari, Glenwick, & Cecero, 2014).

Murr (2013) describes a qualitative investigation of lesbian and bisexual women who grew up in nonaffirming Christian environments. Their stories illustrate the spiritual journeys from negative experiences with Christianity to enlightened and affirmed lives. Similarly, Hattie and Beagan (2013) report rejection from traditional faith communities to reconfigured spiritual relationship.

Transgender Discrimination

The experience of discrimination and mistreatment seems highest for transgender (trans) persons. Rockenbach (2016) describes the outright and micro aggressions of students in higher education. The legislative and religious doctrines on religious-oriented campuses, as well as non-religious ones, make it difficult. LGBTQI students tend to express more diverse religious experiences and worldviews than others.

Despite the harm connected to religious intolerance of LGBTQI identities, many persons derive benefit from their spiritual connection and their participation in an affirming faith community. This network was associated with more positive psychological health and lower levels of internalized homo-negativity (McGeorge, Carlson, & Toomey, 2014).

There have been shifting attitudes over the past 40 years, and several factors influence these changes (Cragun & Sumerau, 2015). These attitudes and how they may directly or indirectly link discrimination against LGBTQQI persons contribute to the mental health stressors they may experience. Internalized prejudice against sexual minorities may also add to mental health issues. This, along with other identity intersections and the role of spirituality, may influence coping abilities. Some may cope well with adverse attitudes through spiritual identities and strategies. Some sexual minority people may find religion also a source of stress (Brewster, Velez, Foster, Esposito, & Robinson, 2016). Although the results of the Brewster team study found positive religious coping was helpful, it did not totally eradicate psychological symptoms. Pursuing religious and spiritual concepts must be approached cautiously to gain understanding of how the positive and negative dimensions may affect one's psychological health. Further research is needed to address the presence or absence of spirituality in working with a person who holds atheist beliefs.

A study of students in family therapy training assessed students' spiritual or religious beliefs and their practice of reparative and affirmative therapies (McGeorge et al., 2014). More males were likely to practice reparative therapy rather than affirmative. The researchers noted the need for training about integrating spirituality as a resource in therapy; as a way to lead to more positive beliefs about LGBTQQI persons; and to train therapists to use the clients' spiritual beliefs rather than impose their own beliefs.

DIFFERENTLY ABLED

Spirituality plays an important role for many people who have different abilities. For persons who see, hear, move, learn, feel, and experience freedom differently, their ways of participating in certain activities may involve substantive stress and strain. Anxiety may also be experienced because of the discrimination and stigma they often face. There are numerous examples of people who handle their daily lives well or who go on to accomplish high achievements and celebrity. Their resilience comes from the ways in which they make sense of their circumstances and situations and the protection of relationships, their environments, and coping strategies (Eliassen, 2014; Sivadasan & Narayanan, 2016).

Some believe disability should not be connected to religion because of the history of discrimination. The notions of disability of the 17th century associated physical differences as impairments to be the result of sin or mental illness. The discussion about disability has been examined from the viewpoint of the Muslim and Christianity traditions (Hayhoe, 2014) and is posed for more research. Both faiths seem to respect one's piety over their social situations and that developing disability equality should be promoted. His observations indicate some people demonstrate a deeper spirituality when a disability occurs and they show empathy with others with a disability.

DEAF AND HARD OF HEARING

Increasing research among the Deaf community now includes themes regarding the meaning of disability, communication, family dynamics, and representation as it applies to mental health practice (Barclay, Rider, & Dombo, 2012). Increasing research evidence supports the belief that spirituality has a positive impact on health outcomes.

Training health professionals in this area has been minimal, but early empirical results suggest that students and practitioners recognize the relevance of spirituality and religion in members of the Deaf community's (McClain, 2009) lives and their need to become more aware and understanding of its potential uses. The lack of research on disability and spirituality may be attributed to researchers' reluctance to investigate this. The need to broaden the consideration of Deaf spirituality in religions, including Buddhism, Hinduism, Islam, Judaism, indigenous communities, and New Age, is emerging as new territory. Themes connected to spirituality that would be helpful to persons pursuing work in the Deaf community pertain to access and barriers. Organizations interested in reaching out to the Deaf community may offer spiritual and religious information, opportunities for group discussion, parenting, and self-determination.

The paternalistic view that presents a negative frame of Deafness is challenged by the relational features that would be connected to a spiritual basis. Materials about spirituality are published by hearing people rather than the members of the community themselves. Delich (2014) highlights key themes that incorporate the reflection of a relationship and communication with God, connecting through challenges and crises, awakening of self through spirituality, and acknowledging relationships with others. A recent work by Morris (2016), *Theology Without Words*, does include comments from Deaf students in BA and master's programs. He describes the approach to theology without words, using British Sign language as one that does not follow the Western structure and is viable nonetheless.

Research from the census on the Deaf community in India reflects on the nearly 18 million in this population group. Sandhu and Kapoor (2014) explored the spiritual development of children through their drawings and found unique symbolism. By appreciating the macro environment of India's development, these researchers focused on how to integrate students of the Deaf community into the mainstream to push their society forward. Inclusion of their spiritual place and learning needs rests on love, acceptance, and equality.

AGING

Experiencing the decline in able functioning occurs as one advances in age. For some, the stigma of being disabled leads to dissatisfaction and impacts their quality of life as they advance in years and experience the daily manifestations of ongoing health conditions. MacKinlay (2008) reports that effective caregiving relationships and affirming spirituality promote a better quality of life among older persons.

The increasing age expectancy of persons with intellectual and /development disabilities (IDD) has created challenges and service gaps in states trying to address the coordination of disability and aging resources (Coyle, Putnam, Kramer, & Mutchler, 2016). Infrastructure improvement is required to respond to this developing home and community-based context where caregivers and siblings are also aging and not as available for the family member's care.

IMMIGRANTS

The context of spiritual supports is diverse across families and individuals who select immigration as a way to seek financial opportunities in the United States. Their choice of the United States is connected to the perceived economic offerings, the freedom of religion, and the possibility of family members being here.

The impact of a different environment and the presence or absence of strong network ties can influence the development of emotional and behavioral health (Lee & Hwang, 2014). Perceptions of immigrant groups by dominant culture members affects the manner in which they interact. These exchanges may inform whether immigrants feel welcomed or intimidated. Generalized ideas that Muslims pose a threat or people with language differences can't be understood will inform the ways in which the receiving communities engage with one another (Van Acker, Phalet, Deleersnyder, & Mesquita, 2014, p. 2). Religious and spiritual beliefs have a strong role as the coping mechanisms for immigrant persons and families. Mental health professionals are urged to become informed of their beliefs to address their mental health needs and assist positive adaptation (Chaze, Thomson, George, & Gurge, 2015).

Overall, Lewis (2015) notes that in a survey of social workers, spirituality or religion can be helpful but most workers ignore it. Hunter-Hernandez and colleagues (2015) propose that without addressing spirituality practitioners may be missing opportunities to connect to bridges of resilience.

MEZZO LEVEL AND THE WORKING CLASS

Acknowledging the class status of service users, though clearly a reality of service access and service provision quality, is a terrain that has not received much attention. The needs of economic-class groups essentially have emphasized the lower-income groups and access to insurance that provides access to services. Case management typically involves proving eligibility and gaining services.

Ineffective services often reflect neglect, lack of warmth, and absence of outreach. This service reluctance can be associated with service users' economic status as well as membership in minority groups. Mental health services may range from medication only to integrative health care. Services in child welfare and education are frequently described by mistreatment, exclusion, and punitive interventions of children of color, LGBTQI folks, differently abled, and those with immigrant status. Increasing collaborative, culturally affirming, and supportive interventions requires additional work. These are areas that program evaluation and observations of service gaps are focused for improvements. Program evaluation that observed the use of accommodations for differently abled youth (Yamatani, Teixeira & McDonough, 2015) and apprenticeships concludes that these efforts and investments pay off when organizations can be convinced to implement them. An after-school program co-created with African American youth (Bulanda, Tellis, & McCrea, 2015) with a curriculum that includes human rights, human development, trauma and stress management resulted in 43% expressing interest in a future social work career. More effort is also needed to help young people make informed choices about their future careers (Bimrose & Barnes, 2007).

ECONOMICS AND THE SERVICE USER POPULATIONS

The exclusion of people of color, women, LGBTQQI, differently abled, and immigrants is dynamically connected to economics and politics. These dimensions of the social environment essentially shape what the media constructs in messages about these groups. Messages about exclusion typically have not mentioned lower-income white people. Recent literature has begun to reflect that people across all groups are experiencing more challenges—food insecurity, less ability for home ownership (Edin & Shaefer, 2016; Smiley & West, 2013), and less upward mobility. Appalachia represents a cultural group that is somewhat isolated and connected to minimal job opportunities. The media has not presented the strengths of this region either.

The decline of manufacturing jobs and other avenues for consistent employment has impacted the emotional and political status of persons who are earning high incomes. Economic inequality is illustrated in the major gains in income of the top 1%; the income of all others has remained fairly stagnant (Desilver, 2013).

Social workers, health professionals, and others who serve the public often interface with them when their vulnerable status is high. Being aware of the presence or absence of insurance and other fiscal responsibilities is important and should be taken into consideration, as supportive resources may need to be located in the community.

Reports suggest that white people believe the economy is not benefiting them. The gains by the richest 1% have, in fact, diminished earnings by those in lower economic groups. However, according to the Pew Research Center, when looking at gender, race, and ethnicity combined, all groups, with the exception of Asian men, lag behind white men in terms of median hourly earnings (Kochhar, 2013). Despite this, Rhodan (2014) points out those perceptions of scarcity influence people's visual representations of race in ways that promote discrimination.

Porter (2016) suggests what might help is a "broadening of the objectives of competition policy" (para 26). He suggests a discussion that "goes beyond how a decline in competition may hurt consumers, but to also consider the way market concentration affects the distribution of growth benefits" (para 26).

Leaders are exploring ways to re-energize the American economy (Muro, 2016). Some social workers are paying more attention to the economic policy dimension that affects communities. Hodge (2003) reported the value of social workers as members of the knowledge class, could hinder the efficacy of services because of the different values of the professionals and the service users.

THE WORKING CLASS AND STRESSORS

Draut (2016) describes toady's working class to include home health workers, janitors, retail salespeople, and fast-food clerks. These workers include more female and more racially diverse persons and usually do not have the protection of a union. While typical families may be managing all right, many are inundated by the pressures of unexpected expenses, health issues, and relationship dynamics. Providing more information, complementary approaches, and self-help resources can help mitigate the stress. There are cultural variations in support (Wang & Lau, 2015). Church, temple, and synagogue groups for men, women, and children have been used traditionally. But with many people questioning traditional religious institutions, some of these support groups have diminished.

The lack of mental health care in low- and middle-class communities where insurance may be limited has generated alternative resources. According to Encyclopedia of Mental Disorders, (2018), self-help groups are increasing and likely tied to lack of insurance. Voluntary, nonprofit, self-help groups are open to anyone with similar needs or interests. Sometimes spin-off groups are created based on issues. McKay and Bonner (2002) mention the use of women's magazines' qualitative content about dealing with illnesses and grief to be useful for many, especially the elderly and women. Training for local mental health self-help group members has been used in India (Shrinivasa, Janardhana, & Nirmala, 2017).

Group-based, self-help, micro-credit programs are also used globally to provide neighborhood-based savings and lending programs (Davidson & Sanyal, 2017). Some self-help groups include an accountant to address financial matters (Vandewalle, n.d.). Marija and Rozman (2015) evaluated persons' satisfaction with self-help groups. Depending on the types of groups, many people do indicate (Cheung & Sun, 2000) satisfaction and empowerment.

Overall, the concerns about economic justice are relevant to the situations of many persons who seek social and mental health services. The life issues of working-class persons create stressors and health problems for them and their children. Fluctuations in job security and stable housing (Matthews, 2016) impact families more in the lower-middle and low class. Living wage advocates urge (2009) working with activists through civic participation and social work education to expand the profession's relationship with workers. Planning to incorporate mezzo and macro participation should be beneficial.

WORKERS AND DEMOCRACY

Advocates for working-class issues emphasize rebuilding the democratic system. According to Pew Research (Stokes, 2018) 46% of respondents are not satisfied with the way our democracy is working. Demos (2017), a public policy organization, promotes people participating in government and having a say in setting the policies that shape opportunities (www.demos.org). The Center for Working Class Life includes the Democracy Charter (O'Dell, 2015), a publication that proposes several points that would address real citizen needs, including commitments to end homelessness; full employment and livable wages; an environment free of bigotry, violence, and intolerance; human rights, reproductive rights, and the rights of gays and lesbians; education from pre K to college; a farm economy that rests on family and cooperation; improved foreign and military policy; universal health insurance; an account-able prison system; and protection of the quality of our natural environment as a vital social inheritance. Achieving these goals through a democratic presence would certainly enhance the lives of many citizens that helping professionals assist.

WOMEN

Employment by gender has increased and suggests the need for additional methods of child care. Women have increased their presence in the labor force since 1950. As of 2014, about 57% worked outside the home (Status of Women, n.d.).

Ai-jen Poo (2017) describes her advocacy for working women in a media presentation by Race Forward (www.raceforward.org). The impact of public policies on the struggles of lower-income workers directly impacts the potential vulnerability of populations social workers serve. Parents who have nonstandard work schedules are likely to have children who may react to this in ways that display internalizing and externalizing problems, cognitive issues, and body mass (Li et al., 2013). Meaningful work and livable wages play critical roles in personal internal and external regulation (Allan, Autin, & Duffy, 2016) and certainly impact the pressures and responses children and adolescents in the family may experience.

APPALACHIA

Persons in the Appalachian area of the United States are often stereotyped by the perceptions of their economic and social conditions. The images of Appalachia are as full of stereotypes as the images of other excluded groups. The economic despair and major health epidemics do impact the area, but the population is diverse. The region spans land stretching from the mountains of southern New York through northern Alabama. The description the media paints is that the area is all-white and poor. However, the population incudes white, Latino, black, and Native groups (Moses, 2015). The term *Affrilachia*, coined by Kentucky poet laureate Frank X. Walker, has brought together multiracial artists. The word has been added to the *Oxford American Dictionary (Second Edition)*.

The diversity of the region may be simply illustrated by these two examples. Vance shared his memoir, *Hillbilly Elegy: A Memoir of a Family and Culture in Crisis* (2016), of his childhood in Kentucky that depicts the range of experiences that launched him into the world and pushed him into becoming a U.S. Marine and Yale Law School graduate. Martha Redbone, from Tennessee, daughter of Native and African American parents, shared a mixture of Cherokee neo-soul music with lyrics and commentary at a recent performance at the National Museum of the Native American in Washington, DC (2016), that shed light on the context of the region.

IMPACT ON FAMILIES

Assessing the impact of economics on the capacity of families presents areas social workers can target for advocacy for relevant policies and partnerships. Working class issues include the inflexibility of businesses with low-wage workers. The low income and irregular hours cause stress and absence of household providers from their child care time and demands. The family work conflict among middle-class families is also a social work concern. Sánchez-Cabezudo and Peláez (2014) pose this situation within Spanish families. Situations around families with dual workers present problems seen in counseling and mental health services. As parents bear the stresses of accommodating their work and family lives and the conflicts that often develop, families are observed to shift into downward mobility. In this dynamic, families that have been socially included begin to experience problems that may spiral them into socially excluded statuses.

MEZZO: RESILIENCE AND CONTEXT

Despite the sociological depiction of assimilation and acculturation processes, people of various cultural groups are interested in maintaining the knowledge and customs of their ancestral heritage. Literature has continuously expressed people's connections to the land, to one another, and to other stories as they navigate the obstacles and constraints transitioning to new and different geographies that communities bring.

The mezzo level contains examples of people managing their lives through ups and downs and moving through age and family life cycles using structured households, authoritarian parenting, assignment of chores, and homework and other activities to promote secure and responsible child development. The family and social networks provide immediate and backup supports. Determining whether there are relatives, friends, neighbors, or people in organizations available for support can be put into a visual chart to assist persons in visualizing their people and organizational support systems. If there is isolation, that may raise the need to begin steps to improve the system. This level contains access to daily reading, awareness of political and economic realities, literature about their heritage, belief and actions in helping others, religious tenets and scriptures that support loving others, and less emphasis on ego and selfishness. Family meetings offer opportunities for discussions that present observations of the macro systems and micro conditions people experience and how they have recovered.

SOURCES OF KNOWLEDGE AND INFORMATION

If we examine the behaviors, beliefs, and pathways of those who do not typically come for social and mental health services, we are likely to find people who operate from cultural- and spiritual-based life pathways that build developmental assets in their families. The Search Institute has promoted developmental assets since the 1990s. A key finding of their work has been that youth with early spirituality and religious connections tend to progress toward well-being as they grow and mature (Benson & Roehlkepartain, 2008).

Spiritual development is perceived to be a viable component of youth development, along with motivation, focus, and multisector engagement (Benson & Roehlkepartain, 2008). Spirituality and religion have been associated with impacting recovery. Stigma and prejudice often account for substantial resistance to using services provided by governmental entities because they generally have not demonstrated having the well-being of cultural groups at heart.

Witmer (2014) explored the dynamics of living in poverty that include factors that impact daily survival and provide an example of how services do miss things that significantly impact people's survival. The supplemental poverty measures examined in New York how close people are to the poverty line. Their research asked about people's awareness of services in nonprofit agencies that may be of assistance to them, and it questioned why they sometimes didn't follow up on possible options. Many were not aware of nonprofit agency options. Some nonprofits, though able to help with emergency rent funds or health funds, don't advertise a lot to protect their limited funds. Service users, when informed there could be other resources available, admitted sometimes the stress and pressure of continually enduring disappointment, job loss, or child care issues sometimes was just too much to handle. The researchers called this *survivor's fatigue*.

FAMILY DEVELOPMENT KNOWLEDGE

Research suggests that acknowledging the negative circumstances that impact child and family development is important to include in education to influence change. Providing information about what may damage children is needed before a first child is born. Information about adverse experiences and the importance of including dads in a child's life should be included in service delivery conversations (Bouchard & Lee, 2000; World Health Organization, 2015). Helping family members understand the emotions that may exist as people transition through developmental phases and various family blending situations should be put forth. Sometimes parent relationships end. Using information and strategies that tame emotional reactions and plan for the adjustment of the children and adolescents would benefit the whole family.

ADDRESSING THE OBSTACLES TO FAMILY ESTEEM BUILDING

Another level of content that often is not addressed is how to include fathers in service delivery. Given the history and range of impact of internalized negative messages, interventions that speak to the macro influences and behaviors of therapists regarding use of community strengths should be examined. Child welfare and mental health services often do not engage fathers. Brewsaugh and Strozier (2016) describe the absence of information regarding fathers in textbooks and the bias against including fathers.

INCLUDING FATHERS

Sieber (2014) notes the marginalization of fathers by mothers and perhaps unintentional exclusion by clinicians. There is plenty of evidence that strong mothers do provide the structure and support raising young men requires, yet extending opportunities to include fathers is often missed by agency policies and mothers' narratives. Research shows that involved fathers of children with autism (Naseef, 2017) get results in academic progress, behavior, and healthy eating. Policies that may obstruct a father's opportunities to support his children require review and modification.

SOCIAL WORKERS USING SPIRITUAL CONTEXTS

Many social workers and other therapists who connect well to clients or service users are likely integrating cultural awareness and spiritual recognition into their protocols. Warner (2003) discusses using tribal methods in working with groups with Native participants. Several references refer to using cultural strengths and resources in facilitating consumer services (Delgado, 1999; O'Neal & Reid, 1999).

Broadly, Jinpa (2015) discusses the benefits of compassion, and Stickle (2016) relates it to social work practice. Jinpa believes compassion brings purpose to our lives and is an important indicator of personal happiness. He also believes it shifts us from narrow self-agendas to increase understanding and tolerance. Stickle notes it as a core value of social work distinct from empathy (p. 120). She proposes the shifts in social issues and demands on social work have resulted in diminished empathy and a decline in perspective.

Diaconescu (1989) reviewed over 38 articles in a 9-year frame that discussed compassion fatigue. First, noting several social workers come to this work having experienced some trauma of their own, self-care and coping strategies are vital. These include physical and behavioral, relational, and cognitive strategies. Relaxation and meditation are emphasized. Kapoulitsas and Corcoran (2015) explore compassion fatigue and recognize it as a point on the way to practitioner resilience.

The research connected to the positive responses to cultural- and spiritual-based service delivery makes awareness and integration of these resources critical to responding to persons likely to drop out after only one or two sessions (Talmon, 1990). This concept of single session was offered as a strategy because the reality of large numbers of people coming for only one session urged designing an intervention to provide as much as possible in that one and possibly only visit. He suggested this strategy be used with multicultural consumers (Slive & Bobele, 2013). Facilitating inclusion builds on student's awareness of self, knowledge of formal and informal community resources, and community practice skills to engage service users and with business and government entities that fund services.

AFRICAN DESCENT

The history of how communities care for one another includes the ways African American communities have responded to care for the young and the elders in communities where services did not reach out to them. Hill (2003) reflected on the literature that notes how low-income families tend to have stronger kinship ties than middle-income families. His examination, with the Urban League, of census data found that black families were more likely to take in young related family members, and in female-headed homes, there was a higher likelihood of taking in other related children. Black families with elderly women took in an even-higher proportion. There was less absorption of young family relatives in white families. In the review of Hill's book, Katz (1973) summarized the five strengths of black families.

1. Strong kinship bonds (p. 1)
2. Strong work orientation (p. 2)
3. Adaptability of family roles (p. 2)

4. High achievement orientation (p. 2)
5. Religious orientation (p. 2)

The report was distributed by the Urban League and was available in communities and in academic disciplines. It encouraged black families to become more cohesive. Building relationships can benefit from sharing this information for reflection.

LATINO/HISPANIC DESCENT

There is substantial research that refers to the missed opportunities for connecting spirituality to service plans. Hunter-Hernandez's team (2015) notes spirituality as a resource that supports adaptation and resilience and can be helpful to Latinos adjusting to and coping with cancer. African-centered family healing urges social workers to join in this alternative paradigm (Mickel, 2013). Older Latinos and caregivers also operate successfully from spiritual frameworks (Hilton & Child, 2014).

Latino/as are widely diverse groups and report belonging to Protestant, Roman Catholic, Mormon, and Evangelical or Pentecostal religious denominations or to no religious affiliation (Pew Research Center, 2014). Their practices have been described as a "communitarian spirituality" that draws on several spiritual traditions that include those of Native communities in the Americas and Africa. Aponte (2012) agrees that their lived religion expands traditional definitions and includes Latinos who are also Jews and Muslims.

NATIVE DESCENT

Local cultural knowledge, worldviews, values, and theories of change are preferred for service interventions that work to protect against harmful substance use (Rasmus, Allen, Connor, Freeman, & Skewes, 2014). Procedures to deliver care using a different framework require support from the agency. The Native community recognizes that typical interventions focus on individual agency, motivation, and autonomous decision-making. These treatments often have low utilization and retention rates.

The preferred approach would build strength through cultural supports rather than reduce risk. Focusing on strengths is key. The emphasis is placed on structure and rituals for families to have clear roles for each member and rules to follow to be protective. Activities that families do together on a regular basis (Rasmus et al., 2014), such as eating together, going to powwows, going out fishing, and helping at ceremonies and funerals, provide stability and build cohesion.

HELP SEEKING AND STRENGTHS BUILDING

Planning services on the organizational and individual and family levels encompasses the process of help seeking, organizational procedures, and attention to updated approaches. Taking a different approach to issues of past marginalization involves acknowledging that some elements of service delivery have not been the most effective and were not inclusive. This view is presented as the need for syncretism, melding the learning process of children of color in their homes and communities with the classroom experience rather than privileging only the traditional practices (Long et al., 2013). Practitioners can seek information on the methods families may use to protect themselves from the influences of discrimination (Hughes, 2003). Inequitable educational experiences should not be perpetuated. Creative processes, developed through a critical perspective, will welcome contexts that can be enriched through syncretic practices. "here are several programs, institutes, and approaches across disciplines that have integrated positive thoughts and designs to support persons. The L'Arche program, developed for persons with disabilities, addressed the abysmal situations of persons with mental illness who lived in asylums (Thulberry & Thyer, 2014). It began as a Roman Catholic movement in France in 1964. Lectures and more formal development have led to founding L'Arche communities in several countries. The philosophy is to raise up and esteem those who are marginalized. As an intentional community, it emphasizes being together with one another.

DEVELOPING IMPLEMENTATION STRATEGIES

In order to address the knowledge and information pointed to over these chapters, needs may be assessed at various points along the life course and may take any point of entry or prevention frame.

The Council on Social Work Education (CSWE, 2008) Educational Competencies 6 through 9 address engaging, assessing, intervening, and evaluating services. Establishing plans for macro, mezzo, and micro goal setting can help visualize the realm of change and the potential of selecting pathways and coaches. Orienting service users to the levels of work involved and seeking their guidance in determining the choices for becoming the best they can be applies across life phases. Screening, brief interventions, and referrals for several health concerns should be available.

ENTRY POINTS

The application of research addressing the integration of cultural strengths has been shown to be effective. However, the gap in time in the implementation of evidence-based practices is concerning. Proctor (2014) reports that interventions with parents and children at risk for maltreatment and mental health as well as substance use program consumers are receiving less-than-quality care. Assessing the situation and selecting theories (O'Neal, 2010) to frame planning and implementing services provides a foundation for thinking through situations and presenting ideas to collaborators.

BUILDING COMMUNITY CAPACITY

Advancing change includes professionals' addressing service users' learning to build community capacity occurring at various entry points over the life course. As more young children have opportunities to attend preschool, families should be informed of what they can do at home. Community-based prevention offers opportunities to share evidence-informed strategies to address challenges, trauma, and coping with goal setting to build resilience across the life cycle. Practical supports can be integrated into existing structures to offer mezzo-level information about financial, educational, and vocational prerequisites. It is necessary to use various sources of cultural information and pedagogies (Hale, 1994; Hallam, 2010). Using business concepts for project management (Barber, 2013) could provide time frames for setting and working on goals within the household. Study times related to goal setting, determining possible group participation, and using the idea of sprints (Dulock, 2015) to get from one point in the goal lineup to another can guide session assignments.

EARLY CHILDHOOD DEVELOPMENT AND EDUCATION

The role of caregiving for early social and emotional learning is critical to infant and toddler development. Parenting and early childhood educators provide the foundation for emotional wellbeing (Vanderbilt, n.d.). Community education for prevention can help prepare families for phases of development and aggravation as well as strategies to accommodate the stressors. Social work and public health agencies can create opportunities to engage with young parents in communities. As young parents begin the family development process, using community-based prevention can offer information and resources to prepare for the 18-plus-year stretch. Preparing parents for setting up household routines, reviewing first-aid strategies for in-home needs, and informing them of attachment strategies, especially when persons and families are experiencing stressful conditions, benefit the community in the long run. Young mothers facing parenting through stressed relationships may need supports to manage anger and frustration.

ADOLESCENT DEVELOPMENT AND EDUCATION

Services for adolescents are particularly important not only to address immediate health and mental health issues but also to link resources to assist identity development, connect to cultural history, and link them with extracurricular and community activities of some sort. Organizational relationships that can assist teens and families to access current and future workforce participation is crucial. Providing young people with opportunities to be informed of academic course selections tied to their interests, tutoring and mentoring, and vocational apprenticeships should be an essential component of the service goals. Acknowledging the obstacles to employment must be reckoned with early on in any service setting they use. Fact sheets about teen behavior that achieves goals, reading lists and databases that include mentors, cultural examples of achievement, and career inventories and culture-based blogs and websites would be useful.

ADULT DEVELOPMENT AND EDUCATION

Implementing service strategies for adults may be designed for individual or family motivation and goal setting. Screening, brief intervention, and referral related to substance abuse is essential. Psycho-neurobiology behaviors may occur or develop in response to past unresolved traumas or recent and current stressors. The emergence of psychological and emotional stress behaviors may begin in response to relationship discomfort, employment issues, and health. Getting people to understand these physiological changes can help. Interventions to improve diets, stop smoking, and resist substance use are helping people recover. As preventive medicine such as flu shots has moved to local pharmacies, consider partnering with local nonstigmatizing entities to offer alternative ways of helping communities members.

FOLLOW-UP

Checking in with service users after a designated time period is used in some mental health or health service agencies, frequently for collection purposes. Follow-up is useful for continuing a service relationship to support recovery efforts and to resume a process that has been started. Recognizing that a substantial percentage of visits to mental health or counseling agencies often results in only one visit—a single session—follow-up could stretch that out to more than that.

On the other hand, the East Side Family Centre in Calgary, Alberta (Canada) initiated a walk-in, single-session, local therapy service in response to community needs for mental health services at no cost to the client (McElheran, Stewart, Soenen, Newman, & McLaurin, 2012). It is located in a shopping mall in an ethnically diverse low-income area. The single session is designed to cover four components, followed by team debriefing and noting future direction if the client returns. The evaluation results of a sample of 600 sessions noted promising results, with respondents rating the session effective in addressing their stressors. Figure 12.1 offers a trajectory of steps from welcoming to follow-up that have been observed to facilitate service user relationships.

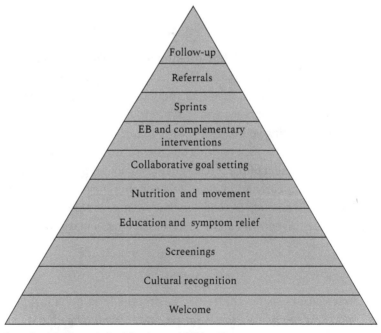

FIGURE 12.1   Stepping Up Through Goal Setting and Achievement

Working with an individual or family can include creating reading resources for different types of information needed to work toward goals. Foeman, Lawton, and Rieger (2015) report that among people of color the intersections of culture are often known and diverse ancestors are recognized. Among some Caucasian participants, the information of additional DNA evidence was resisted or denied, and they didn't want to share the information. These examples are unlike some of the recent TV commercials we have seen by Ancestry.com of people excited about genetic information they were not aware of. For some, gaining information through genograms and family history may prompt other ways of connecting to family and cultural history.

INTERNAL AND EXTERNAL RECOGNITION OF STRENGTHS AND PATHWAYS

Nh'át Hanh (1995, 2007) suggests that understanding ourselves helps us understand others. Compassion is also identified as a mindset, a quality, and a way of being. Lack of self-compassion may allow judgmental thoughts about ourselves and association of self-worth (Jinpa, 2015) with what we do rather than being us at peace with who we are. He shares the steps of moving from compassion to intention, dedication, and motivation as ways to give energy and purpose to our aspirations. Assisting service users to set a vision for themselves by understanding they are capable of doing more can lead to achieving a higher level by tapping into cultural, spiritual, social, and educational resources.

COMMUNITY RESPECT

Respecting communities and affirming their participation in civil responsibilities radiates from the place of humility. Social work recognizes the political and economic influences and the calls for increasing advocacy of policy areas that impact the health of the populations we serve. Hardina (2014) promotes the association of social work activity to organizational development and the roles of community organizing, policy analysis, and development,

Viewing our communities as cities presents a better way of addressing social issues that face us. Acknowledging cultural community beliefs about the natural environment, ceremonies, and interactions is part of some families' intuitive knowledge (Johnson, 1993; Trosper, 2002). The range of service interventions can assist service users in their paths from clients to citizens, homeless to sheltered, depressed to relieved. Fullilove (2013) discusses how fractured cities allow problems to persist. Her observations of collaborative interventions used strategies for design and participation. "What we found interesting was that not only did teams succeed in taking ownership but also people got to know one another. The cooperation among teams led to better interpersonal work relationships across teams" (Fullilove, 2013, p. 256).

An example is provided by Sheehan (2008). Mercado Central believed in the capacity of his neighborhood to activate their collective vision to establish a cooperatively owned marketplace in Minneapolis, Minnesota. The initiative involved local church groups working with new immigrants to integrate worship, skill building, and job development.

Inclusion acknowledges the broad view of geography, the locations of disease, and that remedies must be generated from systems thinking. Senge (2006) proposed that the co-creation of solutions beats trying to convince or influence. As community strengths are recognized, organizations must implement innovation. Workers will need more training to learn to accommodate new ideas and practices. Holbrook, Tennille, and Buck (2017) offer a model for social work educators to use that connects program evaluation and field work with curricular goals.

ROLE OF TECHNOLOGY AND SOCIAL MEDIA

The potential of online, virtual, and webinar information offers challenges and opportunities for connecting with people who are put off by the traditional office setting service. Texting, FaceTime, Google Hangout, and Skype present innovative ways of contact to help clients get through struggles and gain confidence. Social work has an important role in curriculum development, training, and community education to assist professionals, service users, and community residents on the research and behaviors to improve ourselves, our families, and communities.

We know that some young people use three or four screens as they learn, relax, and play. This connection to digital devices and learning pushes helping professionals to generate innovative learning activities for service users on devices online and in locations other than traditional office spaces. Social work can work with others and within their organizational teams to develop service user learning products. These and existing products, webinars, and games, may be incorporated in service sessions or assigned as homework for discussion at subsequent sessions to assist people in learning and addressing community politics as well as their individual emotional needs.

CASE SCENARIO

Day 1. Mariesa and Sasha are in the same sixth-grade class at the local middle school. Mariesa has been absent a day or 2 days each week for the past month. Sasha spoke to the school nurse about her concern for her friend. She knows that Mariesa's mom has recently separated from her husband, and she has had some difficulties at her job. She thinks Mariesa is trying to help her mom, but they haven't spoken this week.

Ms. Jeffries knows the school has a walk-in service for students who want help with navigating home issues. She asks Sasha if she thinks she can bring her by to see her when Mariesa returns to school. Sasha agrees.

Day 2. Sasha brings Mariesa to Ms. Jeffries's office at lunch the next day. Using the pyramid of steps in Figure 12.1, what kind of strategy might they come up with? Consider prevention versus treatment.

- Discuss engagement and goal setting for the 12-year-old.
- How can they uncover issues? Can her friend be involved?
- How might her location or home environment be assessed?

CHAPTER SUMMARY

The mezzo level involves interorganization, intraorganization, and community organization partnerships. Social work students will have opportunities to facilitate conversations to refine professional relationships and facilitate collaborative efforts to meet the consumer in their communities. The geography that families experience influences their sense of place and belonging. Building capacity engages strengths, presents cultural history of connections and principles of support and cohesion for survival and recovery. Students will consider and evaluate multicultural dimensions for considering assessment and establishing collaborative plans with individuals, families, and agency representatives to develop learning organizations capable of promoting growth.

EPAS AND CODE OF ETHICS

CSWE EDUCATIONAL POLICY & ACCREDITATION STANDARDS

Competency 6: Engage with Individuals, Families, Groups, Organizations, and Communities
- 6a) apply knowledge of human behavior and the social environment, person-in-environment, and other multidisciplinary theoretical frameworks to engage with clients and constituencies; and
- 6b) use empathy, reflection, and interpersonal skills to effectively engage diverse clients and constituencies.

Competency 9: Evaluate Practice with Individuals, Families, Groups, Organizations, and Communities
- 9 a) select and use appropriate methods for evaluation of outcomes;
- 9b) apply knowledge of human behavior and the social environment, person-in-environment, and other multidisciplinary theoretical frameworks in the evaluation of outcomes;
- 9c) critically analyze, monitor, and evaluate intervention and program processes and outcomes; and
- 9d) apply evaluation findings to improve practice effectiveness at the micro, mezzo, and macro levels (EPAS, 2015)

NASW CODE OF ETHICS
Value: Importance of Human Relationships
Ethical Principle: Social workers recognize the central importance of human relationships (NASW, n.d.).

DISCUSSION QUESTIONS

1. Select a community of interest. Research the basic ethnic/social group demographics. Locate at least five cultural icons of that community. Select churches, community organizations, businesses, and the like. What do these examples tell you about the culture of this geographic area?
2. What are some steps social workers could take to assist a client's racial or cultural socialization?
3. List two books written by a person of a nondominant cultural group that addresses overcoming serious challenges.

EXERCISES

1. Conduct the Lum self-assessment (Lum, 1999, Chapter 3). What did you think of the results?
2. List two objectives of a session with a service user about identity and community participation. Select a set of readings, film, art, or music to consider in creating the guided conversation with open-ended comments about goals and culture concerns.

MULTICULTURAL RESOURCES

Legend, J. (2016). *Redemption song* [Video file]. TED2016. Retrieved from http://www.ted.com/talks/john_legend_redemption_song? utm_source=newsletter_daily&utm_campaign=daily&utm_medium=email&utm_content=button__2016-07-01

Mohanty, J., & Newhill, C. E. (2011). Asian adolescent and young adult adoptees' psychological well-being: Examining the mediating role of marginality. *Children and Youth Services Review, 33*(7), 1189–1195.

Moses, D. (2015, August). We're off to see Appalachia: The crooked road links rural music communities. *NPR.* Retrieved from http://www.npr.org/2015/08/06/429724724/were-off-to-see-appalachia-the-crooked-road-links-rural-music-communities

Poo, A. J. (2016, Sept. 1). Facing race: Ai-jen Poo and Kai Wright on race, gender, and employment [Podcast]. *Race Forward.* Retrieved from https://www.raceforward.org/media/facing-race-stories-voices

Robbins, M.S., Szapocznik, J., Mayorga, C. C., Dillon, F. R., Burns, M., & Feaster, D. J. (2007). The impact of family functioning on family racial socialization processes. *Cultural Diversity and Ethnic Minority Psychology, 13*(4), 313–32.

FURTHER READING AND RESOURCES

Chou, R. (2016, Oct. 13). *Opioids for chronic pain—Evidence, guidelines, and policy and practice* [Videolecture]. National Center for Complementary and Integrative Health (NIH). Available at https://content.govdelivery.com/accounts/USNIHNCCIH/bulletins/16a8ef0

Congress, E. P., & Gonzalez, M. J. (Eds.). (2013). *Multicultural perspectives in social work practice with families* (Chapter 10). New York, NY: Springer.

Randall, V. (2014). Status of descendants of Africans enslaved in the United States. Available at http://bit.ly/1mzTTOJ

Urban Institute. (2016). How housing matters. Available at http://us11.campaign-archive1.com/? u=2b2f41f0d66eeaa4de409144a&id=f8dccbca6e&e=2725d3f672

Wheeler, D. P., & Dodd, S. J. (2011). LGBTQ capacity building in health care systems: A social work imperative. *Health & Social Work, 36*(4), 307–309.

CHAPTER 13

Facilitating Inclusion

Encouraging Service User Participation and Influencing
Policy for Social and Economic Justice Change / Macro

CHAPTER OVERVIEW

This chapter emphasizes the social work profession's awareness of human and civil rights and the various stages of support for, and pushback against them. Policy areas require knowledge and data for professionals and for service users in order to increase expertise and become more active in their asserting voices.

The range of existing laws and regulations for civil and human rights is reflected in Higginbotham's (1998) words: shades of freedom. It is important for social work practitioners and service delivery personnel to have awareness of relevant rules and regulations regarding issues such as women's rights, educational support for school children in low-wealth communities, Lesbian, Gay, Bisexual, Transgender, Queer, Intersex, Asexual (LGBTQIA) rights, mental health parity, and housing and food security. At a time when many human and civil rights issues appear to be threatened, it is critical to be informed and think calmly and reflectively about the various perspectives. Capacity building among community populations through social work and related professions, alongside others committed to a more peaceful and equitable world, is imperative.

LEARNING OBJECTIVES

- Pursuing policy areas of interest is needed to create career and service agendas.
- Select relevant sources of information and data.
- Understand that partnerships encourage local non-stigmatized locations for self-care and services.
- Understand that community practice involves work with system leadership offices for mutual policy development.
- Facilitate inclusion via citizen participation in agency, government, and business policy, and plan levels that look toward increased stability.
- Appreciate the community network of unique individual, family, and community configurations.
- Understand that ongoing learning, reading, and critical thinking is recommended for service providers and users.

Benchmark: Students will demonstrate the ability to assert their voices, advocate and collaborate with individuals, families, organizations, and communities to promote social justice and human rights.

THE MACRO DIMENSION

Social work in the macro environment involves professionals, service users and the general public. Helping consumers become informed of policy proposals, executive orders and public concerns adds another aspect to the social work landscape. The proliferation of online advocacy about social issues by supportive and opposing entities informs the range of roles where social workers are focusing their time and energy. Addressing the human rights outlined in the United Nations (UN) Declaration of Universal Human Rights is a component of domestic and international social justice and immigration, including the needs of people forced to migrate by governmental conditions.

Providing information to consumers about access to food and water, toxin-free environments, financial literacy, workforce participation, physical and mental health, and parenting and family development skills helps develop awareness and potential participation in service user capacity development. Social workers advancing change collaborate with service users and organizations to "move decisions down the organizational hierarchy" so decisions can be made with attention to the full range of issues intrinsic to advancing and sustaining growth and development (Senge, 1990. p. 287). Senge refers to this localness as the basis of the learning organization. Social work brings together a range of skills for these tasks.

Useful terms for this discussion include

- human rights,

Nadira works for a faith-based organization that serves rural, suburban, and urban communities. She has some experience with legal aid and Planned Parenthood. The agency received inquiries from several young women about their need for family planning and contraception. The group asked to meet with the director of the organization about their concerns. They informed the director that they had generated a petition signed by members of the community. They were aware that some members of their community had been turned away from the agency because of the services the members had requested. Because there were no other agencies within a reasonable distance, they wanted to pursue a legal appeal to urge the agency to address the needs of the community. If the agency's mission was to serve the people, they questioned the agency's right to funds if they were not meeting the community's needs.

Nadira has been asked to meet with the group, along with her supervisor and the agency's director. She will meet with her supervisors to prepare for the meeting. What items should she bring up for discussion?

STUDENT SCENARIO

- social justice,
- civic engagement,
- affirmative action, and
- activism,
- advocacy, and
- policy development.

HUMAN RIGHTS

The Council on Social Work Education (CSWE) "Competency 3: Advance Human Rights and Social, Economic, and Environmental Justice" (cswe.org, p. 7), broadens the scope of social work. Social work in the domestic sphere incorporates social and economic equality issues and promotes dignity and diversity appreciation. The Global Agenda for Social Work and Social Development of 2012 lays out an ambitious plan (Healy & Warire, 2014) for the profession "to contribute to the major human, social and environmental challenges facing the world" (p. 235). The document was developed through a collaboration between representatives from the major international social work associations and consultation with individual social workers in many countries. Issues of workers' rights, food security, justice, and incarceration are of concern around the world, including in the United States. We can incorporate these concepts into social work curricula in ways that connect students' lives to inequality and to the experiences of people living in other geographic locations.

Healy and Warire (2014) present the Millennium Development Goals (MDGs), adopted by the United Nations in 2000, as areas for information awareness at the policy and grassroots levels. The goals identify poverty, maternal and infant mortality, primary education, gender equality, and health outcomes as major concerns for efforts to improve the quality of living for citizens around the world. Through examples, they show how Kenya and the United States address these goals and urge social work educators to structure human rights knowledge in ways that emphasize the language of human rights and illustrate local policies that impact them.

Their discussion raises issues for the US and Kenya and describes the need for further examination of domestic human rights, and to embellish curriculum for practitioners and students interested in pursuing international work. On a foundational level, professional social workers can give people hope of overcoming their unfavorable circumstances by informing them of rights and sharing examples of civic participation and program initiatives that effectively reduce poverty (Healey & Warire, p. 238).

The human rights landscape (Simmons, 2014) in the United States involves service issues concerning inclusion. Unfair consequences frequently result from policies that guide the treatment of women, children, LGBTQIA persons, persons with different abilities, and immigrants in welfare services, the courts, and the labor market (Hertel and Libal, 2011; Human Rights Watch, 2012 in Healy & Warire, 2014). In Kenya, human rights have been violated and challenged since the colonial era. Though the government has relaxed in some ways, it still maintains protections against questioning and change. Efforts by journalists and Non-Governmental Organizations (NGOs) that press for accountability and expose corruption "face hostile rhetoric and restrictions" (Mukoka/Reuters, 2017, para 16).

Human rights is a broad base from which to advocate, to conduct policy evaluation and training, and to conduct research. It also provides a framework for teaching international social work (Mapp, 2014) and economic justice (Simmons, 2014). Helping students become more informed that strategies for poverty reduction and social work roles in prevention and recovery work with families will assist understanding the connections of social justice with political and legal well-being. Sharing this spectrum of resources and information with service users is a component of social work education (Congress, 2014).

The Organization for Economic Cooperation and Development (OECD), established in 1961, is a forum of 35 members who work together to promote prosperity and sustainable development (OECD, 2018). It recommends integrating social services for vulnerable populations with complex service needs, using cost-efficient evaluations, service user satisfaction, and effective preventative care (OECD, 2018). Its perspective on vulnerability requires attention to housing, health, material conditions, and food security as immediate goals. Its report examines these needs for four specific groups: families, frail elderly people, homeless people, and those with complex health needs.

SOCIAL JUSTICE

Social justice is the crux of movements that advocate for what is deemed right and fair (Tyler & Smith, 1995) regarding crimes, and social and economic welfare. Smith & Hayes (2016) identify the need for students to examine their ideas of criminal justice from various points for reflection and critical thinking. Considering the connection of philosophical definitions of freedom and virtue to sociological definitions of inequality, crime and victimization requires critical thinking about policies on policing, surveillance and sentencing. The application of contemporary laws regarding drug possession, white collar crime and other infractions urges students to evaluate ideas of what is ethical and how they would apply standards of justice. Social and economic justice elicits the need for conversations that critically contemplate perspectives about the impact of social policies on low income, working class families, or vulnerable citizens.

People interested in helping others generally bring compassion and are also interested in social and economic justice. Bell (2013) defines social justice as a process and a goal. With this is mind, social workers bring themselves as compassionate beings to organizations and social environments with communities and diverse citizens. They participate in learning, acting, and evaluating behaviors and attitudes that transact with others to determine and achieve specific goals.

Compassion allows sensitivity to another's suffering. It moves us to ameliorate conditions that have contributed to the trauma or injustice experienced by others. Jinpa (2015) illustrates the place of compassion for helpers and for those we seek to assist. He says, "Self-compassion makes us more resilient in the face of challenges" (p. 41). Progress toward social justice requires personal development and self-care. Shifting to paradigms of strength instead of pathology includes an emphasis on encouraging positive emotions and mindsets. Training for the use and application of compassion is being explored. Jinpa's (2015) research on compassion cultivation training explored measures of emotion suppression and regulation. Enhancing compassion practices, expressing and regulating emotional reactions personally and in schools and businesses were connected to increases in positive emotions, stronger sense of community, and improvements in conflict resolution.

Addressing social injustices requires multiple social work skills across the macro, mezzo, and micro domains. While Zerden, Sheely and Despard (2016) note that some social work educators and practitioners foster a belief that social work occurs mainly at the micro level, most practitioners' work actually requires a variety of macro skills. An examination of the scope of social work that incorporates multicultural awareness, culturally affirming strategies, and policy advocacy results in individual, family and organizational benefits. Many social work programs have expanded their curriculum to more strongly reflect the significance of macro practice, management, policy advocacy, community organizing, to the profession (Coyle, 2016). Macro practice also presents analyses of social welfare dynamics that expose some domestic policy adoptions that violate human rights (Hertel & Libal, 2011).

Organizational cultures present structures that may either allow or obstruct opportunities for responding to service users in supportive ways. Students often report they would like to do more for some of their cases but their supervisors don't support it. The path to implementing change is marked with many realities including apathy, politics, and media. Social work can lead by thinking through elements in ways that include the many players and perspectives present. As we lead, accountability for results is a required companion.

Senge (1990) points out that organizations benefit from individuals who learn. By perusing historical sources of strengths across ancestral groups' social workers bring cultural affirmation and role representation to collaborative assessment and goal setting for individuals, families, and communities from a macro perspective. New learning may influence the goals and objectives within social services, behavioral health and related organizations, the social welfare system, to become more inclusive in planning ways to reduce disparities and improve outcomes.

Friedman (2005) writes that political debates more often have to do with the means rather than the ends. Social work students often express beliefs that we all want children to receive a good education, live in safe communities, and enjoy a clean environment. However, we are also aware of attitudes, beliefs, and choices that manipulate poor outcomes for many. Examples of bureaucratic choices that deny federal money for Medicaid, mental health and recovery services often reveal use of monies that benefit those with resources. Stephenson (2016, para 12) asks, "Does sentencing poor people to receiving little or no mental health care truly motivate them to find money they don't have in order to provide them with the dignity to pay for their own health insurance?" The message often sent by legislators appears to be that they have malice for low income citizens or lack training on how to collaborate across constituents to operate for the benefit of democracy. Social justice advocacy urges new learning to improve communication and fiscal allocations.

SYSTEMS THINKING

Systems thinking involves moving the helping disciplines to the next level for innovation and implementation of attitudes, behaviors, and choices that incorporate cultural and community strengths. Senge (1990) called it the fifth discipline and describes it as the discipline "that integrates disciplines" (p. 12). He recognizes a need to look at the big picture in order to get to a shared vision. He observes the need for organizations to become open to new learning. This is expected to occur as members of learning organizations come to terms with seeing ourselves as part of the world rather than separate from it. To get there requires conversations that promote teamwork and team learning. The discussion needs to include short-term goals and the gradual processes that brought us to the present point of major challenges and concerns—a history of terrorism against people of color (Cone, 2011), a damaged public school system, environmental toxicity, and disparities—and the steps that can lead us forward.

Senge (1990) goes on to suggest we only need to read *The March of Folly* (Tuchman, 1985) to see how the status of short-sighted thinking is revealed in a history of policies that led to devastating consequences when there were alternative paths. There are other theories that may explain how day-to-day operations fit into various frames. However, as we continue to explore a frame of systemic thinking to facilitate inclusion and move away from discriminatory actions, the paradigms we choose must contain options to co-create within organizations, so that we can simultaneously build systemic thinking with service users, their families, and communities.

Using systems and people in their environments as a fundamental viewpoint, macro work involves economics, politics, and social interactions, especially in the education and criminal justice areas. What issues and questions can social workers pose to assist those vulnerable to policies that create obstacles?

SOCIAL WORK EDUCATION AND SOCIAL JUSTICE

Social work curriculum development must provide knowledge and skills compatible with our values that offer strategies to engage with diverse communities, collaborate with various stakeholders, and deliver effective interventions that result in positive change. Several areas of knowledge impact student learning and application. The integration of culturally affirming resources with health and emotional health evidence of environmental and social determinant influences contributes to ongoing strategizing for prevention (Surgeon General, 2011). Political awareness and advocacy, citizen participation, technology and evaluation should benefit the welfare of our communities (Iachini, Clone, DeHart, et al., 2016). The National Prevention Strategy is an example of shifting the focus on wellness instead of pathology. Outreach and leadership development through partnerships for universal learning play important roles in talking through issues to establish mechanisms for social justice.

Social work's responsibility to population health is addressed via knowledge building, research, and evidence informed strategies that include perspectives of representatives from all groups impacted by service delivery.

Working across populations involves assessing cultural views and using knowledge on macro, mezzo, and macro levels. Field placements provide opportunities to work with supervisors and a range of service users in local and regional service sites. These settings present opportunities to collaborate with service users and implement through practice and supervision community education and development, trauma informed and complementary approaches, to promote recovery and resilience.

ECONOMICS AND SOCIAL DEVELOPMENT

Economics as the standpoint from which oppression occurs exposes historical restrictions on opportunities. This view connects improved access to capital with a path to social development. Students pursuing social work careers are interested in a range of career opportunities. For those with macro, community practice, and organizational development interests, further study of economics and policy formulation are important.

Governmental tax policy and regulations, educational funding, and workforce equity impact citizens and their capacity to care for families. Policy areas that impact jobs creation and affect citizens who seek assistance from agencies attract social workers and students who have analytical and interpersonal skills to address disparities and effectiveness. State regulations may impose educational requirements where on the job training could be sufficient (Abdul-Jabbar, 2016). Integrating social development goals with economic considerations may not typically occur, but because social work emphasizes addressing the grand challenges in our social environment, innovative partnerships and opportunities for dialog are needed.

Unions need protection to safeguard jobs and benefits. Recent efforts to break unions have resulted in an overall decline in wages (Rosenfeld, Denice, & Laird, 2016). The average minimum wage earner is more educated today and more productive than in 1968, but paid less (Rosenfeld, Denice, & Laird, 2016). The repeal of the pay transparency rule will make it easier to discriminate against women and people of color (EPI, 2017). This rule protects an applicant or employee's questions, comments and disclosures about compensation (United States Department of Labor, n.d.).

The media's lens on Appalachia depicts a cultural group that is somewhat isolated, with minimal job opportunities. Despite the dim view some may have of this region, it has cultural strengths, as does every region, that could be enhanced with innovative community-sensitive policy development. Transportation is one of the infrastructure issues that, with improved policy formulations, could enhance medical access and lead to incremental economic progress. Transportation resources impact health seeking behaviors (Ruggiano, Shtompel, Whiteman, & Sias, 2017) and often reduce work options. Municipal governments and public health agencies should collaborate (Masotti, Fick, & O'Connor, 2010) to remedy obstacles that people without vehicles face.

Stiglitz suggests our current economic policy impedes the growth of people with lower incomes. He urges reform of corporate and personal income taxes to restore economic vitality (Stiglitz, 2014). His ideas include closing corporate tax loopholes, implementing a progressive tax on personal income, and encouraging socially beneficial behavior.

SOCIAL WORK PARTICIPATION IN POLITICS

Social work political participation has been espoused in ethics (NASW Code of Ethics, n.d.) and competencies (CSWE.org, 2015) but actual social work advocates in politics, related to poverty, housing, criminal justice, workforce needs, and other issues that affect service user populations, has been limited. According to Rome & Hoechstetter (2010) about 50 % of social work respondents report active participation in the policy process. Ritter (2008) points out that social work education provides opportunities to practice clinical skills but opportunities for macro work, advocacy, and organizing skills have been restrained. A strong participatory component is needed to encourage social workers' psychological engagement with politics. A strong participatory component is also required to model that participation obligation in our political democracy. Cabiati and Raineri (2016) present an example showing that students respond to specific events designed to help members of different groups engage and take steps toward reducing notions of stigma.

The literature notes a need for social work participation in politics. Social workers' low participation in social protest is described as an under-researched field. Makaros and Grodofsky (2016) describe an Israeli protest movement that speaks to the complexities of political engagement. Participation in protest has been reported to vary in different locations and regarding different tasks. This study identified three themes: daily operations, engagement of the social protests at the national level, and assistance to protesting individuals in need. Making the decision whether to participate or not on a personal or a professional level was affected by conflicting loyalty to their activist role as a public worker and to their employer.

CAN ELECTED OFFICIALS BE HELD ACCOUNTABLE?

The participation of community members in voting for people who express intentions to enact laws that assist working people and others, and not prioritize benefits to wealthy people, is how we expect democracy to work. Including residents in discussions about their communities and ways to improve employment for those who need assistance can lead to better circumstances for middle-class and lower-income citizens. Beck (2017) points out that being held accountable should make people consider other points of view. The expectation is that having to answer to someone, for your actions and your decisions (e.g. your constituency) should make you think more carefully about what you decide or how you vote. Recent observations of political activity that removes protections give us reasons to pause. Simultaneously, activism is occurring that raises questions, that encourages others to participate, and that exposes situations and officials that should be resisted and held accountable.

The role of hometown politics is an example of context regarding economic pathways for potential immigrants. Andrews (2016) contemplates the impact of participatory governance and resource redistribution to protect community residents from the worst agricultural jobs in small rural Mexican communities. Two communities in Mexico were observed. One town was sensitive to residents' needs and allocated resources in a way to provide local employment opportunities other than farm work. The other town did not address the local need for employment and ultimately people had to leave to seek whatever they could find. Political operations could help residents maintain livelihoods in their home areas if communal land distribution and wage labor were shaped to help, rather than push people out.

The work of state level advocacy organizations has potential to influence the government's commitment to low-income families or to negate support (Phinney, 2016). Organizational advocates can help shape state-level policy decisions. People have to continuously question officials and work with advocacy groups to maintain voices that question and urge transparency.

CAPACITY BUILDING

In order to address social and economic injustice, social workers need awareness of the realities of social environments, and how policies drive the challenges people face. In addition, they need knowledge and skill development in capacity building. Awareness of the significance of economics to the social welfare of citizens helps broaden understanding of the systems

> **CRITICAL THINKING**
>
> Select a policy area of concern to you. What do you think social workers could do to encourage community participation to advocate in this area? Compare your ideas with a classmate.

that exclude and diminish capacity. Poverty is just one dimension of exclusion and "poverty does not necessarily lead to exclusion" (Kenyon, Lyons, & Rafferty, 2002, p. 208). The use of virtual technology may present an alternative to assist inclusion beyond mobility-related exclusion. More training for capacity building (Goytia et al., 2013) is needed to help social workers inform community residents and service users of the impact of social environments, leadership, and policies. Strategies for building capacity and resilience go hand in hand to address social issues and injustice.

The fields of community development and social development include social welfare and human development parameters. These subject areas are not limited to visible or geographic locals; they extend to social media and other invisible connections. Invisible connections may include leadership, organization, and evaluation of steps in social change through the lens of place and identity (Green, 2016). Social worker access to socioeconomic and well-being data across communities can lead in capacity building efforts. As social work has expanded its awareness and understanding of communities, population health, and service users' voices, the inclusion of financial capability and asset building (FCAB) has been recognized (Bent-Goodley et al., 2016) as an important area for work.

MATTERS OF ENGAGEMENT: COLLABORATING WITH COMMUNITY ORGANIZATIONS

Community-based prevention services play a critical role in assisting ongoing preparation of community residents for the vicissitudes of life and struggle in rural, suburban, and urban communities. Community development tactics vary across countries and historical time. Establishing community partnerships can be difficult in some places when agencies try to maintain their own spaces and funding. Yet with more focus on resident needs and innovative methods of service delivery, integrated and wrap around approaches have proven effective.

Scaling up system use of evidence-based practice successfully demonstrated the inter-agency collaborative team model (Hurlburt et al., 2013.) The process is complex and takes time, but implementation can lead to solutions for sustained public health benefits.

Community development is linked to business-like procedures in some eras and to more group-work-skills-like negotiation, conflict resolution, or advocacy at other times (Barron & Taylor, 2010). In the context of best practices, the long view that incorporates cultural heritage themes and approaches and prevention frameworks are working to develop more informed communities.

MULTIPLE INTEREST COALITION BUILDING

Yee (2016) suggests that to really get away from the persistent dominance of male hierarchy and to dismantle oppressive practices, processes, and structures, politics needs to move away from the single identity base and pursue transformative steps that "focus on the ways in which privilege and oppression intersect and reinforce, intentionally or not." (p. 497). Tying political processes to race and identity does not address the matrix of domination and it continues to allow those in privileged positions of power to avoid accountability. Yee recommends "multi-co-alition building that relies on shared and ethical responsibility" (p. 497). This represents a move from identity politics that isolates groups, to groups that are diverse and advocate for steps and goals that address mutual needs of the larger group. The multi-coalition is expected to also con-front the tensions of male dominance and privilege in organizations with various roles that race, class, gender and sexual orientation play within the institutional structures. As students engage in community assessment and coalition building, some will likely become more interested in politics. This is a contemporary task of macro practice. Providing clear examples of political (Scott & Scott, 2011) office holders' work may be attractive to some and offer possibilities for leadership. NASW provides a database of social workers in politics (NASW/PACE, 2018).

Opportunities exist for social workers to encourage community members to engage with civic responsibility on governmental, organizational, and community levels. Simultaneously, there are roles for social workers at these levels as participants and as facilitators.

ORGANIZATIONAL DEVELOPMENT AND LEADERSHIP

The role of leaders in various governmental, nonprofit, and private organizations that offer services may be shaped by their application of critical race theory. As a critical theory, it promotes a structural approach to addressing the problems of a diverse society (Ortiz & Jani, 2010). An issue that many students bring involves the reluctance of supervisors to support culturally sensitive approaches that go beyond traditional paradigms.

The history of federal, state, and local policies that encouraged or maintained segregated services in housing (Rothstein, 2014) and medicine have residual influence today. However, as students examine service delivery and promote innovation, they may take innovative program examples and questions to their supervision sessions to explore ways changes might be introduced.

AFFIRMATIVE ACTION

Institutional and organizational policies have evolved as a result of administrators offering opportunities to members of historically excluded groups. Referred to as affirmative action, these guidelines often focus on hiring in organizations and admissions in education (ncsl. org, 2014). Controversy surrounding the constitutionality of affirmative action programs has made the topic one of heated debate. Reasons for using affirming procedures and sharing recruitment information supports inclusion and helps communities navigate educational and employment opportunities.

GRASSROOTS ACTIVITIES

Grassroots organizations can begin with two or more persons and could include hundreds pursuing common interests through an informal, community-based, nonprofit structure. They may begin with volunteers but could grow to incorporate staff and revenue-producing activities.

Some grassroots organizations begin with low levels of formality (Anheier, 2005). However, recent observations indicate the typical views of these organizations will likely change as participants navigate political waters in places around the world.

Grassroots organizations can be characterized by place-based, people-focused, informal structures, collective memberships, and variable lengths of duration (grassrootsgrantmaker. org, 2015). A grassroots level organization (GLO) includes volunteers who support one another (Nair & Guererro, 2014).

ADVOCACY

Advocacy occurs on several levels. It can be practiced on behalf of clients to act on their own behalf or used to obtain resources for clients. Case managers advocate for improved policies and procedures for clients (Nair & Guerrero, 2014), and their voices can lead to improvements. Advocates develop skills like interacting with voters, media relations, coordinating coalition building, research and analysis, processing data, diagnostic programs, and participating in collaborative problem solving (Jansson, 2014).

Dalrymple and Boylan (2013) point to advocacy as a skill central to social work. Independent advocacy has developed as service users have fought to have their voices heard in decisions about service delivery. Advocacy is a social movement that has been influenced by the service user movement. From the United Kingdom's (UK) perspective, social workers can advocate in organizations or independently. The progress from "doing on behalf of" to "working along-side of" service users highlights another dimension of collaboration. Hick's work (2002) offers Canadian perspectives. He proposes taking action, using poetry and creativity, and breaking away from the traditional molds as ways to address the system of classification that ruling groups have imposed on others. Simultaneously, Jansson (2014) provides the basics: knowledge, values, and skills for effective reform through policy practice.

Public health curriculum has not included advocacy as a substantive component in the past. However, as scholars in this area plan for the next generation of public health graduates, they are including online advocacy and mentoring (O'Connell, Stoneham, & Saunders, 2016). The Public Health Advocacy Institute in West Australia implemented a year-long advocacy program that resulted in more proactive engagement in advocacy to guide professional development.

On a micro level, especially where service cut backs occur, individual peer advocacy takes place. Power, Bartlett & Hall (2016) describe the situations of persons with developmental differences being dislocated from supports in the UK. Where personal day services have declined, peer support or peer advocacy increased. When people are in a similar situation, they come together to advocate for themselves. Where some may not be so skilled in speaking up, another may have that ability.

On the macro level, relationships between state advocacy organizations and policy choices are examined for their potential to represent the poor and their ability to gain additional support for low income families (Phinney, 2016). TalkPoverty.org shares data regarding poverty in each state and across selected sets of variables (Visit talkpoverty.org to see interactive maps of this data). The Coalition of Human Needs (CHN) provides data on how federal budget work affects existing programs such as SNAP, work requirements, consumer protections, prevention services for children, and more (chn.org). Click on Outcomes Reports for detailed evidence that these programs work and need to be fully funded. CHN Outcomes fact sheets are compiled from analyses by CHN members and other expert sources and can be shared with the public.

Advocacy voices support many areas of concern to social workers. Workers and citizens who have interests in various disciplinary areas are speaking up through organizations and sometimes individually to address their interpretation of social needs. Prince Ea suggests that immersion in technology is increasing separateness rather than connecting more with others (Ea, 2014). He also encourages a new model for education (2016). Chelsea Shields (TED Talk, 2012) makes a strong case for gender equality in the Mormon religious institution. Her talk identifies the attitudes, behaviors, and fundraising of a group that impacts the lives of many. It offers an important perspective to think about. Using visual discussion to share and promote more conversation gets us thinking.

ADVOCACY ORGANIZATIONS

Advocates often establish organizations when they observe unmet needs, exclusion of some citizens, or existing policies do not offer protection and safety (NewComeryouth.ca). Program evaluation and community survey data are used to build agendas and develop strategies to meet those concerns. Community work in the United Kingdom has a long history in the social work profession. Dalrymple and Boylan (2013) describe advocacy as a social movement that connects service users with social workers. Their social work community supports this view when social workers, due to their institutional connections, cannot advocate for a service user. An independent social work advocate could be an option to overcome that challenge. The issue of social worker loyalty (referred to earlier by the Israeli social workers) or public agency restrictions can pose challenges for workers interested in meeting the needs of service users.

As a component of curriculum design, advocacy also addresses culture. For example, Kiehne (2016) recommends using a Latino critical perspective in social work to assess oppression and promote change. Critical race theory (CRT) evolved following the civil rights movement to challenge the continuing threats to equality. LatCrit developed from this theory to focus on the inequality that disadvantages Latinos. It entails the use of grassroots organizing and promotes systemic change through self-advocacy.

ADVOCACY AND POLICY DEVELOPMENT

Some organizations have been fragmented by the roles of managerialism and marketization and the push to meet the targets set by managers rather than the goals of critical social work practice (Rogowski, 2011). Ferguson (2008) describes how this impacts social work tasks. He states that these changes have eroded the dynamics of social change that attracted people to the profession. The workers he spoke to listed increased paperwork, workloads, bureaucracy, and a mechanistic delivery of services as reasons for work dissatisfaction. Increased insecurity in education, employment, healthcare, housing, and pensions has contributed to an increase in childhood deprivation, worsened relationships with their parents, increased use of substances, and increased unsafe sex. These experiences come to the attention of school officials, juvenile justice workers, mental health professionals, and health agencies, and require evaluation of observable policy modifications.

INTERPROFESSIONAL COLLABORATION

Social workers and other helping professionals can participate in interest areas as individual professionals or as agents of the organizations that employ them. Relationships with other helping professionals can offer guidance for referring service users to opportunities. We all should be sitting at the table to work on the issues facing us (Lewis, 2013). These connections can foster mutual aid around particular issues and serve to initiate collaborative activities.

CIVIC PARTICIPATION

Adequate civic education is absent in schools despite the need to provide it, and obstructions to its implementation need to be addressed (Quigley, 1999). Recent reports lay out recommendations to make students more aware of their roles in sustaining our democracy. Civic learning informs knowledge of our history and should involve opportunities for students to develop civic skills (Herczog, 2016; Lander, 2015). Secretary of Education Duncan remarked that while some people think civics is antiquated, it is in fact, quite necessary for our freedom and for democracy (Duncan, 2011).

Liberal arts education is attracting students returning for education after working or progressing at a slower pace than others. The curriculum needs modification to embrace students from lower income brackets who would benefit from civic engagement activities with more diverse formats (Maurrasse, 2015). There is significant leadership potential for social workers to mediate and facilitate dialogs (Hardina, 2014) regarding civic responsibilities and participation across categories and in various settings. Assisting communities to become more informed of relevant and current legislation and work with one another to improve social conditions speaks to our Code of Ethics (NASW, n.d.) and practice competencies.

STATUS OF VOTING

The electoral voting process allows citizens to cast their support of a person who will participate in planning and developing policy, and implementing leadership on issues that affect citizens.

The status of voting in local communities is marred by obstacles to people of color and denial of voting rights to women and others throughout history. The Voting Rights Act of 1965 was signed by President Lyndon Johnson to address acts of discrimination by those who did not want African Americans to vote (history.com, 2009). Voting rights legislation helped eliminate local obstacles, such as poll taxes and literacy tests, created to keep African Americans away from the polls (history.com, 2018). However, states and local governments have continued to impose challenges to voting and to encouraging people of color and women to run for office. Most recently, Wisconsin, North Carolina and Florida implemented new laws restricting when, where, and how people could vote. These laws harmed students, the poor, and people of color. The lawmakers involved admitted their interest in suppressing Democratic votes (Ollstein, & Lerner, 2016).

Education Secretary John B. King, Jr. recently described voting as the cornerstone of freedom (Heim, 2016). He addressed the role school should play in preparing students for their responsibility to participate in our democracy. He referred to the need for students to be familiar with documents that speak to our history, including the Declaration of Independence; the Constitution; Sojourner Truth's speech, Ain't I a Woman; and Dr. King's letter from a Birmingham jail. A richer history will get students involved in real issues so they can develop solutions and work together to advocate those solutions.

Leadership opportunities exist for social workers and other helping professionals to include service user referrals to community civic organizations and citizenship knowledge

EXISTING POLICIES AND IMPACT ON GROUPS

Policies impact citizen's participation in our democracy. Some obstruct participation. Countries around the world have similar dynamics regarding dominant groups and others (i.e. minority or other nondominant groups).

Policies are developed in organizations that have grown up following single focused management theories. In a presentation on leadership style Maisano (2016), presented three theories for people to select which one they preferred: management science, emotional and social intelligence, and systems. Systems thinking has evolved from distinct concepts of management and emotional intelligence to notions that integrate ideas about achieving better outcomes. The key is co-creation. People must work together to create approaches that may have not been used before. Resilience is needed to address unknowns in organizations. How will an organization respond to creative approaches that integrate culturally different approaches, spirituality, respect for tribal customs, and African folklore, for example? What about an approach that respects the words not spoken by a person who does not hear? Or, one that involves the leadership of a trans person over their life course? A question for students may be, how do I do what I am afraid of? We may also frame this question for clients we work with. How can they work with someone they think may be judging them?

Of the 325,719,178 U.S. residents, 2017 population estimate, (census.gov) about one third are persons of color belonging to an ethnic or racial minority group. In 2013, over 40 million foreign-born persons represented 13% of the population (Dews, 2013).

Multiracial Americans are growing at a rate three times as fast as the population as a whole (Pew Research Center, 2015). Most frequently, those who are informed of cultural strengths are proud of their background. Nevertheless, people of color face barriers to high quality health and mental health care. The absence of people of color in clinical trials accounts in some part for the gap between research and practice for minority group members. Few ethnic specific analyses have been conducted in clinical trials (Jacewicz, 2016). Members of these groups are less likely to receive best evidence based treatment (American Council of Physicians, 2010). Policies and practices often do not offer best strategies for meeting needs of the most vulnerable citizens.

POVERTY DATA

The US's position on the growing gap between the top 20% of households and all others has pushed many citizens to raise their voices for policy review, policy evaluation, and advocacy to promote more justice and equality. The safety net has improved since the 1990s (Tach & Edin, 2017) to the benefit of many working poor parents. However, many have been excluded from benefits and their incomes remain extremely low. Threats to the safety net are continuing. Political support for increasing cuts to benefits that help the poor seems to rely on old mottos and limited analysis that suggest making people poorer will make them better (DeLauro, 2017).

According to a report from the Organisation for Economic Co-operation and Development (OECD) (Gould & Wething, 2012), in the late 2000s, 17.3 percent of the U.S. population lived in poverty—the highest relative poverty rate among OECD peers. Recent reports from several sources indicate rising poverty (Smiley & West, 2013; Edin & Shaefer, 2016; Kneebone, 2014) and inequality in the US. The extent of recovery provided by safety net policies has been shown to be ineffective. Some areas continue to be seriously affected. New Orleans is an example (Berube & Holmes, 2015).

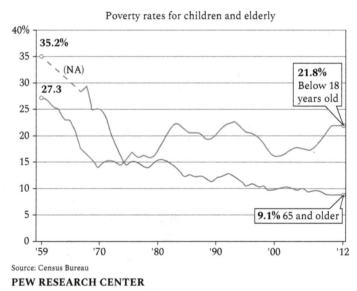

Source: Census Bureau

PEW RESEARCH CENTER

FIGURE 13.1   Poverty Rates for Children and Elderly

According to Pew Research, more poor Americans are in their prime working years. (Desilver, 2014). This impacts more children who are in low wealth families than the elderly. About 21% of all children (15 million children in the United States) live in families with incomes below the federal poverty level (NCCP, 2018). About 14.5% of elderly are poor, based on the Supplemental Poverty Measure (SPM) which allows income to be calculated with addition resources such as food stamps (Cubanski, Orgera, Damico, & Neuman, 2018). The link between economics, physical health, and mental health cannot be ignored when analyzing strategies to improve quality of life in families with children.

GENDER EQUALITY

Policies regarding women and working class groups have particular influence on how they deal with stressors in their lives. Abdul-Jabbar (2016) points out a need to have laws and the motivation to enforce them. Public pressure creates motivation for agencies to enforce laws that protect vulnerable people and address discrimination. Abdul-Jabbar gives the example of Iceland's Women's Day Off, a day when women chose not to cook, clean, or go to work and men are responsible for child care, as an example of a public action that promoted gender equality. Subsequently, the government established reasonable policies that supported women.

Yet, some politicians and others in leadership roles elevate the rights of women and the rights of people with nonconforming gender roles to be themselves and be protected above the rights of others. Rights to a sound education, adequate health care, and individual reproductive decision making should not be obstructed. Audi (n.d.) recommends that among other tenets, "for the sake of the flourishing of citizens, democracies should observe a protection of identity principle" (para 10). Respect of human rights should include representation of citizens of all genders.

In a world of multiple diverse identities, addressing human rights and elevating the poor and the oppressed should be an agreed upon goal for an intelligent society. This should be approached using the most advanced planning methods at our disposal, rather than mandated by a punitive-based perspective. Gerzema and D'Antonio (2013) think more women's thinking is needed in today's organizations. They observed feminine traits of flexibility, empathy, and honesty in their survey to resolve conflicts and increase profits.

ACTIVISM FOR SOCIAL JUSTICE

Social Justice involves process and goals (Bell, 2013). The process includes small steps, from initiating organizational meetings, planning discussion formats, to active campaigning for social change.

Activism occurs on college campuses and in many other arenas, including organizations created by low income youth groups (McClelland & Rizga, 2007) that may not get much media attention. Environmental activism by members of Youth United for Community Action, an organization created by youth of color in the California Bay Area, won a lawsuit to shut down a hazardous waste-handling company. The March 24, 2018, protest march to advocate for changes in gun law influenced some states to change their gun control laws, and is the most recent and remarkable example of youth-organized activism (Visit marchforourlives.com).

Foster youth are also advancing a grassroots movement that includes youth with foster care experiences as participants in Foster Youth in Action. The organization was founded by California Youth Connection in 2008 and is currently engaging participants through training and leadership opportunities, including shared leadership across the country (fosteryouthaction.org).

Gil (1998) offered insight from history on the impact of strategies to overcome injustice and oppression. He looked for associations between the strategies of long- and short-term goals and the likelihood of achieving social change. Calling on prevention theory, he highlighted the need to eradicate causes of injustice linked to an emphasis on inequality, selfishness, competition, and disregard for community. The long-term goal of a shared vision must involve common interests between individuals and social groups in meeting basic human needs, including biological, material, social-psychological, productive, creative, security, self-actualization, and spiritual needs.

In 1998, Gil, a proponent of radical social work, proposed specific ways to challenge existing unjust and oppressive institutions by claiming values of social justice and human liberation. His analysis of social status, which blamed individuals rather than acknowledge the structural system's manipulation of adults, called for principles and values that the broad social work profession is calling for now. These principles include human rights, rejecting political neutrality, insight into one's personal role in oppression, efforts to transform the style and form of practice relationships, and administrative transparency and accountability. He proposed the use of support and study groups to help social workers affirm the integrity of their perspectives, and promote the integration of political activism into everyday life.

Activism can also be connected to other areas that groups want to call attention to. They may include students (Grande, 2001), workers, and other categories of people choosing to protest for change. A group of Black women wanting to encourage occupations in medicine have initiated a media relations project to do that. The "Changing the Face of Medicine Initiative (CFMI) is a groundbreaking multimedia project that includes an educational tour, a biographical photo-essay book, and a documentary film. This initiative celebrates the history and current status of Black women in medicine, while designing diversity and inclusion solutions to change outcomes for the future" (RobbinsList, 2017, para 2).

ACTIVIST SKILLS

Social workers practice activist skills on behalf of clients through grassroots, nonprofit, or corporate organizations, and the activism can be directed by individuals or groups and aimed at organizations for particular outcomes. Activists use a range of community practice techniques to raise awareness, inform, translate research, and motivate others to participate in the democratic process. Skills include asset mapping, organizing across communities and organizations, goal setting, evaluation, negotiation, and mediating. According to Pippard and Bjorkland (2003) the key techniques that help implement strategies to schedule, solicit participation, and prioritize community concerns include force field analysis (FFA), program evaluation review techniques (PERT), nominal group technique (NGT), Delphi, and Q-sort. Organizers and persons pursuing leadership roles should also be familiar with parliamentary procedure.

These techniques are useful for data gathering and setting up sequential meetings to determine and implement strategies. Ongoing activist and advocacy work contribute to the development of capacity to pursue community and social development goals.

Research on the effect of activist practices is also useful in planning community development strategies. Analysis of the impact of activist targets and nontarget organizations illustrates how activists and others shape organizational decisions. Adoption of evidence-based and socially responsible policy appears to be more successfully received than disruption-linked tactics (Briscoe, Gupta & Anner, 2015). The use of disruption-based strategies results in getting attention for the campaign. The results of the evidence-based approaches seem to be more broadly linked to cases for internal changes.

Opportunities for social work students to participate in macro strategies for activism may be developed further as social work highlights evidence of social change strategy intervention results.

POLICYMAKING: SOCIAL WELFARE ISSUES

Policy formulation and development concerning employment, workforce development, and economics are connected to social welfare. According to the Coalition of Human Needs, progress has been made on reducing poverty (chn.org). The goal is to continue making progress and to improve policies to reduce financial distress and social exclusion. Approaches to education in the helping professions, including social work, public health, and counseling, will influence how new professionals work to strengthen and transform existing systems.

Providing effective service delivery embraces organizational policy review and evaluation and promotion of policies that address poverty and working-class conditions. Steps in the process promote strengths identification, resources access, and management skill development.

The Hamilton Project identified several policy areas that can enhance positive outcomes in areas intrinsic to transforming disparities. The major components included early childhood education, support for distressed youth, apprenticeship programs for workforce development, and improvements in safety net legislation (Kearney & Harris, 2014).

International and domestic capacity building involves policy making for legislation that protects and provides opportunities to improve the social welfare of citizens. Organizational decisions based on collaborative approaches that include representatives across groups and using data to drive scenarios that have demonstrated effectiveness and respect for all, call for strong leadership and mediator skills. Policies that impact the social environments of children, need extreme attention, as they are our most important citizens.

CHILDREN

Collaborating across disciplines to promote culturally affirming strategies and supports for physical and mental health care providers and education personnel is critical. Addressing the dynamics that build social divisions should begin with providing educational curricula in the primary grades that establish the cultural strengths of all people, and that engage children in learning environments that promote mutual respect. Teaching the truth about history and employing instructional methods that engage children in ways that permit oral, written, art, and music formats would be a step toward improving academic performance.

Many children across economic, racial, and ethnic groups face adverse circumstances. Trauma-informed professionals are needed to integrate creative universal learning designs into daily routines to help young people become connected to supportive adults. All young people need exposure to techniques to calm themselves and develop habits or hobbies to occupy free time in constructive ways. Children with different learning abilities need culturally relevant and linguistically appropriate services (Utley, Obiakor, & Bakken, 2011), and role representatives that look like them and demonstrate that successful outcomes are reached by people who persist through structured practice and study.

The Kids Count Data Center (kidscount.org) advocates for children. Some states have less poverty and some states have more. Child poverty rates are lowest in Minnesota (8%), Maine (9%), and Wyoming (9%) and highest in California (24%), Florida (22%), and Georgia (21%). People in parts of the US with high poverty rates are involved in promoting goals for change.

Circumstances and impact of discrimination and competition impede learning and promotion of healthy nutrition. The Harlem Children's Zone is one of several models to consider and work from to help children succeed (hcz.org).

HOUSING

Rothstein's *The Color of Law* (2017) clarifies the government's deliberate imposition of racial segregation. Rothstein describes the planned segregation of American cities by personnel in federal, state, and local agencies. Policies were modified to reshape naturally existing configurations of residential neighborhoods to zones that favored wealthy White families and excluded diverse citizens.

The impact of similar policies in Ferguson, Missouri, created an environment that negatively impacts many communities (Rothstein, 2014). Federal, state, and local policies established communities like Ferguson and St. Louis, Missouri, that had restrictive covenants, denied adequate municipal services, and promoted zoning and other designs to obstruct potentially positive endeavors by community residents.

Transportation policy impacts the potential of a community's citizens. Lack of mobility impedes access to myriad opportunities for people with low income, but exclusion occurs for other reasons as well. In addition, low wealth neighborhoods are often affected by the negative community, environmental, health, and safety effects of increased car use (Kenyon, Lyons, & Rafferty, 2002). Heavy traffic areas, limited safe crossings, and lead from emissions cause accidents and respiratory conditions.

EDUCATION

Community members, advocates, students, and other stakeholders question the quality of education for many children and youth served by social workers. School districts across the country tackle academic, social, and emotional issues daily.

CHALLENGES

Issues of disproportionate suspensions, truancy rules, or and low academic performance often paint a grim picture of the public education system. Research by the National Center for Education Statistics (NCES, 2018) estimates that about 16% of public school students do not finish high school (a recent improvement from 19%) and more than 70% do not qualify to enroll for a college degree. In addition to the challenges for the approximately 51% of students who fall into low income categories, quality of teaching, funding shortages, lack of classroom space, building maintenance needs, family hardships, lack of technology, educator morale, and student behavior also present barriers to higher student achievement.

Schreider (2017) questions how the public evaluates the quality of schools. His report indicates the existing data may not be adequate to answer the question.

When actual data were used to evaluate schools, ratings were better than respondents' perceptions indicated. As we contemplate the polices we are concerned about, recognizing that specific kinds of data are needed, and having accurate data is critical for evaluation and planning.

IMPACT ON VULNERABLE POPULATIONS

The challenges just described indicate potential limits on the academic performance of children from vulnerable groups. Longstanding research indicates that when young mothers receive early information and support, children have better starts in school. However, ingrained racial and economic stigmatizing via teacher behavior toward young children of color can begin early as well.

It seems imperative that teacher education increase efforts to implement curricula that inform children in the primary grades the true history of the US and incorporate books written by and about authors of color, as 11-year-old Marley Dias advocates for (McGrath, 2017). Marley wants to see books with Black girls on the cover.

The relevance of incorporating authors who identify from diverse groups has gained attention. Graduate social work students at Columbia University School of Social Work (CSSW Demands, 2016) called for 30% of their curriculum to reflect content and resources written by multicultural writers, researchers, scientists, and other role models to respect people who are often a substantial proportion of service users.

Addressing the needs of different and multiple intelligences and identities, and different abilities and interests, requires considering widespread design of inclusive systems (Langdon et al., 2016). The evaluation of inclusion identifies needs for bus travel, public spaces, and blogging platforms for users who are blind or visually impaired, older people, and those with dementia.

Students and families with disabled members (Wills, Chenoweth, & Ellen, 2016) experience some anxiety around transitioning from state support to connecting with local and community resources. These community members would benefit from more coordinated planning as they transition through different life cycle phases.

POSITIVE STEPS

The politics of education set the stage for debate over educational strategies. There are power struggles over what should be taught, instructional methods, and cost (Spring, 2011). There are data about what teachers think, what media thinks, what powerful people think, and some of what parents think. But there is virtually no data on what students think. From a systems thinking frame, childism needs to be addressed. Childism has been compared to other isms-racism, sexism (Young-Bruehl, 2013). It may also be considered as prejudice about the views of children; they aren't allowed to evaluate teachers. Making improvements in institutions that serve children and youth should include their perspectives through the use focus groups, visual and digital storytelling and other techniques and methods that engage and respect them (Stein, 2012).

The Zinn Education project is a model for teaching the history of all people (zinnproject. org). In reaction to a Texas school board that wanted to use texts that narrowly define history, a parent responded that our culture is diverse and the school board should acknowledge that not everybody has the same religion or the same views (Hobson, 2015).

Analysis from a systems thinking perspective requires teachers and their educational procedures to be viewed from a "why doesn't the classroom process work" approach. Parents should be encouraged to engage with teachers over the school year to help plan for their children. Some teachers are setting up ways to connect at times parents will find convenient. Perhaps Saturday hours once per quarter could be added for parents who work during the week. A former principle offers tips for a collaborative, rather than confrontational, exchange (Schweizer, n.d.). Social workers could also be helpful by working with teachers to establish classroom strategies that meet emotional concerns.

SOCIAL WORK, PHYSICAL HEALTH, AND MENTAL HEALTH

Concerns about health and mental health range from a human rights platform that urges health and emotional care for all, to the behavior of healthcare workers providing appropriate and adequate services. To a large extent, these concerns depend on the insurance that a person has, which offers access to services across the life course.

Experiences of discrimination impose stressors on sexual minority members (Lick, Durso, & Johnson, 2013). Transgender persons have many physical health problems and the additional stress and risk of being denied services at points of access (Lewis, 2016).

Physical and mental health care needs vary across the life course. Mothers-to-be need prenatal care and nourishment for the mother and the unborn. They also need information about how to care for the physical and emotional needs of infants, toddlers, children, and teens as they grow and develop.

A first step includes education in the art of self-care, for professionals and for service users. Relaxation and stress relief can be initiated through structured awareness and use of one's breath. Using breathing to calm the nervous system in any situation under any condition is fairly easy. "Take a deep breath, expanding your belly. Pause. Exhale slowly to the count of five. Repeat four times" (Alderman, 2016, para 1).

CHALLENGES

Addressing the impact of economic and social conditions on physical and mental health requires leadership and collaboration to make information available in nonstigmatizing community locations, presented in ways people are receptive to. Developing effective interventions also requires the participation of representatives from children and teenage groups. We can help children overcome trauma by providing safe space and attention in ways that help them walk through and recover from their experiences.

While we are well aware of the impact trauma can have on people, Myers (2016) examined the impact on social workers counseling people about their experiences. In a sample of 15 social workers, all of the social workers described positive reactions, growth, and satisfaction connected to their level of confidence in working with the clients. It appears that their work actually contributed to building their resilience. More experienced workers were moved to do trauma counseling with large groups.

Despite many inroads made by women in the US and other countries, there remains considerable denigration and continuous assaults against women. One in three women around the world suffer some form of physical or sexual violence at some point in their lives. In the U.S 65% have been assaulted, 23% touched inappropriately, 20% stalked, and 9% coerced to have sex (Bhattacharyya, 2016). Women continue to report incidents of rape, gang rape, and assault on college campuses and the remedies offered by institutional structures in the workplace and in schools offer context for these scenarios. Bhattacharyya (2016, p. 311) identifies "failure of governance" as the central cause of street violence against women in India.

Addressing issues in social service settings cannot be expected to completely remedy the situation. The response requires attention in the household and community, as well as in schools and community organizations, and through policy formulations that put child development at the center of service delivery.

IMPACT ON VULNERABLE POPULATIONS

Trauma and other mental health services are particularly limited to incarcerated women and women veterans. There are efforts to complete more in-depth assessments on inmates.

Although a discussion of undocumented people from other countries tends to bring negative comments to light, the reality is that they require health care like everybody else. Sanctuary cities provide inclusive health policies such as establishing city health insurance and healthcare programs (Aboii, 2014). These services help bridge the gap in health outcomes between documented and undocumented individuals. Efforts on their behalf extend care and inform new directions that address specific conditions. Aboii encourages local and federal government to pursue inclusive health policies.

PARENTING

Ramirez (2014) introduces readers to parenting by pointing out the need for vision in raising children. Parents should embrace their sacred role as guardian to help children realize their identity within a family and teach them to thrive. For Ramirez, the spiritual connection is intrinsic to the parenting role.

Trauma and resilience, when recognized as facts of life (Levine and Kline, 2008) become knowledge that assists capacity and helps children move through the experiences. Social workers engage with many children to address trauma issues (Myers, 2016).

Parents need to project self-control in order to provide support and guidance to children, to minimize stress, maintain calm and balance, and seek appropriate resources. Davis (2016) shares his adverse early childhood experience and family and community came to be a support system. The video, "From the Streets to the Stage" (Velasco, 2016) documents his awareness of his environment and the dynamics that challenged and brought him confidence.

Social workers have opportunities to collaborate with young people and parents and emphasize establishing warmth, calmness, structure and discipline early with infants and toddlers and throughout the growing process. Siblings play significant roles within families and should also be incorporated in family conferences.

POSITIVE STEPS

Notions of task shifting (Patel, 2012) and task sharing (Hanlon, et al., 2016) encourage teaching mental health interventions to community members, and collaborating with health and mental health specialists for consultation, supervision, training and referral Hanlon, et al., 2016, para 6).

Culturally competent services promote advocacy for population-specific interventions. Research that examined patient involvement (Kimerling, Pavao & Wong, 2016) indicated higher participation for women through the use of female providers, women-only settings, and women-only groups. These findings add to a growing literature documenting that better engagement of service users through specific outreach strategies leads to positive outcomes.

SOCIAL WORK AND CRIMINAL JUSTICE

Criminal justice involves the application of laws to the maintenance of order. Generally, criminal justice is discussed in an historical context that involves ideas of deviance and punishment. Social work is connected to many justice variables. The criminalization of substance use conditions instead of connecting these to healthcare has influenced rising incarceration rates. The treatment of low income persons, those with mental health disorders, domestic violence, sex trafficking, and older inmates adds the layer of human rights to criminal offenses. When the concept of rights is applied, behavioral variations should be examined with respect to persons' rights to shelter, food, healthcare, etcetera, and legality. Social work has the opportunity to advocate for healthcare services rather than prison time (American Addiction Centers, 2018), to participate in designing prevention to help people avoid incarceration (Drucker, 2018), to urge school based restorative justice models (Gonzalez, 2012), and assist in efforts to apply restorative justice in creative and innovative ways that heighten the visibility of community accountability (Kim, 2010).

Issues of justice include observations of increased acts of intimidation and harassment in public spaces and in schools. Public order offenses include drug crimes, prostitution, disorderly conduct, public drunkenness, and other alcohol-related crimes. According to the LegalMatch.com, (Tran, 2018) public order crimes may or may not have a particular victim. They are based on social norms of the community. In some jurisdictions, public order crimes may or may not include the following: underage sex, disrupting funeral services, pornography-related crimes, and private recreational drug use (Tran, 2018). Figure 13.2 illustrates trends in the rates of these offenses.

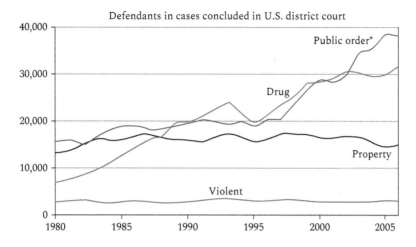

FIGURE 13.2 Trends in Rates of Offenses

Source: Dorsey & Middleton (n.d.). Drugs and Crime Facts. Bureau of Justice Statistics (BJS). *Note:* Public order offenses include weapons and immigration offenses. *Source:* BJS, Compendium of Federal Justice Statistics, Annual and Federal Justice Statistics 2006, Statistical Tables, NCJ 225711, May 2009. p. 29.

CHALLENGES

Attention to social justice has revealed more evidence that people with low incomes, women, and minority group members experience higher penalties from the justice system (Patterson, 2012) than the general population. Punitive attitudes and discrimination mean that people of color and related intersectional identities experience higher incidences of profiling, stop and frisk encounters, fines, detention without recourses, stiffer sentencing, and fewer opportunities for community service.

In addition to the high incarceration rates, shootings of Black individuals by White persons, including law officers, are deemed justified by law enforcement and justice officials at high rates. In cases with a White shooter and a White victim, the shooting is ruled to be justified less than 2% of the time. If the shooter is Black and the victim is White, the rate of justifiable homicide rulings drops to almost 1%. However, if the shooter is White and the victim is Black, it is ruled justified in 9.5% of cases in non-Stand Your Ground (SYG) states. In SYG states, the rate is even higher (Roman, 2013). When returning to their families or communities with limited resources, post incarceration obstacles create challenges to developing support that can assist people with maintaining their livelihoods. Coordinating across educational and mental health care services is needed to prevent young people from moving toward the criminal justice system (Wilson, 2014).

IMPACT ON VULNERABLE POPULATIONS

Challenges to implementing evidence-based practices in criminal justice settings include the politics of administrators and organizational cultures that resist change. In addition, lack of funding, variations from the controlled environment protocol, and ethical issues also need to be addressed (Patterson, 2012).

Ongoing disparities, maintained by the attitudes and beliefs of officials in charge, increase fear in children, youth, and college students of diverse ancestry. Since the 2016 election people express fear and report racial and religious discrimination (Eversley, 2016). From children being intimidated in classrooms and on school property to college students who are documented but have family members at risk of intimidation and deportation, many who observe these situations, are concerned.

Social workers have opportunities to participate in the development of evidence-based strategies to protect and serve people from other countries and to work in criminal justice arenas that address the challenges we face.

POSITIVE STEPS

Several states have begun adjusting laws to assist people trying to make restitution for crimes they committed. Pennsylvania has established Act 5 which allows persons to apply to have old criminal records sealed (newsworks.org, 2016). "This applies to second- and- third-degree misdemeanors. The most common offenses include simple drug possession, drunken driving, prostitution, low-level retail theft and disorderly conduct" (Moselle, 2016, para 19).

Some states are working to keep children out of adult court. The Campaign for Youth Justice has led 30 states passing 55 pieces of legislation making it more difficult to prosecute, house, and/or sentence children as adults. Several states are continuing to reform juvenile justice sentencing procedures. However, there is evidence that while many youth are not transferred a higher percentage of Black youth continue to be placed in adult prisons (Thomas, 2017, p. 9).

Police in the Philadelphia area have formed a Police Youth Alliance (Wolfman-Arent, 2016) to connect with local children engaged in recreation, including chess, dance, and play groups, to meeting and gaining understanding of one another. Community policing is not a new idea. Docobo (2005) notes the introduction of community policing after September 11, 2001, to address local policing and homeland security. In 2001, the U.S. Conference of Mayors commissioned a 281-city survey that encouraged adoption of community policing strategies (Basu, 2017). Evidence that some communities are working to understand the psychology of neighborhoods (Fullilove, 2014) and how to revitalize them attracts professionals who are interested in approaches to the intersections (of neighborhood crime, academic performance, health, and mental health data), that impact communities and their residents (Pendall, Hendey, et al., 2016). Fullilove describes fractures in city planning that contribute to community distress and need to be addressed.

Efforts and reforms at the federal, state, and local levels are reducing the prison population and maintaining public safety, creating a more equitable and effective justice system. The Urban Institute provides reports on the impact of state reforms (King, Peterson, Elderbroom, & Pelletier, 2015).

In a survey of crime victims and survivors, respondents urged more prevention and rehabilitation, mental health treatment, drug treatment, community supervision, and community service (Pelletier, 2016).

Data and legislative information is available and can be shared with individuals, families, and communities interested in advocating for legislation that supports housing and healthcare for urban and rural community development. Using systems thinking to revise our work for solving complex problems (Stroh, 2015) can lead to more informed and improved results.

SOCIAL WORK AND THE ENVIRONMENT: WATER, SOIL, AIR, CLIMATE, AND FOOD SECURITY

Several areas of policy formulation and development affect the ability of citizens to live in communities with clean resources and safe neighborhoods.

Environmental justice issues include policies that allow the impact of toxins, pollutants, and neglect of natural resources to affect the quality, or potential quality, of health on human and other creatures of the world. According to Anson and Paulson (2016), "Environmental activism traditionally focuses on two categories: (1) disproportionate harm or environmental injustices to marginalized communities and (2) the responses by activists within those communities" (p. 426).

The impact of various procedures, regulated and unregulated, may result in poorer quality natural resources across air, soil, and water (Mundaca, Neij, Markandya, & Hennicke, 2016). The discussion within the social network is informed by the social capital differences in visions of community organizing and activism that resist existing forces and push forward to address environmental problems.

Environmental situations can be associated with the quality, status, and availability of shelter for individuals and families. Natural and man-made conditions often impact community residents who may be referred to social, health, mental health, and related services.

WATER

Flint, Michigan, is a primary example of pipeline infrastructure that has become old and eroded through neglect by officials, in part due to attitudes of exclusion toward some citizens, and to cost cutting measures. The result was dangerous toxins in the water supply. According to Michael Moore (2016), several other critical concerns are linked to this disaster, but few have been exposed by the corporate media outlets. These concerns include providing a clean water hookup for General Motors but toxic water to community residents; disease exposure; eroded housing values; use of Flint for unannounced military exercises; private water owners' conflicts of interest with the public good; and penalization of schools and communities with majority people of color to give tax breaks to the wealthy (michaelmoore.com).

SOIL

Children can be exposed to several infections that occur through soil infestations. Frequently, children who play outside are exposed to soil contaminated by various pathogens. Toxins, water runoff, vehicle emissions, and other sources of pollutants are found in samples from international locations with sanitation issues. School children playing outside may be exposed to these conditions in many different geographic locations. Young children, aged 5–9 years, are more likely to be under closer supervision by parents, guardians, or caregivers, than children aged 10–14 (Alelign, et al., 2015). These children capable of playing away from school or residential environments could be exposed to abandoned properties considered brownfields. A *brownfield* is property that may have been previously used in a way that could have allowed it to be affected by pollutants, contaminants, or other hazardous substances, or contaminated by fecal residue. Children could contract hookworms and other infections. Parents may not have awareness because they may or may not receive information about potential health hazards in local areas.

AIR

The impact of various activities, such as fracking and the effects on air quality of phosphorus pollution and subsequent blue-green algae blooms is of concern. Anson and Paulson (2016) report this as an increasingly significant socio-environmental problem. Using social network theory as a point of reference, their article offers insight into social networks of activists who work alongside government agencies on this issue in the Red Cedar Basin of Wisconsin. Their analysis informs and encourages a perspective of civic engagement.

Runoff off from pollution affects water quality. A major contributor to air pollution comes from vehicle emissions. In Philadelphia, the 2016 public transportation strike by SEPTA (Southeastern Pennsylvania Transportation Authority) resulted in more people driving cars. Emissions from the cars resulted in a 400% increase in air pollution over four days (Zhorov, 2016).

CLIMATE

Climate change incorporates impact of warming temperatures on agriculture, fish and other marine life, energy use, low-carbon use, among other concerns. Policy initiatives aimed at low-carbon technology, like carbon capture and storage (CCS), nuclear energy, clean coal, fracking, and others have been proposed, yet there remains uncertainty about these options (Green, 2016).

Research on animals that can or cannot tolerate environmental temperature changes offer insight into how the planet may be saved and the impact of deforestation (Barnosky and Hadly, 2016). The bigger picture can be described based on years of environmental research: "These are the tipping points, and they happen because, in all walks of life, gradual change accumulates slowly until it hits a certain threshold, and then all hell breaks loose" (Hannibal, 2016, para 3).

Environmental issues impact our well-being. Social work has not paid much attention to this arena in the past. However, there is evidence that environmental justice is directly connected to social justice issues that affect power, privilege, and oppression (Beltrán, Hacker, & Begun, 2016).

FOOD

Connecting the impact of climate change to the quality of animal livestock is an area of concern that has received limited attention (Livestock health, 2016). The potential to harm livestock health, and through ingestion impact humans, is a trajectory that warrants examination.

Efforts to protect farm animals have had some success. The Humane Farming Association (hfa.org) advocates against the misuse of antibiotics, hormones, and other chemicals used on factory farms. They provide educational materials for classroom and home activities to inform young people about environmental issues and animals.

The use of genetic modifications in agriculture raised concerns about the safety (livestock health) of the food. Research suggests that the expected yield increases have not been attained. It was expected that crops made resistant to weed killers and pests would grow more robustly (Hakim, 2016). Over twenty years the technology has fallen short. The bottom line in Figure 13.3 shows the growth rate of the genetically modified organisms (GMO). The top line shows the growth rate of crops without modifications. In some ways these modifications have obstructed natural processes (e.g., pollination by bees) that produce and sustain natural growth.

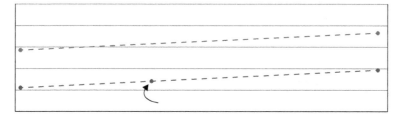

FIGURE 13.3   Growth rate of Genetically Modified Organisms

Source: The New York Times| Sources: Food and Agriculture Organization of the United Nations | *Note:* Western Europe is France, Germany, Belgium, Luxembourg, Switzerland, the Netherlands and Austria. https://www.nytimes.com/interactive/2016/10/30/business/gmo-crops-pesticides.html

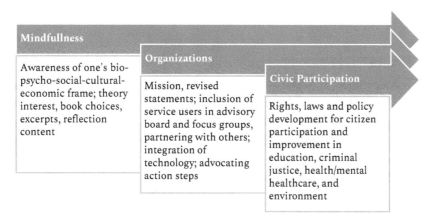

FIGURE 13.4   Moving from Self, to Groups, to Community

Social work's inclusion of this information in their educational curricula and how this history has impacted communities make it imperative to advocate for remedies.

Professional development and capacity building draw on the strengths of our diverse social networks, our knowledge base and backgrounds, and opportunities to listen to multiple perspectives. This foundation has promoted more relevant paradigms and models to assist especially those excluded and oppressed.

Social work's awareness of multiple identities, its cultural and service user strengths, and its organizational potential to address service needs builds competency and capacity with families and communities. This process starts and continues with self-assessment, self-care, reading, and discussion. Our work builds on our predecessors and it is expanding with those who agree that it is a good thing to seek a more just world.

CHALLENGES

The challenges of environmental impact predominantly come from officials of organizations that benefit from their past and current access to, and use of, our natural resources. Policies that set up access and respond to situations resulting from these man-made or natural disasters tend to impact persons living with few financial resources more than it impacts those with more resources.

Protests against the Dakota pipeline illustrate how those who want to protect natural resources, water, and the river—sacred resources—are intimidated by those who have more profit-oriented interest. Those who support reducing man-made interferences that impact climate are opposed by business interests who lobby for their preferences.

IMPACT ON VULNERABLE POPULATIONS

The impact of past and existing environmental and climate-related policies affects not only people of color, LGBTQI people, those with different abilities, and people from other countries, but also everyone across planet Earth. An increase in temperatures has led to observed changes in the sizes of glaciers, earlier break up of winter ice on lakes and rivers, shifting plant and animal life processes, increasing sea levels, and increased heat waves (Walsh & Wuebbles, 2016). Continued warming temperatures are expected to affect droughts, increase potential for fires, and create more impact on plant and animal life. Perhaps advancing science will mitigate the impact, but recommendations for addressing these changes are encouraged now.

POLICY CHALLENGES ACROSS SERVICE AREAS

The National Association of Social Workers (NASW) examines issues that affect Americans from economic inequality to family violence. Social work leaders collaborated to design a set of 12 grand challenges (Pace, 2016). These challenges offer students and professionals areas of focus and avenues of participation. The intent is to focus on these areas and create measurable progress. The challenges are:

- Ensure healthy development for all youth

- Close the health gap
- Stop family violence
- Advance long and productive lives
- Eradicate social isolation
- End homelessness
- Create social responses to a changing environment
- Harness technology for social good
- Promote smart decarceration
- Reduce extreme economic inequality
- Build financial capability for all
- Achieve equal opportunity and justice (American Academy of Social Work & Social Welfare, n.d.)

Since the 1800s, the social work profession in the UK and the US has responded in organized ways to persons with limited incomes, those in need of basic survival resources, and those in vulnerable situations (McNutt, 2013; Skehill, 2010). Bonnie (2016) points out that social work "attracts champions" (para 3). Throughout this history, there are examples of helpers, caregivers, and professionals showing high levels of empathy and altruism in serving people. There are also those who help, but reflect or demonstrate attitudes of privilege that discriminate and diminish people who may be visibly different. There are those who feel the work is too hard and are frustrated or get burned out.

Yet overall, as the social environment evolves and the strengths and contributions of all people are acknowledged, social work has developed awareness in the pursuit of social and economic justice for those who have been excluded. Evaluating this broad terrain from the past to the present urges social workers to advance the dialog for human rights by facilitating the inclusion of everyone.

POSITIVE STEPS

An increase of advocacy groups who support environmental sustainability brings attention to the macro dimension of social work. Lysack (2015) urges social work to encourage citizens to protect the environment. In Canada where coal emissions are tremendous, community partnerships have been arranged to address respiratory health. A study presented information to the community about risks to health from burning coal to generate electricity (Lysack, 2015).

Key social work skills that are useful for effective environmental policy advocacy include community organizing, increasing knowledge of climate science, and community support for "transforming social and political priorities and policy making regarding climate change" (Lysack, 2015, p. 86). Dominelli (in Lysack, 2015) refers to process skills and building capacity to be critical.

CASE:

Jeffrey has been truant from school since the winter holidays, for over three weeks. His name popped up in the counselor's office when she began to review the absentee list and she remembered that he was scheduled to see her last week but did not show up. She contacted the social worker, a young man the students looked up to, and asked if he would help her work with Jeffrey. The counselor called Jeffrey's home number and Jeffrey answered. The counselor referred to his absence and asked how she could help him get back to school. He mentioned his mom had lost her job and he was working to help out. The counselor got him to agree to come in and talk with her and Mr. Jonas (the social worker).

Subsequently, Jeffrey began to work with Mr. Jonas and their planning resulted in problem resolution, a part-time job with better hours, participation in new endeavors, and schoolwork performance improvements. Use the worksheet to identify areas they probably worked on and say why they chose those areas. Discuss with a peer partner.

CONCLUSION

The theoretical foundations of systemic thinking, contextual fluidity, and social exchange seem to embody the concepts that position social work to continue and advance leadership for social and economic justice. The educational competencies and professional standards support the trajectory to move forward to facilitate inclusion of ideas, advocacy and partnering with service users, community citizens, and other disciplines to generate social change. There are other theoretical mixtures and configurations of disciplinary knowledge and interprofessional and interdisciplinary relationships. Professionals, organizations and service users can select relevant theory for different entry points to shape participation and actions that improve our environments and support human rights.

The social work profession is already embedded in local, state, federal and international nonprofit, profit, governmental, and community based organizations. Conversations with our colleagues, our community planners and officials, and service users can lead to partnerships that establish innovative and non-stigmatizing opportunities for macro practice. Collaborations with libraries, businesses, churches, temples, mosques, synagogues, schools, recreation centers, neighborhood associations, welcoming centers, and others will benefit the social welfare of our communities.

In the current atmosphere of mixed positions—political representatives who want to withdraw or restrict citizen tax revenues from aiding those in need—and citizen advocacy for justice and human rights, social work's core concepts, regardless of which country we live in, emphasize human rights and social justice (Jeyapal, 2017). As social work programs address the accreditation standards with multicultural materials and service user participation, social workers have opportunities to facilitate proactive, inclusive, and innovative dialogs.

CHAPTER SUMMARY

As students pursue social and economic justice issues of their interest, the starting point is self-assessment regarding social work values. This advances to identifying policy areas that require attention from social workers, service users, and community participants. Students can research and locate regulations and laws that impact the social welfare of our citizens. Students will be able to provide service to their communities of interest with respect for all.

EPAS AND CODE OF ETHICS

CSWE EDUCATIONAL POLICY & ACCREDITATION STANDARDS

Competency 3: Advance Human Rights and Social, Economic, and Environmental Justice
- 3a) apply their understanding of social, economic, and environmental justice to advocate for human rights at the individual and system levels; and
- 3b) engage in practices that advance social, economic, and environmental justice (EPAS, 2015)

NASW CODE OF ETHICS

Value: Social Justice
Ethical Principle: Social workers challenge social injustice. (NASW, n.d.)

DISCUSSION QUESTIONS

1. Select a policy area you would consider for a future career.
2. Locate a website that provides information about your area of interest. Visit these websites: the National Conference of State Legislatures (nscl.org), the Economic Policy Institute (epi.org) and Coalition of Human Needs (chn.org). Compare the information about your policy area available on these websites. What did you learn?
3. Gather information about your policy interest area and its impact on children and adolescents in your state. Take a look at kidscount.org and mentalhealthamerica.net. Examine the data pertaining to different cultural groups. Using this information, what would you be interested in advocating for?

EXERCISES

1. Research the public meetings in your area (e.g., school boards, university trustees, mental health practitioners, city or township councils). Some organizations post their meetings online. Attend one. How could you share information about local civic participation opportunities with your agency or your service users?

2. Select an environmental issue (e.g., water, air, soil). Research the quality of that resource in your area.

3. As a citizen of your community, are you satisfied with the information you found? Why or why not? Discuss with a classmate.

4. Search the TedTalks website (ted.com) for a topic related to your policy interest area.

5. Watch the talk. List two key points. Was it in line with your ideas? Did it raise questions? Did you agree or disagree with it? If you had an opportunity to create a talk what would your message be?

RELATED LEGISLATIVE ISSUES

The Dream Act, DACA, and other Policies Designed to Protect Dreamers. American Immigration Council. https://www.americanimmigrationcouncil.org/research/dream-act-daca-and-other-policies-designed-protect-dreamers.

The Women's Health Protection Act of 2013—Summary: S.1696—113th Congress (2013-2014). https://www.congress.gov/bill/113th-congress/senate-bill/1696

Affordable Care Act—https://www.healthcare.gov/

Youth Justice: http://www.campaignforyouthjUStice.org/documents/CFYJ_State_Trends_Report.pdf

MULTICULTURAL RESOURCES

Davis, (2016). From the streets to the stage: Frederick Davis, a ballet dancer. Retrieved from http://www.pbs.org/program/streets-stage-journey-fredrick-davis/.

Ea, Prince—Can we auto correct humanity? https://www.youtube.com/watch?v=dRl8EIhrQjQ

Ea, Prince—I just sued the school system https://www.youtube.com/watch?v=dqTTojTija8

Tracy Chapman, CD—Listen to activism songs of the past.

Sotomayor, S. (2014). *My beloved world*. New York: Knopf

Vance, J. (2016). *Hillbilly Elegy: A Memoir of a Family and Culture in Crisis*. New York: Harper.

TED TALKS

Chelsea Shields—How I'm working for change inside my church. https://www.ted.com/talks/chelsea_shields_how_i_m_working_for_change_inside_my_church

Hilary Cottam—Social services are broken: How to fix them. https://www.ted.com/talks/hilary_cottam_social_services_are_broken_how_we_can_fix_them

Jonathan Haidt—Can a divided America heal? http://www.ted.com/talks/jonathan_haidt_can_a_divided_america_heal?utm_source=newsletter_daily&utm_campaign=daily&utm_medium=email&utm_content=button__2016-11-08

Lemn Sissay—Child of the state. https://www.ted.com/talks/lemn_sissay_a_child_of_the_state

Vikram Patel—Community mental health model. https://www.ted.com/talks/vikram_patel_mental_health_for_all_by_involving_all

FURTHER READING

Pinker, S. (2018). *Enlightenment now: The case for reason, science, humanism, and progress*. New York: Viking.

Zakaria, F. (2007). *The future of democracy: Illiberal democracy home and abroad*. New York: NW.W. Norton & Company.

References

Abbott, A. A. (1987). *Professional choices: values at work.* Washington, DC: NASW.

ABC News. (2013). Top 10 facts you don't know about girls' education. Retrieved Jan17, 2018 from http://abcnews.go.com/International/10-facts-girls-education/story?id=20474260

Abdul-Jabbar, K. (2016). Writings on the wall: Searching for a new equality beyond black and white. New York, NY: Liberty Street.

Abel, R., Deitz, R., & Su, Y. (2014). Are recent college graduates finding good jobs? *Current Issues in Economics & Finance, 20*(1), 1–8.

Aboii, S.M. (2014). Undocumented immigrants and the inclusive health policies of sanctuary cities. *Harvard Public Health Review, 7.* Retrieved from http://harvardpublichealthreview.org/undocumented-immigrants-and-the-inclusive-health-policies-of-sanctuary-cities/

Abramowitz, M. (1996). *Regulating the lives of women: Social welfare policy from colonial times to the present.* Brooklyn, NY: South End Press.

Abrams, D. A. (2013). *Diversity and inclusion: The big six formula for success.* North Charleston, SC: CreateSpace Independent Publishing Platform.

Abrams, L. S. (2002). Social context, gender and youth development: An exploratory study of sociocultural variations among at-risk adolescent girls. *Journal of Human Behavior in the Social Environment.* 6(2), 47–60.

Achari, S.R. (Ed.) (2012). The principles of Hindu ethics. M.A. Buc, Hathi, Pole, Baroda, 27-9-1921. Retrieved from https://www.australiancouncilofhinduclergy.com/uploads/5/5/4/9/5549439/principlesofhinduethics.pdf.

Achebe, C. (2010). *Things fall apart.* Penguin Books.

Achinstein, B. Curry, M.W., Ogawa, R.T., & Athanases, S.Z. (2016). Organizing high schools for Latina/o youth success boundary crossing to access and build community wealth. *Urban Education,* 51(7), 824–854.

Acs, G., Braswell, K., Sorensen, E., & Turner, M.A. (2013). The Moynihan Report Revisited. Retrieved from https://www.urban.org/research/publication/moynihan-report-revisited.

Adams, M. H. (2016, May 29). The end of black Harlem: Gentrification is destroying the capital of African American culture. *The New York Times,* Sunday Review.

Adenika-Morrow, T. J. (1995). Building self-esteem in at-risk minority youth through creative approaches to teach math and science. *Equity & Excellence, 28*(3), 32–38.

Adherents.org. (2017). Retrieved from www.adherents.com

Adiche, C. N. (2009). *The danger of a single story* [Video file]. Retrieved from https://www.ted.com/talks/chimamanda_adichie_the_danger_of_a_single_story

Adiele, F., & Frosch, M. (Eds.). (2007). *Coming of age around the world: A multicultural anthology.* New York, NY: New Press.

African American Registry (AAR) (1966). Black Panther Party founded. Retrieved from https://aaregistry.org/story/black-panther-party-founded/

Afua, Q. (2002). *Heal thyself for health and longevity.* Buffalo, NY: Eworld.

Akhtar, F. N. (2013). *Mastering social work values and ethics.* eBook.

Al Gharaibeh, F. M. (2016). Debating the role of custom, religion and law in 'honour' crimes: Implications for social work. *Ethics and Social Welfare, 10*(20), 122–139.

Alderman, L. (2016, November 9). Breathe. Exhale. Repeat: The Benefits of controlled breathing. *The New York Times.* Retrieved from https://www.nytimes.com/2016/11/09/well/mind/breathe-exhale-repeat-the-benefits-of-controlled-breathing.html.

Alegria, M., Atkins, M., Farmer, E., Slaton, E., & Stelk, W. (2010). One size does not fit all: Taking diversity, culture and context seriously. *Administrative Policy in Mental Health, 37*(1–2), 48–60.

Alegria, M., Lin, J. Y., Green, J. G., Sampson, N. A., Gruber, M. J., & Kessler, R. C. (2012). Role of referrals in mental health service disparities for racial and ethnic minority youth. *Journal of American Academy of Child and Adolescent Psychiatry,* 51(7), 703-711.

Alegria, M., Vallas, M., & Pumariega, A. (2010). Racial and ethnic disparities in pediatric mental health. *Child & Adolescent Psychiatric Clinics of North America, 19*(4), 7549–7772.

Aleign, T., Degarege, A., & Erko, B. (2015). Soil transmitted Helminth infection & associated risk factors among school-children in Durbete Town, Northwestern Ethiopia. *Journal of Parasitology Research,*

Alexander, M. (2012). The new Jim Crow: Mass incarceration in the age of colorblindness. Revised Edition. New York, NY: New Press.

Alexie, S. (2007). *The absolutely true diary of a part-time Indian.* Boston, MA: Little, Brown.

Alexie, S. (2009). *War dances.* New York, NY: Grove Press.

Ali, A. H. (2007). *Infidel.* New York, NY: Free Press.

Ali, A., McFarlane, E., Hawkins, R., & Udo-Inyang, I. (2012). Social justice revisited: Psychological recolonization and the challenge of anti-oppression advocacy. *Race, Gender & Class, 19*(1/2), 322–335.

Al-Jahiz, U. (n.d.). The pride of the blacks over the whites. Retrieved Jan. 8, 22018 from https://selfuni.wordpress.com/tag/al-jahiz-superiority-of-blacks-over-whites/

Al-Krenawi, A., & Jordan, S. O. (2014). Arab American marriage: Cultural tradition, religion & the social worker. *Journal of Human Behavior in the Social Environment, 24*(2), 115–137. Special issue: Social work, ethnicity & marriage.

Allan, B. Autin, K.L., Duffy, R.D. Self-Determination and Meaningful Work: Exploring Socioeconomic Constraints *Frontiers of Psychology,* 2016; 7: 7

Allende, I. (2015). *House of spirits.* New York, NY: Atria Books.

Allport, G. (1954). *The nature of prejudice.* New York, NY: Doubleday.

Alperin, R.M. (2016). Jewish self-hatred: The internalization of prejudice. *Clinical Social Work Journal, 44*(3).

Alvarez, A.N., Juang, J. & Liang, C.T. (2006). Asian Americans and racism: when bad things happen to "model minorities." *Cultural Diversity & Ethnic Minority Psychology, 12*(3), 477–92.

Alvarez, J. (2010). *How the Garcia girls lost their accents.* Chapel Hill, NC: Algonquin Books.

Ambrosino, B. (2017). Supreme Court hears wedding cake case: here's what you need to know. The Washinsgton Post. Retrieved Jan 12, 2018 from ttps://www.washingtonpost.com/news/acts-of-faith/wp/2017/12/05/wedding-cake-what-you-need-to-know-about-the-hi

Ambrosio, J. (2014). Teaching the psychosocial subject: White students and racial privilege. *International Journal of Qualitative studies in Education, 27*(10), 1376–1394.

Amen, N. A. (1999). *The ankh: African origin of electromagnetism.* Buffalo, NY: Eworld.

America Tonight Digital Team. (2014). The school-to-prison-pipeline: By the numbers [Blog post]. Retrieved from http://america.aljazeera.com/watch/shows/america-tonight/america-tonight-blog/2014/1/23/school-to-prisonpipelineblackstudents.html

American Academy of Social Work & Social Welfare (n.d.). Grand challenges for social work. Retrieved from http://aaswsw.org/grand-challenges-initiative/12-challenges/.

American Addiction Centers (2018). How other countries deal with addiction and treatment.

American Association of Group Psychotherapy (AAGP). (2017). Statement on Inclusion, 2017.

American Civil Liberties Union. (2017). Retrieved from https://www.aclu.org/your-right-religious-freedom

American College of Physicians. (2010). Racial and ethnic disparities in health care, updated.

American College of Physicians, 190 N. Independence Mall West, Philadelphia, PA 19106.

American Folklore, (n.d.). American Folklore. Retrieved from http://www.americanfolklore.net/

amhistory.si.edu. (n.d.). Japanese Americans and the U.S. Constitution. Retrieved Jan 10, 2018 from http://amhistory.si.edu/perfectunion/non-flash/index.htm.l

Amnesty International. (2015). The state of LGBT human rights worldwide. Retrieved from http://blog.amnestyusa.org/africa/the-state-of-lgbt-rights-worldwide/

Ananthram, S., & Chan, C. (2013). Challenges and strategies for global human resource executives: Perspectives from Canada and the United States. *European Management Journal, 31*(3), 223–233.

Anaya, R. (1972). *Bless me, Ultima.* New York, NY: Warner Books. Retrieved from http://www.neabigread.org/books/blessmeultima/readers-guide/

Anderson, E. (1999). *Code of the street: Decency, violence, and the moral life of the inner city.* New York, NY: W. W. Norton.

Anderson, I. M., Adeney, K. L., Shinn, C., Safaranek, S., Buckner-Brown, J., Krause, L. K. (2015). Community coalition-driven interventions to reduce health disparities among racial and ethnic minority populations. Cochrane Database of Systematic Reviews, 6.

Anderson, R. L., & Gittler, J. (2005). Child and adolescent mental health: Unmet need for community-based mental health and substance use treatment among rural adolescents. *Community Mental Health Journal, 41*(1), 35–45.

Andrews, A.L. (2016). Legacies of inequity: How hometown political participation and land distribution shape migrants' paths into wage labor. *World Development, 87*, 348-332.

Androff, D. (2016), *Practicing rights: Human rights-based approaches to social work practice.* London, England: Routledge.

Anheier, H. L. (2005). *Nonprofit organizations: Theory, management, policy.* London, England: Routledge. Retrieved from http://citeseerx.ist.psu.edu/viewdoc/download?doi=10.1.1.452.6420&rep=rep1&type=pdf.

Anonymous. (2015). *The cloud of unknowing.* CreateSpace Independent Publishing Platform.

Anson, A., & Paulson, N. (2016) An exploratory study of social networks and environmental activism. *Humanity & Society, 40*(4), 424-441.

Anspach, R. R. (1979). From stigma to identity politics: Political activism among the physically disabled & former mental patients. *Social Science & Medicine. Part A: Medicaid Psychology & Medical Sociology.*

Anyikwa, V. A, Chiarelli-Helminiak, C. M., Hodge, D., & Wells-Wilbor, R. (2015). Women empowering women. *Journal of Social Work Education, 51*, 723-737.

Anyon, Y., Nicotera, N., & Vech, C. A. (2016) Contextual influences on the implementation of a schoolwide intervention to promote students' social, emotional, and academic learning. *Children & Schools, 38*(2), 81-88.

Aponte, E. D. (2012). *Santo! Varieties of Latino/a spirituality.* Ossining, NY: Orbis Books.

Appel, H., Ai, A.L., Huang,B., Nicado, E. (2014). Detrimental effects of discrimination on mental health in asian americans: counteracting roles of religious involvement. *International Journal for the Psychology of Religion.* Jan-Mar2014, Vol. 24 Issue 1, p. 28-46. 19

Aptheker, H. (1983). *American Negro slave revolts.* New York, NY: International. Retrieved Jan. 9, 2018 from https://archive.org/stream/in.ernet.dli.2015.533101/2015.533101.American-Negro#page/n53/mode/2up

Aptheker, H. (2006). *Nat Turner's slave rebellion including the 1831 confessions.* Mineola, NY: Dover Books.

Archer, D. (2015). Slurs, insults, (backhanded) compliments and other strategic face work moves. *Language Sciences, 52*, 82-87.

Arfelis, G. (1997). The effects of acculturation on the ethnic and gender identities of immigrant, college-educated Latin American women: A qualitative study. *Dissertation Abstracts International, 58*, B.

Asakura, K., & Craig, S. L. (2014). It gets better, but how? Exploring resilience development in the accounts of LGBTQ adults. *Journal of Human Behavior in the Social Environment, 24*, 253-266.

Asian-nation.org. (n.d.). The first Asian Americans. Retrieved June 25, 2017, from http://www.asian-nation.org/first.shtml

Associated Press. (2016). State of the Flint water crisis. Retrieved from http://flintwaterstudy.org/articles-in-the-press/

Atkinson, A. B., & Stiglitz, J. (2014) Introduction to public economics. Lecture 1. Princeton University.

Atkinson, C., & Woods, K. (2017). Establishing theoretical stability and treatment integrity for motivational interviewing. *Behavioural & Cognitive Psychotherapy, 45*(4), 337-350. doi:10.1017/S1352465817000145.

Atwood, N. C. (2014). Experiencing inequality: Memoirs, hardship, and working-class roots. *Smith College Studies in Social Work, 84*, 484-501.

Audi, R. (n.d.). Church-state separation, healthcare policy, and religious liberty. *The Journal of Practical Ethics.* Retrieved from http://www.jpe.ox.ac.uk/papers/church-state-healthcare-policy-and-religious-liberty/.

Augoustinos, M., & Every, D. (2010). Accusations and denials of racism: Managing moral accountability in public discourse. *Discourse & Society, 21*(3), 251-256.

Augoustinos, M., Tuffin, K., & Every, D. (2005) New racism, meritocracy and individualism: Constraining affirmative action in education. *Discourse & Society, 16*(3), 315-340.

Austin, A. (2013). Native Americans and jobs: The challenge and the promise. *Economic Policy Institute Briefing Paper.*

Austin, A. (2016). There I am: A grounded theory study of young adults navigating a transgender or gender nonconforming identity within a context of oppression and invisibility. *Sex Roles,* 75:215-230

Australian Psychological Society. (2010). *Evidence-based psychological interventions: A literature review* (3rd ed.). Reference chart of disorders and evidence-based treatments for children and adolescents. Retrieved July 3, 2017, from http://www.ohiomindsmatter.org/documents/5c%20Evidence-bbased%20Treatments.pdf

Ayalon, L. (2014). Perceived age, gender and racial/ethnic discrimination in Europe: Results from the European social study. *Educational Gerontology, 40*, 499-517.

Aydelott, B. (1863). *Prejudice against colored people.* Cincinnati, OH: American Reform Tract & Book Society.

Ayvazian, A. (2010). The role of allies as agents of change. In M. Adams, W. J. Blumenfeld, C. Castañeda, H. Hackman, M. L. Peters, & X. Zúñiga (Eds.), *Readings for diversity and social justice* (p. 625). Abingdon, United Kingdom: Routledge.

AZ quotes.com. (n.d.) Poitier's quote. http://www.azquotes.com/quote/504373

Babcock, L. (2016). Morgan Freeman series: "The story of God" to air on National Geographic Channel. *Inquisitor*. Retrieved from http://www.inquisitr.com/2955950/morgan-freeman-series-the-story-of-god-to-air-on-national-geographic-channel/

Badger, E. (2013, Sept. 29). The real cost of segregation. *The Atlantic*.

Bailey, R., & Brake, M. (1975.). *Radical social work*. New York, NY: Pantheon.

Baines, D. (2006). "If you could change one thing": Social service workers and restructuring. *Australian Social Work*, *59*(1).

Baldwin, J. (1949). Preservation of innocence. In M. Blasius & S. Phelan (Eds.), *We are everywhere: A historical sourcebook of gay and lesbian politics*. New York, NY: Routledge.

Baldwin, J. (1956). *Giovanni's Room*. New York: The Dial PressBerry, W. (2014). *Hannah Coulter*. Emeryville, CA: Shoemaker & Hoard.

Baldwin, J. (1963). *The fire next time*. Dial Press.

Balsa, A. & McGuire, T. G. (2003). Prejudice, clinical uncertainty and stereotyping as sources of health disparities. *Journal of Health Economics*, *22*(1), 89–119.

Balsam, K. F., Molina, Y., Beadnell, B., Simoni, J., & Walters, K. (2011). Measuring multiple minority stress: The LGBT people of color microaggressions scale. *Culturally Diverse Ethnic Minority Psychology*, *17*(2), 163–174.

Banks, M. E. (2015). Whiteness and disability: Double marginalization. *Women & Therapy*, *38*(3–4), 220–231.

Banks, S. (2016). Everyday ethics in professional life: social work as ethics work. *Ethics and Social Welfare*, *10*(1), 35–52.

Barclay, D. A., Rider, M. A., & Dombo, E. A. (2012). Spirituality, religion & mental health among Deaf and hard of hearing people: A review of the literature. *Journal of the American Deafness & Rehabilitation Association*, *46*(1), 399–414.

Barlow, F. (2001). Adolescents with leaning disability & psychiatric illness: Two case reports. *Clinical Child Psychology & Psychiatry*, *6*(1), 125–135.

Barnes, A. (2017). How can we help young people to make career enhancing decisions? Cegnet. Retrieved from http://www.cegnet.co.uk/uploads/resources/Making_career_enhancing_decisions.pdf

Barnes, B. (2016). Portland special needs students not getting full school day, civil rights complaint says. Retrieved from http://www.oregonlive.com/education/index.ssf/2016/09/portland_special_needs_student.html.

Barnett, K., Dailey, C. & Polis, S.P. (2017). How cities can support & finance a culture of health. National League of Cities. Retrieved from http://www.nlc.org/article/how-cities-can-support-finance-a-culture-of-health.

Barnett, S.E. (2015). The impact of religious beliefs on professional ethics: A case study of a new teacher. *Canadian Journal of Education*, *38*(3), 1–22.

Barnosky, A.D., & Hadly, E.A. (2016). *Tipping point for planet earth. How close are we to the edge?* New York: Thomas Dunne Books.

Barrera, A. G. (2017). Mexican lawful immigrants among the least likely to become U.S. citizens. *Pew Research Center*. Hispanic Trends.

Barrett, S. E. (2015) The impact of religious beliefs on professional ethics: a case study of a new teacher. *Canadian Journal of Education / Revue canadienne de l'éducation* 38:3, 1–22.

Barron, C., & Taylor, B.J. (2011). The right tools for the right job: Social work students learning community development. *Social Work Education*, *29*(4), 372–385.

Barrow, F. H., Armstrong, M. I., Vargo, A., & Boothroyd, R. A. (2007). Understanding the findings of resilience-related research for fostering the development of African American adolescents. *Child Adolescent Clinical North America*, *16*(2), 393–413.

Barry, E. (2016). Desperate for slumber in Delhi, homeless encounter a "sleep mafia." *The New York Times*.

Barth, R. P., Chung Kwon, L., Wildfire, J., & Guo, S. (2006). A comparison of the governmental costs of long-term foster care and adoption. *Social Service Review*, *80*(1), 127–158.

Bartlett, T. (2017). Can We Really Measure Implicit Bias? Maybe Not. *The, add info to complete entry Chronicle of Higher Education*.

Bartlett, T. (2017, May 26). The intersectionality wars. *The Chronicle of Higher Education, 63*(37).

Bartmess, E. (2015). Review: *The curious incident of the dog in the night by Mark Haddon*. Retrieved from http://disabilityinkidlit. com/2015/04/04/review-the-curious-incident-of-the-dog-in-the-night-time-by-mark-haddon/

Bascsu, J., Jeffrey, B., Novik, N., Abonyi, S., Osman, S., Johnson, S., & Marti, D. (2014). Policy community & kin: Interventions that support rural healthy aging. *Activities, Adaptation & Aging, 38*, 138–153.

Basu, C. (2017). *Effectiveness of community policing*. Retrieved from https://bizfluent.com/info-7912265-effectiveness-community-policing.html.

Bayerl, P.S., Horton, K., Jacobs, G., Rogiest, S., Reguli, Z., Gruschinske, M., Costanzo, P., Trpe Stojanovski, T., Vonas, G., Gascó, M., Elliott, K., (2014). Perspectives on the police profession: an international investigation. *Policing: An International Journal,* 37(4), 728–745

Baynton, (2014). Disability and the justification of inequality. In P. Rothenberg with K. Mayhew (Eds.), *Race, class and gender* (9th ed., p. 94). Duffield, United Kingdom: Worth.

BBC News. (2014, Mar. 20). Freedom 2014: What stands in the way of women being equal to men? Retrieved from http:// www.bbc.com/news/av/magazine-26651162/freedom-2014-what-stands-in-the-way-of-women-being-equal-to-men

Beagan, B. L., & Hattie, B. (2015) Religion, spirituality, and LGBTQ identity integration. *Journal of LGBT Issues in Counseling, 9*(2), 92–117. doi:10.1080/15538605.2015.1029204

Beck, J. (2017, January 12). The tricky psychology of holding government accountable. *The Atlantic.*

Bee, P., Brooks, H., Fraser, C., & Lovell, K. (2015). Professional perspectives on service users & care involvement in mental health care planning: A qualitative study. *International Journal of Nursing Studies, 52*, 1834–1845.

Beets, M. W., Weaver, R. G., Turner-McGrievy, G., Huberty, J., Moore, J. B., Ward, D. S., Freedman, D. A., & Beighle, A. (2017). Two year eating outcomes: An RCT in afterschool programs. *American Journal of Preventive Medicine, 53*(3), 316–326.

Begun, A., Early, T., & Hodge, A. (2016). Mental health and substance abuse service engagement by men and women during community reentry following incarceration. *Administrative Policy & Mental Health, 43*, 207–218.

Behrmann, G., & Tebb, S. (2009). The use of complementary and alternative interventions as a holistic approach with older adults. *Journal of Religion & Spirituality: Social Thought, 28*(1–2), 127–140.

Bell, L. A. (2010). *Readings for diversity and social justice*. In M. Adams, W. J. Blumenfeld, C. R. Castaneda, H. W. Hackman, M. L. Peters, & X. Zúñiga (Ed.). Abingdon, United Kingdom: Routledge.

Bell, L.A. (2010). Theoretical Foundations. I n M. Adams, W. J. Blumenfeld, H.W. Hackman, M. L. Peters, X. Zuniga (Eds.) *Readings for diversity and social justice*, pp. 21–25. New York: Routledge.

Bellafante, G. (2018). Criminal justice reform empties cells, parole fills them up again. *New York Times.*

Beltrán, R., Hacker, A., & Begun, S. (2016). Environmental justice is a social justice issue: Incorporating environmental justice into social work practice curricula. *Journal of Social Work Education, 52*(4), 493–502.

Benard, B. (1991). Fostering resiliency in Kids: Protective factors in the family, school, and *community*. Washington, DC: Department of Education.

Benedict, B. S. (n.d.). Communication considerations A to Z: Deaf culture and community. *Hands & Voices.* Retrieved from http://www.handsandvoices.org/comcon/articles/deafculture.htm

Benson P. L., & Roehlkepartain, E. C. (2008). Spiritual development: A missing priority in youth development. *New Directions in Youth Development, 118*, 13–28.

Bent-Goodley, T., Sherraden, M.S., Frey, J.J., Birkenmaier, J., Callahan, C., & McClendon, G.G. (2016). Celebrating six decades of social work and advancing financial capability and asset development. *Social Work,* 61(4), 293–295.

Benz, T. (2013). Gentrification. *Encyclopedia of Street Crime* (pp. 174–177).

Berchini, C. (2014). Teachers constructing and being constructed by prevailing discourses and practices of whiteness in their curriculum, classroom, and school community: A critical inquiry of three first-year English teachers. (Unpublished doctoral dissertation). Michigan State University, East Lansing, MI.

Berger, M. (2014, Sept. 9). Black fathers, present and accountable. *New York Times Magazine.* Retrieved from http://lens. blogs.nytimes.com/2014/09/19/black-Fathers-present-and-accountable/

Berkowicz, J., & Meyers, A. (2017, May 28). What is cyberbullying? *Education Week.* Retrieved from https://www.stopbullying.gov/cyberbullying/what-is-it/

Berman, J. (2016). 3 proposals from Elizabeth Warren and other Senate Dems to fix student debt. Retrieved from https://www.marketwatch.com/story/3-proposals-from-elizabeth-warren-and-other-senate-dems-to-fix-student-debt-2016-01-21

Berry, W. (n.d.) Quotes, Goodreads. Retrieved Jan9, 2018 from https://www.goodreads.com/quotes/7272037-living-without-expectations-is-hard-but-when-you-can-do

Berube, A., & Holmes, N. (2015, August 27). Concentrated poverty in New Orleans 10 years after Katrina. *Brookings*. Retrieved from https://www.brookings.edu/blog/the-avenue/2015/08/27/concentrated-poverty-in-new-orleans-10-years-after-katrina/?utm_campaign=Brookings%20Brief&utm_source=hs_email&utm_medium=email&utm_content=13660613&_hsenc=p2ANqtz--rbuGoAX-4SXMdIdr4USLX-ZhSWAN5BMgUnIoAyfhumjtK75u83j7BKyYRUi4j4kcce1CPeErgF-QM9f8eATAfvbP5mfQ&_hsmi=13660613#/M10420.

Best, H. (2007). New challenges, new elites? Changes in the recruitment and career patterns of European representative elites. *Comparative Sociology*, 6, 85–113.

Bezusko, A. (2013). Criminalizing motherhood: How the war on welfare was won. *Souls: A Critical Journal of Black Politics, Culture, and Society*, 5(1–2), 39–55.

Bhatnagar, G.V. (2017). Disability activists and EC work to make assembly polls more accessible. Retrieved from https://thewire.in/110842/disability-activists-and-ec-polls-accessible/

Bhattacharyya, P. (2016). Street violence against women in India: Mapping prevention strategies. *Asian Social Work and Policy Review*, 10, 311–325.

Bicakci, B. (2013, Aug. 23). The border protection-asylum industry. Retrieved from https://overland.org.au/2013/08/the-border-protection-asylum-industry/

Bimrose, J. & Barnes, S.A. (2007). Navigating the labour market: Career decision making & the role of guidance. Institute for Employment Research, University of Warwick. Retrieved from https://www2.warwick.ac.uk/fac/soc/ier/publications/2007/egreport08.pdf

Bishop, K. (2014). Challenging research: Completing participatory social research with children and adolescents in a hospital setting. *HERD: Health Environmental research & Design Journal*, 7(2), 76–91.

Bissinger, B. (2015, July 1). Caitlyn Jenner: The full story. *Vanity Fair*. Retrieved from http://www.vanityfair.com/hollywood/2015/06/caitlyn-jenner-bruce-cover-annie-leibovitz

Bivens, J., Costa, D., McNicholas, C, Shierholz, H. & von Wilpert, M. (2018). Ten actions that hurt workers during Trump's first year. *Economic Policy Institute*. Retrieved from www.epi.org/publication/ten-actions-that-hurt-workers-during-trumps-first-year

Bizumic, B., & Duckitt, J. (2012). What is and is not ethnocentrism? A conceptual analysis and political implications. *International Society of Political Psychology*, 33(6), 887–909.

Blair, E. (2015, Sept. 23). Anne-Marie Slaughter's *Unfinished Business*. The New York Times. Book Review.

Blaisdell, B. (Ed.). (2000). *Great speeches by Native Americans*. Mineola, NY: Dover.

Blancato, R. B., & Ponder, M. (2015). The public policies we need to redress ageism. *Generations, 39*(3), 91–95.

Blanchard, A. (2011, Nov. 4). *TEDxHouston 2011—Angela Blanchard* [Video file]. Retrieved from https://www.youtube.com/watch?v=TaX5DUGC1CU

Blanchard, J. (2004). NAACP sues Kent schools over disciplinary tactics. *The Seattle Times*. Retrieved from http://old.seattletimes.com/html/education/2002083784_kent06m.html

Blankertz, L. & O'Neal, G. (2010). The challenges of co-occurring disorders, pp. 171–208, in AA. Abbott, *Alcohol, tobacco and other drugs: challenging myths, assessing theories, individualizing interventions*. NASW Press.

Blasius, M., & Phelan, S. (Eds.). (1997). *We are everywhere: A historical sourcebook of gay and lesbian politics*. Abingdon, United Kingdom: Routledge.

Block, P. (2008). *Community: The structure of belonging*. San Francisco, CA: Berrett-Koehler.

Blomberg, H., Kallio, J., Kroll, C., & Niemelä, M. (2015). What explains frontline worker's views on poverty? A comparison of three types of welfare sector institutions. *International Journal of Social Welfare, 24*, 324–334.

Bloom, M., Fischer, J., & Orme, J. (2009). Evaluating practice: Guidelines for the accountable professional (6th ed.). Boston, MA: Allyn & Bacon.

Blow, C. (2014). *Fire shut up in my bones*. Boston, MA: Houghton Mifflin.

Blumenthal, R. (2015). NASA adds to evidence of mysterious ancient earthworks. *The New York Times,* Science section. Retrieved Nov. 7, 2015, from http://www.nytimes.com/2015/11/03/science/nasa-adds-to-evidence-of-mysterious-ancient-earthworks.html?_r=0

Bochanski, A. (n.d.). Training helps police in interactions with mentally ill people.Retrieved from https://whyy.org/articles/training-helps-police-in-interactions-with-mentally-ill-people/

Boff, L. & Boff, C. (2000). Introduction to liberation theology. Maryknoll, NY: Orbis Books.

Bogosian, A., Hadwin, A., Hankins, M., & Moss-Morris, R. (2015). Parents' expressed emotion and mood, rather than their physical disability are associated with adolescent adjustment: A longitudinal study of families with a parent with multiple sclerosis. *Clinical Rehabilitation, 30*(3), 303–311.

Bole, V. (1995). Financial sector and high interest rates. In. M. Blejer & Skreb, M. (Eds*), Financial sector transformation: lessons from economies in transition.* Cambridge University Press.

Bonds, M., & Farmer-Hinton, R. L. (2008). Empowering neighborhoods via increased citizen participation or a Trojan horse from city hall: The neighborhood strategic planning (NSP) process in Milwaukee, Wisconsin. *Journal of African American Studies, 13,* 74–89.

Bonilla-Santiago, G. (1998). Breaking ground and barriers: Hispanic women developing effective leadership:; Organizing Puerto Rican migrant farmworkers—the experience of Puerto Ricans in New Jersey. New York, NY: St. Martin's Press.

Bonilla-Silva, E. (2010). *Racism without racists: Color-blind racism and the persistence of racial inequality in America* (3rd ed.). Lanham, MD: Rowman & Littlefield.

Bonilla-Silva, E. (2011). The sweet enchantment of color-blind racism in Obamerica. *The ANNALS of the American Academy of Political and Social Science,* 634(1).

Bonnie, C. (2016, October 17). Sitting in: A new look at social work. *Wicked Local.*

Booze, K. (2017). What's right with our schools: Unified PE program strengthens relationships within the school. *41WMGT.* Retrieved from http://www.smartbrief.com/s/2017/08/students-build-relationships-unified-pe-0

Born, P. (2014, July). Creating positive community identity. *Utne Reader.* Retrieved from http://www.utne.com/community/creating-positive-community-identity-ze0z1407zhou.aspx? newsletter=1&utm_source=Sailthru&utm_medium=email&utm_term=UTR%20eNews&utm_campaign=7.14.14%20Utne%20e

Bornstein, D. (2007). *How to change the world: Social entrepreneurs and the power of new ideas.* New York, NY: Oxford University Press.

Bornstein, D. (2017). When families lead themselves out of poverty. *The New York Times.* Opinion pages.

Bosisio, R. & Ronfani, P. (2016). 'Who is in your family?' Italian children with non-heterosexual parents talk about growing up in a non-conventional household. *Children in Society,* 30, 455–466.

Bost, S., & Aparicio, F. R. (Eds.). (2013). *The Routledge companion to Latino/a literature.* New York, NY: Routledge.

Boswell, J. (1980). *Christianity, social tolerance and homosexuality.* Chicago, IL: University of Chicago Press.

Bothamley, J. (1993). *Dictionary of theories.* Farmington Hills, MI: Gale Research.

Bouchard, G., & Lee, C. (2000). The marital context for father involvement with their preschool children: The role of partner support. *Prevention & Intervention in the Community, 20*(1/2), 37.

Bowen, E. & Murshid, N.S. (2016). Trauma-informed social policy: a conceptual framework for policy analysis and advocacy. *American Journal of Public Health,* 106(27), 223–229.

Boxer, A. (2009). Native Americans and the federal government. Retrieved June 24, 2017, from http://www.historytoday.com/andrew-boxer/native-americans-and-federal-government

Boyd, D. (2016, July 24). Why social science risks irrelevance: David Cutler for the *Chronicle Review.*

Boyer, L. B. (1979). *Childhood and folklore: A psychoanalytic study of Apache personality.* New York, NY: The Library of Psychological Anthropology.

Boynton, C.W. (2009). Singing & rapping for their rights as adoptees. *New York Times,* 4.12.2009, 158(54643), p. 6.

Boynton-Jarrett, R. D. (2017, July 24). Data driven change at the community level: Emerging research on urban child health. DataSpeak [Webinar].

Bracy, N. L. (2010). Circumventing the law: Student rights in schools with police. *Journal of Contemporary Criminal Justice,* 26(3), 294–315.

Bradbury, D. E. (2016) Part I—Four decades of action for children (1912-1952). In M. Barger (Ed.), *Children's Bureau Part I.* Retrieved from http://www.socialwelfarehistory.com/programs/child-welfarechild-labor/childrens-bureau-part-i-2/

Bradley, E. H., & Taylor, L. A. (2013). *The American health care paradox: Why spending more is getting us less*. New York, NY: Public Affairs.

Brainwrap. (2015).*The Republican rape advisory chart tracking the republican party's disturbing obsession with all things rape-related*. http://goprapeadvisorychart.com/explanation. Retrieved 1.6.2018.

Bransford, C. L. (2011). Integrating critical consciousness into direct social work practice: A pedagogical view. *Social Work Education*, 30(8), 932–947.

Branson, M.S. (1998). The role of civic education: A forthcoming education policy task force position paper from the communitarian network. Retrieved from http://www.civiced.org/papers/articles_role.html

Brave Heart, M. Y, Elkins, J., Tafoya, G., Bird, D., & Salvador, M. (2012). Wicasa Was'aka: Restoring the traditional strength of American Indian boys and men. *American Journal of Public Health*, 102(S2), 177–182.

Brendtro, L. K., & Mitchell, M. L. (2013). Deep brain learning: Healing the heart. *Reclaiming Children and Youth*, 22(1), 5–12. Burrell, T. (2011). Q & A with Tom Burrell. Retrieved from http://arresteddevelopmentmusic.com/qa-with-tom-burrell-brainwashed/#.Vm8VQkorLIU

Brennan, M. (2016). Opening the door for early childhood education. Retrieved from www.housingmatters.org/articles

Breton, M. (1993). Liberation theology, group work, and the right of the poor and oppressed to participate in the life of the community. *Social Work With Groups*, 15(2–3), 257–269.

Brewsaugh, K., & Strozier, A. (2016). Fathers in child welfare: What do social work textbooks teach our students? *Children & Youth Services Review*, 60(1), 34–41.

Brewster, M. E., Velez, B. L., Foster, A., Esposito, J., & Robinson, M. A. (2016). Minority stress and the moderating role of religious coping among religious and spiritual sexual minority individuals. *Journal of Counseling Psychology*, 63(1), 119–126.

Brewster, V. (2013). Interview with Reeta Wolfsohn, CMSW: Center for Financial Social Work [Blog post]. Retrieved from http://www.socialjusticesolutions.org/2013/11/15/interview-reeta-wolfsohn-cmsw-center-financial-social-work-founder/

Bride, B. E. (2007). Prevalence of secondary traumatic stress among social workers. *Social Work*, 52(I), 63–70.

Briscoe, F., Gupta, A., & Anner, M.J. (2015). Social activism and practice diffusion: How activist tactics affect non-targeted organizations. *Administrative Science Quarterly*, 60(2), 1–33.

Britannica Editors (n.d.). New York slave rebellion of 1712. Retrieved Jan. 9, 2018 from https://www.britannica.com/event/New-York-slave-rebellion-of-1712.

Britton, J. (2013). Researching white mothers of mixed parentage children: The significance of investigating whiteness. *Ethnic & Racial Studies*, 36(8), 1311–1322.

Brodish, A. B., Cogburn, C. D., Fuller-Rowell, T. E., Peck, S., Malanchuk, O., & Eccles, J. S. (2011). Perceived racial discrimination as a predictor of health behaviors: The moderating role of gender. *Race & Social Problems*, 3(3), 160–169.

Broner, N., Franczak, M., Dye, C., & McAllister, W. (2001). Knowledge transfer, policymaking and community empowerment: A consensus model approach for providing public mental health and substance abuse services. *Psychiatric Quarterly*, 72(1), 79–102.

Brookings.edu. (n.d.). Immigration. Retrieved from https://www.brookings.edu/topic/immigration/

Brooks, D. (2016). Three views of marriage. *Psychology Today.com*.

Brooks, M. (2016, April 28). Racial, ethnic heath disparities persist in US, CDC says. *Medscape*.

Brooks, O. (2012). The dangerous usefulness of theorising about race and racism in psychotherapy. https://www.tandfonline.com/doi/abs/10.1080/14753634.2012.664872

Brown, C. (2014, July 22). Linking together the fight for girl's rights *The Washington Post*. Retrieved from http://www.washingtonpost.com/opinions/gordon-brown-the-world-unites-to-fight-for-girls-rights/2014/07/21/3b055718-1019-11e4-98ee-daea85133bc9_story.html? wpisrc=nl_politics

Brown, J. L. C., Eubanks, C., & Keating, A. (2017). Yoga quality of life anxiety and trauma in low income adults with mental health. *Social Work in Mental Health*, 15(3), 308–330.

Brown, L. X. Z. (2013). How "differently abled" marginalizes disabled people [Blog post]. Retrieved from http://www.autistichoya.com/2013/08/differently-abled.html

Brown, M. K., Carnoy, M., Currie, E., Dusts, T., Oppenheim, D. B., Shulz, M. M., & Wellman, D. (2005). *Whitewashing race: The myth of a colorblind society*. Berkeley: University of California Press.

Brown, R. T., Thomas, M. L., Cutler, D. F., & Hinderlie, M. (2013). Meeting the housing and care needs of older homeless adults: A permanent supportive housing program targeting homeless seniors. *Seniors Housing & Care Journal, 21*(1), 125–132.

Browne, C. H. (2014). *Youth thrive: Advancing healthy adolescent development and well-being.* Washington, DC: Center for the Study of Social Policy.

Bruni, F. (2015). Bigotry, the Bible and the lessons of Indiana. *The New York Times.com.* Retrieved from http://www.nytimes.com/2015/04/05/opinion/sunday/frank-bruni-same-sex-sinners.html?src=xpseligions

Brunson, R. K., & Miller, J. (2006). Young black men and urban policing in the United States. *British Journal of Criminology, 46*, 613–640.

Bryan, A., Hyun-Jun, K., & Fredriksen-Goldsen, K. (2017, Supplement). Factors associated with high-risk alcohol consumption among LGB older adults: The roles of gender, social support, perceived stress, discrimination, and stigma. *Gerontologist, 57*, S95–S104.

Buchman, D. D. (2005). A*ncient healing secrets. Practical cures from Egypt, China, India, South America, Russia, Scandinavia, and more.* New York, NY: Black Dog & Levanthal.

Buck, P. D. (2014). Constructing race, creating privilege. In P. Rothenberg with K. Mayhew (Eds.), *Race, class and gender* (9th ed., p. 33). Duffield, United Kingdom: Worth.

Buildiaf.org. (2017). Baltimoreans united in leadership development. Retrieved from www.buildiaf.org

Bulanda, J.J., Tellis, D., & McCrea, K.T. (2015). Cocreating a social work apprenticeship with disadvantaged African American youth: A best-practices after school curriculum. *Smith College Studies in Social Work, 85*(3), 285–310.

Bureau of Justice Statistics. (2016). Crime type. Retrieved from http://www.bjs.gov/index.cfm? ty=tp&tid=3

Bureau of Labor Statistics, (2018). Occupational outlook handbook. Social workers job outlook. Retrieved from https://www.bls.gov/ooh/community-and-social-service/social-workers.htm#tab-6.

Burke, L., Teague, M., Ward, D., & Worrall, A. (2016). Probation occupational cultures for the future? A focus group discussion. *British Journal of Community Justice, 14*(1), 29–43.

Burrell, T. (2010). *Brainwashed: Challenging the myth of black inferiority.* New York, NY: Smiley Books.

Burton, L. M., Kemp, S., P., Leung, M., Matthews, S., & Takeuchi, D. T. (2011). *Communities, neighborhoods, and health: Expanding the boundaries of place, social disparities in health and health care.* Berlin, Germany: Springer.

Bush, M. E. L. (2004). *Breaking the code of good intentions: Everyday forms of whiteness.* Lanham, MD: Rowman & Littlefield.

Businessdictionary.com (n.d.). Ethics.

Buzzfeed Video. (2014). *Students learn a powerful lesson about privilege.* Retrieved from https://www.youtube.com/watch?v=2KlmvmuxzYE

Byrd, J. (2011). *The transit of empire: Indigenous critiques of colonization (First peoples: New directions in indigenous studies).* Minneapolis: University of Minnesota Press.

Cabiati, E., & Raineri, M.L. (2016). Learning from service users' involvement: A research about changing stigmatizing attitudes in social work students. *Social Work Education, 35*(8), 982–996.

Cabrera, N. L. (2012). Exposing whiteness in higher education: White male college students minimizing racism, claiming victimization, and recreating white supremacy. *Race, Ethnicity and Education, 17*(1), 30–55.

Cadet, D. (2014, June). Five lies we should stop telling about black fatherhood. *The Huffington Post.* Retrieved Nov. 21, 2015, from http://www.huffingtonpost.com/2014/06/13/black-fatherhood-statistics_n_5491980.html

Caldwell, B. (2012). Addressing intersectionality in the lives of women in poverty: Incorporating core components of a social work program into legal education. *Journal of Gender, Social Policy and the Law, 20*(4), 823–833.

Caldwell, P. (2015, Nov. 18). Elizabeth Warren on the persistent wage gap that has to stop. *Mother Jones.* Retrieved Jan. 4, 2016, from http://www.motherjones.com/politics/2015/11/elizabeth-warren-women-equal-pay-wage-gap.

California Mental Health. (2016). A new state of mind: Ending the stigma of mental illness. Retrieved from https://vimeo.com/67439197

Callahan, L., Gardner, N., Mendonca, L., & Scott, D. (2014, November). What social sector leaders need to succeed. *McKinsey.com.*

Camfielo, D. (2016). Racism finds a thousand ways to kill, scar & oppress. *Canadian Dimension, 50*(1), 18–21.

Campbell, A.F.(2017). How the fight for a $15 minimum wage in Baltimore fell apart. Retrieved from https://www.vox.com/policy-and-politics/2017/4/10/15224078/fight-for-15-minimum-wage-baltimore.

Campbell, B. M. (2000). *Successful women, angry men.* New York, NY: Berkley Trade.

Campbell, B. M. (2005). *72-hour hold.* New York, NY: Anchor.

Campos, P. F. (2017). White economic privilege is alive and well. *The New York Times, Sunday Review.*

Canda, D., & Furman, L. D. (2009). *Spiritual diversity in social work practice: The heart of helping.* New York, NY: Oxford University Press.

Caplan, S., Paris, M., Whittemore, R., Desai, M., Dixon, J., Alvidrez, J., Escobar, J., & Scahil, L. (2011). Correlates of religious, supernatural and psychosocial causal beliefs about depression among Latino immigrants in primary care. *Mental Health, Religion & Culture, 14*(6), 589–611.

Carey, B. (2015, Dec. 28). Programs expand schizophrenic patients' role in their own care. *The New York Times.*

Carey, B. (2016, April 13). Aid groups aim to put mental health on world agenda. *The New York Times,*

Carlson, L. (2001). Cognitive ableism and disability studies: Feminist reflections on the history of mental retardation. *Hypatia, 16*(4), 124–146.

Carlyle, E. (2013). Power woman Helene Gayle: How to make the greatest impact on the most people.

Carnevale, N., Smith, N., & Strohl, J. (2010). Help wanted: Projections of jobs & education requirements through 2018. *Center on Education & the Workforce.*

Carroll, A.E. (2018). Preventive care saves money? Sorry, it's too good to be true. *New York Times.*

Carroll, J., & Minkler, M. (2000). Freire's message for social workers. *Journal of Community Practice, 8* (1), 21–36.

Carson, R. (2002). *Silent spring.* Boston, MA: Houghton Mifflin.

Carter, J. (2005). *Endangered values: Call to action.* Retrieved from http://www.religionnews.com/2015/05/01/jimmy-carters-essay-on-cutting-his-southern-baptist-ties-goes-viral/

Carter, J. (2014). *A call to action: Women, religion, violence, and power.* New York, NY: Simon & Schuster. Retrieved Nov. 22, 2015, from http://www.dailykos.com/story/2015/4/23/1379812/-Jimmy-Carter-Losing-My-Religion-For-Equality

Carter, S. M., Rychetnik, L., Lloyd, B., Kerridge, I. H., Baur, L., Bauman, A., Hooker, C., & Zask, A. (2011). Evidence, ethics, and values: A framework for health promotion. *American Journal of Public Health, 101*(3), 465–472.

Cartwright, M. (2013). Olmec civilization. *Ancient History Encyclopedia.* Retrieved 1.6.2018 from Retrieved 1.6.2018 from https://www.ancient.eu/Olmec_Civilization/.

Casey Foundation. (2016). Juvenile justice. Retrieved from http://www.aecf.org/work/juvenile-justice/

Cast.org. (n.d.). Universal design for learning. Retrieved June 24, 2017, from http://www.cast.org/

Castro, F. G., Barrera, M., & Stelker, L. K. H. (2010). Issues and challenges in the design of culturally adapted evidence-based interventions. *Annual Review of Clinical Psychology, 6,* 213–239.

Cates, J.T., Schaefle, S.E., Smaby, M.H., Maddux, C.D., & LeBeauf, I. (2007). Comparing multicultural with general counseling knowledge and skill competency for students who completed counselor training. *Journal of Multicultural Counseling and Development,* 35, 27–39.

CBSNews.com. (2016). Grand jury indicts activists behind Planned Parenthood attack videos. Retrieved from http://www.cbsnews.com/news/grand-jury-indicts-activists-behind-planned-parenthood-videos/

CBSNews.com. (2018). African-American unemployment hits record low.

Census.gov. (2017). American Fact Finder. 2017 Population estimate. Retrieved from https://factfinder.census.gov/faces/nav/jsf/pages/index.xhtml

Center for American Progress Immigration Team & Nicholson, M. (2017). The Facts on Immigration Today: 2017 Edition. *Center for American Progress.*

Center for Behavioral Health Statistics and Quality. (2012, Nov. 7). Almost half of American Indian and Alaska Native adult substance abuse treatment admissions are referred through the criminal justice system. *Data Spotlight.* Treatment Episode Data Set.

Center for Disease Control. (2015). *Suicide: Facts at a glance.* Retrieved from https://www.cdc.gov/violenceprevention/pdf/suicide-datasheet-a.pdf

Center for Substance Abuse Treatment (US). Trauma-Informed Care in Behavioral Health Services. Rockville (MD): Substance Abuse and Mental Health Services Administration (US); 2014. (Treatment Improvement Protocol (TIP) Series, No. 57.) Chapter 1, Trauma-Informed Care: A Sociocultural Perspective. Available from: https://www.ncbi.nlm.nih.gov/books/NBK207195

Chandler, S. K. (2009). Working hard, living poor: Social work and the movement for livable wages. *Journal of Community Practice, 17,* 170–183.

Chang, E.C., Yu, E.A., Yu, T., Kahle, E.R, Hernandez, V. Jean M. Kim, J.M., Jeglic, E.L., & Hirsch, J.K., (2016). Ethnic variables and negative life events as redictors of depressive symptoms and suicidal behaviors in Latino college students: on the centrality of receptivo a los Demás. *Hispanic Journal of Behavioral Science*, 38(2), 206–221.

Chang, S. Y., Fleming, T., Luccassen, M., Fenaughty, T., Clark, T., & Denny, S. (2017). Mental health status of double minority adolescents: Findings from national cross-sectional health surveys. *Journal of Immigrant & Minority Health, 19*(3), 499–510.

Change.org. (2014). McMillon, J. *Include more history and insight on the Moorish and African presence/influence on modern European civilization for the AP European History curriculum.* Lynchburg, VA. http://www.change.org/petitions/the-college-board-include-more-history-and-insight-on-the-moorish-and-african-presence-influence-on-modern-european-civilization-for-the-ap-european-history-curriculum?utm_medium=email&utm_source=notification&utm_campaign=new_petition_recruit#share

Chang-Muy, F., & Congress, E. (Eds.). (2009). Social work with immigrants and refugees: Legal issues, clinical skills and advocacy. New York, NY: Springer.

Chao, C.M. (1992). The inner heart: Therapy with Southeast Asian families, pp 157-181. In L.A. Vargas & J.D. Koss-Chiono (Eds.), Working with culture: Psychotherapeutic interventions with ethnic minority children and adolescents. San Francisco, CA: Jossey-Bass.

Chapman, P. (2018). How access to justice helps in the fight against poverty. *Open Society Foundations.*

Charles Colson Task Force on Federal Corrections. (2016). Transforming prisons, restoring lives: Final recommendations of the Charles Colson task force on federal corrections. Retrieved from https://www.urban.org/research/publication/transforming-prisons-restoring-lives?

Chaze, F., Thomson, M.S., George, U., & & Guruge, S. (2015). Role of cultural beliefs, religion, and spirituality in mental health and/or service utilization among immigrants in Canada: A scoping review. *Canadian Journal of Community Mental Health, 34*(3), 87–101.

Chengu, G. (2014, October 12). Before Columbus: How Africans brought civilization to America. *Global Research Newsletter.* Retrieved April 6, 2015, from http://www.globalresearch.ca/before-columbus-how-africans-brought-civilization-to-america/5407584

Cheruvu, R., Souto-Manning, M., Lencl, T., & Chin-Culubaquib, M. (2015). Race isolation and exclusion: What early childhood educators need to know about the experiences of pre-service teachers of color. *Urban Review, 47,* 237–265.

Chesler, P. (1972). *Women and madness. When is a woman mad and who is it that decides?* New York, NY: Doubleday.

Cheung, M., & Leung, P. (2009) Multicultural practice & evaluation: A case approach to evidence based practice. Denver, CO: Love.

Cheung, S.-K., & Sun, S. Y. K. (2000). Effects of self-efficacy and social support on the mental health condition of mutual-aid organization members. *Social Behavior and Personality, 28*(5), 413–422.

Chiao, J. Y. (2015, April 7). Cultural neuroscience and health: Developing an international cultural neuroscience consortium [Blog post]. *Behavioral and Social Sciences.* Retrieved from https://obssr.od.nih.gov/cultural-neuroscience-and-health-developing-an-international-cultural-neuroscience-consortium/

Children's Defense Fund. (2015). *Children in the States Fact Sheets 2015.* Retrieved from http://www.childrensdefense.org/library/data/state-data-repository/cits

Children's Defense Fund. (2016). Retrieved from o http://www.childrensdefense.org/library/data/cradle-to-prison-pipeline-overview-fact-sheet-2009.pdf

Children's Defense Fund.com. (2007). *A report of the Children's Defense Fund: America's cradle to prison pipeline.* Retrieved from http://www.childrensdefense.org/library/data/cradle-prison-pipeline-report-2007-full-lowres.pdf

Childress, S. (2014) A return to school segregation in America? *Frontline.* Retrieved June 24, 2017, from http://www.pbs.org/wgbh/frontline/article/a-return-to-school-segregation-in-america/

Childress, S. (2016). More states consider raising the age for juvenile crime. *Frontline Enterprise Journalism Group.*

Chin, M. H. (2005). Populations at risk: A critical need for research, funding, and action *Journal of General Internal Medicine, 20*(5), 448–449.

Chinn, S. (2010). *The other side of paradise.* New York, NY: Scribner.

Chinn, S. (2010). Performative identities: From identity politics to queer theory. In M. Wetherell & C. T. Mohanty (Eds.), *The SAGE handbook of social identities.* Thousand Oaks, CA: SAGE.

Chung, L. S., Raymond, C. W. S., & Hew, K. F. (2011). Critical thinking in asynchronous online discussion: An investigation of student facilitation techniques. *New Horizons in Education, 59*(1), 52–65.

Chiono (Eds.), Working with culture: Psychotherapeutic interventions with ethnic minority children and adolescents (pp. 157–181). San Francisco, CA: Jossey-Bass.

Choi, N. G., DiNitto, D. M., Marti, C. N., & Nathan, S. P. (2017). Adverse childhood experiences and suicide attempts among those with mental and substance use disorders. *Child Abuse & Neglect, 69*, 252–262.

Chopra, D. & Tanzi, R.E.(2018). *The healing self*. New York: Harmony Books.

Choudhury, H., & Mahood, A. (2008). Introduction: Immigrant residential experience—An overlooked area in environmental design research. *Journal of Architectural and Planning Research, 25* (1),

Christian, J. (2011). *God of the empty-handed: Poverty, power & the kingdom of God.* (2nd ed.). Sydney, Australia: Acorn Press.

Chronicle of Social Change. (2016). GIS and child welfare: A map is worth more than a thousand words. *Chronicle.*

Chung, K. Y. S., & Singh, A. A. (2010). The bisexual youth of color intersecting identities development model: A contextual approach to understanding multiple marginalization experience. *Journal of Bisexuality, 10*, 429–451.

Cihodaru, M., & Dumitrescu, L. Ş. (2013). The motives and rationalizations of the European right-wind discourse on immigrants: Shifts in multiculturalism? *Journal of Comparative Research in Anthropology and Sociology, 4*(2), 51–70.

Cisneros, J., Stakeman, C., Joyner, M., & Schmitz, C. (2008). *Critical multicultural social work.* Chicago, IL: Lyceum.

Cisneros, S. (1991). *The house on Mango Street.* New York, NY: Vintage Books.

Cladoosby, B. (2015). State of the Indian Nations Address. National Congress of American Indians. C-Span. Retrieved from https://www.c-span.org/video/?323936-1/state-indian-nations-address

Clark, R. (2001). Efficacy of racism-specific coping styles as predictors of cardiovascular functioning. *Ethnicity & Disease, 11*(2), 286–295.

Clarke, J. H. (1992). *Christopher Columbus and the Afrikan holocaust: Slavery and the rise of European capitalism.* Brooklyn, NY: A & B Publishers.

Clarke, J. H. (1998). Christopher Columbus and the Afrikan holocaust: Slavery and the rise of European capitalism (Reprint). Buffalo, NY: Eworld, Inc.

Clarke, J. H. (Ed.). (1968). *William Styron's Nat Turner: Ten black writers respond.* Boston, MA: Beacon Press.

Clasp.org. (2017). *Census data on poverty.* Retrieved from http://www.clasp.org/resources-and-publications/publication-1/2016.09.13-Poverty-Day-infographic-sheet-FINAL.pdf

Claxton, N. (2014). What's wrong vs. what happened? *ACEs Connection: A community of practice social network.* Retrieved from http://www.acesconnection.com/printer-friendly-topic/what-s-wrong-v-what-happened.

Cleland, J. A. (2014). Working together through sport? Local authority provision for ethnic minorities in the UK. *Sport in Society, 17*(1), 38–51.

Clevenger, C., Derr, A.S., Cudge, W.,Curran, S. (2014). How do social service providers view recent immigrants? Perspectives from Portland, Maine, and Olympia, Washington. *Journal of Immigration & Refugee Studies, 12*, 67–86.

Clevenger, R.J. (2015). Georgetown University's Ferguson Syllabus and Dr. Marcia Chatelain. Retrieved Jan. 9, 2018 from http://www.pupnmag.com/article/georgetown-universitys-ferguson-syllabus-and-dr-marcia-chatelain/.

Coalition for Evidence-Based Policy (Laura and John Arnold Foundation). (2015). Retrieved from http://evidencebased-programs.org/about/full-list-of-programs

Coalition for Evidence-Based Policy (n.d.). Full list of programs. Retrieved July 10, 2017, from http://evidencebasedpro-grams.org/about/full-list-of-programs

Coalition of Human Needs. (2018). About CHN. Retrieved from chn.org

Coates, T. (2014). *Between the world and me.* New York, NY: Spiegel & Grau.

Coates, T. (2015). The Black family in the age of mass incarceration. *The Atlantic*, October. Retrieved Jan 11, 2018 from https://www.theatlantic.com/magazine/archive/2015/10/the-black-family-in-the-age-of-mass-incarceration/403246/.

Code of Ethics. (2017). Code of Ethics of the National Association ofo Social Workers. NASW.

Coe, M. D. (1968). *America's first civilization: Discovering the Olmec.* New York, NY: American Heritage. Columbia.edu. (2015). Timeline of Chinese history and dynasties. Retrieved Nov. 7, 2015, from http://afe.easia.columbia.edu/timelines/china_timeline.htm

Cohen, L., Chavez, V., & Chehimi, S. (Eds.). (2007). *Prevention is primary: Strategies for community well-being.* Hoboken, NJ: Jossey-Bass.

Cohn, D. (2016). Federal officials may revamp how Americans identify race, ethnicity on census and other forms. *Pew Research Center.*

Coles, R. (1972). Book review: William Ryan's blaming the victim. *American Journal of Sociology. 78*(2), 448–450. collaborative model for capacity building to scale up evidence based practice. *Children and Youth*

Collins, C. B., & Sapiano, T. N. (2016). Lessons learned from dissemination of evidence-based interventions for HIV prevention. *American Journal of Prevention Medicine, 51*(4S)2, S140–S147.

Collins, L. M. (2015). U.S. marriage rate hits new low & may continue to decline. *National Digest News.*

Collins, M., & Haley, A. (1990). *Marva's Way* (2nd ed.). New York, NY: Tarcher Perigee.

Collins, P. Y., Patel, V., Joestl, S. S., March, D., Insel, T. R., & Daar, A. S. (2011). Grand challenges in global mental health. *Nature, 475*(7354), 27–30. doi:10.1038/475027a

Columbia School of Social Work Student Demands. (2016). Demands to improve curriculum. Personal correspondence, October 12, 2016.

Combi, S. (2013, May 12). What is the safety net? Retrieved September 14, 2016, from http://www.urban.org/urban-wire/what-safety-net

Comboni Missionaries. (2016). Native American tribes against North Dakota oil pipeline [Blog post]. Retrieved from https://www.combonimissionaries.org/index.php/latestnews/fr-pezzi-blog-news/285-native-american-tribes-against-north-dakota-oil-pipeline.html

Community Guide.org. (n.d.). Online guide to what works for healthy communities. Retrieved from http://www.thecommunityguide.org/alcohol/index.html

Compellingtruth.org. (2017). What is Hinduism? Retrieved from http://www.compellingtruth.org/what-is-Hinduism.html

Conan, N. (2010, March 18). Negative images "brainwash" African Americans. *NPR.org.* Retrieved May 28, 2017, from http://www.npr.org/templates/story/story.php?storyId=124828546

Cone, J.H. (2010). *A Black theology of liberation.* New York: Orbis Books.

Cone, J.H. (2011). *The cross and the lynching tree.* New York: Orbis Books.

Congress, E. (2014). Developing a curriculum based on human rights and social justice. In K.R. Libal, M. Berthold, R.L. Thomas, R.L. & L.M. Healy (Eds.), *Advancing human rights in social work education,* pp. 77–102. Alexandria, VA: CSWE.

Constantine, M. G., Richardson, T. O., Benjamin, E. M., & Wilson, J. W. (1998). An overview of black racial identity theories: Limitations and considerations for future theoretical conceptualizations. *Applied & Preventive Psychology, 7,* 95–99.

Conway, P. & Lassiter, K. (2011). Opportunity knocks: the intersection of community social work and food justice praxis. Pdf. *Arete* 3–32.

Cook, D. A. (2015). Shifting the center in teacher education: An introduction to the special issue on critical race theory and teacher education. *Urban Review, 47,* 233–236.

Cook, L. (2015). U.S. Education: Still separate and unequal. *USNews.com.* Retrieved from http://www.usnews.com/news/blogs/data-mine/2015/01/28/us-education-still-separate-and-unequal

Cooper, D., & Kroeger, T. (2017). Employers steal billions from workers' paychecks each year. Economic Policy Institute. Retrieved from http://www.epi.org/publication/employers-steal-billions-from-workers-paychecks-each-year-survey-data-show-millions-of-workers-are-paid-less-than-the-minimum-wage-at-significant-cost-to-taxpayers-and-state-economies/

Cooper, T., & McCord, D. (Eds.). (2014). An act for the better ordering and governing of Negroes and Slaves, South Carolina, 1712. In P. Rothenberg with K. Mayhew (Eds.), *Race, class and gender* (9th ed., p. 506). Duffield, United Kingdom: Worth.

Cordero-Guzmán, H. R. (2015). Worker centers, worker center network, & the promise of protection for low wage workers. *Working USA: The Journal of Labor & Society, 18,* 31–57.

Cordova, D., Parra-Cardona, J. R., Blow, A. Johnson, D. J., Prado, G., & Fitzgerald, H. E. (2015). "They don't look at what affects us": The role of ecodevelopmental factors on alcohol and drug use among Latinos with physical disabilities. *Ethnic Health, 20*(1), 66–86.

Cormes, M., Peardon, J., Manthorppppe, J. & 3YO Project Team. (2008). Wise owls and professors: the role of older researchers in the review of the national service framework for older people. *Health Expectations: An International Journal of Public Participation In Health Care And Health Policy.*

Corrigan, P. W. (2007). How clinical diagnosis might exacerbate the stigma of mental illness. *Social Work, 52*(1), 35–38.

Cottam, H. (2015). Social services are broken. How can we fix them [Video file]? Retrieved from https://www.ted.com/talks/hilary_cottam_social_services_are_broken_how_we_can_fix_them

Council on Accreditation (2018). The Cornerstone of COA Accreditation. Retrieved from http://coanet.org/standards/standards-overview/

Council on Social Work Education (CASW). (2016). Retrieved from http://www.cswe.org/About/57763.aspx

Council on Social Work Education, (cswe.org). (2015). Council on Social Work Education. Commission on Accreditation Commission on Educational Policy. Retrieved from https://www.cswe.org/getattachment/Accreditation/Standards-and-Policies/2015-EPAS/2015EPASandGlossary.pdf.aspx.

Council on Social Work Education. (2015). 2015 Educational Policy and Accreditation Standards for Baccalaureate and Master's Social Work Programs. Retrieved Dec. 1, 2015, from www.cwse.org

Courlander, H. (1962). *The king's drum and other African stories.* San Diego, CA: Harcourt Brace, & World.

Courtney, M., & Specht, H. (1994). *Unfaithful angels: How social work has abandoned its mission.* New York, NY: Free Press.

Covarrubias, R., Hermann, S. D., & Fryberg, S.A. (2016). Affirming the interdependent self: Implications for Latino student performance. *Basic and Applied Social Psychology, 38*(1), 47–57.

Coward, H., Neufeldt, R., & Neumaier, E. K. (2006). *Readings in Eastern Religions.* Ontario, Canada: Wilfrid Laurier University Press.

Cowrie, J. (2016).Why are economists so small minded? *The Chronicle of Higher Education.*

Coyle, C.E., Putnam, M., Kramer, J., & Mutchler, J.E. (2016). The role of aging and disability resource centers in serving adults aging with intellectual disabilities and their families: Findings from seven states. *Journal of Aging & Social Policy, 28*(1), 1–14.

Coyle, S. (2016). Trends in macro social work education. *Social Work Today, 16*(2), 16, para 7. Retrieved from http://www.socialworktoday.com/archive/032216p16.shtml.

Cragun, R. T., & Sumerau, J. E. (2015). The last bastion of sexual and gender prejudice? Sexualities, race, gender, religiosity, and spirituality in the examination of prejudice toward sexual and gender minorities. *Journal of Sex Research, 52*(7), 821–834.

Crampton, D. D., Crea, T. M., Abramson-Madden, A., & Usher, C. L. (2008). Challenges of street-level child welfare reform and technology transfer: The case of team decision-making. *Families in Society: The Journal of Contemporary Social Services, 89*(4) 512.

Crawford, E. (2015, Dec. 9). Students learn life skills through Trooper Kitchen. *Educational News,* Journal.com.

Credit Suisse. (2014). Research institute: Global wealth report. Retrieved from https://publications.credit-suisse.com/tasks/render/file/?fileID=60931FDE-A2D2-F568-B041B58C5EA591A4

Crettaz, E., & Jacot, C. (2014). Do family policies matter for educational outcomes? Patterns of educational mobility and family services in Europe. *European Societies, 16*(5), 645–665.

Crisp, B. R. (2008). Social work and spirituality in a secular society. *Journal of Social Work, 8*(4), 363.

Crite, A. R. (2015). Art images. Retrieved from https://www.google.com/search?q=Allan+Rohan+Crite&tbm=isch&imgil=cFt3G-Hp3GU7zM%253A%253B3Fhc-

Crockett, E. (2015). Transgender sex workers are mistreated by the institutions that are supposed to help them. Retrieved Jan. 3, 2016, from http://www.vox.com/2015/12/27/10669996/transgender-sex-workers-report

Cross, W. E. (1978). The Thomas and Cross models of psychological Nigrescence: A literature review. *Journal of Black Psychology, 4,* 13–31

Crow Dog, M., & Erdoes, R. (1990/2011). *Lakota woman.* New York: Grove Weidenfeld Press.

CSPAN 3, (2015). Understanding the Ferguson Protests January 5, 2015 last aired January 25, 2015. Retrieved Jan. 9, 2018 from https://www.c-span.org/search/?sdate=01%2F25%2F2015&edate=01%2F25%2F2015&searchtype=Videos&sort=Best+Match&text=0&formatid%5B%5D=24

CSWE.org. (n.d.). Shared decision making with people who are justice involved and have a serious mental illness. Retrieved July 7, 2016.

Cubanski, J., Orgera, K, Damico, A., & Neuman, T. (2018). How many seniors are living in poverty? National and state estimates under the official and supplemental poverty measures in 2016.

Cui, R., Tate, S.R., Cummins, K., Skidmore, J.R., Brown, S.A. (2015). Chronic physical health problems moderate changes in depression and substance use among dual diagnosed individuals during and after treatment. *Substance Use& Misuse.* 50(2), 174–83.

Cullen, F. T., Vose, B. A., & Lero Jonson, C. N. (2007). Public support for early intervention: Is child saving a "habit of the heart"? *Victims and Offenders, 2,* 109–124.

Cunningham, M. J., & Diverse, M. (2016). Aging out: Youth perspectives on foster care and the transition to independence. *Qualitative Social Work, 12*(5), 587–602.

Cwik, M., Tingey, L., Lee, A., Suttle, R., Lake, K, Walkup, J., & Barlow, A. (2016). Development and piloting of a brief intervention for suicidal American Indian adolescents. *American Indian & Alaska Native Health Research, 23*(2), 248.

Da Silva, D. F. (2001). Towards a critique of the socio-logos of justice: The analytics of raciality and the production of universality. *Social Identities, 7*(3), 421–454.

Dacres, S. (2016). Impact of cultural competence in the delivery of disability services and supports [Webinar]. New Jersey Department of Health.

Daggett, L. M. (2013). Book 'em?: Navigating student privacy, disability, and civil rights and school safety in the context of school–police cooperation. *The Urban Lawyer, 45*(1), 203–233.

Dahinden, J., Duemmler, K., Moret, J. (2014). Disentangling religious, ethnic and gendered contents in boundary work: How young adults create the figure of "the oppressed Muslim woman." *Journal of Intercultural Studies, 35*(4), 329–348.

Dalai Lama. (2013). *The basic sources of happiness.* Berkeley, CA: Parallax Press.

Daley, D.C. (2013). Introduction: Special Issue: The role of social works in the prevention and treatment of substance use disorders. *Social Work in Public Health,* 28(3/4), 159–46. Philadelphia: Routledge.

Dalrymple, J. & Burke, B. (2006). *Anti-oppressive practice: Social care & the law.* Open University Press;

Dalrymple, J., & Boylan, J. (2013). *Effective advocacy in social work.* Thousand Oaks, CA: SAGE

Daniel, A. E. (2004). Commentary: Decision-making by front-line service providers-attitudinal or context. *The Journal of the American Academy of Psychiatry and the Law, 32,* 386–389.

Danielle, B. (2014). Black fatherhood myth: Report finds black dads just as involved in childrearing as other races. Retrieved March 21, 2018 from http://clutchmagonline.com/2014/01/black-fatherhood-myth-report-finds-black-dads-just-involved-childrearing-races/.

Dank, M., Yu, L., & Yahner, J. (2016). Access to safety: Health outcomes, substance use and abuse, and service provision for LGBTQ youth, YMSM, and YWSW who engage in survival sex. Urban Institute, Adolescents and Health. Retrieved from http://www.urban.org/sites/default/files/alfresco/publication-pdfs/2000119-Surviving-the-Streets-of-New-York.pdf.

Darkwah, N. B. (2014). *The Africans who wrote the Bible.* Orlando, FL: HBC Publications

Dart, J. (2016). Australia's disturbing health disparities set Aboriginals apart. Bulletin of the World Health Organization. Retrieved from http://www.who.int/bulletin/volumes/86/4/08-020408/en/

Dash, G. (2015). On field testing of methods, the Egyptians may have used to find cardinal directions. *Journal for the History of Astronomy, 46*(3), 351–364.

Data Spotlight. (2012). Almost half of American Indian and Alaska Native adult substance abuse treatment admissions are referred through the criminal justice system. *Center for Behavioral Health Statistics and Quality.* SAMSHA.

Davidson, B. (1966). *African Kingdoms.* New York: Time-Life Books

Davidson, B. (1969). *The African genius.* Boston, MA: Little, Brown & Company.

Davidson, L. (2012). *Cultural genocide: Genocide, political violence, human rights.* New Brunswick, NJ: Rutgers University Press.

Davidson, T., & Sanyal, P. (2017). Associational participation and network expansion: Microcredit self-help groups and poor women's social ties in rural India. *Social Forces, 95*(4), 1695–1724.

Davies, J. (2013). *Cracked: Why psychiatry is doing more harm than good.* London, England: Icon Books.

Davis, A. (1998). Masked racism: Reflections on the prison industrial complex. *Colorlines.* Retrieved from http://www.colorlines.com/articles/masked- racism-reflections-prison-industrial-complex

Davis, A. (2016). *Freedom is a constant struggle: Ferguson, Palestine and the foundations of a movement.* Chicago, IL: Haymarket Books.

Davis, A., & Gould, E. (2015). Closing the gap & beyond. *Economic Policy Institute.* Retrieved from https://www.epi.org/publication/closing-the-pay-gap-and-beyond/

Davis, S. (2017). China's emerging role in social innovation for global good. *Stanford Social Innovation Review.* Retrieved from https://ssir.org/articles/entry/chinas_emerging_role_in_social_innovation_for_global_good

Davis-Maye, D., Davis, D. J., & Jones, T. B. (2013). Who's got next: SOTA's Kemet Academy as a model to improve the community college to PHD pipeline. *The Journal of Negro Education, 82*(3), 243–254.

De Camargo, O. K (2011). Systems of care: transition from the bio-psycho-social perspective of the international classification of functioning, disability and health. *Child: Care, Health and Development, 37*(6), 792–799.

De Graaf, M. (2016). Revealed: How the sugar industry paid prestigious Harvard researchers to say fat (NOT sugar) caused heart disease. Dailymail.com.

de Haan, A. M., Boon, A. E., de Jong, J. V., Geluk, C. A., & Vermeiren, R. R. (2014). Therapeutic relationship & dropouts in youth mental health care with ethnic minority children and adolescents. Clinical Psychologist, 9(8), 1–9.

De la Merced, M.J. & Fandos, N. (2017). Fox's unfamiliar but powerful television rival: Sinclair. *New York Times.com.* Retrieved Jan 7, 2018 from https://www.nytimes.com/2017/05/03/business/dealbook/sinclair-media-expansion-fox-conservative-media.html?_r=0

de Montigny, G. (2013). The essentialism of whiteness: Abandoning empirical engagement. *Journal of Social Work, 13*(6), 633–651.

Deafnewstoday.com. (2017). Retrieved from http://deafnewstoday.blogspot.com/

Dean, K. L., & Fornaciari, C. J. (2014). Creating masterpieces: How course structures and routines enable student performance. *Journal of Management Education, 38*(1), 10–42.

Delgado, M. (1999). *Community social work practice in an urban context: The potential of a capacity-enhancement perspective.* Oxford University Press

Deaux, K., Bikmen, N., Gilkes, A., Ventuneac, C., Payne, Y., & Steele, C. (2007). Becoming American: Stereotype threat effects in Afro-Caribbean immigrant groups. *Social Psychology Quarterly, 70*(4), pp. 384–404.

Deaux, K., Waters, M. C., Steele, C., & Thomas, E. (1999). *Ethnic identification and stereotype threat: The case of West Indians.* New York, NY: Russell Sage Foundation.

Dee, R. (1991). *Tower to heaven.* New York, NY: Henry Holt.

Degenhardt, L., Saha S, Lim CCW, Aguilar-Gaxiola S, Al-Hamzawi A, Alonso J, Andrade LH, Bromet EJ, Bruffaerts R, Caldas-de-Almeida JM, de Girolamo G, Florescu S, Gureje O, Haro JM, Karam EG, Karam G, Kovess-Masfety V, Lee S, Lepine JP, Makanjuola V, Medina-Mora ME, Mneimneh Z, Navarro-Mateu F, Piazza M, Posada-Villa J, Sampson NA, Scott KM, Stagnaro JC, Ten Have M, Kendler KS, Kessler RC, McGrath JJ; WHO World Mental Health Survey Collaborators (2017). The associations between psychotic experiences, and substance use and substance use disorders: Findings from the World Health Organisation World Mental Health Surveys. *Addictions,* doi: 10.1111/add.1414

Degner, J., Essien, I., Reichardt, R. (2016). Effects of diversity vs segregation on automatic approach and avoidance behavior towards own and other ethnic groups *European Journal of Social Psychology* 46, 783–791.

DeGrury, J. (2005). *Post traumatic slave syndrome: America's enduring legacy of enduring injury and healing.* Portland, OR: Joy DeGrury.

DeGrury, J., & Johnson, U. (2016). *What is cognitive dissonance* [Video file]? Retrieved from https://www.youtube.com/watch?v=ucN12khyfSU

Deines, H. (2014, Nov. 7). *Preferential option for the poor: foundation for social work identity.* Paper presented at the 2014 Convention of the North American Association of Christians in Social Work, Annapolis, MD.

DeLauro, R. (2017). *The least among us: Waging the battle for the vulnerable.* New York, NY: The New Press.

Delgado, M. (1999). *Social work practice in nontraditional urban settings.* New York: Oxford University Press.

Delgado, M. (2007). *Social work with Latinos: A cultural assets paradigm.* New York, NY: Oxford University Press.

Delgado, M. (2016). *Celebrating urban community life: Fairs, festivals, parades & community.* New York, NY: Oxford University Press.

Delich, N. A. M. (2014). Spiritual direction and deaf spirituality: Implications for social work practice. *Journal of Religion & Spirituality in Social Work: Social Thought, 33*(3–4), 317–338.

Demby, G. (2013). How code-switching explains the world. NPR. Retrieved from https://www.npr.org/sections/codeswitch/2013/04/08/176064688/how-code-switching-explains-the-world

Demos.org. (2017). An equal say and an equal chance for all. Retrieved Aug. 31, 2017, from www.demos.org

Department of Education, Office of Special Education Program's (OSEP). (2016). 37th Annual Report to Congress on the Implementation of the Individuals with Disabilities Education Act.

Department of Education. (2016). Ten facts about K–12 funding. Retrieved from http://www2.ed.gov/about/overview/fed/10facts/index.html? exp

DePaulo, B. (2018). There's never been a better time to be single. *CNN, the Cut.* Retrieved Jan.7, 2018 from http://www.cnn.com/2018/01/05/health/single-people-partner/index.html

Deruy, E. (2016). Bringing brain science to early childhood. *The Atlantic.*

Desai, K. (1999). *Hullabaloo in the guava orchard.* New York, NY: Grove Press.

DeSilver, D. (2013). Black unemployment rate is consistently twice that of whites. Fact Tank. *Pew Research Center.*

DeSilver, D. (2014, January 13). Who's poor in America? 50 years into the 'War on Poverty,' a data portrait. *Pew Research Center*, FactTank. Retrieved from http://www.pewresearch.org/fact-tank/2014/01/13/whos-poor-in-america-50-years-into-the-war-on-poverty-a-data-portrait/.

DeSilver, D. (2015). The many ways to measure economic inequality. *Pew Research Center, Fact Tank.*

DeSipio, L. (2017). American Latino theme study: Struggles for inclusion demanding equal political voice ... and accepting nothing less. National Park Service. Retrieved May 28, 2017, from https://www.nps.gov/articles/latinotheme-struggles.htm

Desmond, M. (2017). *Evicted: Poverty and profit in the American city.* New York, NY: Broadway Books.

Devinatz, V. (2013). The significance of the living wage for US workers in the early twenty-first century. *Employee Responsibilities & Right Journal, 25*, 125.

DeWitt, P. (2016). Why collaboration doesn't work. *Education Week.com.*

Dews, F. (2013). What Percentage of U.S. Population Is Foreign Born? *Brookings Institute.* https://www.brookings.edu/blog/.../what-percentage-of-u-s-population-is-foreign-born/

Diaconescu, M. (1989). Burnout, secondary trauma and compassion fatigue in social work. *Revista Asistenta Social, 14*(3), 57–63.

Diament, M. (2015). Feds take aim at sheltered workshops. *Disability Scoop.* Retrieved Jan. 4, 2016, from https://www.disabilityscoop.com/2015/04/14/feds-aim-sheltered-workshops/20216/

Diament, M. (2017). More businesses embracing inclusion. *Disability scoop.com.*

Diament, M. (2017, May 19). Trump budget guts Medicaid, disability programs: Lawmakers propose wider access to community-based services. *Disability Scoop.*

Diamond Sutra Recitation Group. (Ed.). (2007). Chung Hyo Ye: Tales of filial devotion, loyalty, respect and benevolence from the history and folklore of Korea. Flushing, NY: Yong Hwa.

Diaz, J. (1996). *Drown.* New York, NY: Riverhead Books.

Diaz-Rios, Muzaffar, Meline, & Chapman-Makowski. (2016). Talk, heart, hands: A culturally sensitive approach to nutrition education for Latinos with young children. *Journal of Nutrition Education and Behavior, 48*(6),425.

Díaz-Stevens, A. M. (1999, January). Memory, imagination and tradition: Diasporic Latino spirituality. *Union Seminary Quarterly*, 1–19.

Dictionary.com (n.d.). Ethics.

Dictionary.com, (n.d). Ideology.

Digital History ID 2908 (n.d.). Overview of the First Americans. Retrieved Jan. 9, 2018 from http://www.digitalhistory.uh.edu/era.cfm.

Dill, B. T., & Zambrana, R. E. (2009). Critical thinking about inequality: An emerging lens. In B. T. Dill & R. E. Zambrana (Eds.), *Emerging intersections: Race, class, and gender in theory, policy, and practice* (pp. 1–21). Piscataway, NJ: Rutgers University Press.

Dilworth-Anderson, P., Pierre, G., & Hilliard, T. S. (2012). Social justice: Health disparities, and culture in the care of the elderly. *Journal of Law, Medicine & Ethics, The Graying of America: Challenges and controversies*, 26–36.

Diversitybestpractices.com. (2017). Retrieved from http://www.diversitybestpractices.com/news-articles/top- native-american-organizations-to-know

Docobo, J. (2005). Community policing as the primary prevention strategy for homeland security at the local law enforcement level. *Homeland Security Affairs* 1, Article 4. https://www.hsaj.org/articles/183

Docteur, E., & Berenson, R. A. (2014). In pursuit of health equity: Comparing U.S. and EU approaches to eliminating disparities—Timely analysis of immediate health policy issues. *Urban Institute.* Retrieved from https://www.rwjf.org/content/dam/farm/reports/issue_briefs/2014/rwjf414060

Doel, M., & Kelly, T. (2014). *A-Z of groups and groupwork.* London, England: Palgrave Macmillan.

Doherty, C. (2015). Most say government policies since recession have done little to help middle class, poor. *Pew Research Center, U.S. Politics & Policy.*

Domonosoke, C. (2016). For first time in 130 years, more young adults live with parents than with partners. *NPR.org.*

Donnella, L. (2016). The Standing Rock resistance is unprecedented (it's also centuries old). *Codeswitch.* NPR.org. Retrieved May 28, 2017, from http://www.npr.org/sections/codeswitch/2016/11/22/502068751/the-standing-rock-resistance-is-unprecedented-it-s-also-centuries-old

Dorsey, T.L., & Middleton, P. (n.d.). *Drugs and crime facts.* U.S. Department of Justice. Retrieved from https://www.bjs.gov/content/pub/pdf/dcf.pdf.

Dottolo, A. L., & Kaschak, E. (2015). Whiteness and white privilege. *Women & Therapy, 38,* 179–184.

Douglass, F. (1845/2002). *Narrative of the life of Frederick Douglass.* Boston, MA: Bedford/St. Martin.

Dovidio, J., Hewstone, M., Glick, P., & Esses, V. (Eds.). (2010). *SAGE handbook of prejudices, stereotypes and discrimination.* Thousand Oaks, CA: SAGE.

Drabble, L., Trocki, K. F., & Klinger, J. L. (2016). Religiosity as a protective factor for hazardous drinking and drug use among sexual minority and heterosexual women: Findings from the National Alcohol Survey. *Drug and Alcohol Dependence, 161,* 127–134.

Drachman, D. (1996). Immigration statuses and their influence on service provision, access, and use in Ewalt, P., Freeman, E. M., Kirk, S., Poole, D. L. (Eds.). (1996). *Multicultural issues in social work.* Washington, DC: NASW.

Draut, T. (2016). *Sleeping giant: How the new working class will transform America.* New York, NY: Doubleday.

Drescher, J. (2015). Out of DSM: Depathologizing Homosexuality. *Behavioral Science, 5*(4), 565–575.

Dressel, P. L. (1992). Patriarchy and social welfare work, 205–219; and Power in Social Work Practice, 259–275, in Y. Hasenfeld (Ed.). *Human services as complex organizations,* Newbury Park, CA: Sage

Driscoll, C. (2015). Uncertain humanism and the water of whiteness. *The Humanist,* July–August, 14.

Drisko, J. W., & Grady, M. D. (2015). Evidence-based practice in social work: A contemporary perspective. *Clinical Social Work Journal, 43,* 274–282.

Drucker, E. (Ed.) (2018). *Decarcerating America: From mass punishment to public health.* New York: New Press.

Du, N. (1987). *The tale of Kieu* (H. S. Thong, Trans.). New Haven, CT: Yale University Press.

DuBois, W. E. B. (1903/1994). *Souls of black folk.* Mineola, NY: Dover Press.

DuBois, W. E. B. (2014). The Black Codes. In P. Rothenberg with K. Mayhew (Eds.), *Race, class and gender* (9th ed., p. 532). Duffield, United Kingdom: Worth.

DuBois, W.E.B. (1899). The *Philadelphia Negro: A social study.* University of Pennsylvania Press; Reprint edition (December 1, 1995.

Duhaney, P. (2010). Why is our educational system still guilty of whiteness? *Canadian Social Work Review, 27*(1), 95–99.

Dulock, M.J. & Long, H. (2015). Digital collections are a sprint, not a marathon: adapting scrum project management techniques to library digital initiatives. Information Technology for Librarians, 34(4), 5–16.

Dunbar-Ortiz, R. (2014). *An indigenous peoples' history of the United States.* Boston, MA: Beacon Press.

Duncan, A. (2011). The next generation of civics education. U.S. Department of Education. Retrieved from https://www.ed.gov/news/speeches/next-generation-civics-education

Dunlop, J. M., & Holosko, M. J. (2016). *Increasing service user participation in local planning: A how to manual for macro practitioners.* Chicago, IL: Lyceum.

Dunn, K. M., Forrest, J., Burnley, I., & McDonald, A. (2004). Constructing racism in Australia. *Australian Journal of Social Issues,* 39(4), 409–412.

Dunn, L., White, M., & Bailey, P. (1975). Shining star [Recorded by Earth, Wind & Fire]. On *That's the Way of the World* [CD]. New York, NY: Columbia. (Autumn 1974)

Dupper, D. R., Forrest-Bank, S. & Lowry-Castillo, A. (2014). Experiences of religious minorities in public school settings: Findings from focus groups involving Muslim, Jewish, Catholic, and Unitarian universalist youths. *Children & Schools, 37*(1), 37–43.

Durrheim, K., Greener, R., & Whitehead, K. A. (2015). Race trouble: Attending to race and racism in online interaction. *British Journal of Social Psychology, 54*, 84–99.

Dweck, C. (2007). *Mindset: The new psychology of success.* New York, NY: Ballantine Books.

Dwyer, O. J., & Jones, J. P., III. (2000). White socio-spatial epistemology. *Social & Cultural Geography, 1*(2).

Ea, P. (2014). Prince Ea—Can We Auto-Correct Humanity? Retrieved from https://www.huffingtonpost.com/2014/10/01/prince-ea-video_n_5916354.html

Easterbrook, A., Bulk, L., Ghanouni, P., Lee, M., Opini, B., Roberts, E., Parbar, G., & Jarus, T. (2015). The legitimization process of students with disabilities in health and human service educational programs in Canada. *Disability & Society, 30*(10), 1505–1520.

Eastman, C. (2014). *The soul of the Indian.* New York, NY: SMK Books.

Eckstrand, K. L., & Sciolla, A. F. (2014). Using medical education to address disparities. In A. D. Hollenbach, K. L. Eckstrand, & A. Dreger. (Eds.), *Implementing curricular and institutional climate changes to improve health care for individuals who are LGBT, gender nonconforming, or born with DSD: A resource for medical educators* (p. 22). Washington, DC: Association of American Medical Educators.

Edin, K., & Shaefer, H. L. (2016). *$2.00 a day: Living on almost nothing in America.* Boston, MA: Mariner Books.

Editorial Board. (2016, Feb. 20). The crisis of minority unemployment. *The New York Times.* Retrieved from http://www.nytimes.com/saved?module=MySavedItems&action=Click&region=TopBar&WT.nav=shell&pgtype=Homepage

Edsall, T. (2016). Finding the hidden Trump voters. *The New York Times,* Sunday Review, p. 2.

Edsall, T. B. (2012, Aug. 3). Separate and unequal: *The price of inequality* by Joseph Stiglitz. *The New York Times Book Review.*

Edsall, T. B. (2012b, Dec. 12). The reproduction of privilege. *The New York Times,* Opinion Pages.

Eggers, D. (2006). *What is the what?* New York, NY: Vintage.

Eisenberg, A. K. (2011). Incarceration incentives in the decarceration era. *Vanderbilt Law Review, 69*(1), 249–259.

Elder, C., Nidich, S., Colbert, R., Hagelin, J., Grayshield, L., Oviedo-Lim, D., Nidich, R., ... & Gerace, D., (2011). Reduced psychological distress in racial and ethnic minority students practicing the transcendental meditation program. *Journal of Instructional Psychology, 38*(2), 109–116.

Eliassen, A. H. (2014). Religious involvement and readiness to confirm reported physical disability. *Journal of Religion and Health, 53*, 1427–1439.

Eliot, S. (1921). Hinduism and Buddhism. *The Spectator Archive.* Retrieved from http://archive.spectator.co.uk/article/12th-november-1921/19/hindulsm-and-buddhism

elizabethwarren.com. (n.d.). Jobs & the economy: Elizabeth Warren for Senate. Retrieved July 9, 2017, from https://elizabethwarren.com/issues/jobs-and-the-economy.%2017

Elk v. Wilkins. (2014). From Elk v. Wilkins, 112 United States Reports: Cases Adjudged in the Supreme Court (New York: Banks & Brothers) In Rothenberg, P.S., *Race, class and gender in the United States: An integrated study,* pp. 545–546. Worth Publishers.

Elliot, J. (2006). Blue eyes/brown eyes exercise. Retrieved from http://www.janeelliott.com/index.htm

Ellis-Petersen, H. (2016). Unity gives Jerusalem a prayer: Jews, Muslims and Christians join for worship. *The Guardian.* Retrieved from https://www.theguardian.com/world/2016/sep/24/unity-gives-jerusalem-a-prayer-jews-muslims-and-christians-join-for-worship

Elwyn, G., Frosch, D., Thomson, R., Joseph-Williams, N., Lloyd, A., Kinnersley, P., ... & Barry, M. (2012). Shared decision-making: A model for clinical practice. *Journal of General Internal Medicine, 27*(10), 1361–1367.

Emdin, C. (2010). Affiliation and alienation: Hip-hop rap & urban science education. *Journal of Curriculum Studies, 42*(1), 1–25.

Emdin, C. (2016). *For white folks who teach in the hood ... and the rest of y'all too: Reality pedagogy and urban education.* Boston, MA: Beacon Press.

Emery, D. (2017). Pushing propaganda on local news: Critics complain that Sinclair, the nation's largest owner of local television stations, requires its affiliates to insert conservative commentary in local newscasts. Retrieved from http://www.snopes.com/2017/07/11/sinclair-broadcast-group-propaganda/

Encyclopedia of Children & Childhood in History & Society. (2015). Wh–Z (and other topics). Retrieved from http://www. faqs.org/childhood/Wh-Z-and-other-topics/White-House-Conferences-on-Children.html

Encyclopedia of Mental Disorders, (2018). Self help. Retrieved from http://www.minddisorders.com/.

Engler, M. (2014). Why America's 99% have rebelled [Blog post]. Retrieved from https://www.commondreams.org/ views/2011/12/22/why-americas-99-have-rebelled#.TvRtyW_uDb4.blogger

EPAS (2015). CSWE Educational Policy & Accreditation Standards. Retrieved from https://www.cswe.org/getattachment/ Accreditation/Standards-and-Policies/2015-EPAS/2015EPASandGlossary.pdf.aspx

EPAS (2015). Educational Policy and Accreditation Standards for Baccalaureate and Master's Social Work Program. Retrieved from https://www.cswe.org/getattachment/Accreditation/Standards-and-Policies/2015-EPAS/2015E-PASandGlossary.pdf.aspx

Erasmus, D. (2008). *A handbook on good manners for children*. New York, NY: Random House.

McLeod, S. (2018). Erik Erickson's Stages of Psychosocial Development. Retrieved from http://www.simplypsychology. org/Erik-Erikson.html

Erickson, E. (1994). *Identity and the life cycle*. New York, NY: W.W. Norton.

Ermann, L. S., Lawson, G., & Burge, P. I. (2016). Feminists, spirituality and the twelve steps of alcoholics anonymous. *The American Journal of Drug and Alcohol*.

Eugenides, J. (2002). *Middlesex*. New York, NY: Picador.

European Commission. (2009). Solidarity in health: Reducing health inequalities in the EU. Retrieved from http://ec. europa.eu/health/ph_determinants/socio_economics/documents/com2009_en.pdf

Evans, K.L., Millsteed, L., Richmond, J.E., Falkmer, M., Falkmer, T.,Girder, S.J. (2016). Working sandwich generation women utilize strategies within and between roles to achieve role balance. *PLOS ONE* 11(6): e0157469. https:// doi.org/10.1371/journal.pone.0157469

Evans-Campbell, T., Walters, K.L., Pearson, C.R., & Campbell, C.D. (2012). Indian boarding school experience, substance use, and mental health among urban two-spirit American Indian/Alaska natives. *American Journal of Drug & Alcohol Abuse*, 38(5), 421–427.

Eversley, M. (2015). 9 dead in shooting at black church in Charleston, SC. *USA Today.com*. Retrieved from http://www. usatoday.com/story/news/nation/2015/06/17/charleston-south-carolina-shooting/28902017/

Eversley, M. (2016). Post-election spate of hate crimes worse than post-9/11, experts say. Ruidoso, *USA Today News Network*. Retrieved from https://www.ruidosonews.com/story/news/2016/11/12/post-election-spate-hate-crimes-worse-than-post-911-experts-say/93681294/.

Ewalt, P. L., Freeman, E., Kirk, S., & Poole, D. (1996). *Multicultural issues in social work*. Washington, DC: NASW Press. Ewing, R. (2014). Campaign celebrates food stamps' half century protecting public health. Drexel Now. Retrieved from http://drexel.edu/now/archive/2014/October/snap4SNAP-Celebrates-Food-Stamps/.

Eyre, C. (Director). (1998). *Smoke Signals* [Film].

Farber, N. & Shinkle, D. (2011). Aging in place: A state survey of livability policies and practices. AARP and National Conference of State Legislatures.

Farmakopoulou, N. (2002). What lies underneath? An interorganizational analysis of collaboration between education and social work. *British Journal of Social Work, 32*, 1051–1066.

Farnham, B. C. (2008). When professionals weep: Emotional & countertransference responses in end-of-life care. *Journal of Social Work in End-of-life & Palliative Care*.

Farrell, A. L., & Krahn, G. (2014). Family life goes on: Disability in contemporary families. *Studies in Family Relations, 63*(1), 1–6.

Farruggio, P. (2010). Latino immigrant parents' views of bilingual education as a vehicle for heritage preservation. *Journal of Latinos and Education, 9*(1), 3–21.

Feagin, J. R. (2013). *The white racial frame: Centuries of racial framing and counter framing* (2nd ed.). Abingdon, United Kingdom: Routledge.

Feagin, J. R., Vera, H., & Batur, P. (2001). *White racism: The basics*. New York, NY: Routledge.

Federal Reserve Bank of St. Louis, (2015). How Asian families are catching white families in wealth. Retrieved from https://www. stlouisfed.org/on-the-economy/2015/april/how-asian-families-are-catching-white-families-in-wealth.

Fell, A. (2016). Using urban pigeons to monitor lead pollution. *Phys.org*. Retrieved from https://phys.org/news/2016-07-urban-pigeons-pollution.html

Ferber, A. L. (2013). Whiteness studies and the erasure of gender. In S. Ferguson (Ed.), *Race, gender, sexuality, and social class: Dimensions of inequality* (pp. 577–590). Thousand Oaks, CA: SAGE.

Ferguson, I. (2008). *Reclaiming social work: Challenging neo-liberalism and promoting social justice.* Thousand Oaks, CA: SAGE.

Fernández, L., Aggarwal, N. K., Bäärnhielm, S., Rohlof, H., Kirmayer, L. J., Weiss, M. G., Jadhav, S., ... & Lu, F. (2014). Culture and psychiatric evaluation: Operationalizing cultural formulation for *DSM-5*. *Psychiatry, 77*(2), 130–154. doi:1521/psyc.2014.77.2.130

Ferris, J. (2004). *Of sound mind.* New York, NY: Farrar, Straus & Giroux.

Fields, K. E. (2014). *Racecraft: The soul of inequality in American life.* New York, NY: Verso Books.

Financial Times, ft.com/lexicon. (n.d.). Definition of cultural agility. Retrieved from http://lexicon.ft.com/Term?term=cultural-agility

Fine, M., Weis, L., Pruitt, L. P., & Burns, A. (2004). *Off white: Readings on power, privilege & resistance* (2nd ed.). New York, NY: Routledge.

Fischl, J. (2013). Almost 82% of social workers are female and this is hurting men. *MIC Daily.* Retrieved from https://mic.com/articles/30974/almost-82-percent-of-social-workers-are-female-and-this-is-hurting-men#.oaqIjjbwS

Fisher, A. K., Moore, D. J., Simmons, C., & Allen, S. C. (2017). Teaching social workers about microaggressions to enhance understanding of subtle racism. *Journal of Human Behavior in the* Social Environment, 27(4), 346–350.

Fisher, C. B. (2016). #BioethicsSoWhite. Fordham University Center for Ethics Education. *Social Justice Solutions.org.* Retrieved from http://www.socialjusticesolutions.org/? s=bioethicssowhite

Fisher-Borne, M., Cain, J.M., & Martin, J.L. (2015). From mastery to accountability: cultural humility as an alternative to cultural competence. *Social Work Education, 34*(2), 165–181.

Fitzgerald, M. W. (2004). Political reconstruction 1865–1877. In J. A. A. Boles (Ed.), *A companion to the American south.* Hoboken, NJ: Blackwell.

Flake, S. G. (2010). *You don't even know me: Stories and poems about boys.* New York, NY: Disney Hyperion.

Fleischer, A.V. (2013). *Blacks in America before Columbus.* Amazon Digital Services LLC.

Fletcher, T. V., & Navarretee, L. A. (2003). Learning disabilities or difference: A critical look at issues associated with the misidentification and placement of Hispanic students in special education programs. *Rural Special Education Quarterly, 30*(1), 30–36.

Floyd, I., Pavetti, L. & Schott, L. (2017). TANF reaching few poor families. Center on Budget & Policy Priorities.

Foeman, A., Lawton, B. L., & Rieger, R. (2015). Questioning race: Ancestry DNA and dialog on race. *Communication Monographs, 82*(2), 271–290. doi:10.1080/03637751.2014.972966

Foner, E. (2015, Mar. 28). Why reconstruction matters. *The New York Times,* Sunday Review/Opinion. Also see: *Gateway to freedom: The hidden history of the Underground Railroad.* New York, NY: W. W. Norton.

Foo, L. J. (2002). Asian American women: Issues, concerns, and responsive human and civil rights advocacy. Ford Foundation. Retrieved from https://fordfoundcontentthemes.blob.core.windows.net/media/1716/2002-asian_american_women.pdf

Ford, A. (2014). 9 states with anti-gay laws that aren't that different from Russia's. Retrieved from thinkprogress.org/lgbt/2014/02/03/3241421/9-state-gay-propaganda-laws/

Ford, K. A., & Malaney, V. K. (2012). "I now harbor more pride in my race": The educational benefits of inter- and intra-racial dialogues on the experiences of students of color and multiracial students. *Equity & Excellence in Education, 45*(1), 14–35.

Ford, M. (n.d.). A brief history of homosexuality in America. Retrieved from https://www.gvsu.edu/allies/a-brief-history-of-homosexuality-in-america-30.htm.

Forrest-Bank, S., & Jenson, J. (2015). Differences in experiences of racial and ethnic microaggression among Asian, Latino/Hispanic, black, and white young adults. *The Journal of Sociology & Social Welfare, 42*(1). Retrieved from http://scholarworks.wmich.edu/jssw/vol42/iss1/8

Foster, K. (2017). For Harriet [Blog].

Foster, S., & Duke, J. (2000). *A field guide to medicinal plants and herbs of eastern and central North America.* New York, NY: Houghton Mifflin.

FosteryouthinAction.org (2017). Foster youth transforming themselves into powerful leaders and advocates. Retrieved from http://www.fosteryouthaction.org.

Frączkiewicz-Wronka, A. & Wronka-Pośpiech, M. (2013). The use of ICT for achieving the objectives of the business model: social enterprise perspective. *Polish Journal of Management Studies*, 10(2), 33–42.

Fram, M. S., Frongillo, E. A., Fishbein, E. M., & Burke, M. P. (2014). Roles for schools and school social workers in improving child food security. *Children & Schools*, 36(4), 231–238.

Francis, L. (Ed.). (1999). *When the rain sings: Poems by young Native Americans*. New York, NY: Simon & Schuster.

Franklin Law Group. (2015). Over-medication of psychotropic drugs & African-American girls in foster care. Submission to the United Nations Working Group of Experts on People of African Descent. Retrieved Jan 12, 2018 from http://tbinternet.ohchr.org/Treaties/CAT/Shared%20Documents/USA/INT_CAT_NHS_USA_18527_E.pdf

Franklin, C., Harris, M.B., & Allen-Meares, P. (2013). *The School Services Sourcebook: A Guide for School-Based Professionals*. New York: Oxford University Press

Frazier, E. F. (1966). *The Negro Family in the United States*. University of Chicago.

Frederiksen, L. (2015. The top 10 benefits of using social media marketing for business. Hinge. Retrieved from https://hingemarketing.com/blog/story/the-top-10-benefits-of-using-social-media-marketing-for-business.

freedictionary.com. (n.d.). Mindset. Retrieved from http://www.freedictionary.com/resources/search?w=mindset

Freidman, T.L. (2005). *The world is flat: A brief history of the twenty first century*. New York: Farrar, Strauss, Giroux.

Freire, P. (1997). *Pedagogy of the oppressed*. New York, NY: Continuum Press.

French, G. (2007). *Children's early learning and development: A research paper*. Aistear, National Council on Curriculum & Assessment.

Freyd, J. J. (2013). Institutional betrayal and betrayal blindness. Retrieved June 25, 2017, from http://dynamic.uoregon.edu/jjf/institutionalbetrayal/

Friedman, B. D., & Allen, K. N. (2010). Systems theory. In J. R. Brandell (Ed.), *Theory & Practice in Clinical Social Work* (pp. 3–20). Thousand Oaks, CA: SAGE.

Friedman, M. (2005). *Trying hard is not good enough: How to produce measurable improvements for customers and communities*. FPSI Publishing.

Friedman, R. A. (2017, June 30). What cookies and meth have in common. *The New York Times, Sunday Review*.
from https://nces.ed.gov/programs/coe/indicator_coi.asp.

Frost, A. (2013). High-context and low-context cultures. Retrieved from http://restaurantkyoto.dk/blog/en/high-context-and-low-context-cultures/

Frye, M. (2014). Oppression. In P. Rothenberg (Ed.), *Race, class and gender*. Duffield, United Kingdom: Worth.

Fu, M. (2015). I don't see color, all people are the same: Whiteness and color-blindness as training and supervisory issues. *Women & Therapy, 38*(3–4), 279–294.

Fuller, J., Edwards, J., Procter, N., & Moss, J. (2000). How definition of mental health problems can influence help seeking in rural and remote communities. *Australian Journal of Rural Health*, 8, 148–153.

Fuller-Rowell, T., Cogburn, C. D., Brodish, A., Peck, S., Malanchuk, O., & Eccles, J. (2011). Racial discrimination and substance use: Longitudinal associations and identity moderators. *Journal of Behavioral Medicine, 35*(6), 581–590.

Fuller-Thomson E, & Dalton, A.D. (2015) Gender differences in the association between parental divorce during childhood and stroke in adulthood: findings from a population-based survey. *International Journal of Stroke*. 10(6), 868–75.

Fullilove, M. (2015). *Empowering adaptable communities' summit*. 2014: Mindy Fullilove https://www.youtube.com/watch?v=IvyAh-iGmxc

Fullilove, M. T. (2013). *Urban alchemy: Restoring joy in America's sorted-out cities*. New York, NY: New Village Press.

Funders for Lesbian and Gay Issues (2009). Directory of LGBTQ people of color organizations and projects in the U.S. Retrieved from https://www.lgbtfunders.org/wp-content/uploads/2016/05/FLGI_POC_Dirctry_2009.pdf

Furness, S., & Gillian, P. (2014). It never came up: Encouragements and discouragements to addressing religion and belief in professional practice—What do social work students have to say? *British Journal of Social Work, 44*, 763–781.

Gabler, N. (2016). The mainstream media's big disconnect: Why they don't get the middle America? *Moyers & Community*. Retrieved from http://billmoyers.com/story/the-mainstream-medias-big-disconnect-why-they-dont-get-middle-america/

Gadanho, P. (2014). *Uneven growth: Tactical urbanisms for expanding megacities.* New York, NY: Museum of Modern Art.

Gaines, J. (2017). Baltimore schools skip detention for meditation & yoga. *Upworthy.* https://efficientgov.com/blog/2017/06/23/baltimore-schools-skip-detention-meditation-yoga/

Gale Group, (2004). Children and adolescents, impact of the great depression on. Encyclopedia.com. Retrieved from https://www.encyclopedia.com/economics/encyclopedias-almanacs-transcripts-and-maps/children-and-adolescents-impact-great-depression

Gallardo, M. E. (2013). *Developing cultural humility: Embracing race, privilege, and power.* Thousand Oaks, CA: SAGE.

Gallo, L., & Matthews, K. A. (2003). Understanding the association between socioeconomic status and physical health: Do negative emotions play a role? *Psychological Bulletin, 129*(1), 10-51.

Galloway, S. (2008). *The cellist of Sarajevo.* New York, NY: Riverhead Books.

Gambrill, E. (2008). Evidence-based (informed) macro practice: Process and philosophy. *Journal of Evidence-Based Social Work, 5*(3-4), 423-452.

Ganim, S. (2016). 5,300 U.S. water systems are in violation of lead rules. *CNN.com.* Retrieved from http://www.cnn.com/2016/06/28/us/epa-lead-in-u-s-water-systems/

Garb, G. (Ed.) (2005). Directory of organizations and agencies serving deaf and hard of hearing people in the Philadelphia area. Deaf and Hard of Hearing Council of Southeastern Pennsylvania. Retrieved from http://www.captionlit.com/resource/directory.pdf. Revised in 2008.

Garcia, A. R., Gupta, M., Greeson, J. K. P., Thompson, A., & DeNard, C. (2017). Adverse childhood experiences among youth reported to child welfare: Results from the national survey of child & adolescent well-being, *Child Abuse & Neglect 70*, 292-302.

Gary, L. (1996). African American men's perceptions of racial discrimination: A sociocultural analysis. In P. Ewalt, E. Freeman, S. Kirk, & D. L. Poole (Eds.), *Multicultural issues in social work.* Washington, DC: NASW Press.

Gascoigne, B. (2003). *The dynasties of China: A history.* Philadelphia, PA: Running Press.

Gayle, H. (2007, June 12). National Press Club Luncheon with Helene Gayle, President and CEO of CARE, and Sheila Johnson, National Press Club Ballroom. Washington, DC. Retrieved June 1, 2017, from https://www.press.org/sites/default/files/070612hgayle.pdf

Gayle, H. (2013). Speech. CARE. Retrieved from http://ar2013.care.org

Geary, D. (2015). The Moynihan report: An annotated edition. *The Atlantic.* Retrieved Jan11, 2018 from https://www.the-atlantic.com/politics/archive/2015/09/the-moynihan-report-an-annotated-edition/404632/.

Geronimo (Goyahkla Chiricuhua), Dembeck, C. (Ed.) (2011-2013). *Through apache eyes verbal history of the apache struggle.* CreateSpace Independent Publishing Platform

Gerzema, J., & D'Antonio, M. (2013). *The Athena doctrine.* San Francisco, CA: Jossey-Bass.

Gewertz, K. (2007, April 12). Albert Einstein, civil rights activist. *Harvard Gazette.* Retrieved from http://news.harvard.edu/gazette/story/2007/04/albert-einstein-civil-rights-activist/

Giamportone, K. E. (2015). Countertransference in the face of compassionate care. *Journal of Social Work in End-of-life &Palliative Care, 11*, 220-223,

Gibbs, L. E. (2003). Evidence-based practice for the helping professionals: A practical guide with integrated multimedia. Pacific Grove, CA: Brooks/Cole-Thompson.

Gibson, P. A., & Haight, W. (2013). Caregivers' moral narrative of their African American children's out-of-school suspensions: Implications for effective family-school collaboration. *Social Work, 58*(3).

Gibson, P. A., Wilson, R., Haight, W., Kayama, M., & Marshall, J. M. (2014). The role of race in the out of school suspensions of black students: The perspectives of students with suspensions, their parents and educators. *Children and Youth Services Review, 47*, 274-282.

Gichuhi, S. (2016). 13 appalling images of Europeans putting Africans in human zoos. Retrieved from http://ontheblacklist.net/13-appalling-images-of-europeans-putting-africans-in-human-zoos/?utm_source=rss&utm_medium=rss&utm_source=On+The+Black+List&utm_campaign=90eca67a76-OTBL_MC_DAILY_CAMPAIGN&utm_medium=email&utm_term=0_a3fec71fa1-90eca67a76-103652841

Giddings, P. (1984). *When and where I enter: The impact of black women on race and sex in America.* New York, NY: William Morrow.

Gil, D. (1998). "Social change strategies to overcome injustice and oppression", Chapter 3. *In Confronting justice and oppression*, pp. 33-63. New York: Columbia University Press.

Gil, D. (1998). *Confronting injustice and oppression: Concepts and strategies for social workers.* New York, NY: Columbia University Press.

Gilens, M., & Page, B. I. (2016, May 23). Critics argued with our analysis of U.S. political inequality: Here are 5 ways they're wrong. *The Washington Post.*

Gille, E. (2007). Shadows of a childhood: A novel of war and friendship. In F. Adiele & M. Frosch (Eds.), *Coming of age around the world: A multicultural anthology.* New York, NY: Free Press.

Gilligan, R. (2012). Promoting a sense of "secure base" for children in foster care: Exploring the potential contribution of foster fathers. *Journal of Social Work Practice, 26*(4), 473–486.

Ginibi. R. L. (2007). *All Ginibi's Mob: Our voices collected.* Charnwood, Australia: Ginninderra Press.

Girlhood Studies: *An Interdisciplinary Journal*, (2017). Special Issue: technologies of nonviolence: reimagining mobile and social media practices in the lives of girls and young women 10(2), Summer.

Glenn, E. N. (2013). The social construction and institutionalization of gender and race: An integrative framework. In S. Ferguson (Ed.), *Race, gender, sexuality & social class: Dimensions of inequality* (pp. 125–139). Thousand Oaks, CA: SAGE.

Glicken, M. D. (2004). *Using the strengths perspective in social work practice.* Boston, MA: Pearson.

Glover, J.A, Galliher, R.V., & Lamere, T.G. (2009). Identity development and exploration among sexual minority adolescents: examination of a multidimensional model. *Journal of Homosexuality,* 56(1)77–101.

Gold, M., & Richards, H. (2012). To label or not to label: The special education question for African Americans. *Educational Foundations,* 26(1/2), 143–155.

Goldemberg, J. (1990). How to stop global warming. *MIT Technology Review, 19*(1), 88.

Golden, L. (2015). Irregular work scheduling and its consequences. *Economic Policy Institute.*

Goldman-Schatell, J. (2015). Livingstone resident gives voice in world of fashion to differently abled. Retrieved from https://www.tapinto.net/articles/livingston-resident-gives-voice-in-world-of-fashion

Goldstone, L. (2005). *Dark bargain: Slavery, profits and the struggle for the Constitution.* Walker Books

Golombok, S. (2015). *Modern families: Parents and children in new family forms.* Cambridge, United Kingdom: Cambridge University Press.

Gomez, J. M. (2015). Microaggressions and the enduring mental health disparity: Black Americans at risk for institutional betrayal. *Journal of Black Psychology, 41*(2), 121–143.

Gomez, J.M., Smith, C.P., Gobin, R.L., Tang, S.S. & Freyd, J.J. (2015). Collusion, torture, and inequality: Understanding the actions of the American Psychological Association as institutional betrayal. *Journal of Trauma Dissociation,* 17(5), 527–544.

Gonzales, L., Davidoff, K. C., Nadal, K. L., & Yanos, P. (2015). Microaggressions experienced by persons with mental illness: An exploratory study. *Psychiatric Rehabilitation Journal,* 38(3), 234–241.

Gonzalez, R. (2006). *Butterfly boy: Memories of a Chicano mariposa.* Madison: University of Wisconsin Press.

González, T. (2012). Keeping kids in schools: Restorative justice, punitive discipline, and the school to prison pipeline. *Journal of Law & Education* 41(2), 281–334.

Goodman, A. (2013). Air pollution increases dry eye syndrome. American Academy of Ophthalmology Annual Conference. *Medscape.*

Goodtherapy.org (n.d.). Transference. Retrieved from https://www.goodtherapy.org/blog/psychpedia/transference

Gopnik, A. (2012). The caging of America. *The New Yorker.* Retrieved from https://www.newyorker.com/magazine/2012/01/30/the-caging-of-america

Gordon, S. (2015). China's hidden children. *Thediplomat.com*

Gottfried, M. A., & Conchas, E. (Eds.). (2016). *When school policies backfire: How well-intentioned measures can harm our most vulnerable student.* Cambridge, MA: Harvard University Press.

Gough, M., & Noonan, M. (2013). Review of the motherhood wage penalty in the United States. *Sociology Compass, 7*(4), 228–342.

Gould, E., & Wething, H. (2012, July 24). U.S. poverty rates higher, safety net weaker than in peer countries. *Economic Policy Institute.* Retrieved from https://www.epi.org/publication/ib339-us-poverty-higher-safety-net-weaker/

Governing the States and Localities (2011–2012). State high school graduation rates by race, ethnicity. Source: National Center for Education Statistics, Common Core of Data State Dropout and Graduation Rate Data. Retrieved from http://www.governing.com/gov-data/education-data/state-high-school-graduation-rates-by-race-ethnicity.html.

Goytia, C.N., Todaro-Rivera, L., Brenner, B., Shepard, P., Piedras, V., & Horowitz, C. (2013). Community capacity building: A collaborative approach to designing a training and education model. *Progress in Community Health Partnerships, 7*(3), 291–299.

Graham, C. (2015). The high cost of being poor in America: Stress, pain and worry. *Social Mobility Memos.* Brookings.

Graham, C. (2017). The unhappiness of the U.S. working class. *Brookings.* Retrieved from https://www.brookings.edu/opinions/the-unhappiness-of-the-us-working-class/

Grande, D., & Srinivus, S. (2001). Student leadership & activism for social change in the US: Education for healthcare. *Education for Health, 14*(2), 198–206.

Grandhi, K. (2015). Credit Suisse: 1% of the population now owns half the world's wealth. *International Business Times.* Retrieved from http://www.ibtimes.co.uk/credit-suisse-1-population-now-owns-half-worlds-wealth-1523953.

Grandin, T. (1984). *Emergence: Labeled autistic.* New York, NY: Warner Books.

Grant, B. F., Chou, S. P., Saha, T. D., Pickering, R. P., Kerridge, B. T., Ruan, W. J., Huang, B., ... Hasin, D. S. (2017, August). Prevalence of 12-month alcohol us, high risk drinking and *DSM-IV* alcohol use disorder in the United States US 2001–2002 to 2012–2013. *JAMA Psychiatry.*

Grant, C. A., & Sleeter, C. E. (2013). *Turning on learning: Five approaches to multicultural teaching plans—Race, class, gender and disability* (5th ed.). New York, NY: Wiley.

Grassrootsgrantmakers.org (2015). Tools for grassroots grant making. Retrieved from http://www.grassrootsgrantmakers.org/about-us/our-identity-statement/

Gray, L. A., & Price, S. K. (2014). Partnering for mental health promotion: Implementing evidence based mental health services within a maternal and child home health visiting program. *Clinical Social Work, 42,* 70–80.

Green, A. (2014). *True tarot card meanings: Learn the secrets of tarot professionals.* Amazon Digital Services LLC.

Green, E. R., & Patterson, E. N. (2003). LGBTQI terminology. Retrieved Jan. 2, 2015, from http://www.lgbt.ucla.edu/documents/LGBTTerminology.pdf

Green, J. J. (2016). Community development and social development: informing concepts of place and intentional social change in a globalizing world. *Research on Social Work Practice, 26*(6), 605–608.

Green, L.S. (n.d). Stonewall and its impact on the gay liberation movement. Primary Source Set. Retrieved Jan 12, 2018 from https://dp.la/primary-source-sets/sets/stonewall-and-its-impact-on-the-gay-liberation-movement/.

Greenagle, F. (2016). *Life after incarceration* [NAADAC Webinar].

Greene, S., & McGinty, J. (2016). What if cities could create a truly inclusive local sharing economy? Retrieved from http://www.urban.org/research/publication/what-if-cities-could-create-truly-inclusive-local-sharing-economy

Greenstone, M. & Looney, A. (2011). How do recent college grads really stack up? employment and earnings for graduates of the great recession. Brookings.edu. Retrieved from https://www.brookings.edu/blog/jobs/2011/06/03/how-do-recent-college-grads-really-stack-up-employment-and-earnings-for-graduates-of-the-great-recession/

Greenwald, A., & Krieger, L. (2006). Implicit bias: Scientific foundations. *California Law Review, 94*(4), 945–967.

Grimes, E. K., & Slaughter, B. (2006). *Why our children hate us: How black adults betray black children.* Chester, PA: Grimes & Slaughter, LLC.

Grimké, A. (1836). American Slavery as it is. Appeal to the Christian Women of the South. Major Problems in the Early Republic Ch.13: "Abolitionism, Anti abolitionism, and Proslavery" (497–503, 515–521).

Griscom, J.L., The case of Sharon Kowalski and Karen Thompson: Ablesim, heterosexism, and sexism, p. 472 in Rothenberg P. S. with Kelly S. Mayhew (Eds.), *Race, class and gender in the United States.* Gordonville, VA: Worth

Grünenfelder, J., & Schurr, C. (2015). Intersectionality: A challenge for development research and practice? *Development in Practice, 25*(6), 771–784.

Guerin, L. (2016). Language and accent discrimination in the workplace. Retrieved September 14, 2016, from http://www.nolo.com/legal-encyclopedia/language-accent-discrimination-workplace-33464.html

Guerrero, E. G., Aarons, G. A., & Palinkas, L. A. (2014). Organizational capacity for service integration in community-based adduction health services. *American Journal of Public Health, 104*(4), e40.

Guerrero, M., & Nair, E. (2014). *Evidence-based macro practice in social work.* Wheaton, IL: Gregory.

Guibord, A. (n.d.). Science in transition: Understanding the biology behind gender identity. Retrieved Jan 17, 2018 from https://www.theglobeandmail.com/life/science-in-transition-understanding-the-biology-behind-gender-identity/article25553156/.

Guillem, S. M. (2014). Going "global," (re)locating privilege: A journey into the borders of whiteness, foreignness, and performativity. *Journal of Multicultural Discourses, 9*(3), 212–226.

Gutiérrez, D. (n.d.). An historic overview of Latino immigration and the demographic transformation of the U.S. In *American Latinos and the making of the United States*. National Park System Advisory Board. Retrieved from http://www.nps.gov/history/heritageinitiatives/latino/latinothemestudy/pdfs/Immigration_web_final.pdf.

Gutiérrez, G. (1973). *A theology of liberation: History, politics, and salvation*. Maryknoll, NY: Orbis.

Gutiérrez, G. (2012). *The theology of liberation* [Video file]. Retrieved by https://www.youtube.com/watch?v=9FS2UYhLzc8

Gutman, H.G. (1977). *The Black family in slavery and freedom: 1750–1925*. New York, NY: Vintage.

Guy, R. (1995). *Friends*. New York, NY: Laurel Leaf.

H.R.2978—Voting Rights Advancement Act of 2017.

Haddish, T. (2017). *The last black unicorn*. Kore.

Haddon, M. (2003). *The curious incident of the dog in the night*. New York, NY: Vintage Contemporaries.

Hagner, D., Malloy, J. M., Mazzone, M. W., & Cormier, G. M. (2016). Youth with disabilities in the criminal justice system: Considerations for transition and rehabilitation planning. *Journal of Emotional and Behavioral Disorders, 16*(4), 240–247.

Haidt, J. (2012). *The righteous mind: Why good people are divided by politics and religion*. New York, NY: Vintage.

Hakim, D. (2016, October 29). Doubts about the promised bounty and genetically modified crops. *New York Times*. Retrieved from https://www.nytimes.com/2016/10/30/business/gmo-promise-falls-short.html.

Hale, J. (1994). *Black children: Their roots, culture, and learning styles*. Baltimore, MD: Johns Hopkins University.

Hall, E. (1976). *Beyond culture*. New York, NY: Anchor Books.

Hall, R. (2002). *The quiet storm*. New York, NY: Simon & Schuster.

Hallam, S. (2010). The power of music: Its impact on the intellectual, social and personal development of children and young people. *International Journal of Music Education, 28*(3), 269–289.

Hamilton, C. V. (1968). Education in the black community: An examination of the realities. *Freedomways, 8*, 319–324.

Hamilton, V. (1993). *The people could fly: American black folktales*. New York, NY: Knopf Books for Young Readers.

Hancock, T. U., Kiedaras, C. G., & Waites, C. (2012). Facing structural inequality: Students' orientation to oppression and prctice with oppressed groups. *Journal of Social Work Education, 48*(1), 5–10.

Handley, C., & McAllister, M. (2007). Elements to promote a successful relationship between stakeholders interested in mental health promotion in schools. *Australian Journal of Advanced Nursing, 34*(4).

Hanh, T. N. (1995, 2007). *Living Buddha, living Christ*. New York, NY: Riverhead Books.

Hanlon, C., Alem, A., Medhin, G., Shibre, T.,Ejigu, D.A., Negussie, H., Dewey, M., Wissow, L., Prince, M., Susser, E., Lund, C., and Fekadu, A. (2016). Task sharing for the care of severe mental disorders in a low-income country (TaSCS): study protocol for a randomised, controlled, non-inferiority trial. *Trials*, 17, 76.

Hanna, F. J., Talley, W., & Guindon, M. (2000). Power of perception: Toward a model of cultural oppression and liberation. *Journal of Counseling & Development, 78*(4), 430–442.

Hannibal, M.E. (2016, June 17). Tipping point for earth by Barnosky and Hadly. *San Francisco Chronicle*. Retrieved from https://www.sfgate.com/books/article/Tipping-Point-for-Planet-Earth-by-Barnosky-8307445.php.

Harari, E., Glenwick, D. S., & Cecero, J. J. (2014). The relationship between religiosity/spirituality and well-being in gay and heterosexual Orthodox Jews. *Mental Health, Religion & Culture, 17*(9), 886–897.

Harari, Y. N. (2017). *Homo deus: A brief history of tomorrow*. New York, NY: HarperCollins.

Hard Earned. (2015). [Documentary]. Chicago, IL: Kartemquin Films and Al Jazeera America. Retrieved from https://kartemquin.com/films/hard-earned

Hardiman, Jackson, and Griffin (2007). Conceptual foundations for social justice education. In. M. Adams, L. A. Bell, P Griffin (Eds), *Teaching for Diversity and Social Justice, 2nd edition*. New York: Routledge. pp. 35–66.

Hardina, D. (2014). Interpersonal social work skills for community practice. Book Review by L. Pyles in *Journal of Teaching in Social Work*, 34(1), 111–112.

Hardina, D. (2014). *Interpersonal social work skills for community practice*. New York, NY: Springer.

Harlem Children's Zone (n.d.) Retrieved from https://hcz.org/news

Harrell, J. P., Hall, S., & Taliaferro, J. (2003). Physiological responses to racism and discrimination: An assessment of the evidence. *American Journal of Public Health, 93*(2), 243–248.

Harris, D. M. (2011). *Ethics in health services and policy: A global approach*. Wiley.

Harris, K. (2015). Children's spirituality and inclusion: Strengthening a child's spirit with community, resilience and joy. *International Journal of Children's Spirituality, 20*(2–4), 161–177.

Harrison, J., Spybrook, J., Curtis, A., & Cousins, L. (2017, June). Integrated dual disorder treatment: Fidelity and implementation over time. *Social Work Research, 41*(2), 111–119.

Harrison, R. A. (n.d.). Holistic & natural approach to your healthcare. Retrieved from http://www.drnatura.com/natural-health/alternative-health/Retrieved 5.5.16

Harvard.edu (2002). A brief history of the living wage debate at Harvard. Retrieved from https://www.hcs.harvard.edu/~pslm/livingwage/timeline.html

Harvey, A. R., Loughney, G. K., & Moore, J. (2002). A model program for African American children in the foster care system. *Journal of Health & Social Policy, 16*(1/2), 195–206.

Harvey, A., & Coleman, A. A. (1997). An Afrocentric program for African American males in the juvenile justice system. *Child Welfare, 79*(1), January/February, 197–211.

Harvey, A., McCullough-Chavis, A., Littlefield, M. B., Phillips, A. D., & Cooper, J. D. (2010). A culturally competent family enhancement and empowerment model for African American parents. *Smith College Studies in Social Work, 80*, 70–87.

Hastie, B., & Cosh, S. (2013). What's wrong with that? Legitimating and contesting gender inequality. *Language & Social Psychology, 32*(4), 369–389.

Hastie, B., & Rimmington, D. (2014). 200 years of white affirmative action: White privilege discourse in discussions of racial inequality. *Discourse & Society, 25*(2), 186–204.

Hattie, B., & Beagan, B. L. (2013). Reconfiguring spirituality and sexual/gender identity: It's a feeling of connection to something bigger, it's part of a wholeness. *Journal of Religion & Spirituality in Social Work: Social Thought, 32*, 244–268.

Haupt, C. (2016). Mindfulness in schools: When meditation replaces detention. Retrieved from http://health.usnews.com/wellness/mind/articles/2016-12-08/mindfulness-in-schools-when-meditation-replaces-detention

Hauser, C. (2017, May 24). Nevada and Connecticut are latest to ban discredited "conversion therapy." *The New York Times.*

Hawkins, J. (2014). 7 lessons to be learned from the Trayvon Martin and Michael Brown cases. Townhall.com. Retrieved Jan9, 2018 from https://townhall.com/columnists/johnhawkins/2014/11/29/7-lessons-to-be-learned-from-the-trayvon-martin-and-michael-brown-cases-n1925106.

Hawkins, J. D., Shapiro, V. B., & Fagan, A. A. (2010). Disseminating effective community prevention practices: Opportunities for social work education. *Research on Social Work Practice, 20*(5), 518–527.

Hawkins, R. (2016). Degree of freedom. The McSilver Institute for Poverty Policy and Research at NYU Silver School of Social Work.

Hawthorne, J. (2015). Federal housing policy leaves poor kids at risk of lead poisoning. *Chicago Tribune.* Retrieved from http://www.chicagotribune.com/news/ct-cha-lead-paint-hazards-met-20151231-story.html

Hayhoe, S. (2014). Towards a greater dialogue on disability between Muslims and Christians. *Journal of Disability & Religion, 18*, 242–263.

Health Disparities, (2011). Health Disparities Examples,www.patientnavigatortraining.org381 × 282 Search by image

Healthy People 2020. (n.d.). Retrieved from https://www.healthypeople.gov/sites/default/files/HP2020Framework.pdf

Healy, L., & Wairire, G. G. (2014). Educating for the global agenda: Internationally relevant conceptual frameworks and knowledge for social work education. *International Social Work, 57*(3), 235–247.

Heape, R. (Exec. Producer), & Richie, C. (Director). (2009). *The trail of tears* ; Our spirits don't speak English:Indian boarding school.[Documentary]. Retrieved from www.richheape.com.

Heasley, S. (2016). Feds allocate millions for special ed training. *DisabilityScoop.com.*

Heasley, S. (2017). Speechless creator urges casting of actors with disabilities. Disability Scoop. Retrieved from https://www.disabilityscoop.com/2017/06/13/speechless-creator-actors/23804/Holley, L. C., Stromwall, K. K., & Tavassoli, K.Y. (2015). Teaching note—Oppression of people with mental illnesses;: Incorporating content into multiple-issue diversity courses. *Journal of Social Work Education, 51*(2), 398–406.

Heasley, S. (2018). Down Syndrome reality show wins critics' choice award. *Disability Scoop*. Retrieved Jan15, 2018 from https://www.disabilityscoop.com/2018/01/12/down-syndrome-critics-choice/24582/

Heathfield, S. M. (2016). Advantages and disadvantages of flexible work schedules? Employers need to see their advantages when they offer flexibility. *The Balance*. Retrieved July 12, 2017, from https://www.thebalance.com/advantages-and-disadvantages-of-flexible-work-schedules-1917964

Heathy People.gov. (2018). Development of the National Health Promotion and Disease Prevention Objectives for 2030 Retrieved from https://www.healthypeople.gov/

Hedayat, S. (1990). *The blind owl*. Princeton, NJ: Princeton University Press.

Hehrlich, H. (2015). The diversity gap in children's publishing. Retrieved June 1, 2017, from http://blog.leeandlow.com/2015/03/05/the-diversity-gap-in-childrens-publishing-2015/

Heim, J. (2016, October 19). Education secretary says civics education should encourage activism. *Washington Post*. Retrieved from https://www.washingtonpost.com/local/education/education-secretary-says-civics-education-should-encourage-activism/2016/10/19/ec66a5b4-9610-11e6-bb29-bf2701dbe0a3_story.html?noredirect=on&utm_term=.a8b1e5d8fd06.

Held, M. L., Mallory, K. C., & Cummings, S. (2017). Preparing social work students for integrated health care: Results from a national study. *Journal of Social Work Education, 53*(3), 435–448.

Helpguide.org (2017). Learning Disabilities and Disorders: Types of Learning Disorders and Their Signs HELPGUIDE. ORG Trusted guide to mental & emotional health. Retrieved from https://www.helpguide.org/articles/autism-learning-disabilities/learning-disabilities-and-disorders.htm

Henderson, E., Kunitz, S. J., & Levy, J. E. (2001). The origins of Navajo youth gangs. In C. Trafzer & D. Weiner (Eds.), *Medicine ways: Disease, health, and survival among Native Americans* (pp. 222–234). Lanham, MD: Rowman & Littlefield.

Herczog, M. (2016). Next generation citizens: Promoting civic engagement in schools. *Leadership, May/June*, 24–29. Retrieved from https://view.joomag.com/leadership-magazine-may-june-2016-v45-no-5/0038662001461879864?page=5.

Hertel, S. & Libal, K. (2011). *Human rights in the U.S.: Beyond exceptionalism*. New York: Cambridge Press.

Herz, B. & Sperling, G.B (2003). *What works in girls' education: Evidence & policies for the developing world*. Council on Foreign Relations.

Hess, E. D., & Ludwig, K. (2017). *Humility is the new smart: Rethinking human excellence in the smart machine age*. Oakland, CA: Berrett-Koehler.

Hessini, L. (2016, Spring/Summer). Reclaiming and reframing sexual rights in Muslim majority contexts: The role of individual and collective movements in shifting patriarchal discourse and practice. *Brown Journal of World Affairs, 22*(2), 69–80.

HHS.gov. (n.d.). National CLAS Standards National Standards for Culturally and Linguistically Appropriate Services (CLAS) in Health and Health Care. Retrieved from https://www.thinkculturalhealth.hhs.gov/clas

Hibbing, J. B., Smith, K. B., & Alford, J. R. (2014). Differences in negativity bias underlie variations in political ideology. *Behavioral and Brain Sciences, 37*(3), 297–307.

Hick, S.T. (2002). Introduction to anti-oppressive practice: Challenges for social work. *Critical Social Work* 3(1). Retrieved from http://www1.uwindsor.ca/criticalsocialwork/introduction-anti-oppressive-practice-challenges-for-social-work.

Hickert, A. O., & Taylor, M. J. (2011). Supportive housing for addicted, incarcerated homeless adults. *Journal of Social Service Research, 37*, 136–151.

Higginbotham, A.L. (1998). *Shades of freedom: Racial politics and presumptions of the American legal process*. Oxford, UK: Oxford University Press.

Higgins, E. S. (2017). Is mental health declining? *Scientific American Mind*, January/February, 20–21.

Hildebrandt, E. & Stevens, P. (2009). Impoverished women with children and no welfare benefits: The urgency of researching failures of the temporary assistance for needy families program. *American Journal of Public Health, 99*(5), 793–80.

Hill, N. S., Jr. (Ed.). (2013). *Words of power: Voices from Indian America*. Golden, CO: Fulcrum.

Hill, R. (2003). *The strengths of African American families: Twenty-five years later.* Lanham, MD: United Press of America. Chapter 1.

Hill, R. B. (1997, July 21). A strengths perspective on black families. *The Baltimore Sun.*

Hilliard, A. (1997). *SBA: The reawakening of the African mind.* Gainesville, FL: Makare.

Hilliard, A. G., III, Williams, L., & Damali, N. (1987). *The teachings of Ptahhotep: The oldest book in the world.* Atlanta, GA: Blackwood Press.

Hilliard, A. G., III. (1998). *SBA: The reawakening of the African mind.* Gainesville, FL: Makare.

Hillier, A. E. (2007). Why social work needs mapping. Retrieved from http://repository.upenn.edu/spp_papers/86ttp://repository.upenn.edu/spp_papers/86

Hilton, J.M. & Child, S.L. (2014). Spirituality and the successful aging of older Latinos. *Counseling and Values, 59,* 17.

Hinson, E. K. (2015). Mainstreaming equality in federal budgeting: Addressing educational inequities with regard to the states. *Michigan Journal of Race & Law, 20,* 377–385.

Hinton, L., Tran, J. N., Tran, C., & Hinton, D. (2008). Religious and spiritual dimensions of the Vietnamese dementia caregiving experience. *Hallym International Journal of Aging, 10*(2), 139–160.

History.com (2009). *Voting rights act of 1965.* Historian Yohuru Williams video. Retrieved from https://www.history.com/topics/black-history/voting-rights-act Access date 5.21.2018.

History.com Staff. (2010). Manifest Destiny. *A+E Networks.* Retrieved Nov. 28, 2015, http://www.history.com/topics/manifest-destiny

History.com. (n.d.). Freedmens' bureau. Retrieved Jan. 11, 2018 from http://www.history.com/topics/black-history/freedmens-bureau.

Historynet.com. (n.d.) Abolitionist Movement, The Abolitionist Movement spreads, paragraph 11.

Hobson, J. Co-Host of *Here and Now.* (2015, June 25). Controversial new textbooks go into use this fall in Texas. WBUR, 90.9. Retrieved from http://www.wbur.org/hereandnow/2015/06/25/controversial-textbooks-texas.

Hockenberry, J. (2011). Public transit. In C T. Ibrahim (Ed.), *An anthology of disability literature.* Durham, NC: Carolina Academic Press.

Hodge, D.R. (2003). Value differences between social workers and members of the working class & middle class. *Social Work,* 48(1), 107–19.

Hodge, D. R. (2004). Working with Hindu clients in a spiritually sensitive manner. *Social Work,* 49(1), 28–37.

Hodge, D.R., Andereck, K., & Montoya, K. (2007). Spiritual/religious lifestyle profiles and community substance abuse perceptions: An exploratory study among predominantly Hispanic sample in the American southwest. *Journal of Social Service Research, 34*(1), 43–53.

Hoeft, T. J., Fortney, J. C., Patel, V., & Unutzer, J. (2016). Task-sharing approaches to improve mental health care in rural and other low-resource settings: A systematic review. *Journal of Rural Health, 00,* 1–15.

Hoffman, A., & Spengler, D. (2014). Review: DNA memories or early social life. *Neuroscience, 264,* 74–75.

Hogler, R., Henle, C., & Gross, M. (2013). Ethical behavior and regional environments: the effects of culture, values, and trust. *Employee Responsibilities and Rights Journal,* 25, 109–121

Holbrook, A., Tennille, J., & Buck, P. (2017). Building capacity for evidence-based practice together. *Social Work in Public Health, 32*(7), 421.

Holland, K., Blood, R. W., Thomas, S. L., & Lewis, S. (2015). Challenging stereotypes and legitimating fat: An analysis of obese people's views on news media reporting guidelines and promoting body diversity. *Journal of Sociology, 51*(2), 431–445.

Hollenbach, A. D., Eckstrand, K. L., & Dreger, A. (2014). Implementing curricular and institutional climate changes to improve health care for individuals who are LGBT, gender nonconforming, or born with DSD: A resource for medical educators. Washington, DC: Association of American Medical Educators.

Holocaust Museum. (2017). Retrieved from https://www.ushmm.org/wlc/en/article.php?ModuleId=10005201

Hoover, T. (1980). *The Zen experience.* New York, NY: Penguin.

Horn, G. (2000). *The book of ceremonies: A native way of honoring and living the sacred.* Novato, CA: New World Library.

Hostetter, C., Sullenberger, C. W., & Wood, L. (2015). "All these people who can do things that I can't": Adolescents' reflections on class, poverty, and the American dream. *The Journal of Poverty, 19*(2), 133–152.

Houston, J.B. & First, J.M. (2017). The mental health impact of major disasters like Harvey and Irma.

Howarth, C., & Andreouli, E. (2015). Changing the context: Tackling discrimination at school and in society. *International Journal of Educational Development, 41*, 184–191.

Howarth, S., Morris, D., Newlin, M., Webber, M., & Newlin, M. (2014). Health and social care interventions which promote social participation for adults with learning disabilities: a review. *British Journal of Learning Disabilities, 44*, 3–15.

Howell, E. (2015). *How long have humans been on earth?* Retrieved Nov. 6, 2015, from http://www.universetoday.com/38125/how-long-have-humans-been-on-earth/

Howland, C., & Gibavic, E. (2010). Learning disability identity development and social construct: A two-tiered approach. In M. Adams, W. J. Blumenfeld, H. W. Hackman, M. L. Peters, & X. Zuniga (Eds.), *Readings for diversity and social justice*. New York, NY: Routledge.

http://datacenter.kidscount.org/data/tables/9010-young-children-not-in-school#detailed/1/any/false/1491,1443,1218,1049,995/any/17975,17976

http://www.asheweb.net/files/Download/HEOFall2013FinalRevised-Jan9.pdf

https://michaelmoore.com/10FactsOnFlint/

https://www.census.gov/quickfacts/fact/table/US/PST045217.

https://www.urban.org/sites/default/files/publication/23856/412873-Race-Justifiable-Homicide-and-Stand-Your-Ground-Laws.PDF

Hu, C., & Esthappan, S. (2017). Asian Americans and Pacific Islanders, a missing minority in criminal justice data. Urban Institute. Retrieved June 16, 2017, from http://www.urban.org/urban-wire/asian-americans-and-pacific-islanders-missing-minority-criminal-justice-data

Huang, H. L. (2007). From the Asian boyz to the Zhu Lian bang (the bamboo union gang): A typological analysis of delinquent Asian gangs. *Asian Criminology, 2*, 127–143.

Hubbard, K., & Hegarty, P. (2014). Why is the history of heterosexuality essential? Beliefs about the history of sexuality and their relationship to sexual prejudice. *Journal of Homosexuality, 61*, 471–490.

Hubbard, R. (2014). The social construction of sexuality. In P. Rothenberg with K. Mayhew (Eds.), *Race, class and gender* (9th ed., p. 104). Duffield, United Kingdom: Worth.

Huberty, J.L., Matthews, J., Leiferman, J., Hermer, J., & Cacciatore, J. (2017). When a baby dies: a systematic review of experimental interventions for women after stillbirth. *Reproductive Science, 24*(7), 967–975.

Hudson, M. K., & Casey, E. M. (2016). Assessing and planning for second language literacy success with middle level refugee children. *Childhood Education, 92*(2), 158–160,

Hughes, D. (2003). Correlates of African American and Latino parents' messages to children about ethnicity and race: A comparative study of racial socialization. *American Journal of Community Psychology, 31*(1/2), 15.

Hughes, P. (2016). Using symbolic interactionism insights as an approach to helping the individual with Asperger's syndrome overcome barriers to social inclusion. *British Journal of Special Education, 43*(1), 65–75.

Human Rights Watch. (2016). *Like walking through a hailstorm: Discrimination against LGBT youth in U.S. schools.* Retrieved from https://www.hrw.org/report/2016/12/07/walking-through-hailstorm/discrimination-against-lgbt-youth-us-schools

Humane Farming (2017). Humane farming: Campaign against factory farming. Retrieved from http://www.hfa.org/

Humphreys, M. L. (2012). Intergroup dialogue: A pedagogical model for integrating cultural competence within a social justice framework. *International Journal of Interdisciplinary Social Sciences, 6*(5), 199–213.

Hunt, G. G., & Reinhart, S. C. (2015). The impact of America's changing family upon federal & state family caregiving policy. *Generations, 39*(4), 73–79.

Hunt, V., Layton, D., & Prince, S. (2015). Why diversity matters: New research makes it increasingly clear that companies with more diverse workforce perform better financially. *McKinsey.com.*

Hunter-Hernandez, M., Costos-Muñíz, R., & Gary, F. (2015). Missed opportunity: Spirituality as a bridge. *Journal of Religious Health, 54*, 2367–2375.

Huong, D. T. (2002). *Paradise of the blind.* New York, NY: William Morrow.

Hurlburt, M., Aarons, G.A., Fettes, D., Willging, C., Gunderson, L., & Chaffin, (2013). Interagency

Husseini, R. (2009). *Murder in the name of honor: The true story of one woman's heroic fight against an unbelievable crime.* London, England: Oneworld.

Hutchinson, E. (2015). *Dimensions of human behavior: The changing life course* (5th ed.). Thousand Oaks, CA: SAGE.

Hutchinson, E. D. (2015). *Dimensions of human behavior: The changing life course.* Thousand Oaks, CA: SAGE.

Huyghe, P. (1992). *Columbus was last: From 200,000 b.c. to 1492, a heretical history of who was first.* Anomalist Books.

Hyde, B. (2013). Mutual aid group work: social work leading the way to recovery-focused mental health practice. *Social Work with Groups,* 36, 43–58.

Iachini, A.L., Clone, S., DeHart, D.D., Seay, K.D., & Browne, T. (2016). Project STRONG: A capacity–building intervention to improve grant writing among substance abuse organizations. *Journal of Social Work Practice in the Addictions, 16,* 403–420.

Ibrahim, C. T. (Ed). (2011). *An anthology of disability literature.* Durham, NC: Carolina Academic Press.

Iglehart, A. P. & Becerra, R.M. (1997). *Social services and the ethnic community.* Boston, MA: Allyn and Bacon.

Iglehart, A. P., & Becerra, R. (2010). *Social services and the ethnic community: History and analysis.* Long Grove, IL: Waveland Press.

Iglehart, A. P., & Becerra, R. M. (1995). *Social services and the ethnic community.* Long Grove, IL: Waveland Press.

Illanes, P., Lund, S., Mourshed, M., Rutherford, S., & Tyreman, M. (2018). Retraining and reskilling workers in the age of automation. *McKinsey Global Institute.*

Imbery, L. (2016). Fact of the week: Lower-income renters spend nearly half of income on rent. *Pew Research Center.*

Infographics.com. LGBT rights in the United States. Retrieved from https://infogalactic.com/info/LGBT_rights_in_the_United_States

Ingle, B. & McClure, S. (2010). *The Soprano state: New Jersey's culture of corruption.* New York, NY: St. Martin's Griffin.

Inness, S. A. (Ed.). (1998). *Millennium girls: Today's girls around the world.* Lanham, MD: Rowman & Littlefield.

Institute of Medicine. (1999). The unequal burden of cancer: An assessment of NIH research and programs for ethnic minorities and the medically underserved. Washington, DC: National Academies Press.

Institute of Medicine. (2003). Unequal treatment: Confronting racial and ethnic disparities in health care. Washington, DC: National Academies Press.

Interfaith Calendar. (2016). Retrieved from http://www.interfaithcalendar.org/

International Federation of Social Work. (2017). Retrieved from http://ifsw.org/

International Federation of Social Workers (n.d.). What we do. Retrieved from http://ifsw.org/what-we-do/

International Federation of Social Workers. (2012). Statement of ethical principles. Retrieved from ifsw.org/what-we-do/; http://ifsw.org/policies/statement-of-ethical-principles/http://ifsw.org/get-involved/global-definition-of-social-work/ Retrieved 7/29/2015

International Federation of Social Workers. (2014). Global definition of social work. Retrieved from http://ifsw.org/get-involved/global-definition-of-social-work/

Irin. (2013, Feb. 3). At risk because they don't exist. *The Asia Magazine.* Retrieved from http://www.theasiamag.com/patterns/risk-because-they-dont-exist.

Irwin, N. (2017). Can more jobs heal race relations? *The New York Times,* Sunday Business.

Irwin, N., Miller, C. C., & Sanger-Katz, M. (2014, Aug. 9), America's racial divide, charted. The upshot: Persistent inequality. *The New York Times.*

Isaacs, L. (2012*).* Report: the end of the segregated century: Racial separation in America's neighborhood. *Journal of Housing & Community Development,* 69(2), 20–20.

Isasi-Diaz, A. M. (1993) Mujerista theology: A theology for the twenty-first century. *Journal of the American Academy of Religion, 66*(4), 953–955.

Itani, F. (2003). *Deafening.* New York, NY: Grove Press.

Jabr, F. (2017). Headstrong: For many people with depression, exercise may be the most effective, least expensive and safest treatment. *Scientific American, January/February, 31*(1–2), 27.

Jacewicz, N. (2016, June 16). Why Are Health Studies So White? *The Atlantic.* Retrieved from https://www.theatlantic.com/health/archive/2016/06/why-are-health-studies-so-white/487046/

Jackson, J., Williams, D., & VanderWeele, T. (2016). Disparities at the intersection of marginalized groups. *Social Psychiatry & Psychiatric Epidemiology,* 51(10), 1349–1359.

Jackson, M. (2009) *They don't care about us* [Video file]. Retrieved from https://www.youtube.com/watch?v=QNJL6nfu__Q

Jacobson, M. (2012). Breaking silence, building solutions: The role of social justice group work in the retention of faculty of color. *Social Work with Groups, 35,* 267–286.

James, B. (2014). Princeton study: U.S. no longer an actual democracy. *TPM,* Retrieved from talkingpointsmemo.com

Jansson, B. S. (2014). Becoming an effective policy advocate: From policy practice to social justice. Belmont, CA: Brooks/ Cole, Cengage.

Jardine, A. (2016, Mar. 14). Kids' drawings reveal gender stereotypes in an eye-opening spot. Retrieved from http://creativity-online.com/work/inspiring-the-future-redraw-the-balance/45935

Jarman, M. (2011). Coming up from underground: Uneasy dialogues at the intersections of race, mental illness, and disability studies. Retrieved from http://www.uwyo.edu/wind/_files/docs/jarman/coming%20up%20from%20underground.pdf

Jeffrey, D. (2005). 'What good is anti-racist social work if you can't master it?': Exploring a paradox in anti-racist social work education. *Race, Ethnicity and Education, 8*(4), 409–425.

Jeltsen, M. (2015). Chris Christie just vetoed a bill that would have forced domestic abusers to surrender their guns. *HuffPost Politics.*

Jeyapal, D. (2017). The evolving politics of race and social work activism: a call across borders. Social Work, Volume 62, Issue 1, 1 January 2017, Pages 45–52, https://doi.org/10.1093/sw/sww069 Published: 23 December 2016 OR LINK

https://academic.oup.com/sw/article-abstract/62/1/45/2452300?redirectedFrom=fulltext

Jiang, Y., Ekono, M., & Skinner, C. (2015, Jan.). *Basic facts about low-income children, aged 12 through 17 years, 2013.* National Center for Children in Poverty. Retrieved from http://www.nccp.org/publications/pub_929.html

Jinpa, T. (2015). A fearless heart: How the courage to be compassionate can transform our lives. Toronto, Ontario: Hudson Street Press.

Johannson, E. (2017). Wages, hours and scheduling: An issue brief. *Jobs with Justice.org.* Retrieved from http://www.jwj.org/wages-and-hours-101

Johnson, C., & Miteva, M. (2017). Alopecia areata on vertex as a potential pitfall for misdiagnosis of central centrifugal cicatricial alopecia in African-American Women. *International Journal of Trichology,* 202.

Johnson, E. A. (1993). *Women, earth and the creator spirit.* (Madeleva lecture in spirituality). New York, NY: Paulist Press.

Johnson, M. (2013). Why America's women of color have lost ground since the great recession. See more at http://www.scholarsstrategynetwork.org/brief/why-americas-women-color-have-lost-ground-great-recession#sthash.fxv8BRMx.dL9IPd0o.dpuf

Johnston, K. E., Swim, J. K., Saltsman, B. M., Deater-Deckard, K., & Petrill, S. A. (2007). Mothers' racial ethnic, and cultural socialization of transracially adopted Asian children. *Family Relations, 56*(4), 390–402.

Jolanki, O. (2016). To work or to care? Working women's decision-making. *Community Work & Family, 18*(3), 268–283. Retrieved from http://dx.doi.org/10.1080/13668803.2014.997194

Jones, B. (2016). Americans' views of immigrants marked by widening partisan, generational divides. Pew Research Center. Retrieved from http://www.pewresearch.org/fact-tank/2016/04/15/americans-views-of-immigrants-marked-by-widening-partisan-generational-divides/.

Jones, B., & Phillips, F. (2016). Social work and interprofessional education in health care: A call for continued leadership. *Journal of Social Work Education, 52*(1), 18–29.

Jones, J. (2013, Aug. 28). Albert Einstein called racism "a disease of white people" in his little known fight for civil rights. Retrieved from www.openculture.com

Jones, J., & Mosher, W. D. (2013). *Fathers' interactions with their children: United States 2006–2010.* National Health Statistics Reports, Center for Disease Control, #71.

Jones, M. (2015). Why a generation of adoptees is returning to South Korea. *The New York Times Magazine.*

Jones, M. L., & Galliher, R. V. (2015). Daily racial microaggressions and ethnic identification among Native American young adults. *Cultural Diversity and Ethnic Minority Psychology, 21*(1), 1–9.

Jones, R. P. (2014). Self-segregation: Why it's so hard for whites to understand Ferguson. *The Atlantic.* Retrieved from http://www.theatlantic.com/national/archive/2014/08/self-segregation-why-its-hard-for-whites-to-understand-ferguson/378928/

Jordan, R., Mireles, A., & Popkin, S. (2013, October). *HOST youth: The challenges of growing up in low income-housing.* Retrieved from https://www.urban.org/sites/default/files/publication/24186/412953-HOST-Youth-The-Challenges-of-Growing-up-in-Low-Income-Housing.PDF

Jorm, A. F., Patten, S. B., Brugha, T. S., & Mortubai, R. (2017). Has increased provision of treatment reduced the prevalence of common mental disorders? Review of the evidence from four countries. *World Psychiatry, 16*(11), 90–99.

Jost, J., Glaser, J., Kruglanski, A. W., & Sulloway, F. J. (2003). Political conservatism as motivated social cognition. *Psychological Bulletin, 129*(3), 339–375.

Jouejati, R. (2013, Oct. 3). Syrian women organize for security. *Utne Reader.* Retrieved from http://www.utne.com/politics/syrian-women-organize-for-security.aspx

Júlíusdóttir, S. (2006). The emerging paradigm shift in social work: In the context of the current reforms of European social work education. *Social Work & Society International Online Journal, 4*(1). Retrieved May 25, 2017, from http://www.socwork.net/sws/article/view/175/566

Jurkowski, J. M., Rivera, Y., & Hammel, J. (2009). Health perceptions of Latinos with intellectual disabilities: The results of a qualitative pilot study. *Health Promotion Practice, 10*(1), 144–155.

Jutel, A. G., & Dew, K. (2014). *Social issues in diagnosis: An introduction for students and clinicians.* Baltimore, MD: Johns Hopkins University.

Kahn, A. (1969). *Theory and practice of social planning: Companion volume to studies in social policy and planning.* New York, NY: Russell Sage Foundation.

Kaltreider, K. (2003). *American Indian prophecies: Conversations with Chasing Deer.* Carlsbad, CA: Hay House.

Kamenetsky, S.B., Dimakos, C., Aslemand, A., Amani Saleh, A., & Ali-Mohammed, S. (2016). Eliciting help without pity: The effect of changing media images on perceptions of disability, *Journal of Social Work in Disability & Rehabilitation, 15*:1, 1–21, DOI: 10.1080/1536710X.2016.1124251

Kanaʻiaupuni, S., Ledward, B., & Jensen, U. (2010). *Culture-based education and its relationship to student outcomes.* Retrieved from http://www.ksbe.edu/_assets/spi/pdfs/CBE_relationship_to_student_outcomes.pdf

Kanashiro, P., & Starik, M. (2016). Business efforts, opportunities and limits addressing the poor: A Brazilian case study. *Business Horizons, 59*(5), 471–479.

Kanellos, N. (2002). *Recovering the U.S. Hispanic literary heritage.* Houston, TX: Arte Püblico PR.

Kanellos, N. (2011). *Hispanic immigrant literature: El sueño del retorno.* Austin: University of Texas.

Kanno, H. & Giddings, M. (2017). Hidden trauma victims: Understanding and preventing traumatic stress in mental health professionals. *Social Work in Mental Health, 15*(33), 331–353.

Kantowitz, B. H. (1974). Information processing theory. In J. Bothamley (Ed.), *Dictionary of theories.* Washington, DC: Gale Research Group.

Kapoulitsas, M. & Corcan, T. (2014). Compassion fatigue and resilience: A qualitative analysis of social work practice. *Qualitative Social Work, 14*(1), 86–101.

Karenga, M. (1984). *Selections from the Husia: Sacred wisdom of ancient Egypt.* Los Angeles, CA: University of Sankore Press.

Karger, H. (2015). Curbing the financial exploitation of the poor: financial literacy and social work education. *Journal of Social Work Education, 51*(3), 425–438.

Karp, S. (2015). A tale of two districts: The long reach and deep pockets of corporate reform. *Rethinking Schools, 29*(3), 36–41.

Karsten, J. & West, D.M. (2015). Who protects workers in the on-demand economy? Brookings.edu. Retrieved from https://www.brookings.edu/blog/techtank/2015/08/27/who-protects-workers-in-the-on-demand-economy/.

Kattari, S. K. (2015). Examining ableism in higher education through social dominance theory and social learning theory. *Innovative Higher Education, 40,* 375–386.

Katz, J. (2012). Violence against women is a men's issue [TED Talk]. Retrieved from https://www.ted.com/talks/jackson_katz_violence_against_women_it_s_a_men_s_issue

Katz, W. (1973). The strengths of Black Families. Book Review. *Equal Opportunity Review.* Retrieved from https://files.eric.ed.gov/fulltext/ED085430.pdf.

Katznelson, I. (2017). Making affirmative action white again. *The New York Times,* Sunday Review.

Kaye-Tzadok. A. & Spiro, S.E. (2014). Evaluation capacity building: Can a classroom-based course make a difference? *Research on Social Work Practice, 26*(5), 565–571.

Kearny, M.S., & Harris, B.H. (Eds), (2014). Policies to address poverty in America. For *The Hamilton Project, Brookings.* Retrieved from https://www.brookings.edu/interactives/policies-to-address-poverty-in-america/

Keene, D. E., & Geronimus, A. T. (2011). Community-based support among African American public housing residents. *Journal of Urban Health: Bulletin of the New York Academy of Medicine, 80*(1), 41–52.

Keesee, T. (2016). Police and Community Trust, A webinar of the Office of Justice Programs, January 26.

Keeton, A. (2012). Strip searching in the age of colorblind racism: The disparate impact of *Florence v Board of chosen freeholders of the county of Burlington. Michigan Journal of Race & Law, 21*(55), 55–90.

Kelley, A., & Small, C. (2015). Establishing the reliability and validity of the sources of strength in one American Indian community. *American Indian and Alaska Native Mental Health Research, 84.*

Kelley, M. (2011). On the social construction of place: Using participatory methods and digital tools to reconceive distressed urban neighborhoods. In Sutton & Kemp (Eds.), *The paradox of urban place: Inequality and transformation in marginalized communities* (pp. 206–220). New York, NY: Palgrave Macmillan.

Kelley, M., James, C., Kraft, A. S., Korngiebel, D., Wijangco, I., Rosenthal, E., Joffe, S., & Lee, S. S. (2015). Patient perspectives on the learning health system: The importance of trust and shared decision making. *The American Journal of Bioethics, 15*(9), 4–17.

Kellogg, C. (2015). Junot Diaz on reading, writing, & America's amnesia about race. *Los Angeles Times.* Retrieved Nov. 10, 2015, from http://www.latimes.com/ December.books/jacketcopy/la-et-jc-junot-diaz-occidental-20150919-story.html

Kelly, J. (2016). Why women should tell the story of humanity [TED Talk]. Retrieved from https://www.ted.com/talks/jude_kelly_why_women_should_tell_the_stories_of_humanity.

Kelly, L. (2017). Reconceptualizing professional knowledge: The changing role of knowledge and evidence in social work practice. *Social Work Education, 36*(3), 245–256.

Kelto, A. (2015). John Oliver says U.S. students learn virtually nothing about Africa. NPR. Retrieved from http://www.npr.org/sections/goatsandsoda/2015/09/09/438672718/john-oliver-says-u-s-students-learn-virtually-nothing-about-africa

Kentucky Center for Women and Families. (2017). Retrieved from https://www.thecenteronline.org/education/education-https://www.thecenteronline.org/education/education-resources/

Kenyon, S., Lyons, G., & Rafferty, J. (2002) Transport and social exclusion: investigating the possibility of promoting inclusion through virtual mobility. *Journal of Transport Geography, 10*(3), 207–219.

Kessler, S. (2017). We've been worrying about the end of work for 500 years. *Quartz Media.* Retrieved from https://qz.com/1019145/weve-been-worrying-about-the-end-of-work-for-500-years/?mc_cid=ce3cb55747&mc_eid=bf05644be9

Kids Count (n.d.). Children in immigrant families. Retrieved Jan 16, 2018 from http://datacenter.kidscount.org/data/tables/115-children-in-immigrant-families#detailed/2/40/false/573,869,36,868,867/any/445,446

Kids Count. (2016). The kids count index. Retrieved from http://www.aecf.org/work/kids-count/kids-count-data-center/ [See http://datacenter.kidscount.org/]

Kids Count.org. (2014). Retrieved from http://datacenter.kidscount.org/data/Map/6795-children-living-in-areas-of-concentrated-poverty?loc=40&loct=2#2/any/false/1201/any/13892/Orange

KidsCount.org. (2017, July 27). Another Look at Child Poverty: The Supplemental Poverty Measure. Retrieved from https://datacenter.kidscount.org/updates/show/164-supplemental-poverty-measure-2017

Kiehl, J. T. (2016). *Facing climate change: An integrated path to the future.* New York, NY: Columbia University Press.

Kiehne, E. (2016). Latino critical perspective in social work. *Social Work, 61*(2), 119–126.

Kiel, P. (2016, Jan. 3). Debt and the racial wealth gap. *The New York Times,* Sunday review, p. 7.

Killiam, K. (2015). A hug a day keeps the doctor away: Research demonstrates cold fighting power of hugging. *Scientific American.* Retrieved from https://www.scientificamerican.com/article/a-hug-a-day-keeps-the-doctor-away/

Kim, G. (2017). *How co-housing can make us happier (and live longer)* [Video file]. Retrieved from https://www.ted.com/talks/grace_kim_how_cohousing_can_make_us_happier_and_live_longer

Kim, H. H. (2012). Asian feminist theology. Retrieved from https://www.drew.edu/theological/2012/03/30/asian-feminist-theology/

Kim, J. (2014). Building coalitions and learning together: A Korean-American community organization. *Community Development Journal, 49*(3), 473–488.

Kim, M.E. (2010). Moving beyond critique: creative interventions and reconstructions of community accountability. Social Justice, 37(4), 14–35.

Kimerling, R., Pavao, J., & Wong, A. (2016). Patient activation and mental health care experiences among women veterans. *Administration and Policy in Mental Health and Mental Health Service Research, 43*(4), 506–513.

King, L. H., Aguinaga, N., O'Brien, C., Young, W., & Zgonc, K. (2010). Disability in higher education: A position paper. *Annals of the Deaf, 155*(3), 386–391.

King, R., Peterson, B., Elderbroom, B., & Pelletier, E. (2015). Reducing mass incarceration requires far-reaching reforms. *Urban Institute.* Retrieved from http://webapp.urban.org/reducing-mass-incarceration/

Kingsolver, B. (1998). *The poisonwood Bible.* New York, NY: Harper Collins.

Kinney, A. B. (2014). *Exemplary women of early China: The Lienüzhuan of Liu Xiang.* New York, NY: Columbia University Press.

Kirby, A. (2014). Adapting cities, adapting the curriculum. *Geography, 99,* Part 2, 90.

Kircher, M. M. (2016, Feb. 15). Stevie Wonder just made a powerful statement at the Grammys about people with disabilities. *Huffington Post.* Retrieved from http://www.techinsider.io/stevie-wonder-just-made-a-powerful-statement-about-kids-with-disabilities-2016-2

Kirp, D. (2015). What do the poor need? Try asking them. *New York Times.* Retrieved Jan 12, 2018 from https://www.nytimes.com/2015/08/09/opinion/sunday/david-l-kirp-what-do-the-poor-need-try-asking-them.html

Kirst-Ashman, K. (2014). *Human behavior in the macro social environment* (4th ed.). Pacific Grove, CA: Brooks/Cole.

Klijs, B., Nusselder, W. J., Looman, C., & Mackenbach, J. P. (2014). Educational disparities in the burden of disability: Contributions of disease prevalence and disabling impact. *American Journal of Public Health, 104*(8), 141–147.

Knappertsbusch, F., Milbradt, B., & Kelle, U. (2013). Qualitative research on prejudice. *International Journal of Conflict & Violence, 7*(1), 50–56.

Knauer, N. (2009). LGBT elder law: Toward equity in aging. *Harvard Journal of Law & Gender, 32.* Temple University Legal Studies Research Paper #2009-5.

Kneebone, E. (2014, July 31). The growth and spread of concentrated poverty, 2000 to 2008-2012, *Brookings.* Retrieved from https://www.brookings.edu/interactives/the-growth-and-spread-of-concentrated-poverty-2000-to-2008-2012/.

Knickmeyer, L., Hopkins, K., & Meyer, M. (2003). Exploring collaboration among urban neighborhood associations. *Journal of Community Practice,* 11(2), 13–26.

Kochar, R. (2013, Dec. 11). How Pew Research measured the gender pay gap. Retrieved from http://www.pewresearch.org/fact-tank/2013/12/11/how-pew-research-measured-the-gender-pay-gap/

Kochhar, R., & Fry, R. (2014). Wealth inequality has widened along racial, ethnic lines since end of great recession. *Pew Research Center.* Retrieved from http://www.pewresearch.org/fact-tank/2014/12/12/racial-wealth-gaps-great-recession/

Kolata, G. (2015, Nov. 2). Death rates rising for middle-aged white Americans, study finds. *The New York Times.*

Kolata, G., & Cohen, S. (2016). Drug overdoses propel rise in mortality rate of young whites. *The New York Times.*

Kosslyn, S. M., & Rosenberg, R. S. (2010). *Introducing psychology: Brain, person, group* (4th ed.). Upper Saddle, NJ: Pearson Education.

Kozol, J. (2005). *The shame of the nation: The restoration of apartheid schooling in America.* New York, NY: Broadway Books.

Kozol, J. (2014). Still separate, still unequal. In P. S. Rothenberg & K. S. Mayhew (Eds.), *Race, class and gender in the United States* (9th ed., p. 627). Duffield, United Kingdom: Worth.

Kozol. J. (2005). Still separate, still unequal. *Harper's Magazine.* https://harpers.org/archive/2005/09/still-separate-still-unequal

Kreindler, S.A., Dowd, D.A., Star, N.D., & Gottschalk, T. (2012). Silos and social identity: the social identity approach as a framework for understanding and overcoming divisions in health care. *Milbank Quarterly,* 90(2), 347–374.

Kreisberg, N. & Marsh, J.C. (2016). Social Work knowledge production and utilisation: An international comparison. *British Journal of Social Work,* 46, 599–618.

Kreitzer, L., McLaughlin, A. M., Elliott, G., & Nicholas, D. (2016). Qualitative examination of rural service provision to persons with concurrent developmental and mental health challenges. *European Journal of Social Work, 19*(1), 46–61.

Kristof, N. D., & WuDunn, S. (2010). *Half the sky: Turning oppression into opportunity for women worldwide.* New York, NY: Alfred A. Knopf.

Kristof, N. (2017, July 30). Motherhood is deadlier in America. *The New York Times.*

Krumer-Nevo, M., Monnickendam, M., & Weiss-Gall, I. (2009). Poverty-aware social work practice: A conceptual framework for social work education. *Journal of Social Work Education, 45*(2), 225–229.

Krupa, T., & Lysaght, R. (2016). Perspectives on how social business can engender work identity among people with mental illness. *Journal of Policy Practice, 15*(1–2), 36–57.

Kujawa-Holbrook, S. A. & and Montagno, K.B. (Eds.) (2009). *Injustice and the care of souls: Taking oppression seriously in pastoral care.* Minneapolis, MN: Fortress Press.

Kumpfer, K., Magalhães, C., & Xie, J. (2016). Cultural adaptation and implementation of family evidence-based interventions with diverse populations. *Prevention Science, 18,* 649–659.

Kunen, J. S. (2017). Opening minds behind bars: What happens when you bring college classes to incarcerated men and women? *Columbia Magazine,* Summer, 21–27.

Kunjufu, K. (1978). *Developing positive self-images & discipline in black children.* Chicago, IL: African American Images.

Kushner, M. (2014). Why buildings of the future will be shaped by you [Video file]. Retrieved from https://www.ted.com/talks/marc_kushner_why_the_buildings_of_the_future_will_be_shaped_by_you

Kusisto, L. (2015, July 8). New HUD rules take aim at segregated housing: Government can withhold money from communities that fail to address historical segregation. *Wall Street Journal.*

Kwanzaawebsite.org, (2017) Kwanzaa, A celebration of family, community and culture. Retrieved from http://www.officialkwanzaawebsite.org/NguzoSaba.shtml

Kyung, C.H. (1988). "Han-pu-ri": Doing theology from Korean women's perspective. *The Ecumenical Review, 40(1),* 27–39.

Laferriere, D. (2008). *I am a Japanese writer.* Vancouver, British Columbia: Douglas & McIntyre.

Lai, Z., & Zhou, H. (2017). Making strides in social innovation. *Stanford Social Innovation Review.* Retrieved from https://ssir.org/articles/entry/making_strides_in_social_innovation

Lakerveld, J., Loyen, A., Schotman, N., Peeters, C., Brug, J., Cardon, G., van der Ploeg, H. P., ... & Brug, J. (2017). Sitting too much: A hierarchy of socio-demographic correlates. *Preventive Medicine, 101,* 77–83.

Lamar, K. (2015). Alright. M. Kuhle & P. Williams (Producers). *To Pimp a Butterfly* [album].

Lamb, H. R., & Weinberger, L. E. (2014). Decarceration of U.S. jails and prisons: Where will persons with serious mental illness go? *Journal of American Academy of Psychiatric Law, 42*(4), 489–456.

Lander, J. (2015, April 18). Teach civics in schools—but do it right. *The Boston Globe.*

Langdon, P., Clarkson, J., Robinson, P., Lazar, J., & Heylighen, A. (Eds.). (2012). *Designing inclusive systems: Designing inclusion for read world application.* London, England: Springer.

Langellier, B. A., Garza, J. R., Gilk, D., Prelip, M. L., Brookmeyer, R., Roberts, C. K., Peters, A., & Ortega, A. N. (2012). Immigration disparities in cardiovascular disease risk factor awareness. *Journal of Immigration Health, 14,* 918–925.

Lantz, P.M., Lichtenstein, R.L., & Pollack, H.A. (2007). Health policy approaches to population health: the limits of medicalization. *Health Affairs, 26*(5),

Lappin, J. (2016, Oct. 31). Complex homeless problem needs a subtle fix. *Wall Street Eastern Edition.*

Lara, D., Greene, D., & Bejarano, C. (2010). A critical analysis of immigrant advocacy tropes: How popular discourse weakens solidarity and prevents broad, sustainable justice. *Social Justice, 36*(2), 21.

Lareau, A. (2011). *Unequal childhoods: Class, race, and family life* (2nd ed.). Berkeley: University of California Press.

Larmer, B. (2012, June). Terra-cotta army. *National Geographic.*

Larson, K. C. (2004). *Bound for the Promised Land: Harriet Tubman—Portrait of an American hero.* New York, NY: Ballantine Books.

Law Library of Congress (2016). Decriminalization of narcotics. Retrieved from https://www.loc.gov/law/help/decriminalization-of-narcotics/decriminalization-of-narcotics.pdf.

Lawler, A. (2007, March/April). Beyond the family feud. *Archaeology,* 20–25.

Lbgt-rights-hrw.silk.com. (n.d.). #outlawed. Retrieved July 3, 2015, from https://lgbt-rights-hrw.silk.co/

LeCook, B., Manning, W., & Alegria, M. (2013). Measuring disparities across the distribution of mental health care expenditures. *Journal of Mental Health Policy Economics, 16*(1) 3–12.

Lee, A. R. (2003). *Multicultural American literature: Comparative Black, Native, Latino/a and Asian American fictions.* Oxford, MS: University Press of Mississippi.

Lee, AJ, Kane, S, Ramsey, R, Good, E, Dick, M, (2016). Testing the price and affordability of healthy and current (unhealthy) diets and the potential impacts of policy change in Australia. *BMC Public Health, 12*(16), 315.

Lee, D. (2017). *Single mother statistics.* Retrieved Jan. 7, 2018 from https://singlemotherguide.com/single-mother-statistics/

Lee, E., & Bhuyan, R. (2013, March). Negotiating within whiteness in cross-cultural clinical encounters. *Social Service Review,* 98–130.

Lee, H. S. (2015). The ethical dilemma of abstinence-only service delivery in the United States. *Journal of Social Work Values & Ethics, 12*(1), 61–72.

Lee, K.H. & Hwang, M.J. (2014). Private religious practice, spiritual coping, social support, and health status among older Korean adult immigrants. *Social Work in Public Health,* 29, 228–443.

Lee, M. & Lam, B.O. (2016). The academic achievement of socioeconomically disadvantaged immigrant adolescents: a social capital perspective. *International Review of Sociology*—Revue Internationale de Sociologie, 26(1), 144–173. https://www.tandfonline.com/doi/abs/10.1080/03906701.2016.1112528

Lee, O., & Buxton, A. (2010). *Diversity and equity in science education: Research, policy and practice.* New York, NY: Teachers College Press.

Lefmann, T., Combs-Orme, T., & Orme, J. G. (2017). Examining the inter-correlated effects of low income, life stress, and race on birth outcomes: A representative state study. *Social Work in Health Care, 56*(6), 450–469.

Lehigh.edu. The Chinese Exclusion Act (1882): Brief overview. Retrieved from https://www.lehigh.edu/~ineng/Virtual-Americana/chineseimmigrationact.html

Lehrman, S. (2006). The implicit prejudice. *Scientific American.* Retrieved Dec. 28, 2015, from http://www.scientificamerican.com/article/the-implicit-prejudice/

Lemkin, R., Schabas, W.A., & Power, S. (1944, 2008). *Axis rule in occupied Europe: Laws of occupation, analysis of government, proposals for redress (Foundations of the laws of war). 2nd edition.* The Lawbook Exchange, Ltd.

LePoire, B.A. (2006), Family communication: Nurturing and control in a changing world. Thousand Oaks, CA: SAGE.

Leslau, C., & Leslau, W. (1985). *African proverbs.* New York, NY: The Peter Pauper Press.

Leung, C. K. Y., Sarpça, S., & Yilmaz, K. (2012). Public housing unites vs. housing vouchers: Accessibility, local public goods, and welfare. *Journal of Housing Economics, 21,* 310–321.

Levasseur, M. D. (2015). Gender identity defines sex: Updating the law to reflect modern medical science is key to transgender rights. *Vermont Law Review, 39,* 953–1005.

Levine, P. & Kline, M. (2008). *Trauma-proofing your kids: A parents' guide for instilling confidence, joy and resilience.* Berkeley, CA: North Atlantic Books.

Levintova, H. (2015, Nov. 17). Up to 240,000 women have tried to give themselves abortions in Texas and clinic closures may make it worse. *Mother Jones.* Retrieved from http://www.motherjones.com/politics/2015/11/thousands-texas-women-are-trying-self-induce-abortions/#

Levitin, D. (2007). *This is your brain on music: The science of a human obsession.* Penguin.

Levitin, D. (2015). *The organized mind: Thinking straight in the age of information overload.* New York, NY: Dutton Books.

Levitsy, S. R. (2014). *Caring for our own: why there is no political demand for new American social welfare rights.* Oxford, United Kingdom: Oxford University Press. Retrieved from http://www.oxfordscholarship.com/view/10.1093/acprof:oso/9780199993123.001.0001/acprof-9780199993123-chapter-3

Lewinson, T., & Bryant, L. O. (2012). There's no fresh air there: Narrative of smoke exposure. *Health & Social Work, 40*(2), 77–83.

Lewis, A. G. (2012). Ethics, activism and the anti-colonial: Social movement research as resistance. *Social Movement Studies, 11*(2), 227–240.

Lewis, C., Jr. (2013, August 7). A place at the policy table for social workers. Retrieved from http://www.socialjUStices-olutions.org/2013/08/07/a-place-at-the-policy-table-for-social-workers/

Lewis, C.P. (2017, February 1). The road to trans-inclusive health care: Policy implications and the critical role of social work. *Health & Social Work, 42*(1),60–62 doi: 10.1093/hsw/hlw056.

Lewis, T. (2015). For social workers, religion is the elephant in the room: Religion and spirituality can be helpful but are seldom discussed. *Consumer Affairs.*

Lewis, T. O. (2015). LGBT-affirming black churches' responses to the HIV/AIDS crisis. *Journal of Religion & Spirituality in Social Work & Social Thought, 34*(2), 140–157.

Li, J., Johnson, S. E., Han, W.-J., Andrews, S., Kendall, G., Strazdins, L., & Dockery, A. (2014). Parents' nonstandard work schedules and child well-being: A critical review of the literature. *Journal of Primary Prevention, 35*(1), 53–73.

Li, L., Lei, Y., Pan, D., Yu, C., & Si, C. (2016). Economic evaluation of the air pollution effect on public health in China's 74 cities. *SpringerPlus*, 5, 402.

Libal, K. R., Berthhold, S. M., Thomas, R. L., & Healy, L. M. (2014). *Advancing human rights in social work education.* Washington, DC: CSWE.

Liboro, R. M. (2015). Community-level interventions for reconciling conflicting religious and sexual domains in identity incongruity. *Journal of Religious Health, 54*, 1206–1220.

Lick D., Durso, L.E., & Johnson, K.L. (2013). Minority stress and physical health among sexual minorities. *Perspectives on Psychological Science, 8*(5), 521–548.

Life. (2015). Terracotta Army, 94, in Secrets of the Ancient World. Time Specials.

Liggan, D. Y., & Kay, J. (1999). Race in the room: Issues in the dynamic psychotherapy of African Americans. *Transcultural Psychiatry, 36*, 195.

Lightburn, A. & Sessions, P. (2005). *What is community-based clinical practice, in Handbook of Community-based clinical practice.* Oxford University Press.

Lima, A. (2017). President IFSW Europe, Ana Lima, welcome speech at European Conference of Social Work. Retrieved June 2, 2017, from http://ifsw/org/wp-content/uploads/2017

Lincoln, C. E., & Mamiya, L. H. (1990). *The black church in the African American experience.* Durham, NC: Duke University Press.

Lind, M. (2013). *Land of promise: An economic history of the US.* New York, NY: HarperCollins.

Lind, M. (2016). Is there too much democracy in America or too little? *The New York Times, Sunday Review*, 6–7.

Ling, A. (2016). Asian gangs & why join one? Retrieved from https://web.stanford.edu/class/e297c/poverty_prejudice/gangcolor/asiangang.htm

Lion, K. C., & Raphael, J. L. (2015). Partnering health disparities research with quality improvement science in pediatrics. *Pediatrics, 35*(2), 354–361.

Lipkin, E. (2009). *Girls' studies.* Berkeley, CA: Seal Press.

Liu, A. (2016). *Remaking economic development.* Brookings Institution.

Livestock Health, (2016). Livestock and animal health. Retrieved from http://www.fao.org/ag/againfo/themes/en/animal_health.html

Livingstone, G. (2014). *Fewer than half of U.S. kids today live in a traditional family.* Pew Research Center, Fact Tank. Retrieved from http://www.pewresearch.org/fact-tank/2014/12/22/less-than-half-of-u-s-kids-today-live-in-a-traditional-family/

Locke, K. (2015). Intersectionality and reflexivity in gender research: disruptions, tracing lines and Shooting arrows. *International Studies in Sociology of Education, 25*(3), 169–187.

Logan, S., & Freeman, E. (2004). Reconceptualizing the strengths and common heritage of Black families: Practice, research and policy issues. Springfield, IL: Charles Thomas.

Long, S., Volk, D., Baines, J., Tisdale, C. (2013). 'We've been doing it your way long enough': Syncretism as a critical process. *Journal of Early Childhood Literacy* 13(3) 418–439

Longden, E. (2013). *The voices in my head* [Video file]. Retrieved from https://www.ted.com/talks/eleanor_longden_the_voices_in_my_head

Lopez, G. (2016). Mass incarceration in America, explained in 22 maps and charts.Vox. Retrieved from https://www.vox.com/2015/7/13/8913297/mass-incarceration-maps-charts

Lopez, G., & Gonzalez-Barrera, A. (2016). Afro-Latino: A deeply rooted identity among U. S. Hispanics. Pew Research Center. Retrieved from http://www.pewresearch.org/fact-tank/2016/03/01/afro-latino-a-deeply-rooted-identity-among-u-s-hispanics/

Lopez, G., Ruiz, N.C., & Patten, E., (2017). Key facts about Asian Americans, a diverse and growing population. Pew Research Fact Tank. Retrieved Jan 9, 2018 from http://www.pewresearch.org/fact-tank/2017/09/08/key-facts-about-asian-americans/.

Luce, S. (2005). Lessons from living-wage campaigns. *Work & Occupations, 32*(4), 423–440.

Lugo-Ocando, J. (2014). *Blaming the victim: How global journalism fails those in poverty.* London, England: Pluto Press.

Lui, M., et al. (2014). The economic reality of being Asian American. In P. Rothenberg (Ed.), *Race, class and gender in the United States* (9th ed.). Duffield, United Kingdom: Worth.

Lukens, J.M. & Solomon, Pl (2013). Thinking through recovery: resolving ethical challenges and promoting social work values in mental health services. *Journal of Social Work Values & Ethics,* 10(1), 61–71.

Lum, D. (1986). *Social work with people of color: A process stage approach.* Pacific Grove, CA: Brooks/Cole.

Lum, D. (1999). *Culturally competent practice: A framework for growth and action.* Pacific Grove, CA: Brooks/Cole.

Ly, A., & Crowshoe, L. (2015). Stereotypes are reality: Addressing stereotyping in Canadian Aboriginal medical education. *Medical Education, 49,* 612–622.

Lyman, B. (2015, Oct. 20). Alabama will reopen closed DMV offices in black counties. *Governing.* Retrieved from http://www.governing.com/topics/politics/drivers-license-offices-will-reopen-on-limited-basis.html

Lynch, W. (2010). The Willie Lynch letter and the making of a slave. LaVergne, TN: BN Publishing.

Lysack, M.L. (2015). Effective policy influence and environmental advocacy; health, climate change and phasing out coal. *International Social Work, 58*(3), 436–447.

M'Bantu, A. (2012). *Unmistakably black: Sculpture and paintings from the world's first civilization.* London, England: Pomegranate.

M'Bantu, A. (2012a). *The ancient black Arabs.* London, England: Pomegrante Publishing.

M'Bantu, A. (2012b). *Unmistably Black: Sculpture and paintings from the world's first civilization.* London, England: Pomegrante Publishing.

Macgillis, A., & Propublica. (2016). The original underclass. *The Atlantic.* Retrieved from https://www.theatlantic.com/magazine/archive/2016/09/the-original-underclass/492731/

Mackenzie, I., Meyer, C., & Noble, S. (2013). How retailers can keep up with consumers. Retrieved from http://www.mckinsey.com/industries/retail/our-insights/how-retailers-can-keep-up-with-consumers

MacKinlay, E. (Ed.) (2008). *Ageing, disability and spirituality: addressing the challenge of disability in later life.* London, England: Jessica Kingsley Publishers.

Maclean, M., Sims, S., Bowen, C., Leonard, H., Stanley, F. J., & O'Donnell, M. (2017). Maltreatment risk among children with disabilities. *Pediatrics, 139*(4), 1–10.

MacLeod, J. (2009). *Ain't no makin' it: Aspirations & attainment in a low-income neighborhood.* Boulder, CO: Westview Press.

Madaniyazi, L., Guo, Y., Yu, W., & Tong, S. (2015). Projecting future air pollution-related mortality under a changing climate: Progress, uncertainties and research needs. *Environmental International, 75,* 21–32.

Madrigal, A.C. (2014). The racist housing policy that made your neighborhood. *The Atlantic.*

Magaña, L. (2013). SB 1070 and negative social constructions of Latino immigrants in Arizona. *Aztlán: A Journal of Chicano Studies, 38*(2), 151–159.

Maisano, N. (2016, October 8). Creating your personal leadership brand. Panelist. *Columbia University Alumni Leaders Conference,* New York.

Makaros, A., & Grodofsky, M.M. (2016). Social workers' conflict of loyalty in the context of social activism: The case of the 2011 social protests in Israel. *Journal of Community Practice, 24*(2), 147–165.

Makowski, A. C., Mnich, E. E., Ludwig, J., Daubmann, A. Bock, T., Lambert, M., & Knesebeck, O. V. (2016). Changes in beliefs and attitudes toward people with depression and schizophrenia—Results of a public campaign in Germany. *Psychiatry Research, 237,* 27–287.

Malhi, R. L., & Boon, S. P. (2007). Discourses of "democratic racism" in the talk of South Asian Canadian women. *Canadian Ethnic Studies, 39*(3).

Mallett, C. A. (2015). The school to prison pipeline: A critical review of the punitive paradigm shift. *Child & Adolescent Social Work Journal, 33,* 15–24.

Mallett, C. A., & Boitel, C. (2016). From juvenile offender institutions to residential treatment centers: Evidence of the shifting paradigm to improved youth and community outcomes *Journal of Evidence Informed Social Work, 13*(2).

Mander, M. S. (Ed.). (1999). *Framing friction: Media and social conflict*. Champaign: University of Illinois Press.

Mann, M., Hosman, C. M. H., Schaalma, H. P., & de Vries, N. K. (2004). Self-esteem in a broad-spectrum approach for mental health promotion. *Health Educational Research, 19*(4), 357–372.

Mapp, S. (2014). Human rights as a framework for teaching international social work. In K.R. Libal, M. Berthold, R.L. Thomas, & L.M. Healy, (Eds.), *Advancing human rights in social work education*, pp. 103–119. Alexandria, VA: Council on Social Work Education.

Marchforourlives.com. (2018). Mission Statement. Retrieved from https://marchforourlives.com/mission-statement/

Margolin, L. (1997). *Under the cover of kindness: The invention of social work*. University of Virginia Press.

Marija, M., & Rozman, K. (2015). Differences in the perceived benefits of membership among types of self-help and support groups. *Ljetopis Socijalnog Rada/Annual of Social Work, 22*(3), 351–370.

Marshall, F. (2014). *Quotable Elizabeth Warren*. New York, NY: Skyhorse.

Marshall, P. (Director). (1990). *Awakenings* [Film].

Marsiglia, F. F., & Kulis, S. (2015). *Diversity, oppression, and change* (2nd ed.). Chicago, IL: Lyceum Books, Inc.

Martin, D. (2008). Maat and order in African cosmology: A conceptual tool for understanding indigenous knowledge. *Journal of Black Studies, 38*(6), 951–967.

Martin, K. W. (2010). *Isabel Allende's House of the spirits trilogy (Narrative geographies)*. Rochester, NY: Tamesis Books.

Martinez, O., Wu, E., Sandfort, T., Dodge, B., Carballo-Dieguez, A., Pinto, R., … & Chavez-Baray, S. (2015). Evaluating the impact of immigration policies on health status among undocumented immigrants: A systematic review. *Journal of Immigrant Minority Health, 17*, 947–970.

Martinson, M. L., & Reichmann, N. G. (2016). Socioeconomic inequalities in low birth weight in the United States, the United Kingdom, American Canada, and Australia. *American Journal of Public Health, 106*(4), 748–758.

Mason, E., Williams, A., & Elliott, K. (2016, July 1). The dramatic rise in state efforts to limit LGBT rights. *The Washington Post*.

Mason, T., Caulfield, M., Hall, R., & Melling, K. (2010). Perceptions of diagnostic labels in forensic psychiatric practice: a survey of differences between nurses and other disciplines. *Issues in Mental Health Nursing, 31*, 336–344.

Masotti, P.J., Fick, R. & O'Connor, K. (2010) Healthy naturally occurring retirement communities: the need for increased collaboration between local public health agencies and municipal government. *Journal of Housing and the Elderly, 24*(3–4), 249–266.

Matejkowski, J. C., Johnson, T., & Severson, M. E. (2016). Prison social work. *The Encyclopedia of Social Work*. New York, NY: NASW and Columbia University Press.

Mathias, J. (2015). Thinking like a social worker: Examining the meaning of critical thinking in social work. *Journal of Social Work Education, 51*(3), 457–474.

Matthews, D. (2016). *Evicted: Poverty and Profit in the American City*. Crown Publishing.

Matthews, L., & Mahoney, A. (2005). Facilitating a smooth transition for immigrant Caribbean children: The role of teachers, social workers and related professional staff. *Journal of Ethnic & Cultural Diversity in Social Work, 14*(1/2), 69.

Maurrasse, D.J. (2016). *Beyond the campus: How colleges and universities form partnerships with their communities*. New York: Routledge.

Mayer, J. (2016). *Dark Money: The hidden history of billionaires behind the rise of the radical right*. Doubleday.

Mazumder, B. (2014). Black–white differences in intergenerational economic mobility in the United States. *Federal Reserve Bank of Chicago*, 1Q/Economic Perspectives, 1–19.

McBride, J. (1995). *The color of water: A black man's tribute to his white mother*. New York, NY: Riverhead Books.

McCabe, H.A. & Wahler, E.A. (2016). The affordable care act, substance use disorders, and low-income clients: Implications for social work. *Social Work, 61*(3), 227–232.

McCarthy, J. (2016). Americans' concerns about water pollution edge up. *Gallup News*.

McCarty, D. (2008). The impact of public housing policy on family social work theory and practice. *Journal of Family Social Work, 11*(1), 74–88.

McClain, R. (2009). *The role of spirituality, religiosity in the lives of people who are hearing impaired*. California State University, Long Beach, ProQuest Dissertations Publishing, 2009. 1466289.

McClelland, N., & Rizga, K. (2008, January 7). Top 10 youth activism victories in 2007. *The Nation*

McCoy, C., Woo, R., Anderson, C., & Lotfipour, S. (20 Race-related healthcare disparities among California workers: public health considerations for immigration reform, *Public Health in Emergency Medicine, 50(1), 159–166*.

McCoy, T. (2017). In former coal country, the working poor show open contempt for neighbors who seek handouts. *The Washington Post*. Retrieved from http://www.msn.com/en-us/news/us/in-former-coal-country-the-working-poor-show-open-contempt-for-neighbors-who-seek-handouts/ar-AAoxvtQ? li=BBnbfcL&ocid=mailsignout

McDaid, D., Oliveira, M. D., Jurczak, K., Knapp, M., & The Mheen Group. (2007). Moving beyond the mental health care system: An exploration of the interfaces between health and non-health sectors. *Journal of Mental Health, 16*(2), 181–194.

McDaniel, M., Simms, M., Monson, W., & Fortuny, K. (2013). Imprisonment and disenfranchisement of disconnected low-income men—Issue Brief 4. *Urban Institute*.

McDonough, W., & Braungart, M. (2002). *Cradle to cradle: Remaking the way we make things*. New York, NY: Farrar, Strauss, and Giroux.

McElheran, S. N., Soene, D., Newman, J., & McLaurin, D. (2012). Capturing the moment: The inaugural symposium on single session in therapy & walk in services on Phillips Island in Victoria, Australia.

McGaa, E. E. M. (1990). *Mother earth spirituality: Native American paths to healing ourselves and our world*. San Francisco, CA: Harper.

McGee, M. G. (2014). Lost in the margins? Intersections between disability and other nondominant statuses with regard to peer victimizations. *Journal of School Violence, 13*, 396–421.

McGeorge, C. R, Carlson, T. S., & Toomey, R. B. (2014). The intersection of spirituality, religion, sexual orientation and gender identity in family therapy training: An exploration of students' beliefs and practice. *Contemporary Family Therapy, 36*, 497–506.

McGovern, J. & Vinjamuri, M.K. (2016). Intergenerational practice with different LGBTQ cohorts: a strengths-based, affirmative approach to increasing well-being. *International Journal of Diverse Identities*, 16(3), 11–20.

McGrath, M. (2017, June 13). From activist to author: How 12-year-old Marley Dias is changing the face of children's literature. *Forbes*. Retrieved from https://www.forbes.com/sites/maggiemcgrath/2017/06/13/from-activist-to-author-how-12-year-old-marley-dias-is-changing-the-face-of-childrens-literature/#17526b744ce0

McIntosh, P. (2014). White privilege: Unpacking the invisible knapsack. In P. S. Rothenberg & K. S. Mayhew (Eds.), *Race, class and gender in the United States* (9th ed., p. 126). Gordonville, VA: Worth. (Original work published 1988)

McIntyre, J., Daley, A., Rutherford, K., & Ross, L. E. (2011). Systems-level barriers in accessing supportive mental health services for sexual and gender minorities: Insights from the provider's perspective. *Canadian Journal of Community Mental Health, 30*(2), 173.

McKay, S., & Bonner, S. (2002). Evaluating illness in women's magazines. *Journal of Language & Social Psychology, 21*(1), 53.

McKean, B.L. (2001). Harvard's shame. *The Nation*. Retrieved from http://www.hcs.harvard.edu/~pslm/livingwage/05_21_tn.html

McKnight, U. (2010). *The everyday practice of race in America: Ambiguous privilege*. New York, NY: Routledge.

McKown, C. & Strambler, M.J. (2009). Developmental antecedents and social and academic consequences of stereotype-consciousness in middle childhood. *Child Development*, 80(6), 1643–59.

McLaughlin, H., Brown, D., & Young, A. M. (2004). Consultation, community and empowerment: Lessons from the Deaf community. *Journal of Social Work, 4*(2), 153–165.

McLaughlin, K. (2005). From ridicule to institutionalization: Anti-oppression, the state and social work. *Critical Social Policy, 25*(3), 283–305.

McLuhan, M. (1964). *Understanding media*. Cambridge, MA: The MIT Press.

McMahon, Kenyon, & Carter. (2013). My culture, my family, my school, me: Identifying strengths and challenges in the lives and communities of American Indian youth. *Journal of Child & Family Studies, 22*, 694–706.

McMillin, S. E. (2014). Translating social work research for social justice: Focusing translational research on equity rather than the market. *Journal of Evidence Based Social Work, 11*(1–2), 148–156.

McNoll, A. (2016). Watch: Eileen Munro on bureaucracy, blame and building a better future for social work. *Community Care.co.uk*. Retrieved from http://www.communitycare.co.uk/2016/05/03/watch- eileen-munro-bureaucracy-blame-building-better-future-social work/

McNutt, J. (2013). Social work practice: History and evolution. *Encyclopedia of Social Work*. Retrieved from http://social-work.oxfordre.com/view/10.1093/acrefore/9780199975839.001.0001/acrefore-9780199975839-e-620

McNutt, J.G. (2013). History of social work. *Encyclopedia of Social Work*. Retrieved from http://socialwork.oxfordre.com/search?siteToSearch=oresw&q=history+of+social+work&searchBtn=Search&isQuickSearch=true

McQuiston, & McQuiston. (Creators & Producers). (1994). *Nature in Native American Art*. San Francisco, CA: Chronicle Books.

McWhirter, E. H., & McWhirter, B. T. (2016). Critical consciousness and vocational development among Latina/o high school youth: Initial development and testing of a measure. *Journal of Career Assessment, 24*(3), 543–558.

McWhirter, J. (2013). Juvenile delinquency and youth violence. In *At-risk youth: A comprehensive response—For counselors, teachers, psychologists, and human service professionals* (5th ed., p. 229). Belmont, CA: Brooks/Cole, Cengage Learning.

Meares, W. L., & Riggs, W. (2016). Walkability and the benefits of place-based housing: An examination of Louisville's HOPE VI neighborhoods. *Housing & Society, 43*(2), 103–125.

Medicare Henry J. Kaiser Family Foundation. Retrieved from https://www.kff.org/medicare/issue-brief/how-many-seniors-are-living-in-poverty-national-and-state-estimates-under-the-official-and-supplemental-poverty-measures-in-2016/

Mehrotra, N. (2016). *A resource book on disabilities studies in India*. Centre for the Study of Social Systems, School of Social Sciences. Jawaharlal Nehru University.

Mendes, P., Baidawi, S., & Snow, P. (2013). Young people transitioning from out-of-home care: A critical analysis of leaving care policy, legislation and housing supporting the Australian state of Victoria. *Child Abuse Review, 23*, 402–414.

Merriam-Webster.com. (2017). Homophobia. Retrieved from http://www.merriam-webster.com/dictionary/homophobia

Meyer, I. (2013). Prejudice, social stress, and mental health in lesbian, gay, and bisexual populations: Conceptual issues and research evidence. *Psychology of Sexual Orientation & Gender Diversity, 1*(S), 3–26.

Meyer, J, (2006). *Battlefield of the mind*. New York, NY: FaithWords.

Meyer, J. (2011, July 21). *Love out loud: Daily devotionals*. Hachette Book Group.

Meyers, J. (2015). Daily Devotional. Battlefield of the Mind.

Michael, A., & Bartoli, E. (2014). What white children need to know about race? *Independent School, 73*(4), 56–62.

michaelmoore.com (2016). 10 things they won't tell you about the Flint water tragedy. But I will. Retrieved from https://michaelmoore.com/10factsonflint/

Michaels, S. (2015). Maps: 10 years after Katrina, NOLA's poor neighborhoods are still largely abandoned: The Lower Ninth Ward only has a fraction of its pre-storm population. *Mother Jones*. Retrieved Jan 14, 2018 from http://www.motherjones.com/politics/2015/08/maps-10-years-after-hurricane-katrina-uneven-recovery-new-orleans/.

Mickel, E. (2002). African centered family healing: an alternative paradigm. *Journal of Health & Social Policy, 16*(1/2), 185–193; and Disability and the black community. In S. D. Miller (Ed.), *The Haworth Press* (pp. 185–193).

Mickel, E. (2013). African-centered reality therapy parenting: An alternative paradigm. *Journal of Human Behavior in the Social Environment, 23*(2), 278–286.

Micula, A. (2014. Social perception on social integration of people with disabilities. *Revista de Asistenț\ Social\, 3*, 57–68.

Middaugh, E., & Perlstein, D. (2005). Thinking and teaching in a democratic way: Hilda Taba. *Journal of Curriculum & Supervision, 20*(3), 234–256.

Middleton, J. (2015). Hands-on: Special education student learns life skills, confidence through jobs. Texarkana Gazette.com.

Miller, C. C., & Bui, Q. (2016, Feb. 27). Equality in marriage grows & so does class divide. *The New York Times*. The Upshot.

Miller, D. (2015). *The neighborhood tutoring program (NTP): A guide for establishing neighborhood tutoring programs*. WestBow Press.

Miller-Lachmann, L., & Taylor, L. S. (1995). *Schools for all: Educating children in a diverse society*. New York, NY: Delmar.

Milner, H. R., & Laughter, J. C. (2015). But good intentions are not enough: Preparing teachers to center race and poverty. *Urban Review, 47*, 341–363.

Minds Matter. (2014). Evidence-based treatments. Retrieved from http://www.ohiomindsmatter.org/documents/5c%20Evidence-Based%20Treatments.pdf

Mintz, S. & McNeil, S. (2013). Overview of the colonial era. Digital History, Bartleby.com. Retrieved Jan. 9, 2018 from https://www.bartleby.com/essay/Comparing-American-Slavery-and-the-Holocaust-FKG2SS57KU4Y.

Mishel, L. (2015). Causes of wage stagnation. *Economic Policy Institute.* Retrieved from http://www.epi.org/publication/causes-of-wage-stagnation/

Mishel, L. (2017). $15 minimum wage under attack. *Economic Policy Institute.*

MIT Open Courseware. (2017). Retrieved from http://ocw.mit.edu/courses/brain-and-cognitive-sciences.

Mitchum, P. (2013). 4 years later: Examining bias-motivated crimes against LGBT people. Center for American Progress. Retrieved from https://www.americanprogress.org/issues/lgbt/news/2013/10/31/78518/4-years-later-examining-bias-motivated-crimes-against-lgbt-people-after-the-shepard-byrd-act/

Mitman, H. (2016). Lawsuit alleges Philadelphia knew of and concealed lead contamination in drinking water. *Philly Voice.* Retrieved from http://www.phillyvoice.com/city-sued-over-concerns-lead-philadelphias-drinking-water/.

Mock, G. (2015). Tweedy and Brodhead on the many consequences of race in medicine. Retrieved from https://today.duke.edu/2015/10/tweedyrhbtalk

Mohanty, J. (2013). Ethnic & racial socialization and self-esteem of Asian adoptees: The mediating role of multiple identities. *Journal of Adolescence, 36*(1), 161–172.

Monchalin, R., Flicker, S., Wilson, C. Prentice, T., Oliver, V., Jackson, R., Larkin, Mitchell, C., Restoule, J.P., (2016). "When you follow your heart, you provide that path for others": indigenous models of youth leadership in HIV prevention. *International Journal of Indigenous Health,* 11(1), 135–158.

Mongeau, L. (2017). What happens when a regular high school decides no student is a lost cause? *High School Reform.*

Monroe, C. R. (2013). Discipline and diversity in the suburban U.S. south. *Race, Ethnicity and Education, 16*(2), 182–202.

Monrouxe, L & Poole, G. (2013). An onion: Conceptualizing and researching identity. *Medical Education,* 47, 425–429.

Moodley, R. (2005). Maat: An African centered paradigm for psychological & spiritual healing. *Integrating traditional healing practices into counseling & psychotherapy.* 210.

Moody, H. R. (Ed.). (2005). Religion, spirituality and aging: A social work perspective. *Haworth Social Work Practice & Journal of Gerontological Social Work, 45(1–2).*

Mooney, C. (2014). Scientists are beginning to figure out why conservatives are ... conservative [Blog post]. *Mother Jones.* Retrieved from http://www.motherjones.com/politics/2014/07/biology-ideology-john-hibbing-negativity-bias

Moore M, Cristofalo M, Dotolo D, Torres N, Lahdya A, Ho L, Vogel M, Forrester M, Conley B, Fouts S. (2017). When high pressure, system constraints, and a social justice mission collide: A socio-structural analysis of emergency department social work services. *Social Science & Medicine,* 178, 104–114.

Moreno, G., Lin, E. H., Change, E., Johnson, R. L., Berthoud, H., Solomon, C. C., & Morales, L. S. (2015). Disparities in the use of internet and telephone medication refills among linguistically diverse patients. *Journal of General Internal Medicine, 31*(30), 282–288.

Morgan, O., & Skelton, K. (Eds). (2014). *The Shriver report: A woman's nation pushes back from the brink—A study by Maria Shriver and the Center for American Progress.* Basingstoke, United Kingdom: Macmillan.

Morrow, A. (2003). Breaking the curse of Willie Lynch: The science of slave psychology. Rising Sun Publications.

Moselle, A. (2016). Pa. law allows sealing some old criminal records—and new sense of hope for the future. WHYY. Retrieved from https://whyy.org/articles/pa-law-allows-sealing-some-old-criminal-records-and-new-sense-of-hope-for-the-future/.

Mosley, W. (2006). *Fortunate son: A novel.* New York, NY: Back Bay Books.

Mowbray, C. T., Robinson, E. A. R., & Holter, M. (2002). Consumer drop-in centers: Operations, services and consumer involvement. *Health & Social Work,* 248–261.

Moyers, B. (1996). *Healing and the mind.* St. Charles, MO: Main Street Books.

Mueller. B. (2016.). Westbury schools agree to alter enrollment policies for immigrants. *The New York Times.*

Muhammad, K. (2012). Retrieved from http://billmoyers.com/segment/khalil-muhammad-on-facing-our-racial-past/

Mukoka/Reuters (2017). Kenya: Events of 2017. Human Rights Watch. Retrieved from http://africanarguments.org/2018/02/27/how-and-why-the-us-should-intervene-in-kenya/

Mundaca, L., Neij, L., Markandya, A., & Hennicke, P. (2016). Towards a soil energy economy? Assessing policy choices, strategies and transitional pathways. *Applied Energy*, 179, 1283–1292.

Munnell, A. H. (2004). Why are so many older women poor? Just the facts on Retirement Issues. Center for Retirement Research at Boston College.

Muravyev, A., & Oshchepkov, A. (2016). The effect of doubling the minimum wage on employment: Evidence from Russia. *IZA Journal of Labor & Development*, 5, 6.

Muro, M. (2016) Why noncompete pacts are bad for workers—and the economy. *Wall Street Journal*.

Murr, R. (2013). "I became proud of being gay and proud of being Christian": The spiritual journeys of queer Christian women. *Journal of Religion & Spirituality in Social Work: Social Thought*, 32, 349–372.

Murray, K. (2015). Social workers save lives. We are not child-snatchers or do-gooders. *The Guardian*. Retrieved from https://www.theguardian.com/society/2015/dec/08/social-workers-survey-not-child-snatchers-love-jobs-leave-sector

Museum of disABILITY History. (2014). About us. Retrieved from http://museumofdisability.org/virtual-museum/

Musgrave, C. F., Allen, C. E., & Allen, G. J. (2002). Spirituality and health and women of color. *Rural Health and Women of Color, American Journal of Public Health*, 92(4), 557–560.

Myers, J. S., & Caruso, C.C. (2016). Towards a public food infrastructure: Closing the food gap through state-run stores. *Geoforum, 72*, 30–33.

Myers, Meg A., (2016). *Climbing the mountain together: Social workers' constructions of positive reactions from trauma work* (Doctoral dissertation). Doctorate in Social Work (DSW) Dissertations. Paper 85. Retrieved from http://repository.upenn.edu/edissertations_sp2/85

Nadal, K. L., Davidoff, K. C., Davis, L. S., Wong, Y., Marshall, D., & McKenzie, V. (2015). A qualitative approach to intersectional microaggressions: Understanding influences of race, ethnicity, gender sexuality, and religion. *Qualitative Psychology, 2*(2), 147–163.

Nadal, K. L., Wong, Y., Sriken, J., Griffin, K., & Fuji-Doe, W. (2015). Racial microaggressions and Asian Americans: An exploratory study on within-group differences and mental health. *Asian American Journal of Psychology, 6*(2), 136–144.

Nadal, K., Davidoff, K. C., Davis, L. S., Wong, Y., Marshall, D., & McKenzie. (2015). Qualitative approach to intersectional microaggressions: Understanding influences of race, ethnicity, gender, sexuality and religion. *Qualitative Psychology, 2*(2), 147–163.

Nafizi, A. (2008). *Reading* Lolita *in Teheran*. New York, NY: Random House.

Nair, M. D., & Guerrero, E. G. (2014). *Evidence based macro practice in social work*. Wheaton, IL: Gregory Publishing

NAMI.org (n.d.). National Alliance of Mentally Ill. About us.

Narine, L., & Shobe, M. A. (2014). Making sense of housing disparities research: A review of health and economic inequities. *Social Work in Public Health, 29*, 35–41. Retrieved from https://surface.syr.edu/cgi/viewcontent.cgi?referer=https://www.google.com/&httpsredir=1&article=1004&context=nsd

Naseef, R. (2017). Fathers around the world are stepping up and raising children with autism. Retrieved from https://drrobertnaseef.wordpress.com/2017/06/14/fathers-are-stepping-up-around-the-world-and-raising-children-with-autism/

Nash, G.B. (1970). *Red, white & black: The Peoples of early America*. Englewood, NJ: Prentice-Hall.

NASW. (n.d.). NASW Code of Ethics. Retrieved from https://www.socialworkers.org/About/Ethics/Code-of-Ethics/Code-of-Ethics-English

NASW. (n.d.). *Cultural competence standards*. Retrieved from www.naswdc.org

NASW. (2013). NASW statement on Supreme Court's same-sex marriage rulings. Retrieved from http://www.naswdc.org/pressroom/2013/062613.asp

NASW. (2016). Women's access. Retrieved from http://www.socialworkblog.org/advocacy/2016/03/the-national-association-of-social-workers-supports-womens-access-to-birth-control/

NASW/PACE. (2018). Social Workers in State and Local Office. Retrieved from https://www.socialworkers.org/Advocacy/Political-Action-for-Candidate-Election-PACE/Social-Workers-in-State-and-Local-Office.

National Alliance on Mental Illness. (2010). National alliance on mental illness advocacy 2010: State statistics PA. Retrieved from http://www.nami.org

National Association of Social Work. (2017). Retrieved from https://www.socialworkers.org/

National Center for Child Poverty (NCCP). (2018). Child Poverty. Retrieved from http://www.nccp.org/topics/childpoverty.html.

National Center for Children in Poverty (NCCP). (2016). Columbia University. Retrieved from http://www.nccp.org/media/releases/release_34.html

National Center for Complementary and Alternative Medicine. (2017). Retrieved from https://nccih.nih.gov/health/integrative-health

National Center for Education Statistics (NCES). (2018). Public high school graduation rates. Retrieved from https://nces.ed.gov/programs/coe/indicator_coi.asp

National Coalition for the Homeless. (2009). Mental illness and homelessness. Retrieved from http://nationalhomeless.org/wp-content/uploads/2014/06/Mental_Illness-Fact-Sheet.pdf

National Conference of State Legislatures. (2017). Retrieved from http://www.ncsl.org/

National Conference of State Legislatures.org (2016). *Improving the health system.* Retrieved from http://www.ncsl.org/blog/2016/09/27/ncsl-report-details-state-strategies-to-improve-health-systems.aspx)

National Council on Disabilities. (2003). Understanding disabilities in American Indian & Alaska Native communities: Toolkit guide.

National Education Association. (2017). About National Education Association. Retrieved from nea.org.

National Geographic. (n.d.). The genographic project. Retrieved from https://www.nationalgeographic.org/education/genographic/

National Humanities Center.org. (2017). The making of African American Identity, Vol. 1, 1500–1865: African American community during slavery.

National Institute of Health (NIH). (n.d.). National Center for Complementary and Integrative Health. https://nccih.nih.gov/health/integrative-health

National Institute of Mental Health. National Institute of health. (2016). Grand Challenges in Global Mental Health. Retrieved from http://www.nimh.nih.gov/research-priorities/scientific-meetings/2016/grand-challenges/solving-the-grand-challenges-in-global-mental-health-maintaining-momentum-on-the-road-to-scale-up.shtm

National League of Cities. (2017). Land use and planning. Retrieved Aug. 25, 2017, from http://www.sustainablecitiesinstitute.org/topics/land-use-and-planninghttp://www.sustainablecitiesinstitute.org/topics/land-use-and-planning

National League of Cities. (2017, July 26). Addressing housing and health: How cities are making a difference [Webinar].

National Museum of the Native American. (2017). Martha Redbone. You tube, https://www.youtube.com/watch?v=TA5YR4MtBKU

National Network of Libraries of Medicine. (2017). Health literacy. Retrieved from https://nnlm.gov/professional-development/topics/health-literacy

National Scientific Council on the Developing Child. (2005/2014). *Excessive stress disrupts the architecture of the developing brain: Working paper 3.* Retrieved from http://www.developingchild.harvard.edu.

Native Partnerships. (n.d.). nrcprograms.org. Northern Plains Reservation Aid (NPRA). Formerly American Indian Relief Council (AIRC). Retrieved from http://nrcprograms.org/site/PageServer? pagename=airc_hist_boardingschools

Natland S., & Celik, H. D. (2015). Service users' self-narratives on their journey from shame to pride: Tales of transition. *Journal of Evidence-Informed Social Work, 12,* 50-63.

Navarro, M. (2014). For many Latinos, racial identity is more culture than color. In P. Rothenberg (Ed.), *Race, class and gender in the United States* (9th ed.). Duffield, United Kingdom: Worth.

Nebraska Studies.org. (n.d.). Native American citizenship: A long history of treaties. Retrieved from http://www.nebraskastudies.org/0700/stories/0701_0141.html

Neese, B. (2016). Intercultural communication: High- and low-context cultures. Posted August 17th, 2016 on http://online.seu.edu/high-and-low-context-cultures/

Neff, H. (2006). The Olmec and the origins of Mesoamerican civilization. *Antiquity* 80 (2006), 714–716.

Nelson, C., & McPherson, D. (2004). Contextual fluidity: An emerging model of helping, *Rural Social Work, 9,* 199-205.

Nelson, J. E. (1994). *Healing the split: Madness or transcendence? A new understanding of the crisis and treatment of the mentally ill.* New York, NY: Tarcher.

Neporent, L. (2015). Gender identity is biological, endocrine practice. *Good Morning America*. Retrieved from http://abcnews.go.com/Health/gender-identity-biological-study/story? id=29335854

Nesteruk, C., Helmstetter, N. M., Gramesu, A., Siam, M. H., & Price, C. (2015). Development of ethnic identity in young adults from immigrant families: "I want to hold onto my roots, but I also want to experience new routes." *Marriage & Family Review, 51*(5), 466–487.

Netting, F., & O'Connor, M. (2008). Recognizing the need for evidence-based macro practice in organizational and community settings. *Journal of Evidence-Based Social Work, 5*(3–4), 473–496.

Nevaer, L.E.V. (20210). Characteristics of Mexican & Caribbean Hispanics, Section 1. Excerpted from *Managing Hispanic and Latino Employees: A Guide to Hiring, Training, Motivating, Supervising, and Supporting the Fastest Growing Workforce Group*. San Francisco, CA: Berrett-Koehler.

New York Amsterdam News. (2009). Block association reclaims territory (p. 9).

Neweditionnet (n.d.) The white cane—clearing the way to independence. Retrieved Jan9, 2018 from http://www.neweditions.net/index.php/blogs/white-cane-clearing-way-independence.

Newsworks.org. (2016). *Pa. law allows sealing some old criminal records—and new sense of hope for the future*. Philadelphia Reentry Reporting Initiative. Retrieved from http://www.newsworks.org/index.php/local/harrisburg/98984-pa-law-allows-sealing-some-old-criminal-records-and-new-sense-of-hope-for-the-future-

Ng, S. L., Lingard, L., Hibbert, K., Regan, S., Phelan, S., Stooke, R., Meston, C., Schryer, C., Manamperi, M. & Friesen, F. (2015) Supporting children with disabilities at school: implications for the advocate role in professional practice and education, *Disability and Rehabilitation*, 37, 24.

Ngai F.W., Wong P.W., Chung K.F., & Leung K.Y. (2017). The effect of a telephone-based cognitive behavioral therapy on quality of life: a randomized controlled trial. *Archive of Women's Mental Health, 20*(3), 421–426.

Nguyen, V. T. (2015). The sympathizer. Grove Press.

NHMC-National Hispanic Media Coalition. (n.d.). Powerful Hispanic Heritage Tradition Launches in Orange County, CA. Retrieved from http://myemail.constantcontact.com/Powerful-Hispanic-Heritage-Tradition-Launches-in-Orange-County--CA.html?soid=1101346166756&aid=Dy-H9ijxjqQ&utm_content=bufferdf2f5&utm_medium=social&utm_source=twitter.com&utm_campaign=buffer.

Nickels, S. V., Arvaiza, F N. A., & Valle, M. S. R. (2016). A qualitative exploration of a family self-help mental health program in El Salvador. *International Journal of Mental Health Systems*, 10–26.

Nie, P. (2015). A monopoly of pollution emissions. *Journal of Environmental Planning & Management, 55*(6), 705–711.

Nielson, P. (2015). Making sense of implementation theories, models and frameworks *Implementation Science, 10*, 53–57.

NIH Reporter. (2015). Retrieved from https://projectreporter.nih.gov/reporter_searchresults.cfm

NIMH.com. (2015). Autism. Retrieved from http://www.nimh.nih.gov/health/topics/autism-spectrum-disorders-asd/index.shtml

Nomeland, M. M. & Nomeland, R. E. (2012). *The Deaf community in America: History in the making*. Jefferson, NC: McFarland.

Norris, J. (2012). State efforts to reduce racial disparities in criminal justice: Empirical analysis and recommendations for action. *Gonzaga Law Review, 47*, 493–530.

Norton, D. (1978). *Dual perspective*. New York, NY: Council on Social Work Education.

NPR. (2011). Comparing hate speech laws in the u.s. and abroad. Retrieved from https://www.npr.org/2011/03/03/134239713/France-Isnt-The-Only-Country-To-Prohibit-Hate-Speech

NPR. (2016). When 'Your Heart Is A Muscle,' Empathy Is A Revolutionary Act. Interview with Sunil Yapa.

NPR. (2016). America's "lead wars" go beyond Flint, Mich.: "It's now really everywhere." [Radio interview]. *Fresh air*. Retrieved from https://www.npr.org/sections/health-shots/2016/03/03/469039064/americas-lead-wars-go-beyond-flint-mich-its-now-really-everywhere

Nurius, P., Coffey, D.S., Fong, R., Korr, W.S., McCoy, R. (2017, Spring). Preparing professional degree students to tackle grand challenges: a framework for aligning social work curricula. *Journal of the Society for Social Work & Research, 8*(1), 99–118.

Nybell, L., Shook, J. J., & Finn, J. (2009). *Childhood, youth and social work in transformation: Implications for policy and practice*. New York, NY: Columbia University Press.

O'Connell, E. O., Stoneham, M., & Saunders, J. (2016). Planning for the next generation of public health advocates: Evaluation of an online advocacy mentoring program. *Health Promotion Journal of Australia, 27*, 43–47.

O'Dell, J. (2015). 10 steps to transform American society an outline for social transformation in the United States, inspired by South Africa's freedom charter. *The Nation*. Retrieved from https://www.thenation.com/article/beginning-see-light/.

O'Donnell, J. T. (2017, May 17). If employees trash your reputation online, science says do this. *Inc.com*.

O'Leary, M. (2017). Sen. Chris Murphy introduces act to help get mental health care for veterans. *New Haven Register*.

O'Leary, M. E. (2012). Coming to America: Mistreatment of immigrants is nothing new. *New Haven Register*. Retrieved from http://www.nhregister.com/article/NH/20120128/NEWS/301289921

O'Neal, E. S. S. (2013*). Indigosm music beats* [Video file]. Retrieved from http://pitchfork.com/tv/6-selector/732-the-underachievers-break-down-indigoism-beast-coast/? utm_campaign=search&utm_medium=site&utm_source=search-ac

O'Neal, G. S. (1984, Summer). Leaderstyle and community involvement. *Community Mental Health Journal, 20*(2).

O'Neal, G. S. (1998). *Hypersegregation*. Pasadena, CA: Salem Press.

O'Neal, G. S. (2010). Selecting perspectives and theories for ATOD practice. In A. Abbott (Ed.), *Alcohol, tobacco, and other drugs* (p. 31). Washington, DC: NASW Press.

O'Neal, G. S. (2012). Teaching note: Self-assessment and dialogue as tools for appreciating diversity. *Journal of Social Work Education, 48*(1), 159–165.

O'Neal, G. S. (2017). Multicultural resources database. West Chester University. Retrieved from http://subjectguides.wcupa.edu/c.php? g=61434&p=395263

O'Neal, G. S., & Reid, J. C. (1999). Parent education groups: Using cultural literature in the engagement phase. *Groupwork, 11*(2), 138–141.

O'Neal, G.S. (2009). Civic awareness: Student opinions about political participation. Unpublished manuscript.

O'Toole, C. J. (2004). The sexist inheritance of the disability movement. In B. G. Smith & B. Hutchison (Eds.), *Gendering disability* (p. 294). New Brunswick, NJ: Rutgers University Press.

Offermann, L. R., Basford, T. E., Graebner, R., Jaffer, S., De Graf, S. B., & Kaminsky, S. E. (2014). See no evil: Color blindness and perceptions of subtle racial discrimination in the workplace. *Cultural Diversity and Ethnic Minority Psychology, 20*(4), 499–507.

Office of Minority Mental Health. (2017). Cultural and linguistic competency. Retrieved from https://minorityhealth.hhs.gov/

Oh, J. S., & Au, T. K. (2005). Learning Spanish as a heritage language: The role of sociocultural background variables. *Language, Culture and Curriculum, 18*(3), 229–241.

Ohmer, M. (2008). Assessing and developing the evidence base of macro practice interventions with a community and neighborhood focus. *Journal of Evidence-Based Social Work, 5*(3–4), 519–547.

Okeke-Adeyanju, N., Taylor, L.C., Craig, A.B., Smith, R.E., Thomas, A., Boyle, A.E., & DeRosier, M.E.(2014). Celebrating the strengths of black youth: Increasing self-esteem and implications for prevention. *Journal of Primary Prevention*, 35(5), 357–369.

Oklahoma, T. (2013). Native Americans before European civilization [Video file]., Retrieved 6/14/15from https://www.youtube.com/watch? v=7FItlStGMY4https://www.youtube.com/watch? v=7FItlStGMY4.

Olivier, C. (2003). Population health: A potential approach for progressive social work. *Canadian Social Work Review*, 20(1), 25–38.

Ollstein, A. (2015). Alabama Addresses Voter Suppression by Keeping Rural DMVs Open One Day A Month. Thinkprogress.org.

Ollstein, A.M. & Lerner, K. (2016, November 15). Republicans were wildly successful at suppressing. opposition. *Thinkprogress*. Retrieved from https://thinkprogress.org/2016-a-case-study-in-voter-suppression-258b5f90ddcd/

Omer, A. (2015). The cry of the forgotten stones: The promise and limits of a Palestinian liberation theology as a method for peacebuilding. *Journal of Religious Ethics*, 43(2), 369–407.

Operario, D., Smith, C.D., Arnold, E., & Kegeles, S. (2010). The Bruthas Project: Evaluation of a community-based HIV prevention intervention for African American men who have sex with men and women. *AIDs Education Preview*, 22(1), 37–48.

Organization for Economic Cooperation & Development, (2018). About the OECD.

Ortiz, L., & Jani, (2010). Critical race theory: Transformational model for teaching diversity. *Journal of Social Work Education*, 46(2), 175–191. DOI: 10.5175/JSWE.2010.200900070 175

Ortiz, L., Garcia, B., & Hernandez, S. H. (2012). Why it is important for social work education to oppose racist-based anti-immigration legislation. *Journal of Social Work Education, 48*(2), 197.

Orwat, J., Caputo, N., Key, W., & De Sa, J. (2017). Comparing rural and urban cervical and breast cancer screening rates in a privately insured population, *Social Work in Public Health*, 32(5), 1-13.

Orwell, G. (1949). *1984*. London, England: Harvill Secker.

Otsuka, J. (2002). *When the emperor was divine*. New York, NY: Alfred Knopf.

Oxhandler, H. K., & Pargament, K. I. (2014). Social work practitioners' integration of clients' religion and spirituality in practice: A literature review. *Social Work, 59*(3), 271.

Paasche-Orlow, (2004). The ethics of cultural competence. *Academic Medicine, 79*(4), 347-50

Pace, P. R. (2016, November 1). Grand challenges meeting focuses on policy. *National Association of Social Workers News*. Retrieved from http://digitaledition.qwinc.com/publication/?i=355494#{%22issue_id%22:355494,%22page%22:2}

Padden, C., & Humphries, T. (1988). *Deaf in America: Voices from a culture*. Cambridge, MA: Harvard University Press.

Padela, A., Pruitt, L., & Mallick, S. (2017). The types of trust involved in American Muslim healthcare decisions: an exploratory qualitative studies. *Journal of Religion & Health*, Springer.

Pande, R. (2009). Women in a woeful world: Coming to terms with oppression. *Harvard Magazine*, September/October. Retrieved from http://harvardmagazine.com/2009/09/book-review-half-the-sky

Papouli, E. (2016). Using the critical incident technique (CIT) to explore how students develop their understanding of social work values and ethics in the workplace during their final placement. *Journal of Social Work Values & Ethics, 13*(2), 56-72.

Parisi, R. (2015). Practices and rhetoric of migrants' social exclusion in Italy: Intermarriage, work & citizenship as devices for the production of social inequalities. *Identities, 22*(6), 739-756.

Parry, M. (2012). The neighborhood effect. *The Chronicle of Higher Education*.

Parsell, C., Petersen, M., & Mouton, O. (2016). Single site supportive housing: Tenant perspectives. *Housing Studies, 30*(8), 1189-1209.

Patel, V. (2012). Vikram Patel: Mental health for all by involving all [TED Talk]. Retrieved from http://www.ted.com/talks/vikram_patel_mental_health_for_all_by_involving_all.

Pateman, C. (1970). *Participation and democratic theory*. Cambridge, United Kingdom: Cambridge University Press.

Patterson, G.T. (2008). Police social work Police Social Work: NASW. Retrieved from http://www.naswnyc.org/?Page=77.

Patterson, T. (2012). *Social work practice in the criminal justice system*. New York: Routledge.

Patton, S. (2007). *That mean old yesterday*. New York, NY: Washington Square Press.

Paul, R., & Elder, L. (1999). *Critical thinking: Concepts & tools (Thinker's Guide series)*. Tomales, CA: Foundation for Critical Thinking.

Pelletier, E. (2016). *What do victims want from criminal justice reform?* Retrieved from http://www.urban.org/urban-wire/what-do-victims-want-criminal-justice-reform

Peña, R. P. (2015, July 31). St. Louis county biased against black juveniles, justice department finds. *The New York Times*.

Pendall, R., & Hendey, L. (2016, October 26). *Revitalizing neighborhoods*. Urban Institute.

Pérez, L. M., & Martinez, J. (2008). Community health workers: Social justice and policy advocates for community health and well-being. *American Journal of Public Health, 98*(1), 11-14.

Perry, A.M. (2018). Who deserves credit for African American employment? Brookings.edu. Retrieved from https://www.brookings.edu/blog/the-avenue/2018/02/01/who-deserves-credit-for-african-american-employment/?utm_campaign=Brookings%20Brief&utm_source=hs_email&utm_medium=email&utm_content=60420238

Perry, S. (2013). *Magnet school principal: Steve Perry, a rebel with a cause*. Retrieved from http://articles.courant.com/2013-11-24/news/hc-steve-perry-education-reform-1123-20131124_1_school-reform-efforts-diane-ravitch-hartford

Persell, C. H. (1990). Becoming a member of society through socialization. In *Understanding society: An introduction to sociology* (3rd ed., pp. 98-107). New York, NY: Harper & Row.

Petersen, J. L. (2015). White privilege chaos sweeps schools nationwide. Experts slam transition from education to racial indoctrination. *WND, 52*(3), 409-416. Retrieved from http://www.wnd.com/2015/06/white-privilege-chaos-sweeps-schools-nationwide/

Peterson, B., Fontaine, J., Kurs, E., & Cramer, L. (2015). Children of incarcerated parents framework. *Urban Institute.*

Petry, A. (1997). *The street.* Boston, MA: Houghton Mifflin.

Pew Research Center. (2013). Economies of emerging markets better rated during difficult times. Retrieved from http://www.pewglobal.org/2013/05/23/economies-of-emerging-markets-better-rated-during-difficult-times/

Pew Research Center. (2013). The rise of Asian Americans. Retrieved from http://www.pewsocialtrends.org/2012/06/19/the-rise-of-asian-americans/

Pew Research Center. (2014). How Americans feel about religious groups. Retrieved from http://www.pewforum.org/2014/07/16/how-americans-feel-about-religious-groups/

Pew Research Center. (2014). The shifting religious identity of Latinos in the United States nearly one-in-four Latinos are former Catholics. Retrieved from http://www.pewforum.org/2014/05/07/the-shifting-religious-identity-of-latinos-in-the-united-states/.

Pew Research Center. (2015, June 11). *Multiracial Americans.* Pewresearch.org. Retrieved from http://www.pewsocialtrends.org/2015/06/11/multiracial-in-america/.

Pew Research Center. (2015). Parenting in America. *Social and Demographic Trends.* Retrieved from http://www.pewsocialtrends.org/2015/12/17/1-the-american-family-today/

Pew Research Center. (2016b) Discrimination and racial inequality. http://www.pewsocialtrends.org/2016/06/27/3-discrimination-and-racial-inequality/.

Pew Research Center. (2016). On views of race and inequality, blacks and whites are worlds apart: About 4 in 10 blacks are doubtful that the U.S. will ever achieve racial equality. Retrieved from http://www.pewsocialtrends.org/2016/06/27/on-views-of-race-and-inequality-blacks-and-whites-are-worlds-apart/

Pew Research Center. (2016). Table 7.2. A majority of blacks say they have faced racial discrimination; Table 7.3 Naturalization of Mexicans. Retrieved from http://www.pewsocialtrends.org/2016/06/27/5-personal-experiences-with-discrimination/

Pew Research Center. (2016). The gender gap in religion around the world. Retrievd from http://www.pewforum.org/2016/03/22/the-gender-gap-in-religion-around-the-world/

Pew Research Hispanic Center. (2007). National survey of Latinos.

Pham, A. X. (2007). From Catfish and Mandala: A two-wheeled voyage through the landscape and memory of Vietnam, "Last Gamble." In F. Adiele & M. Frosch (Eds.), *Coming of age around the world: A multicultural anthology.* New York, NY: The New Press.

Pharr, S. (2010). Reflections on liberation. In M. Adams, W. J. Blumenfeld, C. Castañeda, H. W. Hackman, M. L. Peters, & X. Zúñiga (Eds.), In *Readings for diversity and social justice* (2nd ed.; p. 591). New York, NY: Routledge.

Phinney, J. S. (1989). Stages of ethnic identity development in minority group adolescents. *Journal of Early Adolescence.* 9(1/2), 34–49.

Phinney, R. (2016). Advocacy for the poor: Organized interests and social policymaking in the American states. *American Politics Research, 44*(5), 903–938.

Pickerill, J., & Krinsky, J. (2012). Why does Occupy matter? *Social Movement Studies, 11*(3–4), 279–287.

Pickering, D. (2012). *Dictionary of Superstitions.* Buckingham, UK: Cassell.

Piepzna-Samarasinha, L. L. (2002). browngirlworld. In D. Hernández & B. Rehman (Eds.), *Colonize this! Young women of color on today's feminism.* Berkeley, CA: Seal Press.

Piketty, T. (2014). New thoughts on capital in the twenty-first century [Video file]. Retrieved from https://www.ted.com/talks/thomas_piketty_new_thoughts_on_capital_in_the_twenty_first_century

Pilkington, E. (2009). Police arrest prominent black history scholar for breaking into own home. Retrieved from https://www.theguardian.com/world/2009/jul/21/henry-louis-gates-jr-arrest-harvard

Pinsky, H.T., Shepard, M.E., Bird, E.R., Gilmore, A.K., Norris, J., Davis. K.C., George, W.H. (2016). Differences in mental health and sexual outcomes based on type of nonconsensual sexual penetration. *Violence Against Women,* 23(9), 1039–1054.

Pinto, P.E. Sahur, N. (2001). Working with people with disabilities: an Indian perspective. Retrieved from http://cirrie-sphhp.webapps.buffalo.edu/culture/monographs/india.php

Pippard, J., & Bjorkland, R. (2003). Identifying essential techniques of community practice. *Journal of Community Practice.* 11(4), 101–115.

Plessy v. Ferguson, 1896. (2014). In P. Rothenberg with K. Mayhew (Eds.), *Race, class and gender in the United States* (pp. 547–549). Duffield, United Kingdom: Worth.

Plucinska, J. (2015). Study says white extremists have killed more Americans in the U.S. than Jihadists since 9/11. *Time.com*

Pointer, N. I. (2010). *The history of white people*. New York, NY: W. W. Norton.

Poitier, D. (2007). *The measure of a man: A spiritual autobiography*. San Francisco, CA: Harper.

Policy Press. (2009). Lesson from the literature. *Evidence & Policy, 5*(3), 305–326.

Pols, H. (2007). August Hollingshead and Frederick Redlich: Poverty, socio-economic status & mental illness. *American Journal of Public Health, 97*(10), 17–55.

Poo, A. J. (2016, Sept. 1). Facing race: Ai-jen Poo and Kai Wright on race, gender, and employment [Podcast]. *Race Forward*. Retrieved from https://www.raceforward.org/media/facing-race-stories-voices

Pooley, K. (2015). Segregation's new geography: the Atlanta metro region, race, and the declining prospects for upward mobility. *Southern Spaces.com*

Pope Francis. (2015, Sept. 26). Speech. Retrieved from http://www.phillyvoice.com/transcript-pope-francis-festival-families-speech/

Porter, A. (1997). Cultural imperialism' and protestant missionary enterprise, 1780–1914. *The Journal of Imperial & Commonwealth History. 25*(3), 367–391.

Porter, E. (2016). We've seen the Trump phenomenon before. *New York Times.*

Porter, E. (2016). With competition in tatters, the rip of inequality widens. *New York Times.com*

Portes, A. (2014). Immigration's aftermath. In P. Rothenberg with K. Mayhew (Eds.), *Race, class and gender in the United States* (p. 397). Duffield, United Kingdom: Worth.

Posey-Maddox, L. (2016). Beyond the consumer: Parents, privatization, and fundraising in US urban public schooling. *Journal of Education Policy, 31*(2), 178–197.

Poussaint, A. (1974). Building a strong self-image in black children. *Ebony Magazine,* 138–143.

Powell, A., Davies, H., & Nutley, S. (2017). Missing in action? The role of the knowledge mobilisation literature in developing knowledge mobilisation practices. *Evidence & Policy: A Journal of Research, Debate & Practice, 13*(2), 201–223.

Power, A., Bartlett, R., & Hall, E. (2016). Peer advocacy in a personalized landscape: The role of peer support in a context of individualized support and austerity. *Journal of Intellectual disabilities, 20*(2), 183–193.

Prizant, B. B. (2015). *Uniquely human: a different way of seeing autism.* New York, NY: Simon & Schuster.

Probst, B. (2010). Implicit and explicit use of the strengths perspective in social work education. *Journal of Teaching in Social Work,* 30, 648–484.

Project Implicit. (2011). About the IAT. Retrieved from https://implicit.harvard.edu/implicit/iatdetails.html

Project Implicit. (2011). Implicit association test. Retrieved from https://implicit.harvard.edu/implicit/demo/copyright.html

Project Implicit (2017). Retrieved 1.7.2018 from https://implicit.harvard.edu/implicit/.Rampell, C. (2013). U.S. women on the rise as family breadwinner. *The New York Times.*

Psychodynamic Practice Individuals, Groups and Organisations, 18(2), 181–194.

Ptashnick, M., & Zuberi, D. (2015) Certifying voluntary living wage employers, International Journal of Sociology and Social Policy, 35(9/10), .618–634, https://doi.org/10.1108/IJSSP-09-2014-0070

Puett, M., & Gross-Loh, C. (Trans.). (2016). *Confucius, Mencius, Laozi, Zhuangzi, Xunzi: Selected passages from the Chinese philosophers in the path.* New York, NY: Simon & Schuster.

Putnam, R. (2015). *Our kids: The American dream in crisis.* New York, NY: Simon & Schuster.

Putrie, J. (2014). How to turn "What's wrong with you?" into "What happened to you?" *Philadelphia Inquirer.* Retrieved Nov. 28, 2015, from http://www.philly.com/philly/blogs/public_health/How-to-turn-Whats-wrong-with- you-into-What-happened-to-you.html

Quélin, B., Kivleniece, I., & Lazzarini, S. (2017). Public–private collaboration, hybridity and social value: Towards new theoretical perspectives. *Journal of Management Studies, 54*(6), 763–792.

Quigley, D. (2016). Applying "place" to research ethics and cultural competence/humility training. *Journal of Academic Ethics*, published online 13 January, SPringer.

Radio Times. (2016, May 20). How poverty affects health [Podcast]. Retrieved from http://whyy.org/cms/radiotimes/2016/05/25/how-poverty-hurts-kids-health/

Ramakrishnan, U., & Cerisola, M. (2004). Regional economic disparities in Australia. *International Monetary Fund*, WP/04/144.

Ramanathan, G. (2012). *Locating gender in modernism: The outsider female.* New York, NY: Routledge.

Ramirez, L. M. (2004). *Keepers of the children: Native American wisdom and parenting.* Chicago, IL: Walk in Peace Productions.

Randall, M. (2012). Six exercises for mastering cultural agility. *FastCompany.com.*

Ranesh, R. (2011). Income equality growing faster in the UK than any other rich country. *The Guardian.com.*

Rapaport, L. (2016). Many depressed teens don't get needed treatment. *Reuters Health News.*

Rasmus, S., Allen, J., Connor, W., Freeman, W., & Skewes, M. and the Native Tribal Council Action Board. (2014). Native transformations in the Pacific Northwest: A strength-based model of protection against substance use disorder. *American Indian & Alaska Native Mental Health Research*, 159.

Rasmussen, D. (2012). *The untold story of America's largest slave revolt.* New York, NY: Harper.

Ratner, A. R., & Kalman, J. S. (2016). Breakers, benders, and obeyers. *Education Policy Analysis Archives, 24*(35), 2–25.

Rauscher, L., & McClintock, J. (1996). Ableism curriculum design. In M. Adams, L. A. Bell, & P. Griffen (Eds.), *Teaching for Diversity and Social Justice* (pp. 198–231). New York, NY: Routledge.

Razgale, I., Kokarevica, A., & Bolsteina, G. (2014). Importance of social work intervention: Social and economic benefits, SHS Web of Conferences. 10, 00036 DOI: 10.1051/shsconf/20141000036

Razza, R. A., Bergen-Chen, D., & Raymond, K. (2015). Enhancing preschooler's self-regulation via mindful yoga. *Journal of Child and Family Studies, 24*, 372–385

Reamer, F. C. (2005). Social work values & ethics: Reflections on the profession's odyssey. *Advances in Social Work, 6*(1), 24–32.

Reeves, R. V. (2017). *Dream hoarders: How the American upper middle class is leaving everyone else in the dust, why that is a problem and what to do about it.* Washington, DC: Brookings Press.

Reeves, R., & Rodriguez, E. (2016). Black wealth barely exists in one terrible chart. *Brookings.* Retrieved from http://www.huffingtonpost.com/entry/black-opportunity-wealth_us_568c44cee4b0c8beacf4a391 (See also Social Mobility Blog, http://www.brookings.edu/blogs/social-mobility-memos)

Reference Chart Of Disorders And Evidence-Based Treatments, http://vcoy.virginia.gov/documents/collection/Reference%20Chart%20of%20Disorders%20and%20Evidence-based%20Treatments_1.pdf

Reid-Merritt, P. (2010). *Righteous self- determination: The Black social work movement in America.* Baltimore, MD: Imprint.

Reisch, M. (2009). Social worker, unions and low wage workers: A historical perspective. *Journal of Community Practice, 17*, 50–72.

Reisch, M. (2014). The boundaries of social justice: Addressing the conflict between human rights and multiculturalism in social work education. In K. Libal & S. M. Berthold (Eds.), *Advancing human rights in social work education.* Alexandria, VA: CSWE.

Resnick, D. B. (2015). What is ethics in research and why is it important? National Institution of Environmental Health Sciences. Retrieved from htttp://www.niehs.nih.gov/research/resources/bioethics/whatis/

Retrieved 1.6.2018 from https://www.forbes.com/sites/erincarlyle/2013/05/22/power-woman-helene-gayle-how-to-make-the-greatest-impact-on-the-most-people/#2f33d65b354f

Retrieved from http://reading.wickedlocal.com/news/20161017/sitting-in-new-look-at-social-work

Retrieved from http://rooseveltinstitute.org/reforming-taxation-promote-growth-and-equity/

Retrieved from http://www.oecd.org/about/

Retrieved from http://www.socialjusticesolutions.org/2016/10/20/denying-poor-people-health-care-defies-logic/

Retrieved from https://deserthopetreatment.com/drug-abuse/other-countries-treatment/.

Retrieved from https://www.bostonglobe.com/opinion/editorials/2015/04/17/teach-civics-schools-but-right/uZ7CAOtKwrpLDZXOxi06BI/story.html.

Retrieved from https://www.dol.gov/ofccp/regs/compliance/faqs/PayTransparencyFAQs.html#Q0.

Retrieved from https://www.theatlantic.com/education/archive/2017/07/the-education-perception-gap/533898/.

Retrieved from https://www.theatlantic.com/science/archive/2017/01/government-accountability-psychology/512888/.

Retrieved from https://www.thenation.com/article/top-10-youth-activism-victories-2007/

Retrieved from https://www.urban.org/research/publication/revitalizing-neighborhoods

Retrieved Jan. 9, 2018 from http://www.historynet.com/abolitionist-movement.

Retrieved on 1.7.2018 from https://www.chronicle.com/article/Can-We-Really-Measure-Implicit/238807.

Reuters. (2015). Surgery and sterilization scrapped in Malta's benchmark LGBTI law. *The New York Times*.

Rhodan, M (2014). Study: Hard times can make people more racist. Time.com. Retrieved from http://time.com/2850595/race-economy/

Rich, M. (2016). Charter schools suspend black and disabled students more, study says. *The New York Times*.

Rienzi, E. S. (2009). A part yet apart: Exploring racial and ethnic identities for adult Asian transracial adoptees. Conference Papers. American Sociological Association, 2163.

Riera, A., Borrell, N., Argudo, J. L., Pérez, A., Ricart, N., & García, J. J. (2016). Challenges and achievements in integrated care: Different health and social care providers working together–Successful projects that show that this is the way. 16th International Conference on Integrated Care, Barcelona.

Rigard, T.J, Laracy, S.D., DuPaul, G.J., Shapiro, E.S., & Power, T.J. (2015). Trauma-informed care in schools: a social justice imperative. *Communique*, 44(2).

Riggs, M. (Director). (1986). *Ethnic notions*.

Rios, V. (2011). *Punished: Policing the lives of black and Latino boys—New perspectives of crime, deviance & law*. New York: New York University Press.

Ritter, J.A. (2016). A national study predicting licensed social workers' levels of political participation: The role of resources, psychological engagement, and recruitment networks. *Social Work*, 53(4), 347–357.

Robbie, S. (2017). Random act of Mendez. Retrieved from https://www.randomactofmendez.us/?%20utm_campaign=8.17%2BRandom%2BE-Blast&utm_medium=email&utm_source=8.17%2BE-Blast%2BRandom%2BAct

Robbins, K. G. (2017, June 23). The media narrative around families is racist and homophobic. It needs to stop. *talkpoverty.org*. Retrieved from https://talkpoverty.org/2017/06/23/media-narrative-around-families-racist-homophobic-needs-stop/

Robbins, T. (2012, August). The American food revolution: A call to action from James Robbins. *Utne Reader*.

RobbinsList (2017). *Black women in medicine* documentary by local filmmaker—airs Wednesday on public television. URU the right to be, Inc. https://urutherightobe.org/. Retrieved from http://www.changingthefaceofmedicine.org

Roberto, C. A., Pomerantz, J. L., & Fisher, J. O. (2014). The need for public policies to promote healthier food consumption: A comment on Wansink and Chandon. *Journal of Consumer Psychology*, 24(3), 438–445.

Roberts-DeGennaro, M. (2008). Evidence-based (informed) macro practice paradigm: Integration of practice expertise and research. *Journal of Evidence-Based Social Work*, 5(3–4), 407–422.

Robertson, D. (2000). *Denmark Vesey: The buried story of America's largest slave rebellion and the man who led it*. New York, NY: Vintage.

Robertson, S. (2015). The production of the Indian student: Regimes and imaginaries of migration, education citizenship and class. *Cosmopolitan Civil Societies Journal*, 7(3), 4508–4511.

Robinson, L. (2012). Identity development and transracial/ethnic adoption: Some challenges for practice. *Asia Pacific Journal of Social Work & Development*, 22(1–2), 116–126.

Robinson, R. (1999). *Defending the spirit: A black life in America*. New York, NY: Plume.

Robinson-Wood, T. L. (2011). "It makes me worry about her future pain": A qualitative investigation of white mothers of non-white children. *Women & Therapy*, 34(4), 331–344.

Rocco, T. S., & Delgado, A. (2011). Shifting lenses: A critical examination of disability in adult education. In T. S. Rocco (Ed.), *Challenging ableism, understanding disability, including adults with disabilities in workplaces and learning spaces* (pp. 1–20). San Francisco, CA: Jossey-Bass.

Rock, C. (Creator, Producer), & LeRoi, A. (Creator). (2005). *Everybody Hates Chris!* [Television series]. Hollywood, CA: CR Enterprises.

Rockenbach, A.N., & Crandall, R.E. (2016). Faith and LGBTQ inclusion: Navigating the complexities of the campus spiritual climate in Christian higher education. *Christian Higher Education*, 15(1–2), 62–71. doi:10.1080/15363759.2015.1106355

Rodriquez, A. (2001). *The Buddha book: A novel.* New York, NY: Picador Press.

Rodriquez, L. J. (1993). *Always Running: La Vida Loca, Gang Days in L.A.* Willimantic, CT: Curbstone Press.

Roediger, D. R., & Esch, E. D. (201). *The production of difference: Race & management of labor in US history.* New York, NY: Oxford University Press.

Roediger, D. R., & Esch, E. D. (2012). *The production of difference: Race & management of labor in US history.* Oxford, United Kingdom: Oxford University Press.

Roets, G., Rutten, K., Roose, R., Vandekinderen, C., & Soetaert, R. (2015). Constructing the "child at risk" in social work reports: A way of seeing is a way of not seeing. *Children & Society, 29,* 198–208.

Rogowski, S. (2011). Managers, managerialism and social work with children and families: The deformation of a profession? *Practice-Social Work in Action,* 23(3), 157–167.

Rohter, L. (2013). *Captivity as a mirror of society: Liao Yiwu's "For a Song and a Hundred Songs." New York Times* Books. Retrieved Nov. 16, 2015, from http://www.nytimes.com/2013/07/03/books/liao-yiwus-for-a-song-and-a-hundred-songs.html?_r=0

Rollins, C. (1731). The ancient history of the Egyptians, Carthaginians, Assyrians, Babylonians, Medes and Lydians. Retrieved from https://www.gutenberg.org/files/28558/28558-pdf.pdf

Roman, J.K. (2013, July 26). Race, justifiable homicide, and stand your ground laws: analysis of FBI supplementary homicide report data. Washington, D.C: Urban Institute. Retrieved from https://www.urban.org/research/publication/race-justifiable-homicide-and-stand-your-ground-laws

Rome, S.H. & Hoechstetter, S. (2010). Social work and civic engagement: The political participation of professional social workers. *Journal of Sociology and Social Welfare.* 37(3), 107–12.

Romero, J. (2011). American holocaust of Native American Indians. Retrieved from American holocaust of Native American Indians.

Romilă, D., & Roman, A. M. (2015). The social worker—A major player in the integration of students with mental disabilities in mainstream schools. *Revista de Asistenţă Socială, 24*(3), 163–171.

Rönnlund, A. R. (2017). See how the rest of the world lives, organized by income. [TED Talk]. Dollar Street

Roozen, D. A. (2015). American congregations, 2015: Thriving and surviving. Retrieved from www.faithcommunitiestoday.org

Rosenfeld, J., Denice, P., & Laird, J. (2016, August 30). Union decline lowers wages of nonunion workers: The overlooked reason why wages are stuck and inequality is growing. *Economic Policy Institute.* Retrieved from https://www.epi.org/publication/union-decline-lowers-wages-of-nonunion-workers-the-overlooked-reason-why-wages-are-stuck-and-inequality-is-growing/.

Rosenkoetter, S. E., Hains, A. H., & Dogaru, C. (2007). Successful transitions for young children with disabilities and their families: Roles of school social workers. *Children & Schools, 29*(1), 25–34.

Rosenthal, B.M. & Barned-Smith, S.J. (2016). Denied: Houston schools systematically block disabled kids from special ed. *Houston Chronicle.*

Roser, M., & Ortiz-Ospina, E. (2017). Global extreme poverty. Retrieved from https://ourworldindata.org/extreme- poverty/

Ross, E. L. (1978). *Black heritage in social work: 1860 to 1930.* Lanham, MD: Scarecrow Press.

Ross, H. (2016). *Everyday bias: Identifying & navigating unconscious judgments in our daily lives.* Lanham, MD: Rowman & Littlefield.

Rossatto, C. A. (2014). Global activism and social transformation vis-á-vis dominant forms of economic organization: Critical education within Afro-Brazilian and transnational pedagogical praxis. *Perspectives on Global Development and Technology, 13,* 151–175.

Rothenberg, P. S. (2014). Introduction. In P. Rothenberg with K. Mayhew (Eds.), *Race, class and gender,* (9th ed., pp. 7–12). Duffield, United Kingdom: Worth.

Rothstein, R. (2013). For public schools, segregation then, segregation since. Education and the unfinished march. *Economic Policy Institute.*

Rothstein, R. (2014, October 15). The making of Ferguson public policies at the root of its troubles. *Economic Policy Institute.* Retrieved from https://www.epi.org/publication/making-ferguson/

Rowe, W., Hanley, J., Moreno, E. R., & Mould, J. (2000). Voices of social work practice: International reflections on the effects of globalization. *Social Work and Globalization,* Special Issue, July, 65–87.

Ruggiano, M., Shtompel, N., Whiteman, K. & Sias, K. (2017). Influences of transportation on health decision making and self-management behaviors among older adults with chronic conditions. *Behavioral Medicine, 43*:1, 61–70, DOI:10.1080/08964289.2015.1065788.

Rukmini, S. (2014). India's staggering wealth gap in 5 charts. *TheHindu.com.* Retrieved from http://www.thehindu.com/data/indias-staggering-wealth-gap-in-five-charts/article6672115.ece

Rupp, G. (2016, Mar. 4). Tripodi lecture by Dr. George Rupp, President Emeritus of Columbia University.

Ruscio, J. (2004). Diagnoses and the behaviors they denote: A careful evaluation of the labeling theory of mental illness. *The Scientific Review of Mental Health Practice, 3*(1), 5–11.

Russell, L. (1988). *Inheriting our mothers' gardens: Feminist theology in Third World perspective.* Louisville, KY: Westminster John Knox Press.

Ruth, B. J., Marshall, J. W., Velasquéz, E. E. M., & Bachman, S. (2015). Teaching note-educating public health social work professionals: Results from a MSW/MPH program outcome study. *Journal of Social Work, 5,* 186–194.

Ryan, W. (1970). *Blaming the victim.* New York, NY: Vintage.

Ryder, A., & Cemlyn, S. (2016). Monoculturalism, austerity & moral panics: Assessing government progress on addressing gypsy, travelers & Roma exclusion. *Journal of Poverty & Social Justice, 24*(2), 143–155.

Saandal, M., Cook, J., Poblacion, A., Sheward, R., Coleman, S., Viveieros, J., & Sturtevant, L. (2016). Housing as a health care investment. Children's Healthwatch: National Housing Conference. *Insights from Housing Policy Research.*

Sáenz, B. A. (2009) *Last night I sang to the monster.* El Paso, TX: Cinco Punto Press. (Listen to the first pages read by the author at https://www.youtube.com/watch? v=i5I7flSOF6M)

Safety Net Almanac. (2015). Retrieved from http://safetynet.urban.org

Saffigna, M., Church, A., & Tayler, C. (2011). *Evidence paper practice principle 3: High expectations for every child.* Melbourne Graduate School of Education. Retrieved from http://www.education.vic.gov.au/Documents/childhood/providers/edcare/highexpect.pdf

Sajan.com. (2013, Jan. 2). High context & low context cultures: Gaining an edge in website localization. Retrieved from https://www.sajan.com/high-context-and-low-context-cultures-gaining-an-edge-in-website-localization/

Sakala, L. (2014). Breaking down mass incarceration in the 2010 census: State-by-state incarceration rates by race/ethnicity. Prison Policy Initiative. Retrieved from https://www.prisonpolicy.org/reports/rates.html

Salcido, R. (2008). Incorporating evidence-based practice into the macro practice curriculum. *Evidence Based Social Work, 5*(3–4), 623–645.

Saleebey, D. (2012) *The Strengths Perspective in Social Work Practice (6th Edition) (Advancing Core Competencies).* Pearson.

Saleem, M. (2016, Spring). Muslim stereotyping in the media. *Race & Difference Colloquium Series.* Emory University, Atlanta, GA.

Salkas, K., Magaňa, S., Marques, I., & Mirza, M. (2016). Spirituality in Latino families of children with autism spectrum disorder. *Journal of Family Social Work, 19*(1), 38–55.

Salon. Retrieved from https://www.salon.com/2017/09/15/the-mental-health-impact-of-major-disasters-like-harvey-and-irma_partner/.

Salty Current. (2015). James Baldwin's existentialist critique of gender, misogyny, and homophobia and its value today, Part 2 [Blog post]. Retrieved from http://saltycurrent.blogspot.com/2015/08/james-baldwins-existentialist-critique.html

Salzillo, K. (2015). Jimmy Carter: 'Losing My Religion For Equality', Kos Media LLC. https://www.dailykos.com/stories/2015/4/23/1379812/-Jimmy-Carter-Losing-My-Religion-For-Equality

Salzillo, L. (2015, July 30). Catholic nun explains pro-life in a way that will stun many (especially Republican lawmakers). *Daily Kos.* Retrieved Jan. 1, 2016, from https://www.dailykos.com/story/2015/07/30/1407166/-Catholic-Nun-Explains-Pro-Life-In-A-Way-That-May-Stun-The-Masses? detail=emailclassic

SAMSHA, (2016). Behavioral Health Treatments and Services. Retrieved from https://www.samhsa.gov/treatment.

SAMSHA, (2017). Health disparities. https://www.samhsa.gov/health-disparities

SAMSHA, Recovery. (2017). Recovery and Recovery Support. Retrieved https://www.samhsa.gov/recovery

SAMSHA. (2017). Cultural competence. Retrieved from https://www.samhsa.gov/capt/applying-strategic-prevention/cultural-competence

SAMSHA. (2018). Health disparities. Retrieved from https://www.healthypeople.gov/2020/about/foundation-health-measures/disparitie

Samuels, C. (2016). What's really happening with special education enrollment. *EdWeek.com.*

Sánchez-Cabezudo, S. S., & Peláez, A. L. (2014). Social work with middle class Spanish families: The challenge of the work-family conflict. *International Journal of Social Welfare, 23,* 100–111.

Sandberg, S. (2013). *Lean in: Women, work and the will to lead.* New York, NY: Alfred A. Knopf.

Sanders, M. (2016). *Counseling African Americans with substance use disorders* [Webinar]. ATTC Network. Retrieved from www.attcnetworkoffice.org

Sandhu, T., & Kapoor, S. (2014). Symbolism as an expression of religious spiritual development amongst the deaf. *International Journal of Children's Spirituality, 19*(2), 97–111.

Santow, R., & Rothstein, R. (2012). A different kind of choice: Educational inequality and the continuing significance of racial segregation. *Economic Policy Institute.*

Saper, R. B., Lemaster, C. M., Elwy, A. R., Paris, R., Herman, P.M., Plumb, D., ... & Weinberg, J. (2016). Yoga versus education for veterans with chronic low back pain: Study protocol for a randomized controlled trial. *Trials, 17,* 224.

Sarana, A. K. (2017, April 11). Sessions announces "new era" in treatment of undocumented immigrants. *foreignpolicy.com.* Retrieved from http://foreignpolicy.com/2017/04/11/sessions-announces-new-era-in-treatment-of-undocumented-immigrants-trump-crackdown-illegal-border-wall/

Sarquello, Henderson, Faba, Mead, Salanese, & Plaza. (2016). Health and Social integrated care in practice. Local Partnerships in action. *International Journal of Integrated Care.* 16(6):, A64. DOI: http://doi.org/10.5334/ijic.3015

Satrapi, M. (2004). *The story of a childhood.* New York, NY: Pantheon Books.

SBIRT. (2017). SBIRT: Screening, Brief Intervention, and Referral to Treatment. Retrieved from https://www.integration.samhsa.gov/clinical-practice/sbirt

Schaffner, L. (1998). Do bad girls get a bum rap? Sexual solutions and state interventions. In S. Inness (Ed.), *Millennium girls: Today's girls around the world* (pp. 269–296). Lanham, MD: Rowman & Littlefield.

Scharrer, E., & Ramasubramanian, S. (2015). Intervening in the media's influence on stereotypes of race and ethnicity: The role of media literacy education. *Journal of Social Issues, 71*(1), 171–185.

Schiffer, M. (Writer), & Avildsen, J. G. (Director). (1989). *Lean on me.* Burbank, CA: Warner Bros.

Schiller, F. (2016). Urban transitions: Scaling complex cities down to human size. *Journal of Cleaner Production, 112,* 4273–4282.

Schlosser, E. (1998). The prison industrial complex. *The Atlantic Monthly. December-January.* Retrieved from http://www.theatlantic.com/magazine/toc/1998/12/crimes

Schmoker, M. J. (2011). *Focus: Elevating the essentials to radically improve student learning.* Alexandria, VA: Association for Supervision & Curriculum Development.

Schoen, D., Hurtado, S., Sevig, T., Chester, M., Sumida, S. H. (2001). 'Intergroup Dialogue: Democracy at Work in Theory and Practice', in Schoem, D., Hurtado, S. (Eds), *Intergroup Dialogue: Deliberative Democracy in School, College, Community and Workplace.* Ann Arbor, MI: University of Michigan Press, pp. 1–21.

Schon, D. A. (1983). *The reflective practitioner: How professionals think in action.* New York, NY: Basic Books.

Schreider, F. R. (1973/2009). *Sybil.* New York, NY: Grand Central.

Schreider, J. (2017, September 6). Why Americans think so poorly of the country's schools. *Atlantic.com*

Schulman, S. (2013). *The gentrification of the mind: Witness to a lost imagination.* University of California Press.

Schumacher, /r. (2013). Building communities that help your child & family thrive. A national survey by early childhood-LINC: A learning & innovative network for communities. Center for the Study of Social Policy.

Schwartz, P. (2014). Why more women choose not to marry. CNN.com. Retrieved from http://www.cnn.com/2014/10/15/opinion/schwartz-single-women/

Scooters.com. (n.d.). History of the wheelchair. Retrieved from www.mobilityscooters.co.nz/history/wheelchairs

Scott, C. A., & O'Neal, G. S. (1981). *Supplying a critical need: Preparing ethnic minority doctoral social work students for leadership roles in mental health.* New York, NY: Council on Social Work Education.

Scott, D. M. (n.d.). "The religious origins of manifest destiny." Divining America. TeacherServe©. National Humanities Center. Retrieved June 29, 2017, from http://nationalhumanitiescenter.org/tserve/nineteen/nkeyinfo/mandestiny.htm

Scott, D.L. & Scott, R. (n.d.). Social worker as political candidate: Seeking a seat at the table. *Arete*, 87–104. Retrieved from file:///E:/Scott,%20Social%20Worker%20as%20Political%20Candidate.pdf.

Scott, R. E. (2016). The Trans-Pacific Partnership would hurt black and Hispanic workers even more than white workers. *Economic Policy Institute*.

Scott, S. (2015, Winter). A hard look at how we see race. *Utne Reader*. Retrieved from http://www.utne.com/politics/social-psychology-racial-disparity-zm0z15wzdeh.aspx

See, L. (2009). *Snow flower and the secret fan*. New York, NY: Random House.

Segal, R. (2002). *Islam's Black slaves: The other Black diaspora*. New York, NY: Farrar, Strauss & Giroux.

Seif, H. (2009). The civic education and engagement of Latina/o immigrant youth: Challenging boundaries and creating safe spaces. Retrieved from www.wilsoncenter.org/migrantparticipation

Shiffrin, R. M., & Schneider, W. (1977). Controlled & automatic human information processing. *Psychology Review, 84*(2), 127–190.

Seita, J. (2014). Reclaiming disconnected kids. *Reclaiming Children & Youth.* 23(1), 27–31. https://search.proquest.com/openview/a55881cb1215293d943413493bf10c40/1?pq-origsite=gscholar&cbl=33810

Selyukh, A., Hollenhorst,M., & Park, M. (2017). Big media companies and their many brands—in one chart. *NPR. org* . Retrieved Jan 7, 2018 from https://www.npr.org/sections/alltechconsidered/2016/10/28/499495517/big-media-companies-and-their-many-brands-in-one-chart

Semega, J.L., Fontenot, K.R., & Kollar, M.A. (2017 pp. 60–259). Income and poverty in the United States: 2016. U.S. Census Bureau, Current Population Reports, U.S. Government Printing Office, Washington, DC.

Sen, S. (Director). (2015). *Cities of sleep* [Documentary].

Senden, M. G., Sikström, S., & Lindholm, T. (2015). "She" and "he" in news media messages: Pronoun use reflect gender biases in semantic contexts. *Sex Roles, 72*, 40–49.

Senge, P. (2006). *The fifth discipline: The art and practice of the learning organization (2nd ed.).* New York, NY: Random House Business.

Sengupta, S. (2016). *The end of karma: Hope and fury among India's young.* New York, NY: W.W. Norton.

Sentencing Project. (2017). *Policy brief: Racial disparities in youth commitments and arrests.* Retrieved from file:///C:/Users/75GONEAL/Downloads/Racial-Disparities-in-Youth-Commitments-and-Arrests.pdf

Serres, C. (2016, Sept. 1). Subminimum wage changes catch states "flat-footed." *Disability scoop.com.*

Severson, K. (2017). Protest or party? *The New York Times.* Pride 2017, p. 3.

Shaddox, C. (2016). Cultural hurdles limit medical care for LGBTs. Health I Team Connecticut. Retrieved from http://c-hit.org/2016/03/27/cultural-hurdles-limit-medical-care-for-lgbts/

Shaefer, L., & Edin, K. (2015). *$2.00 a day: Living on almost nothing in America.* Boston, MA: Houghton Mifflin.

Shah, A. (2011). Public protests around the world. *Global Issues.* Retrieved from http://www.globalissues.org/article/45/public-protests-around-the-world

Shakur, T. (2000). Thank God how? Track 12.

Shakur, T. (2009). The rose that grew from concrete. New York; Pocket Books.

Shank, C. (2016, Jan. 7). *What the what? Strategies for critical self-reflection and assessment.* Tulsa Community College Leap Day Breakout Session.

Shaw, M. (2003, Oct. 24). Black pupils helped to reach much higher. *The Times Educational Supplement.*

Sheehan, G. (2008). Building the Mercado Central: Asset-based community development and community entrepreneurship in the USA. 63–83. In A. Mathie & G. Cunningham (Eds.), From clients to citizens: Communities changing the course of their own development (pp. 63–83). Rugby, United Kingdom: Practical Action.

Shelby, H., Jr. (1957). *Last exit to Brooklyn.* New York, NY: Grove Press.

Shelton, K., & Delgado-Romero, E. A. (2011). Sexual orientation microaggressions: The experience of lesbian, gay, bisexual, and queer clients in psychotherapy. *Journal of Counseling Psychology, 58*(2), 210–221.

Shemmings, D. Shemmings, Y. & Cook, A. (2012). Gaining the trust of 'highly resistant' families: Insights from attachment theory and research. *Child & Family Social Work,* 17(2), 130–137._

Shierholz, H., Cooper, H., Wolfe, J. & Zipperer, B. (2018). Women would lose $4.6 billion in earned tips if the administration's 'tip stealing' rule is finalized. *Economic Policy Institute.*

Shields, A. (2015). *How I'm working for change inside my church* [Video file]. Retrieved from https://www.ted.com/talks/chelsea_shields_how_i_m_working_for_change_inside_my_church

Shields, C. (2015). Ted Talk. Retrieved from https://www.ted.com/talks/chelsea_shields_how_i_m_working_for_change_inside_my_church]

Shin, K. S. (2011). *Please look after Mother*. New York, NY: Vintage.

Shmoop Editorial Team. (2008, November 11). *Native American history timeline of important dates*. Retrieved January 1, 2018, from https://www.shmoop.com/native-american-history/timeline.html

Shoji, M. M., Haskins, A. R., Rangel, D. E., & Sorensen, K. N. (2014). The emergence of social capital in low income Latino elementary schools. *Early childhood Research Quarterly, 29*, 600-613.

Shonkoff, J. P., Boyce, W. T., & McEwen, B. S. (2009). Neuroscience, molecular biology and the childhood roots of health disparities: Building a new framework for health promotion and disease prevention. *Journal of the American Medical Association, 301*(21), 2252-2259.

Shrestha, L. B., & Heisler, E. J. (2011). *The changing demographic profile of the United States*. Washington, DC: Congressional Research Service.

Shrinivasa, B., Janardhan, N., & Nirmala, B. P. (2017). Mental health orientation for self-help group members: A feasibility study. *Journal of Neuroscience in Rural Practice, 8*, 395-400.

Shriver, M. (2014). *The Shriver report: A woman's nation pushes back from the brink—A study by Maria Shriver*. Washington, DC: The Center for American Progress.

Shyamalan, M. K. (2013). *I got schooled: The unlikely story of how a moonlighting movie maker learned the five keys to closing America's education gap*. New York, NY: Simon & Schuster.

Siddiqui, S. (2011). Critical social work with mixed-race individuals: Implications for anti-racist and anti-oppressive practice. *Canadian Social Work Review, 28*(2), 255-265.

Sieber, D. (2014). Engaging absent fathers in the treatment of children. *Clinical Social Work Journal, 36*, 333-340.

Silber, R., Subramanian, R., & Spotts, M. (2016). Justice in review: New trends in state sentencing and corrections, 2014-2015. *Vera Institute of Justice.* www.vera.org.

Silberman, S. (2015). *Neuro tribes: The legacy of autism and the future of neurodiversity*. New York, NY: Avery.

Simmons, L. (2014). Economic justice, social work education and human rights. In K.R. Libal, M. Berthold, R.L. Thomas, & L.M. Healy, (Eds.), *Advancing human rights in social work education*, pp. 213-230. Alexandria, VA: Council on Social Work Education.

Simmons, S. & Harding, L. (2009). Economic justice, labor and community practice. *Journal of Community Practice, 17*(1-2), 1-10.

Simon, B. L. (2015, April). Keynote address, Columbia University Alumni Conference, New York, NY.

Simon, R. (2011). *The story of beautiful girl*. New York, NY: Grand Central.

Simpson, A. (2014). *Mohawk interruptus: Political life across the borders of settler states*. Durham, NC: Duke University Press.

Singer, L. (2012). Immigrant workers in the U.S. labor force. Brookings. Retrieved from https://www.brookings.edu/research/immigrant-workers-in-the-u-s-labor-force/

Singhai, S., Latko, B. & Martin, C.P. (2018). The future of healthcare: Finding the opportunities that lie beneath the uncertainty. *McKinsey.com*

Sisneros, J. (2003). I don't think a Latino should teach about whiteness: A story about essentialism and Latino/a multiplicity. *Reflections.* 4-12.

Sisneros, J., Stakeman, C., Joyner, M., & Schmitz, C. (2008). *Critical multicultural social work*. Chicago, IL: Lyceum.

Sitshange, M. (2012). Social workers' perceptions of inter-organisational collaboration in child and family welfare. *Social Work, 48*(2), 159-171.

Sivadasan, L., & Narayanan, A. (2016). Factors of resilience among physically disabled: An interpretative phenomenological analysis. *Indian Journal of Positive Psychology, 7*(1), 113.

Skehill, C. (2010). *History of social work in the United Kingdom*. Oxford Bibliography.

Slaughter, A. M. (2015). *Unfinished business: Women, men, work, family*. New York, NY: Random House.

Slive, A., & Bobele, M. (2013). *Single sessions with children & families*. Institute #103. Paper presented at American Association for Marriage and Family Therapy.

Smieetana, B. (2015). Sunday morning in America still segregated – and that's ok with worshipers. Lifeway Research. Retrieved from http://lifewayresearch.com/2015/01/15/sunday-morning-in-america-still-segregated-and-thats-ok-with-worshipers/

Smiley, T., & West, C. (2013). *The rich and the rest of us: A poverty manifesto (8th ed.)*. New York, NY: SmileyBooks.

Smit, A. L. (2010). Spiritual life of Deaf people in South Africa. *American Annals of the Deaf, 155*(4).

Smith, A. (2013). Civic engagement in the digital age. Retrieved from www.pewinternet.org

Smith, A. N., Brief, A.P., & Colella, A. (2010). Bias in organizations. In J. Dovido, M. Hewstone, P. Glick, & V. M. Esses (Eds.), *The SAGE handbook of prejudice, stereotyping, and discrimination*. Thousand Oaks, CA: SAGE.

Smith, B. (2007). Student ratings of teaching effectiveness: An analysis of end-of-course faculty evaluations. *College Student Journal, 41*(4).

Smith, C. (2017, March 21). Personal correspondence. CIT Project coordinator.

Smith, C. (2017, April). Policy Development and Collaboration with Police. in Chester County. Class presentation.

Smith, D. (1997). Diversity works: The emerging picture of how students benefit. Washington, DC: Association of American Colleges and Universities.

Smith, D.H. (2000). *Modern tribal development: paths to self-sufficiency and cultural integrity in Indian country*. AltaMira Press.

Smith, J. M. & Hayes, R. (2016) Integrating philosophy, sociology, and dialog-based instruction in the social & criminal justice classroom. *Contemporary Justice Review, 19*:1, 3–18, DOI: 10.1080/10282580.2015.1101684

Smith, L.T. (2012). *Decolonizing methodologies: research and indigenous peoples*. London, England: Zed Books, Ltd.

Smith, M. B. (2013). Critical trans politics as a framework for addressing the needs of intersectionally oppressed transgender, intersex, and gender non-conforming people. Retrieved from http://globalmigration.web.unc.edu/files/2013/09/Critical-Trans-Politics-as-Framework-for-Addressing-the-Needs-of-Intersectionally-Oppressed-Transgender-Intersex-and-Gender-Non-conforming-People.pdf

Smith, M., Wilkes, N., & Bouffard, L. A. (2016). Rape myth adherence among campus law enforcement officers. *Criminal Justice and Behavior, 43*, 539–556. Southern Poverty Law Center, (2017). Fighting hate. https://www.splcenter.org/fighting-hate

Smith, P. (2010). The origin of contextual fluidity. Retrieved Jan. 14, 2018 from http://meeting.knet.ca/mp19/mod/forum/discuss.php?d=2808

Smith, S. (2007). Projective processes on the frontline. *Journal of Social Work Practice*.

Smithsonian Institution: National Museum of the Native American. (2016). Strong women/strong nations: Opening song and introduction. Retrieved from https://www.youtube.com/watch? v=XTGQ8PrEYKA

—*Social Work, 62*(1), 45–52.

Social workers.org. (n.d.). Retrieved June 26, 2017, from https://www.socialworkers.org/pubs/code/code.asp

Solomon, A. (2012). *Far from the tree: Parents, children and the search for identity*. New York, NY: Scribner.

Sommerfeld, P. (2014). Social work as an action science: A perspective from Europe, Special section—Science in social work roundtable. *Research on Social Work Practice, 24*(5), 586–600.

Sotomayor, S. (2013). *My beloved world*. New York, NY: Vintage.

Southern Poverty Law Center (SPLC). (2016). Trump effect. Retrieved from https://www.splcenter.org/20160413/trump-effect-impact-presidential-campaign-our-nations-school

Southern Poverty Law Center (SPLC). (2018). Retrieved from https://www.splcenter.org/hate-map

Southern Poverty Law Center. (2016). *SPLC Report*, Fall, *46*(3).

SPAN, Statewide Parent Advocacy Network of New Jersey (2018). Family Wrap, Wisdom, Resoures, advocacy, parent to parent support. Retrieved from http://www.spannj.org/familywrap/

Sparks, S. D., & Viadero, D. (2016). How students' emotions affect their schooling: Simple steps prevent slide in well-being. *Education Week, 35*(28), 7.

Specht, H., & Courtney, M. E. (1994). *Unfaithful angels: How social work abandoned its mission*. New York, NY: Free Press.

Spector, A. (2014). Racism and capitalism-crisis and resistance: Exploring the dynamic between class oppression and racial oppression. *Humanity & Society, 38*(2), 116–131.

Spirited Thinking. (2013). Now trending: Candler dean looks to future of seminary education. *Emory News Center*. (See also Faith3.org)

Spolander G. Linda Martin, L., Kingsley, J. Barber, C. (2013). Successful project management in social work and social care by Gary Spolander and Linda Martin Jessica Kingsley. *Child & Family Social Work, 18*(2), 241–242.

Sprague, J. R., Vincent, C., Tobin, T. J., & CHiXapkaid. (2013). Preventing disciplinary exclusions of students from American Indian/Alaska Native backgrounds. *Family Court Review, 51*(3), 452–459.

Spring, J. (2010). *The politics of American education (sociocultural, political, and historical studies in education)*. New York: Routledge.

Staff, CBI and Life Skills program. (2013). Ninety-three percent of young people are not receiving adequate careers information. *Education Journal, 25*(182), 4. November 25, 2013

Stagman, S., & Cooper, J. L. (2010). *Children's mental health: What every policymaker should know*. New York, NY: Columbia University, National Center for Children in Poverty.

Stallworth, B. J. (2006). It's not on the list: An exploration of teacher's perspective on using multicultural literature. *Journal of Adolescent & Adult Literacy, 49*(6), 478–489.

Stanford, S., & Taylor, S. (2013). Welfare dependence or enforced deprivation? A critical examination of white neoliberal welfare and risk. *Australian Social Work, 66*(4), 476–494.

Stanhope, V., & Dunn, K. (2011). The curious case of housing first: The limits of evidence based policy. *International Journal of Law and Psychiatry, 14*, 275–282.

Stanton, B. (2016). Humans of New York. Retrieved from http://www.dailymotion.com/video/x3y5e4q

Stanton-Salazar, R. (1997). A social capital framework for understanding the socialization of racial minority children and youths. *Harvard Educational Review, 67*(1), 1–41.

Staples, B. (2016). Donald Trump & reconstruction era politics. *The New York Times*. Opinion Page.

Staples, R. (2011). White power, black crime, and racial politics. *The Black Scholar, 41*(4), 31–41.

Starbuck, D., Howell, J. C., & Lindquist, D. J. (2001). Into the millennium: Hybrids and other modern gangs. Juvenile Justice Bulletin, Youth Gang Series. Washington, DC: U.S. Department of Justice.

State of Working America Data Library (2016). Economic Policy Institute. Retrieved from https://www.epi.org/data/#about.

Statewide Parent Advocacy Network. (n.d.). About SPAN. Retrieved from http://www.spanadvocacy.org/content/about-span

Status of Women in the States. (n.d.). Employment and earnings. Retrieved from https://statusofwomendata.org/explore-the-data/employment-and-earnings/#section-b

Stavans, I. (Ed.). (1998). *Prospero's mirror: A translator's portfolio of Latin American short fiction*. Evanston, IL: Curbstone Press.

Steele, C. M., & Aronson, J. (1995). Stereotype threat & the intellectual test performance of African Americans. *Journal of Personality & Social Psychology, 69*(5), 797–811.

Stein, J. C. (2011). The case for collaboration. Integrating information on English learners and special education in teacher preparation program. Diversity and Special Education. *Multicultural Education*, 35–40.

Stein, P. (2012). *Multimodal pedagogies in diverse classrooms: Representation, rights and resources (2nd edition)*. New York: Routledge.

Stein, P., & Bever, L. (2017, July 1). The opioid crisis is straining the nation's foster care systems. *The Washington Post*.

Steinberg, D. M. (2009). *A mutual aid model for social work with groups*. Abingdon, United Kingdom: Routledge.

Steinmetz, K. (2014). Kansas bill allowing refusal of service to gay couples moves forward. *Time.com*. Retrieved from http://nation.time.com/2014/02/11/kansas-bill-allowing-refUSal-of-service-to-gay-couples-moves-forward/?%20xid=newsletter-weekly

Stephenson, F.D. (2016). Denying poor people health care defies logic. *Social Justice Solutions*, October.

Stephenson-Davidowits, S. (2015, June 6). Talking red state blues. *The New York Times*.

Sternthal, M., Williams, D. R., Musick, M. A., & Buck, A. C. (2012). Religious practices, beliefs, and mental health: Variations across ethnicity. *Ethnicity and Health, 17*(1–2), 171–185.

Stetzer, E. (2015). The most segregated hour of the week. *The Exchange*. Retrieved from www.christianitytoday.com/edstetzer/2015/january/most-segregated-hour-of-week.html

Stevens-Watkins, D., Perry, B., Pullen, E., Jewell, J., & Oser, C. B. (2014). Examining the association of racism, sexism, & stressful events on psychological distress among African American women. *Cultural Diversity & Ethnic Minority Psychology, 20*(4), 561–569.

Stickle, B. (2016). A national examination of the effect of education, training and pre-employment screening on law enforcement use of force. *Justice Policy Journal*, Spring, 13(11), 1–15.

Stiffman, N. R., Brown, E., Freedenthal, S., Hone, L., Ostman, E., & Yu, M. S. (2007). American Indian youth: Personal, familial, and environmental strengths. *Journal of Child & Family Studies, 16*, 331–346.

Stiglitz, J. E. (2012). *The price of inequality: How today's divided society endangers our future.* New York, NY: W. W. Norton.

Stiglitz, J.E. (2014, May 28). Reforming taxation to promote growth and equity. *Roosevelt Institute.*

Stiglitz, J. E. (2015). *The great divide: unequal societies and what we can do about them.* New York, NY: W. W. Norton.

Stiglitz, J. E. (2015). *Rewriting the rules of the American economy: An agenda for growth and shared prosperity.* New York, NY: W.W. Norton.

Stoesser, S., & Good, C. (2005). Stereotype threat: An overview of excerpts and adaptations. Reducing Stereotype Threat. org. Retrieved June 13, 2017 from http://diversity.arizona.edu/sites/diversity/files/stereotype_threat_overview. pdf

Stokes, B. (2018). Many Americans going to the polls are not happy with our democracy. Pew Research

Stokes, J., & Schmidt, G. (2011). Race, poverty and child protection decision-making. *British Journal of Social Work, 41*, 1105–1121.

Stokoe, W. C. (2005). Sign language structure: An outline of the visual communication systems of the American deaf. *Journal of Deaf Studies and Deaf Education, 10*(1), 1–35.

Stolker, T. (2015). Conference to Explore Economic and Health Issues for Girls and Women. Retrieved from https://news.fordham.edu/colleges-and-schools/graduate-school-of-social-service/conference-to-explore-economic-and-health-issues-for-girls-and-women/

Stop solitary confinement. Aclu.org/stopsolitary

Stotzer, R. (2008). Gender identity and hate crimes: Violence against transgender people in Los Angeles County. *Sexuality Research and Social Policy, 5*(1), 43–52.

Stotzer, R., & Hossellman, E. (2011). Hate crimes on campus: Racial/ethnic diversity and campus safety. *Journal of Interpersonal Violence, 27*(4), 644–661.

Stoute, S. (2011). *The tanning of America: How hip hop culture created a culture that rewrote the rules of the economy.* New York, NY: Penguin.

Strayhorn, T. (2015). National symposium on student retention 2015: Keynote address [Video file]. Retrieved from https://www.youtube.com/watch? v=eZXRjsUIwXI

Strier, R., & Bershtling, O. (2016). Professional resistance in social work: Counter practice assemblages. *Social Work, 61*(2), 111–116.

Strier, R., & Binyamin, S. (2013). Introducing anti-oppressive social work practices in public social services: Rhetoric to practice. *British Journal of Social Work, 44*, 2095–2112.

Stroh, D.P. (2015). *Systems thinking for social change: A practical guide to solving complex problems, avoiding unintended consequences, and achieving lasting results.* Chelsea, Vermont: Chelsea Green Publishing.

Strong, P. (2009). The history of the white cane. Tennessee Council of the Blind. Retrieved from http://www.acb.org/tennessee/white_cane_history.html

Styron, W. (1967). *Confessions of Nat Turner.* New York, NY: Vintage Books.

Suarez, E., & Gadalla, T. M. (2010). Stop blaming the victim: A meta-analysis on rape myths. *Journal of Interpersonal Violence, 25*(11), 2015–2029.

Sue, D. W. (2010). *Microaggressions in everyday life: Race, gender, and sexual orientation.* Hoboken, NJ: Wiley & Sons.

Suk, J. (2016, Feb. 19). *Incarceration nation* by Baz Dreisinger. *The New York Times.*

Sullivan, L. W., & Eagel, B. A. (2005). Leveling the playing field: Recognizing and rectifying disparities in management of pain. Pain Medicine, 6(1), 5–14.

Sullivan, S.P. (2016). Christie vetoes N.J. domestic violence gun bill – again. Retrieved from http://www.nj.com/politics/index.ssf/2016/05/christie_vetoes_nj_domestic_violence_gun_bill_agai.html

suppression-258b5f90ddcd/

Supreme Court History. (n.d.). Landmark cases. *Pbs.org.* Retrieved June 12, 2017, from http://www.pbs.org/wnet/supreme-court/rights/landmark_brown.html

Surgeon General (2018, May 21). National Prevention Strategy, Prevention Matters. Retrieved from https://www.surgeongeneral.gov/priorities/prevention/strategy/infographic/index.html

Sutter, M., & Perrin, P. B. (2016). Discrimination, mental health, and suicidal ideation among LGBTQ people of color. *Journal of Counseling Psychology, 63*(1), 98–105.

Sutton, S. E., & Kemp, S. P. (Eds.). (2011). *The paradox of urban space: Inequality and transformation in marginalized communities.* New York, NY: Palgrave Macmillan.

Sutton, S., & Kemp, S. (2011). Introduction: Place as marginality and possibility. In S. E. Sutton & S. P. Kemp (Eds.), *The paradox of urban space: Inequality and transformation in marginalized communities.* Basingstoke, United Kingdom: Palgrave Macmillan.

Swanson, J. (2004, Aug. 14). Torn together: America's struggle for integration in the midst of segregation. (Conference papers). American Sociological Association.

Swignoski, M. (2006). Violence, hates crimes and hate language. In D. F. Morrow & L. Messinger (Eds.), *Sexual orientation and gender expression in social work practice working with gay, lesbian, bisexual, and transgender people* (pp. 365–372). New York, NY: Columbia University Press.

Symon, G., Buehring, A., Johnson, P., & Cassell, C. (2008). Positioning qualitative research as resistance to the institutionalization of the academic labour process. *Organization Studies, 29*(10), 1315–1336.

Symonds, J., Chow, A., Dietrich, J., & Salmela-Aro, K. (2016). Mental health improves after transition from comprehensive school to vocational education or employment tin England: A national cohort study. *Developmental Psychology, 52*(4), 652–665.

Szasz, T. (1970/2011). *The myth of mental illness: Foundations of a theory of personal conduct.* New York, NY: Harper Collins.

Szulanski, G. (1999). *The process of knowledge transfer: A diachronic analysis of stickiness.* Philadelphia: University of Pennsylvania.

Tach, L. and Edin, K. (2017). The social safety net after welfare reform: recent developments and consequences for household dynamics (July). *Annual Review of Sociology,* 43, 541–561. Available at SSRN: https://ssrn.com/abstract=3018064 or http://dx.doi.org/10.1146/annurev-soc-060116-053300.

Tajima-Peña, R., & Portillo, L. (Producers). (2004). *My journey home.* Washington, DC: WET.

Takaki, R. (1989). *Strangers from a different shore: A history of Asian Americans.* New York, NY: Little, Brown.

Talen, E. (2005). Land use zoning and human diversity: Exploring the connection. *Journal of Urban Planning and Development,* December, 214.

Talkpoverty.org. (2018). Poverty data. Center for American Progress Retrieved from https://talkpoverty.org/category/first-person/

TallBear, K. (2014). Indigenous scientists constitute knowledge across cultures of expertise and tradition: An indigenous standpoint research project. In J. Gärdebo, M.-B. Öhman, & H. Maryuama (Eds.), *RE: MINDINGS: Co-constituting indigenous/academic/artistic knowledge.* Uppsala Multiethnic Papers 55, 173–191.

TallBear, K. (2018). Native American DNA; Belonging and the false promise of genetic science. Minneapolis: University of Minnesota. Retrieved from http://www.kimtallbear.com/research.html

Talmon, M. (1990) *Single session therapy: Maximizing the effect of the first (and often only) therapeutic encounter.* San Francisco, CA: Jossey-Bass.

Tan, A. (2001). *The opposite of fate.* London, United Kingdom: Penguin Books.

Tan, A. (2006). *The kitchen god's wife.* New York, NY: Penguin Books.

Tangenberg, K. M. (2005). Faith-based human services initiatives: Considerations for social work practice and theory. *Social Work, 50*(3), 197–206.

Taplin, J. (2017). *Move fast and break things: How Facebook, Google, and Amazon cornered culture and undermined democracy.* Boston, MA: Little, Brown.

Tator, C., & Henry, F. (2009). *The color of democracy: Racism in Canadian society* (4th ed.). Toronto, Ontario: Nelson.

Taylor, B. (2015). The ADA and return to work issues. *Legal Briefings, Employment.* Brief No. 2015.

Tea, M. (2004). *Without a net: The female experience of growing up working class.* New York, NY: Seal Press

Teixeira, S., & Krings, A. (2015). Sustainable social work: An environmental justice framework for social work education. *Social Work Education, 34*(5), 513–527 doi:10.1080/02615479.2015.1063601

Tendolini, C. (2018). Why Latin America is a hotbed of political innovation. *Open Society Foundations.*

Teología de la liberación (Gustavo Gutiérrez). (2013). Peru cultural. Retrieved from http://www.theopedia.com/liberation-theology

Texas Trails (Ed.). (2014). *Magical folktales from old Mexico: A collection of 14 famous Mexican legends and myths.* Retrieved from http://americanfolklore.net/folklore/2010/07/the_armadillos_song.html

The Sentencing Project. (2000). Reducing racial disparities in the criminal justice system: A manual for practitioners and policymakers. Retrieved from http://www.sentencingproject.org/doc/publications/rd_reducingracialdisparity.pdf

The Sentencing Project. (2017). Fact sheet: Trends in U.S. Corrections. Retrieved Jan9, 2018 from https://sentencingproject.org/wp-content/uploads/2016/01/Trends-in-US-Corrections.pdf

Theodos, B., & Seidman, E. (2016). Housing counseling should help with more than just home buying. Retrieved from http://www.urban.org/urban-wire/housing-counseling-should-help-more-just- home buying.

Theopedia.com. (n.d.). Liberation theology. Retrieved from http://www.theopedia.com/liberation-theology

Thoits, P.A. (2016). I'm not mentally ill: Identity deflection as a form of stigma resistance. *Journal of Health & Social Behavior.* 57(2), 135–131.

Thomas, J.M. (2017). Raising the bar: state trends in keeping youth out of adult courts (2015-2017), Washington, DC: Campaign for Youth Justice. Retrieved from http://cfyj.org/images/A-StateTrends_Report-Web.pdf.

Thompson, D. (2013). Bending energy: ADHD kids benefit from yoga. Retrieved from www.everyhealth.com

Thompson, K. J., Switky, B., & Gilinsky, A. (2012). Impromptu presentations: Boosting student learning & engagement through spontaneous collaboration. *Journal of Education for Business, 87*, 14–21.

Thoms, S. (2015). *First-episode psychosis gets early intervention under Michigan pilot program.* Retrieved from http://www.mlive.com/news/grand-rapids/index.ssf/2015/08/first-episode_psychosis_gets_e.html

Thornberg, R. (2015). School bullying as a collective action: Stigma processes and identity struggling. *Children & Society.* 28(4), 310–320.

Thulberry, S. C., & Thyer, B. (2014). The L'Arche program for persons with disabilities. *Journal of Human Behavior in the Social Environment, 24*, 348–353.

Thurber, A. (2015, Feb. 2). Personal correspondence. College Board AP exam content.

Thyer, B. (2008). Evidence-based macro practice: Addressing the challenges and opportunities. *Journal of Evidence-Based Social Work, 5*(3–4), 453–472.

Timander, A. C., Grinyer, A., & Möller, A. (2013). The study of mental distress and the reconstruction of identities in men and women with experience of long-term mental distress. *Disability & Society, 30*(3), 327–339.

Tindall, G. B., & Shi, D. E. (2012). America: A narrative history (9th ed.). U.S. Census Bureau. Chart & data compiled by Russ Long. Retrieved from http://dmc122011.delmar.edu/socsci/rlong/data/Inequality/PerCapitaIncomeUS2000.htm

Todd, S., & Coholic, D. (2007). Christian fundamentalism and anti-oppressive social work pedagogy. *Journal of Teaching in Social Work, 27*(3/4), 5–22.

Toikko, T. (2016). Becoming an expert by experience: An analysis of service users' learning process. *Social Work in Mental Health, 14*(3), 292–312.

Toppo, G. (2016). GAO study: Segregation worsening in U.S. schools. *USA Today.*

Torres, L., & Taknint, J. T. (2015). Ethnic microaggressions, traumatic stress symptoms, and Latino depression: A moderated mediational model. *Journal of Counseling Psychology, 62*(1), 393–401.

Tough, P. (2009). *Whatever it takes: Geoffrey Canada's quest to change Harlem & America.* Boston, MA: Mariner Books.

Trafzer, C. E., & Weiner, D. (Eds.). (2001). *Medicine ways: Disease, health, and survival among Native Americans.* Lanham, MD: Altimara Press.

Tran, J. (2018, May 6). *What are crimes against public order?* LegalMatch. Retrieved from https://www.legalmatch.com/law-library/article/crimes-against-public-order.html.

Travis, J. (2002). *Invisible punishment: An instrument of social exclusion.* Urban Institute. Retrieved from https://www.urban.org/sites/default/files/publication/59901/1000557-Invisible-Punishment-An-Instrument-of-Social-Exclusion.PDF

Treanor, J. (2015). Half of world's wealth now in hands of 1% of population. *The Guardian.* Retrieved from https://www.theguardian.com/money/2015/oct/13/half-world-wealth-in-hands-population-inequality-report

Trevithick, P. (2011). Understanding defences and defensiveness in social work Hidden trauma victims: Understanding and preventing traumatic stress in mental health professionals. *Journal of Social Work Practice, 25*(4), 389–412.

Trine, R. W. (1933). *The higher powers of mind and spirit*. Glasgow, Scotland: The University Press. (Original work published 1918)

Troncoso, S. (1999) *The last tortilla and other stories*. Tucson, AZ: The University of Arizona Press.

Trosper, R. L. (2002). Northwest coast indigenous institutions that supported resilience and sustainability. *Ecological Economics, 41*(2), 329–344.

Tuchman, B.W. (1985). *The march of folly: From Troy to Vietnam*. New York: Random House Trade Paperbacks.

Ture, K. (formerly Carmichael, S.), & Hamilton, C. (1992). *Black power: The politics of liberation*. New York, NY: Vintage Books.

Turner, M.A. (2003). Strengths and Weaknesses of the Housing Voucher Program. Urban Institute. Congressional Testimony of Margery Austin Turner, Director, Metropolitan Housing and Communities Policy Center, The Urban Institute, prepared for the Committee on Financial Services, Subcommittee on Housing and Community Opportunity, United States House of Representatives, June 17, 2003.

Turner, W. L. (2000). Cultural considerations in family-based primary prevention programs in drug Abuse. *Journal of Primary Prevention, 21*(2), 285–295.

Tyler, T.R., & Smith, H. (1995). Social justice and social movements. *Institute of Industrial Relations Working Paper No. 61*. Retrieved from http://irle.berkeley.edu/files/1995/Social-Justice-and-Social-Movements.pdf.

Tzu, S. (2006). *The art of war*. Minneapolis, MN: Filiquarian.

U.S. Census Bureau. (n.d.). Retrieved from https://www.census.gov/

U.S. Commission on Human Rights. (2014). Indian Tribes: A continuing quest for survival. In P. Rothenberg with K. Mayhew (Eds.), *Race, class and gender in the United States* (p. 501). Duffield, United Kingdom: Worth.

U.S. Department of the Interior—Indian Affairs. (n.d.). Frequently asked questions. Retrieved June 6, 2015, from http://www.bia.gov/FAQs/

U.S. Global Change Research Program. (2016). *The impacts of climate change on human health in the United States: A scientific assessment*. Retrieved from https://s3.amazonaws.com/climatehealth2016/low/ClimateHealth2016_FullReport_small.pdf

U.S. History. (2016). America in the Second World War. Retrieved from http://www.ushistory.org/us/51e.asp

U.S. News http://www.USnews.com/news/blogs/data-mine/2015/01/28/US-education-still-separate-and-unequal

Uebelacker, L. A., Tremont, G., Gillette, L. T., Epstein-Lubow, G., Strong, D. R., Abrantes, A. M., Tyrka, A. R., ... & Miller, I. W. (2017). Adjunctive yoga v. health education for persistent major depression: A randomized controlled trial. *Psychological Medicine, 47*(12), 2130–2142.

Uehara, E. S., Sohng, S. S. L. Bending, R.L., Seyfried, S., Richey, C., Morelli, P., ... & Kanyha, V. (1996). Towards a values-based approach to multicultural social work research. *Social Work, 41*(6), 613–621.

Umich.edu, (2011). Emperor Qin's terra cotta army: A place that will blow your mind. Retrieved from http://www.umich.edu/~ssgchem/BPCtravel/2011September/D5.1.TerraCotta/index.html

Umrigar, T. (2007). *The space between us*. New York, NY: Harper Perennial.

UNESCO. (2009). *The UNESCO world report on cultural diversity*. Retrieved from http://www.unesco.org/new/en/culture/resources/report/the-unesco-world-report-on-cultural-diversity/

UNESCO.org. (n.d.). Social transformation. Retrieved June 1, 2017, from http://www.unesco.org/new/en/social-and-human-sciences/themes/international-migration/glossary/social-transformation/

UNICEF (2018). UNICEF data: monitoring the situation of children and women. Current Status + Progress Updated: February 2018. Retrieved https://data.unicef.org/topic/education/primary-education/

United Nations. (1964). *Universal Declaration of Human Rights* Retrieved from https://ourdocuments.gov/doc.php?flash=true&doc=100

United States Department of Health and Human Services (USHHS). (2017). Work Requirements Restored for TANF. Administration for Children & Families. Retrieved from https://www.acf.hhs.gov/media/press/tanf-work-requirements-restored.

United States Department of Labor. (n.d.) Frequently Asked Questions Pay Transparency Regulations.

University of Medicine & Dentistry, Rutgers Newark. (1985). Multicultural prevention project [Handout]. *Cultural Assessment Guidelines*.

Upenn.edu. (1990). What is Kwanzaa, *Akwansosem African Studies Program*. Retrieved from https://www.africa.upenn.edu/K-12/Kwanzaa_What_16661.html University Of Pennsylvania—African Studies Cente.

Urban Institute. (2016). *Effective partnerships for family-focused reentry services* [Webinar]. Retrieved from http://www.urban.org/events/effective-partnerships-family-focused-reentry-services

Urban Institute. (2016). Sentencing reform projects. Retrieved from https://www.urban.org/research/publication/reforming-sentencing-and-corrections-policy

Urban Institute. (2016a). The US partnership on mobility from poverty.

Urban Institute. (2016b). Reducing poverty and increasing opportunity: Envisioning the next 20 years.

Urban Wire. (2016, Feb. 23). Race, ethnicity, and gender: Talk about structural racism. Retrieved from www.urbaninstitute.org

Uretsky, M. C., & Stone, S. A. (2016). Factors associated with high school exit exam outcomes among homeless high school students. *Children & Schools, 38*(2), 91–98.

USA.com. (2015). Arson, hate crimes may be behind black church fires across US. Retrieved from https://www.rt.com/usa/270457-black-churches-fires-south/

ushistory.org. (2018). Japanese-American internment. *U.S. History Online Textbook.* Retrieved Jan. 1, 2018, from http://www.ushistory.org/us/51e.asp

Utley, C.A., Obiakor, F.E., & Bakken, J.P. (2011). Culturally responsive practices for culturally and linguistically diverse students with learning disabilities. *Learning Disabilities: A contemporary Journal, 9*(1), 5–18.

Valdeón, R. A. (2013). The use of Latin American Hispanic & Latino in U.S. academics articles, 2000–2015. *Terminology, 19*(1), 112–137.

Valiente, C., Swanson, J., & Eisenberg, N. (2012). Linking students' emotions and academic achievement: When and why emotions matter. *Child Development Perspectives, 6*(2), 129–135.

Vallas, R., Fremstad, S., & Ekman, L. (2015). A fair shot for workers with disabilities. *Center for American Progress.* Retrieved from https://www.americanprogress.org/issues/poverty/report/2015/01/28/105520/a-fair-shot-for-workers-with-disabilities/

Van Acker, K., Phalet, K., Deleersnyder, J., & Mesquita, B. (2014). Do "they" threaten "us" or do "we" disrespect "them": Majority perceptions of intergroup relations and everyday contacts with immigrant minorities. *Group Processes & Intergroup Relations, 17*(5), 617–628.

Van der Kolk, B. (2017). The body keeps score: Dr. Bessel van der Kolk, today's leading trauma treatment expert [Video file]. Eau Claire, WI: PESI.

Van Sertima, I. (1997). *Blacks in science.* New Brunswick, NJ: Rutgers University Press.

Van Wormer, K. (2004). *Confronting oppression, restoring justice: From policy analysis to social action.* Alexandria, VA: CSWE.

Vance, J. D. (2016). *Hillbilly elegy.* New York, NY: Harper Collins.

Vanderbilt. (n.d.). Infant mental health and early care and education providers. The Center on the Social and Emotional Foundations for Early Learning. Retrieved from http://csefel.vanderbilt.edu/documents/rs_infant_mental_health.pdf

Vandewalle, L. (2017). The role of accountants in Indian microfinance groups: a trade-off between financial and non-financial benefits. Retrieved from https://ideas.repec.org/p/nam/wpaper/1118.html

Vanhanen, S. & Heikkilà, E. (2017). Multi-professional work practices in the field of immigrant integration – examples of collaboration between the police and social work. *Migration Letters, 14*(2), 273–284.

Vega, W. A., & Wallace, S. P. (2016). Affordable housing: A key lever to community health for older Americans. *American Journal of Public Health, 106*(4), 4–5.

Velasco, X.J., (Aired 2016, 6.30.). Frederick Davis performs original choreography in front of the Brooklyn Bridge in New York: About the Show. Produced by WTCI, PBS. Retrieved from http://www.pbs.org/program/streets-stage-journey-fredrick-davis/.

Venkatesh, S. (2008). *Gang leader for a day: A rogue sociologist takes to the street.* New York, NY: Penguin Books.

Vera, E., & Kenny, M. (2013). *Social justice and culturally relevant prevention.* Thousand Oaks, CA: SAGE.

Vice Essentials. (2017). Maternity leave [Television series episode]. In *Ovary Action.* Retrieved from https://video.vice.com/en_us/video/ovary-action-maternity-leave/56afd1501f8f224341d4947a

Victor, B.G., Hodge, D.R., Perron, B.E., Vaughan, M.G., Salas-Wright, C. (2017). The Rise of Co-Authorship in social work scholarship: a longitudinal study of collaboration and article quality, 1989-2013. *British Journal of Social Work, 47*(8), 2201-2214.

Villavicencio, K.C. (2018). The Americans left behind by deportation. *New York Times.*

Virginia Commonwealth University. (n.d.). Social welfare history project. Retrieved from https://socialwelfare.library.vcu.edu/organizations/National-Association-of-Social-Workers/

Vivekananda, S. (1896). *Karma yoga*. Retrieved from http://www.vivekananda.net/PDFBooks/KarmaYoga.pdf

Vö, L. T., & Bonus, R. (2002). *Contemporary Asian American communities: Intersections and divergences.* Philadelphia, PA: Temple University Press.

Voborníková, P. (2014). Divided we live: Racial and ethnic segregation in housing in the U.S. *The Scientific Journal of Humanistic Studies, 6*(10), 43–51.

Vol 2015. Retrieved from http://dx.doi.org/10.1155/2015/641602.

Volkow, N. D. (2015). Can the science of addiction help reduce stigma? *Advances in Addiction Recovery, 3*(3).

Wah, L. (Director). (1994). *Color of fear.* Oakland, CA: Sitr-Fry Seminars.

Wakefield, J. (1997). Foucauldian fallacies: An essay review of Leslie Margolin's *Under the Cover of Kindness.* Chicago, IL: University of Chicago Press.

Walker, A. (2006). *The color purple.* New York: Mariner Books.

Wallis, V. (2013). *Two old women: An Alaska legend of betrayal, courage and survival.* New York, NY: Harper Perennial.

Walsh, J.D. & Wuebbles, K. (2016). *Climate change and risk to food security.* Retrieved from http://reports.weforum.org/global-risks-2016/climate-change-and-risks-to-food-security/

Walsh, S. (2016). The hidden epidemic of teen hunger. *The Atlantic.*

Walters K. L. (1999). Urban American Indian identity attitudes and acculturation styles. *Journal of Human Behavior in the Social Environment.* 2, 163–178.

Wang, H. L. (2014). A tale of Asian gangs unleashed in *Green Dragons* film. Retrieved from http://www.npr.org/sections/codeswitch/2014/10/24/357622138/a-tale-of-asian-gangs-unleashed-in-green-dragons-film

Wang, H. L. (2014). Not just a black thing: An Asian American's bond with Malcolm X. NPR.org. Retrieved from http://www.npr.org/sections/codeswitch/2013/08/19/209258986/the-japanese-american-internee-who-met-malcolm-x

Wang, H.L. (2018). No middle eastern or north African category on 2020 census, bureau says. NPR.org. Retrieved from https://www.npr.org/2018/01/29/581541111/no-middle-eastern-or-north-african-category-on-2020-census-bureau-says.

Wang, S., & Lau, A. S. (2015). Mutual and non-mutual social support: Cultural differences in the psychological, behavioral, and biological effects of support seeking. *Journal of Cross-Cultural Psychology, 46*(7), 916–929.

Warner, J. (2015). *Emotional politics of social work and child protection.* Bristol, United Kingdom: Policy Press.

Warner, J.C. (2003). Group therapy with Native Americans: understanding essential differences. *Groupwork, 27*(4), 191–202.

Warren, E. (2014). *A fighting chance.* New York, NY: Metropolitan Books.

Warren, J. R., Hoffman, E., & Andrew, M. (2014). Patterns and trends in grade retention rates in the United States. *Educational Researcher, 43*(9), 433–443.

Watkins, D.C. & Jefferson, S.O. (2013). Recommendations for the use of online social support for African American Men. *Psychological Services, 10*(3), 323–332.

Watt, S. K. (2007). Difficult dialogues, privilege and social justice: Uses of the privileged identity exploration (PIE) model in student affairs practice. *The College Student Affairs Journal, 26*(2), 114–125.

Watts, A. (1975). *Psychotherapy East and West.* New York, NY: Vintage.

Wayman, R. H. (n.d.). *Innovation: Rethinking approaches to LGBTQ homeless youth.* Retrieved from http://www.endhomelessness.org/section/policy/focusareas/youth

Wearing, M. (2011). Strengthening youth citizenship and social inclusion practice—The Australian case: Towards rights based and inclusive practice in services for marginalized young people. *Children and Youth Services Review, 33,* 534–540.

Weaver, H. N. (1999). Indigenous People and the Social Work Profession: Defining Culturally Competent Services. Social Work, 44(3), 217–226.

Weick, A. (2009, Summer). Issues in overturning a medical model of social work practice. *Reflections.* Retrieved from https://pdfs.semanticscholar.org/25e7/c96eecd5d73f0a55a498ff955f61a05a40c1.pdf

Weiner, M. (Writer), & Lionsgate (Producer). (2007). *Mad Men* [Television series]. New York, NY: AMC.

Weis, L. (2006). Masculinity, whiteness, and the new economy: An exploration of privilege and loss. *Men and Masculinities*, *8*(3), 262–272.

Wells-Barnett, I. (2014). *On lynchings*. New York, NY: Dover.

Wells-Wilborn, R., Jackson, N. D., & Schiele, J. H. (2010). Lessons from the Maafa: Rethinking the legacy of a slain hip-hop icon Tupac Amaru Shakur. *Journal of Black Studies*, 509–526.

Wessels, A. (2003). Displacing mothers from work and welfare. *International Social Science Journal*, 55(175), 79–88.

Wessler, S. F. (2015). Class in America: Who do you think you are? *NBC News*. Retrieved from http://www.pewresearch.org/daily-number/asian-americans-lead-all-others-in-household-income/

West, C. (1996). *Race matters*. Boston, MA: Beacon Press.

West, D. (2010). Political ads: Fear and loathing on immigration. CNN.com Retrieved from http://www.cnn.com/2010/OPINION/10/28/west.immigration/index.html.

West, D. M. (2016). *Megachange: Economic disruption, political upheaval, and social strife in the 21st century*. Washington, DC: Brookings Institution Press.

Westby, C., Burda, A., & Mehta, Z. (2003). Asking the right questions in the right ways: Strategies for ethnographic interviewing. *The ASHA Leader*, 8, 4–17. doi:10.1044/leader.FTR3.08082003.4

Wetherill, M., & Mohanty, C. T. (Eds.). (2012). *SAGE handbook of social identities*. Thousand Oaks, CA: SAGE.

WGAC. (2017). Women and gender advocacy center at Colorado State University. Retrieved from http://www.wgac.colostate.edu/

What this means for the effort to grow wages and reduce inequality. Economic Policy Institute. Retrieved from http://www.epi.org/publication/the-changing-demographics-of-americas-working-class/#epi-toc-2

Wheeler, C. H., & Olson, L. M. (2015). Racial differences in mortgage denials over the housing cycle: Evidence from U.S. metropolitan areas. *Journal of Housing Economics*, *30*, 33–49.

Wheeling, K. (2017). The justice department wants to end solitary confinement of juveniles — for now. *Pacific Standard*. Retrieved 1Jan. 11, 2018 from https://psmag.com/news/the-justice-department-wants-to-end-solitary-confinement-of-juveniles-for-now.

White House conference on children. (n.d.). Encyclopedia.com. Retrieved May 27, 2017, from http://www.encyclopedia.com/children/encyclopedias-almanacs-transcripts-and-maps/white-house-conferences-children

White, G. (2015). Rural America's silent jousting crisis. *The Atlantic*.

White, G. (2015). The invisible work that women do around the world. The Atlantic.com According to the UN, women take on three of every four hours of unpaid laborRetrieved Jan9, 2018 from https://www.theatlantic.com/business/archive/2015/12/the-invisible-work-that-women-do-around-the-world/420372/.

Whitehead, A., & Gould, F. S. (2017). Yoga treatment for chronic non-specific low back pain. *Explore New York, 13*(4), 281–284.

Whiteside, M., Klieve, H., Millgate, N., Webb, B., Gabriel, Z., McPherson, L., & Tsey, K. (2016). Connecting and strengthening young Aboriginal men: A family wellbeing pilot study. *Australian Social Work*, 69(2), 241–252.

Whiting, R. (2015). Gestures of mutuality: Bridging social work values and skills through Erasmian humanism. *Ethics and Social Welfare*, 9(4), 328–342.

Whitley, R. (2012). Religious competence as cultural competence. *Transcultural Psychiatry*, 49(2), 245–260.

Whitmore, D., Schanqenbach, D. B., Mumford, M., & Nantz, G. (2015, Mar. 24). Fourteen economic facts on education and economic opportunity. Brookings. Retrieved from https://www.brookings.edu/research/fourteen-economic-facts-on-education-and-economic-opportunity-2/

WHO.org. (2017). World conference on social determinants of health: Fact file on health inequities. Retrieved from http://www.who.int/sdhconference/background/news/facts/en/

Whyy.org (n.d.). Training helps police in interactions with mentally ill people. Retrieved Jan. 12, 2018 from https://whyy.org/articles/training-helps-police-in-interactions-with-mentally-ill-people/

Whyy.org. (2016). The pursuit. Retrieved from http://www.whyy.org/specials/pursuit.php

Whyy.org. (2016, May 20). Sign language in the age of technology [Podcast]. *Radio Times*. Retrieved from http://whyy.org/cms/radiotimes/2016/05/20/sign-language-in-the-age-of-technology/

Wikipedia.org. (n.d.). Diagnostic and statistical manual of mental disorders. Retrieved from https://en.wikipedia.org/wiki/Diagnostic_and_Statistical_Manual_of_Mental_Disorders#DSM-I_.281952.29

Wilcox, S. (Ed.). (1989). *American deaf culture: An anthology*. Burtonsville, MD: Linstok Press.

Wilkerson, I. (2010). *The warmth of other suns: The epic story of America's great migration.* New York, NY: Vintage.

Williams, A.R. (2016). Discoveries may rewrite history of China's terra-cotta warriors.National Geographic.com Retrieved on Jan. 8, 2018 from https://news.nationalgeographic.com/2016/10/china-first-emperor-terra-cotta-warriors-tomb/

Williams, D. J. (2015). The future of effective social work practice: Broadening multidisciplinary collaboration and increasing flexibility social work. *Social Work, 61*(4), 363–365.

Williams, D. R., Neighbors, H. W., & Jackson, J. S. (2003). Racial/ethnic discrimination and health: Findings from community health. *American Journal of Public Health, 93*(2), 200–208.

Williams, D. S. (1987). Womanist theology: Black women's voices. Retrieved from http://www.religion-online.org/articl Escaping the Disability Trap e/woanist-theology-black-womens-voices/

Williams, H. A. (2015). How slavery affected African American families. TeacherServ. Chapel Hill: University of North Carolina. Retrieved from https://whyy.org/articles/training-helps-police-in-interactions-with-mentally-ill-people/.http://nationalhumanitiescenter.org/tserve/freedom/1609-1865/essays/aafamilies.htm

Williams, J. (2000). Thurgood Marshall: American Revolutionary.

Williams, L. N. (2017, July). Issues: trending topics. *Essence Magazine,* 72.

Williams, M. (2016). Special Olympics Let Me Be Myself—A Champion [TED Talk].

Williams, M. T. (2011, Dec. 27). Colorblind ideology is a form of racism: Culturally speaking a colorblind approach allows us to deny uncomfortable cultural differences. Retrieved from https://www.psychologytoday.com/blog/culturally-speaking/201112/colorblind-ideology-is-form-racism

Williams, P. (2018). Supreme Court allows Mississippi anti-LGBT law to stand. nbcnews.com. Retrieved from https://www.nbcnews.com/feature/nbc-out/supreme-court-allows-mississippi-anti-lgbt-law-stand-n835721

Wills, R., Chenoweth, L., & Ellem, K. (2016). Disability and transition from state education to community life: Next steps for parents. *International Journal of Inclusive Education, 20*(5), 552–567.

Wilson, A. (1978). *The developmental psychology of the black child.* New York, NY: African Research Publication.

Wilson, A. N. (1992). *Awakening the natural genius of black children.* New York, NY: Afrikan World InfoSystems.

Wilson, H. (2014). Turning off the school-to-prison pipeline. *Reclaiming Children and Youth. Journal,* 23(1), 49–53.

Wilson, J. (2016, June 9) People of color will be a majority of the American working class in 2032. *Economic Policy Institute.* Retrieved from https://www.epi.org/publication/the-changing-demographics-of-americas-working-class/

Wilson, V. (2017, August 30). Repeal of pay transparency rule will make it easier to discriminate against women and people of color. *Economic Policy Institute.* Retrieved from https://www.epi.org/blog/repeal-of-pay-transparency-rule-will-make-it-easier-to-discriminate-against-women-and-people-of-color/

Wilson, W. J. (1996). *When work disappears: The world of the new urban poor.* New York, NY: Vintage.

Wiltz, T. (2015). State struggles with hidden rural homelessness. *Pew Charitable Trust, Stateline.*

Wimer, C. (2016) Population research report. Retrieved from http://socialwork.columbia.edu/news/according-to-latest-poverty-tracker-data-new-york-city-fails-to-meet-needs-of-poorest-residents/

Windsor, L., Pinto, R. M., Benoit, E., & Jessell, L. (2014). Community wise: The development of an anti-oppression model to promote individual and community health. *Journal of Social Work Practice in the Addictions, 14,* 402–420.

Windsor, L., Pinto, R. M., Benoit, E., Jessel, L., & Jemal, A. (2014). Community wise: The development of an anti-oppression model to promote individual and community health. *Journal of Social Work Practice in the Addictions, 14,* 402–420.

Wines, M., & Schwartz, J. (2016). Safe lead levels in tap water not limited to Flint. *The New York Times.*

Wingfield, A. H., & Feagin, J. R. (2010). *Yes we can? White racial framing and the 2008 presidential campaign.* New York, NY: Routledge.

Wise, T. (2012). *Dear white America: Letter to a new minority.* San Francisco, CA: City Lights.

Wise, T. (2015, Dec. 5). *400 years head start and how white wealth was created* [Video file]. Retrieved from https://www.youtube.com/watch?v=PV-JqtiQijk

Witmer, C. (2014). Robin Hood foundation poverty tracker. Retrieved from http://povertytracker.robinhood.org/

Witten, T. M. (2014). End of life, chronic illness, and trans-identities. *Journal of Social Work in End-of-Life & Palliative Care, 10,* 34–58.

Wo, J., Hipp, J. R., & Boessen, A. (2016). Voluntary organizations and neighborhood crime: A dynamic perspective. *Criminology, 54*(2), 212–241.

Wolfman-Arent, A. (2016). *Clubs run by Philly cops: A recipe for harmony.* newsworks@Whyy.org

Wolkstein, D. (Ed.).(1980). *The magic orange tree and other Haitian folktales.* New York, NY: Schocken Books.

Wong, A. (2016). Escaping the disability trap. *The Atlantic.* Retrieved from https://www.theatlantic.com/education/archive/2016/06/escaping-the-disability-trap/487070/

Wood, M. D. (2003). Willingboro, the other Levittown: Integration and the politics or race and class in South Jersey. Paper presented at the annual meeting of the American Sociological Association, Atlanta Hilton Hotel, Atlanta, GA.

Wood, S. D., Jakubek, J. T., & Kelly, K. (2015). You've got to fight to be white: The rural foundation of the new militia for race control. *Contemporary Justice Review, 18*(2), 215–230.

Woodruff, J. and Honig, E. (n.d.). The post overdose response team. Pbs.org. Retrieved from https://www.pbs.org/newshour/show/to-stop-overdose-deaths-this-response-team-brings-treatment-options-to-your-doorstep

Woodson, C. G. (2010). *The mis-education of the Negro.* Amazon Digital Services LLC. (Original work published 1933)

Woodson, J. (Ed.). (1996). *A way out of no way: Writings about growing up Black in America.* New York: Henry Holt and Company.

World Bank Group. (2016). Poverty. Retrieved from http://www.worldbank.org/en/topic/poverty/overview

World Health Organization. (2015, Oct. 7). Family included: Engaging fathers and families in maternal and infant health. Retrieved from http://www.who.int/pmnch/media/news/2015/fathers/en/

World Health Organization. (2014, May 14). WHO calls for stronger focus on adolescent health. Retrieved from http://www.who.int/mediacentre/news/releases/2014/focus-adolescent-health/en/

Wozniacka, G. (2014). Undocumented immigrants find paths to college, careers. In P. Rothenberg with K. Mayhew (Eds.), *Race, class and gender in the United States.* Duffield, United Kingdom: Worth.

Wroe, L. (2015). Social workers have a duty to speak up about the humanitarian crisis. Retrieved from https://www.theguardian.com/social-care-network/2015/aug/04/social-workers-humanitarian-crisis-calais

Wsj.com. (2017). How to increase workplace diversity [Blog post]. *Wall Street journal.com.*

Wynn, M. (1992). *Empowering African-American males to succeed: A 10-step approach for parents and teachers.* South Pasadena, CA: Rising Sun.

Xue, C. (1997). *The embroidered shoes.* New York, NY: Henry Holt & Co.

Yamatani, H., Samantha Teixeira, S., & McDonough, K. (2015). Employing people with disabilities: a preliminary assessment of a start-up initiative. *Journal of Human Behavior in the Social Environment* 25(8).

Yan, M. C., & Wong, Y. L. R. (2005). Rethinking self-awareness in cultural competence: Toward a dialogic self in cross-cultural social work. *Families in Society, 86*(2), 181–188.

Yancy, G., & Feagin, J. (2015). American racism in the white frame. *The New York Times.* Retrieved from http://opinionator.blogs.nytimes.com/2015/07/27/american-racism-in-the-white-frame/

Yapa, S., (2016). *Your Heart Is a Muscle the Size of a Fist.* Boston, MA: Little, Brown and Company.

Yasui, M., Pottick, K., & Chen, Y. (2017, March). Conceptualizing culturally infused engagement and its measurement for ethnic minority and immigrant children and families. *Clinical Child & Family Psychological Review,* 1–83.

Yates, M. (2008). The injuries of class. Monthly Review. *An Independent Socialist Magazine,* 59(8).

Yee, J.Y. (2016) A paradox of social change: How the quest for liberation reproduces dominance in higher education and the field of social work. *Social Word Education: The International Journal, 35*(5), 495–505.

Yellow Horse Brave Heart (n.d.). Historical trauma and unresolved grief: implications for clinical research and practice with indigenous peoples of the Americas. Native American & Disparities Research Center for Rural & Community Behavioral Health. University of New Mexico. Retrieved from https://www.ihs.gov/telebehavioral/includes/themes/newihstheme/display_objects/documents/slides/historicaltrauma/historicaltraumaintro0113.pdf

Yiwu, L. (2013). *For a song and a hundred songs: A poet's journey.* New York, NY: Harcourt.

Yliruka, L., & Karvinen-Niinikoski, S. (2013). How can we enhance productivity in social work? Dynamically reflective structures, dialogic leadership and the development of transformative expertise. *Journal of Social Work Practice, 27*(2), 191–206.

Young, A. (1992). *A way out of no way: The spiritual memoirs of Andrew Young*. Nashville, TN: Thomas Nelson.

Young, S. (2014). *I'm not your inspiration* [Video file]. Retrieved from https://www.ted.com/talks/stella_young_i_m_not_your_inspiration_thank_you_very_much

Yousafzai, M. (2013). *I am Malala: The girl who stood up for education and was shot by the Taliban*. Boston, MA: Little, Brown.

Zanoni, P., & Mampaey, J. (2011). Achieving ethnic minority students' inclusion: A Flemish school's discursive practices countering the quasi-market pressure to exclude. *British Educational Research Journal, 39*(1), 1–21.

Zerden, LS., Sheely, A., & Despard, M.R. (2016). Debunking macro myths: findings from recent graduates about jobs, salaries, and skills. *Social Work Education*, 35(7), 752–766.

Zhang, L., Nathan, A. J., Link, P., & Schell, O. (2008). *The Tiananmen papers*. Available at https://katateag.files.wordpress.com/2014/10/the-tiananmen-papers.pdf

Zhao, Y. (2016). From deficiency to strength: shifting the mindset about education inequality. *Journal of Teaching in Social Work*, 30, 648–684.

Zhorov, I. (2016, March 25). Location of lead water pipes is often anybody's guess. *The Allegheny Front*. Retrieved from https://www.alleghenyfront.org/location-of-lead-water-pipes-is-often-anybodys-guess/

Zia, Helen. (2000). *Asian American dreams: The emergence of an American people*. New York, NY: Farrar, Straus and Giroux

Zinn Education Project. (2018). Teaching a people's history. A collaboration between Rethinking Schools and Teaching for Change. Retrieved from https://zinnedproject.org/

Zinn, H. (2003). *A people's history of the United States: Teaching edition*. New York, NY: New Press.

Zinn, H. (n.d.). A people's history of the United States: 1492–present. Retrieved Jan. 9, 2018 from https://tzmvirginia.files.wordpress.com/2013/12/zinn-a-peoples-history-of-the-united-states-1492-present.pdf.

Zinn, H., adapted by Stefoff, R. (2009). *A young people's history of the U.S.: 1492 to present*. New York, NY: Harper Collins.

zinnedproject.org. (n.d.). *If we knew our history* [Series]. Retrieved from https://zinnedproject.org/why/if-we-knew-our-history-series/

Zivanovic, R., Omura, J., Wood, E., Nguyen, P., Kerr, T., & DeBeck, K. (2016). Eviction and loss of income assistance among street involved youth in Canada. *Journal of Public Health Policy, 37*(2), 244–259.

Zorigian, K., & Job, J. (2013). Minority representation in special education classrooms. *Learn NC*. Retrieved from http://www.learnnc.org/lp/pages/6799

Zuckerman, I. H., Ryder, P.T. Simoni-Wastila, L., Shaffer, T., Sato, M., Zhao, L., & Stuart, B. (2008). Racial and ethnic disparities in the treatment of dementia among Medicare beneficiaries. *Journal of Gerontology, 63B*(5), S3328–3333.

Zufferey, C. (2012). Not knowing that I do not know and not wanting to know: Reflections of a white Australian social worker *International Social Work, 56*(5) 659–673.

Züñiga, X. (2013). Bridging differences through intergroup dialogue, 635–637. In Adams, M., Blumenfeld, W.J., Castañeda, C., Hackman, H.W., Peters, M. L., & Zúñiga, X., *Readings for diversity and social justice*. (3rd edition.). New York: Routledge.

INDEX

N

CPSIA information can be obtained
at www.ICGtesting.com
Printed in the USA
LVHW050022101220
673745LV00002B/3